A Reader for Developing Writers

A Reader for Developing Writers

Santi V. Buscemi

Middlesex County College

McGraw Hill

Boston Burr Ridge, IL Dubuque, IA Madison, WI New York
San Francisco St. Louis Bangkok Bogotá Caracas Kuala Lumpur
Lisbon London Madrid Mexico City Milan Montreal New Delhi
Santiago Seoul Singapore Sydney Taipei Toronto

McGraw-Hill Higher Education

A Division of The **McGraw-Hill** Companies

A READER FOR DEVELOPING WRITERS

Published by McGraw-Hill, an imprint of The McGraw-Hill Companies, Inc. 1221 Avenue of the Americas, New York, NY, 10020. Copyright © 2002, 1999, 1996, 1993, and 1990 by The McGraw-Hill Companies, Inc. All rights reserved. No part of this publication may be reproduced or distributed in any form or by any means, or stored in a database or retrieval system, without the prior written consent of The McGraw-Hill Companies, Inc., including, but not limited to, in any network or other electronic storage or transmission, or broadcast for distance learning.

Some ancillaries, including electronic and print components, may not be available to customers outside the United States.

 This book is printed on acid-free paper.

4 5 6 7 8 9 0 DOC/DOC 0 9 8 7 6 5 4 3

ISBN 0-07-243264-0

Vice President and editor in chief: *Thalia Dorwick*
Editorial director: *Phillip A. Butcher*
Exeutive editor: *Lisa Moore*
Editorial coordinator: *Victoria Fullard*
Marketing manager: *David Patterson*
Project manager: *Ruth Smith*
Production supervisor: *Susanne Riedell*
Coordinator freelance design: *Gino Cieslik*
Supplement coordinator: *Vicki Laird*
Media technology producer: *Todd Vaccaro*
Cover design: *Kay Fulton*
Interior design: *Kay Fulton*
Compositor: *Shepherd Incorporated*
Typeface: *10/12 Berkeley Book*
Printer: *R. R. Donnelley & Sons Company*

Library of Congress Cataloging-in-Publication Data

Buscemi, Santi V.
     A reader for developing writers / Santi V. Buscemi.—5th ed.
         p. cm.
     Includes index.
     ISBN 0-07-243264-0 (alk. paper)
     1. College readers. 2. English language—Rhetoric—Problems, exercises, etc. 3. Report writing—Problems, exercises, etc. I. Title.
PE1417 .B855 2002
808'.0427—dc21

2001030149

*For **Joseph** and **Theresa Buscemi** and for all the other Sicilian heroes who came to this country to make a better life for their children*

About the Author

Santi V. Buscemi teaches reading and writing and chairs the English Department at Middlesex County College in Edison, NJ. He is the author of *AllWrite! 2.0 with Online Handbook,* McGraw-Hill's interactive electronic writing program, and co-author of *The Basics* and *75 Readings Plus.* He has lectured on developmental education at national conferences in the United States and South Africa.

To the Instructor

Now in its fifth edition, *A Reader for Developing Writers* has evolved into a complete rhetoric and reader that can be used by both developmental and freshman writers. Used in many colleges across the United States and in other parts of the world, the text has been far more successful than I could have predicted when I completed the first edition in 1990. Thus, as I have said before, no matter what the future brings, I will always be grateful for the support that so many teachers and students have given me in the ten years since *A Reader for Developing Writers* was first published.

As in the past, this edition aims at helping students read carefully, react thoughtfully, and use those reactions as creative springboards for writing. Research in reading, rhetoric, and composition continues to affirm the close relationship among these skills. College writers, whether developmental or freshman, need a program of critical and committed reading that increases their appreciation of language, provides inspiration for their own creative efforts, and reinforces the teaching of basic rhetorical strategies. In short, no composition program in English—at any level—makes sense without the integration of reading and writing.

I have chosen reading selections with the intention of helping students use their own experiences and perceptions as sources of information and insight in writing that explores questions suggested by—if not drawn directly from—the reading. More than ever, the paragraphs, essays, and poems I have included reflect a diversity of cultural and academic interests, and many of them speak about phenomena, cultures, and lifestyles with which some students may be unfamiliar. For example, the new fifth edition contains an essay by a student who writes about her suffering during the Pol Pot regime in Cambodia. Another new student essay—which moved a state government to pass new legislation—argues for increased compensation to victims of violent crime. Two other new student essays explore the relationship between part-time work and full-time college study.

In the fourth edition, I added a letter by Elie Wiesel, which addresses the Master of the Universe about the question of evil in the context of the Holocaust. In the latest edition, I included two new moving pieces written by medical doctors discussing the physical and psychological effects of disease. Both show that scientists can write passionate, fascinating, and moving prose while including hard scientific data presented factually and objectively. At the suggestion of the reviewers, I have also expanded the number of sustained pieces to include selections by Dr. Martin Luther King, Jr., Gordon Parks, Michael Barone, Paul Simon, and Nat Hentoff.

As in previous editions, introductory materials illustrate important principles and techniques, and reading selections demonstrate variety in length, subject matter, and purpose. Included in most chapters is at least one short, readily accessible piece designed to promote confidence in beginning writers and readers and to prepare them for longer, more challenging selections.

The fifth edition continues to emphasize the notion that writing is a process of discovery to be approached with care, commitment, and energy. The "Getting Started" section, which opens the book, traces the evolution of an essay from prewriting through the final draft, with each stage fully explained and illustrated via samples taken from the work of a first-year college student. In addition, materials to help students learn to gather information for and plan their writing have been added, as has been complete coverage of purpose, audience, and style as they relate to academic writing. Another major feature new to the fifth edition is thorough coverage of writing research papers using Modern Language Association style, complete with coverage of the Internet and other electronic sources. The Appendix in which this material appears also contains a fully documented student research paper with accompanying marginal notations to help students learn from this model. A third major feature of the fifth edition is the new, two-chapter section entitled Argumentation/Persuasion, containing a total of ten student and professional selections and complete coverage of techniques relevant both to argumentation and to persuasion. At the suggestion of several reviewers, the Looking Ahead sections, which preceded each selection, have been strengthened so as to encourage more pre-reading, and they have been renamed "Preparing to Read." Finally, parts of speech have been indicated in the Vocabulary section.

As before, chapter introductions compare excerpts from rough and revised drafts of a student essay that appears a few pages later. Comments in the margins relevant to techniques and skills covered in the chapter demonstrate the riches revising can yield. Again, the belief that writing is a process is reinforced in the Suggestions for Sustained Writing, which appear near the end of each chapter. Most suggestions refer to journal entries students make after reading the selections, and they encourage the use of this information to begin and to develop full-length essays and letters. Each and every Suggestion for Sustained Writing also reminds students that composing is more than simply gathering information and arranging it on a page. Indeed, woven into the fabric of each item is a reminder that successful writing demands careful planning, the creation of multiple drafts, frequent reorganization and revision, and painstaking editing. Other important features retained from the earlier editions include introductions to the reading process and to taking notes. These appear in "Getting Started," the opening section of the book. A form of the SQ3R (Survey, Question, Read, Recite, Review) method, taught in many developmental reading classes, is explained clearly and concisely. This material also offers students suggestions— complete with easy-to-follow illustrations—on how to keep a double-entry notebook and to make notes in the margins. Again, there are even special tips on how to read this text.

The emphasis on careful reading and thinking is carried through the rest of the text in Thinking Critically, a pedagogical subsection accompanying each selection. Thinking Critically offers students questions for writing and discussion by which they can practice a variety of important critical skills. For example, some items ask students to practice techniques learned in the reading and note-taking sections of "Getting Started." Others ask them to extend or respond to the discussion of ideas or opinions found in what they have just read. Still others require them to make comparisons between two or more selections in the text. Also retained in the fifth edition are the "Writing to Learn" group activities. These assignments take student groups through a step-by-step process of discussion, research, writing, and revision that culminates in a major collaborative project. Students are encouraged to research and discuss trends, problems, events, and figures from a variety of disciplines by interviewing professors, using the college library, and searching the Internet.

The list of readings continues to address a variety of academic disciplines and a wide range of social, political, economic, and scientific concerns. As in the first four editions, I have chosen selections appropriate to the reading abilities of first-year students, but I have also included several that promote healthy intellectual stretching. However, the text continues to offer easy-to-follow aids designed to foster comprehension. While most selections are non-fiction prose, poetry plays a prominent role. More important, every chapter boasts at least one student piece. This is also true of the Appendix on research paper writing, which contains a student paper that was so well researched and so convincing that it prompted the New Jersey State legislature to pass measures increasing compensation to victims of violent crime. Once again, I have made it a point to show that the student essays are products of careful, sustained effort through which the writers' forceful and distinctive voices address engaging topics via various modes of discourse. Thus, each chapter introduction contains samples of rough and corrected drafts of student essays appearing in that chapter. Including such material has been effective in emphasizing the importance of adhering to the writing process through careful drafting, revising, and editing.

Behind the design of the text remains a conviction that there should be a natural connection between what students are asked to read and what they are asked to write. This is not to say that the reading selections have been chosen to serve as blueprints or models for the students' own writing. However, they do illustrate important principles and techniques clearly, and they inspire students to use writing as a way to explore their own values, ideas, concerns, and opinions. The connection between reading and writing is fostered by the text's instructional apparatus. Section and chapter introductions discuss fundamental principles of rhetoric and composition illustrated in the reading selections. In addition, graphic illustrations help students see as well as read about principles and techniques they can apply in their own work.

As in the past, each selection is accompanied by materials that help students practice techniques explained in chapter introductions and illustrated in the reading selections. Helpful features for each selection include Preparing to Read (comments and questions that help students preview their reading), Vocabulary, Questions for Discussion, Suggestions for Journal Entries, and Suggestions for Sustained Writing. As mentioned earlier, each chapter ends with a collaborative writing activity entitled "Writing to Learn: A Group Activity." Since beginning writers often find collecting detail difficult, special attention is paid to the early stages of the writing process. In this regard, the book's opening section, "Getting Started," which has been expanded significantly in the fifth edition, is especially helpful and important. This introduction to the text delineates the evolution of a student essay from beginning to end. It explains several prewriting strategies that are often recommended or referred to in the Suggestions for Journal Entries and that help students gather information they can use to launch longer projects described in the Suggestions for Sustained Writing. "Getting Started" addresses issues and presents techniques important to reading and outlining, with clear and comprehensive examples of the techniques, as well as a full range of prewriting techniques including brainstorming, clustering, drawing a subject tree, and freewriting. Finally, in the fifth edition, "Getting Started" provides comprehensive coverage of the crucial issues of purpose, audience, and academic style.

The instructional apparatus remains fully integrated. Questions and comments under Preparing to Read and the Vocabulary section help students preview the contents and structure of each selection. At the same time, they prepare students for the Questions for Discussion and the items under Thinking Critically. The clear connection between the Suggestions for Journal Entries and the Suggestions for Sustained Writing has been maintained. The latter make direct reference to details, insights, and ideas students have recorded in their journals, and they encourage the use of such materials as springboards for longer projects.

No textbook is the product of one person, even a book that carries a single byline. I am indebted to several good friends and fellow teachers whose counsel, direction, and encouragement helped make this book what it is. For their careful reviews, I would like to thank several of my teaching colleagues from across the country: Robert Canter, Virginia Tech; Stephen E. Hudson, Portland Community College; James Allen, College of DuPage; William O. Boggs, Slippery Rock University; Patricia Jenkins, University of Alaska–Anchorage; Marie Iglesias-Cardinale, Genesee Community College; Roy Neil Graves, University of Tennessee at Martin; Ernest J. Smith, University of Central Florida; Brennan Enos, Palm Beach Community College; Jeffrey T. Andelora, Mesa Community College; Michael Punches, Oklahoma City Community College

Among my friends and colleagues at Middlesex County College, I want to thank Betty Altruda, Jamie Daley, Sallie DelVecchio, Barry Glazer, James Keller, Jack Moskowitz, Georgianna Planko, Renee Price, Yvonne Sisko, Sonia Bokalo, and Mathew Spano for their support. Special thanks goes to Emanuel diPasquale for his splendid advice and encouragement. I also want to express my thanks to Laura Barthule and Lisa Moore of McGraw-Hill and to Fran Hannify of Luzerne County Community College. Finally, I want to thank my wife, Elaine, for putting up with my "imperfections" and for granting me her patience and support during the writing of this and of earlier editions.

Santi V. Buscemi

Getting Started

CHAPTER 7

Sentence Structure: Creating Emphasis and Variety 227

SECTION   THREE

Description   263

CHAPTER   8

Describing Places and Things   267

C H A P T E R   9

Describing People   305

SECTION FOUR

Narration   341

CHAPTER 10

Personal Reflection and Autobiography   345

CHAPTER 11

Reporting Events   373

SECTION FIVE

Exposition 405

CHAPTER 12

Illustration 409

CHAPTER 13

Comparison and Contrast 449

CHAPTER   14

Process Analysis   479

CHAPTER 16

Persuasion 551

A Reader for
Developing Writers

Getting Started

A Reader for Developing Writers is a collection of short reading selections by professional and student authors. Each paragraph, essay, and poem, is accompanied by discussion questions, suggestions for short and sustained writing, and other instructional aids. The reading selections use techniques you will want to learn as you develop your reading and writing skills. Some even serve as models for writing you do in other college courses.

Most important, the reading selections will act as springboards to your own writing. Some supply facts and ideas you can include and make reference to in your own work. Others will inspire you to write paragraphs, letters, or essays about similar subjects by drawing details from what you know best—your own experiences, observations, and reading. In short, this book will help you make connections between your reading and your writing, and it will show you ways to improve both.

The rest of this introduction offers advice about getting started. It discusses:

How to use this book

Making the most of your reading

Taking notes

Learning the writing process

Gathering information

Writing an outline

The making of a student essay: From prewriting to proofreading

How to Use This Book

The most important parts of this book are the reading selections—paragraphs, essays, poems, and stories—which your instructor will assign. These are accompanied by instructional aids such as Questions for Discussion and Suggestions for Sustained Writing. They will help you make the most of your reading and get started on your own writing projects. Here's one way to use *A Reader for Developing Writers* (your teacher may suggest others):

1. The book is divided into six sections; each contains at least two chapters. Always begin a section by reading the introduction. Section introductions aren't long, but they provide important information. The introduction to Section One begins on page 31.

1

2. Next, read the chapter introduction. It explains principles and strategies illustrated by the reading selections that follow. The introduction to Chapter 1 begins on page 33.

3. When you get to the reading selections in a chapter, you will see that each is preceded by an author's biography, a preview section called Preparing to Read, and a vocabulary section. These are instructional aids. Read them first; then read the selection itself at least twice. The first selection begins on page 43.

4. Read and answer the Questions for Discussion that follow the selection. It's a good idea to put your answers in writing, perhaps in a notebook reserved for this class.

5. Next, read and complete the short Thinking Critically exercise following Questions for Discussion after a selection. In most cases you can write your responses to the exercises in the text itself—on blank pages or in the margins. Completing these exercises will also provide you with ideas for longer writing projects.

6. Now, respond to the Suggestions for Journal Entries, which follow Thinking Critically. Write your responses in a notebook (journal) kept for this purpose only. Making regular journal entries is critical to developing your writing skills. First, like any skill, writing is mastered only through frequent practice, and keeping a journal provides this practice. Second, a journal contains your response to the readings, so it helps you understand and use what you read. Finally, responding to Suggestions for Journal Entries is an easy way to gather information for longer projects. In fact, almost all of the Suggestions for Sustained Writing (found at the end of each chapter) refer to journal entries. So, keeping a journal means you will have already taken the first step in completing major writing assignments.

7. Finally, respond to one of the Suggestions for Sustained Writing at the chapter's end. Read each suggestion carefully; then, choose one you know a lot about. Almost all Suggestions for Sustained Writing refer to earlier journal suggestions. If you haven't made a journal entry like the one referred to, go back and do so.

8. Important terms are defined in the Glossary at the end of the book. Refer to it if you have questions about a term used to define a writing technique, rule, or principle.

Making the Most of Your Reading

READING IN COLLEGE

Reading and writing are closely related. The more you read, the better writer you will become. The more you write, the easier reading will be.

Like writing, reading is an active process. It should be done conscientiously—with a questioning and curious mind. Don't just accept what someone else writes. Don't just ignore what at first you don't understand. Reading is a struggle, but it will make you a better thinker and writer.

Some students get frustrated when they read challenging material. Fortunately, there are many simple methods to make your reading more successful and, simultaneously, to use it as a tool for improving your writing. However, all require careful preparation and review. Here's a five-step process based on one developed by Professor Francis P. Robinson of Ohio State University. Apply it to any text and especially to paragraphs and essays in this book:

(1) **Survey:** First, pay careful attention to the title. Next, scan the entire selection. Look for words or phrases in bold; they reveal important ideas and give clues about organization. Then, read the introduction (first few sentences or paragraphs); try to spot the central or main idea.

(2) **Question:** Now, ask yourself questions like these:
- What do I think is the author's subject?
- What main point is he or she making about the subject?
- How is the piece organized? What major points will the author make and in what order?
- What do subheadings and words in bold or italics reveal?
  You don't have to answer all such questions immediately. However, asking intelligent questions (try making up some of your own) is a good way to warm up the mind, just as stretching is a good way to warm up the body before exercising.

(3) **Read:** Questions like those above will give your reading purpose and focus. Try to answer them as you read through the material.

(4) **Reread and take notes:** You will learn that the key to good writing is rewriting. The same is true of reading. Never read an assignment just once. The second time around, make sure to take notes. (You will soon learn two good ways to take notes for selections in this book.)

(5) **Review:** Always read your notes at least once. If possible, write a short response based on them, in which you can summarize what you have read, question, add to, argue against, or make some other response. The Suggestions for Journal Entries after each selection will help you do this.

SPECIAL TIPS FOR READING SELECTIONS IN THIS BOOK

1. Prepare for a selection by first reading the author's biography, the vocabulary words, and the Preparing to Read section, which come before it.

2. Take notes while you read. You can do this in many ways, such as listing or outlining ideas on a notepad. Two especially good methods are to make notes in the margins of the text and to keep a double-entry notebook. Both are explained below.

3. Answer the Questions for Discussion that appear after each selection in this textbook. Then, complete at least one of the Suggestions for Journal Entries and the Thinking Critically exercise.

Taking Notes

Two good ways to take notes are by making them in the margins and by keeping a double-entry notebook. Try these techniques as you read this book:

MAKING NOTES IN THE MARGINS

A simple but effective way to react to what you read is by jotting down short notes anywhere in the text you can find space. Doing so will help you better understand what you read and inspire you to write on similar subjects. The left and right margins are convenient places to put notes, but the bottom of the page or a blank page will also do. Here are tips for making notes in the margins:

- Never read a textbook without a pen or marker in your hand. Your college books are your own; mark them up. Francis Bacon said, "Some books are to be tasted, others to be swallowed, and some few to be chewed and digested." So chew, digest, and enjoy them.
- Underline central ideas of essays and paragraphs. (You will learn more about central ideas later.) If the central idea isn't stated, make one up and write it in the margin.
- Circle or highlight words, phrases, or sentences that are moving, convincing, or otherwise effective.
- Ask questions about the writer's ideas or opinions.
- Agree or disagree with the author's facts and opinions.
- Place a question mark (?) next to an unfamiliar word, phrase, name, or fact. You can look it up later.
- Most important, add information of your own. Relate ideas to yourself or people you know. This will inspire you to write on this subject yourself.

Now read the introduction to Gina K. Louis-Ferdinand's "Is Justice Served?" (You can read the complete essay in Chapter 2.) Note these comments a reader has made in the margins.

Americans love a juicy story. We want   *Grabs your attention!*

intimate details, and the media is happy to

comply, but what we forget is that people's

lives are at stake. A crime is not a form of

macabre entertainment from which to derive   *? (look up in dictionary)*

perverse pleasure. It is the failure of a

person to live up to his or her obligations

Could be essay's central idea.

as a law-abiding citizen, and the media should report it as such.

    Recently, several crimes have been *Yes! Especially TV.*

And how! Remember the Tanya Harding case.

sensationalized. As far as the <u>media</u> is concerned, the more gruesome the crime, the better. Take the Menendez brothers' case or the trial of the policemen who beat Rodney King. If a famous person is accused, members of the <u>press appear to smack their lips and</u> *Too strong an accusation?*

<u>wring their hands in anticipation.</u> Insert sex or race, as in the O.J. Simpson murder trial, and the <u>journalist's</u> fondest dreams *All journalists?*

Effective word.

come true. But such exploitation <u>is not</u> */agree 100%.*

<u>harmless</u> entertainment; it tears at the core of the American judicial system: a fair trial by an impartial jury.

This is central idea.

KEEPING A DOUBLE-ENTRY (SUMMARY/RESPONSE) NOTEBOOK

There are several ways to keep a double-entry notebook. Here's one of the easiest:

1. Before you begin a selection, draw a line from top to bottom down the middle of a notebook page.
2. Label the left column *Summary:* the right column, *Response.*
3. As you read the poem, story, or essay, summarize the major ideas in each paragraph or stanza (a paragraph in a poem) under the left column. A summary condenses (puts briefly) what you have read into your own words.
4. After you have finished reading and made summary comments, write brief responses to those summaries in the right column. (You may have to reread sentences or even whole paragraphs to do this.) Your personal responses can take any form you want, but they will probably be similar to notes you might write in the margins. For example:

- Ask a question.
- Agree or disagree with an opinion.
- Identify the central and other important ideas.
- Identify a word or phrase you especially like.
- Add information to show how the reading relates to you or your world. Doing this might inspire you to write on a similar subject.

As an example, here is Alfred Lord Tennyson's poem "The Eagle," followed by a sample notebook entry:

The Eagle
He clasps the crag with crooked hands;
Close to the sun in lonely lands,
Ring'd with the azure world, he stands.

The wrinkled sea beneath him crawls;
He watches from his mountain walls,
And like a thunderbolt he falls.

Summary

Stanza 1—Grasping a large rock, an eagle stands on a high and lonely cliff.

Stanza 2—The eagle looks down at the sea and drops quickly, furiously.

Response

The eagle is so high he is surrounded by sky.
He is given human qualities—"hands."

He is so high the sea seems wrinkled. What is he going after? Food? An enemy? "Thunderbolt" is a great word. This is a wonderful picture of a majestic animal.

Learning the Writing Process

Like reading, writing is a process. The writing process can be divided into four major steps: prewriting, drafting, revising, and editing/proofreading. The next few paragraphs outline the writing process. To understand it even better, read pages 8 through 30. They detail the process more fully and give you many suggestions for being successful as you complete each stage.

PREWRITING

Prewriting consists of three important steps:

- Considering purpose, audience, and style.
- Gathering information.
- Outlining.

Don't skip this important stage. Also called invention, prewriting helps you to decide on considerations like purpose and audience, to gather information, and to set up a plan for organizing your ideas.

Here's what Gilbert Muller and Harvey Wiener, two experienced professors and authors, have to say about prewriting:

> Few writers begin without some warm-up activity. Generally called prewriting, the steps they take before producing a draft almost always start with thinking about their topic. They talk to friends and colleagues; they browse in libraries . . . ; they read newspaper and magazine articles. Sometimes they jot down notes and lists in order to put on paper some of their thoughts in very rough form. Some writers use free-association; they record as thoroughly as possible their random, unedited ideas. . . . Using the raw, often disorganized materials produced in this preliminary stage, many writers try to group related thoughts with a scratch outline. ("On Writing")

DRAFTING

Begin drafting the first version of any document by reviewing what you have decided is the purpose of your project, its intended audience, and the style you should use. Then read the information you have gathered in your journal and look over the preliminary outline you made. As you begin drafting, you will probably decide on your preliminary or working central idea, and then you will start expressing your thoughts in the sentences and paragraphs of your project. You can read more about drafting later in "Getting Started" and in Chapter 1. For now, remember that, once you have completed a first draft—also known as the working draft—you are not at the end of the process. You have made a good start, but only a start.

REVISING THE FIRST DRAFT

Revising means rewriting the working draft of your document, then rewriting it, and rewriting it some more. Don't be satisfied with just one quick revision. Take this stage in the writing process as seriously as the rest. In the back of your mind, keep repeating the old saying "all writing is really just rewriting." With each revision your writing will improve. Revising helps you clarify your purpose and central idea, reorganize confusing sentences and paragraphs, add details, combine short, choppy sentences, and improve word choice. So, make at least three or four revisions of your work!

EDITING AND PROOFREADING

Editing means reading the best of your drafts to correct errors in grammar, punctuation, sentence structure, and mechanics. Proofreading involves the final check for spelling, punctuation, and typographical errors.

These steps seem neatly defined, but they are not always distinct from each other. For example, while editing, you might have to make major revisions to correct important language or organizational problems. If this happens, don't worry. It's the way the process is supposed to work.

Prewriting: Considering Purpose, Audience, and Style

As you read above, there are three things you must do in the prewriting stage to help your writing project succeed: (1) consider purpose, audience, and style; (2) gather information; and (3) outline.

Even before you begin taking notes, you should give some thought to the purpose, audience, and style of your writing. *Purpose* is the task or objective that a piece of writing aims to accomplish. The term *audience* refers to the intended reader or readers. *Style* has to do with the level of language—informal, familiar, or formal—that is appropriate to the purpose and audience of a piece of writing. Of course, you can change your mind about each of these considerations once you have begun taking notes or even after you have begun drafting your project. However, thinking about purpose, audience, and style from the very beginning of the writing process is always a good idea.

DETERMINE YOUR PURPOSE

Writing is a practical activity. It always serves a purpose, whether the writer is producing a technical report that explains an electronic process, an argumentative essay on a current social issue, a thank-you letter to a business client, a review of a film or book, a pamphlet that describes a beautiful vacation resort, or simply an entry in a diary. The purpose of the writing determines the major approach or method that the writer uses and the form that the document will take. For example, in order to explain the workings of a cellular phone system, you might use a technique called *process analysis* to list steps required for the transmission of voice and fax messages over a wireless system. If you are trying to convince the state legislature to increase assistance to victims of violent crime, you would probably use techniques associated with *argumentation* and *persuasion*. If you are simply recording the day's events in a diary, narration (recalling events in time order) might be the most useful tool.

Keep in mind, however, that pieces of writing rarely rely on only one method or approach to accomplish their purpose. For instance, a *process analysis* explaining how cellular phones transmit messages might also use *definition* to explain what a cellular phone or a transmission tower is. It might even *contrast* a cellular phone to the more traditional, wired models. An argument attempting to convince legislators to increase aid to crime victims might also include paragraphs of pure *narration* to tell the history of recent crime legislation or recall a particular experience of a crime victim the writer knows. A simple diary entry that relies heavily on narration might also include a *description* of what the writer heard or saw during the course of the day.

In short, even though a piece of writing relies on one major approach, it may also use a variety of other approaches to achieve its purpose. The choice of approaches or methods depends, of course, on the writer's objective, his or her purpose.

For students enrolled in first-year college writing classes, the assignment an instructor makes might indicate a specific purpose and even require a definite approach. However, this is not always the case. With some assignments, an instructor might ask students to determine their own purposes and then decide for themselves how best to achieve them. This is part of a process intended to help developing writers grow and gain experience. Although we sometimes think of effective writing as a matter of sticking to the rules of grammar and mastering the techniques of rhetoric, mature and effective writing also demands an ability to make judgements. For example, writers must decide on a topic's particular focus, gather information appropriate to that focus, define their purpose, and determine ways to fulfill that purpose. No textbook can do these things for them.

A writer develops judgment only by experience, and, as with any other craft, this is a process of trial and error. So, don't get discouraged if you suddenly discover that you have chosen the wrong approach or that you haven't defined your purpose clearly enough. Most new writers—and many experienced writers—often have the same problems. Simply go back and rethink your purpose and your approach; then, start again. Of course, this might require doing more information gathering by using some of the prewriting tools explained in the next few pages. It might also require you to get rid of information you gathered earlier simply because it is no longer relevant to your new purpose. However, all of this is normal—writing is a process of discovery and revision.

The best time to think about your purpose for an academic essay is *before* you begin gathering facts, ideas, and insights about your topic through *listing, clustering,* or some other method explained below. After carefully considering the assignment you have been given, you might write a statement of purpose (a sentence or two should do) on an index card. However, keep in mind that you might revise this statement of purpose later in the process, after you have gathered information, after you have made an outline, or even after you have written a first draft of the essay. You will learn more about purpose in Chapter 1.

CONSIDER THE AUDIENCE

The audience for any piece of writing is its reader or readers. It is certainly important to consider the readers before you begin writing a first draft, but you should also do so even before you begin gathering information. Let's say your purpose is to convince your classmates to use the library's new online periodical database to find recent information on their majors. You might first have to define "professional journals" and distinguish such publications from "weekly news magazines." You might also have to define "periodical," "database," and even "online." Finally, you might want to explain ways in which students can find relevant articles so as to convince them of the ease with which this new tool can be used.

On the other hand, what if you are writing to the members of the library staff to convince them that your college should subscribe to a particular database? You probably would not have to explain such basic things to get your point across. Indeed, taking time to do so would probably bore these readers.

The primary audience for academic essays is usually the professor. Often, however, your classmates will also be asked to read your work, especially if you discuss papers in small writing groups. In such cases, you must consider your whole audience—both instructor and students—and you might need to include explanatory information and definitions of specialized terms in addition to what you would have included had you been writing for your instructor alone.

Even if you are writing for the instructor alone, evaluating the needs of your reader can get tricky. Many instructors of first-year composition classes have advanced degrees in English or related disciplines. Therefore, you can assume that they are well trained in their field and intelligent. But does that mean that they will be acquainted with other specialized fields of knowledge? Would they know the process by which atoms are split, the most effective methods for tracking economic growth, or the latest theories on criminology and prison reform? If you were writing on recent developments in American music, would your instructor be able to distinguish "hip-hop" from "rap" music? Would he or she be familiar with the "boy-band sound"? If not, you would have to define these specialized terms and provide explanatory information that would be obvious to an expert in these subjects.

As in determining your purpose, considering your audience requires the use of your judgment as a writer. Try evaluating your audience's needs before you begin to gather information, but again, remember that you may later revise your understanding of your readers and their needs at any time in the writing process.

You will learn more about evaluating an audience in Section Six.

Use Formal Style in Academic Writing:

Style refers to the level of language you use. Essentially there are three levels of language you can use in writing, but *formal* style—the third of these—is preferable in academic writing.

Informal Style   You use this style when writing to a very limited audience—yourself, a close friend, a classmate—in short notes or personal letters. Such writing may use *colloquialisms,* or conversational expressions used only in certain locales or by a familiar group. Informal style also allows *slang,* or language that has a special meaning within a limited group and that changes rapidly. Such style sometimes makes reference to people, events, or things that have special meaning only to the reader and writer. Consider the terms "tanking" and "Geek Patrol," for example, in this paragraph that uses informal style from a student's personal letter to a former high school classmate:

```
Most dudes in my college fraternity seem to

be pretty brainy, and they hit the books

real hard. But they aren't that stuck up,

not like the Geek Patrol we knew at

Jefferson High. In fact, they're all right!

They even tutor kids whose grades are

tanking.
```

Familiar Style   You might use a familiar style in a short business memo, in a letter to the editor of your college newspaper, or in a letter to a relative or acquaintance. Here is a sample from a student's letter about his first year in college, which he sent to the boss he worked for during the summer:

```
You would like the students in my

fraternity. They are fairly smart, but they

often burn the midnight oil when they want

to ace a big exam. However, they're not

snobby eggheads. In fact they often tutor

other kids who are having trouble with

school work.
```

This version is somewhat more formal than the last, and it resembles everyday conversation among intelligent people. It does not include slang or private language, but it does use colloquialisms such as "ace a big exam" and "snobby eggheads." For the sake of easy communication, it also includes a cliché (a phrase that lacks originality): "burn the midnight oil." In the familiar style, it addresses the reader directly by using the word "you."

Formal Style   This is the kind of language that belongs in academic papers, in answers to essay questions, in business letters, and in business, technical, and government reports. Notice that the writer now replaces all colloquialisms, slang, and clichés, and that he no longer addresses the reader directly by using "you." The vocabulary he uses is more sophisticated than the more relaxed choice of words he used in the two versions above.

```
Students in my fraternity are quite likable.

They are intelligent, but they are also
```

diligent, studying hard especially when it

comes to major examinations. However, they

are not snobs. In fact they often tutor

other students who are having difficulty

with their studies.

It is best to use a formal style from the moment you begin drafting your paper. However, you can always check for and eliminate clichés, slang, colloquialisms, and other less-than-formal elements when you edit your work.

Prewriting: Gathering Information

Another important aspect of prewriting is gathering information. You can use the following seven techniques to gather facts, ideas, and opinions for any assignment, especially for journal entries. A good way to start a journal entry is to read the notes you made on a reading selection. This should get you mentally set for writing. Then, follow the Suggestions for Journal Entries, which often recommend using the information-gathering techniques that follow.

LISTING

You can use your journal to make a list of details by recording what you think is most important, most startling, or most obvious about your topic. Sometimes, in fact, you can compile a useful list of details simply by putting down whatever comes to mind about your topic. Here's a list that student writer Aggie Canino made when she was asked to describe a recent storm and its effects on her community:

Cloged rain sewers overflowing

Giant tree limbs across the road

Flooding

Strong winds

Birch trees bent duble in the wind

Cracked utility poles

Downed power lines

Loss of electric

Lasted only one hour

Dog hidding under bed

```
Flooded basements

Thunder/lightening

Loss of power

Frightening sounds—howling of the wind, crash of

thunder

Complete darkness in the middle of the day

Old oak on corner struck by lightening—bark ripped

off
```

This list is repetitious and has spelling errors, but don't worry about such problems at first; you can correct them later. Just concentrate on your topic, and record the details as fast as they pop into your head.

Make sure to read your list after—but only *after*—you run out of things to say. Doing so will allow you to eliminate repetition and correct obvious errors. More important, it will help you make various items more specific and even come up with a few new details. For instance, Aggie expanded her mention of "cracked utility poles" by describing the "white sparks that flew from downed power lines" and by detailing the terror she felt as she heard the "splintering of a utility pole struck by lightning."

FOCUSED FREEWRITING

Freewriting is a very common technique to help overcome *writer's block,* a problem that results in staring at a blank piece of paper while trying unsuccessfully to come up with something to say. Freewriting involves writing nonstop for 5 or 10 minutes and simply recording ideas that come into your mind at random. Focused freewriting is similar, but it involves concentrating on a predetermined topic.

Let's say that you want to do some focused freewriting on a storm. The results might look like this:

```
The clogged rain sewers were overflowing,

and there was a lot of flooding with strong

winds knocking down power lines. Thunder

crashed, and lightning flashed. Giant tree

limbs fell across the road and a birch was

bent double, and there were lots of flooded

basements. Even so, the storm lasted only
```

```
one hour. Several downed power lines threw
threatening sparks and flashes across the
road. My street was blocked; a large oak had
fallen across it. We lost our electricity.
The crash of thunder shook me to my bones.
My dog hid under the bed. We were terrified.
```

Again, don't worry about grammar and other such errors at this point in the process. Simply try to focus on your topic and record your ideas quickly and completely.

As always, read your journal entry as soon as possible after you've recorded your ideas. Doing so will help you cut out repetition, rework parts that require clarification, and add more details that come to mind in the process.

CLUSTERING

Clustering is a good way to turn a broad subject into a limited and more manageable topic for a short essay. Also called *mapping* and *webbing*, it is another effective way to gather information for an essay.

Like focused freewriting, which you just read about, clustering uses free association. To cluster ideas, begin with a blank sheet of paper. In the center, write and circle the word or phrase that expresses the broad subject you want to write about. Let's say your broad subject is dancing. Think of ideas and details related to this subject. Write down whatever pops into your mind. For example, you might think of subheadings such as ballet, ballroom dancing, dancing as exercise, modern dance, dancing in the movies, and folk/ethnic dancing. If you arrange these subheadings in circles around your general subject, you might create a kind of diagram that looks like this:

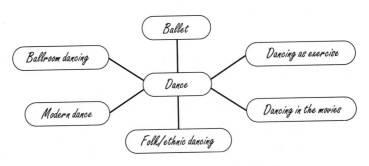

Now write down ideas and details related to these subheadings, and continue in this way until you have run out of ideas. Circle each word or phrase, and draw lines between each of your subheadings and the ideas and details that relate to them. Here's what your paper might look like when you are finished:

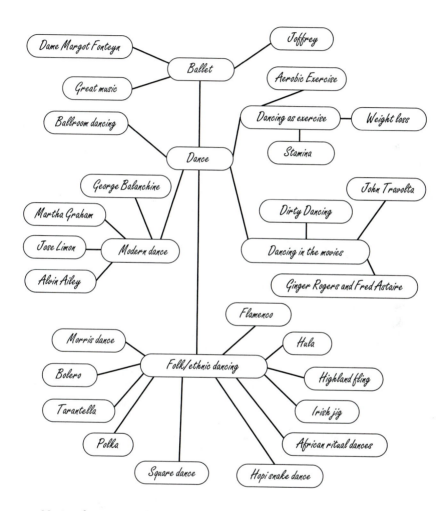

Notice that some subheadings have been given more attention than others. That just means that you may know more or have more to say about folk/ethnic dancing than about ballroom dancing. In fact, then, clustering has helped you focus on the topic that you know most about or that you are most interested in.

Of course, you can stop at this stage, review your notes, and begin planning a preliminary thesis statement (and even an outline) for a paper on ethnic dancing. On the other hand, you might want to focus your topic even further by getting more specific. Let's say you know a lot about African ritual dancing or are interested in learning more about it through some library research. You might then want to extend your clustering by focusing in on that subtopic. Here's what yet another cluster might look like:

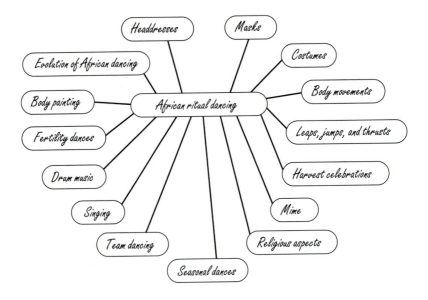

DRAWING A SUBJECT TREE

Still another way to settle on a manageable topic and to gather information is to draw a subject tree. As with clustering, start with a broad subject. Then, divide it into two or three subheadings, or branches. Next, subdivide each of these branches, and so on, until you feel comfortable that your topic is limited enough and that you have enough information to begin writing an outline or a rough draft of your paper. On the next page is an example that begins with "uses of computers" as a general subject.

As you create a subject tree, you will almost naturally put down more details and ideas under subheadings with which you are most familiar or in which you have the greatest interest. For example, the writer who created the subject tree for "uses of computers" would probably feel most comfortable writing about ways in which computers help both students and teachers.

BRAINSTORMING

Unlike most other ways to gather information, brainstorming usually results in a collection of words and phrases scribbled across a page randomly. Another difference is that brainstorming is done with friends or classmates. Using this method, a small group can come up with many more interesting questions and answers about a topic than someone working alone.

You can begin brainstorming in a variety of ways. One of the most effective is to ask journalists' questions. Reporters ask these when they plan their stories: *What happened? When did it happen? Where did it happen? Who was in-*

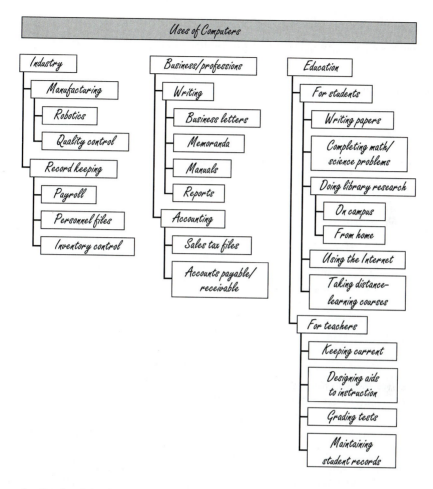

volved? *Why did it happen?* and *How did it happen?* (An easy way to remember the six questions journalists use is to think of them as the 5Ws and the H.)

Questions like those above work best if you want to tell a story or explain how or why something happens or should happen. However, you will probably have to think of different questions if you have other purposes in mind. Say you want to describe your Uncle Charlie. You might ask: What does he look like? How old is he? Who are his friends? Where does he live? What kind of job does he have? In any case, remember that prewriting is also called *invention,* so be creative and invent as many kinds of questions as you like.

Not all the questions you ask will yield useful information. However, the answers to only one or two might suggest ideas and details to other members of your brainstorming group. In a little while, a mental chain reaction will occur, and you will find yourself discussing ideas, facts, and opinions that seem to pop up naturally. Working together, then, you will inspire each other to produce information for a fine journal entry and even for a longer piece of writing based on that entry.

INTERVIEWING

Asking appropriate questions of people who know about your topic is an excellent way to gather detail. Like brainstorming, interviewing gives you other perspectives from which to view your topic, and it often yields information that you might otherwise never have learned.

The kinds of questions you ask should be determined by your purpose. If you are trying to learn why something happened, what someone did, or how something works, for example, you might begin your interview with a group of questions like those journalists rely on and that you read about under Brainstorming. As you just learned, they have to do with the *who, what, when, where, why,* and *how* of a topic. Again, however, you might have to decide on your own set of questions.

Just make sure that the person you interview is knowledgeable about your subject and willing to spend enough time with you to make your interview worthwhile. People who can give you only a few minutes might not be good sources of information. When you make the appointment to meet with the person you want to interview, tell him or her a little about your topic, your purpose, and the kinds of questions you will ask. This will give your subject a chance to think about the interview in advance and prepare thoughtful responses to your questions.

Finally, come to the interview prepared. Think carefully about the questions you need answered ahead of time. Write them down—at least those you feel are most important—in your journal or on a piece of notebook paper. Bring them to the interview, and use them to get your subject talking. If your questions are clear and interesting, you should gather more information than you bargained for. On the other hand, don't get upset if the interview doesn't go exactly as you planned. Your subject might not answer any of your questions but simply discuss ideas as they come to mind. Such interviews sometimes provide a lot of useful information. Just take good notes.

SUMMARIZING

This prewriting method involves condensing another writer's ideas and putting them into your own words. It is especially effective if you want to combine information found in your reading with details you have gathered from your own experiences or from other sources. Just be sure to use your own language throughout the summary. In addition, if you plan to use any of this information in an essay, make certain to tell your readers that it comes from the work of another writer by mentioning the writer's name. For instance, if you decide to summarize Bertrand Russell's "Three Passions I Have Lived For" (a selection in Chapter 1), you might begin: "As Russell explained in his autobiography . . ."

Prewriting: Writing an Outline

After gathering information and deciding on a working central idea, some writers construct an outline for the essay. Although not always necessary, an outline can often make the writing of a working draft of your paper easier. Think of an outline as a sort of a blueprint, which will guide you through the beginning of the drafting process.

For most short essays, an informal or scratch outline is sufficient. However, if you are writing a lengthy essay, such as a library research paper, you might want to use a formal outline, which can also serve as a table of contents. Ask your instructor if you should submit an outline as part of the assignment and, if so, which type is required. In any event, your essay will be more successful if you spend a few minutes constructing a working thesis statement, the central idea of your essay, and then jotting down a scratch outline of the main points you want to make in the body of your essay. (You will learn more about writing thesis statements and developing ideas in the body of your essay in Chapters 1 and 3.)

WRITING A SCRATCH OUTLINE

Let's say you have just reviewed the notes you took when you completed a clustering exercise about African ritual dancing (page 16). Realizing that the most important aspect of what you know about such dancing is that it is dramatic, colorful, and exciting, you decide to write an essay showing this. Your thesis might be: "African ritual dances are the most dramatic, colorful, and exciting folk dances I have ever witnessed."

As you review your notes a second time, you realize that several of the ideas you have put down in your clusters do not relate to your working thesis. For example, the fact that some African dances are seasonal does not relate to—develop or support—your working thesis. So you decide to leave it out and focus on aspects of the dances that are dramatic, colorful, and exciting. Here's what your scratch outline might look like:

> **Working thesis:** African ritual dances, which I observed on my visit to Zimbabwe, are the most dramatic, colorful, and exciting folk dances I have ever seen.
>
> 1. Colorful masks.
> 2. Frightening costumes.
> 3. Bodies painted in bright colors, eye-catching patterns.
> 4. Joyful music.
> 5. Vivid body movements.

As you can see, this scratch outline is no more than a brief list of details—most of them just words and phrases—pulled from the clustering exercise completed earlier. However, it is enough to provide a pattern that the writer can follow to construct a successful first, or working, draft.

WRITING A FORMAL OUTLINE

A formal outline differs from a scratch outline in that it is more complete and more consistent in structure. A formal outline for an essay on African ritual dancing might look like this:

I. Introduction.
    A. Folk dances differ in form and purpose from culture to culture.
    B. Many European and American folk dances reveal much about the cultures in which they originated.
    C. Thesis: African ritual dances, which I observed on my visit to Zimbabwe, are the most dramatic, colorful, and exciting folk dances I have ever seen.
II. Many dancers wear bizarre masks intended to startle and even frighten the audience.
    A. Patterns painted on these masks are varied and vivid.
    B. They take odd shapes and are often very large.
        1. Many are triangular or pointed; others resemble shields used in warfare.
        2. Some triple the size of the wearer's face so as to make him appear monstrous.
        3. Some look like the faces of animals; others suggest that the dancer has come from another planet.
III. The costumes are rich, complex, and colorful.
    A. Some are made of animal skins; others are woven from native vegetable fibers.
    B. All are extremely colorful.
    C. The costumes make great use of fascinating geometric patterns.
    D. Huge headdresses are worn, some resembling the heads of animals.
IV. Drum music gets the heart pounding; the air is sometimes filled with song.
    A. The musicians keep the pace energetic, often adding to the dramatic effect.
    B. A chorus of women singing sweetly often accompanies the dancers.
V. The real spectacle comes in the dancers' acrobatics.
    A. Each dancer conveys a message or vivid story through movement.
    B. Performers run, stomp, and leap high into the air.
    C. Some prance around on huge stilts, standing 15 feet tall.
    D. They even approach members of the audience, pretending to threaten them with lunges and howls.

Though not very long, this formal outline is still quite different from the scratch outline that might be used for this essay:

1. It contains major sections, each of which is subdivided into more specific subheadings. Therefore, it contains far more detail than the scratch outline.
2. Each heading is expressed as a complete sentence. As a result, the writer might be able to use each of these sentences as the topic sentence of the

major paragraphs of the essay. A topic sentence expresses a paragraph's main or central idea. (You will learn more about it in Chapters 1 and 2.)

3. Various sections of the formal outline are identified by number or letter. Notice that the major headings have Roman numerals (I, II, III, IV). These are subdivided into items with capital letters (A, B, C, D), and these are followed by Arabic numerals (1, 2, 3).

4. It is not necessary to divide each major heading into as many subheadings as you divide another. For example, IV is divided into two subheadings, but V is subdivided into four. Sometimes you might want to divide a subheading as in IIB, but you need not do so all the time. Actually, the pattern to follow in a formal outline is straightforward:

I. (Roman numeral)
   A. (Capital letter)
      1. (Arabic numeral)
         a. (Lowercase letter)

5. Notice that each unit in the outline is divided into at least two subunits. If you can't divide a heading into two or more subheadings, leave it alone.

Not	But	Or
I.	I.	I.
A.	A.	II.
II.	B.	
	II.	

Whether you make a scratch or a formal outline, remember that outlines are intended only to guide you through the task of drafting your essay and to get you started. No outline is written in stone. As you begin your first draft, stick to your outline as closely as you can. However, don't be afraid to add new information that pops into your head, make changes in organization, replace or delete parts of the outline, or revise your working thesis. Of course, if you are writing a long paper and want your outline to serve as a table of contents, you will have to revise it to reflect changes you have made. But this can be done after the essay itself has been completed. Just remember that writing is a process of discovery; the deeper you get into it, the better you will understand what you have to say.

The Making of a Student Essay: From Prewriting to Proofreading

The rest of "Getting Started" traces the writing of a full-length essay by Deborah Diglio, who was a first-year nursing student when she wrote it. Diglio's work shows that she sees writing as a process of five important steps:

- Prewriting to gather information.
- Making a scratch outline.
- Writing a working draft.
- Revising the working draft.
- Editing and proofreading.

PREWRITING TO GATHER INFORMATION

The process began when Diglio was inspired by Carl Sandburg's "Child of the Romans," a poem in Chapter 11 about the difficult life of an immigrant laborer. She responded to one of the Suggestions for Journal Entries that recommended using focused freewriting to gather details about a job she once held. Here's what she wrote in her journal about waitressing:

```
People ordering food. The night was going
by fast. Nervous. First nights can be
scarry. Keep a pleasant attitude. I could
do the job easily. Training period over, I
was on my own. I needed this job. We needed
the money. I felt confident, too confident.
I can now laugh at it. Not then. Society
may not place waitressing high on the
social ladder, but you have got to be
surefooted, organized, you have to have a
sense of humor, and a pleasant personality.
You have to be able to learn from your
mistakes. Eventually, I did learn but then
I thought I would die. This old woman left
her walker in the corner. How did I know it
wasn't a tray stand? Still I should have!
Why didn't I just look more closely. Why
did'nt my brain take over. And the old
folks didn't mind. We should look back at
ourselves and laugh sometimes.
```

As you can see, there is no particular order to Diglio's notes, and like most freewriting, it uses quick phrases as much as full sentences. Nonetheless, an event that might make interesting reading is coming through. So is the idea that Diglio learned something from the experience and can now look back at it with a smile.

MAKING A SCRATCH OUTLINE

After discussing her journal entry with her teacher, Diglio decided to tell her story in a full-length essay. She reviewed what she had written in her journal and thought more about the central idea, the point she wanted her essay to make. After adding notes to her original journal entry, she made a scratch outline to organize and begin drafting her essay. Here is her scratch outline for that working draft:

> **Working thesis:** Sometimes, we need to look
>
> back at ourselves and laugh.
>
> **1.** Describe the restaurant, set the stage.
>
> **2.** State the thesis.
>
> **3.** Describe the job.
>
> **4.** Tell what happened that first night:
>
> How well it went first--thought I was a
>
> "born natural."
>
> The old couple and their walker.
>
> I wanted to crawl into a hole.
>
> **5.** What I learned from my mistake.

WRITING A WORKING DRAFT

Diglio used her scratch outline as a blueprint for her first draft. As you will see, each of the paragraphs in that draft corresponds roughly to the five major headings in her scratch outline. However, the act of writing inspired her. As she wrote, more and more details and ideas came to mind, and she included them wherever she could.

All of this goes to prove an important point: an outline—especially a quick, scratch outline—can be used only to get started. You need not be a slave to your outline, and if the act of writing adds brand new details or takes you in a new direction, so be it. Remember, writing is a process of discovery, and good writers can and often do change their minds at many points along the way.

When Diglio stopped writing, she read her draft, a process that helped her recall even more details, which she squeezed in between paragraphs and sentences and in the margins of her paper. The result was messy, so she retyped the working draft as shown below. This is the first version of her paper. It contains more detail and is better written than her journal entry or her outline, but it is only a working draft. (Note: This first draft contains numerous, unacceptable spelling errors. No one would suggest that these are right at any stage, merely that first drafts like this one may have them.)

Waitressing

It was a typical Saturday night. I was standing there, paying no attention to the usual racket of the dinner crowd. The restaurant was crowded. I was waiting for my next table. I try to listen to the sounds around me. I hear the stereo.   1

In come my eight oclock reservation, fifteen minutes late. There is an elderly woman with them. She reminded me of something that happened when I started working there many years before. Recalling that story taught me to look back and laugh at myself.   2

When my second child was born. it became clear that I needed to find a part-time job to help make ends meet. A friend said I should waitress at the restaurant where she worked. I thought about it for a few days. I decided to give it a try. I bluffed my way thru the interview. A new chapter in my life began. Since then, I have learned from many mistakes like the one I am going to   3

describe. My friends told me that, someday,
I would look back and laugh at that night. I
guess after fifteen years that day has come!

I followed another waitress for a few
days and then I was released on my own. All
went well that first week. When Saturday
night came, I had butterflies in my stomache.
I was given four tables not far from the
kitchen. It was an easy station. Oh, God, was
I happy, however I still felt awkward
carrying those heavy trays. Before I new it,
the restaurant was packed resembling mid-day
on wall street. I moved slowly organising
every move. I remember the tray stand in my
station. It looked a little different than
the one I was trained on. It had nice grips
for handles of which made it easier to move
around. I was amazed at how well things were
going. I was too confident. I remember
thinking that I was a born natural. Than,
this jovial looking old man came over, and
taped me on the shoulder, and said "Excuse
me, dear, my wife and I loved watching you
work. It seems your tray stand has been very
handy for you, but we are getting ready to
leave now, and my wife needs her walker
back." I wanted to crawl into a hole and
hide. What a fool I had made of myself. I was
so glad when that night ended.

4

Since then, I have learned from many   5

mistakes such as the one I just described.

REVISING THE WORKING DRAFT

The essay above makes for entertaining reading. But Diglio knew it could be improved, so she revised it *several times* to get to the last draft (but not final version) of her paper, which appears below. Although this draft is not perfect, it is more complete, effective, and polished than the one you just read. Note, again, the unacceptable errors that *must* be corrected in the editing stage.

Lessons Learned

It was a typical Saturday night at   1

Carpaccio's Restaurant. I was standing

there, paying no attention to the usual

merrymaking of the dinner crowd. Just two of

the restaurant's twenty-five tables were

vacant. As I waited for my next table, I

absorbed a few of the sounds around me:

clanging trays, the ringing of the cash

register. I could even hear Dean Martin

belting out a familiar Italian song in the

background.

Finally, in come my eight o'clock party.   2

As they were seated, my attention was drawn

to an elderly woman with a walker slowly

shuffling behind the others. She brought back

a memory I had locked away for fifteen years.

After the birth of my second child, I   3

needed a part-time job to help make ends

meet. A friend suggested I apply for a

waitressing job at a new restaurant where

she worked. I decided to give it a shot. I

bluffed my way through the interview and was hired. A new chapter in my life began the next evening.

After trailing an experience waitress for a few days, I was allowed to wait tables on my own. All went well that first week. When Saturday night came, the butterflies in my stomach were set free. I was given the apprentice station that night, four tables not far from the kitchen. Oh, God, was I relieved, however I still felt awkward carrying the heavy trays.

4

Before I new it, the restaurant was packed; it resembled mid-day on wall street. I moved slowly, organising every step. I remember how impressed I was with the tray stand in my station, it looked different than the one I was trained on. It had nice grip-like handles, of which made it easier to manuver. I was amazed at how well things were going. I began to believe I was a natural at this job.

5

Then, a jovial, old man approached, tapped me on the shoulder, and said, "Excuse me, dear, my wife and I loved watching you work. It seems your tray stand has been very handy for you, but we are getting ready to leave now, and my wife needs her walker back."

6

At first his message did not register.   7
"What was he talking about!" Then, it sank
in. I had set my trays on his wife's
orthopedic walker. I stood there frozen as
ice, but my face was on fire. I wanted to
crawl into a hole; I wanted to hibernate.

Since then, I have learned from many   8
mistakes such as the one I just described. I
have learned to be more observant and more
careful. I have learned to guard against
overconfidence, for no matter how well
things are going, something will come along
eventually to gum up the works. Most of all,
I have learned that the best way to get over
honest embarrassment is to look back and
laugh at yourself.

As this last draft shows, Diglio made several important changes to improve her essay:

1. She changed the title to make her purpose clearer; "Waitressing" didn't say much about the point of her story.

2. She moved the central idea—the point she wants it to make—to the end. This allows her to tell her story first and then to explain its importance in a way that is both clear and interesting. It also makes her conclusion more effective and memorable.

3. She added details to make her writing exact and vivid. Just compare the beginning of each draft. In the later version, Diglio names the restaurant, and she explains that just two of its "twenty-five tables were vacant," not simply that it was "crowded." She even mentions that "Dean Martin [was] belting out a familiar Italian song."

4. She reorganized paragraph 4 into several new paragraphs. Each of these focuses on a different idea, makes a new point, or tells us another part of the story. Thus, the essay becomes easier to read.

5. She removed unnecessary words to eliminate repetition and make her writing more direct.

6. She replaced some words with more exact and interesting substitutes. In paragraph 1, the dinner crowd's "racket" is changed to "merrymaking"; in paragraph 4, "I was happy" becomes "I was relieved."

7. She combined short, choppy sentences into longer, smoother ones to add variety and interest.

8. She corrected some—but not all—problems with spelling, verb tense, punctuation, sentence structure, and mechanics.

EDITING THE FINAL DRAFT

Although Diglio's last version is much better than the draft with which she began, she owed it to her readers to review her paper once more. She wanted to remove annoying errors that could interfere with their appreciation of her work. Using a pencil, a dictionary, and a handbook of college writing skills recommended by her instructor, she corrected problems in grammar, spelling, punctuation, capitalization, and style in her final draft. Here's what just two paragraphs from that draft looked like after she edited them. (If you want to practice you own editing skills, you can go back and correct the rest of Diglio's paper after you review her changes in what follows.)

¶ ⟶

After trailing an experience_d waitress for a   4
few days, I was allowed to wait tables on my
own. All went well that first week. When
Saturday night came, the butterflies in my
stomach were set free. I was given the
apprentice station that night, four tables
not far from the kitchen. Oh, God, was I
relieved/; however, I still felt awkward
carrying the heavy trays.

     Before I _knew it, the restaurant was   5
packed; it resembled mid-day on _Wall _Street.
I moved slowly, organi_zing every step. I
remember how impressed I was with the tray
stand in my station/; it looked different
<s>then</s> ^{from} the one I was trained on. It had nice
grip-like handles, <s>of</s> which made it easier

```
to maneuver. I was amazed at how well things

were going. I began to believe I was a

natural at this job.
```

Of course, an entire paper full of such corrections is too sloppy to submit in a college composition class. Therefore, after correcting her final draft in pencil, Diglio prepared one last, clean copy of her paper. It was this copy that she gave her instructor.

Each person is unique in the way he or she writes. The methods you use to put together a paper may be different from those Deborah Diglio used. They also may be different from the ways your friends or classmates choose to write. And no one says any step outlined above has to be done separately from the others. In fact, some folks revise while they edit. Some continue to gather information as they write their second, third, and even fourth drafts. Nevertheless, writing is serious business. Completing just one or two drafts of an essay will never allow you to produce the quality of work you are capable of. You owe it to your readers and to yourself to respect the process of writing and to work hard at every step in that process, regardless of the way or the order in which you choose to do so. (If you want to learn more about the process of writing, read Richard Marius's "Writing and Its Rewards" in Chapter 2.)

Organization and Development

In "Getting Started" you learned several ways to gather facts, ideas, and opinions about the subjects you choose to write about. Collecting sufficient information about your subject—making sure that you know as much about it as you need to—is an important first step in the writing process.

Next, you will need to determine what it is about your subject that you wish to communicate and how to use your information to get your point across clearly and effectively. Learning how to make such decisions is what the four chapters of Section One are all about.

In Chapter 1 you will learn that two of the most crucial steps early in the writing process are *focusing and limiting* the information you've collected so that you can begin to decide upon a *central idea.* Sometimes referred to as the *main* or *controlling* idea, the central idea of a paragraph or essay expresses the main point its writer wishes to develop.

The process of deciding on a central idea begins with a review of information you collected in your journal through focused freewriting, brainstorming, and the other prewriting techniques explained in "Getting Started." You can then evaluate these details to determine what they say about your subject and to decide exactly what you want to tell your readers about it. Always keep your journal handy. The more information you collect about a subject, the easier it is to find an interesting central idea. Once you have found it, the central idea will help you choose the kinds and amounts of detail needed to develop your writing effectively.

Chapter 2 introduces you to *unity* and *coherence,* two key principles to observe in organizing information. The section on unity explains how to choose details that best accomplish your purpose and relate most directly to your central idea. The section on coherence shows you how to create connections in and between paragraphs to maintain your reader's interest and to make your writing easy to follow.

Chapter 3, "Development," shows you how to determine the amount of detail a paragraph or essay should contain. It also explains ways to arrange these details and develop ideas. Chapter 4, "Introductions and Conclusions," suggests techniques to create effective openings and closings in essays.

The reading selections in Section One contain examples of the important principles of organization and development explained in the chapter introductions. They are also a rich source of interesting topics to develop in your own writing. However, like the other selections in *A Reader for Developing Writers,* each has a value all its own. Whether written by professionals or by college students like you, these paragraphs and essays discuss people, places, or ideas you are sure to find interesting, informative, humorous, and even touching. Here's hoping they will inspire you to continue reading and writing about a variety of subjects, especially those you care about most!

CHAPTER 1

The Central Idea

An important concern for any writer is the ability to organize information in a form that is easy to follow. The best way to do this is to arrange, or focus, the details you've collected around a central idea.

Identifying the Central Idea

The central idea is often called the *main idea* because it conveys the writer's main point. It is also called the *controlling idea,* for it controls (or determines) the kinds and amounts of detail that a paragraph or essay contains.

The central idea is the focal point to which all the other ideas in an essay or paragraph point. Just as you focus a camera by aiming at a fixed point, you focus your writing by making all the details it contains relate directly to the central idea. Everything you include should help prove, illustrate, or support the central idea. You might also think of a central idea as an umbrella. It is the broadest or most general statement in an essay or paragraph; all other information fits under it. The diagrams on page 34 illustrate these two concepts.

Read these next two paragraphs; their central ideas (in italics) act as focal points to which everything else points. Notice that the central ideas are broader than the details that support them.

> *Talk about bad days: today is a classic.* First, I woke up to hear my parents screaming in my ear about a bill I have to pay. Then I went to school to find out I had failed my art project. After that, I called home to learn that I might have my license revoked, and the accident wasn't even my fault. Finally, while walking out of the cafeteria, I tripped over somebody's book bag and made myself look like an ass. And it's only two in the afternoon! (Donna Amiano, "Bad Days")

> *My life is full of risks.* As a stair builder who works with heavy machinery, I risk cutting off a finger or a limb every day. Each Monday and Thursday, I risk four or five dollars on the state lottery. Every time I take my beat-up, 1981 Chevy Caprice Classic for a drive, I risk breaking down. However, the biggest risk I've ever taken was my decision to attend DeVry Institute this year. (Kenneth Dwyer, "Risks")

In most cases the central idea of a paragraph is expressed in a *topic sentence,* and the central idea of an essay is expressed in a *thesis statement.* In some pieces of writing, however, the central idea is so obvious that the author does not need to state it in a formal topic sentence or thesis statement. In

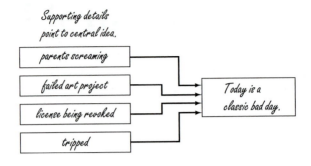

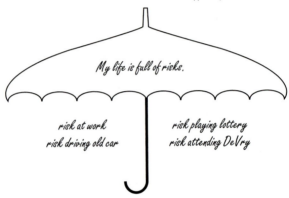

such cases, the central idea is said to be implied. This is often true of narration and description, the kinds of writing you will read in Sections Three and Four. However, it can apply to all types of writing. In this chapter, for example, a paragraph in which the central idea is only implied appears on page 44; it is entitled "The Way We Were."

Nonetheless, as a developing writer, you should always state the central idea outright—as a topic sentence when you write a paragraph or as a thesis statement when you tie several paragraphs together in an essay. Doing so will help you focus on specific ideas and organize information.

Often, authors state the central idea early, placing the topic sentence or thesis at the very beginning of a paragraph or essay. However, this is not always the best place for it. For example, you first might have to give readers explanatory details or background materials. In such cases, you can place your topic sentence or thesis somewhere in the middle or even at the end of a paragraph or essay. Delaying the central idea can also create suspense. Finally, it is a good way to avoid offending readers who at first may be opposed to an opinion you are presenting.

Writing a Preliminary Topic Sentence or Thesis Statement

As a developing writer, make sure you have a good grasp of the central ideas that will control the paragraphs and essays you write. You can do this early in the writing process by jotting down a working version of your central idea on a piece of scratch paper or in your journal. This will be your *preliminary* topic sentence or thesis statement. It is called *preliminary* because you can and often should make significant changes in this version of your topic sentence or thesis statement after you've begun to write your paragraph or essay.

Of course, before you draft a preliminary topic sentence or thesis, you must choose a subject to write about. Keep in mind that by its very nature a subject represents a kind of thinking that is abstract, general, and incomplete. A central idea, on the other hand, is a concrete, specific, and complete expression of thought. For example, notice how much more meaningful the subject "waterskiing" becomes when you turn it into a central idea: "Waterskiing can be *dangerous.*"

To turn any subject into a central idea, whether it winds up as the topic sentence of a paragraph or the thesis of an essay, you will have to *focus* and *limit* your discussion of a subject by saying something concrete and specific about it. Focusing and limiting are important thinking processes that will help you begin to organize the information you've collected about your subject. Here's how they work.

FOCUS YOUR DISCUSSION

A good time to think about focusing on a central idea and drafting a working thesis or topic sentence is immediately after you have reviewed your journal for facts, ideas, and opinions that you gathered through prewriting as explained in "Getting Started." While these important details are still fresh in your mind, ask yourself three questions:

1. *Purpose:* What do I want this piece of writing to accomplish?
2. *Main point:* What is the main point I wish to communicate about my subject?
3. *Details:* What details can I use to develop this main point?

Purpose   As well as you can at this stage in the writing process, determine your purpose—what you want your essay or paragraph to do. For instance, it may be to entertain the reader with a humorous story, to explain a natural process, to compare two types of music, to warn readers of a health hazard, or to convince them to adopt your position on a social issue. You can read more about purpose in "Getting Started."

Once you have determined your purpose, you will be able to decide on your main point more easily, for you will already have begun determining which of the details you have gathered will be useful and which will not.

Let's say your purpose is to describe a forest you hiked through last fall. You review your notes and decide to include details about the colors—brilliant reds, burnt oranges, bright yellows—against which you saw a small herd of white-tailed deer. You also consider describing other things you saw, such as the old truck tire dumped on the side of the trail or the two hunters dressed in green and orange camouflage gear. On the other hand, you decide not to tell readers that you traveled three hours in an old pickup to get there, that you bumped into a high school friend as you were leaving, or that you met a forest ranger who had dated Aunt Bertha. None of these facts describe the forest.

Main Point The next step is to determine exactly what you want to say about your walk through the woods. Ask yourself what for *you* is the most interesting or important aspect of the subject. This will be your *main point,* the point that will help you tie all the details together logically.

In short, you can turn a subject into a central idea by making a main point about the subject. If you decide that the most interesting or important aspect of your walk in the forest is that it was *inspiring,* your central idea might read: "The forest I hiked through this autumn was inspiring."

As you learned earlier, focusing lets the writer turn an abstract, general, incomplete subject into the central idea for a paragraph or essay. Notice how much clearer, more specific, and more complete the central ideas on the right are than the abstract subjects on the left:

Subject	Central Idea
My fall walk in the forest	My fall walk in the forest was inspiring.
Aunt Isabel	Aunt Isabel was a hero.
Rock music	Rock music can damage your hearing.
Electric cars	Electric cars can replace gasoline models.
The Battle of Gettysburg	The Battle of Gettysburg was the turning point of the Civil War.
Homeless children	The government should guarantee homeless children proper nutrition, education, and health care.
The Brooklyn Bridge	The Brooklyn Bridge is an engineering marvel.
The Spanish influenza epidemic of 1917	The Spanish influenza epidemic of 1917 killed more people than did World War I.

As you can see, focusing on a main point helps change an abstract idea into something specific and concrete—into a central idea.

Details   Focusing also provides a starting point for a first draft of an essay because it helps you choose between the details to include and those to discard. If you decide to focus on the inspirational aspects of the forest, for example, you ought to include a description of the changing leaves and of the deer, but should you also mention the old tire and the hunters? They are certainly part of the experience, but do they relate to the notion that your hike was inspirational? Probably not.

LIMIT YOUR DISCUSSION TO A MANAGEABLE LENGTH

Typically, students are asked to write short essays, usually ranging between 250 and 750 words, with paragraphs seldom longer than 75 words. That's why one of the most important things to remember when writing a thesis statement or topic sentence is to limit your central idea as much as you can. Otherwise, you won't be able to develop it in as much detail as will be necessary to make your point clearly, effectively, and completely.

Let's say you are about to buy a car and want to compare two popular makes. In a short essay it would be foolish to compare these automobiles in more than two or three different ways. Therefore, you might limit yourself to cost, appearance, and comfort rather than discuss their performance, handling, and sound systems as well. You might even limit your central idea to only one of these aspects—cost, for instance. You can then divide cost into more specific subsections, which will be easier to organize when it comes time to write your first draft. The thesis for such an essay might read: "I chose the 2001 Mountain Marauder over the 2001 Cross-Country Schooner because it costs less to buy, to operate, and to repair."

SOME TIPS ON WRITING TOPIC SENTENCES AND THESIS STATEMENTS

1. Make sure your topic sentence or thesis is a complete sentence. A complete sentence contains a subject and a verb, and it expresses a complete thought.

   Not: Computers and being a successful college student.
   Or: Using computers to succeed in college.
   Or: How computers can help students succeed in college.
   But: Computers can help students succeed in college.

2. State your main point directly; don't announce it.

   Not: I am going to write about how computers can help students succeed in college.
   Or: This paper will discuss the fact that computers help students succeed in college.
   But: Computers can help students succeed in college.

3. In most cases, readers will naturally assume that what you are writing about is your own opinion or is what you believe. There is no need to explain that.

   Not: I believe that computers can help students succeed in college.

> **Or:** It is my opinion that computers can help students succeed in college.
>
> **But:** Computers can help students succeed in college.

4. Make sure your topic sentence or thesis clearly states the point you want to make about your subject.

> **Not:** Computers affect student performance in college.
>
> **But:** Computers can help students succeed in college.

Controlling Unity and Development

At the beginning of this chapter, you read that the central idea can be called the *controlling idea* because it helps the writer determine the kind and amount of information a paragraph or essay contains. This is explained further in Chapters 2 and 3.

For now, remember that the kinds of details a piece of writing contains determine whether it is unified. A paragraph is unified if its sentences relate directly to its central idea, whether or not that idea is expressed formally in a topic sentence. An essay is unified if its paragraphs relate directly to its central idea, whether or not that idea is expressed in a thesis statement.

The amount of detail a piece of writing contains determines whether it is well developed. A paragraph or essay is well developed if it contains all the detail it needs to prove, illustrate, or otherwise support its central idea.

Revising the Central Idea

One last and very important bit of advice: Always revise the working, or preliminary, versions of your thesis statements and topic sentences during the writing process. Like taking notes or writing a first draft of a paper, writing a preliminary version of a thesis statement or topic sentence is intended only to give you a starting point and a sense of direction. Don't be afraid to reword, edit, or completely rewrite your central idea at any point. Like all processes, writing involves a series of steps or tasks to be completed. However, there is no rule that prevents you from stopping at any point along the way, looking back at what you've done, and changing it as thoroughly and as often as you like. What's more, the process of writing always includes discovery. The more you discover about your subject, the more likely you are to understand it better and to revise what you *thought* you had wanted to say about it.

As an example, study three drafts of the introductory paragraphs from Maria Cirilli's essay "Echoes." Each time she revised her work, Cirilli came to a clearer understanding of her subject and of what she wanted to say about it. This can be seen best in the last sentence, which is Cirilli's thesis statement. A complete version of "Echoes" appears at the end of this chapter.

Cirilli—Draft 1

I hardly remember my grandmother except for the fact that she used to bounce me on her knees by the old-fashioned brick fireplace and sing old songs. I was only four years old when she died. Her face is a faded image in the back of my mind.

In contrast, I remember my grandfather very well. He was 6'4" tall. He possessed a deep voice, which distinguished him from others whether he was in the streets of our small picture-perfect town in southern Italy or in the graciously sculptured seventeenth-century church. He appeared to be strong and powerful. In fact he used to scare all my girlfriends away when they came to play or do homework. <u>Yet, I knew that there was nothing to be afraid of.</u>

Is this thesis clear? Does it tell what the essay will say about Cirilli's grandfather?

Cirilli—Draft 2

I hardly remember my grandmother except for the fact that she used to bounce me on her knees by the old-fashioned brick fireplace and sing old songs. I was only four years old when she died.

The last sentence of draft 1 has been removed.

In contrast, I remember my grandfather very well. He was 6'4" tall, a towering man with broad shoulders and a pair of mustaches that I watched turn from black to grey over the years. He possessed a deep voice, which

Detail added to describe him better.

distinguished him from others whether he was in the streets of our small picture-perfect town in southern Italy or in the graciously sculptured seventeenth-century church. He appeared to be strong and powerful. <u>In fact, he used to scare all my girlfriends away when they came to play or do homework, yet he was the most gentle man I have ever known.</u>

The thesis is clearer. But, will essay also discuss fear?

Cirilli—Draft 3

I hardly remember my grandmother except for the fact that she used to bounce me on her knees by the old-fashioned brick fireplace and sing old songs. I was only four years old when she died. <u>Her face is a faded image in the back of my mind.</u>

Cirilli reuses this sentence from draft 1.

In contrast, I remember my grandfather very well. He was 6'4" tall, a towering man with broad shoulders and a mustache that I watched turn from black to grey. His voice was deep, distinguishing him from others in our small picture-perfect town in southern Italy. To some, my grandfather appeared very powerful, and he used to scare my girlfriends away when they came to play or do homework. <u>In fact, he was strong, but he was the gentlest and most understanding man I have ever known.</u>

Detail about church removed; not needed.

Thesis is expanded; now includes "most understanding."

Thesis stands alone in its own sentence; much clearer.

Practicing Writing Central Ideas

To turn a subject into a central idea, you must express a main point about the subject. In the left column are subjects you might discuss in a paragraph or essay. Turn them into central ideas by writing your main point in the spaces provided. To think of an effective main point, ask yourself what is most interesting or most important about the subject. When you join your subject and main point, be sure to create a complete sentence. A complete sentence has a subject and a verb. The first item is done for you as an example.

┌──────────── **Central Idea** ────────────┐

Subject	Main Point
1. A successful diet	*requires much will power.*
2. College textbooks	
3. Computers	
4. My family	
5. Noise pollution	
6. Listening to music	
7. Professional athletes	
8. AIDS (or another disease)	
9. Learning to drive (swim, play tennis, use a computer, cook, fix cars, etc.)	
10. Studying mathematics (science, accounting, a foreign language, etc.)	

The reading selections that follow illustrate the organizational principles just discussed. Read them carefully, take notes, and respond to the Questions for Discussion and the Suggestions for Journal Entries that accompany them. Doing so will give you an even better understanding of the central idea and its importance to organization.

Four Paragraphs for Analysis

The four paragraphs that follow show the importance of focusing on a central idea. Written by various authors, they discuss four different ideas, but each focuses clearly on a main point developed through detail.

Barbara Dafoe Whitehead is a noted social historian and author. Her writing has appeared in several American magazines and professional journals. Gen X is an abbreviation for Generation X, a term that, roughly speaking, includes people in their late teens to late twenties. "The Girls of Gen X" first appeared in The American Enterprise *magazine (1998).*

Stephen Fox is the author of "The Education of Branch Rickey," one of many essays published in 1995 to mark the fiftieth anniversary of Jackie Robinson's breaking of professional baseball's color barrier. Branch Rickey was the owner of the Brooklyn Dodgers at the time. The paragraph included here is from that essay.

Ernest Albrecht is a professor of English, a drama critic, and the author of two books on the circus.

Lewis Lord writes for U.S. News & World Report. *The paragraph he wrote appeared as part of a history of the year 1000 AD, published in that magazine in the summer of 1999.*

Preparing to Read

1. As the following four paragraphs show, a writer who wants to express a central idea in a topic sentence need not start with that sentence. Depending on the paragraph's purpose, he or she might provide a few sentences of background or explanation first. To create emphasis, a writer might even wait until the end of a paragraph before stating the central idea. In fact, as you will see in Lewis Lord's paragraph from "The Way We Were," sometimes writers choose not to express central ideas in a topic sentence at all. Instead, they allow readers to draw their own conclusions. In such cases the central idea is said to be "implied."

2. As you read the first sentence of paragraph 1, try to identify Whitehead's main point. Keep this in mind as you read the details in the rest of the paragraph, which relate to that point.

3. Paragraphs 2, 3, and 4 contain several personal and place names, such as Branch Rickey, Brooklyn Dodgers, Jackie Robinson, Madison Square Garden, and Roman Empire. Be on the lookout for them. If you are unsure about what they contribute to the meaning of the paragraph, look them up in an encyclopedia or on the Internet. In fact, if you have never heard of these people or places, look them up now.

Vocabulary

adolescence (noun)	The stage of growth between childhood and maturity, roughly from 10 to 18 years.
binge (adjective)	Excessive, uncontrolled.
controversial (adjective)	Causing disagreement; disputable, arguable.
debris (noun)	Waste, litter.
depression (noun)	A psychological disorder in which the patient feels sad, hopeless.
dialects (noun)	Various forms of the same language.
enigmatic (adjective)	Puzzling, mysterious.
harbinger (noun)	Sign of things to come, forerunner.
hippodrome (noun)	Arena for horses.
innovate (verb)	Invent, create something new.
lathe (noun)	Machine for shaping wood.
millennium (noun)	One thousand years, ten centuries.
novel (adjective)	New.
ordeals (noun)	Trials.
relics (noun)	What's left of, remnants.
roustabouts (noun)	Workers, laborers.
venereal (adjective)	Relating to sexual indulgence, most commonly as in a disease resulting from sexual contact.
replete with (adjective)	Full of.
wary	Careful, cautious.

The Girls of Gen X

Barbara Dafoe Whitehead

ALL IS NOT well with the women of Generation X. Consider the evidence: Close to 40 percent of college women are frequent binge drinkers, a behavior related to date rapes and venereal disease. Young women suffer higher levels of depression, suicidal thoughts and attempts than young men from early adolescence on. Between 1980 and '92, the rate of completed suicides more than tripled among white girls and doubled among black girls. For white women between 15 and 24, suicide is the third leading cause of death.

The Example of Jackie Robinson*

Stephen Fox

FIFTY YEARS ago this fall, Branch Rickey announced that Jackie Robinson had signed a contract to play with the Brooklyn Dodgers organization, thus breaking the "color line" that had kept African-Americans out of white organized baseball in the 20th century. With that single stroke, the crafty, enigmatic 63–year-old white man and the wary, explosive 26-year-old black man helped spark a social revolution. Intensely controversial at the time, the signing of Robinson now seems a harbinger of the postwar civil-rights movement: three years before the integration of the armed forces, nine years before the Supreme Court's *Brown* decision, ten years before the Montgomery, Alabama, bus boycott.

Sawdust

Ernest Albrecht

AS A TEN year old, I watched as miniature mountains of the magical debris took shape around my father's lathe or his table saw, and with hardly any effort at all I imagined three rings and a hippodrome track sprinkled with the stuff in various colors. Having once conjured that, it didn't take much more effort to envision the ropes and cables that the circus roustabouts spun into a fantastic web transforming the old Madison Square Garden on Eighth Avenue and 49th Street (New York) into an exotic world of wonder and fantasy. That is why, of all the changes that progress has wrought upon the circus, I lament the loss of the sawdust the most. Rubber mats may be practical, but they have no magic.

The Way We Were

Lewis Lord

ONE MILLENNIUM AGO, the best roads in Europe were several centuries old, the neglected relics of the Roman Empire. Most routes were so bad that the well-to-do chose to travel by horseback. Only the poor and sick bumped along in wagons. Perhaps 19 of every 20 people lived in villages, typically surrounded by forests replete with wolves, bears, and outlaws. The outside world was everything beyond the village fence, and local dialects often could not be understood by people residing only a few miles away. Generations of

---

*Editor's title.

villagers lived their 30 or 40 years unaware of important events elsewhere: floods, wars, and deaths of popes, kings, and emperor. Few ever saw a single thing that was both significant and novel. With learning scorned, hardly anyone knew how to innovate. What existed was deemed God's way, and those who dared change it risked suspicion and possible ordeals by fire and water to prove their innocence.

Questions for Discussion

1. What are the topic sentences in the first three paragraphs?
2. What in your own words is the central idea of Lord's paragraph from "The Way We Were"?
3. Would "The Girls of Gen X" have been as effective and easy to read had the topic sentence appeared in the middle of the paragraph? At the end of the paragraph?
4. What important information does Fox provide before the topic sentence in "The Example of Jackie Robinson"?
5. What is the main point of "Sawdust?" Why does Albrecht wait until the end of the paragraph to reveal it"?

Thinking Critically

Remember that a central idea acts as an umbrella under which all the details and other, more limited, ideas in a paragraph or essay fit. The central idea for the following paragraph is unstated. Read the paragraph; then, in your journal, write your own central idea for it in a complete topic sentence. Remember, the idea in a topic sentence is broader than any other idea in a paragraph.

> The planet Mars takes its name from the Roman god of war. Mercury is the Roman god of commerce; and Venus, the goddess of love. Pluto is named for the Greek god of the underworld, Neptune rules the sea, and Jupiter reigns as king of the gods. Even the planets Saturn and Uranus borrow their names from ancient deities.

Suggestion for a Journal Entry

This journal entry is in three parts:

First, pick a limited subject you know a lot about. Here are some examples: waiting on tables, last year's Fourth of July picnic, your bedroom at home, feeding a baby, your car, studying math, your Uncle Mort, going to a concert, watching baseball on television.

Second, decide what are the most interesting or important points you can make about that subject. Choose *one* of these as the main point of a central idea. Write that central idea down in the form of a topic sentence for a paragraph you might want to write later.

Third, do the same with three or four other limited subjects you know about. Here's what your journal entry might look like when you're done:

1. **Limited subject:** Feeding a baby
   Main points: Sometimes messy, always fun
   Topic sentence: Feeding a baby can be messy.

2. **Limited subject:** Uncle Mort
   Main points: Old, handsome, outgoing, considerate
   Topic sentence: My Uncle Mort was one of the most considerate people in my family.

3. **Limited subject:** Last year's Fourth of July picnic
   Main points: Much food, many people, lots of rain
   Topic sentence: Last year's Fourth of July picnic was a washout.

Still on the Point

George Bush

George Bush (1924–) served as U.S. ambassador to the United Nations, ambassador to China, director of the Central Intelligence Agency, vice president of the United States under Ronald Reagan, and forty-first president of the United States from 1989 to 1993. During his administration, the United States invaded Panama and removed the government of Manuel Noreiga, a corrupt dictator involved in the illicit drug trade. Bush also sent troops to the Persian Gulf to lead a successful international alliance against the aggression of Iraq's Saddam Hussein, whose army had occupied Kuwait. The following essay appeared in Newsweek *shortly before Bush spoke along with several other American presidents at a meeting in Philadelphia in 1997 to launch a nationwide campaign for volunteers to help solve problems facing America's youth.*

Preparing to Read

1. During the Panama and the Persian Gulf campaigns, General Colin Powell served as chairman of the Joint Chiefs of Staff.

2. At the 1988 Republican convention, Bush accepted his party's nomination for president with a speech that emphasized the role citizen volunteers can play in helping others and in addressing many important social problems. He referred to such volunteers as "a thousand points of light." Think about the meaning of "point" as Bush used it in his speech and in this essay.

Vocabulary

bickering (noun)	Squabbling, arguing in a petty way.
cynical (adjective)	Suspicious, scornful, skeptical.
commitment (noun)	A desire to fulfill a pledge, keep a promise, or meet an obligation.
nonpartisan (adjective)	Impartial, neutral, not supporting a particular political party or philosophy.
plague (verb)	To trouble, attack, harass.
transcends (verb)	Goes beyond.

Still on the Point

George Bush

COLIN POWELL and I have been in battle together before—we're old com- 1
rades in arms, from Panama to the Gulf. Now, with the general's heart-
felt, nonpartisan leadership, America is opening a new front at home: volunteer service to help save a generation of young people. It's a campaign
founded on the fact that more and more people are realizing that the answers
to our kids' problems—illiteracy, fatherless families, teenage pregnancy,
drugs, whatever—lie not in Washington but in our own neighborhoods. Barbara Bush likes to say that what happens in your house is more important
than what happens in the White House, and she's right.

Volunteerism isn't an excuse for government to be completely rolled 2
back. But the public sector can't do it all—the old view was that if a federal
program didn't work, double the spending and see if it will work then. That's
not the way to do things. When I was in the White House, some critics used
to charge that our emphasis on "a thousand points of light" was just a dodge,
a way of saying that encouraging volunteerism could justify spending cuts.
That wasn't the case at all: our thinking then, and the philosophy behind the
Philadelphia Summit, is that fixing the country requires our time, not just our
tax dollars. It takes both. Somewhere in the country at this very minute the
problems that plague us nationally are being solved at a local level through
volunteers.

People sometimes say, "Well, George Bush, he's a man of privilege— 3
what does he know about real-life problems?" It's true that I was blessed.
During the Depression, if we'd gotten sick, my dad could have paid the hospital bills. And I was given a good education. But I was more blessed in a
different way: that my mother and dad taught us that no life is complete unless you serve others. Following their example, I became what you might call
a tiny point of light: headed up the United Negro College Fund Drive at
Yale, pitched in to start a YMCA in Midland, Texas. Barbara's passion is family literacy.

So many Americans share this commitment to help out. It transcends 4
politics—people are tired of the bickering, and there's a crying need for less
partisanship. But no matter what the media (they sometimes seem to live for
conflict) tells you, don't be cynical about the gathering in Philadelphia. It's
not about sweeping promises and no follow-through: it's about going to work
in our hometowns.

I hope that the fact that presidents of very different political views and 5
experiences—me, President Clinton, and former Presidents Reagan, Carter,
and Ford—are coming together to back this wonderful movement will send a
signal that this is more than politics. This is serious stuff. It's about service,
the future, and our children's well-being. Nothing could be more serious. Or
more important.

Questions for Discussion

1. Bush expresses the essay's central idea in the first paragraph. Find the essay's thesis statement.
2. Explain how the ideas in paragraphs 2, 3, and 4 relate to and support the thesis.
3. Where in this essay does Bush restate his thesis? Why does he restate it?
4. What is the purpose of this essay? In what paragraph or paragraphs does Bush make that purpose most clear?

Thinking Critically

1. Write a short paragraph in which you answer the following question: Why does Bush talk about his wife, Barbara, his childhood, and his own volunteer service?
2. Do you agree with Bush that "the public sector can't do it all" (paragraph 2)? Write down your reasons for agreeing or disagreeing.
3. Make a list of problems affecting young people that you think the private sector (volunteers, families, businesses, etc.) and not the government should solve. Then make a list of such problems that you believe only government can solve.

Suggestions for Journal Entries

1. Bush is committed to the idea of volunteerism, and so he can make an impassioned and convincing plea for our taking up the challenge. Think of a cause or an activity that you are committed to, believe in, or wish to recommend to others. Then, list some reasons why you support this cause or activity. Here are two examples of what your journal entry might look like:

Activity	Reasons for Support
Volunteering at a homeless shelter	Makes me appreciate what I have. Teaches me humility. Makes me more tolerant of others. Introduces me to new friends. Allows me to help my community.
Swimming	Provides a good aerobic workout. Strengthens the heart and lungs. Is inexpensive. Is fairly safe. Helps keep my weight down.

2. Review the list you made for suggestion 1. Then write two sentences, each of which summarizes *all or most* of the reasons you think the activity you are writing about is worth pursuing. You may want to make one of these the working thesis statement (statement of a central idea) of an essay you write later. Remember that a thesis contains a subject and expresses a main point about that subject. For example, for the subjects above you might write:

Subject	**Main Point**
Volunteering at a homeless shelter	has enriched my life.
Swimming	is a practical way to stay in shape.

You probably recall reading on page 34 that a central idea can be compared to an umbrella. Well, the main points being made about these two subjects summarize or include all of the reasons in the lists above. In other words, these main points act as umbrella statements under which all those reasons can be placed.

Remember: A thesis statement must be a complete sentence. Make sure that it has a subject and verb and that it expresses a complete idea.

Suffering
Siu Chan

Siu Chan was born in Cambodia of Chinese parents. Her father owned a small business in Phnom Penh, the capital, where Siu lived with her parents and her five brothers and sisters. In 1975 her life changed drastically. That was the year that the Khmer Rouge, the movement headed by communist leader Pol Pot, took control of the country. The atrocities committed by this group resulted in the extermination of millions of native Cambodians and other people with millions more displaced from their homes and sent to live in work camps. In fact, the communists nearly evacuated the city of Phnom Penh and redistributed the people in rural areas.

This essay tells of Siu Chan's experience during the four years she lived under the tyranny of the Khmer Rouge. In 1979, she and three younger brothers and sisters escaped from Cambodia into Vietnam traveling by bus, boat, bicycle, and on foot. They spent five years in Vietnam before immigrating to the United States, where an uncle who sponsored them was waiting. Today, Siu works two jobs to help support her family and attends college part-time, hoping to major in accounting. As she explained to her writing instructor, she works seven days a week and has not had a day off in over three years.

Preparing to Read

1. Chan states a thesis in her first paragraph. It contains three main points. Make sure you understand each before going on to the rest of the essay.

2. This is a five-paragraph essay. Paragraph 1 is the introduction, with the essay's thesis statement. Each of the three main points in Chan's thesis is the basis for the topic sentence you will find in each body paragraph—2, 3, and 4. Paragraph 5 is the essay's conclusion.

3. Think about the significance of Chan's title. Doing so makes reading her essay easier.

4. The horrors that the Khmer Rouge created in Cambodia are documented in *The Killing Fields*, a film that you can find on videotape.

Vocabulary

authorities (noun)	People in charge.
craved (verb)	Desired.
malnutrition (noun)	Lack of proper food, inadequate diet.
nourishment (noun)	Proper food, sustenance.
tyranny (noun)	Oppression, dictatorship.

Suffering

Siu Chan

WHENEVER I THINK about the word "suffering," the first thought that comes 1
to mind is the time I lived under the dictatorship of the Khmer Rouge
from 1975 though 1979 in my homeland of Cambodia. It was the worst time
in my life: I was allowed very little personal freedom, I witnessed the death of
my family, and I nearly died of starvation.

Starting in 1975, when the communists under Pol Pot took over, the 2
government destroyed nearly all personal freedom. Families were split apart,
with each member being forced to live separately. Even my two-year-old
brother was taken away to live with a group of children the same age. We
were never able to visit each other, and when my parents passed away I
wasn't even able to see them for a final goodbye. In addition, the communists
forced me into slave labor. I got up at 3:00 AM every day, sometimes to work
on a road-building project for which I carried water and earth and sometimes
to dig a hole for an artificial pond. Our work day sometimes ended at 11:00 PM.
Moreover, I was allowed to speak only one language: Cambodian. At home,
we had spoken Chinese. The authorities would not allow any criticism of the
government, and I had to be very careful about what I said and did. Otherwise, they would kill me.

During those four years, I lost six members of my family. First my grand- 3
parents passed away about two months apart. They were old and ill. Because
my country had experienced war and tyranny for many years, they could not
get the medicines they needed. Approximately four months later, my uncle
died; he was overworked and did not have enough food to eat, so he became
ill. There was no medicine to help him either. One year later, my little
brother died after suffering from a fever for one full week. Again, no medication was available. After another six months, my parents also died one month
apart. They starved to death.

I had to eat food that the communist government gave me whether it was 4
good or not. Usually it was just plain white rice, sometimes with a few wild
vegetables mixed in, but it was never enough to fill me up. I can still remember a three-month period during which I nearly starved to death. The rice
crop had failed because of flooding, so I had to go into the woods to search
for tree roots and other wild foods. But they satisfied me only temporarily,
and they did not have enough nourishment to keep me healthy. I began to
suffer from malnutrition, and my body became swollen. In fact, I was so hungry for real food that I sometimes burst into tears. I craved food all the time. I
even dreamt about it. I would have been very satisfied with only a bowl of
plain rice or a slice of bread.

Throughout those four years, I suffered a great deal. I cannot find the ap- 5
propriate words to describe that horror. However, having gone through it, I
can appreciate the life I have now. My spirit and my mind get stronger each
day. I learned not to waste anything—especially food—when I was in Cam-

bodia, and I am doing well in the United States. I work hard and I have even started going to college. What's more I feel confident about the future. My suffering has prepared me to face any obstacle.

Questions for Discussion

1. What is Chan's thesis? What are the three main points found in that thesis?
2. Identify each of the topic sentences Chan uses in paragraphs 2, 3, and 4.
3. Explain how the details in paragraphs 2, 3, and 4 relate to their topic sentences.

Thinking Critically

1. Why do you think the authorities allowed people to speak only Cambodian?
2. What questions might you ask Chan if you had the opportunity? Write those questions in the margins.
3. Compare the structure of this essay with the structure of Russell's "Three Passions I Have Lived For," which follows.

Suggestions for Journal Entries

1. Recall a personal experience in which your freedom was limited and/or your well-being was threatened because of the power someone had over you. Use clustering, a subject tree, or listing to record details.
2. Recall a battle with serious illness from which you or someone you know well suffered. What caused it? What were its symptoms? What kind of suffering did it cause? Was the illness ever overcome? How?

Three Passions I Have Lived For

Bertrand Russell

One of the most widely read philosophers and mathematicians of the twentieth century, Bertrand Russell (1872–1970) is even better remembered as a social and political activist. For many years, he was considered an extremely unorthodox thinker because of his liberal opinions on sex, marriage, and homosexuality. Politically, Russell was a socialist and pacifist. In the 1950s and 1960s he became one of the leaders of the ban-the-bomb movement in Europe, and later he helped organize opposition to U.S. involvement in Vietnam.

Among his most famous works are Principles of Mathematics, A History of Western Philosophy, *and a three-volume autobiography in which the selection that follows first appeared. Russell won the Nobel Prize in literature in 1950.*

Preparing to Read

1. The first paragraph contains Russell's thesis. Read it carefully; it will give you clues about the topic sentences on which he develops three of the paragraphs that follow.

2. The word *passions* should be understood as deep, personal concerns that Russell developed over the course of his life and that had a significant influence on the way he lived.

Vocabulary

abyss (noun)	Deep hole.
alleviate (verb)	Lessen, soften, make less harsh or painful.
anguish (noun)	Grief, sorrow, pain.
consciousness (noun)	Mind, intelligence.
mockery (noun)	Ridicule, scorn.
prefiguring (adjective)	Predicting, forecasting.
reverberate (verb)	Resound, repeatedly echo.
unfathomable (adjective)	Unmeasurable.
verge (noun)	Edge.

Three Passions I Have Lived For

Bertrand Russell

THREE PASSIONS simple, but overwhelmingly strong, have governed my life: the longing for love, the search for knowledge, and unbearable pity for the suffering of mankind. These passions, like great winds, have blown me hither and thither, in a wayward course over a deep ocean of anguish, reaching to the very verge of despair. 1

I have sought love, first, because it brings ecstasy—ecstasy so great that I would often have sacrificed all the rest of my life for a few hours of this joy. I have sought it, next, because it relieves loneliness—that terrible loneliness in which one shivering consciousness looks over the rim of the world into the cold unfathomable lifeless abyss. I have sought it, finally, because in the union of love I have seen, in a mystic miniature, the prefiguring vision of the heaven that saints and poets have imagined. This is what I sought, and though it might seem too good for human life, this is what—at last—I have found. 2

With equal passion I have sought knowledge. I have wished to understand the hearts of men. I have wished to know why the stars shine. . . . A little of this, but not much, I have achieved. 3

Love and knowledge, so far as they were possible, led upward toward the heavens. But always pity brought me back to earth. Echoes of cries of pain reverberate in my heart. Children in famine, victims tortured by oppressors, helpless old people a hated burden to their sons, and the whole world of loneliness, poverty, and pain make a mockery of what human life should be. I long to alleviate the evil, but I cannot, and I too suffer. 4

This has been my life. I have found it worth living, and would gladly live it again if the chance were offered me. 5

Questions for Discussion

1. The title gives us a clue about why Russell wrote this selection. What was his purpose?

2. Russell expresses the central idea—the thesis—in paragraph 1. What is his thesis?

3. In your own words, explain each of the central ideas—topic sentences—in paragraphs 2, 3, and 4. In other words, what three passions did Russell live for?

4. How do these three passions relate to the thesis?

5. What details does Russell use to develop the topic sentence in paragraph 2? In paragraph 3? In paragraph 4? Explain how these details relate to their topic sentences in each case.

6. You've learned in this chapter how to limit your discussion to a manageable length. In what ways did Russell make sure to limit his essay's length?

Thinking Critically

Russell lists reasons for seeking love and knowledge. What *other* reasons might someone have for seeking them? In your journal, write a paragraph of between 50 and 100 words explaining why you are seeking love or knowledge, or are pursuing some other personal passion. Focus on only one of these. Start your paragraph with a topic sentence modeled after the ones Russell uses.

Suggestions for Journal Entries

1. In your own words, summarize the three reasons Russell has "sought love."

2. In Preparing to Read you read that Russell used the word *passions* to describe the deep, personal concerns that determined the way he lived. Using Russell's essay as a model, write a series of topic sentences for paragraphs that describe the passions—at least three of them—that *you* live for. The kinds of passions you mention should be personal and real. Remember to limit each topic sentence to one and only one passion. If you're embarrassed to write about yourself, write about someone else's passions. Here are some examples:

    One of the most important concerns in my life is getting a good education.

    My religion is the cornerstone of my existence.

    My brother lives to eat.

    My grandmother's most important concern was her children.

    Mother Teresa's sole purpose in life was to serve the poor.

Echoes
Maria Cirilli

Born in a small town in southern Italy, Maria Cirilli immigrated to the United States in 1971. She earned her associate's degree in nursing from a community college and is now an assistant head nurse at the Robert Wood Johnson University Hospital in New Brunswick, New Jersey. Cirilli has completed her bachelor's in nursing from the University of Medicine and Dentistry of New Jersey. Since writing "Echoes" for a college composition class, she has revised it several times to add detail and make it more powerful.

Preparing to Read

1. Cirilli chose not to reveal the central idea of this essay—her thesis statement—in paragraph 1. However, the first paragraph is important because it contains information that we can contrast with what we read in paragraph 2.
2. The two main points in the thesis (paragraph 2) are important because they give us clues about the topic sentences in the body paragraphs, which follow.

Vocabulary

distinguishing (adjective) Making different from.
exuberance (noun) Joy, enthusiasm.
manicured (adjective) Neat, well cared for.
mediator (noun) Referee, someone who helps settle disputes.

negotiating (adjective) Bargaining, dealing.
placate (verb) Pacify, make calm.
siblings (noun) Sisters and brothers.
solemnly (adverb) Seriously.
tribulation (noun) Trouble, distress.
vulnerable (adjective) Open, without defenses.
with a vengeance (adverb) Skillfully, earnestly.

Echoes

Maria Cirilli

I HARDLY REMEMBER my grandmother except for the fact that she used to 1
bounce me on her knees by the old-fashioned brick fireplace and sing old
songs. I was only four when she died. Her face is a faded image in the back of
my mind.

In contrast, I remember my grandfather very well. He was 6'4" tall, a 2
towering man with broad shoulders and a mustache that I watched turn from
black to grey. His voice was deep, distinguishing him from others in our
small picture-perfect town in southern Italy. To some, my grandfather appeared very powerful, and he used to scare my girlfriends away when they
came to play or do homework. In fact, he was strong, but he was the gentlest
and most understanding man I have ever known.

I still see him weeping softly as he read a romantic novel in which his fa- 3
vorite character died after many trials and much tribulation. And I will never
forget how carefully he set the tiny leg of our pet bird, Iario, who had become
entangled in a fight with frisky Maurizio, our cat. Once, my brother and I accompanied him to our grandmother's grave at a nearby cemetery that was
small but manicured. As we approached the cemetery, my tall grandfather
bent down from time to time to pick wild flowers along the road. By the end
of the journey, he had a dandy little bouquet, which he placed solemnly at
my grandmother's grave while bountiful tears streamed down his husky, vulnerable face.

My grandfather was always available to people. Mostly, he helped senior 4
citizens apply for disability or pension benefits or file medical-insurance
claims. Several times, however, he was asked to placate siblings who had
quarreled over a family inheritance. Many angry faces stormed into our home
dissatisfied with what they had received, but they usually left smiling, convinced by my grandfather that their parents had, after all, distributed their
possessions fairly.

At times, he could even play Cupid by resolving disputes between cou- 5
ples engaged to be married. Whether the problem concerned which family
would pay for the wedding or who would buy the furniture, he would find a
solution. As a result, our family attended many weddings in which my proud
grandfather sat at the table of honor.

On Sundays, there was always a tray of fresh, homemade cookies and a 6
pot of coffee on our oversized kitchen table for visitors who stopped by after
Mass. Seeking advice about purchasing land or a house, they asked my
grandfather if he thought the price was fair, the property valuable, the land
productive. After a time, he took on the role of mediator, negotiating with a
vengeance to obtain the fairest deal for both buyer and seller.

I remember most vividly the hours we children spent listening to our 7
grandfather's stories. He sat by the fireplace in his wooden rocking chair and

told us about the time he had spent in America. Each one of us kids would aim for the chair closest to him. We didn't want to miss anything he said. He told us about a huge tunnel, the Lincoln Tunnel, that was built under water. He also described the legendary Statue of Liberty. We were fascinated by his stories of that big, industrialized land called America.

As I grew up and became a teenager, I dreamt of immigrating to America and seeing all the places that my grandfather had talked about. His exuberance about this land had a strong influence on my decision to come here.

8

A few months before I arrived in America my grandfather died. I still miss him very much, but each time I visit a place that he knew I feel his presence close to me. The sound of his voice echoes in my mind.

9

Questions for Discussion

1. What important information does Cirilli give us in paragraph 1?
2. What is her thesis? Why does she wait until paragraph 2 to reveal it?
3. Pick out the topic sentences in paragraphs 4 through 7, and explain what each tells us about Cirilli's grandfather.
4. What evidence does the author give to show that her grandfather was "gentle?" How does she prove he was "understanding?"
5. What about the fact that Cirilli's grandfather scared her girlfriends? Why does the author give us this information?
6. Why is "Echoes" a good title for this essay?

Thinking Critically

1. Reread the three drafts of Cirilli's introduction, which appear earlier in this chapter (pages 39 and 40). Then, in your journal, write a paragraph that explains the major differences you see among the versions. Use the notes in the margins as guides, but write the paragraph in your own words. If you read carefully, you will find even more differences than those described in the margins.
2. Cirilli tells us that her grandmother's "face is a faded image in the back of [her] mind." Why did she put this line back into the third version after taking it out of the second (page 39)? Explain in two or three sentences why keeping this line is important to Cirilli's essay.

Suggestions for Journal Entries

1. Use focused freewriting to gather information that shows that someone you know practices a particular virtue. Like Cirilli's grandfather, your subject might be gentle or understanding. Then again, he or she might

be charitable, hardworking, generous, or considerate of others. Reread paragraph 3 or 4 in "Echoes" to get an idea of the kind of details you might put in your journal. After completing your entry, read it carefully and add details if you can. Finally, write a sentence that expresses the main point you have made and that might serve as a topic sentence to a paragraph using this information.

2. Think of someone special in your life, and write down a wealth of details about this person. Use brainstorming, interviewing, or any other information-gathering techniques discussed in "Getting Started." Then, discuss this special person in three or four well-written sentences. Like the topic sentences in "Echoes," each of yours should focus on only one main point you want to make about your subject or about your relationship with this person.

Suggestions for Sustained Writing

1. Recall what you have read about writing central ideas at the beginning of this chapter: a central idea contains a subject and makes a point about that subject, a point that is focused and specific. Think about a subject you know a great deal about. Then write four or five sentences that express different points about that subject. Let's say your subject is Thanksgiving dinner. You might write the following central ideas:

Subject	Main Point
Thanksgiving dinner at my house	is always very noisy.
In my family, Thanksgiving dinner	means eating a lot and watching football.
Our Thanksgiving dinners	are not very traditional.
A typical Thanksgiving dinner	can kill a diet.
Preparing a Thanksgiving dinner	takes a lot of work.

Next, use each of these sentences as the topic sentence for a different paragraph. When you write each paragraph, remember to include details that support or explain the paragraph's central idea as expressed in its topic sentence. Here's what one of the paragraphs you are going to write might look like:

Preparing a Thanksgiving dinner takes a lot of work. First you'll have to prepare the stuffing. This means peeling and cutting up the apples, chopping up and soaking the bread, mixing in the raisins and the spices. After you're done, you'll have to stuff the turkey with this gooey mixture. While you're waiting for the bird to roast, you should peel, boil, and mash the potatoes, and cook any other vegetables you will serve. You'll also have to bake the biscuits, set the table, pour the cider, and put the finishing touches on the pumpkin and apple pies you spent three hours preparing the night before.

As you learned in "Getting Started," don't be satisfied with the first draft of your work; rewrite it several times. Then, correct spelling, grammar, punctuation, and other distracting problems.

2. If you haven't done so already, complete the Suggestion for a Journal Entry after "Four Paragraphs for Analysis." Use *each* of the topic sentences you were asked to write as the beginning of a paragraph in which you explain the main point you are making in that topic sentence. You should wind up with the rough drafts of four or five paragraphs, each of which is several sentences long.

Rewrite these rough drafts until you are satisfied that your topic sentences are clear and that you have included enough information to help your readers understand the main point in each paragraph easily. Complete the writing process by editing your work just as student writer Deborah Diglio did with her paper in "Getting Started."

3. If you haven't completed both of the Suggestions for Journal Entries for George Bush's "Still on the Point," do so now. If you have completed these assignments, read your journal notes carefully.

Write an essay that uses one of the sentences you wrote for suggestion 2 as its thesis statement. You will recall that you wrote two sentences summarizing the reasons you think a particular activity you engage in is worth pursuing.

A good way to start outlining the essay is to express each of the reasons you like this activity in its own sentence. These sentences can then become the topic sentences of your body paragraphs. Here's what an outline for such an essay might look like:

Working thesis/introduction:	Volunteering at a homeless shelter has enriched my life.
Topic sentence/paragraph 2:	It has made me appreciate what I have.
Topic sentence/paragraph 3:	Working with the homeless has taught me humility.
Topic sentence/paragraph 4:	Through this experience I have learned to tolerate those different from me.
Topic sentence/paragraph 5:	It has enabled me to make many new friends.

Try one or more of the several prewriting techniques that you read about in "Getting Started" to gather details to use in developing each of your essay's body paragraphs. Remember to write several drafts of your paper. Before you hand it in, make sure to edit and proofread carefully.

4. Have you ever lived under the tyranny of a government, organization, or person? If so, explain how this experience affected you in two or three ways. Like Siu Chan, ("Suffering," page 51) begin your essay with an introductory paragraph that contains a thesis statement. Make sure that the two or three main points in this thesis statement express the effects that living under this oppression caused you. Then, make these main points the basis of the topic sentences you use in your essay's body paragraphs. Again, use Chan's essay as your model.

    Begin by reviewing the notes you made in your journal after reading Chan's essay. They might provide you with materials with which you can get started. Then, do some more prewriting to gather even more information. Next, write a preliminary thesis statement, which might appear in your introductory paragraph. Also write a preliminary or working topic sentence for each of your essay's body paragraphs. Again, base each topic sentence on one of the main points stated in your thesis. Next, make a rough outline of your essay.

    Write a rough draft and several revisions of your essay. Don't be afraid to revise your working thesis and topic sentences if you need to. End your essay with a conclusion, such as the one Chan used. Finally, edit and proofread the whole paper carefully.

5. In "Three Passions I Have Lived For," Bertrand Russell explains three deep, personal concerns that have "governed" his life. If you responded to item 2 in the Suggestions for Journal Entries following this essay, you have probably written a few topic sentences about the passions you or someone you know well lives for.

    Use each of your topic sentences as the basis or beginning of a fully developed paragraph about each of these passions. Next, take the main points expressed in your topic sentences and combine them into a sentence that might serve as the thesis statement to an essay made up of the paragraphs you have just written.

    Refer to Russell's essay as a model. Remember that his thesis statement mentions three passions: "the longing for love, the search for knowledge, and unbearable pity for the suffering of mankind." These three passions are used individually as the main points in each of the topic sentences of the paragraphs that follow and develop his thesis.

    You should end up with the draft of an essay that contains a thesis statement followed by a few paragraphs, each of which develops one of the points mentioned in that thesis. Don't forget to revise and edit this draft.

6. Write a short essay in which you explain three reasons that you are doing something important in your life. Include these three reasons in a central idea that you will use as your thesis statement. Let's say that you decide to explain three of your reasons for going to college. You might write: "I decided to attend Metropolitan College to prepare for a rewarding career, to meet interesting people, and to learn more about music and literature." Put this thesis somewhere in your introductory paragraph.

Next, use *each* of the reasons in your thesis as the main point in the topic sentences of the three paragraphs that follow. In keeping with the example on the previous page, you might use the following as topic sentences for paragraphs 2, 3, and 4. The main point in each topic sentence is in italics:

Paragraph 2: The most important reason I decided to attend Metropolitan College was *to prepare myself for a rewarding career.*

Paragraph 3: *The opportunity to meet interesting people* was another reason I thought that going to college would be a good idea.

Paragraph 4: My decision to continue my schooling also had a lot to do with my desire to *learn more about literature and music.*

Try to develop each of these in a paragraph of three or four sentences that will help you explain the main point of your topic sentence completely and effectively. Finally, as with other assignments in this chapter, revise and edit your work thoroughly.

7. In item 2 of the Suggestions for Journal Entries after Maria Cirilli's "Echoes," you were asked to write three or four sentences, each of which was to focus on a single aspect or characteristic of someone special in your life. Make each of these the topic sentence of a paragraph that describes or explains that aspect or characteristic. If necessary, reread "Echoes." Many of the paragraphs in the body of this essay will serve as models for your writing.

Next, write an appropriate thesis statement for an essay containing the three or four paragraphs you've just written. Make sure that your thesis statement somehow reflects the main points found in the topic sentences of the three or four paragraphs in your essay. Make this thesis part of your essay's first or introductory paragraph.

Again, approach this writing assignment as a process. Complete several drafts of your paper, and don't submit your final product until you are satisfied that you have dealt with problems in grammar, spelling, punctuation, and the like.

Writing to Learn: A Group Activity

THE FIRST MEETING

Meeting in a group of three or four classmates, reread Stephen Fox's paragraph, "The Example of Jackie Robinson" on page 44. Ask each member of the group to research a person, place, event, or thing that played an important role in the struggle to secure civil rights for African-Americans. Here are some examples.

continued

Martin Luther King, Jr.'s "I Have a Dream" Speech

Rosa Parks

Medgar Evers

Malcolm X

Jesse Jackson

The Montgomery, Alabama, bus boycott

The U.S. Supreme Court's Brown v. the Board of Education decision

The 1965 Civil Rights Law

The Ku Klux Klan

RESEARCH

You can learn about the subject you choose by looking it up in a current encyclopedia or on the World Wide Web or by interviewing someone, such as a history, political science, law, or other professor, who knows a great deal about the civil rights movement.

Find out why your subject is important to the struggle for civil rights for African-Americans. After completing your research, summarize what you have learned in a paragraph of about 100 of your own words. A good way to start is with a topic sentence that explains your subject's importance to the civil rights movement. Then, fill your paragraph with details that prove, support, or explain that idea. Finally, in another, shorter paragraph, explain the steps you took to gather information.

THE SECOND MEETING

When you meet with your group again, give each member a copy of your paragraph. As you discuss each other's work, make suggestions that will help each student revise and edit his or her writing.

CHAPTER 2

Unity and Coherence

Chapter 1 explained the importance of focusing on a central idea. The central idea is also called the controlling idea. It controls, or determines, the kind of information a writer uses in an essay or paragraph.

Deciding how much information to include in a piece of writing has to do with development, a principle discussed in the next chapter. Deciding what kinds of information to include and making sure such information fits together logically relates to two principles of organization discussed in this chapter: unity and coherence.

Creating Unity

A piece of writing is unified if it contains only those details that help develop—explain or support—the central idea. You probably remember from Chapter 1 that a central idea contains both a subject and a main point the writer wishes to make about that subject. The following paragraph by Dorian Friedman describes the much discussed weather-maker El Niño. To maintain unity, the author has included only those details that support or explain the central idea, which he has put into the first sentence, the paragraph's topic sentence. Its subject is "the child"; its main point is "appears unusually cranky."

> It was South American fishermen who first dubbed [named] the December arrival of warm coastal currents "El Niño"—for the baby Christ—and this year, *the child appears unusually cranky.* Scientists tracking a mass of warm water building along the equatorial Pacific say it may signal the most pronounced El Niño of the century. The cyclical phenomenon—El Niño visits every two to seven years—occurs when trade winds and ocean currents change course for reasons still not understood. Already this year's system is scrambling climatic conditions worldwide, causing droughts in Asia and Brazil and torrential rains in Peru. Meanwhile, Californians are bracing [preparing] for rains and flooding this winter [1997–1998] that could match the 1982–83 El Niño.

Sometimes, beginning writers lose focus on the main point of a paragraph or essay, and they include irrelevant information—information that does not help explain or support the writer's central idea. Including such information sidetracks readers by drawing their attention to ideas that don't serve the writer's purpose. Make sure to check for unity when you revise your rough drafts. Writing that lacks unity makes it difficult for readers to determine exactly what you are trying to say.

The following paragraph is based on one written by Geoffery Ward from a *National Geographic* article that commemorates the fiftieth anniversary of India's independence. However, it has been rewritten so that it now contains details unrelated to its central idea. The material was added to show that irrelevant details destroy the focus of a piece of writing.

[1] Indian civilization has an astonishingly long history, and Delhi has witnessed a good deal of it. [2] There have been at least eight cities here in the past 3,000 years, beginning with Indraprastha, the capital mentioned in the Hindu epic [heroic poem], the *Mahabharata*. [3] Some scholars believe that if all the smaller settlements and fortifications and military outposts whose remnants are scattered across the landscape were taken into account, the actual number would be closer to 15. [4] Today, remnants of several old civilizations can also be found in Rome, Italy. [5] Monuments, ruins, and relics of the rich past are everywhere. [6] The high-rise office buildings that have gone up near Connaught Place in recent years cast their reflections into the green waters of a 14th-century steppe well. [7] In fact, as one of the world's fastest growing countries, India is experiencing a great deal of urban construction. [8] Traffic on one of New Delhi's busiest thoroughfares has to swerve around the masonry slab that marks a Muslim saint's grave. [9] Under the Independence Act of 1947 the Muslim state of Pakistan emerged as a separate country. [10] Even on the fairways on the New Delhi Golf Club . . . royal tombs offer unique hazards.

Ward establishes his focus in the first sentence. His subject is "Delhi"; his main point is that this city "has witnessed a good deal" of Indian civilization's "long history." This is what he sets out to prove. Therefore, each sentence and each detail that he includes should relate directly to that point. With the added information, however, that is not the case.

Sentence 1, the topic sentence, expresses the central idea.

Sentence 2 tells us about cities that existed on this site as far back as 3,000 years ago, so it helps explain the "long history" mentioned in the topic sentence.

Sentence 3 continues the idea begun in sentence 2, so it too is relevant to the topic sentence.

Sentence 4 makes an interesting comparison between Rome and Delhi. However, it does not help convince the reader that Delhi has witnessed a great deal of Indian history. It should be removed.

Sentence 5 mentions the city's "rich past" and even mentions a particular artifact from a much earlier century. Therefore, it belongs in the paragraph.

Sentence 6 tells us about a 600-year-old well, another sign of Delhi's "long history." It too belongs.

Sentence 7 makes no reference to the past; it is entirely about the present. It is irrelevant and should be removed.

Sentence 8 is relevant; it explains that a modern highway has been designed in such a way as to preserve a historical site, in this case the grave of a Muslim saint.

Sentence 9 is irrelevant. It has nothing to do with Delhi, the paragraph's subject, or about the long history that the city has witnessed. It doesn't belong.

Sentence 10 is relevant to the topic sentence. The royal tombs are more evidence that Delhi has seen much of the country's history.

This analysis shows that details added to Ward's original paragraph are irrelevant. Compare the disunited version above with the correct version below.

> Indian civilization has an astonishingly long history, and Delhi has witnessed a good deal of it. There have been at least eight cities here in the past 3,000 years; beginning with Indraprastha, the capital mentioned in the Hindu epic [heroic poem], the *Mahabharata*. Some scholars believe that if all the smaller settlements and fortifications and military outposts whose remnants are scattered across the landscape were taken into account, the actual number would be closer to 15. Monuments, ruins, and relics of the past are everywhere. The high-rise office buildings that have gone up near Connaught Place in recent years cast their reflections into the green waters of a 14th-century steppe well. Traffic on one of New Delhi's busiest thoroughfares has to swerve around the masonry slab that marks a Muslim saint's grave. Even on the fairways on the New Delhi Golf Club . . . royal tombs offer unique hazards.

Maintaining Coherence

The second principle important to organization is coherence. A paragraph is coherent if the sentences it contains are connected clearly and logically in a sequence (or order) that is easy to follow. An essay is coherent if the writer has made sure to create logical connections between paragraphs. The thought expressed in one sentence or paragraph should lead directly—without a break—to the thought in the following sentence or paragraph.

Logical connections between sentences and between paragraphs can be created in two ways: (1) by using transitional devices and (2) by making reference to words, ideas, and other details the writer has mentioned earlier.

USE TRANSITIONAL DEVICES

Transitional devices, also called *transitions* or *connectives,* are words, phrases, and even whole sentences that establish or show definite relationships in and between sentences and paragraphs. As seen in the following, transitional devices can be used for many different purposes.

To Indicate Time   You would be describing the passage of time if you wrote: "Henry left home just before dawn. *After a short while*, sunlight burst over the green hills." Other connectives that relate to time include:

After a few minutes	Back then
Afterward	Before
All the while	Before long
Already	Before that time
As soon as	Now
At that time	Prior to
During	Right away
Immediately	Soon
In a few minutes (hours, days, etc.)	Still
In a while	Subsequently
In the meantime	Suddenly
Meanwhile	Then
	Thereafter
	Until
	When
	While

To Indicate Similarities or Differences   You can also use transitions to show that things are similar or different: "Philip seems to be following in his sister's footsteps. *Like* her, he has decided to major in engineering. *Unlike* her, he doesn't do very well in math." Other transitions that indicate similarities and differences include:

Similarities	**Differences**
And	Although
As	But
As if	Even though
As though	However
In addition	In contrast
In the same way	Nevertheless
Like	Nonetheless
Likewise	On the other hand
Similarly	Still
	Though
	Unless
	Yet

To Introduce Examples, Repeat Information, or Emphasize a Point You would be using a transition to introduce an example if you wrote: "Mozart displayed his genius early. *For example,* he composed his first symphony when he was only a boy."

You would be using a transition to repeat information if you wrote: "At the age of 21, Mozart was appointed court composer for the emperor of Austria. This event was *another* indication of how quickly the young man rose to fame."

You would be using a transition to emphasize a point if you wrote: "The end of Mozart's career was hardly as spectacular as its beginnings. *In fact,* he died in poverty at age 35."

Other transitional devices useful for these purposes include:

Introducing Examples	Repeating Information	Emphasizing a Point
As an example	Again	As a matter of fact
For instance	Once again	Indeed
Specifically	Once more	More important
Such as		To be sure

To Add Information If you wanted to add information by using a transition, you might write: "When Ulysses S. Grant and Robert E. Lee met at Appomattox Courthouse in 1865, they brought the Civil War to an end. *What's more,* they opened a whole new chapter in U.S. political history." Here are some other connectives you will find useful when adding information:

Also	Furthermore
And	In addition
As well	Likewise
Besides	Moreover
Further	Too

To Show Cause and Effect If you wanted to explain that an action or idea led to or was the cause of another, you could indicate this relationship by using a transitional device like *consequently,* the word that draws a connection between the two thoughts in these sentences: "During the early days of the Revolution, General George Washington was unable to defend New York City. *Consequently,* he was forced to retreat to Pennsylvania." Other transitional devices that show cause-effect relationships are:

As a result	So that
Because	Then
Hence	Therefore
Since	Thus

To Show Condition   If you need to explain that one action, idea, or fact depends on another, you might create a relationship based on condition by using words like *if*, as in these sentences: "Professor Jones should arrive in a few minutes. *If* she doesn't, we will have to go on without her." Some other transitions that show condition include:

As long as	In order to
As soon as	Provided that
Even if	Unless
In case	When

Make Reference to Material That Has Come Before

Two other effective ways to connect details and ideas in a sentence or paragraph with what you have discussed in earlier sentences or paragraphs are (1) to use pronouns to link details and ideas and (2) to restate important details and ideas.

Using Pronouns to Link Details and Ideas   A good way to make reference to material that has come before is to use *linking pronouns,* pronouns that point clearly and directly to specific names, ideas, or details you've mentioned earlier. Such pronouns direct the reader's attention to nouns in earlier sentences or paragraphs; these nouns are called *antecedents*. Relying on pronouns to maintain coherence also helps you avoid mentioning the same noun over and over, a habit that might make your writing repetitious.

The most important thing to remember about using linking pronouns is to make sure they refer directly and unmistakably to the nouns you want them to. In other words, all pronouns of reference should have antecedents that the reader will be able to identify easily and without question.

Read this paragraph, from the writings of Mother Teresa, the Roman Catholic nun who dedicated her life to the poor of Calcutta. Pronouns used to maintain coherence appear in italics:

> Here in Calcutta, we have a number of non-Christians and Christians *who* work together in the house of the dying and other places. There are also *some who* offer *their* care to the lepers. One day an Australian man came and made a substantial donation. But as *he* did *this he* said, "*This* is something external. Now I want to give something of *myself.*" *He* now comes regularly to the house of the dying to shave the sick men and to converse with *them. This* man gives not only *his* money but also *his* time. *He* could have spent it on *himself,* but what *he* wants is to give *himself.*

The paragraph above includes only a few of the pronouns you might want to use to make your writing more coherent. Here are others:

Personal Pronouns. These are pronouns that refer to people and things:

I (me, my, mine)   We (us, our, ours)
He, she, it (him, his; her, hers; its)   You (your, yours)
                                                   They (them, their, theirs)

Relative Pronouns. These are pronouns that help describe nouns by connecting them with clauses (groups of words that contain nouns and verbs):

Who (whose, whom)   Whatever
That   Which
What   Whichever

Demonstrative Pronouns. These are pronouns that precede and stand for the nouns they refer to. Sentences like "*Those* are the best seats in the house" or "*That* is my book" make use of demonstrative pronouns. The most common demonstrative pronouns are:

This   These
That   Those

Indefinite Pronouns. These are pronouns used for general rather than specific reference. You can make good use of these pronouns as long as you are sure the reader can identify their antecedents easily. For instance: "Both Sylvia and Andrew were released from the hospital. *Neither* was seriously injured." In this case, the antecedents of *neither* are Sylvia and Andrew. Here are other indefinite pronouns:

All	Either	Nobody	Several
Another	Everybody	None	Some
Both	Everyone	No one	Someone
Each	Neither	Others	

Restating Important Details and Ideas

The second way to make reference to material that has come before is to restate important details and ideas by repeating words and phrases or by using easily recognizable *synonyms*, terms that have the same (or nearly the same) meaning as those words or phrases.

The following paragraph is from a pamphlet by Shen C. Y. Fu, who was curator of Chinese Art for the Freer Gallery of the Smithsonian Institute in Washington, DC. Fu uses the word *calligraphy* four times, but for the sake of variety he also uses recognizable synonyms (italics added):

> *Calligraphy* is generally defined as beautiful *writing*. In the West the *term* applies to *decorative writing* or may simply mean *good penmanship*. In China, however, *calligraphy* is regarded as the ultimate artistic expression, requiring years of training, discipline, and dedication before mastery can be achieved. Like music and dance, *calligraphy* is an art of performance. But unlike music and

dance, each performance of *calligraphy* results in a tangible [material] creation that both captures the artist's technical skills at the time and provides concrete evidence of his or her immediate mood and innate [inborn] personality.

Visualizing Unity and Coherence

The following paragraph is from Gerald Parshall's "Freeing the Survivors," which tells what U.S. soldiers saw in 1945 when they liberated inmates of Nazi concentration camps, where millions of people had been murdered.

Notes in the margins explain how the paragraph is unified. Shaded words and phrases show how the writer maintained coherence.

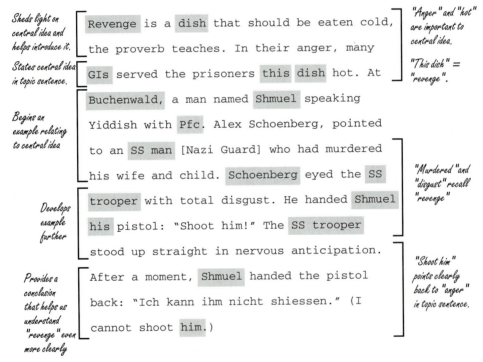

Sheds light on central idea and helps introduce it.

States central idea in topic sentence.

Begins an example relating to central idea

Develops example further

Provides a conclusion that helps us understand "revenge" even more clearly

Revenge is a dish that should be eaten cold, the proverb teaches. In their anger, many GIs served the prisoners this dish hot. At Buchenwald, a man named Shmuel speaking Yiddish with Pfc. Alex Schoenberg, pointed to an SS man [Nazi Guard] who had murdered his wife and child. Schoenberg eyed the SS trooper with total disgust. He handed Shmuel his pistol: "Shoot him!" The SS trooper stood up straight in nervous anticipation. After a moment, Shmuel handed the pistol back: "Ich kann ihm nicht shiessen." (I cannot shoot him.)

"Anger" and "hot" are important to central idea.

"This dish" = "revenge".

"Murdered" and "disgust" recall "revenge"

"Shoot him" points clearly back to "anger" in topic sentence.

Revising to Improve Unity and Coherence

Read these two versions of paragraphs from "Is Justice Served?" which appears later in this chapter. Then read notes in the margins of the second version to see how student author Gina K. Louis-Ferdinand revised her essay to improve unity and coherence.

Louis-Ferdinand—Rough Draft

Today, the big story is the O.J. Simpson murder trial, which has been splashed across newspapers and televisions all over the world. The media has made it nearly impossible to select an impartial jury

Needs a transition — because of its lack of responsibility in reporting this case. The press reported that a sock soaked with Nicole Simpson's blood

Add transitions? — had been found in O.J.'s bedroom. The judge, defense, and prosecution all denied that any such evidence existed. The media stood by the story. They retracted the story without the fanfare that had accompanied the first report. An explosive book was published by Nicole Simpson's self-proclaimed best

New idea. Create new paragraph?

Add transitions?

Add information? — friend. The author discusses her second-hand knowledge of Nicole and O.J.'s life. She claims Nicole told her that one day O.J. would kill her. The author has become a highly sought-after commodity on the talk-show circuit. The judge in the case personally contacted the networks airing shows that were scheduled to interview her and asked that the interviews be postponed until after a jury had been selected and sequestered. All but one refused.

When the media treats crimes in this manner, how can an impartial jury be found? In a trial, a judge has the power to allow or disallow information based on the legality of the item. His job is to make sure a trial is fair for all parties involved and that it is based on fact and not hearsay or false information. The media have no such restrictions and can report practically anything they wish, fact or fiction.

Is this relevant to central idea?

Louis-Ferdinand—Final Draft

Today, the big story is the O.J. Simpson murder trial, which has been splashed across newspapers and televisions all over the world. The media has made it nearly impossible to select an impartial jury

Adds transitions to introduce example and indicate time.

because of its lack of responsibility in reporting the case. For example, early in the investigation, the press reported that a sock soaked with Nicole Simpson's blood had been found in O.J.'s bedroom. The judge, defense, and prosecution all denied that any

Adds transitions to indicate time.

such evidence existed. At first, the media stood by the story. Two days later, they retracted it but without the fanfare that had accompanied the first report.

Adds transitions to show difference.

Adds transitions to show time and introduce another example.

More recently, an explosive book was published by Nicole Simpson's self-proclaimed best friend, who claims Nicole told her that one day O.J. would kill her.

Creates new paragraph to discuss second example.

Adds transitions to show cause/effect.

As a result, the author has become a highly

Adds transitions to emphasize a point.

sought-after commodity on the talk-show circuit. In fact, upon learning of her intent to be interviewed, the judge in the case personally contacted the networks airing such shows and asked that the interviews be postponed until after a jury had been selected and sequestered. All but one network refused. When the media treats crimes in this manner, how can an impartial jury be found?

Unnecessary information about the judge has been removed.

Practicing Unity and Coherence

Read this paragraph—written by Stacy Zolnowski for a first-year writing class—to learn more about paragraph unity. Then, using complete sentences, answer the questions that follow in the spaces provided:

[1] Throughout history, left-handedness has been deemed a nasty habit, a social infraction, a symptom of neurosis, or even a sign of mental retardation. [2] More recently, however, its social, educational, and psychological implications have acquired a more enlightened appreciation. [3] Nonetheless, left-handers continue to be discriminated against in an environment that conforms to the needs and prejudices of a right-handed society. ("The Left-Handed Minority")

1. Assume that the paragraph's topic sentence is the third sentence. What, in your own words, is the paragraph's central idea?

_____

_____

_____

_____

2. How do sentences 1 and 2 relate to the central idea?

_____

_____

_____

3. What transitional devices does the writer use to maintain coherence?

_____

_____

_____

4. In what other ways does the writer maintain coherence?

_____

_____

_____

This chapter has introduced you to two important principles of organization: unity and coherence. A paragraph or essay is *unified* if all its ideas and details relate to and contribute to the central idea. A paragraph or essay is *coherent* if the reader can move from sentence to sentence and paragraph to paragraph easily because the writer has connected the ideas logically.

Look for signs of unity and coherence as you read the following selections. More important, apply these principles in your own writing as you respond to the Suggestions for Journal Entries and the Suggestions for Sustained Writing.

Frank Sinatra

Pete Hamill

Pete Hamill has been a reporter, editor, and freelance writer for a number of important newspapers and periodicals since the 1960s. He has written several novels and collections of short stories as well as a memoir entitled A Drinking Life *(1994), which was a national best-seller for several months. This paragraph on Frank Sinatra was published in* Piecework, *a collection of Hamill's essays.*

Sinatra, who was a singer, movie actor, and nightclub entertainer, is one of the best-known figures in American entertainment. He died in 1999. Hamill's portrait is based on a meeting with Sinatra in 1980.

Preparing to Read

1. Hamill begins with his topic sentence. He restates that idea in different words at the end of the paragraph. As such, he gives the structure of the paragraph added strength and emphasis.
2. As you read Hamill's topic sentence, try to figure out the kinds of details he will use in the rest of the paragraph to support that idea.
3. This paragraph mentions the titles of two of Sinatra's works: a movie and a three-volume record set. You can spot these titles because they are in italics.
4. Look up Frank Sinatra on the Internet, and read a little about him before you start Hamill's paragraph.

Vocabulary

incidental (adjective)	Almost unrelated, not an essential part of.
intensity (noun)	Strength.
lapse (noun)	Fall, drop, decrease.
prose (noun)	Common form of writing or speaking, as opposed to poetry.
stature (noun)	Reputations, standing.
unleash (verb)	Let loose.

Frank Sinatra

Pete Hamill

AT 64, Francis Albert Sinatra is one of that handful of Americans whose deaths would certainly unleash a river of tearful prose and much genuine grief. He has worked at his trade for almost half a century and goes on as if nothing at all had changed. He is currently in New York making his first feature film in ten years, *The First Deadly Sin.* His first new studio album in five years is in the record stores, a three-record set called *Trilogy,* and despite one astonishing lapse in taste, . . . it reveals that what Sinatra calls "my reed" is in better shape than it has been in since the 1960s. In concert halls and casinos he packs in the fans, and the intensity of their embrace remains scary. But his work and its public acceptance are now almost incidental to his stature. Frank Sinatra, from Hoboken, New Jersey, has forced his presence into American social history; when the story of how Americans in this century played, dreamed, hoped, and loved is told, Frank Sinatra cannot be left out. He is more than a mere singer or actor. He is a legend. And the legend lives.

Questions for Discussion

1. In your own words, state the paragraph's central idea.
2. What use of repetition does Hamill make to maintain coherence?
3. What transitional devices does the author use?
4. Is this paragraph unified? Name two details that show Sinatra is "a legend."
5. What is Hamill saying about Sinatra's "stature?"

Thinking Critically

Think of an entertainer (other than Sinatra), a sports figure, a politician, or another well-known personality who "has forced his [or her] presence" into our "social history." In other words, think of another "legend." Write a short paragraph explaining why this person is important to us. In the process, you might list the qualities you think a legend should have.

Suggestion for a Journal Entry

Make a list of qualities you think someone should have in order to be effective as *one* of the following:

Father or mother

Husband or wife

Employer or supervisor

Civil servant/politician

Teacher

Police officer

Doctor, nurse, or other medical professional

A subject of your own choosing

Writing and Its Rewards

Richard Marius

Richard Marius directed the expository writing program at Harvard University. He began his career as a historian and has authored biographies of Thomas More and Martin Luther. He also wrote four novels and several books on writing, including The McGraw-Hill College Handbook, *which he co-authored with Harvey Wiener. "Writing and Its Rewards" is from* A Writer's Companion, *Marius's splendid guide for both experienced and developing writers. Richard Marius died in 1999.*

Preparing to Read

1. Writing is a process of drafting and revising, Marius tells us. As you probably learned in "Getting Started," *drafting* means putting down facts and ideas in rough form, no matter how disorganized your paragraph or essay might seem at first. *Revising* involves rewriting, reorganizing, adding to, deleting from, and correcting earlier drafts to make them more effective and easier to read.

2. In paragraph 5, Marius mentions three writers whose work you may want to read: Geoffrey Chaucer, Leo Tolstoy, and W.H. Auden. To learn more about them, look up their names in an encyclopedia or reference book recommended by your college librarian.

Vocabulary

eighteenth century (adjective and noun)	The 1700s.
embodied (adjective)	Contained.
enduring (adjective)	Lasting.
lexicographer (noun)	Writer of a dictionary.
parable (noun)	Story with a lesson or moral.
profound (adjective)	Deep, extreme.
weighing (adjective)	Carefully considering.

Writing and Its Rewards

Richard Marius

WRITING IS hard work, and although it may become easier with practice it is seldom easy. Most of us have to write and rewrite to write anything well. We try to write well so people will read our work. Readers nowadays will seldom struggle to understand difficult writing unless someone—a teacher perhaps—forces them to do so. Samuel Johnson, the great eighteenth-century English writer, conversationalist, and lexicographer, said, "What is written without effort is in general read without pleasure." Today what is written without effort is seldom read at all.

Writing takes time—lots of time. Good writers do not dash off a piece in an hour and get on to other things. They do not wait until the night before a deadline to begin to write. Instead they plan. They write a first draft. They revise it. They may then think through that second draft and write it once again. Even small writing tasks may require enormous investments of time. If you want to become a writer, you must be serious about the job, willing to spend hours dedicated to your work. 2

Most writers require some kind of solitude. That does not mean the extreme of the cork-lined room where the great French writer Marcel Proust composed his huge works in profound silence. It does mean mental isolation—shutting yourself off from the distractions around you even if you happen to be pounding a computer keyboard in a noisy newspaper office. You choose to write rather than do other things, and you must concentrate on what you are doing. 3

In a busy world like ours, we take a risk when we isolate ourselves and give up other pursuits to write. We don't know how our writing will come out. All writers fail sometimes. Successful writers pick themselves up after failure and try again. As you write, you must read your work again and again, thinking of your purpose, weighing your words, testing your organization, examining your evidence, checking for clarity. You must pay attention to the thousands and thousands of details embodied in words and experience. You must trust your intuitions; if something does not sound right, do it again. And again. And again. 4

Finally you present your work to readers as the best you can do. After you submit a final draft, it is too late to make excuses, and you should not do so. Not everybody will like your final version. You may feel insecure about it even when you have done your best. You may like your work at first and hate it later. Writers wobble back and forth in their judgments. Chaucer, Tolstoy and Auden are all on record for rejecting some of their works others have found enduring and grand. Writing is a parable of life itself. 5

Questions for Discussion

1. Reread Marius's introduction. What is his thesis? What is the main point in this thesis?
2. This essay is unified because each paragraph clearly develops the essay's central idea (thesis). Explain how each topic sentence in paragraphs 2, 3, and 4 relates to Marius's thesis.
3. Reread paragraphs 2 and 3. Which techniques does Marius use to maintain coherence?

4. Reread paragraph 4. Which words and phrases are used to repeat ideas and, thus, to maintain coherence?
5. What does Marius mean by writing "is a parable of life itself" (paragraph 5)? Why is this conclusion effective?

Thinking Critically

One assumption Marius makes is that all educated people need to be competent writers. Is that true of you? Will you need strong writing skills for the job you take after college? Contact someone practicing in that field or profession. Ask her or him about the need for good writing skills. Then write a short report of your interview.

Suggestions for Journal Entries

1. Marius says "Most writers require some kind of solitude." Do you? Use your journal to describe the place in which you write or study most often. Is it comfortable? Can you concentrate there? Should you find another place to work?
2. "Writing and Its Rewards" contains advice to make us better writers. Use your journal to list three or more specific pieces of advice to help you or a classmate become better at an important activity you know a lot about. Here are examples of such an activity: studying or doing homework; dressing for school or work; driving in heavy traffic or bad weather; communicating with parents, children, teachers, or classmates; maintaining a car; losing weight; sticking to a nutritious diet; or treating members of a different race, age group, religion, or sex with respect.

   Express each piece of advice in a complete sentence, the kind that can serve as the topic sentence to a paragraph you might write later on to explain that piece of advice more fully.

Study Calculus!

William J. Bennett

Secretary of education and chairman of the National Endowment for the Humanities in the Reagan administration, William J. Bennett holds a doctorate in political philosophy from the University of Texas and a law degree from Harvard University. Under President Bush, Bennett directed the war on drugs as head of the Office of National Drug Control Policy. This essay, which reveals much about Bennett's thinking when he was secretary of education, is taken from The De-Valuing of America: The Fight for Our Children. *Bennett is also the author of the best-selling* Book of Virtues: A Treasury of Great Moral Stories *as well as several other books.*

Preparing to Read

1. Bennett maintains coherence in and between paragraphs well. Look for linking pronouns and other connective words and phrases as you read his essay.

2. In paragraph 2, Bennett reports that some of Escalante's colleagues claimed "his plan to teach calculus was a quixotic fantasy." The word *quixotic* is taken from the name of the title character of Miguel de Cervantes's seventeenth-century Spanish novel *Don Quixote*. Although admirable in many respects, Cervantes's hero was a dreamer who often got himself into trouble by attempting the impossible. Therefore, the term *quixotic,* has come to mean "foolish," "silly," or "totally impractical."

3. The essay ends with several one-sentence paragraphs. Although not often found in formal writing, such paragraphs are useful here because they convey dialogue, conversation between two or more people.

4. The title of this essay provides a strong hint about its thesis. Why was "Calculus" and not "math" or "arithmatic" used?

Vocabulary

calculus (noun)	A branch of mathematics important to science, engineering, and other disciplines.
canard (noun)	False belief, principle, rule, or story.
ethic (noun)	Principle, belief in.
pedagogy (noun)	Education, schooling, teaching.
skepticism (noun)	Doubt, distrust, disbelief.

Study Calculus!

William J. Bennett

PRINCIPAL HENRY Gradillas at Garfield High School in East Los Angeles let   1
Jaime Escalante teach. And did the students ever learn. Escalante, a Bolivian immigrant, arrived at the school in 1974 to teach math. Now perhaps America's most famous teacher, he wanted to return something to the country that had taken him in and given him opportunity.

His plan to teach calculus to disadvantaged Hispanic youngsters was   2
greeted with skepticism and laughter by his colleagues, and he encountered resistance from his students. But he told me that the greatest resistance came not from the students but from others in the profession, other teachers and counselors who urged him not to push so hard. They told him that his plan to teach calculus was a quixotic fantasy. "If you try," some told him, "the students will fail. They can't do it. They will be embarrassed, and their self-esteem will suffer. What you want to do—teach calculus—will be dangerous."

Escalante told me what he told his critics: "If you are fifteen or sixteen   3
years old, in the barrio of East Los Angeles, there are a lot of things that are dangerous. But calculus isn't one of them." His principal, Henry Gradillas, encouraged him to proceed.

Escalante persisted, and in 1982 eighteen of his students took the Advanced Placement (AP) calculus test. By 1991, 160 students from Garfield   4
took the test. According to Jay Mathews, author of *Escalante: The Best Teacher in America,* Escalante has given Garfield the most successful inner-city mathematics program in the United States. In recent years only four or five secondary schools in the country have prepared more students for the AP calculus examination (tests so difficult that fewer than 2 percent of American students even attempt them). Because of Escalante's efforts, about a fourth of all the Mexican-American students in the country who pass AP calculus come from Garfield.

Escalante's methods and approach (celebrated in the movie *Stand and   5
Deliver*) are in marked contrast to the theory and practice of pedagogy as taught in most American schools of education. He consistently violates the canard that a teacher shouldn't "impose his values on students." Indeed, he seeks every opportunity to impose his ethic of achievement, success, and hard work on them. His reason, as expressed to me, is simple: "My values are better than theirs." His way of doing this is direct, manly, no nonsense. In the early days of his career at Garfield, he asked a student whether he wanted to study calculus. "No," said the student, "I want to see my girlfriend."

"Well, then," responded Escalante, "go over to woodworking class on   6
your way out."
"Why," the student asked.   7

"So you can learn how to make shoeshine boxes so you can have a career   8
shining the shoes for Anglos as they pass through Los Angeles International
Airport on their business trips."

"I don't want to shine Anglos' shoes," protested the student.   9

"Then study calculus," was Escalante's reply.   10

Questions for Discussion

1. What is the essay's thesis?
2. What is the topic sentence in paragraph 4? Explain how each of the sentences it contains relates to or develops that topic sentence.
3. What does the dialogue in paragraphs 6–10 contribute to the essay?
4. Why didn't Bennett combine paragraphs 6–10 into one paragraph?
5. Explain how Bennett uses linking pronouns to maintain coherence in paragraph 2.
6. Find two transitional words or phrases in paragraph 1. Find at least three more in the rest of the essay.
7. What use does Bennett make of repetition to maintain coherence within paragraphs?

Thinking Critically

1. Do you agree with the way in which Escalante challenged his students? Think of another way that you might motivate students to study a difficult subject if you were a teacher. Explain this in a paragraph or two.
2. What kind of values is Escalante talking about in paragraph 5? Should teachers be allowed to impose other values—social, political, or moral, for example—on students? On a separate sheet of paper list the advantages and disadvantages of allowing them to do so.
3. Why do you think some teachers had a low opinion of the abilities of students whom Escalante helped? What connection, if any, is there between a teacher's attitude and student success?

Suggestions for Journal Entries

1. Use clustering or listing to come up with several characteristics or qualities of a good teacher. You might begin by thinking about the best teacher or teachers you have had. Consider those qualities that caused you to admire them or that made them effective instructors. For example you might write that:

Ms. Jones challenged students.

Mr. Mendoza graded homework and tests carefully.

Dr. Patel inspired confidence in you.

Ms. Fernandez made geometry interesting and easy to understand.

By the way, you don't need to limit yourself to teachers you have had in school. Family members, employers, neighbors, coaches, and members of the clergy often teach us a lot as well.

2. Freewrite for about 10 minutes to gather information about the teacher who has influenced you most. Again, don't limit yourself to teachers you have had in school.

Is Justice Served?

Gina K. Louis-Ferdinand

Gina K. Louis-Ferdinand grew up in Southfield, Michigan, and is planning to pursue a career as a writer. She works full-time and takes college courses in the evening. When the instructor of her first-year composition class invited students to write on a topic about which they had strong feelings, Louis-Ferdinand knew immediately that she would explain her concern over the effects of the media on our justice system.

Preparing to Read

1. Louis-Ferdinand organizes her essay around examples relating to three of the crimes she believes the media has sensationalized. She mentions these three cases early in the essay, then develops each one in detail in the body paragraphs. This pattern makes her essay easy to follow:

   Paragraph 1: Provides introductory information and gets the reader interested.

   Paragraph 2: Expresses the essay's central idea in a thesis statement. It also introduces three examples that support the thesis and that are developed in the essay's body paragraphs, which follow.

   Paragraph 3: Fully discusses the first example mentioned in paragraph 2: the Menendez case.

   Paragraph 4: Fully discusses the second example mentioned in paragraph 2: the Rodney King incident.

   Paragraph 5: Uses an example from the O. J. Simpson trial to support the thesis.

   Paragraph 6: Uses a second example from the O. J. Simpson trial to support the thesis.

   Paragraph 7: Concludes the essay by reminding us of the thesis.

2. This essay is fairly easy to read because Louis-Ferdinand has done a masterful job of maintaining coherence by using transitions and other devices discussed in this chapter. Look for them especially in paragraphs 3, 4, 5, and 6.

3. The title of this essay is a question. What will the answer be?

Vocabulary

allegations (noun)   Charges.
commodity (noun)   Object, article of trade.

exploitation (noun)	Abuse, unethical or unfair use of.
impartial (adjective)	Fair, objective.
perverse (adjective)	Evil, distorted, sinful.
preconceived (adjective)	Biased, having been made before the evidence was heard.
retracted (verb)	Took back, corrected.
sequestered (verb)	Isolated, separated.

Is Justice Served?

Gina K. Louis-Ferdinand

AMERICANS LOVE a juicy story. We want intimate details, and the media is happy to comply, but we forget that people's lives are at stake. A crime is not a form of entertainment from which to derive perverse pleasure. It is the failure of a person to live up to his or her obligations as a law-abiding citizen, and the media should report it as such.

1

Recently, several major crimes have been sensationalized. As far as the media is concerned, the more gruesome the crime, the better. Take the Menendez brothers' case or the trial of the policemen who beat Rodney King. If a famous person is accused, members of the press appear to smack their lips and wring their hands in anticipation. Insert sex or race, as in the O. J. Simpson murder trial, and the journalist's fondest dreams come true. But such exploitation is not harmless entertainment; it tears at the core of the American judicial system: a fair trial by an impartial jury. A juror is supposed to be objective and have no preconceived opinion about the guilt or innocence of the accused. However, the media's bombarding the public with information about a crime—true or otherwise—makes finding twelve people who have no opinion about it nearly impossible.

2

In the Menendez case, for example, two brothers were accused of murdering their parents. Initially, this case received media attention because the victims' children were accused of the murders. However, when the brothers claimed they killed their parents because they had been molested by them, the press really went wild. For months before the trial, every paper and news program contained something about the crime. Only then was the jury selected. Thus, even though no proof was ever found to support the brothers' allegations of molestation, their [first] trials ended in hung juries.

3

The Rodney King incident gained national attention when a videotape of the racially motivated beating was shown on television. In the beginning, just the facts about the incident were reported, but as time went on information on Rodney King's personal life was publicized. Mr. King was portrayed as a sleazy ex-convict from the ghetto who deserved what happened to him because he had resisted arrest. In reality, Rodney King was the victim in this crime, and his personal life had nothing to do with his being so severely beaten. However, the press chose to make his personal life an issue. As a

4

result, at the end of the first trial, the police officers, who had been caught on videotape kicking and punching Mr. King and against whom a fellow police officer had testified, were set free.

Today, the big story is the O. J. Simpson murder trial, which has been 5 splashed across newspapers and televisions all over the world. The media has made it nearly impossible to select an impartial jury because of its lack of responsibility in reporting the case. For example, early in the investigation, the press reported that a sock soaked with Nicole Simpson's blood had been found in O. J.'s bedroom. The judge, defense, and prosecution all denied that any such evidence existed. At first, the media stood by the story. Two days later, they retracted it but without the fanfare that had accompanied the first report.

More recently, an explosive book was published by Nicole Simpson's 6 self-proclaimed best friend, who claims Nicole told her that one day O. J. would kill her. As a result, the author has become a highly sought-after commodity on the talk-show circuit. In fact, upon learning of her intent to be interviewed, the judge in the case personally contacted the networks airing such shows and asked that the interviews be postponed until after a jury had been selected and sequestered. All but one network refused. When the media treats crimes in this manner, how can an impartial jury be found?

Though our judicial system is far from perfect, it is the best one in the 7 world. Our Constitution seeks fairness for all citizens, victim and accused alike, and what makes this system so effective is the jury. Our legal system cannot work if a jury makes a decision based upon anything other than simple facts, and that is not what happens when the media reports a crime as if it were dramatic entertainment. Did Rodney King or Mr. and Mrs. Menendez receive justice? Can O. J. Simpson get a fair trial? Those are the kinds of questions a journalist should ask before exploiting a story just to "scoop" another network or paper. Those are the kinds of questions we as a society should ask before we get taken in by one of these "juicy" stories. And, if we find ourselves answering such questions with anything other than a resounding "yes," we should not say "shame on the media" for publishing them. Rather, we should say "shame on ourselves" for listening.

Questions for Discussion

1. What sentence in this essay best expresses Louis-Ferdinand's central idea? In other words, what is her thesis?

2. Why does the author introduce the Menendez brothers, Rodney King, and O. J. Simpson early in the essay (paragraph 2)? Why didn't she simply introduce them when discussing their cases later on?

3. The central idea in paragraph 3 is not stated in a topic sentence. It is only implied. How would you express that central idea in your own words?

4. Is this essay unified? If so, explain how paragraph 4 relates to the thesis?

5. What is the topic sentence in paragraph 5?

6. Reread paragraph 4. Circle transitions and other elements the author uses to maintain coherence.

7. Reread paragraph 6. Circle transitions and other elements the author uses to maintain coherence.

Thinking Critically

1. The policemen accused of beating Rodney King were tried a second time in federal court for violating King's civil rights. Two of them were given long-term jail sentences. Write a paragraph that explains the effect this fact has on Louis-Ferdinand's argument that the media's treatment of Rodney King interfered with justice. Does it strengthen or weaken her argument? Does it have any effect at all? Why or why not?

2. Some say the O. J. Simpson murder trial captured the public's attention like no other trial since the Lindbergh kidnapping case in the 1930s. What are the causes of the public's fascination with the Simpson case? What has the media done to keep our attention? What other factors account for the public's interest in this trial?

3. Different people have different opinions about O. J. Simpson's guilt or innocence. Is it fair to judge Simpson when you were not in the courtroom hearing arguments from both the defense and the prosecution? Why or why not?

Suggestions for Journal Entries

1. Think of a crime, trial, scandal, or other incident that the news media has sensationalized. (Try not to pick one of the examples Louis-Ferdinand used.) Then use listing to gather facts and ideas that might later help you discuss the media's handling of this event. If possible, do some brainstorming with a friend or classmate about the topic before you begin putting down information.

2. Use freewriting or listing to gather information about a sensitive event you believe the media reported accurately, fairly, and professionally. To get started on this assignment, recall what you learned about the event from television or radio; then read three or four accounts of it in different newspapers or magazines.

Suggestions for Sustained Writing

1. If you completed the Suggestion for a Journal Entry after Pete Hamill's paragraph on Frank Sinatra, then you have listed several qualities you believe are necessary for someone to be an effective father/mother, husband/wife, employer/supervisor, civil servant/politician or other. Read your list. Then, write a topic sentence that includes one or two of those qualities to describe a particular type of person. It might go like this:

    A good mother is both forgiving and patient.

    Now, using examples of real people you know well, write a paragraph that supports and develops this topic sentence. For example, you might discuss incidents in which your mother has been unexpectedly forgiving and/or in which a relative or neighbor has demonstrated exceptional patience with her family.

    Be as detailed as you can. Write several drafts of the paragraph so as to add information as needed. Then edit for grammar, punctuation, and spelling. If you are ambitious, try writing another paragraph, but this time focus on another type of person.

2. If you responded to item 2 in the Suggestions for Journal Entries after Marius's "Writing and Its Rewards," you have probably listed three or four sentences that give advice on a particular activity you know a lot about. Use *each* of these sentences as the topic sentence of a paragraph that explains the advice you are giving in detail. For example, if you are trying to help a friend lose weight, one thing you might suggest is that he or she get a lot of exercise. That would make a good topic sentence of a paragraph that goes like this:

    Get a lot of exercise. Wake up early and jog two or three miles. Use the weight room in the college gymnasium several times a week or ride one of the stationary bicycles you will find there. If all else fails, walk the three miles to school every day, do sit-ups in your room, or jump rope in your backyard.

    After you have written three or four such paragraphs, decide on a thesis statement that might express the central idea of the essay in which these paragraphs will appear. Make your thesis broad enough to include the main points you made in all three or four of your topic sentences. Use the thesis statement as the basis of a paragraph that comes before and introduces the three or four body paragraphs you have just completed.

    Now, rewrite your paper several times. Make sure it is clear and well organized. Check to see that you have included enough transitional devices to maintain coherence as explained in this chapter.

3. Review the notes you made for the first journal entry following Bennett's "Study Calculus!" If you have not responded to that journal prompt yet, do so now. Use this information to write the thesis statement for an essay that might be entitled "The Ideal Teacher." In that thesis, mention at least

three qualities that make for excellent teaching. Here's how such a thesis might read:

The best of teachers challenge their students, inspire confidence in them, and work harder than anyone else in class.

Place this thesis statement in your first paragraph, your introduction. Now use each of the three or four characteristics of good teaching in your thesis as the basis for the topic sentences of your essay's body paragraphs. Here's how each of the topic sentences for paragraphs 2, 3, and 4 or your essay might read:

Paragraph 2: The best teachers challenge their students.

Paragraph 3: Inspiring confidence in students is another sign of good teaching.

Paragraph 4: Good teachers work harder than their students.

Develop each of these body paragraphs with examples relating to a teacher or teachers you have known. You need not discuss the same teacher in each paragraph. If you completed the second journal suggestion after Bennett's essay, you might have already gathered some information you can use.

After writing several drafts of your paper, check that you have maintained coherence in and between paragraphs by using techniques explained in this chapter. Finally, remember that the best essays are those that are reviewed and edited carefully.

4. Read the journal entry you made after completing Louis-Ferdinand's "Is Justice Served?" (If you haven't responded to this essay in your journal, do so now.)

What does your journal tell you about your opinion of how the news media handles sensitive events? Make your answer to this question the thesis statement of a short essay discussing at least three events, like those used by Louis-Ferdinand, to support that thesis.

If you followed the Suggestions for Journal Entries after "Is Justice Served?" carefully, you already have one of the three examples you will use in your essay. Now, do some prewriting to gather information about two other events the media has handled badly or well.

As you draft your essay, make sure that all three events relate to and help prove your thesis. Place your thesis in your introductory paragraph. Then, following Louis-Ferdinand's model, explain each example in a body paragraph. End your essay with a short paragraph that reminds your readers of your thesis.

Here's an outline you might follow:

Paragraph 1: Contains thesis; captures readers' interest.

Paragraph 2: Discusses first example, which you wrote about in your journal.

Paragraph 3: Discusses second example.

Paragraph 4: Discusses third example.

Paragraph 5: Reminds readers of your thesis.

As you revise your first draft, make sure to check coherence. Repeat ideas and insert transitions and linking pronouns as needed. Finally, edit and proofread your work.

Writing to Learn: A Group Activity

THE FIRST MEETING

Pretend you and several others have been asked to contribute to a brochure that will help students choose an academic major. (For inspiration, reread Bennett's "Study Calculus!") Meet in a group of three or four students and ask each to research one (only one) major, perhaps from the list below or from a list that the group makes for itself:

Accounting	Dental hygiene	Nursing
Anthropology	Economics	Pharmacy
Architecture	History	Physical education
Biology	Journalism	Political science
Business	Literature	Psychology
administration	Mathematics	Rehabilitation science
Chemistry	Mechanical	Sociology
Computer science	engineering	Speech therapy
Civil engineering	Modern languages	Theater
Criminal justice		

RESEARCH

Make sure each member covers a different major. Search the Internet, do some research in your college's career placement center, or interview professors who teach courses in the assigned areas of study. Find out:

- What courses are required of students who major in this area.
- What careers are open to students who graduate with this major.
- What are the employment opportunities in one or two of these careers (make sure to focus on only one or two).
- What rewards (monetary and other) do these careers offer.
- What are some of the negative aspects of these careers.

WRITING

Then, write an essay that discusses most or all of these points for the major each of you chose. In your second group meeting, share early drafts (not first drafts) of each other's papers and suggest revisions. Be especially concerned with changes that will help the writer improve unity and coherence as explained in this chapter. In your third group meeting, distribute final versions of your papers. Finally, ask everyone to write a paragraph that explains whether the reading of these essays has influenced his or her choice of a major.

CHAPTER 3

Development

By now you know from practice that you use the central idea to focus your writing on a main point and to keep it unified. You do so by making sure that all the information in your paragraphs and essays relates clearly to the central idea. This chapter explains how the central idea also controls *development*—how much information a piece of writing contains and how this information is organized.

A paragraph or essay is well developed if it contains all the details it needs to prove, support, or illustrate its central idea. You should provide enough details to make your point clearly and convincingly. You should also arrange these details in a way that fits your purpose and allows readers to follow your train of thought easily.

Determining How Much a Paragraph or Essay Should Contain

There is no simple rule to tell how long a piece of writing should be. Depending on your thesis, you might be able to develop an essay in only a few paragraphs. But in some cases, your central idea will require that you write several more paragraphs of explanation and support.

Something similar is true for paragraphs. In some, you will have to supply many concrete details, illustrations, and other information important to your topic sentence. In others, you will be able to make your point clearly with only one or two supportive details. In a *few,* you might find that one sentence is all you need to achieve your purpose. (Keep in mind, however, that using too many one-sentence paragraphs can make your writing seem choppy.)

It is a good idea to rely on your central idea as a guide for development. After all, the central idea contains the main point you want to make. Therefore, it can give you a good clue about the kinds and amount of detail you should use to develop that point effectively.

Let's say you want to explain that there are *several* career opportunities for people majoring in biology. You might start by discussing teaching and medicine. But you will also have to include other fields (such as laboratory research, environmental management, and forestry) if you want your reader to understand all of what you meant when, in your topic sentence or thesis, you wrote, "Majoring in biology can provide a good foundation for *several* careers."

The subject in the sentence above is "Majoring in biology." The main point you want to make about this subject is that it can lead to "*several* careers." To write a paragraph or essay that develops this point fully, therefore, you will have to discuss *several*—at least three—careers.

In short, you can think of the central idea as a promise you make to your readers at the beginning of a paragraph or essay—a promise to discuss your main point in as much detail as is appropriate. If you start off by writing that "Three types of birds visit your backyard regularly during the winter," make sure to discuss all *three* birds. If you set out to explain that "There are many ways to decrease cholesterol in the bloodstream," discuss *many* ways, not just one or two. If you want to prove that your brother is not neat, don't be content to describe his closet and leave it at that. Talk about the mess of papers and books he often leaves scattered across the floor, and mention the jumble of sporting equipment and dirty clothes on the back seat of his car.

Deciding how many details are enough to develop a paragraph or essay fully is not always easy. However, the more experienced you become, the easier it will be to determine how much to include. For now, remember that providing too much detail is better than not providing enough. Too much information might bore your readers, but too little might leave them unconvinced or even confused. The first of these sins is forgivable; the second is not.

Just how much detail to include is what physician Lewis Thomas had to decide when he wrote this paragraph:

> Everyone must have had at least one personal experience with a computer error by this time. Bank balances are suddenly reported to have jumped from $379 into the millions, appeals for charitable contributions are mailed over and over to people with crazy-sounding names at your address, department stores send the wrong bills, utility companies write that they're turning everything off, that sort of thing. If you manage to get in touch with someone and complain, you then get instantaneously typed, guilty letters from the same computer, saying, "Our computer was in error, and an adjustment is being made in your account." ("To Err Is Human")

Obviously, Thomas could not include an example of every computer error he had ever heard of. So, he limited himself to those that would make his point most effectively and that his readers would recognize. His decision to include a specific number of examples—four in this case—is not important. We know without counting that Thomas has provided enough information to get his point across.

Choosing the Best Method of Development

You can develop an idea in many ways. The method you choose depends on your purpose—the point you wish to make and the effect you want your writing to have on your readers. Your purpose can be descriptive, narrative, explanatory, persuasive, or any combination of these.

DESCRIPTION

If your purpose is to introduce your reader to a person, place, or thing, you might *describe* your subject in concrete detail. The easiest way to gather detail for this kind of paragraph or essay is to use your five physical senses. Sight, smell, hearing, taste, and touch provide details that make writing vivid and effective. Description is also discussed in Chapters 8 and 9.

NARRATION

If you want to tell a story—to explain what happened—you will likely *narrate* a series of events as they occurred in time, explaining each event or part of an event in the order it took place. Narration is also discussed in Chapters 10 and 11.

EXPLANATION AND ARGUMENT

If your purpose is to *explain* an idea (expository writing) or to *argue* that an opinion or belief is correct (argumentative writing), you can choose from several methods to develop your ideas. Among these, of course, are narration and description, as well as the simple method called *conclusion and support,* which allows you to defend an opinion or explain an idea by using concrete and specific details that relate to it directly. However, you may want *to explain* or *to argue* by choosing from seven other methods:

- Illustration: Develop an idea with examples.
- Definition: Explain a term or concept.
- Classification: Distinguish between types or classes.
- Comparison and contrast: Point out similarities and differences.
- Analogy: Compare an abstract or difficult idea to something that is concrete and that the reader knows; usually, the subjects being compared seem unrelated at first.
- Cause and effect: Explain why something happens.
- Process analysis: Explain how something happens or how to do something.

Deciding which method of development is best for your purpose depends on the idea you are explaining or the point you are making. Let's say you want to persuade your readers that the best way to clean up the rivers in your town is to fine polluters. The cause-and-effect method might work well. If you decide to explain that the daily routine you followed in high school is quite different from the one you follow in college, you might choose contrast. If want to prove how serious a student you are, you can support your opinion with specific details that show how often you visit the library, how infrequently you miss class, or how seldom you go to parties on nights before important tests.

Various methods of development appear in the sample paragraphs and essays that follow in this chapter. You will learn even more about exposition in Section Five of this book. There you will find separate chapters on three very common and useful methods of development: illustration, comparison and contrast, and process analysis. Section Six contains two chapters on techniques useful in argument and persuasion. For now, just remember that any method of development can be used by itself or in combination with others to develop paragraphs and essays that explain, that persuade, or that do both.

Deciding How to Arrange the Ideas and Details in a Paragraph

FOR NARRATIVE AND DESCRIPTIVE WRITING

Often, the best way to organize narration or description is simply to recall details naturally—just as you saw or experienced them. When *narrating,* you can arrange events in the order they happened, from beginning to end; this is called *chronological order,* or order of time. In the following narrative paragraph, John Steinbeck tells of a young man who is being chased by the police in the wilderness. Words that relate to time or that show action are in italics:

> Pepé *stumbled* down the hill. His throat was almost closed with thirst. *At first* he *tried to run,* but immediately he *fell* and *rolled. After that* he *went* more carefully. The moon *was just disappearing* behind the mountains *when* he *came* to the bottom. He *crawled* into the heavy brush *feeling* with his fingers for water. There was no water in the bed of the stream, only damp earth. Pepé *laid* his gun *down* and *scooped up* a handful of mud and put it in his mouth, and *then* he *spluttered* and *scraped* the earth from his tongue with his finger, for the mud *drew* at his mouth like a poultice [plaster dressing]. He *dug* a hole in the stream bed with his fingers, *dug* a little basin to catch water; but *before* it was very deep his head *fell forward* on the damp ground and he *slept.* ("Flight")

When *describing,* you can put concrete details into a *spatial* pattern, according to any arrangement you think best. For example, you might describe a place from east to west or from left to right; an object from top to bottom or from inside to outside; and a person from head to toe. In the following paragraph, John Steinbeck introduces a character from his short story "The Chrysanthemums" by telling us about both her facial and physical characteristics and then by describing what she wore:

> Elisa watched [the men] for a moment and then went back to her work. She was thirty-five. Her face was lean and strong and her eyes were as clear as water. Her figure looked blocked and heavy in her gardening costume, a man's black hat pulled low down over her eyes, clodhopper shoes, a figured print dress almost completely covered by a big corduroy apron with four big pockets to hold the snips, the trowel and scratcher, the seeds and the knife she worked with. She wore heavy leather gloves to protect her hands while she worked.

FOR EXPOSITORY AND ARGUMENTATIVE WRITING

Again, several choices are available when trying your hand at exposition—writing that explains—and at argument—writing that proves a point or defends an opinion. Here are a few patterns of arrangement you can use.

From General to Specific   Starting with a general statement and supporting it with specific details or ideas is a common way to organize a paragraph. Each of the following paragraphs has a different purpose and uses a different method of development. However, all begin with a general statement (the topic sentence) that is followed and developed by specific information.

Conclusion and Support: Use Details That Explain or Prove

Columbine. For years, it was simply the name of a big high school in Littleton, Colo. But last April, it became a code word for a kind of killing disease that has been sweeping America's schools. When students Eric Harris and Dylan Klebold massacred a teacher and 12 classmates (as well as themselves), they set a new standard for the bloody horror that may confront teenagers showing up for class each day. Columbine capped a long season of school killings in Pearl, Miss.; Paducah, Ky.; and Springfield, Ore.; and left the nation in a state of confusion and grief. Despite a national outbreak of finger pointing at everyone from gun manufacturers to Hollywood to uninvolved parents, the rampages have continued. Just last month, a 13-year-old boy opened fire and wounded five classmates in Fort Gibson, Okla., with a semiautomatic handgun. (Editors of *US News & World Report*)

Comparison and Contrast: Point Out Similarities and Differences

Grant and Lee were in complete contrast, representing two diametrically opposed elements in American life. Grant was the modern man emerging: behind him, ready to come on the stage, was the great age of steel and machinery, of crowded cities and a restless, burgeoning [blossoming] vitality. Lee might have ridden down from the old age of chivalry, lance in hand, silken banner fluttering over his head. Each man was the perfect champion of his cause, drawing both his strengths and his weaknesses from the people he led. (Bruce Catton, "Grant and Lee: A Study in Contrasts")

Classification: Distinguish between Types or Classes

Many religions have definite beliefs regarding hell. Some Christians see it as a fiery pit—much like what Dante described in the Inferno—where sinners suffer eternal damnation. Islamic texts describe it as a lake of fire spanned by a bridge over which souls must travel to get to heaven. Evil doers, who fall off the bridge, are cast into the lake, there to spend eternity. Buddhism and Hinduism describe many hells through which a soul must pass in order to be cleansed of any evil so as to be reincarnated and eventually to reach a state of perfection. For the ancient Greeks and Romans, Hades, or the underworld, was populated by the shades or shadows of people who had once walked the earth. Few ever escaped this miserable place. In Judaic theology, hell was once a real place, but for most modern Jews, hell is merely an idea discussed in the scriptures so as to help people understand evil. (Karen Staples, "Deep Down Under")

Analogy: Compare an Abstract or Difficult Idea to Something that Is Concrete and That the Reader Knows

Time is like a river made up of the events which happen, and a violent stream: for as soon as a thing has been seen, it is carried away, and another comes in its place, and this will be carried away too. (Marcus Aurelius, "Meditations")

From Specific to General Beginning with specific details and moving toward a general conclusion (the topic sentence) that relates to these details is another way to arrange information. Although the following paragraphs use different methods of development, all move from specific to general.

Illustration: Develop Ideas with Examples

The ancient Chinese thought they were celestial brooms wielded [operated] by the gods to sweep the heavens free of evil. In the West they were believed to presage [foretell] the fall of Jerusalem, the death of monarchs and such anomalies as two-headed calves. The Norman Conquest of England was attributed to the 1066 flyby of Halley's, history's most famous comet, which has been linked to everything from Julius Caesar's assassination to the defeat of Attila the Hun. Told that Earth would pass through Halley's tail during its 1910 visit, many Americans panicked and bought gas masks and "comet pills." Alan Hale calls these waves of fear and mysticism "comet madness," and as co-discoverer of Comet Hale-Bopp, he's seen more than his share. (Leon Jaroff, "Crazy about Comets")

Comparison and Contrast: Point Out Similarities and Differences

In *The Expression of the Emotions in Man and Animals,* Darwin made a systematic study of how animals look when they are afraid. In both humans and animals, he found, some or all of the following may occur: the eyes and mouth open, the eyes roll, the heart beats rapidly, hairs stand on end, muscles tremble, teeth chatter, and the sphincter loosens. The frightened creature may freeze in its place or cower. These rules hold true across a remarkable array of species. Somehow it is surprising to learn that when dolphins are terrified, their teeth chatter and the whites of their eyes show, or that a frightened gorilla's legs shake. Such familiar behavior in a wild animal is a reminder of our ultimate kinship. Melvin Konner has written, "We are—not metaphorically, but precisely, biologically—like the doe nibbling moist grass in the predawn misty light; chewing, nuzzling a dewy fawn, breathing the foggy air, feeling so much at peace; and suddenly, for no reason, looking about wildly." (Jeffrey M. Masson and Susan McCarthy, *When Elephants Weep*)

You learned earlier that various methods of development can be used together. The paragraph above uses both comparison and description.

Analogy: Compare an Abstract Idea to Something that Is Concrete and that the Reader Knows

Perhaps El Hoyo, its inhabitants, and its essence can best be explained by telling a bit about a dish called capirotada. Its origin is uncertain. But, according to the time and the circumstance, it is made of old, new or hard bread. It is softened with water and then cooked with peanuts, raisins, onions, cheese, and panocha. It is fired with sherry wine. Then it is served hot, cold, or just "on the weather" as they say in El Hoyo. The Sermeños like it one way, the Garcias another, and the Ortegas still another. While it might differ greatly from one home to another, nevertheless it is still capirotada. And so it is with El Hoyo's chicanos. While being divided from within and from without, like the capirotada, they remain chicanos. (Mario Suarez, "El Hoyo")

From Question to Answer   A good way to begin a paragraph is with an interesting question. You can then devote the rest of your paragraph to details that develop an effective answer to that question.

Definition: Explain a Term or Concept

What does it mean to be poor in America? We can offer no single description of American poverty. But for many, perhaps most, it means homes with peeling paint, inadequate heating, uncertain plumbing. It means that only the very lucky among the children receive a decent education. It often means a home where some go to bed hungry and malnutrition is a frequent visitor. It means that the most elementary components of the good life in America—a vacation with kids, an evening out, a comfortable home—are but distant and unreachable dreams, more likely to be seen on the television screen than in the neighborhood. And for almost all the poor it means that life is a constant struggle to obtain the merest necessities of existence, those things most of us take for granted. We can do better. (U.S. Senator Paul Wellstone, "If Poverty Is the Question . . .")

Analogy: Compare an Abstract or Difficult Idea to Something that Is Concrete or that the Reader Knows

How can a telescope provide information about the beginning of the Universe? The answer is that when we look out into space, we look into the past. If a galaxy is five billion light-years away, it takes five billion years for the light from this galaxy to reach the earth. Consequently, our telescopes show the galaxy not as it is today, but as it was five billion years ago, when the light we are receiving now had just left that galaxy on its way to the earth. A telescope is a time machine; it carries us back to the past. (Robert Jastrow, *Journey to the Stars*)

The paragraph above is another that uses more than one method of development. Here, analogy combines with process analysis.

From Problem to Solution   Organizing a paragraph by stating a problem and explaining how to solve it in the sentences that follow is much like asking a question and answering it. It is especially effective when you are explaining a process or analyzing causes and effects. But it can be used with other methods of development as well.

Process Analysis: Explain How to Do Something

For most people, being overweight is not simply a matter of vanity. Excess weight is a threat to health and longevity. You should start losing weight by getting a thorough physical examination, then begin following a regular exercise program prescribed by your doctor. Next, start counting calories; read labels or look up the caloric content of your favorite foods in diet guides available at most supermarkets and drugstores. Finally, stay away from high-fat animal products and rich desserts. Fill up on fruits, vegetables, natural grains and other high-fiber foods. (Diana Dempsey, "Tightening Our Belts")

By Order of Importance   Writers of fiction often place the most important bit of information last. This makes their work suspenseful and creates a more effective climax. If arranged in this pattern, an expository or argumentative paragraph can help you create emphasis by guiding your readers to the details and ideas you believe are most important.

Cause and Effect: Explain Why Something Happens

The greatest moral imperative [obligation] we face is replacing the welfare state with an opportunity society. For every day that we allow the current conditions to continue, we are condemning the poor—and particularly poor children—to being deprived of their basic rights as Americans. The welfare state reduces the poor from citizens to clients. It breaks up families, minimizes work incentives, blocks people from saving and acquiring property, and overshadows dreams of a promised future with a present despair born of poverty, violence, and hopelessness. (former Speaker of the U.S. House of Representatives Newt Gingrich, *To Renew America*)

Around a Pivot   The pivoting pattern begins with one idea, then changes direction—pivots—by presenting a different or contrasting idea. The topic sentence normally appears in the middle of the paragraph and announces the shift. Often, but not always, the topic sentence is introduced by a transition such as *but, however,* and *nonetheless.*

Illustration: Develop an Idea with Examples

I sometimes hear people who should know better saying that we would be healthier if we depended solely on herbal remedies and refused to take the synthetic drugs purveyed [supplied] by modern scientific medicine. Browse through a pharmacopoeia [list of medicines] and see how many of the medicines prescribed by doctors and sold by druggists are prepared from plants. Quinine for malaria, ephedrine for asthma, cascara for constipation, digitalis for heart conditions, atropine for eye examinations and a great host of other valuable medicines in constant use came directly from folk herbal medicines, and are still prepared from wild plants or those recently brought under cultivation. (Euell Gibbons, *Stalking the Wild Asparagus*)

Visualizing Paragraph Development

The following paragraphs are from "Which Side of the Fence?" freshman Dan Roland's essay that recalls a honeymoon trip to Jamaica. The first uses the conclusion-and-support method of development and a general-to-specific pattern of organization. The second, which is arranged in the specific-to-general pattern, illustrates three methods of development: description, cause/effect, and contrast.

Topic sentence expresses a conclusion.

Paragraph moves from general to specific.

Arriving at the resort is like stepping into another world. This ultra-modern hotel is surrounded by a golf course; tennis courts; a huge swimming pool; outdoor lounges complete with palm trees, calypso bands, and elegant bamboo cages that hold parrots and other exotic birds; and a beach that features water skiers, wind surfers, yachts, and hundreds of tourists wearing the latest summer fashions and sipping numerous fruit and rum drinks with little umbrellas in them.

Specific details support conclusion.

Paragraph moves from specific to general.

All of the luxury in this hotel is surrounded by a barbed-wire fence, with only one entrance on each side patrolled by armed security guards. This protects the tourist from a constant bombardment of sales pitches

Description

from native Jamaicans, who can feed their families for weeks by selling just a few of their homemade souvenirs. Hotel guests are

Cause/effect

allowed to go out through the gate, but natives may not come in. Many of them live in small shacks right next to the fence, so as never to miss a selling opportunity. The symbolism is staggering: on one side are wealth and luxury, on the other poverty and

Contrast

hunger. The fence is a barrier to the good life.

Topic sentence

Revising to Improve Development

Read these two versions of paragraphs from "Exile and Return," an essay appearing later in this chapter, which discusses the author's return to his high school after many years. Compare the second version with the first to learn how James Keller added to, corrected, and clarified his rough draft to improve the effectiveness of his essay.

Keller—Rough Draft

Eventually my eyes come to rest on the chalkboards. I remember staring at them

Why faces?

bored at what I was listening to. Faces turn and face me from seats in front and to my side. They are only shadows from the past,

Why was he "bored"?

Check meaning?

only memories. They're looking for me. And through me. They've left. Some gone to school, some gone to the world. Others gone quite <u>literally</u> to hell, not soon to return.

Choppy, vague, and weak. Needs detail.

Vague. What "places" are these?

Out of the building, I walk on grassy playing fields that were greener then. . . . <u>Places</u> where many of us found brief, <u>insignificant glory</u>. I no longer remember who won and who lost. Only that somehow we all walked away winners and losers to the same heart. It is more than I can bear.

Explain this term?

I leave now, maybe forever, if I ever existed at all.

Keller—Final Draft

Eventually my eyes come to rest on the chalkboards. Old habits die hard. I remember staring at them through teachers whose words

Adds quotation to explain why he was "bored."

Identifies "faces."

"had forked no lightning." My <u>teachers</u> and <u>classmates</u> are gone, but many faces remain.

Adds narrative and descriptive details.

From seats in front and to my side, they turn and stare. They are shadows of the past, bloodless visions, returned from long exile to mock my exile and return. They're looking for me and through me. But they're only memories. They've left, you know—some gone to school, some gone to the world,

Has removed "literally."

others gone to their own private hells.

Smoother and developed more fully.

Faces that laughed, young and innocent, now cry, worn and haggard. Their expressions hide lives that were true and alive but now are neither.

Adds information about classmates.

Out of the building, I walk on grassy playing fields where so many of us found brief insignificant glory. They were greener in another spring. The empty stands play sentinel to the lonely track and football field, and a thousand ghosts applaud a hundred athletes only I can see. I no longer remember who won and lost, only that somehow we all walked away winners and losers to the same heart, veterans of so much happiness and so much pain. It is more than I can bear.

Identifies "places" with specific information.

Adds information to explain "insignificant glory."

I leave now, maybe forever. I wonder if I ever existed and was ever here at all. To say good-bye is to die a little. And so I do.

A stronger conclusion: adds detail to convey his emotional reaction.

Practicing Methods of Development

Complete the paragraphs begun below. Include information based on your own observations and experiences. Use whatever method of development you think the topic sentence, which begins each paragraph, calls for.

1. My family provides me with a great deal of emotional support. For example,

_____

_____

_____

_____

_____

_____

_____

2. There are three types of students at my college. The first _____

_____

_____

_____

_____

3. If you want to flunk a test, do the following:

_____

_____

_____

_____

4. Most people gain weight because _____

_____

_____

_____

_____

5. My sister (brother, best friend) is a _____ type of person. I, on the other hand, am

_____

_____

_____

_____

_____

_____

_____

As you read the following selections, remember what you've just learned about (1) the methods that writers use to develop their ideas and (2) the patterns they use to organize their paragraphs. Approach each selection carefully, and devote as much effort to determining *how* the author has organized and developed the material as you do to understanding what the essay means. Doing so will help you develop your own writing more effectively.

The Last Safe Haven

Joannie M. Schrof

"The Last Safe Haven" appeared in the December 26, 1994, issue of U.S. News and World Report, *a weekly news magazine. It analyzes the spread of violence to the small town, once considered a refuge from the kinds of crime found in the city.*

Preparing to Read

1. This essay was printed in an end-of-year column called "Farewells: Faces We Knew, Ways We Were: Now They Are Gone." This information is important in understanding the author's purpose.

2. Schrof makes good use of transitions and other devices to maintain coherence. Read her essay twice. The second time, circle words and phrases that make it coherent.

3. What does the first sentence of the essay tell us about what is to come?

Vocabulary

hamlet (noun)	Small town, village.
maelstrom (noun)	Storm.
mayhem (noun)	Violence.
palpable (adjective)	Obvious, plain, evident.
recital (noun)	Speech, reading, presentation.
refuge (noun)	Safe place, shelter.
relentless (adjective)	Without end, unceasing.
sanctuary (noun)	Holy place, haven, refuge.
seared (verb)	Burned.

The Last Safe Haven

Joannie M. Schrof

NINETEEN NINETY-FOUR SEARED a series of disturbing images into the American memory: a mother drowning her sons, children shooting each other, a 5-year-old boy thrown from a high-rise window. The relentless recital of mayhem added to the fear, to the feeling—however illusory—that there was once true refuge, and that it has disappeared.

Nowhere is this sense more palpable than in the nation's small towns. While cities have always battled crime, the small town has been celebrated as a sanctuary, where doors are left unlocked and children roam freely. But even the smallest towns are growing more dangerous, often at the hands of the very children they are famous for protecting.

Geneseo, Ill. (population 5,990), is one such place. A decade ago its quiet streets won the state's "Hometown Award." This year, after a series of violent incidents, the police department created a gang investigation unit. Every other week now, it seems, a teenager is badly beaten in gang-related violence: Recently, a local boy was clubbed to death in a nearby town. Stolen cars, burglarized homes and vandalism are on the rise. And nightfall brings the sound of doors locking all around town.

City dwellers have long imagined that if things got too bad, they could pack up and move to a place like Geneseo, a cozy, self-enclosed hamlet far from the maelstrom. It was probably always a fantasy. Now that we know it, the only alternative left is to stand and fight back.

Questions for Discussion

1. Identify the essay's thesis.
2. In Preparing to Read, you read that the title of the column in which this essay appeared, "Faces We Knew, Ways We Were: Now They Are Gone," tells us something about the author's purpose. Explain.
3. What is the chief method of development used in paragraphs 1 and 4?
4. What is the chief method of development used in paragraphs 2 and 3?
5. What pattern of organization does Schrof use in paragraphs 2 and 4? In paragraph 3?
6. Explain the function of paragraph 2's first sentence in terms of maintaining coherence.
7. Find places in which Schrof uses transitions to maintain coherence.

Thinking Critically

1. In paragraph 2, Schrof writes: "even the smallest towns are growing more dangerous, often at the hands of the very children they are famous for protecting." Are children getting more and more violent? If so, what do you think is causing this?
2. Schrof concludes by saying that "the only alternative left is to stand and fight back." What are some ways we can combat the growing trend toward violence?
3. Explain in what way the tragedy at Columbine High School supports Schrof's thesis.

Suggestions for Journal Entries

1. Whether you come from a city or small town, do you think your community is a safe haven? Ask yourself whether or not you feel safe walking the streets at night, leaving the front door unlocked, carrying around a lot of cash, parking your car on the street, and so on. Try asking and answering a variety of questions that will help you determine how safe your community is.

2. Many of us have "safe havens," places where we can feel safe and at ease. There we seek advice, safety, sympathy, or encouragement, or just a peaceful atmosphere where we can relax and rejuvenate ourselves ("recharge our batteries"). Where is your safe haven? Freewrite for about 10 minutes to describe this place.

Exile and Return

James Keller

As managing editor for his college newspaper, James Keller wrote many news and feature stories that attracted the attention of professors and fellow students. Today he is a college English professor. "Exile and Return" recalls his visit to his suburban high school several years after graduation. This before-and-after portrait reveals as much about the author as it does about his school.

Preparing to Read

1. Keller's thesis statement appears at the end of his first paragraph. Identify the main point he makes in this essay as you read this sentence.
2. "Had forked no lightning" (paragraph 5) is from "Do Not Go Gentle into That Good Night," a poem by Dylan Thomas.
3. You know what the subject of this essay is. Can you guess Keller's purpose in writing this essay? Who might his primary readers be?

Vocabulary

arcane (adjective)	Secret, known only by a few.
asbestos (noun)	Insulating material now considered a health hazard.
banality (noun)	Boring quality.
predicting (adjective)	Giving signs of, foretelling.
stifling (adjective)	Suffocating.

Exile and Return

James Keller

IT'S ALL DIFFERENT, quiet and grey now, like the sun reflecting on the previous 1 night's darkness or predicting the afternoon's storm. On this stifling summer morning, I scarcely recognize the school I had attended for four years. The life and laughter have died. It is another world.

I walk down the vacant halls, and what light there is shines a path on the 2 mirrored beige floors, leading me past imposing grey lockers that stand erect in columns. At one time, they woke the dead in closing but now remain closed in silence. I remember the faces of people who stood and sometimes slumped before them at day's end. They were friendly faces that looked up and nodded or said "Hello" as I galloped past. Now there are other faces, faces of people I never got to know.

The lockers soon give way to the classrooms, cement cells we once lived in, learned in, and often slept in. Steel I-beams I had once hardly noticed now hang like doom over cracked and peeling walls. The architect left them exposed, for want of talent, I assume. From the color scheme of putrid green to the neutral asbestos ceiling and steel rafters, the banality of the classrooms overwhelms me.

3

The rooms are empty now save the ancient desks. They are yellow clay and steel and much smaller than I remember. I can still read arcane graffiti, its meaning forgotten, on their dull surfaces. The handwriting is my own. I recognize the doodles drawn as every minute ran past like a turtle climbing up a glass wall. Back then, they killed the time. They didn't do much for the furniture either.

4

Eventually my eyes come to rest on the chalkboards. Old habits die hard. I remember staring at them through teachers whose words "had forked no lightning." My teachers and classmates are gone, but many faces remain. From seats in front and to my side, they turn and stare. They are shadows of the past, bloodless visions, returned from long exile to mock my exile and return. They're looking for me and through me. But they're only memories. They've left, you know—some gone to school, some gone to the world, others gone to their own private hells. Faces that laughed, young and innocent, now cry, worn and haggard. Their expressions hide lives that were true and alive but now are neither.

5

Out of the building, I walk on grassy playing fields where so many of us found brief insignificant glory. They were greener in another spring. The empty stands play sentinel to the lonely track and football field, and a thousand ghosts applaud a hundred athletes only I can see. I no longer remember who won and lost, only that somehow we all walked away winners and losers to the same heart, veterans of so much happiness and so much pain. It is more than I can bear.

6

I leave now, maybe forever. I wonder if I ever existed and was ever here at all. To say good-bye is to die a little. And so I do.

7

Questions for Discussion

1. What is Keller's thesis statement? What words in that thesis express his main point? In short, what is he telling us about his high school?

2. In which paragraphs does the topic sentence not appear at the very beginning? Can you find a paragraph in which the central idea is only implied?

3. The author's purpose is to contrast his memories of a place with its present reality. However, he uses other methods of development as well. In which paragraph or paragraphs does he use cause and effect?

4. Where in this essay can you find examples of narration and description?

5. Find an instance in which Keller uses analogy.

6. Which pattern of organization discussed earlier in this chapter does Keller use in paragraph 2?

7. Which pattern of organization does he use in paragraphs 6 and 7?

Thinking Critically

The biographical note on Keller, which appears before the essay, claims that this selection reveals as much about the author as about the place he is discussing. What have you learned about Keller's personality from this essay?

Suggestions for Journal Entries

1. Take a mental stroll through the hallways, classrooms, or athletic fields of your high school. What do you remember most about it and about your classmates, your teachers, and yourself? Use focused freewriting or listing to record these memories in your journal.

   Next, read your journal entry. What main impression about your high school experience can you draw from these details? Did you enjoy it? Were you happy and secure around the teachers and students you met each day? Is the opposite true? Or do you have mixed feelings? Put your main impression into a preliminary thesis statement that might get you started on a longer assignment described in the Suggestions for Sustained Writing at the end of this chapter.

2. "To say good-bye is to die a little," Keller writes. Recall an incident in which you had to say good-bye to someone, something, or some place. Use focused freewriting to write a brief story about the event. Try to reveal why saying good-bye was so hard.

Burger Queen

Erin Sharp

Erin Sharp was a sophomore at Cornell University when she wrote this essay. It first appeared in The American Enterprise Magazine.

Preparing to Read

1. The information in this essay comes from Sharp's employment at a McDonald's restaurant. Before you begin reading, think about the layout and appearance of such a restaurant, the people who might work there, and people who might eat there.

2. If you were writing an essay about your place of employment, what subjects would you discuss to give your readers a good understanding of this place?

3. What do you think Sharp is hinting at in the title?

4. As you read, you might find unfamiliar words not listed in the vocabulary below. If so, try to get at their meanings by using context clues within the essay. For example, in paragraph 4, the author says that some customers have "bickered" with her "for five minutes over a measly ten-cent increase in the price of an Egg McMuffin." What might "bickered" and "measly" mean in this sentence?

Vocabulary

bickered (verb)	Argued over something silly or unimportant.
coveted (adjective)	Desired.
forfeited (verb)	Gave up.
freelance (adjective)	Self-employed, temporary, hired for one-time job.
hoard (verb)	Save, hide away.
quipped (verb)	Answered in a joking or sarcastic way.
pathologist (noun)	Doctor who diagnoses physical changes caused by disease.
perspective (noun)	Point of view.
reimbursement (noun)	Refund.
scam (verb)	To cheat.
stereotypes (noun)	Labels, types.
tackiness (noun)	Bad taste.
tempered	Moderated, lessened, toned down.

Burger Queen

Erin Sharp

WHEN I ANNOUNCED the change of my major from biology with pre-med 1
aspirations to English, my advisor simply raised an eyebrow and asked
if I planned to work at McDonald's for the rest of my life. "Actually," I
quipped, "I've been working at McDonald's for two and a half years, and it's
sort of fun." His surprise was evident, a typical reaction to my shocking side
occupation. I spoke the truth, though; I have held a dozen jobs ranging from
camp counselor to pathologist's assistant (now including, I suppose, freelance
journalism), yet none have been as entertaining as my stints at the Golden
Arches.

My double life as Erin Sharp, Ivy League McDonald's Worker, has re- 2
vealed twin stereotypes to me. People told I go to Cornell view me as bright
and ambitious. Put me behind the counter at McDonald's, however, and I am
usually assumed to be a high school dropout with fifteen unseen piercings.

When I was six years old, McDonald's was my favorite place to eat, and 3
kids have not changed much in the last dozen years. I am often asked
whether I have actually met "The Ronald" McDonald, and have been given
letters to pass along to him, like one of Santa Claus's elves. Among kids, Mc-
Donald's workers rank right up there with policemen and firefighters.

Yet this perspective rarely survives adolescence. Respect for the workers 4
of the fast food industry is lost among most adults, with absurd results. Many
adults seem to assume that McWorkers are stupid, attempting to scam us out
of free food and coupons. The depths of tackiness to which some human beings will stoop in order to save a few pennies at a drive-thru window are worthy of "Candid Camera." Grown men driving Lincoln Town Cars have bickered with me for five minutes over a measly ten-cent increase in the price of
an Egg McMuffin. Perhaps they imagine that I overcharge each patron and
hoard misbegotten dimes in a piggy bank behind the shake machine?

Once, my store even received a phone call at noon from a furious woman 5
demanding reimbursement for the breakfast she had bought that morning via
drive-thru; apparently, it was cold when she arrived at work over an hour
later. Our most famous TIC (Truculent, Irate Customer) lost her temper
when we could not (in her eyes, would not) provide the grilled chicken sandwich she craved in the middle of breakfast rush hour. An entirely new traffic
pattern was created in Drive-thru for the 25 minutes spent in fruitless argument and accommodation attempts by our managers as the grill team thawed
frozen meat, heated a grill to cook on and produced the coveted sandwich for
her. When at last presented with it, she lofted the bag triumphantly and accused us of withholding it from her for the entire time, then zoomed off with
the last words: "I'm never coming back here again!" The effectiveness of this
condemnation was tempered by her license plate, which proclaimed her to be
from Delaware—over an hour away.

A small portion of our patrons are so confused that there is really noth-   6
ing to do but wait for them to leave. My most prominent example of this sort
of "guest" is the infamous Snack Attack Lady, who ordered hotcakes and
sausage during our 90-second-guaranteed-service hour and then ate her
breakfast right outside the drive-thru window. Heedless of the frenzied honk-
ing behind her, she carefully opened the platter, poured a puddle of syrup,
rolled the sausage in a hotcake and dipped both daintily into the syrup. My
co-workers and I watched in speechless amazement. When asked what she
was doing, she rolled her eyes and snapped, "What does it look like I'm
doing? I'm eating my breakfast!" That woman has permanently forfeited all
rights to complain about slow drive-thru service.

And yet, there are some great customers out there, like the Morning   7
Crew: the seven retired men and one active police officer who wait for our
doors to open every day so that they can enjoy their dawn coffee and conversation. If I missed a day of work, I would return to inquiries about my health
and concern that all was well. The greatest customers ever to grace our store
were two deliverymen who drove up to the window one spring afternoon two
years ago with armfuls of roses for my co-worker and me. They were moving
their business out of state, they explained, and wanted to thank us for making their afternoons brighter.

Well, boys, if you are reading this article, thank you again for that fabu-   8
lous surprise. I still have the ribbon which bound them.

Questions for Discussion

1. In which paragraphs does Sharp make use of illustration?
2. Which paragraph uses the cause-and-effect method? Which uses contrast?
3. What method of development can be seen in paragraph 1?
4. Identify the pattern of organization used in paragraphs 1 through 7.
5. What is Sharp's central idea?
6. Why does Sharp tell us that her advisor was surprised when she told him she had worked at McDonald's? How does doing so help introduce her central idea?

Thinking Critically

1. In Preparing to Read, you were asked to use context clues to determine the meaning of some of Sharp's vocabulary. What does she mean by "pre-med," "aspirations," and "stints" in paragraph 1; "truculent," "irate," "fruitless," and "lofted" in paragraph 5; "heedless" and "frenzied" in paragraph 6?

2. What are the Ivy League, "Candid Camera," and McWorkers? You might find more about the first two terms on the Internet or in your college library, but you will have to figure out the third term on your own.

3. What is the pun (play on words) Sharp uses in the title?

Suggestions for Journal Entries

1. Use focused freewriting, listing, or clustering to gather information that describes customers or employees or both at a place at which you work or have worked. Focus on people with the most interesting or distinctive personalities.

2. Sharp's essay is more than a listing of complaints about annoying customers. It is a statement—and a positive one at that—about her role and image as a worker in a fast-food restaurant. Use clustering or any other prewriting method to explain your feelings—be they positive, negative, or mixed—about a job you hold or once held.

A Brother's Dreams

Paul Aronowitz

Paul Aronowitz was a medical student at Case Western Reserve University when he wrote this very sensitive essay comparing his dreams, hopes, and ambitions with those of his schizophrenic brother. Schizophrenia is a mental illness characterized by withdrawal from reality.

Aronowitz's love, compassion, and understanding come across clearly as he unfolds the story of how he learned to deal with the fact that his brother's strange, sometimes violent behavior was the symptom of an illness and not a defect in character. This essay is also Aronowitz's admission and unselfish affirmation that, however "elusive" and "trivial," his brother's dreams might be even more meaningful than his own.

"A Brother's Dreams" first appeared in "About Men," a weekly column in the New York Times Magazine.

Preparing to Read

1. Aronowitz's central idea concerns how he came to understand his brother's illness and to accept the fact that his brother's dreams were meaningful and important. However, the author does not begin to reveal this central idea until near the end of this essay, and he never puts the idea into a formal thesis statement.

2. Many of the paragraphs in this selection are developed through narration and description, but Aronowitz also makes good use of cause and effect, comparison and contrast, illustration, and conclusion and support.

3. Josef Mengele, whom Aronowitz mentions in paragraph 5, was a Nazi medical researcher who conducted unspeakable experiments in which he tortured and maimed or killed thousands of human beings.

Vocabulary

acrid (adjective)	Bitter, harsh, sharp.
aimlessly (adverb)	Without purpose.
alienate (verb)	Make enemies of, isolate oneself from.
delusions (noun)	Misconceptions, fantasies.
depravity (noun)	Immorality, corruption.
elusive (adjective)	Hard to grasp, intangible.
paranoid (adjective)	Showing unreasonable or unwarranted suspicion.
prognosis (noun)	Prediction about the course or outcome of an illness.

resilient (adjective)   Able to bounce back.
siblings (noun)   Sisters and brothers.

A Brother's Dreams

Paul Aronowitz

EACH TIME I go home to see my parents at their house near Poughkeepsie, 1
N.Y., my brother, a schizophrenic for almost nine years now, comes to
visit from the halfway house where he lives nearby. He owns a car that my
parents help him to maintain, and his food and washing are taken care of by
the halfway house. Somewhere, somehow along the way, with the support of
a good physician, a social worker and my ever-resilient parents, he has managed to carve a niche for himself, to bite off some independence and, with it,
elusive dreams that, to any healthy person, might seem trivial.

My brother sits in a chair across from me, chain-smoking cigarettes, try- 2
ing to take the edge off the medications he'll be on for the rest of his life.
Sometimes his tongue hangs loosely from his mouth when he's listening or
pops out of his mouth as he speaks—a sign of tardive dyskinesia, an often-
irreversible side effect of his medication.

He draws deeply on his cigarette and tells me he can feel his mind heal- 3
ing—cells being replaced, tissue being restored, thought processes returning.
He knows this is happening because he dreams of snakes, and hot, acrid
places in which he suffocates if he moves too fast. When he wakes, the birds
are singing in the trees outside his bedroom window. They imitate people in
his halfway house, mocking them and calling their names. The birds are so
smart, he tells me, so much smarter than we are.

His face, still handsome despite its puffiness (another side effect of the 4
medications that allow him to function outside the hospital), and warm
brown eyes are serious. When I look into his eyes I imagine I can see some of
the suffering he has been through. I think of crossed wires, of receptors and
neurotransmitters, deficits and surpluses, progress and relapse, and I wonder,
once again, what has happened to my brother.

My compassion for him is recent. For many years, holidays, once happy 5
occasions for our family of seven to gather together, were emotional torture
sessions. My brother would pace back and forth in the dining room, lecturing
us, his voice loud, dominating, crushing all sound but his own, about the end
of the world, the depravity of our existences. His speeches were salted with
paranoid delusions: our house was bugged by the F.B.I.; my father was Josef
Mengele; my mother was selling government secrets to the Russians.

His life was decaying before my eyes, and I couldn't stand to listen to 6
him. My resentment of him grew as his behavior became more disruptive and
aggressive. I saw him as being ultimately responsible for his behavior. As my
anger increased, I withdrew from him, avoiding him when I came home to
visit from college, refusing to discuss the bizarre ideas he brought up over the

dinner table. When I talked with my sister or other two brothers about him, our voices always shadowed in whispers, I talked of him as of a young man who had chosen to spend six months of every year in a pleasant, private hospital on the banks of the Hudson River, chosen to alienate his family with threats, chosen to withdraw from the stresses of the world. I hated what he had become. In all those years, I never asked what his diagnosis was.

Around the fifth year of his illness, things finally changed. One hot summer night, he attacked my father. When I came to my father's aid, my brother broke three of my ribs and nearly strangled me. The State Police came and took him away. My father's insurance coverage had run out on my brother, so this time he was taken to a locked ward at the state hospital where heavily sedated patients wandered aimlessly in stockinged feet up and down long hallways. Like awakening from a bad dream, we gradually began talking about his illness. Slowly and painfully, I realized that he wasn't responsible for his disease any more than a cancer patient is for his pain.

As much as I've learned to confront my brother's illness, it frightens me to think that one day, my parents gone from the scene, my siblings and I will be responsible for portions of my brother's emotional and financial support. This element of the future is one we still avoid discussing, much the way we avoided thinking about the nature of his disease and his prognosis. I'm still not capable of thinking about it.

Now I come home and listen to him, trying not to react, trying not to show disapproval. His delusions are harmless and he is, at the very least, communicating. When he asks me about medical school, I answer with a sentence or two—no elaboration, no revelations about the dreams I cradle in my heart.

He talks of his own dreams. He hopes to finish his associate's degree—the same one he has been working on between hospitalizations for almost eight years now—at the local community college. Next spring, with luck, he'll get a job. His boss will be understanding, he tells me, cutting him a little slack when he has his "bad days," letting him have a day off here or there when things aren't going well. He puts out his cigarette and lights another one.

Time stands still. This could be last year, or the year before, or the year before that. I'm within range of becoming a physician, of realizing something I've been working toward for almost five years, while my brother still dreams of having a small job, living in his own apartment and of being well. As the smoke flows from his nose and mouth, I recall an evening some time ago when I drove upstate from Manhattan to tell my parents and my brother that I was getting married (an engagement later severed). My brother's eyes lit up at the news, and then a darkness fell over them.

"What's wrong?" I asked him.

"It's funny," he answered matter-of-factly. "You're getting married, and I've never even had a girlfriend." My mother's eyes filled with tears, and she turned away. She was trying her best to be happy for me, for the dreams I had—for the dreams so many of us take for granted.

"You still have us," I stammered, reaching toward him and touching his [14] arm. All of a sudden my dreams meant nothing; I didn't deserve them and they weren't worth talking about. My brother shrugged his shoulders, smiled and shook my hand, his large, tobacco-stained fingers wrapping around my hand, dwarfing my hand.

Questions for Discussion

1. If you wanted to write a formal thesis statement for this essay, what would it be?
2. "A Brother's Dreams" contains at least two paragraphs that are developed through description. Identify one of them. What important idea does this paragraph communicate?
3. The purpose of paragraph 6 is to explain a cause and an effect. What is the paragraph's topic sentence (cause)? What details (effect) does Aronowitz provide to develop the paragraph fully?
4. Which paragraphs use narration?
5. Aronowitz gets specific about his brother's dreams in paragraph 10, which he develops by stating a conclusion and then supporting this conclusion with details. Identify these details.
6. Paragraph 11 contrasts some of Aronowitz's dreams to some of his brother's. In what other paragraph do we see their dreams contrasted?
7. Most paragraphs in this essay are organized in the general-to-specific pattern. However, paragraphs 11 and 13 are organized according to order of importance. What is the most important idea in each of these paragraphs?
8. This is a powerful essay. Which paragraph affects you most strongly? What do the details in this paragraph tell you about the author or his brother or both?

Thinking Critically

Explaining how he came to terms with his brother's illness, Aronowitz says his compassion for his brother is only "recent." Pretend you are interviewing Aronowitz. What would he say is the reason for not feeling compassion earlier? What caused his change in attitude?

Suggestions for Journal Entries

1. Aronowitz writes about a person whose lifestyle and dreams are very different from those of most other people. Do you know someone like this? If so, write a paragraph showing how this person's lifestyle or dreams differ from those of most others. Use one major method of development; for instance, you might *describe* what this individual

looks like (much in the way Aronowitz describes his brother in paragraphs 2 and 4), or you might use *narration* to tell a story about the kind of behavior you have come to expect from the person (as Aronowitz does in paragraphs 3, 5, and 7). You might even want to try your hand at the cause-and-effect method by telling your reader how you normally react to or deal with this person and then explaining what causes you to react in this way.

2. Aronowitz's essay contrasts his brother's dreams to his own. Write a paragraph in which you show how different you are from your brother, sister, or other close relative by contrasting a major goal in your life to one of his or hers.

   Clearly identify the two different goals in your topic sentence, and fill the rest of your paragraph with details showing how different they are; that is, develop the paragraph by contrast. Your topic sentence might go something like this: "My sister Janet intends to move to the city and find a high-paying job, even if she hates every minute of it; I'll be happy earning the modest income that comes with managing our family farm."

Suggestions for Sustained Writing

1. Write a paragraph that uses the cause-and-effect method to explain why you do something habitually. For instance, explain why you are late for work every day, why you take the same road home, why you frequent a particular restaurant or bar, or why you study in the same place every night.

   Arrange the paragraph in a general-to-specific or specific-to-general pattern, provide enough details to develop your central idea clearly and convincingly, and check for unity and coherence. You will find examples of effective cause-and-effect paragraphs in "Exile and Return" and "A Brother's Dreams."

   As with other assignments, revise your work as necessary; never be satisfied with an early draft. Add or remove detail as appropriate, and insert transitions that will make your ideas easy to follow. Then edit carefully for mechanical errors that might reduce your writing's effectiveness.

2. If you responded to the first of the Suggestions for Journal Entries after "The Last Safe Haven," you have begun to gather information on whether or not you believe your community is safe. If you think it isn't, use what you have written thus far as the basis of a longer essay that supports your opinion. Here's a sample outline for the first draft of such an essay:

   Paragraph 1: Thesis: *An increase in serious crime is making my hometown unsafe.* (You might include general information about kinds of crime you have seen, read about, or heard about.)

Paragraph 2: Discusses specific examples of criminal acts you know about. A good way to organize this paragraph is the general-to-specific pattern.

Paragraph 3: Uses cause and effect to explain the increase in crime. A good way to organize this paragraph is the question-to-answer pattern.

Paragraph 4: Uses process analysis to explain what your community should do to combat crime. A good way to organize this paragraph is the order-of-importance pattern.

Paragraph 5: Concludes the essay by referring to the thesis and expressing hope that things will get better.

Make sure to revise your rough draft several times. As you do, practice the techniques for maintaining coherence and unity discussed in Chapter 2. Whenever possible, add detail to make your ideas more convincing. Finally, edit and proofread the final version carefully.

3. After you read Keller's "Exile and Return," you might have used your journal to take a mental stroll through your high school and to write a preliminary thesis statement for an essay explaining your main impression or opinion of the time you spent there. If so, you might also have begun collecting memories that explain that impression.

Read your journal notes carefully. Add information if you can. Then, use your preliminary thesis as the beginning of an essay on your high school experience. Express your main impression or opinion of the experience through the thesis statement's main point.

Next, write three or four paragraphs that explain or support your thesis. Give each paragraph a topic sentence about one aspect of your experience. Make sure the topic sentence expresses a main point, and focus the information in your paragraph on that point.

Here's what an outline for such an essay might look like:

Paragraph 1

Thesis: *The thing I appreciate most about Valley High is that it helped me gain confidence as a student.* (This paragraph might also include information about the kind of high school you attended, your overall impression of the place, and things you most remember about it.)

Paragraph 2

Topic sentence: *My classmates were supportive.*

Method of development: Illustration

Pattern: General to specific

Paragraph 3

Topic sentence: *My teachers taught me to study for tests.*

Method of development: Process analysis or contrast

Pattern: Order of importance

Paragraph 4

Topic sentence: *With the help of math tutors, I finally overcame my fear of algebra.*

Method of development: Cause and effect or contrast

Pattern: Pivot

Paragraph 5:

Conclusion: This paragraph makes reference to the thesis. It also explains that the confidence you developed in high school will help you in college.

Read your rough draft carefully. Add details as needed to make your essay complete and convincing. After completing several drafts, edit and proofread the best of them.

4. Read any journal notes you made after reading Sharp's "Burger Queen." Use as much of this material as you can to write an essay that gives your general impression or opinion of a job you have held or a place at which you have worked. Your opinion might be positive, negative, or mixed, but make sure to state it clearly in your thesis statement, which should appear in your first paragraph.

To practice writing various kinds of paragraphs, try to include at least one of the following:

- A paragraph that defines the kind of business conducted or work performed at this job or place.
- A paragraph that provides examples of your usual duties or tasks.
- A paragraph that describes the physical environment in which you work or have worked—the factory, office building, restaurant, etc. If your job is or was outdoors, describe the kind of locations in which you most often work or worked.
- A paragraph that contrasts this job with another you have held.
- A paragraph that narrates incidents with customers and/or employees to explain the social environment or atmosphere in which you work or worked.

In addition, vary the patterns by which you organize your paragraphs. Try to include at least one that is arranged from general to specific; one that is arranged from specific to general; and one that uses the pivot pattern.

You might want to begin writing by making a formal outline of your paper based on what has been said above. Then, after carefully drafting and revising each paragraph and the paper as a whole, edit and proofread slowly and methodically.

5. After completing Paul Aronowitz's "A Brother's Dreams," you might have written a paragraph in your journal explaining how different your goal in life is from that of your brother, sister, or other close relative. If so, the method by which you developed this paragraph was contrast.

Reread this paragraph. What does it tell you about your subject's character? What kind of person is he or she? Turn your answer into the central idea (thesis statement) of an essay in which you continue to discuss this relative. In fact, make the paragraph you've already written the introduction to your essay.

As you plan this essay, consider writing a paragraph or two in which you describe this individual—the way he walks, the way she dresses, and so on. You might also want to include a narrative paragraph, one in which you tell a story that helps support what you say about him or her in your thesis. Finally, think about using additional methods of development—illustration, and conclusion and support, for example—in other paragraphs to develop your thesis further.

Once again, remember that writing is a process. You owe it to yourself and your readers to produce the most effective paper you can through painstaking rewriting and editing.

Writing to Learn: A Group Activity

The First Meeting

For inspiration, read Joannie M. Schrof's "The Last Safe Haven" aloud. Then, ask each group member to gather information about methods communities (both police and ordinary citizens) are using to prevent crime. Ideally, each member should gather the equivalent of two or three typewritten pages of information.

Research

Start with what you already know about crime prevention. However, interviewing a sociology or criminal justice professor, the head of the campus security force, or even a local police officer might be very worthwhile.

Another way to gather information is library research. Find informative magazine articles by checking recent editions of the *Readers' Guide to Periodical Literature* under headings such as crime, crime prevention, gang violence, vandalism, violent crime, rape, theft, burglary, automobile theft, and homicide. Also, search the Internet or any of your college library's electronic databases (CD-ROM or online). Ask your librarian for assistance.

Make enough photocopies of your interview notes or articles for each member of the group.

The Second Meeting

Begin by exchanging interview notes or articles. Then, take turns reporting and discussing what each of you has found. Next, have each student choose the method of crime prevention he or she wants to make the topic of a paragraph of about 75–125 words. Each of you should write on a different method of crime prevention. Ideally, you should each write your paragraphs using a different pattern of paragraph organization as explained in this chapter: general-to-specific; specific-to-general; question-to-answer; problem-to-solution; order of importance; and around a pivot.

Make enough photocopies of your paragraphs for each member of your group.

THE FINAL MEETING

Share your paragraphs with each other and offer suggestions for revision and editing. Keep these questions in mind as you do so:

• Does the paragraph have a clear topic sentence?

• Is it developed in enough detail?

• Does the paragraph follow a pattern resembling one explained in this chapter?

• Is the paragraph unified and coherent? (Remember what you learned in Chapter 2.)

• Does the writer need to correct errors in grammar, sentence structure, punctuation, and spelling?

CHAPTER 4

Introductions and Conclusions

In the previous chapters you learned important principles to help you focus on the central idea of a paragraph or essay and to express this central idea in a topic sentence or thesis statement. You also learned how to develop paragraphs adequately and to make sure that each paragraph in an essay clearly develops the essay's thesis.

Most effective essays begin with an interesting and informative introduction—a paragraph or a series of paragraphs that reveal the essay's thesis and captures the reader's attention. Similarly, most successful essays end with a paragraph or a series of paragraphs that bring the writer's discussion of the subject to a timely and logical conclusion. Effective conclusions always leave the reader satisfied that everything the writer set out to discuss from the very beginning has been discussed.

Clearly, then, introductions and conclusions have special uses and are important to the success of an essay. That's why this chapter explains how to write them.

Writing Introductions

Before deciding exactly what to include in an introduction, how to organize it, or even how to begin it, ask yourself whether the essay you're writing actually calls for a formal introduction. If you're writing a narrative, for instance, you might simply want to start with the very first event in your story. Of course, you can always begin with colorful details, exciting vocabulary, or intriguing ideas that will spark your readers' interest. But you need not provide a thesis statement, background information, explanatory details, or other introductory material before getting into the story proper. If you feel the need to express your central idea in a formal thesis statement, you can do so later, at a convenient point in the body of your essay or even in its conclusion.

On the other hand, you might decide that your essay needs a formal introduction. If so, remember that the *most important* function of an introduction is to capture the attention of the readers and make them read on. However, you can also use an introduction to:

- Reveal the essay's central idea as expressed in the thesis.
- Guide readers to important ideas in the body of the essay.
- Provide background or explanatory information to help readers understand the essay's purpose and thesis.

Consider these four objectives when you plan your introduction. But if you are unable to decide how to begin, simply write out a preliminary thesis statement and go directly to the body of your essay. You can always get back to your introduction later in the writing process. It certainly does not have to be the very first part of the essay you write.

However you choose to get started, remember that an exciting part of writing is deciding *exactly* what you want to say about your subject. You usually won't make this discovery until after you have completed at least one draft—and often more than one draft—of the middle or body paragraphs of your essay. Once you have done that, your chances of going back and drafting a clearer, more substantial thesis will have improved. So will your chances of writing an interesting and effective introduction.

The simplest and sometimes best way to write an introductory paragraph or series of introductory paragraphs is to state your thesis at the very beginning and follow it with explanatory details that prepare readers for what they will find in the body of the essay. This is the method used by Shimon Peres, former prime minister of Israel, in an essay that appeared in *Civilization* magazine. Peres's thesis appears in italics.

> [A nation's] *strength and wealth today are products of science and technology.* No matter what the size of your land, no matter what the wealth of your natural resources, no matter what the number of your people, what really counts is the level of your scientific effort, your investment in education, your ability to encourage the human mind to flow freely and stimulate new ideas. ("The Bull in the Garden")

However, depending on your purpose, your thesis, and your audience, this may not always be the best way to begin. In Chapter 3, you learned several ways to develop the essay's body paragraphs. Here are several ways to write introductions:

1. Use a startling remark or statistic.
2. Ask a question or present a problem.
3. Challenge a widely held assumption or opinion.
4. Use a comparison, a contrast, or an analogy.
5. Tell an anecdote or describe a scene.
6. Use a quotation.
7. Define an important term or concept.
8. Address your readers directly.
9. Open with a paradox (an apparent contradiction).

Often, beginning writers limit their introductions to one paragraph. Doing so will help you get to the point quickly. On the other hand, you can—and sometimes must—spread your opening remarks over two or three short paragraphs. This may help you increase your readers' interest because it allows you to use a variety of methods to write your introduction. Each method is described below and illustrated by one or more sample paragraphs. In some samples, the central idea is expressed in a formal thesis statement (shown in italics); in others, the central idea is only implied, and no formal thesis statement can be identified.

USE A STARTLING REMARK OR STATISTIC

Some pieces of writing begin with statements or statistics (numbers) that, while true to the author's intent, have an effective shock value—one sure to make readers want to continue. Take this example of a lead paragraph from an essay on the state of the American family:

> Divorce and out-of-wedlock childbirth are transforming the lives of American children. In the postwar generation more than 80 percent of children grew up in a family with two biological parents who were married to each other. By 1980 only 50 percent could expect to spend their entire childhood in an intact family. If current trends continue, less than half of all children born today will live continuously with their own mother and father throughout childhood. *Most American children will spend several years in a single-mother family.* (Barbara Dafoe Whitehead, "Dan Quayle Was Right")

You might find this technique particularly effective if you have to take an unpopular stand on a well-known subject, as did former Philadelphia Phillies pitcher Robin Roberts in the opening of "Strike Out Little League":

> In 1939, Little League baseball was organized by Bert and George Bebble and Carl Stotz of Williamsport, Pa. What they had in mind in organizing this kids' baseball program, I'll never know. But *I'm sure they never visualized the monster it would grow into.*

A startling statement is often followed by details—some of them statistics—that explain the writer's point. In *Victims of Vanity,* a book criticizing laboratory tests on animals, Lynda Dickinson decided that spreading startling remarks and statistics over three short paragraphs would be a better way to capture the readers' attention and prepare them for her thesis than using one long unit:

> Lipstick, face cream, anti-perspirant, laundry detergent . . . these products and hundreds of other personal care and household items have one common ingredient: the suffering and death of millions of animals.
>
> An average of 25 million animals die every year in North America for the testing of everything from new cosmetics to new methods of warfare. Five hundred thousand to one million of these animals are sacrificed each year to test new cosmetics alone.
>
> *Of all the pain and suffering caused by animal research, cosmetic and household product testing is among the least justifiable, as it cannot even be argued that tests are done to improve the quality of human life.*

Ask a Question or Present a Problem

If you begin by asking a question or presenting a problem, you can devote the rest of your essay to discussing that question or problem and, perhaps, to providing answers or solutions. In "Old, Ailing, and Abandoned," an editorial on care of the elderly, which appeared in the *Philadelphia Inquirer,* the writer begins with three thought-provoking questions:

> How would you punish the people responsible for letting 18 hours pass before getting emergency medical help to an epileptic with second- and third-degree burns, while large sections of her skins were peeling off? What justice is there for a man whose amputated foot is allowed to become infested with maggots while he's paying for care in a specialized rooming house? And what's the proper penalty for someone who leaves a mentally ill woman alone for three days with little food and no medication?

In the first paragraph of "The Ambivalence of Abortion," Linda Bird Francke introduces the problem she and her husband faced over an unplanned pregnancy, thus preparing us for her discussion of abortion later in the essay:

> We were sitting in a bar on Lexington Avenue when I told my husband I was pregnant. It is not a memory I like to dwell on. Instead of the champagne and hope which had heralded [announced] the impending [coming] births of the first, second and third child, the news of this one was greeted with shocked silence and Scotch. "Jesus," my husband kept saying to himself, stirring the ice cubes around and around, "Oh Jesus."

Challenge a Widely Held Assumption or Opinion

This can be a direct way to stir your reader's interest. Roger McGrath uses this method to begin "The Myth of Frontier Violence."

> It is commonly assumed that violence is part of our frontier heritage. But *the historical record shows that frontier violence was very different from violence today.* Robbery and burglary, two of our most common crimes, were of no great significance in the frontier towns of the Old West, and rape was seemingly nonexistent.

In "Gen X Is OK," Professor Edward E. Ericson, Jr., writes an introduction that both challenges an opinion and surprises his readers:

> Today's young adults read little. They're poorly prepared for college. They're suckers for the instant gratification of booze and drugs. They're enormously confused about sex and scared to death of marriage. They're all for a woman's right to choose an abortion, especially the men. They force metal rings through the most unwelcoming of facial orifices [openings]. They're so light on civic duty that few vote and fewer still can imagine why one would die for one's country. *And I like them.*

The last line of this paragraph—the author's thesis—captures our attention. We want to learn why in the world Ericson likes people whom he has just described so negatively. So, we read on!

USE A COMPARISON, A CONTRAST, OR AN ANALOGY

Comparison points out similarities; contrast points out differences. Both methods can help you provide important information about your subject, clarify or emphasize a point, and catch the reader's attention.

Donald M. Murray offers students good advice by contrasting the way they sometimes complete writing assignments with the more thorough and careful process used by professionals:

> When students complete a first draft, they consider the job of writing
> done—and their teachers too often agree. *When professional writers
> complete a first draft, they usually feel that they are at the start of the writing
> process.* When a draft is completed, the job of writing can begin. ("The
> Maker's Eye")

In the following paragraph, student Dan Roland uses both comparison and contrast. He begins by likening Kingston, Jamaica, to any city the reader might recognize, only to follow with a stark contrast between the extremes of wealth and poverty found there. The effect is startling and convincing. Roland has prepared his readers well for the thesis at the end of the paragraph.

> From my seat on an American Airlines 727, Kingston, Jamaica, looks like
> any other large urban center to me: tall buildings dominate the skyline, traf-
> fic weaves its way through roadways laid out like long arteries from the
> heart of the city. But Kingston is not like other cities, for it is here that some
> of the most extreme poverty in the world exists. The island of Jamaica was
> founded as a slave colony to help satisfy Europe's great demand for sugar
> cane, and its inhabitants are the descendants of slaves. Despair and poverty
> are part of everyday life and have been for centuries. The leading industry is
> tourism; every year thousands of well-to-do vacationers, mostly Americans
> and Canadians, come to stay in the multitudes of luxurious hotels and re-
> sorts. *Jamaica is one of the most beautiful places on Earth; it is also one of the
> most destitute [poorest].* ("Which Side of the Fence?")

Analogy serves the same purposes as comparison or contrast; the most important of these is, once again, to keep the reader's attention. But analogy also helps explain ideas that are hard to grasp by allowing you to compare them with things readers can understand more easily. Analogy points out similarities between subjects that are unrelated. This is what happens in "The Tapestry" when student Steven Grundy compares his family to a fine wall hanging:

> *My family is an ancient tapestry,* worn in places, faded by the passage of time,
> its colors softened by accumulated dust. It has hung there for so long that

we rarely stop to appreciate its value. Yet beneath the dusty coating lies a precious masterpiece, a subtle composition of woven thread.

TELL AN ANECDOTE OR DESCRIBE A SCENE

Anecdotes are brief, interesting stories that illustrate or support a point. An anecdote can help you prepare readers for the issues or problems you will be discussing without having to state the thesis directly. For example, this anecdote, which begins a *Wall Street Journal* editorial, makes the essay's central idea clear even though it does not express it in a thesis statement:

> We don't know if Janice Camarena had ever heard of *Brown v. Board of Education* when she enrolled in San Bernadino Valley College in California, but she knows all about it now. Mrs. Camarena was thrown out of a class at her public community college because of the color of her skin. When she sat down at her desk on the first day of the semester in January 1994, the instructor asked her to leave. That section of English 101 was reserved for black students only, she was told; Mrs. Camarena is white. ("Affirmative Reaction")

Another way to prepare readers for what follows is to describe a scene in a way that lets them know your feelings about a subject. Take the introduction to "A Hanging," an essay in which George Orwell reveals his view on capital punishment. Orwell does not express his opinions in a thesis statement; the essay's gloomy setting—its time and place—does that for him:

> It was Burma, a sodden [soggy] morning of the rains. A sickly light, like yellow tinfoil, was slanting over the high walls into the jail yard. We were waiting outside the condemned cells, a row of sheds fronted with double bars, like small animal cages. Each cell measured about ten feet by ten and was quite bare within except for a plank bed and a pot for drinking water. In some of them brown silent men were squatting at the inner bars, with their blankets draped around them. These were the condemned men, due to be hanged within the next week or two.

USE A QUOTATION

Quoting an expert or simply using an interesting, informative statement from another writer, from someone you've interviewed formally, or even from someone with whom you've only been chatting can lend interest and authority to your introduction. If you use this method, however, remember to quote your source accurately. Also be sure that the quotation relates to the other ideas in your paragraph clearly and logically.

Philip Shabecoff uses a quotation from world-famous scientist and writer Rachel Carson to lead us to his thesis in the introduction to his essay on pesticides:

> "The most alarming of all man's assaults upon the environment is the contamination of air, earth, rivers, and sea with dangerous and even lethal materials," Rachel Carson wrote a quarter of a century ago in her celebrated book

Silent Spring. Today there is little disagreement with her warnings in regard to such broad-spectrum pesticides as DDT, then widely used, now banned. *But there is still hot debate over how to apply modern pesticides—which are designed to kill specific types of weeds or insects—in ways that do not harm people and their environment.* ("Congress Again Confronts Hazards of Killer Chemicals")

DEFINE AN IMPORTANT TERM OR CONCEPT

Defining a term can explain aspects of your subject that will make it easier for readers to understand and agree with your central idea. But try not to use dictionary definitions. Because they are often limited and rigid, they can make the beginning of an essay flat and uninteresting. Instead, rely on your own knowledge and ingenuity to create definitions that are interesting and appropriate to your purpose. This is what student Elena Santayana has done in the introduction to a paper about alcohol addiction:

> Alcoholism is a disease whose horrible consequences go beyond the patient. Families of alcoholics often become dysfunctional; spouses and children are abandoned or endure physical and emotional abuse. Co-workers suffer too. Alcoholics have high rates of absenteeism, and their work is often unreliable, thereby decreasing office or factory productivity. Indeed, alcoholics endanger the whole community. One in every two automobile fatalities is alcohol-related, and alcoholism is a major cause of violent crime. ("Everybody's Problem")

ADDRESS YOUR READERS DIRECTLY

Speaking to your readers directly is an excellent way to get their attention. Notice how effectively Claudia Wallis does this at the very beginning of an article from *Time* magazine:

> To grasp what it means to be 120 years old, consider this: a woman in the U.S. now has a life expectancy of 79 years. Jeanne Calment of Arles, France, reached that advanced age back in 1954, when Eisenhower was in the White House and Stalin had just passed from the scene. Twenty-two years later, at age 100, Calment was still riding her bicycle around town, having outlived both her only child and grandchild. And 20 years after that, she was charming the photographers and reporters who arrived in droves last week, . . . to mark her 120th birthday. ("How to Live to Be 120")

In "What Is Poverty?" Jo Goodwin Parker has also chosen to address her readers directly, but she begins with a question. Her introduction is both urgent and emphatic:

> You ask me what is poverty? Listen to me. Here I am, dirty, smelly, and with no "proper" underwear on and with the stench of my rotting teeth near you. I will tell you. Listen to me. Listen without pity. I cannot use your pity. Listen with understanding. Put yourself in my dirty, worn out, ill-fitting shoes, and hear me.

OPEN WITH A PARADOX

A paradox is a statement that, while true, seems to contradict itself. Because such statements are interesting in themselves, they make effective beginnings. For example, take this opening paragraph to Angie Cannon's "Crime Stories of the Century," which appeared in a December 1999 issue of *U.S. News & World Report.* Cannon's thesis, which contains a paradox, appears in italics.

> We are at once disgusted and fascinated by crime. First we avert [turn away] our eyes. Then we reach for the newspapers with their grisly headlines and stare for hours at our televisions as the accused villains go on trial. *Every decade, it seems, produces a "crime of the century."* As E. L. Doctorow noted in *Ragtime,* headline writers way back in 1906 had already anointed [labeled] the murder of renowned architect Stanford White the "Crime of the Century," even though there were still 94 more years to go.

Writing Conclusions

Make sure your essay has an effective conclusion. Sometimes, it is on the basis of your conclusion alone that your readers respond to your essay and remember the point it tries to make.

The conclusion's length depends on the essay's length and purpose. For a very short essay, you can simply end the last paragraph with a concluding sentence, which might itself contain details important to developing your thesis. Such is the case in Kenneth Jon Rose's "2001 Space Shuttle." Rose's last paragraph, a description of the shuttle's landing on its return to Earth, also contains his conclusion (shown in italics):

> [T]he sky turns lighter and layers of clouds pass you like cars on a highway. Minutes later, still sitting upright, you will see the gray runway in the distance. Then the shuttle slows to 300 mph and drops its landing gear. Finally, with its nose slightly up like the Concorde SST and at a speed of about 225 mph, the shuttle will land on the asphalt runway and slowly come to a halt. *The trip into space will be over.*

Although one-sentence conclusions are fine for short essays, you will often need to close with at least one full paragraph. Either way, a conclusion should bring your discussion of the thesis to a timely and logical end. Try not to conclude abruptly; always give a signal that you are about to wrap things up. And never use your conclusion to introduce new ideas—ideas for which you did not prepare your readers earlier in the essay.

There are many ways to write conclusions. Here are eight:

1. Rephrase or make reference to your thesis.
2. Summarize or rephrase your main points.
3. Offer advice; make a call to action.
4. Look to the future.

5. Explain how a problem was resolved.
6. Ask a rhetorical question.
7. Close with a statement or quotation readers will remember.
8. Respond to a question in your introduction.

REPHRASE OR MAKE REFERENCE TO YOUR THESIS

In Chapter 1 you learned that it can be appropriate to place the thesis state-ment not in the introduction, but in a later paragraph or even in the conclu-sion. As a beginning writer, however, you might want to use the more tradi-tional pattern of organization, which is to place your thesis at the beginning of the essay. Of course, this doesn't mean that you shouldn't rephrase or refer to the thesis in your conclusion. Doing so can be an excellent way to empha-size your central idea.

Take this three-part conclusion from Professor Edward E. Ericson, Jr.'s "Gen X Is OK," the introduction to which appears on page 132.

> I didn't plan to develop a special fondness for today's young. My students made me do it. Of course I haven't stopped worrying. This generation does not seem headed for greatness. They have suffered too much cultural despo-liation [loss], too much distortion of personhood, for that. It would take a global cataclysm [catastrophe] for them to have any chance of rising to the heights of human valor.
>
> But will they be basically sensible, productive adults? Were I a betting man, I'd put my money on them. And the more intergeneration friendships they form, the better their odds will be.
>
> All in all, I think Gen X is OK.

Ericson rephrases his thesis when he says, "Gen X Is OK." But he also re-states four important points he made in the body of his essay:

1. His students caused him "to develop a special fondness for today's young."
2. Members of Gen X don't seem "headed for greatness."
3. They will become "sensible, productive adults."
4. Friendships between members of different generations will help improve their chances for success.

SUMMARIZE OR REPHRASE YOUR MAIN POINTS

For long essays, restating your thesis can be combined with summarizing or rephrasing each of the main points you have made in the body paragraphs. Doing so will help you write an effective summary of the entire essay and em-phasize important ideas. This is exactly what Robin Roberts has done in his two concluding paragraphs of "Strike Out Little League" (see his introduction on page 131):

> I still don't know what those three gentlemen in Williamsport had in mind when they organized Little League baseball. I'm sure they didn't want par-ents arguing with their children about kids' games. I'm sure they didn't want

young athletes hurting their arms pitching under pressure. . . . I'm sure they didn't want young boys . . . made to feel that something is wrong with them because they can't play baseball. I'm sure they didn't want a group of coaches drafting the players each year for different teams. I'm sure they didn't want unqualified men working with the young players. I'm sure they didn't realize how normal it is for an 8-year-old boy to be scared of a thrown or batted baseball.

For the life of me, I can't figure out what they had in mind.

OFFER ADVICE; MAKE A CALL TO ACTION

An example of a conclusion that offers advice appears in Elena Santayana's "Everybody's Problem," the introduction to which appears on page 135.

> If you have alcoholic friends, relatives, or co-workers, the worst thing you can do is to look the other way. This disease and its effects are simply not theirs to deal with alone. Try persuading them to seek counseling. Describe the extent to which their illness is hurting their families, co-workers, and neighbors. Explain that their alcoholism endangers the entire community. Above all, don't pretend not to notice! Alcoholism is everybody's problem.

LOOK TO THE FUTURE

If you believe the future can bring significant changes or new developments in regard to a topic you have discussed in your essay, you might end by discussing those changes. This is what Barbara Dafoe Whitehead does in "Dan Quayle Was Right." (You will find her introduction on page 131.)

> People learn; societies can change; particularly when it becomes apparent that certain behaviors damage the social ecology, threaten the public order, and impose new burdens on core institutions. Whether Americans will act to overcome the legacy of family disruption is a crucial but as yet unanswered question.

In "Crime Stories of the Century" (its introduction appears on page 136), Angie Cannon concludes with a much darker vision of the future. Given her subject matter and the points she makes in her essay, however, it seems appropriate to her purpose:

> Crime stayed high during the 1970s and 1980s, but demographic [population] changes and widespread prosperity reduced crime in the 1990s to the lowest level since World War II.
>   And in the new millennium? "Oklahoma City, I'm afraid, is the future," says [historian Roger] Lane." At the end of this American century and the beginning of the next, all the world's grievances center on Uncle Sam." Sadly, there will be many more "crimes of the century."

Note that Cannon's conclusion appears in more than one paragraph. In fact, this conclusion uses more than one method. In addition to looking to the future, the author inserts a direct quotation that readers will remember.

All of this is perfectly appropriate. So, when it comes time to writing your own essays—especially those of the longer variety—don't be afraid to combine methods or to spread your conclusion over two or three paragraphs.

EXPLAIN HOW A PROBLEM WAS RESOLVED

In "The Ambivalence of Abortion" (see page 132 for the introduction to this essay), Linda Bird Francke writes about the difficulty she and her husband had in deciding whether to have or abort their fourth child. Francke's conclusion tells us how they resolved the question and, like many effective endings, reveals the author's feelings:

> My husband and I are back to planning our summer vacation and his career switch. And it certainly does make sense not to be having a baby right now—we say to each other all the time. But I have this ghost now. A very little ghost that only appears when I'm seeing something beautiful, like the full moon on the ocean last weekend. And the baby waves to me. And I wave at the baby. "Of course, we have room," I cry to the ghost. "Of course, we do."

ASK A RHETORICAL QUESTION

A rhetorical question (a question whose answer is obvious) asks your readers to participate in your essay's conclusion by answering the question. If you believe the essay has made the answer so obvious that all readers will indeed respond to the question as you want them to, ending with a rhetorical question can be a fine way to make your essay memorable. As a reader, it's hard to forget an essay when you've answered its question in your own words.

Jo Goodwin Parker uses this device to emphasize the seriousness of the problem she describes in "What Is Poverty?" (See her introduction on page 135):

> I have come out of my despair to tell you this. Remember I did not come from another place to another time. Others like me are all around you. Look at us with an angry heart, anger that will help you help me. Anger that will let you tell of me. The poor are always silent. Can you be silent too?

CLOSE WITH A STATEMENT OR QUOTATION READERS WILL REMEMBER

Deciding whether a statement or quotation will stick in readers' memories isn't easy. Just trust your instincts. If a particular remark has made a strong impression on you, it may work for others. As always, however, make your conclusion relate directly to your essay's content. In "How to Live to Be 120," Claudia Wallis closes her discussion with a direct quotation from her fascinating subject, which you read about in the introduction to her essay on page 135.

> As for Jeanne Calment, she seems to embody the calm resilience associated with long life. "I took pleasure when I could," she said. . . . "I acted clearly and morally and without regret. I'm very lucky."

RESPOND TO A QUESTION IN YOUR INTRODUCTION

After asking a question in your introduction, you can fill your essay with information that discusses the question or prepares the reader for an answer in your conclusion, or both. In the introduction to "Old, Ailing, Abandoned," the writer raises serious questions about caring for the elderly (see page 132). Here is the conclusion to that essay:

> Communities, stretched though they may be, need to remember these forgotten elderly living in our midst. What if every church in the region agreed to regularly visit residents at just one [nursing] home? How about local government, or advocate agencies, linking the owners of small facilities more closely with existing services, such as rehab grants that could improve conditions?
>
> One simple question need guide us: How would we want *our* parents treated?

Interestingly, the writer phrases much of this conclusion in questions; but these are rhetorical questions, for which the answers are obvious.

Visualizing Ways to Write Introductions and Conclusions

Read the introduction and conclusion to Michael Ryan's "They Track the Deadliest Viruses," which appear below. Comments in the margins identify effective techniques you might use in your own introductions and conclusions.

Ryan—Introduction

Makes a startling statement and challenges an assumption.

"A disease that's in a faraway place today may be in our own backyard tomorrow," said Dr. James Hughes [of] the Centers for Disease Control and Prevention (CDC) in Atlanta. "We're certainly not immune."

Creates a contrast.

A few years ago, this statement would have surprised many Americans. The advent [coming] of "miracle drugs and vaccines that conquered such plagues as polio, smallpox and even measles led many of us—including some scientists—to believe that the age of killer diseases was coming to an end.

The AIDS epidemic changed that . . . *States essay's thesis*

Ryan—Conclusion

On my visit to Atlanta I . . . met with the associate director of the CDC, Dr. James Curran. He has been involved in the fight against AIDS since 1981. "The first five years, through 1985, was the age of discovery. . . . We discovered the global extent of the epidemic, the virus, antibody tests, AZT. *Refers to thesis.* It was an exciting time, but when it ended, half a million people in the U.S. already were infected.

Today, Dr. Curran said, the Centers for Disease Control and Prevention's response to *Looks to the future.* the AIDS epidemic has changed. "We're trying to help the country evaluate the blood supply, develop test kits and work on prevention and counseling *Makes a call to action.* strategies. . . . Information alone isn't *Uses a quotation readers will remember.* sufficient. We have to find ways to change behavior—especially in young people, who sometimes think they're invulnerable."

Revising Introductions and Conclusions

Later in this chapter, you will read Anita DiPasquale's "The Transformation of Maria Fernandez." DiPasquale knew that the first version of her essay was not the best she could do, so she rewrote her paper several times. Compare the rough and final drafts of the paragraphs she used in her essay's introduction and conclusion.

DiPasquale's Introduction—Rough Draft

Maria's story is a very shocking testimony

A good first try; add stronger details?

to a brutal war. Her country is Nicaragua.
This impoverished yet beautiful land is the
site in which the Reagan Administration
became involved in a series of actions known
as the Iran-Contra fiasco. The only good

Is this essay's thesis?

that has come from our country's involvement
in this dreadful war is that the apathetic
American, hopefully, has finally realized
that Kansas does not mean Central America,
Contra does not mean freedom fighter, and
Sandinista does not mean repressive regime.

We meet Maria on a trip through hell. The
month was June; the year was 1988. Maria is
seventeen, no longer a child, no longer a
woman. She is a soldier in the FSLN.

Is author with someone or does "we" include her readers?

Maria is a thin girl with shoulder-length
raven hair, which she keeps in a braid and
tucks away under her camouflage hat. Her

Will this move the reader?

nose is long, her chin is proud. She is
olive in color, and her cheekbones are high
like those of a *Vogue* model.

DiPasquale's Introduction—Final Draft

Final draft combines sentences for smoothness.

Maria's story is testimony to the horror of
war. Her country is Nicaragua, one of
America's greatest embarrassments and yet
another battleground in what the superpowers

called the "cold" war. In this impoverished, merciless, yet beautiful land, the Reagan Administration became mired in a series of covert operations known as the Iran-Contra fiasco. Ironically, our shame over this dreadful incident may be the only good thing to come from our presence in Nicaragua.

Adds detail; improves word choice.

Perhaps Americans who were once parochial and apathetic will realize that Kansas is not Central America, that *Sandinista* and "repressive" are not synonymous, that *Contra* may not mean "freedom fighter," and that all wars, no matter who the adversaries, are barbarous!

Focuses her essay on a revised, more specific thesis.

My friend Michael and I meet Maria on a trip through hell in Nicaragua's capital, Managua. The month is June, the year 1988.

Adds information to clarify a point.

Maria is seventeen, no longer a child, no longer a woman. She is a soldier in the FSLN (*Frente Sandinista de Liberacion Nacional*), the national liberation front named for Augusto Sandino, a guerrilla fighter martyred in an earlier war of liberation.

Explains important historical information and abbreviation.

Maria is thin, with shoulder-length raven hair, which she braids and tucks away under her camouflage hat. Her nose is long and straight, her chin prominent and proud. A silky olive complexion and cheekbones straight out of *Vogue* magazine reveal a face

Adds a question that startles reader and sets essay's tone.

that is truly delicate. How, then, has it come to harbor the deadest eyes I have ever seen?

DiPasquale's Conclusion—Rough Draft

My stomach grew heavy and sank to a depth I did not know was possible. A truck pulled into the street. It was filled with dead Contra bodies on the way to burial. Another truck pulled up behind, and this one was filled with Sandinista soldiers. My heart sank in desperation. These soldiers were children: eight, ten, fifteen. All toting

Needs to describe in more detail.

rifles, passing cigarettes among the crowd. When I looked in the other truck, I grew ill with fear. This truck was also filled with children, men, and women, but all were dead.

Sentences are choppy.

Needs expansion, stronger detail.

   It is practically impossible to tell the Contras and Sandinistas apart. Their youth, their camaraderie, and dead have a lot in common.

DiPasquale's Conclusion—Final Draft

Uses present tense to create excitement.

As Maria finishes her story, my stomach grows heavy and sinks to a depth I did not think was possible. Suddenly, a truck pulls onto the street. It is filled with dead Contras on the way to burial. Another truck pulls up behind; this one is filled with Sandinista soldiers, none of whom look over twenty. Most are between ten and fifteen. Some might be eight. They are all toting rifles, passing cigarettes out among the

Combines sentences to correct and smooth out sentence structure.

Uses stronger vocabulary and adds stark details.

crowd. When I look into the first truck, I become desperate with fear. Piled one on top of another are men, women, and children. They are all dead.

Adds a new paragraph that refers to someone mentioned earlier in the essay.

Back at the ledge, I slump against Michael. Maria emerges from the daze of her horrid memory and kisses Michael on the cheek. She points to the trucks. "If he [Maria's younger brother] were here, his world would be all too real."

Sometimes it is nearly impossible to tell Contra soldiers and Sandinistas apart. They have a lot in common: their youth, their camaraderie, their mortality. When Salvadoran Archbishop Rivera y Damas spoke of the role of the superpowers in his country's civil war, he could have been

Expands this paragraph with stronger, smoother wording.

Adds quotation readers will remember.

describing the tragedy of Nicaragua: "They supply the weapons, and we supply the dead."

Practicing Writing Introductions

Write a one-paragraph introduction for an essay you might compose on one of the following topics. Try using one of the methods for writing introductions suggested with each topic.

1. **Topic:** A terrifying, tragic, or emotionally charged experience.

   Method: Use a startling remark or statistic.

   _____

   _____

   _____

   _____

   _____

2. **Topic:** Dealing with an allergy or other common health problem.
   Method: Ask a question or present a problem.

   _____

   _____

   _____

   _____

   _____

3. **Topic:** The benefits (or dangers) of physical exercise.

   Method: Tell an anecdote or use contrast.

   _____

   _____

   _____

   _____

   _____

4. **Topic:** Ways to overcome pain other than using drugs.
   Method: Challenge a widely held opinion, use contrast, or present a problem.

   _____

   _____

   _____

   _____

   _____

5. **Topic:** What your clothes (car, home, or room) say about you.
   Method: Describe a scene, use a quotation, or address your readers directly.

   _____

   _____

   _____

   _____

   _____

6. **Topic:** The role of a father or mother in a young family.
   Method: Ask a question or challenge a widely held opinion.

   _____

   _____

   _____

   _____

7. **Topic:** Overcoming a fear of math (heights, closed-in places, water, etc.).
   Method: Address your readers directly, ask a question, or define a term.

   _____

   _____

   _____

   _____

8. **Topic:** Practicing safe sex.
   Method: Present a problem, define a term, or address your readers directly.

   _____

   _____

   _____

   _____

   _____

Read the introductions and conclusions to the following four essays carefully, and take some time to respond to the Questions for Discussion and the Suggestions for Journal Entries that follow each selection. As always, you will also want to try your hand at the Suggestions for Sustained Writing at the end of the chapter. Doing so will help you develop the skills needed to write good introductions and conclusions of your own—the kind that will capture your readers' attention and make them look forward to more of your writing.

I Was Just Wondering

Robert Fulghum

Robert Fulghum wrote All I Really Need to Know I Learned in Kindergarten, *the best-selling collection of essays from which this one is taken. The contents of this funny book are summed up by its subtitle:* Uncommon Thoughts on Common Things. *Fulghum has worked as a cowboy, IBM sales representative, bartender, teacher, artist, and minister. Judging from this selection, he has a curiosity and love for life that make it easy to understand why his writing is so popular.*

Preparing to Read

1. As you read this essay, ask yourself why Fulghum's introduction and conclusion are effective. Identify methods for writing beginnings and endings you learned earlier in this chapter.

2. In paragraphs 1, 5, and 8, Fulghum intentionally uses incomplete sentences, known as fragments, to create emphasis and establish a conversational tone. They are part of a carefully considered style that this experienced writer chose for his essay. As a rule, however, developing writers should avoid fragments.

Vocabulary

curry (verb)	Groom.
epidemic (noun)	Widespread occurrence.
meditate (verb)	Think, ponder, contemplate.
oracle (noun)	Advisor, prophet. (Here, *oracle* is used figuratively; Fulghum describes the habit some folks have of questioning themselves as they look in the mirror.)
Ph.D. (noun)	Advanced academic degree, also known as a doctorate.
potions (noun)	Liquid medicines, remedies.
preen (verb)	Make ready, prepare.
unguents (noun)	Salves, ointments.
spelunking (noun)	Cave exploring.

I Was Just Wondering

Robert Fulghum

I WAS JUST wondering. Did you ever go to somebody's house for dinner or a   1
party or something and then use the bathroom? And while you were in

there, did you ever take a look around in the medicine cabinet? Just to kind of compare notes, you know? Didn't you ever—just look around a little?

I have a friend who does it all the time. He's doing research for a Ph.D. in sociology. He says lots of other people do it, too. And they aren't working on a Ph.D. in sociology, either. It's not something people talk about much—because you think you might be the only one who is doing it, and you don't want people to think you're strange, right?

My friend says if you want to know the truth about people, it's the place to go. All you have to do is look in the drawers and shelves and cabinets in the bathroom. And take a look at the robes and pajamas and nightgowns hanging on the hook behind the door. You'll get the picture. He says all their habits and hopes and dreams and sorrows, illnesses and hangups, and even their sex life—all stand revealed in that one small room.

He says most people are secret slobs. He says the deepest mysteries of the race are tucked into the nooks and crannies of the bathroom, where we go to be alone, to confront ourselves in the mirror, to comb and curry and scrape and preen our hides, to coax our aging and ailing bodies into one more day, to clean ourselves and relieve ourselves, to paint and deodorize our surfaces, to meditate and consult our oracle and attempt to improve our lot.

He says it's all there. In cans and bottles and tubes and boxes and vials. Potions and oils and unguents and sprays and tools and lotions and perfumes and appliances and soaps and pastes and pills and creams and pads and powders and medicines and devices beyond description—some electric and some not. The wonders of the ages.

He says he finds most bathrooms are about the same, and it gives him a sense of the wondrous unity of the human race.

I don't intend to start an epidemic of spelunking in people's bathrooms. But I did just go in and take a look in my own. I get the picture. I don't know whether to laugh or cry.

Take a look. In your own. And from now on, please go to the bathroom before you visit me. Mine is closed to the public.

Questions for Discussion

1. What two ways of writing introductions discussed in this chapter did you find in paragraph 1?
2. Which of the methods for concluding discussed earlier best describes Fulghum's approach in paragraph 8?
3. What method of development that you learned about in the previous chapter does Fulghum use in paragraph 3?
4. What techniques does Fulghum use to maintain coherence in and between paragraphs?

Thinking Critically

1. Pretend you caught someone snooping around in your bathroom, bedroom, closet, or other private part of your home. Write this person a letter explaining your reaction.
2. What does Fulghum mean when he says that bathrooms are places where we go "to meditate and consult our oracle and attempt to improve our lot"?

Suggestions for Journal Entries

1. Are most people "secret slobs"? What about you? Think of a particular place you call your own. Does the way you keep it show how neat or sloppy you are? If so, use focused freewriting to describe what it looks like. A place to write about might be your bedroom, bathroom, car, closet, area in which you study, or location where you spend most of your time at work.
2. Like Fulghum, do some wondering. Focus on someone you know very well. Can you describe or at least imagine what the inside of his or her room, closet, apartment, house, refrigerator, garage, basement, or bathroom looks like? What might you see in such places that would describe this individual's personality?

A Prayer for the Days of Awe

Elie Wiesel

Elie Wiesel was born in Romania in 1928. In 1944, he was imprisoned in Auschwitz and Buchenwald, two of the many infamous Nazi death camps where six million Jews and millions of other people were murdered. This horror is now called the Holocaust, a word derived from the fact that the bodies of many victims of this mass murder were burned in ovens after having been gassed or killed in other ways. Wiesel's autobiographical novel Night *recalls his experience in the camps, and his many other novels, plays, and stories are aimed at making sure the Holocaust is never forgotten. Wiesel was awarded the Nobel Peace Prize in 1986. He now teaches at Boston University.*

Preparing to Read

1. This essay appeared in the *New York Times* shortly before Rosh Hashanah, the Jewish New Year Holiday, which is observed in prayer and begins the Ten Days of Penitence, ending with Yom Kippur, the Day of Atonement. These Days of Awe conclude with the faithful's praying for forgiveness for the previous year's sins.

2. As Wiesel's title indicates, this is not just an essay; it is a prayer. Keep this in mind as you read this selection, for Wiesel is addressing two— and perhaps three—different audiences.

3. How might Wiesel be using the word "awe"? Look this word up in a dictionary.

Vocabulary

annihilate (verb)	Destroy completely, exterminate.
culpability (noun)	Guilt, responsibility.
fervor (noun)	Enthusiasm, eagerness, passion.
Sabbath (noun)	Day of worship.
testimony (noun)	Written or spoken statement that something is true.
theological (adjective)	Having to do with the study of God.
Treblinka (noun)	Another Nazi concentration camp.
tribunal (noun)	Council, court.
Zionism (noun)	A movement that attempted to reestablish the Jewish state in Palestine.

A Prayer for the Days of Awe

Elie Wiesel

Master of the Universe, let us make up. It is time. How long can we go on 1 being angry?

More than 50 years have passed since the nightmare was lifted. Many 2 things, good and less good, have since happened to those who survived it. They learned to build on ruins. Family life was recreated. Children were born, friendships struck. They learned to have faith in their surroundings, even in their fellow men and women. Gratitude has replaced bitterness in their hearts. No one is as capable of thankfulness as they are. Thankful to anyone willing to hear their tales and become their ally in the battle against apathy and forgetfulness. For them every moment is grace.

Oh, they do not forgive the killers and their accomplices, nor should 3 they. Nor should you, Master of the Universe. But they no longer look at every passer-by with suspicion. Nor do they see a dagger in every hand.

Does this mean that the wounds in their soul have healed? They will 4 never heal. As long as a spark of the flames of Auschwitz and Treblinka glows in their memory, so long will my joy be incomplete.

What about my faith in you, Master of the Universe? 5

I now realize I never lost it, not even over there, during the darkest hours 6 of my life. I don't know why I kept on whispering my daily prayers, and those one reserves for the Sabbath, and for the holidays, but I did recite them, often with my father and, on Rosh Hashanah eve, with hundreds of inmates at Auschwitz. Was it because the prayers remained a link to the vanished world of my childhood?

But my faith was no longer pure. How could it be? It was filled with an- 7 guish rather than fervor, with perplexity more then piety. In the kingdom of eternal night, on the Days of Awe, which are the Days of Judgment, my traditional prayers were directed to you as well as against you, Master of the Universe. What hurt me more: your absence or your silence?

In my testimony I have written harsh words, burning words about your 8 role in our tragedy. I would not repeat them today. But I felt them then. I felt them in every cell of my being. Why did you allow if not enable the killer day after day, night after night to torment, kill and annihilate tens of thousands of Jewish children? Why were they abandoned by your Creation? These thoughts were in no way destined to diminish the guilt of the guilty. Their established culpability is irrelevant to my "problem" with you, Master of the Universe. In my childhood I did not expect much from human beings. But I expected everything from you.

Where were you, God of kindness, in Auschwitz? What was going on in 9 heaven, at the celestial tribunal, while your children were marked for humiliation, isolation and death only because they were Jewish?

These questions have been haunting me for more than five decades. You 10 have vocal defenders, you know. Many theological answers were given me, such as "God is God. He alone knows what He is doing. One has no right to question Him or His ways." Or: "Auschwitz was a punishment for European Jewry's sins of assimilation and/or Zionism." And: "Isn't Israel the solution? Without Auschwitz, there would have been no Israel."

I reject all these answers. Auschwitz must and will forever remain a question mark only: it can be conceived neither with God nor without God. At one point, I began wondering whether I was not unfair with you. After all, Auschwitz was not something that came down ready-made from heaven. It was conceived by men, implemented by men, staffed by men. And their aim was to destroy not only us but you as well. Ought we not to think of your pain, too? Watching your children suffer at the hands of your other children, haven't you also suffered?   11

As we Jews now enter the High Holidays again, preparing ourselves to pray for a year of peace and happiness for our people and all people, let us make up, Master of the Universe. In spite of everything that happened? Yes, in spite. Let us make up: for the child in me, it is unbearable to be divorced from you so long.   12

Questions for Discussion

1. What method or methods for writing introductions does Wiesel use?
2. What method does he use to close the essay?
3. Why does the author refer to God as "Master of the Universe" rather than use a more personal form of address?
4. This selection is addressed to at least two audiences: God and the readers of the *New York Times*. Why did Wiesel choose to address both? Why didn't he write it solely for human readers?
5. Is Wiesel also writing to himself? Explain.
6. In paragraph 10, Wiesel tells us that many questions have been "haunting [him] for more than five decades." What are those questions?
7. Reread paragraphs 11 and 12. What do they reveal about the reason or reasons Wiesel wants to make peace with God?

Thinking Critically

1. In a 1998 interview with George Plimpton, Wiesel said: "I rarely speak about God. To God, yes. I protest against Him. I shout at Him. But to open a discourse [discussion] about the qualities of God, about the problems that God imposes . . . , no. And yet He is there, in silence." What light does this quotation shed on "A Prayer for the Days of Awe"? What is Wiesel's purpose in writing this prayer? Has his attitude toward God changed from what it was when he spoke with Plimpton?

2. Do you have a favorite prayer, poem, or hymn? Read it carefully; then, summarize it in your journal. In the process explain why this particular piece is meaningful to you.

Suggestions for Journal Entries

1. Sometimes life seems illogical, and tragedies strike for no apparent reason and with no warning. If such an incident has occurred in your life or in the life of someone you know, write down everything you know about this event.
2. Have you ever been angry with God or with the universe for allowing some difficulty or horror to visit you or others? Record the particulars of this situation. Make sure to explain why you are or were angry.

Code of Denial

Tena Moyer

Like many of the authors whose work appears in this text, Tena Moyer's primary occupation is not writing. However, she is an articulate professional who is passionate enough about a subject to communicate it brilliantly to others. Moyer is a physician practicing in a small town in the mountains of southern California, where she runs a breast-cancer screening clinic. Once having worked for a large health maintenance organization (HMO) in Los Angeles, Moyer moved to a rural community to practice the kind of medicine that allowed her to develop a more personal understanding of her patients and their needs.

First published in Discover *magazine, this selection is taken from a longer essay that describes Moyer's reaction to her sister's getting and dying from breast cancer. But this is no straightforward medical report; Moyer reveals a great deal of herself, not simply as a doctor and sister, but in a variety of roles.*

Preparing to Read

1. Search the Internet to find out all you can about breast-cancer examinations. What are they like? How often should women get them? Why are they so important? Do men get breast cancer? What are the treatments for such an illness?

2. Above you read that the author reveals herself through a variety of roles. Besides recalling this experience through the eyes of a doctor and of a sister, what other ways might she be looking at it? Think about such perspectives as you read this essay.

3. What concerns, fears, plans might run through an author's mind as he or she writes an essay on losing a sister to cancer? Begin thinking about this question by considering the title of this essay.

4. In the conclusion, the author distinguishes medicine as science from medicine as art. Look for clues to this distinction earlier in the essay.

Vocabulary

alien (adjective)	Foreign, strange.
bat mitzvahs (noun)	Ceremonies that celebrate a daughter's coming of age in Judaism.
bereft (adjective)	Deprived of.
biopsy (noun)	Laboratory test on tissue to determine presence of disease.
cataclysm (noun)	Catastrophe.

chemotherapeutic (adjective)	Pertaining to chemotherapy, a treatment for cancer.
desolate (adjective)	Barren.
fitfully (adverb)	Erratically, irregularly.
indelible (adjective)	Nonerasable, permanent.
obfuscate (verb)	Confuse, complicate, bewilder.
palette (noun)	Hand-held board on which a painter places blobs of paint.
pathology (noun)	Study of diseases.
prognosis (noun)	Prediction of the effects or outcome of an illness.
protoplasm (noun)	Basic matter that makes up the cells of living things.
sadistic (adjective)	Taking pleasure from inflicting pain.
sentient (adjective)	Alive and conscious, aware.

Code of Denial

Tena Moyer

Cancer is like a nuclear bomb that detonates in the middle of your family. 1 Before the phone call, the explosion, you go about your life unaware and unconcerned that a cataclysm of such proportion could possibly disrupt your life. Sure, there are the warning signs that scream like air raid sirens—the lump, the unhealed sore, the bloody stool, the shortness of breath. But we have learned to live with denial. After all, we are the generation that learned to duck and cover during the Cold War. And so when the physician, with drawn and serious face, says we need to run a few tests, we hear the siren and shudder at the thought, but we dismiss it just as quickly saying, praying, "It could never happen to me or my family." Duck and cover.

But the phone rings and the bomb falls and in a heartbeat the once famil- 2 iar landscape of your life becomes desolate and devastated, alien and treacherous. All the landmarks, the road signs, you have used to orient and guide yourself are blown away, and suddenly you don't know what to do or where to turn or whom to call or how to feel. You will never forget that moment; it will replay itself over and over again in your thoughts, like a slow-motion scene from some disaster movie.

I remember that instant more clearly and completely than any other mo- 3 ment of my life. My husband, Jim, and I had gone to the Midwest to visit his family, to take a long-overdue vacation from the stress of life and work and moving. I had left for that vacation knowing that my sister's biopsy report was pending. I heard the sirens but was unconcerned. I had seen enough negative biopsy reports to know that this couldn't possibly happen to my family, to my sister, to someone I loved so much. But as we turned into the driveway of my in-laws' home, the bomb exploded. I remember the color of the light—pale yellow and sky blue—on that late May afternoon: the fall of the shadows, the hot sun on my face, the moist air in my nostrils, the smell of hay and freshly turned Iowa farmland. I remember the lines and angles of my nephew Eric's face, drawn tense and tight, when we drove up the driveway and he approached the car. He didn't know how to tell me that my sister had called, that she had cancer. "I'm sorry," he said. "I'm sorry."

That moment is frozen in my memory like a held breath, tattooed into my sensory system in indelible and undeniable ink. Even after I have recovered from the initial shock, the fear and doubt and pain and anger linger night after night, month after month, like radiation slowly and silently consuming my soul.   4

Once I return to California and see my mother, Geraldine, for the first time since the news, she turns to me. I have fulfilled the dreams and fantasies of her own youth: I have become a physician. She has paid almost $100,000 for this, and now she turns to me with her pleading eyes and her beseeching face, asking for a return on her investment. "What does this all mean? Explain it to me." She wants a prognosis, a script for the future, a prescription for a cure. She wants me to save my sister. I cannot look her in the eye; I cannot give her the reassurance she so desperately wants and needs and wishes for. I cannot look myself in the eye, plumb the depths of my own heart, give myself what I desperately need—reassurance—and what I desperately want—ignorance. I have read too many pathology reports, memorized too many statistics.   5

I don't know how to tell my mother that her daughter has cancer, serious cancer. I don't know how to tell myself, and so I retreat to my professional vocabulary and obfuscate, muttering things about chemotherapeutic agents and tissue receptors and treatment outcomes. "Speak English!" she says. The language that she once beamed with pride and pleasure to hear me speak has now become a barrier between us, a barrier between my brain and my heart, my intellect and my emotions.   6

My poor mother. I cannot imagine what it must feel like to know your child has an illness that you cannot defend against. No matter how religious you have been about vaccinations, about nutrition, about safety, you cannot protect your child from this. You cannot protect yourself from this. It is a parent's worst nightmare. Children are supposed to outlive their parents. Children are supposed to weather their parents' illnesses and mourn their passing. Not vice versa.   7

And my sister. Mother of two young children, wife of a physician, painter of magnificent and fantastic landscapes. Andrea tells me that she stands in front of her unfinished canvases without the knowledge of how to complete them, indecisive, not knowing what palette to choose or which brush stroke to use. At night she sits in the doorways of her children's bedrooms and watches them as they sleep, fitfully and restlessly, breathing softly, sometimes crying out in their dreams. As she watches them she cries over the   8 lives she may not see to adulthood, the dance recitals unapplauded, the bat mitzvahs uncelebrated, the graduations unrewarded, the weddings unplanned, the grandchildren unheld. My sister stands in front of the unfinished canvas of her life and wishes for the time to complete it.

My sister's husband, Russell—the doctor—and I look at each other 9 without speaking, yet a silent dialogue passes between us—words we don't want to say and things we don't want to hear. Andrea and Russell's daughters, Sophie, just under 7, and Allie, not quite 4, named for their great-grandmothers, too young to understand and too old to be unaffected, have taken to fighting more during the day and sleeping together at night. "Mommy, are you going to die?" asks Sophie. The younger child angrily hits my sister in the breast.

My poor sister. She cannot protect her children from this, the most hor- 10 rible of children's nightmares. I turn to my husband and say, "I wish it was me instead of her. At least I don't have children."

"Don't say that!" Jim recoils from the thought, afraid someone might hear 11 me, afraid this could happen to his wife, almost as if he's crossing himself or reciting a prayer or fending off the evil eye. Duck and cover.

I am determined that no tumor will escape detection during my breast 12 screening clinic today. So I pinch and press and probe deep into these breasts, searching for the lump or the lymph node or the nipple discharge. I do this because I am a committed and caring physician, but I also do this because I am an angry and frightened and hurting sister. In my mind the tumor is sentient and is purposefully devouring my sister's life with a voracious appetite and sadistic pleasure. I am so angry.

I am angry at the cancer for invading my sister's body. I am angry at her 13 immune system for failing to overwhelm and destroy the disease. I am angry with my sister for getting cancer and causing me so much pain. I am angry with my mother because she is bereft and desperate and I have no words to comfort her. I am angry with the nurse who, when my sister called requesting an appointment because of a lump she felt, told her to wait until after her period was over. Three precious weeks lost. I am angry with the physicians because they don't seem to recognize that my sister is not a pathology report but a living, breathing person with two beautiful young children and plans for the future and a family who loves her absolutely and without reservation.

I am angry with everybody, acquaintance and stranger alike, because 14 they are going about their lives unaware and unconcerned, as if nothing has changed, when my own life has been transformed so terribly and irretrievably. I am angry at the world because nothing in the world can undo the damage or turn back time. I am angry with myself because it is my sister who got cancer and not me, and for the briefest moment I breathed a sigh of relief and said, "Bad luck, bad protoplasm." But today, mostly, I am angry at breasts because they become cancerous, and despite all my education and training there is nothing I can do about it; I cannot make it go away. So I press and probe and pinch maybe a little too hard and a little too aggressively because I hate breasts for what they have done to my family and me.

By the end of the day my hands and fingers are aching and cramped. It has been an exhausting day. The science of medicine may be doing a thorough breast exam, but the art of medicine is talking with your patients, listening to their stories and learning about their lives. Today I have gotten to know 30 women who will become my patients and friends. But there is still one task left, I take a sheet of paper and make circles and scribbles and comments on it. "History of fibrocystic disease," it says. "Status post biopsy times two, family history of breast cancer." I walk down the hall and hand it to the mammographer as I unbutton my blouse.

15

Questions for Discussion

1. What method or methods discussed earlier in this chapter does Tena Moyer use to introduce this essay?

2. Is Moyer's introduction limited to one paragraph? What function does paragraph 2 play?

3. What methods does she use in her concluding paragraph?

4. What is the "task" that Moyer mentions in paragraph 15?

5. Preparing to Read, you were asked to consider the various roles Moyer plays in this essay. What role is she playing in paragraph 15?

6. Why does the author mention the names of her nieces, her mother, and other family members?

7. In most of this essay, the author writes in the present tense, even when she is recalling the past. What is the effect of her doing so? Why does she use the past tense in paragraph 3?

8. Comment on Moyer's title.

Thinking Critically

1. The author tells us that medicine is both an art and a science. Write notes in the margins of this selection to identify places in which Moyer discusses medicine as an art, as a science, or as both. Then, write two or three paragraphs that explain her vision of medicine and her role as a doctor.

2. In Chapter 3, you might have read "A Brother's Dreams," in which medical student Paul Aronowitz describes his brother's mental illness. What does this essay have in common with "Code of Denial"?

3. Read ahead to Gaye Wagner's "Death of an Officer" in Chapter 10. What concerns and characteristics does this essay share with "Code of Denial"?

Suggestions for Journal Entries

1. Many of us play two or more roles in life. We are students, employees, family members, church- or temple-goers, and so on. Does your personality seem to change or do you see things differently when you are asked to play different roles? Use listing or draw a subject tree to gather details that explain differences in your personality, your approach to life, your self-image, or the image you portray to others as you take on different roles.

2. Moyer expresses frustration that she cannot reassure her mother about her sister's prognosis. This frustration is increased when she realizes that no mother can really protect her daughter from this illness. Think about an illnesss or condition that we can attempt to prevent or to lessen the effects of. For example, we can avoid the ill effects of obesity by eating carefully and exercising regularly. We can decrease our chances of contracting lung cancer by not smoking. Use focused freewriting, clustering, or brainstorming with a friend to gather information that you could use if you wanted to advise someone on how to prevent an illness.

The Transformation of Maria Fernandez

Anita DiPasquale

Anita DiPasquale had the rare opportunity to visit Nicaragua near the end of the civil war that devastated that Central American country in the 1980s. She went there with a friend to bring news to relatives of a Nicaraguan child who had been adopted by a family in California. When a college writing instructor asked DiPasquale to narrate an unforgettable experience, she had no trouble deciding what to write about.

The Iran-Contra affair, which is mentioned in paragraph 1, involved the sale of arms to Iran as part of an illegal plan to provide American military aid to the Contras of Nicaragua. The Contras were a group trying to overthrow Nicaragua's communist government led by a group called the Sandinistas. The "superpowers," mentioned twice in this essay, are the United States and the former Soviet Union.

Preparing to Read

1. Think about what the word "transformation" in the title prepares us for in the essay. What is a "transformation"?

2. DiPasquale's introduction is longer than one paragraph, and it uses more than one of the methods for writing introductions explained earlier in this chapter. Read her introduction carefully; make sure you understand what she is saying and how she is saying it.

3. Although her story takes place in the past, DiPasquale writes in the present tense. In paragraph 2, for example, she tells us that Michael and she "meet," not "met" Maria. Using the present tense often adds excitement to a narrative essay and makes it more convincing.

4. The author kept an informal journal of her conversations with Maria by recording what she remembered of their talks from time to time. What we read may not be exactly what she and Maria said, word for word, but it is a fair re-creation of their conversations.

Vocabulary

adversaries (noun)	Opponents, enemies.
apathetic (adjective)	Unconcerned, uninterested.
communal (adjective)	Having to do with a community.
covert (adjective)	Secret, hidden.
defiled (adjective)	Dirtied, violated.
diverse (adjective)	Various, assorted.
eking out (verb)	Struggling to make or get.

eradicate (verb)	Destroy, annihilate.
ironically (adverb)	Contrary to what is expected.
meager (adjective)	Poor, little.
mired (adjective)	Stuck.
parochial (adjective)	Isolated, provincial.
raven (adjective)	Black.
repressive (adjective)	Tyrannical, dictatorial.
synonymous (adjective)	Similar in meaning.

The Transformation of Maria Fernandez

Anita DiPasquale

MARIA'S STORY IS testimony to the horror of war. Her country is Nicaragua, 1
one of America's greatest embarrassments and yet another battleground
in what the superpowers called the "cold" war. In this impoverished, merciless, yet beautiful land, the Reagan Administration became mired in a series
of covert operations known as the Iran-Contra fiasco. Ironically, our shame
over this dreadful incident may be the only good thing to come from our
presence in Nicaragua. Perhaps Americans who were once parochial and apathetic will realize that Kansas is not Central America, that *Sandinista* and "repressive" are not synonymous, that *Contra* may not mean "freedom fighter,"
and that all wars, no matter who the adversaries, are barbarous!

My friend Michael and I meet Maria on a trip through hell in Nicaragua's 2
capital, Managua. The month is June, the year 1988. Maria is seventeen, no
longer a child, no longer a woman. She is a soldier in the FSLN (*Frente Sandinista de Liberacion Nacional),* the national liberation front named for Augusto
Sandino, a guerrilla fighter martyred in an earlier war of liberation.

Maria is thin, with shoulder-length raven hair, which she braids and 3
tucks away under her camouflage hat. Her nose is long and straight, her chin
prominent and proud. A silky olive complexion and cheekbones straight out
of *Vogue* magazine reveal a face that is truly delicate. How, then, has it come
to harbor the deadest eyes I have ever seen?

Maria, Michael and I make our way along the gray and blue cobblestone 4
street and sit on a curb so large it would be considered a ledge in the United
States. The masonry buildings around us are old, bruised, and defiled. Bullet
holes and political graffiti have stained the faces of these tired shelters. Some
still lie battered and tormented by the earthquake that devastated Nicaragua
on December 23, 1972.

A young woman bathes in rain water that has collected in an old metal 5
drum across the street. No one notices; people walk by as if she were invisible. Maria catches me staring: "It's a way of life here; so many people are
without water, without homes."

She is safer here on the street than at the river, I am told. "Listen, haven't 6
you heard the gunfire or seen the blood?" asks Maria.

"Have my eyes and ears deceived me?" I wonder. I have seen no blood and heard no shooting. I know there is a war, but not until many days later will I fully realize what she means.

7

Michael pulls a photograph from his shirt pocket and hands it to Maria. It is a picture of her brother Alberto; he is seated on a bright red Big Wheel. Alberto is seven and lives in Los Angeles with Michael's uncle. The child is smiling; he knows his world is make-believe, like that of most children in countries free of war.

8

"I remember," she proclaims, as she stares at the photo. "I remember when I was a child; we lived in the north, in Matagalpa." Matagalpa is known for its mountains and its hard living. Aside from the small towns every five miles or so, nothing but small shacks dot the landscape. The people of Matagalpa work alone on small plots of land, eking out a meager existence. There are no real communities here as there are in the Pacific culture, which is known for its communal involvement with the land.

9

Maria lights a cigarette and sighs. "We were very poor and lived close to the earth. I can still smell Mama's tortillas cooking in the oven. Our house had two rooms, and the roof was made of corrugated tin. The floor was dirt except for a small area which Papa dug out and covered with wood in order to hide us when the soldiers came through."

10

Her face grows solemn for a moment. But she lifts her strong chin and continues proudly. "As a small girl, I would wear pretty dresses that Mama made from spare pieces of cloth. They always had flowers on them, pink and yellow. I never had a pair of shoes; there was no need for them. My job on the land was to spread the fertilizer." Maria's nose crinkles as if she can still smell the manure.

11

"Once we went on a trip to Puerto Cabezas; Alberto was so small he had just learned to walk. There the Miskito Indians were catching giant sea tortoises on the shore. The tortoises were larger than Alberto," she chuckles. "A Miskito woman gave us a ride on her boat. It was made from a hollowed out tree. That was the last family outing I remember."

12

"How did Alberto come to live in America?" I ask. Michael has never told me, and I know by the look on his face that I should not have asked the question. The story Maria tells is more horrifying than any horror film. It makes the ravages of war real to me. I no longer look on them as someone else's problems. It also explains how a happy little girl in flowered dresses could have become a soldier, a killer, how her eyes can be so dead.

13

"I must go back a few years to help you understand what led to Alberto's departure," began Maria. "In August of 1978, when I was a very small child, before Alberto was born, our world changed forever. The FSLN had seized the National Palace, taking 1,500 hostages. When the attackers and 59 newly freed prisoners drove to the airport to get a flight to Panama, thousands of people lined the streets and cheered their victory. After the Palace assault, there were many attacks on the National Guard throughout Nicaragua—in Matagalpa, Leon, Masaya, Esteli, and Chinandega. The people lifted up arms against President Anastasio Somoza Debayle. So, to stop the rebels, the Guard

14

destroyed our cities from the air. It took about two weeks and left over 4,000 dead. As the Sandinistas withdrew, they took thousands of newly recruited soldiers. My father was one.

"Later, in 1979, Somoza was driven into exile, to America's Miami. We 15 thought there was hope for our country. Your President Carter worked with us, but then Reagan came. He reorganized Somoza's National Guard, which became the Contras. They were given haven in Honduras. The 75,000 Sandinistas had few weapons and little money, so they could not eradicate the 10,000 Contras, who were well equipped with U.S. weapons and money.

"Back to Alberto. The last day I saw my brother started like any other. I 16 was fourteen or so, Alberto about four. We were home alone with my mother. Papa was off fighting in the jungle. It was September, and a wonderful rain had fallen the night before, leaving the air fragrant with a lush tropical scent. However, smoke hovered over the village, casting shadows on houses and streets and plunging the land into a deep, damp calm.

"Suddenly, I heard our neighbor Guillermo run into our house. He was 17 covered with blood. 'Contras,' he screamed before darting into the mist. Mama moved the heavy trunk that covered the hiding place my father had made. She was eight months pregnant, so I helped. First we placed Alberto into the hole, and I climbed on top of him. Mama placed the wood back on top and threw a rug over the floor.

"Just then the soldiers must have arrived. They were yelling and laughing. 18 I covered Alberto's ears and tried to muffle his crying. I heard my mother's screams; I still hear her screams. They were finally silenced by gunfire.

"The soldiers must have stayed about an hour; it felt like an eternity. The 19 house grew quiet. 'I dare not move,' I thought, so we lay there for several hours. Before I climbed out of the hole, I tied a piece of my dress around Alberto's eyes and around his hands so he wouldn't remove the blindfold. When I entered the daylight I was instantly sick. Mama was dead; they had cut my baby sister from her stomach; they lay there in a pool of blood. Both bodies were riddled with bullets.

"The soldiers had stayed there with their dead bodies long enough to eat 20 our breakfast. There was blood everywhere. I don't know how long I stood motionless when a shadow crossed the doorway. It was Chris, a U.S. reporter who often came by to feed his stories and his belly. He buried Mama and the baby, Isabel. That would have been her name.

"Chris told me my father had died the week earlier in a battle in 21 Jinotega. He said he could get Alberto out of Nicaragua, away from the Contras. He knew someone who was smuggling small, light-skinned children into California. He promised he would personally get him a good home as repayment for the help my family had given him. He was crying when he said I was too big to go. I had forgotten how to cry. Right then, at that moment, I was reborn into this world all alone. You do what you have to do in order to survive. I now know the meaning in the smoke. You do what you have to do to survive."

As Maria finishes her story, my stomach grows heavy and sinks to a 22
depth I did not think was possible. Suddenly, a truck pulls onto the street. It
is filled with dead Contras on the way to burial. Another truck pulls up behind; this one is filled with Sandinista soldiers, none of whom look over
twenty. Most are between ten and fifteen. Some might be eight. They are all
toting rifles, passing cigarettes out among the crowd. When I look into the
first truck, I become desperate with fear. Piled one on top of another are
men, women, and children. They are all dead.

Back at the ledge, I slump against Michael. Maria emerges from the daze 23
of her horrid memory and kisses Michael on the cheek. She points to the
trucks. "If he were here, his world would be all too real."

Sometimes it is nearly impossible to tell Contra soldiers and Sandinistas 24
apart. They have a lot in common: their youth, their camaraderie, their mortality. When Salvadoran Archbishop Rivera y Damas spoke of the role of the
superpowers in his country's civil war, he could have been describing the
tragedy of Nicaragua: "They supply the weapons, and we supply the dead."

Questions for Discussion

1. A transformation is a very significant change. What significant change
   has Maria experienced? Has the author experienced a change as a
   result of meeting Maria?
2. What is DiPasquale's thesis? What events in the story support or
   develop that thesis best?
3. The introduction to the essay includes several startling remarks.
   Identify two or three.
4. Where in the introduction does DiPasquale challenge widely held
   assumptions or opinions?
5. How does the question at the end of paragraph 3 help us understand
   her thesis?
6. This essay closes with quotations and statements that might stick in
   your mind long after you have read them. Which of these do you
   think is most memorable?
7. In what way does the scene described in paragraph 22 support the
   essay's thesis?
8. In paragraph 24, DiPasquale mentions the "superpowers," which we
   recall from paragraph 1. What is she trying to accomplish by
   repeating this word at the end of the essay?

Thinking Critically

1. Do a little reading on Nicaragua in a recently published encyclopedia
   or other reference work. Your college librarian can help you find such

resources. Then, write a short explanation of DiPasquale's first paragraph. Make sure to identify the *Sandinistas* and the *Contras* and to explain the significance of her hope that Americans will no longer confuse Central America with Kansas.

2. Read "Growing Up in Romania," another student essay, which appears in Chapter 12. What does it have in common with DiPasquale's work?

Suggestions for Journal Entries

1. Recall a horrifying or dangerous event that showed you the sad or dark side of life. Ask the journalists' questions (you can find these in "Getting Started," under Brainstorming) to collect as many details about it as you can. Examples of such an incident include military combat; a bad automobile or industrial accident; a building fire; a tornado; a bout with a serious illness; a violent crime; a fall from a ledge or down a stairs; a mishap at sea, in a lake, river, or other body of water; or a fight in which someone was seriously hurt. Whatever event you write about, make sure to show why it was horrifying or dangerous.

2. Do you know someone who experienced a tragic or horrifying event like those mentioned above? If so, interview him or her using the techniques described in "Getting Started." Gather as much information as you can about the incident, and determine how it affected the person you interview.

3. Do you have a friend or relative who went through a drastic and sudden personality change as a result of an important event or development in his or her life? Write about this person by making three lists: one that contains details describing your subject before the change; one that describes him or her after the change; and one that explains what caused the change.

Suggestions for Sustained Writing

1. Reread one of the papers you've written this semester. Try to pick the one you or your instructor liked best, but don't limit your choice to papers you've completed for English class. Then, rewrite the beginning and ending to that essay by using techniques for writing introductions and conclusions discussed in this chapter.

2. Do you agree with Robert Fulghum that people's bathrooms tell a lot about them? How about their cars, bedrooms, closets, or refrigerators?

Write an essay in which you introduce your readers to a close friend or relative by describing his or her room, home, apartment, car, work area, or the like. Include details that focus on one and only one aspect of your subject's personality. For example, to show that this person has expensive tastes, mention the brand names and estimate the costs of clothes you saw in his or her closet. Then talk about the luxurious furniture and expensive stereo equipment in his or her living room, and so on. If you responded to the second suggestion for journal writing after "I Was Just Wondering," you have already gathered useful details for this assignment.

When you write your introduction, you might use a startling statement or, like Fulghum, ask a question that helps reveal your thesis. Here's an example of such a question: "How do I know Andy has expensive tastes?"

You can conclude by summarizing your main points, offering advice, or looking to the future. For example:

> Andy spends money faster than he can make it. Unless he gets a better-paying job, cuts back on expensive purchases, or inherits money from a rich relative, the finance company will repossess his furniture.

3. If you responded to either of the suggestions for journal writing after Wiesel's "A Prayer for the Days of Awe," read the notes you made in preparation for the writing of a letter to God or to the Master of the Universe (in other words, a prayer). You might write about your concerns and frustrations over an incident in which someone has been harmed, or you might express your anger to the Creator for allowing evil, sorrow, and injustice to exist either in general or in a particular situation you have observed. Or you might simply discuss some questions that have been bothering you about yourself, about your relationship with God, or about life in general.

Whichever path you choose, remember that your letter/prayer will be read by a human audience, so provide enough details to ensure that your readers will understand the situations, concepts, and emotions you are discussing. In addition, use one or more of the methods for writing introductions and conclusions that you have learned in this chapter. Whether human or divine, your audience deserves interesting and effective openings and closings.

Finally, write several drafts of your paper. Revise and edit it carefully. God may forgive sloppy writing, but other readers won't.

4. Look back at the notes you made in response to either of the journal suggestions following Moyer's "Code of Denial." Use your notes as a springboard for the completion of a piece of writing that contains an interesting and focused introduction and an effective conclusion. Try using more than one technique explained in this chapter to open and close your work.

If you responded to the first of the Suggestions for Journal Entries after Moyer's essay, explain the changes that your personality or self-image undergoes when you take on different roles during a typical day or week. If you responded to the second journal suggestion, write a letter to a relative or friend offering advice on how to prevent contracting an illness or how to detect signs of that illness. In the Preparing to Read section that precedes Moyer's essay, you were advised to learn more about breast-cancer examinations via the Internet. Try using this information if you decide to write about breast cancer. Return to the Internet to find information if you decide to write about another disease.

Again, pay particular attention to your introduction (include an effective thesis statement) and to your conclusion. You may wish to write both your introductory and concluding paragraphs after you have completed a rough draft of the body paragraphs. In any case, remember that writing is a process. So, write and revise several drafts, edit them carefully, and proofread your final copy.

Note: If you take information from the Internet, you must cite (give credit to) your source(s), whether you use a direct quotation or put the information into your own words. The Appendix which appears at the end of this textbook explains how to cite sources using Modern Language Association (MLA) style.

5. "The Transformation of Maria Fernandez" tells of tragic events that Anita DiPasquale witnessed or that she learned about from someone else. If you responded to either of the first two suggestions for journal writing after this essay, you have collected information about a terrifying incident you experienced directly, witnessed, or heard about from another person. Turn these notes into a full-length essay that tells your story in detail. Like the author of "The Transformation of Maria Fernandez," you might quote yourself or others in your story.

DiPasquale opens by making startling statements, challenging popular assumptions, and asking a rhetorical question. Any of these methods is a good way to introduce your essay, but you can also describe a scene, use a quotation, or explain a problem. When concluding, try a memorable quotation from someone in the story, make a call to action, or look to the future.

You can tell from the final product that DiPasquale wrote several drafts of her essay and edited it quite well. Do the same with yours.

6. Have you ever known anyone who, because of a single experience, went through a drastic and sudden change in personality, lifestyle, or attitude like the one you read about in "The Transformation of Maria Fernandez"? Write the story of this transformation by telling your readers about the experience and by explaining how it changed the person you are writing about. First, however, review the notes you made after reading DiPasquale's essay. If you responded to the third journal suggestion, you may have gathered details you can use in this assignment.

A startling statement, an interesting question or analogy, or the vivid description of a place might make an interesting introduction to your story. Quoting your subject, looking to the future, or asking a rhetorical question might make an effective conclusion.

Once again, remember that writing is a process, so draft, revise, and edit!

Writing to Learn: A Group Activity

THE FIRST MEETING

For inspiration, reread and discuss Elie Wiesel's "A Prayer for the Days of Awe" as well as the following short prayer from the Koran, the Islamic holy book:

In the Name of God, the Compassionate, the Merciful

Praise be to God, Lord of the worlds!
The compassionate, the merciful!
King on the Day of reckoning!
Thee *only* do we worship, and to Thee do we cry for help.
Guide Thou us on the straight path,
The path of those to whom Thou has been gracious;—with whom Thou art not angry, and who go not astray. (Sura I)

Now pretend that you have been asked to write a group letter to the Master of the Universe. Brainstorm for at least 20 minutes to come up with three or four questions that you might ask about the nature of life, of the universe, of the afterlife, of God Himself, or of any other relevant issues important to you. Write out each question in a clear and complete sentence. Assign each student of the group—except one—to discuss this question in a fully developed paragraph that he or she will complete for homework. Assign the remaining student the task of writing the introduction and conclusion for an essay that will include the three or four paragraphs written by the other group members. Everyone should bring several copies of his or her work to the next meeting.

THE SECOND MEETING

Distribute the materials everyone has brought. Now decide which paragraphs need to be expanded or revised in any way. Make suggestions as needed. Then decide on the order in which each paragraph should appear in the paper. Rewrite your paragraphs for homework, making enough copies to distribute at the next meeting.

continued

THE THIRD MEETING

Distribute the materials everyone has brought. Arrange all the paragraphs in the order they are to appear in the essay's final version. Collectively, make sure that there are transitions in and between paragraphs, that the paper begins and ends in interesting and logical ways, and that it makes sense over all. Next, edit the paper for grammar, spelling, sentence structure, and other errors. Finally, assign one person the job of typing the paper as a whole and of making enough copies for each member of the group and for the instructor.

Word Choice and Sentence Patterns

In Section One you learned how to approach a subject, to focus on a purpose and central idea, and to organize and develop the information you collected. The three chapters in Section Two explain how to use language and sentence structure to make your writing clearer, more interesting, and more emphatic.

What you will learn in Section Two is just as important as what you learned earlier. In most cases, however, the techniques discussed in this section—refining word choice, creating figures of speech, and reworking sentence structure for emphasis and variety—are things you will turn your attention to after having written at least one version of a paper, not while you are focusing on a central idea, organizing details, or writing your first rough draft.

Keep this in mind as you read the next three chapters. Chapter 5 explains how to choose vocabulary that is concrete, specific, and vivid. You will learn even more about using words effectively in Chapter 6, which explains three types of figurative language: metaphor, simile, and personification. Finally, Chapter 7 will increase your ability to create variety and emphasis through sentence structure.

Enjoy the selections that follow. Reading them carefully and completing the Questions for Discussion, the Suggestions for Journal Entries, and the Suggestions for Sustained Writing will not only help you learn more about the writing process but should also inspire you to continue developing as a writer.

CHAPTER 5

Word Choice: Using Concrete, Specific, and Vivid Language

A writer has three ways to communicate a message: by (1) implying it, (2) telling it, or (3) showing it. Of course, all three types of writing serve specific and important purposes. Usually, however, writing that is the clearest and has the greatest impact uses language that shows what you wish to communicate. Words that show are more concrete, specific, and usually more interesting than those that simply tell the reader what you want to say, and they are always more direct than language that only implies or suggests what you mean.

Although the following two paragraphs discuss the same subject, they contain very different kinds of language. Which of the two will have the greater impact on the reader?

Writing That Tells

Smith's old car is the joke of the neighborhood. He should have gotten rid of it years ago, but he insists on keeping this "antique" despite protests from his family and friends. The car is noisy and unsafe. What's more, it pollutes the environment, causes a real disturbance whenever he drives by, and is a real eyesore.

Writing That Shows

Whenever Smith drives his 1957 Dodge down our street, dogs howl, children scream, and old people head inside and shut their windows. Originally, the car was painted emerald green, but the exterior is so covered with scrapes, dents, and patches of rust that it is hard to tell what it looked like when new. His wife, children, and close friends have begged him to junk this corroded patchwork of steel, rubber, and chicken wire, but Smith insists that he can restore his "antique" to its former glory. It does no good to point out that its cracked windshield and bald tires qualify it as a road hazard. Nor does it help to complain about the roar and rattle of its cracked muffler, the screech of its well-worn brakes, and the stench of the thick, black smoke that billows from its rusty tail pipe.

As you will learn in the chapters on narration and description, language that shows makes for effective and interesting writing, especially when your purpose is to describe a person or place or to tell a story. But such language is important to many kinds of writing, and learning how to use it is essential to your development as a writer.

There are three important things to remember about language that shows: It is concrete, it is specific, and it is vivid.

Making Your Writing Concrete

Concrete language points to or identifies something that the reader can experience or has experienced in some way. Things that are concrete are usually material; they can be seen, heard, smelled, felt, or tasted. The opposite of *concrete* is *abstract,* a term that refers to ideas, emotions, or other intangibles that, while very real, exist in our minds and hearts. That's why readers find it harder to grasp the abstract than the concrete.

Compare the nouns in the following list. The ones on the left represent abstract ideas. The ones on the right stand for concrete embodiments of those ideas; that is, they are physical representations, showing us what such ideas as *affection* and *hatred* really are.

Abstract	Concrete
Affection	Kiss, embrace
Hatred	Sneer, curse
Violence	Punch, shove
Anger	Shout
Fear	Scream, gasp
Joy	Laugh, smile

Here are three ways to make your writing concrete.

USE YOUR FIVE SENSES TO RECALL AN EXPERIENCE

Giving your readers a straightforward, realistic account of how things look, smell, sound, taste, or feel is one of the most effective ways to make your writing concrete. There are examples of how authors appeal to the five senses in the later chapters on description. For now, read the following passage from "Once More to the Lake," in which E. B. White recalls concrete, sensory details about arriving at the camp in Maine where he spent his summer vacations as a boy. The only sense that White does not refer to is taste; see if you can identify details in this paragraph that appeal to the other four:

> The arriving . . . had been so big a business in itself, at the railway station
> the farm wagon drawn up, the first smell of the pine-laden air, the first
> glimpse of the smiling farmer . . . and the feel of the wagon under you for
> the long ten-mile haul, and at the top of the last long hill catching the first

view of the lake after eleven months of not seeing this cherished body of water. The shouts and cries of the other campers when they saw you, and the trunks to be unpacked, to give up their rich burden.

CREATE A CONCRETE IMAGE

An image is a mental picture that expresses an abstract concept in concrete terms. Therefore, it helps readers understand more easily. You can create images by packing your writing with details, usually in the form of nouns and adjectives. The word *image* is related to the word *imagine*. Therefore, a good time to create an image is when you write about something that your readers have never experienced or that they can only imagine from the information you provide. This is what happens in the following paragraph from "Searching for El Dorado," an essay that likens modern-day gold mining in South America to the search for the mythical golden land of El Dorado. Here, author Marc Herman uses an image to explain "a natural paradise."

> The Guiana Shield region of South America is a natural paradise. The moisture from its waterfalls sifts over lush forests, producing daily rainbows that span hundreds of miles at their base and widen into double spectra across cliff faces. Tourists come here to see Angel Falls, the world's highest, or Canaima National Park, a plateau with Wyoming's sky, Yosemite's waterfalls, and New Mexico's mesas. The tallest of these mesas, Mount Roraima, creates its own weather, as clouds slip off the top and twist beside the cliffs like dropped scarves, catching the sunlight and staining the brush below a dense, woven brown the color of a monk's robe. The landscape is studded with Pemon Indian houses shaped like rockets—wood and mud cylinders with conical roofs made of dried leaves.

USE EXAMPLES

Using easily recognizable examples is a very effective way to help your readers grasp abstract ideas, which might otherwise seem vague or unclear. For instance, if you want to explain that your Uncle Wendell is eccentric, you can write that "he has several quirks," that "he is odd," or that "he is strange." But such synonyms are as abstract and as hard to grasp as *eccentric*. Instead, why not provide examples that your readers are sure to understand? In other words, show them what *eccentric* means by explaining that Uncle Wendell never wears the same color socks, that he often cuts his own hair, that he refuses to speak for days at a time, and that he sometimes eats chocolate-covered seaweed for dessert.

In "Less Work for Mother?" Ruth Schwartz Cowan uses a number of examples we are certain to recognize as she explains the idea that technology has transformed the American household:

> During the first half of the twentieth century, the average American household was transformed by the introduction of a group of machines that profoundly altered the daily lives of housewives. . . . Where once there had

been a wood- or coal-burning stove there now was a gas or electric range. Clothes that had once been scrubbed on a metal washboard were now tossed into a tub and cleansed by an electrically driven agitator. The dryer replaced the clothesline; the vacuum cleaner replaced the broom; the refrigerator replaced the ice box and the root cellar. . . . No one had to chop or haul wood anymore. No one had to shovel out ashes or beat rugs or carry water; no one even had to toss egg whites with a fork for an hour to make an angel food cake.

Making Your Writing Specific

As you've learned, writing that shows uses details that are both specific and concrete. Writing that lacks specificity often contains language that is general, which makes it difficult for the writer to communicate clearly and completely. One of the best ways to make your language more specific is to use carefully chosen nouns and adjectives. As you probably know, nouns name persons, places, and things; adjectives modify (or help describe) nouns, thereby making them more exact and distinct. In the following list, compare the words and phrases in each column; notice how much more meaningful the items become as you move from left to right:

General	More Specific	Most Specific
automobile	sports car	Corvette
residence	house	three-bedroom ranch
fruit	melon	juicy cantaloupe
school	college	University of Kentucky
tree	evergreen	young pine
baked goods	pastries	chocolate-filled cream puffs
airplane	jetliner	brand new Boeing 777
beverage	soft drink	caffeine-free diet cola
television show	situation comedy	Seinfeld
public transportation	train	Orient Express

You probably noticed that several of the "Most Specific" items contain capitalized words. These are proper nouns, which name specific persons, places, and things. Use proper nouns that your readers will recognize whenever you can. Doing so will show how much you know about your subject and will increase the readers' confidence in you. More important, it will help make your ideas more familiar and easier to grasp.

At first, you might have to train yourself to use specifics. After a while, though, you will become skilled at eliminating flat, empty generalizations from your writing and at filling it with details that clarify and focus your ideas.

Notice the differences between the following two paragraphs. The first uses vague, general language; the second uses specific details—nouns and adjectives—that make its meaning sharper and clearer and that hold the reader's interest better.

General

The island prison is covered with flowers now. A large sign that is visible from a long way off warns visitors away. But since the early 1960s, when they took the last prisoners to other institutions, the sign has really served no purpose, for the prison has been abandoned. The place is not unpleasant; in fact, one might enjoy the romance and solitude out there.

Specific

Alcatraz Island is covered with flowers now: orange and yellow nasturtiums, geraniums, sweet grass, blue iris, black-eyed Susans. Candytuft springs up through the cracked concrete in the exercise yard. Ice plant carpets the rusting catwalks. "WARNING! KEEP OFF! U.S. PROPERTY," the sign still reads, big and yellow and visible for perhaps a quarter of a mile, but since March 21, 1963, the day they took the last thirty or so men off the island . . . the warning has been only *pro forma* [serving no real purpose]. It is not an unpleasant place to be, out there on Alcatraz with only the flowers and the wind and the bell buoy moaning and the tide surging through the Golden Gate. (Joan Didion, "Rock of Ages")

The differences between these two paragraphs can be summed up as follows:

• The first calls the place an "island prison." The second gives it a name, "Alcatraz."
• The first claims that the prison is covered with flowers. The second shows us that this is true by naming them: "nasturtiums, geraniums," and so on. It also explains exactly where they grow: "through the cracked concrete" and on "rusting catwalks."
• The first tells us about a sign that can be seen "from a long way off." The second explains that the sign is "visible for perhaps a quarter of a mile" and shows us exactly what it says.
• The first mentions that the last prisoners were removed from Alcatraz in the 1960s. The second explains that they numbered "thirty or so" and that the exact date of their departure was March 21, 1963.
• The first tells us that we might find "romance and solitude" on Alcatraz Island. The second describes the romance and solitude by calling our attention to "the flowers and the wind and the bell buoy moaning and the tide surging through the Golden Gate."

Making Your Writing Vivid

Besides using figurative language (the subject of the next chapter), you can make your writing vivid by choosing verbs, adjectives, and adverbs carefully.

1. Verbs express action, condition, or state of being. If you wrote that "Jan *leaped* over the hurdles," you would be using an action verb. If you explained that "Roberta *did not feel* well" or that "Mario *was* delirious," you would be describing a condition or a state of being.

2. Adjectives describe nouns. You would be using adjectives if you wrote that "the *large, two-story white* house that the *young Canadian* couple bought was *old* and *weather-beaten*."

3. Adverbs modify (tell the reader something about) verbs, adjectives, or other adverbs. You would be using adverbs if you wrote: "The *easily* frightened child sobbed *softly* and hugged his mother *very tightly* as she *gently* wiped away his tears and *tenderly* explained that the knee he had *just* scraped would stop hurting *soon*."

Choosing effective verbs, adjectives, and adverbs can turn dull writing into writing that keeps the reader's interest and communicates ideas with greater emphasis and clarity. Notice how much more effective the rewritten version of each of the following sentences becomes when the right verbs, adjectives, and adverbs are used:

1. The old church needed repair.

   The pre–Civil War Baptist church cried out for repairs to its tottering steeple, its crumbling stone foundation, and its cracked stained-glass windows.

2. The kitchen table was a mess. It was covered with the remains of peanut butter and jelly sandwiches.

   The kitchen table was littered with the half-eaten remains of very stale peanut-butter sandwiches and thickly smeared with the crusty residue of strawberry jelly.

3. A pathetic old homeless person was in an alley among some garbage.

   The body of a homeless man, his face wrinkled and blistered, lay in a pile of oil-covered rags and filthy cardboard boxes piled in the corner of a long alley devoid of life and light.

Visualizing Concrete, Specific, and Vivid Details

In the following paragraphs from "Where the World Began," Margaret Laurence describes her small hometown on the Canadian prairie. Comments in the margins of the first paragraph point to examples of the kinds of language you just learned about. After studying the first paragraph, find and circle similar examples of effective language in the second.

Adjectives appeal to senses.

Summers were scorching, and when no rain came and the wheat became bleached and dried before it headed, the faces of farmers and townsfolk would not smile much, and you took for granted, because it never seemed to have been any different, the frequent knocking at the back door and the young men standing there, mumbling or thrusting defiantly their requests for a drink of water and a sandwich if you could spare it. They were riding the freights, and you never knew where they had come from, or where they might end up, if anywhere. The Drought and Depression were like evil deities which had been there always. You understood and did not understand.

Startling image.

Vivid adjectives.

Vivid adverb.

Specific type of train.

Proper nouns.

Yet the outside world had its continuing marvels. The poplar bluffs and the small river were filled and surrounded with a zillion different grasses, stones, and weed flowers. The meadowlarks sang undaunted [courageously] from the twanging telephone wires along the gravel highway. Once we found an old flat-bottomed scow [small boat], and launched her, poling along the shallow brown waters, mending her with

wodges [chunks] of hastily chewed Spearmint,
grounding her among the tangles of yellow
marsh marigolds that grew succulently along
the banks of the shrunken river, while the
sun made our skins smell dusty-warm.

Revising to Include Concrete, Specific, and Vivid Language

Read these two versions of a paragraph from Nancy J. Mundie's ironic (tongue-in-cheek) essay that proposes to use the mentally ill in scientific experimentation. It is clear that, by revising her work, Mundie was able to make her language more concrete, specific, and vivid. You will find a complete version of Mundie's essay—"The Mentally Ill and Human Experimentation: Perfect Together"—later in this chapter.

Mundie—Rough Draft, Paragraph 2

This proposal would have an immediate impact
on the condition of our cities. For the
homeless a dirty, litter-strewn corner would
be replaced by a clean living environment.
Tourism would become more attractive to out-
of-towners, for the mentally ill would be
off the streets. Public transportation would
flourish as bus, train, and subway stations
would be devoid of ranting vagabonds. Houses
of worship would see an increase in
membership, for the "street-corner preacher"
would be unavailable. Crime would decrease,
for police could concentrate on serious
offenders as opposed to acting as street
sweepers of the homeless.

Added detail causes author to create two paragraphs from one.

Mundie—Final Draft, Paragraphs 2 and 3

This proposal would have an immediate impact on the homeless, many of whom are afflicted with mental disorders. For them, a filthy,

Adds concrete details, vivid language.

litter-strewn street corner would be replaced by a sterile environment in a research hospital, sheltered from rains, sleet, and snow, from the heat of summer and

the biting winds of winter. Of course, their absence would improve our cities' landscapes

Adds detail that appeals to senses; creates an image.

as well. Tourism would increase dramatically, for the mentally ill, many of whom walk around encrusted with filth and reeking of their own excrement, would be off the streets. Public transportation would

flourish as bus, train, and subway stations would be devoid of ranting vagabonds.

Houses of worship would see an increase in membership, for "street-corner preachers" would be hauled off to hospitals where,

Adds specifics and a quotation.

while undergoing extensive neurological observation, they could shout that the "world is coming to an end" to their heart's content. Crime would decrease, for police would concentrate on serious offenders as

Expands original to create a startling image.

opposed to acting as street sweepers of the homeless, of beggars, and of vagrants shouting obscenities to passersby or mumbling incoherently to themselves as they lie in dark and dirty doorways.

Practicing Using Concrete, Specific, and Vivid Language

In the spaces provided, rewrite the following sentences to improve word choice. Use techniques you have just read about to turn language that *tells* into language that *shows*. The first item has been completed for you as an example.

1. When the proud, old woman graduated, her classmates showed their approval.

   When the eighty-year-old chemistry major strutted across the stage to get

   her diploma, her classmates stood up and cheered.

2. A construction worker hung from a beam above the street.

   _____

   _____

   _____

3. The woman was overjoyed to be reunited with her lost son.

   _____

   _____

   _____

4. The exterior of the house needed painting.

   _____

   _____

   _____

5. His desk was cluttered.

   _____

   _____

   _____

6. The garden contained a variety of beautiful flowers and trees.

   _____

   _____

   _____

7. The children became frightened when the dog came into the room.

   _____

   _____

   _____

8. The bus was crowded.

_____

_____

_____

9. The supermarket was doing a brisk business.

_____

_____

_____

_____

10. The Greasy Spoon Restaurant was a breeding ground for bacteria.

_____

_____

_____

Word choice is extremely important to anyone who wants to become an effective writer. Using the right kind of language marks the difference between writing that is flat, vague, and uninteresting and writing that makes a real impact on its readers. The following selections present the work of poets and essayists who have written clear and effective explanations of very abstract ideas, ideas they would have been unable to explain without language that is concrete, specific, and vivid.

Those Winter Sundays

Robert Hayden

Robert Hayden (1913–1980) taught English at Fisk University and at the University of Michigan. For years, the work of this talented African-American writer received far less recognition than it deserved. Recently, however, his reputation has grown, especially since the publication of his complete poems in 1985.

"Those Winter Sundays" uses the author's vivid memories of his father to show us the depth and quality of love that the man had for his family. Unlike much of Hayden's other work, this poem does not deal with the black experience as such, but it demonstrates the same care and skill in choosing effective language that Hayden used in all his poetry.

If you want to read more by Hayden, look for these poetry collections in your college library: A Ballad of Remembrance, Words in Mourning Time, Angle of Ascent, *and* American Journal.

Preparing to Read

1. Hayden's primary purpose is to explain his father's love for his family. Look for details that are physical signs of that love.
2. The author says his father "made/banked fires blaze." Wood and coal fires were "banked" by covering them with ashes to make them burn slowly through the night and continue giving off heat.
3. The word *offices* isn't used in its usual sense in this poem. Here, it means important services or ceremonies.

Vocabulary

austere (adjective)   Severe, harsh, difficult, without comfort.
chronic (adjective)   Persistent, unending, constant.
indifferently (adverb)   Insensitively, without care or concern.

Those Winter Sundays

Robert Hayden

Sundays too my father got up early
and put his clothes on in the blueblack cold,
then with cracked hands that ached
from labor in the weekday weather made
banked fires blaze. No one ever thanked him.   5

I'd wake and hear the cold splintering, breaking.
When the rooms were warm, he'd call,
and slowly I would rise and dress,
fearing the chronic angers of that house,

Speaking indifferently to him,
who had driven out the cold
and polished my good shoes as well.
What did I know, what did I know
of love's austere and lonely offices?

10

Questions for Discussion

1. What details in this poem appeal to our senses?
2. In line 2, Hayden uses "blueblack" to describe the cold in his house on Sunday mornings. What other effective adjectives do you find in this poem?
3. Hayden shows us his father in action. What were some of the things this good man did to show his love for his family?
4. What was Hayden's reaction to his father's "austere and lonely offices" when he was a boy? How did he feel about his father when he wrote this poem?

Thinking Critically

Hayden mentions that he feared "the chronic angers of that house." What might he mean by that? Do you associate any "chronic angers" with your home?

Suggestions for Journal Entries

1. In Preparing to Read, you learned that Hayden describes his father's love by using language that is concrete, specific, and vivid. In your own words, discuss the kind of love that Hayden's father showed his family.
2. Do you know someone who demonstrates love for other people day in and day out, as Hayden's father did? In your journal, list the offices (services, tasks, or activities) that he or she performs to show this love. Include as many concrete and specific terms as you can. Then expand each item in your list to a few short sentences, showing that these activities are clearly signs of love.

Jeffrey Dahmer, Cannibal

Angie Cannon

Angie Cannon is a writer for US News & World Report, a weekly news magazine. In December 1999, the magazine ran a multipart feature entitled "Crimes of the Century." This essay was one of the many that made up that feature.

Preparing to Read

1. Consider Cannon's title. Is the author trying to shock us, or is she warning sensitive readers about the gory nature of her subject? What other purposes might this title serve?

2. Given the length of the essay, its introduction is fairly long, but it clearly states the central idea. The thesis is repeated later in the essay. Look for it in both places.

Vocabulary

barbell (noun)	Used in body building, a metal bar with weights at both ends that can be added or removed.
biceps (noun)	Muscle that has two points of origin.
depraved (adjective)	Degenerate, mentally and spiritually twisted.
fetish (noun)	Mania, compulsion, obsession.
forensic (adjective)	Having to do with legal proceedings including criminal investigations and trials.
putrid (adjective)	Disgusting, rotten, rank.
repulsive (adjective)	Horrible, disgusting.
revolting (adjective)	Offensive, disgusting, nauseating.
torso (noun)	Trunk of the body.
zombies (noun)	In folklore, dead bodies that have been taken over by a spirit or outside power.

Jeffrey Dahmer, Cannibal

Angie Cannon

HE WAS A former chocolate factory worker with a fetish for flesh. In his pu- 1
trid, one-bedroom apartment in Milwaukee, he saved painted skulls and severed heads, including one stashed in the fridge next to a box of baking soda. He had a kettle and a freezer of body parts. He stored torsos in a vat of acid. He drilled holes in his victims' heads and had sex with dead bodies. He

chewed on body parts, once using Crisco and meat tenderizer on a biceps. Over 13 years, mostly through the excessive 1980s, Jeffrey Dahmer, alone in his poisoned world, was monstrous, repulsive, depraved. But the most frightening thing about Dahmer is what he was not: insane. He was objectively judged to be sane. He did what he did with his wits intact. "He was a man who made a decision that he would satisfy himself," says E. Michael McCann, the Milwaukee district attorney who put Dahmer away in 1992. "He liked sex with dead bodies. It was the ultimate in self-indulgence."

In an interview with NBC's *Dateline* in March 1994, Dahmer said lust drove him to lure his victims, most of them black and gay, from bars, bus stops, and shopping malls, to his apartment, where he drugged, strangled, and dismembered them. "Once it happened the first time, it just seemed like it had control of my life from there on in," he said. "The killing was just a means to an end. That was the least satisfactory part. I didn't enjoy doing that. That's why I tried to create living zombies with . . . acid and the drill."

2

His killing spree started in 1978 with an 18-year-old hitchhiker whom Dahmer met and brought home for a few beers. Dahmer, who had just graduated from high school, battered him with a barbell, cut up the body, and scattered the crushed bones behind his parents' house. By the time he was arrested on July 22, 1991, after a man he had handcuffed escaped from his apartment and flagged down a police car, Dahmer had killed 17 men and boys. He confessed, saying simply, "I carried it too far, that's for sure."

3

The only issue at his 1992 trial was whether to accept his plea that he was criminally insane—and therefore not responsible for his revolting actions. Dr. Park Dietz, a respected California forensic psychiatrist, determined that he was not insane. "Dahmer was quiet, introverted, and performed his job pretty well until he finally fell asleep and couldn't do his work because he couldn't keep up with his nighttime dastardly deeds," says prosecutor McCann.

4

Dahmer was serving 16 consecutive life terms when inmates beat him to death in a prison bathroom in November 1994. Two years later, a businessman offered more than $400,000 to buy his implements—the refrigerator, the vats, the drills, the saws—to prevent a public auction. They were secretly buried.

5

Questions for Discussion

1. Reread paragraph 1, and identify verbs and adjectives that are particularly vivid. Where else in this essay does Cannon use vivid details?

2. What examples of concrete language appear in paragraph 1? What about paragraph 3?

3. Why didn't Cannon say that Dahmer put vegetable shortening on a body part rather than that he used "Crisco on a biceps"?

4. The journalist who wrote this essay was careful about researching specific facts and statistics. What evidence do you find of such research?

5. Why does Cannon include direct quotations in this essay? Who are the sources for such quotations?

6. What method or methods explained in Chapter 4 does the author use to introduce her essay? To conclude it?

Thinking Critically

1. "The most frightening thing about Dahmer," claims the author, "is what he was not: insane." Consider this statement. Then explain why it was necessary for Cannon to include so many gruesome details in paragraph 1.

2. What does Cannon's concluding paragraph say about our society?

Suggestions for Journal Entries

1. This essay is the portrait of a serial killer, but concrete, specific, and vivid language can be used to discuss anyone's life—unknown or famous, good or evil. Think about an individual you admire or dislike. Your subject can be someone you know personally or someone you have only read or heard about such as an entertainer, a politician, or even an historical figure. Make a list of as many concrete, specific, and vivid details as you can to describe this individual's personality or character.

2. Cannon quotes Dahmer directly so as to help us understand his motives and his character. Freewrite for at least 10 minutes about having done something or having made a decision that you now deeply regret. Explain what it was, why you did it, and why you regret it.

Of Famine and Green Beer

John Leo

John Leo has written for Time *and for the* New York Times, *has been an editor of* Commonweal, *and has worked as a columnist for* Society *and the* Village Voice. *Today, he writes a column called "On Society" for* U.S. News & World Report, *a weekly magazine. Several of these commentaries and satires of trends, fads, and morals in our time have been collected in* How the Russians Invented Baseball and Other Essays of Enlightenment *(1993). "Of Famine and Green Beer" was an "On Society" column for St. Patrick's Day.*

Preparing to Read

1. The British controlled Ireland for many centuries. In 1917, southern Ireland became the Republic of Ireland, with Ulster in the north remaining part of Great Britain.

2. In paragraph 2, Leo mentions the Napoleonic wars and World War I. The Napoleonic wars ended in 1815; World War I broke out in 1914. In paragraph 5, Leo tells us about the "Know-Nothings and other nativists." The Know-Nothings were an American political party of the 1850s. They opposed further immigration and were especially hostile to Roman Catholics.

3. Part of Leo's purpose is to recount a period of history in language that keeps the reader's eyes glued to the page. Pay special attention to the verbs he uses, and underline any you find especially effective.

4. Leo is a master at creating vivid images, pictures in words. Try to spot two or three of these as you read this essay.

5. Consider Leo's unusual title. What signals does it provide about what is to come?

Vocabulary

commemorate (verb)	Honor, celebrate, remember.
genetic (adjective)	Hereditary, handed down from generation to generation.
grudging (adjective)	Resentfully, with ill will.
halting (adjective)	Hesitantly, slowly.
lobbied (verb)	Tried to exert political influence.
nettles (noun)	Thorns from the nettle plant.
psychic (adjective)	Relating to one's mental or emotional makeup.
searing (adjective)	Burning, scorching.
urbanized (adjective)	Citified.

Of Famine and Green Beer

John Leo

THIS WEEK'S ST. Patrick's Day parades commemorate the 150th anniversary 1
of "Black '47," the worst year of the Irish potato famine. "The Great
Hunger" was the most searing event in Ireland's long and sad history. It killed
a million Irish and drove a million and a half more to America. Among them
were Ellen Burke and Thomas Leo, my great-grandparents.

It was the last big famine in Western Europe and the greatest loss of life 2
in the country between the Napoleonic wars and World War I. When a wind-
borne fungus wiped out the potato crop, the Irish died of yellow fever,
dysentery, typhus, and starvation. They ate dogs and rats, often dogs and rats
that had already eaten human corpses. When one English traveler spat out
some gooseberry skins from a passing carriage, a mother raced to pick up the
skins and place them in the mouth of her starving infant. The roadways were
littered with bodies of people with green stains around the mouth, from eating grass as a desperate last meal. Some were found with bark and nettles in
their mouths.

In the beginning, the British made many honest attempts to help, some 3
of them heroic. Later, politics and what we would today call "compassion fatigue" sealed the fate of the Irish. A New York State law requires schools to
teach about the famine, and some of those who lobbied for the law wanted
teachers to say that the British intentionally managed the famine to kill off as
many Irish as possible. It's fairer to say that rescue efforts, often halting and
grudging, were colored by a hands-off, free-market philosophy and the fact
that the Irish were a despised people in a captive society, semi-enslaved for
600 years, and therefore regarded as primitive, stupid, and hopeless.

An ocean of dead. The voyages that brought the dazed and starving 4
Irish to America were a cross between the scramble of the Haitian boat people
and the middle passage of African slaves. Fever broke out, but there were no
medicines. The stench of excrement filled the holds. The Irish were jammed
in like cordwood, gaining a bit more room as dead bodies were heaved over-
board. During one storm 178 immigrants were shoved down among the cattle, where half of them quickly suffocated. If crosses and tombs could be
placed on the water, one American official said at the time, the Atlantic
would look like a huge cemetery stretching from Ireland to America.

In America, the Irish faced the same contemptuous attitudes they had to 5
bear at home, this time centering more on their Catholic religion. The Know-
Nothings and other nativists campaigned against the Irish in much the same
way that the Klan organized against blacks. A few convents and churches
were burned. "No Irish Need Apply" signs appeared in store windows.

The rural Irish, entering an urbanized and industrial culture, arrived in 6
much worse shape than most immigrants and bore the psychic marks of an
increasingly sick and violent society back home. They were quickly identified
in the public mind with poverty, disease, alcoholism, crime, and violence.

Much of this was an accurate portrait of the Irish at the time. Irish violence was often astounding. Bodies floated in New York City's East River almost every day. At one point, the city jail population was 90 percent Irish. Police vehicles that rounded them up were called "paddy wagons," the wagons that carried all the hopeless Paddys to their natural home. Cartoonists drew pictures of the Irish as crazed monkeys, and good citizens wondered about a permanently unfit underclass and the possibility of genetic inferiority. Does any of this sound familiar? 7

Almost in the blink of an eye, the Irish "erupted" out of allegedly permanent underclass status, as one author put it, pouring into the middle class and taking political control of Boston and New York. Along the way, the St. Patrick's Day parade, once a defiant show of strength against Protestant power, gradually declined into a pointless annual march of aging suburbanites and drunken collegians staggering along in funny hats. 8

The good news is that efforts are under way to reconnect the Irish and their parades with their roots in famine, poverty, and despised immigrant status. Commemorations of the famine, both here and in Ireland, have become fund-raisers to combat famine in Africa and Asia. Seminars and conventions on the Irish famine often have surprisingly little material on Ireland and a lot on the problem of world hunger today. "We are allergic to famine," said Mary Robinson, president and national icon of the confident and rapidly changing Irish Republic. She is widely known as a "faminist." 9

Two summers ago my daughter and I climbed halfway up a mountain in the raw and empty west of Ireland to inspect a large Celtic cross, placed strategically in the middle of nowhere. We thought it would be a monument to the famine. But we didn't expect the inscription: "to all those who walked this way in the great famine, and to all those who walk this way now in the Third World." A very nice touch. Congratulations, Ireland. 10

Questions for Discussion

1. Where in paragraphs 2 and 4 does Leo create vivid images? Where else in this essay does he place vivid images?
2. Why did Leo tell us that Irish famine caused the greatest loss of life between the Napoleonic Wars and World War I. Why didn't he just say "in a hundred years"?
3. In paragraph 2, Leo tells us that during the famine, the Irish died of yellow fever, dysentery, and typhus. Why did he mention these specifically? Why didn't he just use the word *disease*?
4. In Preparing to Read, you were advised to underline verbs you found effective. Which ones did you underline and why?
5. Why does Leo mention his great-grandparents in his introduction?
6. Reread paragraphs 8, 9, and 10. What do they tell us about the writer's purpose? Why does he mention famines in Africa and Asia?

7. In what way is Leo's title important to his purpose? Why does he couple the word "famine" with "green beer"?

8. Evaluate the ending of this essay according to what you learned about conclusions in Chapter 4.

Thinking Critically

1. What pun (play on words) is Leo making by telling us that Mary Robinson is known as a "faminist" (paragraph 9)?

2. In a short paragraph that makes specific reference to parts of this essay, explain Leo's attitude about the Irish. Is it one-sided or balanced? Then, write another short paragraph that explains his understanding of the role the British played in "The Great Hunger."

3. At the end of paragraph 7, Leo asks, "Does any of this sound familiar?" In what way does what he says in that paragraph relate to the experience of other immigrant or minority groups?

Suggestions for Journal Entries

1. Leo paints a distinctive picture of the experience of the Irish both during the famine and after they emigrated. If you are a member of a recently arrived ethnic group, explain what convinced you or your family to come to America and explain how you were received. Use listing or clustering or get together with three or four classmates who are members of your group and brainstorm to gather information for this assignment. You might also want to brainstorm with or interview members of your family. In any case, try to include as many concrete nouns, verbs, and adjectives as you can.

2. At the end of this essay, Leo congratulates the Irish for using their memory of the famine to remind us about hunger in the third world today. Think about the ethnic group, religion, culture, family, community, or country you belong to. What about this group makes you proud to be a member? Be specific. For example, don't just say that your family values hard work or that they are kind and generous to those in need. Instead, explain how they demonstrate these values by discussing a family practice or recalling a specific event. Use freewriting, brainstorming, or interviewing to gather information. Whenever possible, record your notes using concrete and specific nouns and vivid verbs and adjectives. Need more inspiration? Read Robert Hayden's "Those Winter Sundays" on pages 184–185 or reread paragraphs 9 and 10 in Leo's essay.

The Mentally Ill and Human Experimentation: Perfect Together

Nancy J. Mundie

Mundie wrote this essay in a composition class after reading Jonathan Swift's "A Modest Proposal," an eighteenth-century essay that uses irony to expose the abuse of the Irish poor by the rich. Irony is a technique writers use to state the opposite of what they really mean. Often, it adds sting to social criticism. For example, Swift suggested ironically that poor children be bred like cattle and sold for food to the rich. His point was that the poor were being "eaten alive" by the economic practices of the powerful and wealthy.

Mundie uses irony to condemn society's treatment of the mentally ill. Thus, although she seems to suggest we use the mentally ill for experimentation, she is arguing just the opposite. As she makes clear at the essay's end, she is a strong advocate for the mentally ill. In fact, Mundie is majoring in psychological/social rehabilitation.

Preparing to Read

Mundie refers to Willowbrook and Salem in paragraph 1. Willowbrook is a psychiatric hospital on Staten Island, New York, which was criticized for its treatment of patients in an investigation by Geraldo Rivera in the 1970s. Salem, Massachusetts, is often remembered for its seventeenth-century trials, as a result of which several people accused of being witches were burned at the stake.

Vocabulary

advocates (noun)	Supporters.
afflicted (adjective)	Adversely affected by, hurt by.
consistent (adjective)	Compatible with, conforming to.
diverse (adjective)	Varied.
incompetent (adjective)	Unfit, incapable.
paramount (adjective)	Most important.
pesky (adjective)	Annoying, troublesome.
psychotropic (adjective)	Affecting one's behavior, changing one's psychological state or mood.
squalor (noun)	Misery, poverty, filth.
suffice (verb)	Be enough.

The Mentally Ill and Human Experimentation: Perfect Together

Nancy J. Mundie

THE HUMAN RACE has always failed at attempting to solve the problem of the   1
mentally ill. In previous generations, this segment of society had been
handled in ways consistent with the thinking of the times. However, whether
burned at the stake in Salem, Massachusetts, or condemned to live in squalor
at Willowbrook, the mentally ill have never fulfilled a constructive purpose.
Therefore, I propose that we begin using the mentally incompetent as test
subjects for scientific and social research.

This proposal would have an immediate impact on the homeless, many   2
of whom are afflicted with mental disorders. For them, a filthy, litter-strewn
street corner would be replaced by a sterile environment in a research hospital, sheltered from rains, sleet, and snow, from the heat of summer and
the biting winds of winter. Of course, their absence would improve our
cities' landscapes as well. Tourism would increase dramatically, for the
mentally ill, many of whom walk around encrusted with filth and reeking
of their own excrement, would be off the streets. Public transportation
would flourish as bus, train, and subway stations would be devoid of ranting vagabonds.

Houses of worship would see an increase in membership, for "street-   3
corner preachers" would be hauled off to hospitals where, while undergoing
extensive neurological observation, they could shout that the "world is coming
to an end" to their heart's content. Crime would decrease, for police would
concentrate on serious offenders as opposed to acting as street sweepers of the
homeless, of beggars, and of vagrants shouting obscenities to passersby or
mumbling incoherently to themselves as they lie in dark and dirty doorways.

Those classified as mentally ill (except women with children, for their   4
behavior mimics that of the unstable) would be housed in a common area
close to the hospital or research center. Public homeless shelters—notorious
for filth, crime, and vermin—would suffice, for the patients' stay would not
be long. This would keep housing costs down.

Moreover, only short-term, unskilled care would be required, for re-   5
search on patients would be unmonitored and as such would probably result
in high fatality rates. Since the patients' stay would be brief, the use of psy-
chotropic drugs would be unnecessary; hence, another cost savings. At the
same time, the housing industry would be stimulated by the need to build
more low-quality public shelters, the medical professions given yet another
opportunity to grow and profit as a result of the need for more research.

The advantages of this proposal to the scientific community are numer-   6
ous. Human experimentation is usually preferred over experimenting with
animals to determine a procedure's or product's effectiveness. However, in
much research as we know it, animal experimentation must precede work on
human beings. Using the mentally ill as guinea pigs, so to speak, would elim-

inate this requirement, thereby saving much time, effort, and money. In addition, a diverse test pool is paramount to reliable and accurate scientific research. Using the mentally ill will enable us to create a large and varied pool, for mental illness knows no social, economic, ethnic, or gender boundaries. Finally, researchers will not be forced to contend with pesky animal-rights activists such as members of the ASPCA. Moreover, there is no need to worry about civil-rights advocates, for the American Civil Liberties Union's attorneys and the like will make up a large portion of the "research pool."

This proposal is of course preposterous and inhumane at best. The mentally ill have a right to decent living conditions and proper care. Because their illness is largely "unseen" in the physical realm and misunderstood in the intellectual sense, they are often undiagnosed, misclassified, or ignored. But the mentally ill are our beloved family members and friends: the aging grandfather with Alzheimer's disease, the teenager battling depression, the daughter suffering from bulimia, the uncle addicted to alcohol, the neighbor victimized by schizophrenia. Mental illness is so widespread, so close to us, that we would do well always to remember the saying "there but for the grace of God go I."

7

Questions for Discussion

1. Mundie begins by saying that we have "failed at attempting to solve the problem of the mentally ill." Why didn't she write "failed at attempting to solve the problem of mental illness"? Would this have meant the same thing?
2. What is Mundie's thesis (or supposed thesis)?
3. Where in this essay do you find proper nouns?
4. Find and explain at least one image Mundie creates.
5. Discuss the language in paragraph 4. Which words contribute most to the effect of this paragraph?
6. What is Mundie proposing at the end of paragraph 6?
7. What type of conclusion does Mundie use? (Recall various types of conclusions you read about in Chapter 4.)

Thinking Critically

1. This proposal is "preposterous," Mundie admits. However, many of the social problems she describes are all too real. Focus on one such problem—say the one mentioned at the end of paragraph 3—and offer a solution you think is both practical and humane. Put your "proposal" in a paragraph of between 75 and 100 words.
2. Reread Paul Aronowitz's "A Brother's Dreams" in Chapter 3. Explain how that selection helps us understand Mundie's essay, especially her conclusion.

Suggestions for Journal Entries

1. Are you concerned about the way victims of poverty, disease, or a social problem are treated by others? If so, use your journal to list your complaints about the way society treats members of any one of these groups.

2. Reread Mundie's last paragraph. Do any of the people she mentions remind you of people you know? If so, use freewriting to describe the effects of their illnesses on themselves or on their families.

Suggestions for Sustained Writing

1. Hayden's "Those Winter Sundays" praises a man who demonstrates his love for others. If you responded to the second journal suggestion after this poem, you have probably made a list of the offices (activities, tasks, or services) that someone you know performs to show his or her love.

   Focus on at least three offices that mean the most to you, and expand your discussion into an essay in which you show how much this individual does for others. Begin with a preliminary thesis that expresses your feelings about your subject, but remember once again that you will probably want to revise this statement after you write your first draft.

   Limit each of the body paragraphs to only one of the offices in your list. Try developing these paragraphs by using methods described in Chapter 3; narration, description, conclusion and support, illustration, and process analysis might work well in such an assignment. Whatever you decide, follow Hayden's lead and use language that is concrete and specific.

   Express your revised thesis in an effective introduction that uses one or more of the techniques for effective openings explained in Chapter 4. Close with a conclusion like one you read about in that chapter. As usual, write several drafts of your paper and edit it carefully.

2. Read the notes you made in response to either of the Suggestions for Journal Entries after Angie Cannon's "Jeffrey Dahmer, Cannibal." Do more listing or freewriting to add concrete and specific nouns and vivid verbs, adjectives, and adverbs to this information. Then use this prewriting to develop an essay that either describes a person's character (Suggestion 1) or that explains the motivations behind your once doing something or making a decision that you now regret (Suggestion 2). After writing the first draft, try gathering direct quotations from others. If you are describing someone's character or personality, interview people who know your subject. (If your subject is well-known, read what others have

said about him or her in newspapers or other sources.) If you are writing about yourself, interview people who witnessed or heard about the action or decision you now regret. Put such quotations into your second draft; they will make your writing more believable, realistic, and convincing. Revise this draft by adding details, refining your thesis statement, and sharpening your introduction and conclusion. Finally, edit the work carefully and systematically, and proofread it before you hand it in.

3. Read what you wrote in response to the second item under Suggestions for Journal Entries after Leo's "Of Famine and Green Beer." Now write a letter to members of a group to which you belong congratulating them on some accomplishment or quality that makes you proud to be associated with them. Start with the notes you made in your journal, but add more detail. If you have begun explaining a specific event, accomplishment, or practice, expand your discussion. If necessary, talk about other events, accomplishments, or practices that will help demonstrate why the group you are writing to deserves congratulations.

    Reread each draft of your essay with an eye toward making your writing more concrete, specific, and vivid. Replace vague, general, and dull language. Like Leo, try to include at least one vivid image. In addition, try opening the letter with one of the methods for writing introductions discussed in Chapter 4. Perhaps using an anecdote, making a startling remark, or just addressing your readers directly would do the trick. You might conclude by looking to the future or, like Leo, by making a statement your readers are sure to remember.

    After you have thoroughly revised your work and are satisfied that it is organized and developed well, edit it. Once again, pay special attention to word choice in light of what you have learned in this chapter. Finally, proofread.

4. In the second suggestion for journal entries after Nancy Mundie's "The Mentally Ill and Human Experimentation: Perfect Together," you were asked to describe the effects of an illness on someone you know or on his or her family. Turn this journal entry into a full-length essay by explaining the causes or symptoms of the illness. Then, in language that is concrete, specific, and vivid, show to what degree it has changed the lives of the people it touches. If appropriate, conclude your essay by looking to the future. Try to predict what will become of the people you are writing about.

    As you revise the first draft of your paper, include language that will show your readers what you mean by using the techniques discussed in this chapter. In other words, try to create forceful images, use concrete and specific nouns, and fill your writing with lively verbs, adjectives, and adverbs.

    After you are satisfied with the result, edit and proofread your work. A great paper deserves a final polishing.

Writing to Learn: A Group Activity

In "Of Famine and Green Beer," John Leo speaks of "The Great Hunger," which occurred more than 150 years ago and nearly 3,000 miles from our shores. Yet famine persists in our country and around the world.

The First Meeting

Assign each member of the group the job of identifying a different example of hunger in your community, in the country, or around the world. For example, one student might research the problem of hunger among the homeless in a nearby city; another might learn more about hunger on Indian reservations or in Appalachia; still another might research famines in North Korea, Burundi, or Rwanda. Ask everyone to write 100 to 150 words discussing a particular example of famine and its effects on its victims.

Also, ask everyone to write a second, shorter paragraph explaining what charities are available for these victims. In other words, each student should provide information helpful to someone interested in donating money or volunteering his or her time to help these hungry people.

Each writer should make enough copies of these paragraphs to distribute to the whole group later on.

Research

If you are researching a local problem, try calling and interviewing the head of a homeless shelter, soup kitchen, or religious organization involved in charity work. You might also telephone your local newspaper to find out more about hunger in your community and about charities that address the problem. If you are researching national or worldwide examples of hunger, check the Internet or the electronic databases in your library under words such as *hunger, hunger relief, famine,* and *malnutrition.* To limit your research, you might try entering phrases such as *famine in Burundi.*

The Second Meeting

Share each other's paragraphs. Make sure that each writer has explained the problem in detail and that he or she has provided enough information to make it easy for people to donate money or time to this cause. (If not, ask the writer to do more research and add information.) Revise and edit each of these paragraphs either at this meeting or for homework.

THE THIRD MEETING

Submit all completed paragraphs to one student whose job it will be to put this material into the body paragraphs of a letter that will be sent to the editor of the student or the local newspaper. The letter's purpose will be to inform the college or the community of the persistence of famine and the need for help locally and around the world. Assign a second student to write the introduction and the conclusion for this letter. Remind everyone to photocopy his or her work for the next meeting.

THE FOURTH MEETING

Collect the introduction, the body paragraphs, and the conclusion, and arrange them in the proper order. Assign a third student to edit the letter, making sure that it contains language that is concrete, vivid, and specific. Assign yet another student to type and proofread the final product.

CHAPTER 6

Word Choice: Using Figurative Language

In Chapter 5 you learned that you can bring to life and clarify abstract ideas by using concrete language. You can engage your reader by filling your writing with specific details and creating verbal images (pictures in words) that appeal to the reader's senses. You also learned that using effective verbs, adjectives, and adverbs can help make your writing vivid. All of these techniques help you *show*—and not simply tell—your readers what you mean.

Another way to make your writing clearer and more vivid is to use figurative language. Such language is called *figurative* because it does not explain or represent a subject directly. A figure of speech works by creating a comparison or other relationship between the abstract idea you want to explain and something concrete that readers will recognize easily. In that way, it can help you explain an idea more clearly and emphatically than if you used literal language alone.

In fact, figures of speech provide a way to create images, mental pictures that allow readers to *see* what you mean. Notice how effective your description of a "clumsy" friend becomes when you compare him to a "bull in a china shop." The concrete image of a bull in a china shop—complete with shattered teacups, bowls, and plates—is sharper and more dramatic than the abstraction *clumsy* can ever be.

The most common figures of speech take the form of comparisons. The three discussed in this chapter are simile, metaphor, and personification.

Simile

A simile creates a comparison between two things by using the words *like* or *as*. For example, say that you're writing your sweetheart a letter in which you want to explain how much you need him or her. You can express your feelings literally and directly by writing "I need you very much." Then again, you can *show* how strongly you feel by writing that you need him or her "as an oak needs sunlight," "as an eagle needs the open sky," or "as the dry earth needs spring rain."

Read the following list carefully. Notice how much more concrete, exciting, and rich the ideas on the left become when they are expressed in similes:

Literal Expression	Simile
She arrived on time.	She arrived as promptly as the sunrise.
Snerdly's face was sunburned.	Snerdly's face was as red as the inside of a watermelon.

Eugene is a fancy dresser.	Eugene dresses like a peacock.
The tires made a loud noise.	The tires screeched like a wounded animal.
The dog moved slowly.	The dog moved like corn syrup on a cold day.

Finally, have a look at "Dream Deferred" by Langston Hughes, an important twentieth-century American poet, who was one of the lights of the Harlem Renaissance, an artistic and cultural flowering of the 1920s. Hughes uses five similes in eleven lines.

What happens to a dream deferred?

Does it dry up
like a raisin in the sun?
Or fester like a sore—
And then run?
Does it stink like rotten meat?
Or crust and sugar over—
like a syrupy sweet?

Maybe it just sags
like a heavy load.

Or does it explode?

Metaphor

A metaphor also uses comparison to show the relationship between things in order to make the explanation of one of these things clearer and livelier. In fact, a metaphor works just like a simile except that it does not make use of *like* or *as*. For instance, you can turn the simile "Eugene dresses like a peacock" into a metaphor by writing "Eugene is a peacock." In neither case, of course, do you actually mean that Eugene is a bird; you're simply pointing out similarities between the way he dresses and the showiness we associate with a peacock.

Remember that, like all figures of speech, similes and metaphors turn abstract ideas (such as "Eugene is a fancy dresser") into vivid, concrete images. In other words, they communicate more emphatically and clearly than if the writer had used literal language alone. Study the following list of similes and metaphors. What effect do they have on you, especially when compared with the literal expressions on the left?

Literal Expression	**Simile**	**Metaphor**
My old car is hard to drive.	My old car drives like a tank.	My old car is a tank!

She works too hard for her family.	She works like a slave for her family.	She is a slave to her family.
During holidays, shopping malls are crowded and noisy.	During holidays, shopping malls are so crowded and noisy that they seem like madhouses.	During holidays, shopping malls are so crowded and noisy that they become madhouses.
The hayloft was hot.	The hayloft was as hot as a blast furnace.	The hayloft was a blast furnace.

Read the following excerpt from Martin Luther King's "I Have a Dream," a speech he delivered at the Lincoln Memorial during the 1963 march on Washington. Identify the metaphors and similes that Dr. King used to captivate the thousands in his audience and to make his message more concrete, vivid, and effective:

> Five score years ago, a great American, in whose symbolic shadow we stand today, signed the Emancipation Proclamation. This momentous decree came as a great beacon light of hope to millions of Negro slaves who had been seared in the flames of withering injustice. It came as a joyous daybreak to end the long night of their captivity.
>
> But one hundred years later, the Negro still is not free. One hundred years later, the life of the Negro is still sadly crippled by the manacles of segregation and the chains of discrimination.

Personification

Personification is the description of animals, plants, or inanimate objects by using terms ordinarily associated with human beings. Like metaphor and simile, personification is an effective way to turn abstract ideas into vivid and concrete realities that readers will grasp easily and quickly.

One common example of personification is Father Time, the figure of an old man trailing a white beard and carrying a scythe and hourglass. Another is the Grim Reaper, the representation of death pictured as a skeleton holding a scythe. Shakespeare often used personification to enrich the language of his poems and plays. In "Sonnet 18," for example, he described the sun as "the eye of heaven." William Least Heat Moon does something similar when, in *Blue Highways,* he describes the saguaro cactus of the southwestern United States:

> Standing on the friable slopes . . . saguaros mimic men as they salute, bow, dance, raise arms to wave, and grin with faces carved in by woodpeckers. Older plants, having survived odds against their reaching maturity of sixty million to one, have every right to smile.

Visualizing Figurative Language

You may recall reading two paragraphs from Margaret Laurence's "Where the World Began" in Chapter 5 (pages 179–180). Here are two more paragraphs from that essay. Read the first paragraph, which is accompanied by notes that identify figures of speech. Then, read the second paragraph and circle or box examples of figurative language you find.

In winter we used to hitch rides on the back
of the milk sleigh, our moccasins squeaking
and slithering on the hard rutted
snow . . . our hands in ice-bubbled mitts   *Metaphor*
hanging onto the box edge of the sleigh for
dear life . . . . Those mornings, rising, there
would be the perpetual fascination of the
Metaphor frost feathers on windows, the ferns and   *Metaphor*
flowers and eerie faces traced there during   *Personification*
the night by unseen artists of the wind.
Evenings, coming back from skating, the sky
would be black but not dark, for you could
see a cold glitter of stars from one side of
the earth's rim to the other. And then the
sometime astonishment when you saw the
Northern Lights flaring across the sky, like
Simile   the scrawled signature of God.

My best friend lived in an apartment
above some stores on Main Street (its real
name was Mountain Avenue, goodness knows
why), an elegant apartment with royal-blue
velvet curtains. The back roof, scarcely
sloping at all, was corrugated tin, of a
furnace-like warmth on a July afternoon, and

```
we would sit there drinking lemonade and
looking across the back lane at the Fire
Hall. Sometimes our vigil would be rewarded.
Oh joy! Somebody's house was burning
down . . . . Then the wooden tower's bronze
bell would clonk and toll like a thousand
speeded funerals in a time of plague, and in
a few minutes the team of giant black horses
would cannon forth, pulling the fire wagon
like some scarlet chariot of the Goths,
while the firemen clung with one hand,
adjusting their helmets as they went.
```

Revising to Include Figurative Language

Read these two versions of a paragraph from Louis Gonzalez's "Music," a student essay that appears at the end of this chapter. As you will see, the revision process has enabled Gonzalez to make his writing stronger, livelier, and more interesting.

Gonzalez—Rough Draft

```
As I became a little older and entered high
school, my interests shifted toward learning
to play a musical instrument.  After a
little experimentation, the bass guitar
became my love.  It produced warm, confident
tones.  They danced around my head.  The
guitar became the implement of my
creativity.  It soon became the center of my
existence.  I felt naked and insecure
without it.  Its weight was a lover's hand
upon my shoulder.
```

Gonzalez—Final Draft

When I entered high school, my interests
shifted toward learning to play a musical

Adds personification by comparing guitar to lover. Creates an image; personifies "tones."

instrument. After a little experimentation,
I fell in love with the bass guitar. It
covered me with warm, confident tones—
blankets of pure ecstasy. They were poised
ballroom dancers waltzing elegantly around

Adds a metaphor; compares guitar to a painter's brush.

my head. The guitar became the implement of
my creativity, the brush with which I
painted portraits of candid love and dark
emotion. I was naked and insecure without

Adds detail to continue personifying guitar as lover.

it. Its weight was a lover's hand upon my
shoulder, and its smooth hourglass body was
a pleasure to hold. It whispered sweet
kisses in my ear.

Practicing Creating Simile, Metaphor, and Personification

In the spaces provided, put the idea you find in the literal expressions into a simile, metaphor, or personification as indicated. The first item is done for you as an example.

1. **Literal expression:** The two men fought hard through the night.
   Simile: <u>The two men fought like gladiators through the night.</u>
2. **Literal expression:** Cheryl treats her mother well.
   Simile: _____

   _____

   _____

3. **Literal expression:** He ran to the end of the street and jumped over the barricade.
   Simile: _____

   _____

   _____

4. **Literal expression:** Modern appliances have made our homes more comfortable and convenient than ever before.
   Simile: _____

   _____

   _____

5. **Literal expression:** I enjoy the sounds of robins in the morning.
   Metaphor: _____

   _____

   _____

6. **Literal expression:** The small boat was overloaded.
   Metaphor: _____

   _____

   _____

7. **Literal expression:** In the last 20 years, medical researchers have produced wondrous cures.
   Metaphor: _____

   _____

   _____

8. **Literal expression:** The wind was strong.
   Personification: _____

   _____

   _____

9. **Literal expression:** We did not feel welcome as we entered the dark house.
   Personification: _____

   _____

   _____

10. Literal expression: The front-page photograph contained a warning about driving drunk.

Personification: _____

_____

_____

The following selections demonstrate very careful uses of language, both literal and figurative. As you read them, identify their similes, metaphors, and personifications and ask yourself if these figures of speech have made the selections clearer, more vivid, and more effective than if their authors had relied on literal language alone.

Joy of an Immigrant, a Thanksgiving *and* Giovanni Iacono

Emanuel di Pasquale

Emanuel di Pasquale immigrated to the United States from Ragusa, Sicily, when he was 14 yeas old. An accomplished poet and teacher of composition, creative writing, and children's literature, he has published in several periodicals including The Nation, The Sewanee Review, *and* Cricket. *His work has been anthologized in college and high school textbooks and in several collections of children's literature.* Genesis, *his first full-length book of poetry, was published in 1989. In 1998, di Pasquale translated into Italian Joseph Salerno's* Song of the Tulip Tree, *for which he won the Bordighera Poetry Prize. In 2000, he published his second full-length book of poetry,* The Silver Lake Love Poems, *and a translation into English of Carlo Della Corte's verse novel* The Journey Ends Here.

"Joy of an Immigrant" and "Giovanni Iacono" reveal di Pasquale's intense love of nature and his talent for creating powerful figures of speech that make his work clear, powerful, and sweet.

Preparing to Read

1. "Joy of an Immigrant" contains an extended metaphor in which the speaker of the poem compares himself to a wandering bird. *Extended metaphors* are metaphors developed over several lines. In this case, the metaphor appears *throughout* the poem.

2. The subtitle of "Giovanni Iacono"—"My Sicilian Brother-in-Law, a Gentle, Kind Man"—tells us a lot about what is to follow.

3. Like "Joy of an Immigrant," "Giovanni Iacono" makes use of extended metaphors to create an image or picture. This is especially true of the first stanza (verse paragraph).

4. The Irminio River runs through southeastern Sicily. "Giovanni" is Italian for "John."

Vocabulary

garnet (noun)	Dark red, semiprecious stone.
rivulets (noun)	Small streams.
shards (noun)	Sharp fragments of pottery or glass.
transfigured (verb)	Transformed, thoroughly changed. A "transfigured" object or person takes on a spiritual quality in the process.

Joy of an Immigrant, a Thanksgiving

Emmanuel di Pasquale

Like a bird grown weak in a land
where it always rains
and where all the trees have died,
I have flown long and long
to find sunlight pouring over branches   5
and leaves. I have journeyed, oh God,
to find a land where I can build a dry nest,
a land where my song can echo.

Giovanni Iacono: My Sicilian Brother-in-law, a Gentle, Kind Man

Emanuel di Pasquale

I

His voice had wings
as when at dawn
small sails are raised
from the bellies of boats
and stretched open for the new sky.   5

II

You could smell pine trees in him,
river water, lemon rind, the sea.
And in his eyes, burning in brown,
you could see the fire of earth
lifting cedar, cornstalk, chestnut.   10

III

All sea-glass was jewelry to him,
green bits of emerald,
white shards of diamonds—
slivers of iodine bottles
transfigured into burning garnet.   15

IV

And in long Summer days,
down the Irminio river,

he knew which rocks
covered soft-shelled crabs
and which covered
spring water rivulets.   20

Watermelons he buried
in river shallows sang red,
and corncob he roasted
turned hickory and honey.   25

Questions for Discussion

1. In "Joy of an Immigrant, a Thanksgiving," di Pasquale compares himself to a bird through an extended metaphor. What details does he use to develop this comparison?

2. Why does di Pasquale subtitle the first of these poems "a Thanksgiving"?

3. What do the metaphors "where I can build a dry nest" and "where my song can echo" show us about the poet's feelings for his new "land"?

4. What is your emotional reaction to the words in the first three lines of "Joy of an Immigrant, a Thanksgiving"? What do they tell you about the place the poet has left?

5. Explain the image that the author uses in the first stanza of "Giovanni Iacono"? Where else in this poem do you find images?

6. What figures of speech appear in stanza III of this poem?

7. To what senses does di Pasquale appeal in stanza IV? What does he mean when he says: "Watermelons . . . sang red"? What did the poet have to do to create this interesting metaphor?

8. Where else does the poet appeal to our senses in "Giovanni Iacono"?

Thinking Critically

1. Write a short paragraph that explains di Pasquale's attitude toward either of the subjects of these poems: his new homeland or Giovanni Iacono.

2. Di Pasquale claims that, for Giovanni Iacono, "slivers of iodine bottles/transfigured into burning garnet." What does the poet's choice of the word "transfigured" rather than "changed" or even "transformed" tell us about Iacono? (Check the meaning of "transfigured" in the vocabulary list om page 209.)

3. Read "Giovanni Iacono" again, and think about the kinds of things and places with which the poet associates his subject. For example,

we learn that Iacono's "voice had wings," which the poet compares to "raised sails." What might such things and places reveal about Iacono? What might they tell us about the poet?

Suggestions for Journal Entries

1. Have you ever experienced a change—any change—in your life that was as dramatic or as important as the one di Pasquale describes in "Joy of an Immigrant, a Thanksgiving"? It need not involve moving from one country or even from one town to another, but it should be something that has had an effect on the person you have become. Describe how this change affected you by listing as many concrete details about it as you can. Try to create similes and metaphors that will help you describe its effects more vividly.

2. Is there a person in your life whom others might find interesting in some way, who stands out from the crowd? Perhaps your subject is "gentle and kind"; perhaps she has a special talent; or perhaps he is noteworthy for the *wrong* reasons. Describe him or her in a paragraph or poem. Follow di Pasquale's lead. Use details that help readers see this person through a vivid word picture. Include concrete and specific nouns, vivid verbs, adjectives, and adverbs, and as many figures of speech as you can. Like di Pasquale, also consider using details taken from nature.

Back from the Brink

Daniel Zanoza

Daniel Zanoza wrote this essay to describe the horrors of drug addiction and to broadcast a warning. Originally published in The American Enterprise *magazine, the essay uses both literal and figurative language to get and maintain the reader's attention. Zanoza lives in Illinois.*

Preparing to Read

1. Besides using metaphors and similes to describe his life as a drug addict, Zanoza assigns human qualities to the addiction itself, thereby creating a kind of ghostly character that haunts the entire essay. He does this through personification.

2. One of Zanoza's objectives in writing this essay is to respond to those who would have us believe that the drug life can be fashionable, "chic" as he puts it. His use of figurative language helps him make his point emphatically, and it shows that such language can be used for a variety of purposes, including persuasion.

3. What does Zanoza mean by "The Brink"?

Vocabulary

accessible (adjective)	Obtainable, available.
anesthetization (noun)	Deadening of the senses.
cross a threshold (verb)	Pass through a doorway.
dastardly (adjective)	Evil, nasty, unscrupulous.
deterrents (noun)	Obstacles, barriers.
dispensary (noun)	Clinic, place where drugs are distributed.
emerging (adjective)	Arising.
euphoria (noun)	Elation, feeling of well-being.
gateway (noun)	Doorway, entrance.
illicit (adjective)	Illegal.
insidious (adjective)	Sneaky, evil.
invincibility (noun)	Indestructibility.
magnitude (noun)	Size, extent.
psychosis (noun)	Madness.
seminal (adjective)	Defining, determining.
urgency (noun)	Necessity.
veritable (adjective)	Genuine, actual.

Back from the Brink

Daniel Zanoza

I NEVER THOUGHT I'd hear the words heroin and chic mentioned in the same   1
sentence. But lately the two have been paired, in movies and other pop culture. This shakes me to my very soul, as I recall the private hell that heroin
brought to my life for over 20 years.

A single decision can determine one's life path. My seminal moment   2
came on my nineteenth birthday. A friend stopped by to help me celebrate.
At the time, I'd been experimenting with all kinds of illicit drugs. Marijuana
had been the first. Soon the world was a veritable candy store: alcohol, up-
pers, downers, psychedelics—there was a pharmaceutical cocktail for every
mood. Combine this with the invincibility of youth, and life became one long
party. Or so it seemed. My true goal was self-anesthetization from the pains
of life.

On my nineteenth birthday, however, I crossed a further threshold. For   3
the first time, I tried heroin, and the drug became my life partner for the next
two decades.

At first, there were no meetings in dark alleys or dingy bars. Drug use   4
was easy and attractive. Heroin was just another adventure. A negative experience might have been the best thing to happen on that nineteenth birthday,
but that wasn't the case. I felt right at home in the sedated euphoria caused
by the drug.

The insidious danger of heroin is that in early use, you're in control. You   5
feel you can take it or leave it; therefore, quitting holds no urgency.

Year after year passed. I went to school and became a social worker. It   6
was all right; I just needed to use responsibly. Can you believe that? A responsible heroin addict.

By age 30, the addiction was a way of life. The pain was great, an all-   7
consuming dull throb of hopelessness and dependence that possessed my
life. Greeting the day was a chore of the greatest magnitude. Sometimes I
would sleep until 5:00 PM because the light was too revealing. I was a creature
of the night, a vampire sucking family and friends for all they were worth.

No, I didn't commit any armed robberies or burglaries, but rarely did a   8
gift or any item of value last for long. Sold or returned for cash. After all,
what was really important? Heroin was my god. It came before parents and
friends. It came before a job. It came before food and shelter. Often, it came
before life itself.

Most current and former drug addicts like me will tell you that legaliza-   9
tion of drugs is a terrible idea—and that includes marijuana. Marijuana was
the first drug used by the vast majority of us, and recent research has shown
it works on the brain in precisely the same ways "harder" drugs like cocaine
and heroin do. That's why scientists now describe marijuana as a natural
"gateway" to stronger narcotics.

Decriminalization or legalization would only create greater access to drugs. With the explosion of teenage drug use during the last four years, the last thing America should be thinking about is making drugs more accessible. One of the strongest deterrents to using drugs today is simply the fact that they are illegal.

Unlike other unhealthful "temptations," drugs actually exert a chemical power over their users. I've asked advocates of drug legalization, "What do we do with people who have been up for three days on a cocaine bender?" There is a psychosis that grips such a person, and their binge ends only when they run out of funds, or consciousness. Some dastardly crimes are committed by people under the influence of drugs. What do we do with such people if there is legalization? Give them a ticket and send them down the road to kill my family or yours? Or create a one-stop dispensary where an abuser can obtain the drug until his heart seizes?

In my own case, even a new faith wasn't enough to break the drug stranglehold at first. I expected a miraculous deliverance. God would do all the work; I would just sit back and wait. But that deliverance never came. It wasn't that easy: recovery takes strenuous effort. A substance abuser, I learned, must make a habit out of being sober.

Eventually, with the help of God and the support of others, I was ready for that commitment—after decades of misery. I've been almost five years in recovery now, living life again. The appreciation of a beautiful sunset has returned, along with my gratefulness for true love and friendship. Silly things make me laugh and sad movies make me cry. The simple pleasures of household chores are no longer unimaginable burdens but welcome responsibilities.

Some of my human relationships were irreparably harmed, but those who cared about me most now care again. I asked for their forgiveness, and they've welcomed back the old me that was lost and nearly forgotten. I have a wife and family who never left my side. I have an emerging new journalism career, and I'm active in public service. I'll never be a literary giant, or president, but I'm looking forward to the future. With God's help, I will be the best friend, husband, and person I can be.

And for me, that's quite an accomplishment.

Questions for Discussion

1. What is Zanoza's thesis?
2. What is the author's purpose for writing this essay? Did he have more than one purpose? Reread paragraphs 9, 10, and 11 before you answer.
3. Explain the metaphors the author uses in paragraph 2.
4. In what other paragraphs does he use metaphors? Explain each example.

5. In paragraph 3, Zanoza uses personification when he refers to his addiction as his "life partner." Where else does he use personification?

6. Paragraph 11 makes good use of concrete and vivid literal language, like the kind you learned about in Chapter 5. Underline or mark such words in this paragraph.

Thinking Critically

1. Do you agree with Zanoza that drugs like heroin and marijuana should be kept illegal? If so, think of at least one reason not mentioned in his essay that supports this opinion.

2. If you disagree with Zanoza, make a list of reasons that support your view. Make sure to answer both the questions that the author asks in paragraph 11.

Suggestions for Journal Entries

1. After reading this essay, what advice might you give to a friend or relative suffering from a drug, alcohol, gambling, food, sex, shopping, or other addiction? Freewrite or use clustering to gather information. Discuss the effects of the addiction on the addict and on his or her loved ones. After you complete this entry, read what you have written. Then, revise it, creating a few figures of speech that will explain your subject more vividly. Say that you write that your cousin's life "has been ruined by alcohol." You might revise this to read that "the demon of alcohol haunts my cousin."

2. Do you know someone suffering from a serious illness? Write a paragraph in which you identify the illness and describe one of its effects on that individual and on his or her family. In the process, include figures of speech such as the ones explained in this chapter.

The Gift

Li-Young Lee

Li-Young Lee is a Chinese-American poet born in Indonesia, where his father had been imprisoned by the government of Sukarno, that country's dictator. After his father's escape, the family left Indonesia and eventually made their home in Pennsylvania. Lee's reputation has grown rapidly over the last several years. He is the author of Rose, *a book of poems published in 1986.*

Preparing to Read

1. Lee's title is especially significant. Keep it in mind as you read this tender poem.
2. Look for examples of both metaphor and personification in "The Gift."

Vocabulary

christen (verb) Give a name to.
shard (noun) Fragment of metal or glass.

The Gift

Li-Young Lee

To pull the metal splinter from my palm
my father recited a story in a low voice.
I watched his lovely face and not the blade.
Before the story ended he'd removed
the iron sliver I thought I'd die from.   5

I can't remember the tale
but hear his voice still, a well
of dark water, a prayer.
And I recall his hands,
two measures of tenderness   10
he laid against my face,
the flames of discipline
he raised above my head.

Had you entered that afternoon   15
you would have thought you saw a man
planting something in a boy's palm,
a silver tear, a tiny flame.

Had you followed that boy
you would have arrived here,
where I bend over my wife's right hand.   20
Look how I shave her thumbnail down
so carefully she feels no pain.
Watch as I lift the splinter out.
I was seven when my father
took my hand like this,   25
and I did not hold that shard
between my fingers and think,
Metal that will bury me,
christen it Little Assassin,
Ore Going Deep for My Heart.   30
And I did not lift up my wound and cry,
Death visited here!
I did what a child does
when he's given something to keep.
I kissed my father.   35

Questions for Discussion

1. What "gift" has Lee received? Is it simply the skill to remove a splinter? Or is there more to it than that?
2. Why does he tell us about removing the shard from his wife's hand? What point does this image help him make about his father? About himself?
3. What other image do you see in this poem?
4. To which of the five senses does Lee appeal?
5. What examples of metaphor do you find in this poem? Of personification?
6. Why does Lee tell us that he didn't "christen" the splinter "Little Assassin" (line 29)? What does "*Death visited here!*" mean (line 32)?

Thinking Critically

Reread Hayden's "Those Winter Sundays" (pages 184–185), which is also about a father's love. In what ways is it similar to Lee's poem? In what ways is it different? Explain these similarities and differences in two or three paragraphs. Before you begin, consider the titles of the poems and the stories they tell. What do they reveal about the authors and their purposes?

Suggestions for Journal Entries

1. Think back to a time when your father, mother, or family member comforted you or made you feel good about yourself. Use freewriting to explain what happened and to discuss your reaction.

2. What Lee is "given . . . to keep" is not material; it is an attitude, an emotional treasure, made plain in his father's voice and gentle touch. Think about similar gifts that your mother, father, or other relative has given you by example and that you will pass on to others. Your father may have shown you a love for gardening, your great-aunt may have taught you to love animals, and through her actions your mother may have taught you that all people, regardless of race or sex, deserve respect. Use focused freewriting to describe one or more of these gifts. Include figures of speech to make your ideas concrete and vivid.

Music

Louis Gonzalez

When asked by his professor to define a concept, idea, or activity that was important to him, Louis Gonzalez knew immediately what he would write about. The challenging part came in making this abstraction real to his readers. He did this by choosing concrete, specific, and vivid vocabulary and by filling his writing with powerful figures of speech. In other words, he showed the reader what he meant.

Gonzalez writes musical reviews for a local magazine and is considering a career as a writer. He was a first-year liberal-arts student when he wrote this essay.

Preparing to Read

1. Pay special attention to paragraph 4. You will recall that the rough draft of this paragraph appears earlier in the chapter with the author's revisions, which show how much care he puts into the process of writing.

2. Gonzalez uses all three figures of speech discussed in this chapter. He also uses hyperbole, or exaggeration. Look for an example of this technique at the end of paragraph 7.

Vocabulary

cathartic (adjective)	Cleansing, purifying.
chaotic (adjective)	Confusing, disorderly.
licks (noun)	Musical phrases created when improvising.
mesmerizing (adjective)	Absorbing, hypnotizing.
obsession (noun)	Passion, fixation.
orgasms (noun)	Sexual climaxes.
oscillating (adjective)	Moving from side to side.
poised (adjective)	Balanced.
preoccupied (adjective)	Absorbed in, wrapped up in.
reverberates (verb)	Echoes.
tangible (adjective)	Able to be touched, felt.
tenacity (noun)	Determination, persistence.
venues (noun)	Places where events take place.
yoke (noun)	Shackle, chain.

Music

Louis Gonzalez

MUSIC IS MY obsession. It reverberates across every fiber of my being. I have spent endless hours of my life creating music, performing it, or even just dreaming about it. My thoughts are filled with the angelic sigh of a bow kissing the string of a violin, or the hellish crash of batons torturing the skin of a kettle drum. But my favorite instrument is the vociferous world around us. The scuff of a penny loafer against a wood floor, the clinking of Crayolas across a child's desk, or the mesmerizing hum of an oscillating fan are all part of this chaotic symphony. It is within this sonic spectrum that I exist.

I have long been preoccupied with the audible world. When I was younger, anything and everything that made a sound became a musical instrument. My mother's pots, empty soda bottles, even the railing on my front porch became part of my private symphony orchestra. Then, for my ninth birthday, I received a Fisher-Price record player. A single tin speaker was built into the base, and the needle was attached to a wooden lid, which I had to shut in order to make the thing work. More often than not, the lid would fall accidentally and cut deep scratches into the record. But to my young ears, it made the sounds of heaven.

Armed with my record player and some old jazz 45s I liberated from my dad's collection, I locked myself in the garage and entered another world. Instead of remaining surrounded by tools and half-empty paint cans, I lowered the lid of that cheap Fisher-Price and transported myself to a smokey club somewhere in the city. As the music played, wrenches became saxophones, boxes became a set of drums, and the workbench became a sleek black piano. I played 'em all, man! I wore those old 45s down until there was nothing left but pops, cracks, and the occasional high note. I spent most of my childhood in that smelly garage listening to Miles Davis and my other patron saints, while other kids played football and video games. Even though my parents said I wasted my time there, the experience instilled in me a burning desire to become a musician.

When I entered high school, my interests shifted towards learning to play a musical instrument. After a little experimentation, I fell in love with the bass guitar. It covered me with warm, confident tones—blankets of pure ecstasy. They were poised ballroom dancers waltzing elegantly around my head. The guitar became the implement of my creativity, the brush with which I painted portraits of candid love and dark emotion. I was naked and insecure without it. Its weight was a lover's hand upon my shoulder, and its smooth hourglass body was a pleasure to hold. It whispered sweet kisses in my ear.

As my skills increased, so did my yearning to play those old jazz songs of 5
my youth. But the harder I tried, the less I succeeded. It seemed as though I
was simply incapable of playing those songs. All those wild bass licks that
poured out of that Fisher-Price record player were ripped from my dreams.

My lust for jazz was then replaced by the desire to perform in a live rock 6
band. So, I joined a local college group and began to play small venues. The
shows were like cathartic orgasms of sweaty bodies undulating as the sensa-
tion of music overwhelmed them. While I was on stage, the power of the
music pierced through the air like a volley of arrows falling upon the flannel-
clad flesh whirling below me. But I felt as though the music was in control
and I was just letting it happen. That feeling began to consume my spirit and
destroy my sense of oneness with the music.

There was definitely something missing. Even though what I played was 7
structurally powerful, it lacked a soul. I also realized that my style of playing
lacked a human quality. So when I came upon my old jazz records, I listened
to them with new ears. I dropped all of my preconceived notions of song
structure. As the records popped and scratched their way around the
turntable, the secrets of the universe were finally revealed to me.

I realized that my approach had been all wrong. All my songs were suffo- 8
cated under the weight of formality. Harnessed to the yoke of "proper" song
structure and arrangement, they were never allowed to grow fully. So, I
picked up my bass with a fresh tenacity and dropped all my inhibitions. Not,
surprisingly, those old jazz songs started to pour out. I played them as if I
had known them all of my life.

I look back on that day and realize that I did know how to play those 9
songs all along. It wasn't a tangible lack of something—like talent or effort—
that held me back. I just needed to *feel* the music—to feel the sweet life a musician blows into, to feel it the way that innocent child felt in the garage all
those years ago.

Questions for Discussion

1. What is Gonzalez's thesis? Has he proved it?
2. How would you describe the introduction of this essay? Is it like one
   or more of the types you learned about in Chapter 4? Which one or
   ones?
3. Find examples of metaphor in paragraphs 3 and 4.
4. Where in this essay does Gonzalez use simile?
5. Find two paragraphs in which the author makes good use of
   personification. Explain these figures of speech.
6. Paragraphs 1, 2, and 3 show that Gonzalez uses concrete and specific
   nouns, like those you read about in Chapter 5. Find examples of such
   nouns.
7. Vivid verbs make paragraph 7 especially interesting. Identify a few of
   them.

Thinking Critically

1. Gonzalez uses a hyperbole, another figure of speech, in paragraph 7. Explain what he means. Is his use of exaggeration effective?
2. If you could speak to Gonzalez, what would you ask him about his experiences with music? Write these questions in the margins of the essay.

Suggestions for Journal Entries

1. What is your obsession? Use freewriting or brainstorming to record facts about your love for an activity or idea that will show how much you are committed to it.
2. Create a list of metaphors, similes, or personifications that might describe how you feel when you are doing a particular activity you really enjoy. For inspiration reread paragraphs 1, 3, 4, and 6 of "Music."

Suggestions for Sustained Writing

1. After reading di Pasquale's "Joy of an Immigrant, a Thanksgiving," you might have made journal notes to begin explaining how a dramatic change in your life affected you. Tell the story of what caused this change. Using "Joy of an Immigrant, a Thanksgiving" as an example, include effective metaphors and similes to help your readers understand the full effect of the change. This is also a good time to continue using concrete nouns—both common and proper—and vivid adjectives, like those you read about in Chapter 5. They will help you create powerful images to communicate your feelings.

   When you finish your story, write an introductory paragraph, complete with a formal thesis statement that states the importance of this change in your life. Describe a scene, use a startling remark, create a contrast or analogy, or try any other method explained in Chapter 4 to write an introduction that captures the readers' attention. Conclude your paper by making reference to your thesis, looking to the future, or using a memorable statement or quotation.

   Now review the completed draft of your essay. Is it the best you can do, or can you add detail, strengthen your focus, and improve your word choice? Write at least one more draft. Then revise and edit this version thoroughly before submitting your work to your instructor.

2. In "Giovanni Iacono," di Pasquale tells us that the man's "voice had wings," that "you could smell pine trees in him, river water, lemon rind, the sea." Write an essay in which you include extended metaphors that use natural

objects (animals, plants, trees, the sea, and so on) to describe the personality, spirit, or soul of someone you know. The verbal portrait you create can be flattering or unflattering. For example, one of the metaphors you use might compare your subject to a garden—fresh, vital, fragrant, and nourishing. On the other hand, if your portrait is unflattering, you might compare your subject to a snake or worm by describing his sneaking behind people's backs or her squirming out of responsibilities.

Whatever you decide, have fun with this project. It's a good chance to create entertaining images of a person about whom you have strong feelings. As usual, check your journal notes for information that will help you get started. Revise your essay several times, and edit it closely.

A word of caution: If your essay criticizes a person, keep his or her real identity secret.

3. The first of the Suggestions for Journal Entries after Daniel Zanoza's "Back from the Brink" asks you to write down advice you might give someone suffering from an addiction. Review your entry carefully and add to it. Make a special effort to create similes and metaphors and to use personification so as to make your writing vivid. Then, put this information into a letter that tries to convince the reader to give up his or her addiction.

After you have written your first draft, read your paper carefully. Ask yourself if you have used vocabulary that is concrete, specific, and vivid enough to convince your reader. If not, use the techniques you learned in this chapter and in Chapter 5 to make your language more effective.

When you are satisfied that you have developed your letter well and that you have expressed your ideas in language that is powerful and convincing, edit and proofread your letter. Then send it.

4. The second journal assignment after "Back from the Brink" by Daniel Zanoza asks you to write a paragraph explaining one effect of a serious illness on someone you know and on his or her family. Review this paragraph. Then, write several more paragraphs, each of which explains another way in which the patient's life or the life of his or her loved ones has been affected. You might introduce this essay with a paragraph that explains how the patient contracted or found out about the illness. Such a paragraph might end with your thesis statement.

As you revise your rough draft, pay special attention to your language. Add figures of speech, like those you read in Zanoza's essay. They will make your writing more effective and convincing. As always, edit and proofread the last draft of your paper.

5. "The Gift" by Li-Young Lee explains how the poet received an emotional treasure that enriched his life and that he can pass on to others. If you read this poem, you may have made journal notes about similar gifts your parents or others have passed along to you through example. For instance, seeing your sister work hard at her studies may have motivated you to do the same; watching your aunt tend her roses may have made you love flowers; or noticing how cheerful your father remains on bad days may have inspired you to keep smiling through sorrow or adversity.

   Use your journal notes as the basis of an essay that discusses one emotional treasure or gift someone in your family (or your family as a whole) has given you. A good way to begin is to explain what that gift is. You might even compare it to the gift Lee discusses in his poem. Then, in the body of your paper, you can provide three or four examples of how your father, mother, or other relative revealed the gift to you. In any case, be specific. Show what difficulties your father has had to face, or describe the long hours and hard work your sister devotes to studying for an exam or completing a paper. A good way to conclude is to explain how you intend to share your gift with someone else.

   Use figures of speech to create images that, like those in Lee's poem, will help readers see what you are trying to explain. As always, write several versions of your paper and edit it carefully. Make sure it is fully developed, easy to follow, and free of distracting errors.

6. Read the journal notes you made after completing Louis Gonzalez's "Music." If you responded to either or both of the Suggestions for Journal Entries, you have a good start on an essay that will discuss an obsession of your own.

   Begin with an introduction that, like Gonzalez's, explains the extent to which you are committed to a particular pursuit, idea, study, activity, hobby, art form, or sport. Then go on to explain how this obsession developed in you. End your essay by looking to the future or by using any of the other types of conclusions discussed in Chapter 4.

   As always, remember that one draft is never enough. When you write your second draft, include concrete and specific nouns and adjectives. Add vivid verbs, adjectives, and adverbs as well. When you revise this draft, try to add figures of speech like those discussed in this chapter. Then, revise your third draft to improve organization, sentence structure, and grammar. The final step is, of course, to edit and proofread your work carefully.

Writing to Learn: A Group Activity

Daniel Zanoza's "Back from the Brink" describes a life nearly lost to drug abuse. Luckily for Zanoza, his wife and family helped him battle his demon. But what about people not lucky enough to have the support of loved ones—where can they seek help?

THE FIRST MEETING

Ask each group member to identify a different community, religious, volunteer, or government agency, group, or organization dedicated to helping people fight their drug habits.

RESEARCH

One of you might call your city or town government to find out what services it offers or to ask for leads about religious or other community groups that provide such services. Another might call the local hospital, board of health, or the college's counseling center, infirmary, or health office for information about health services or drug rehabilitation programs in the community or on campus. Finally, someone might research topics such as drug rehabilitation or drug addiction in the college library or on the Internet.

Ask each member of the group to find out about and take careful notes on one service, agency, or organization—whether public or private—that helps drug addicts. Everyone should photocopy his or her notes and be prepared to discuss them at the next meeting.

THE SECOND MEETING

Distribute, discuss, and critique each other's notes. Don't be afraid to recommend that a particular student find out more about the agency or service he or she has chosen to write about. Then, ask everyone to write two or three well-developed paragraphs explaining what the agency or service he or she researched does to help addicts recover. Again, ask group members to make photocopies of their work so that it can be discussed at the next meeting.

THE THIRD MEETING

Discuss the paragraphs that each member of the group has written and distributed. Make suggestions for revision and editing. Then assign one member of the group the task of incorporating this material into a letter to the editor of your local college newspaper. The purpose of this letter would be, of course, to advise drug addicts on campus or in the community that help is available. Assign one or two other students to use this same information in a poster that could be displayed in your college's student center or in classroom buildings. Ask other members to put this information into a one- or two-page pamphlet that might be displayed and distributed at your college's counseling center.

CHAPTER 7

Sentence Structure: Creating Emphasis and Variety

In Chapters 5 and 6 you learned to express your ideas more effectively by using language that is concrete, specific, and vivid. In this chapter you will learn how to use sentence structure to give your writing emphasis and variety, making it even more interesting and effective.

Emphasis

Communicating ideas clearly often depends on the ability to emphasize, or stress, one idea over another. By arranging the words in a sentence carefully, you can emphasize certain ideas and direct your readers' attention to the heart of your message.

A good way to emphasize an idea is to express it in a short, simple sentence of its own. But you will never develop your writing skills if you stick to a steady diet of such sentences. Even the shortest writing projects require sentences containing two or more ideas. In some cases, these ideas will be equally important; in others, one idea will need to be emphasized over the other or others.

CREATE EMPHASIS THROUGH COORDINATION

Ideas that are *equal* in importance can be expressed in the same sentence by using coordination. The sentence below coordinates (makes equal) three words in a series: *found, pitched,* and *started.*

> We *found* a clearing, *pitched* the tent, and *started* a small fire.

You can also use coordination to join two or more *main clauses* to which you wish to give equal emphasis. A main clause contains a subject and verb and, even when standing by itself, expresses a complete idea. You can join main clauses with a comma and a coordinating conjunction, such as *and, but, or, nor, for,* or *so.* Here are some examples; the main clauses are shown in italics:

> *Wild ponies gallop through the surf,* and *eagles soar quietly overhead.*

> *Robert Frost is famous for poetry set in rural New England,* but *he was born in San Francisco.*

227

The raccoons have not been near our house in days, nor *have they been missed.*

Marlin will take the final exam, or *he will fail the course.*

The area was contaminated with a strange virus, so *the medical team wore protective gear.*

I floss my teeth daily, for *I want to avoid gum disease.*

Note that in the above sentences, the beginning and ending clauses are given equal importance. Another way to coordinate (make equal) main clauses within a sentence is to join them with a semicolon:

Alice's car is an antique; it was built in 1927.

You can use both a semicolon and a conjunction when you want to make sure your readers see the relationship of equality between the ideas you are emphasizing. This is especially important in long sentences:

Hoping to reach Lake Soggy Bottom by noon, we left our house by 6:00 AM and took Interstate 90; but traffic was so heavy that we soon realized we would be lucky to reach the lake before dark.

CREATE EMPHASIS THROUGH SUBORDINATION

The sentences above contain complete ideas—main clauses—that are equal in importance. But what if you decide that one of your ideas is more important than the other? Sometimes, putting the less important idea into a *phrase* or *subordinate clause* helps emphasize the other. A phrase is a group of words without a subject or predicate; a subordinate clause contains a subject and predicate, but, unlike a main clause, it does not express a complete idea. Say you wrote these sentences:

Ethel turned the corner, and she noticed a large truck in her lane.

She was frightened, but she avoided the truck.

When revising, you decide that in each sentence the second idea is more important than the first. Therefore, you *subordinate* the first idea to the second:

Turning the corner, Ethel noticed a large truck in her lane.
(*The first idea has been put into a phrase.*)

Although she was frightened, she avoided the truck.
(*The first idea has been put into a subordinate clause.*)

Here are three of many ways to subordinate ideas.

Use Participles   *Participles* are adjectives formed from verbs. They describe nouns and pronouns. Each of the following sentences has been revised by turning one of its main clauses into a phrase that begins with a participle. Doing so helps put emphasis on the main clause that remains.

Original: Charlotte was visiting her Uncle in Knoxville, and she decided to drive through the Great Smoky Mountains.

(*The sentence contains two main clauses of the same importance.*)

Revised: Visiting her uncle in Knoxville, Charlotte decided to drive through the Great Smoky Mountains.

(*The first idea is expressed in a phrase that begins with the participle "Visiting." It is less important than the second idea, which remains in a main clause, "Charlotte decided" . . .)*

Original: Angel planned to visit Moscow, so he began to study Russian.

(*The ideas are equally important.*)

Revised: Planning to visit Moscow, Angel began to study Russian.

(*The first idea is now less important than the second because it is expressed in a phrase, which begins with the participle "Planning.")*

Use Subordinating Conjunctions
You can turn a main clause into a subordinate clause with words such as *although, after, as, because, even though, if, since, unless, until,* and *while.*

Original: The French military leader Joan of Arc was condemned as a witch, so she was burned at the stake.

(*The ideas are equally important.*)

Revised: Because she had been condemned as a witch, the French military leader Joan of Arc was burned at the stake.

(*The second idea, expressed in a main clause, is emphasized. The first idea is now in a subordinate clause, which begins with "Because.")*

Use Relative Pronouns
Using pronouns such as *who, whom, whose, that,* and *which* is another way to subordinate one idea to another. Subordinate clauses beginning with relative pronouns describe nouns in the sentence's main clause.

Original: My friend's parents once lived in Corsica; Corsica is the birthplace of Napoleon.

(*The ideas are equally important.*)

Revised: My friend's parents once lived in Corsica, which is the birthplace of Napoleon. (*The first idea, expressed in a main clause, is more important than the second idea, which is now in a subordinate clause introduced by "which.")*

Original: Audrey Davis has spent two years in the Marine Corps; she was sent to Saudi Arabia.

Revised: Audrey Davis, who has spent two years in the Marine Corps, was sent to Saudi Arabia.

(*The subordinate clause, introduced by "who," comes in the middle of the main clause.*)

CREATE EMPHASIS BY USING PERIODIC SENTENCES

You can create emphasis by putting the strongest or most important word or idea at the end of the sentence. Such sentences are called *periodic* because the emphasis comes just before the period. Here are three examples:

> Mario forgot the tomato sauce's most important ingredient, garlic!

> India, where over half a billion people have the right to vote, is the world's largest democracy.

> Zora Neale Hurston is remembered not for her work in anthropology, the field in which she was trained, but for her novels.

CREATE EMPHASIS BY USING A COLON

A colon can be used in place of a semicolon in a compound sentence when the second main clause explains the first. The effect is similar to the one created by a periodic sentence.

> Toni Morrison has been busy: she has written eight novels and several books of criticism over the last twenty years.

The second main clause, which follows the colon, explains what the writer means by "busy." Notice that, as with a periodic sentence, emphasis is placed on information at the end of the sentence.

CREATE EMPHASIS BY USING THE ACTIVE OR PASSIVE VOICE

Sentences that use the *active voice* contain subjects—persons, places, or things—that perform an action. Sentences that use the *passive voice* contain subjects that are acted upon. Notice how the structure of a sentence changes when it is put into the passive voice.

> **Active:** The enthusiastic listeners applauded the young guitarist.
> **Passive:** The young guitarist was applauded by the enthusiastic listeners.

Generally, using the active voice rather than the passive voice makes it easier to stress the subject of a sentence. For instance, if you wanted to report that the president of your college announced her decision to resign, it wouldn't make much sense to write, "Her decision to resign was announced by President Greenspan." A clearer and more emphatic version would be "President Greenspan announced her decision to resign."

However, there are times when using the passive voice can create emphasis. In some cases, you might decide that the receiver of an action is more important than the person, place, or thing who completes that action. For example,

> Ann was elected to the Monroe City Council.

is more emphatic than

The residents of Monroe elected Ann to the City Council.

Sometimes, in fact, you might not know who or what is responsible for an action, and you will have to use the passive voice:

Doors and windows were left open; books, furniture, and clothing were scattered across the room; and curtains, sheets, and blankets were torn to shreds.

CREATE EMPHASIS BY REPEATING KEY WORDS AND PHRASES

Repeating important words and phrases, carefully and sparingly, can help you stress important ideas over those that deserve less emphasis. This technique is used in the speeches of President John F. Kennedy and Reverend Martin Luther King, Jr.

In his inaugural address, Kennedy gave a special meaning to his plans for the nation when he said:

All this will not be finished in the first one hundred days. Nor will it be finished in the first one thousand days, nor in the life of this administration, nor even perhaps in our lifetime on this planet. But let us begin.

Dr. King used repetition to communicate a sense of urgency about civil rights to a massive audience at the Lincoln Memorial when he delivered the speech now known as "I Have a Dream":

Now is the time to make real the promises of democracy. Now is the time to rise from the dark and desolate valley of segregation to the sunlit path of racial justice. Now is the time to lift our nation from the quicksands of racial injustice to the solid rock of brotherhood. Now is the time to make justice a reality for all of God's children.

CREATE EMPHASIS THROUGH PARALLELISM

We the people of the United States, in Order to *form* a more perfect union, *establish* Justice, *insure* domestic Tranquility, *provide for* the common defence, *promote* the general Welfare, and *secure* the Blessings of Liberty to ourselves and our Posterity, do ordain and establish this Constitution for the United States of America.

The sentence you have just read begins the United States Constitution; this preamble is one of the most well-known sentences in American history. One reason it is so powerful and memorable has to do with its use of six phrases (the reasons for establishing the Constitution) that follow the same pattern. Each consists of a verb followed by a direct object. This writing technique is called *parallelism.*

Parallelism is a way to connect facts and ideas of equal importance in the same sentence and thereby give them added emphasis. Sentences that are parallel list items by expressing each of them in the same grammatical form.

For instance, Adlai Stevenson's eulogy of Winston Churchill, the great British prime minister, contains several examples of parallelism:

> The voice that led nations, raised armies, inspired victories and blew fresh courage into the hearts of men is silenced. We shall hear no longer the remembered eloquence and wit, the old courage and defiance, the robust serenity of indomitable faith. Our world is thus poorer, our political dialogue is diminished, and the sources of public inspiration run more thinly in all of us. There is a lonesome place against the sky.

In the first sentence, Stevenson placed equal emphasis on Churchill's accomplishments by expressing each through a verb followed by a direct object: "led nations," "raised armies," "inspired victories," and "blew fresh courage into the hearts of men." He created parallelism in the second sentence in a series of adjectives and nouns that describe Churchill's best qualities: "the remembered eloquence and wit," "the old courage and defiance," "the robust serenity of indomitable faith." In the third sentence, he explained the effects of Churchill's death in a series of main clauses: "Our world is thus poorer," "our political dialogue is diminished," and "the sources of public inspiration run more thinly in all of us."

Consistency is the key to making sentences parallel. Express every idea in a list in the same grammatical form. Without a doubt, the eulogy you just read would have sounded awkward and been less emphatic had Stevenson written that Churchill's voice "led nations, raised armies, inspired victories, and it blew fresh courage into the hearts of men." The first three items are verbs followed by objects; the fourth is a main clause.

Here are three other examples of how parallelism creates emphasis:

> The President enjoys *reading* mystery novels, *fishing* in Maine, and *speaking* with young people.
> (*The sentence contains gerunds, nouns formed from verbs by adding* "ing"; *gerunds show activity.*)

> *To master* the piano, *to compose* beautiful music, and *to lead* a symphony orchestra seemed to be her destiny.
> (*The sentence contains infinitives, which are formed by placing* to *before the present tense of the verb. Infinitives act as nouns, adjectives, or adverbs.*)

> They vowed to battle the invaders *on the land, on the sea,* and *in the air.*
> (*The sentence contains* prepositional phrases; *a preposition is a short word—such as* at, in, *or* on—*that shows the relationship of a noun or pronoun to the rest of the sentence.*)

Variety

One sure way to make your readers lose interest in what you have to say—no matter how important—is to ignore the need for variety. Good writers try not to repeat vocabulary monotonously, and they vary the length and structure of their sentences whenever possible.

Create Variety by Changing Sentence Length

A steady diet of long, complicated sentences is sure to put your readers to sleep. On the other hand, relying solely on short, choppy sentences can make your writing seem disconnected and even childish. Therefore, one of the most important things to remember about the sentences you write is to vary their length. You can do this by combining some of them into longer, more complex units and by leaving others short and to the point.

Reread the passage from President Kennedy's Inaugural Address on page 231. One reason it holds our interest is that it contains sentences of different lengths. The last of these leaves a lasting impression, not simply because it comes at the end but because it is so much shorter than the others and carries a special punch.

You can combine two or three short sentences into a longer unit in three ways: coordination, subordination, or compounding.

Coordination   This method is useful if you want to write a longer sentence in which all the main ideas receive equal emphasis. The easiest way to do this is to combine sentences with a comma and the appropriate coordinating conjunction or to use a semicolon, as explained on pages 227–228.

Subordination   As you know, subordination lets you combine two or more sentences to emphasize one idea over another. It also helps you vary sentence length and make your writing more interesting. Say you've just written:

> I had been waiting at the bus stop for 20 minutes. The afternoon air was hot, thick, and humid. I became uncomfortable and soon began to perspire. I wished I were home. I thought about getting under the shower, cooling off, and relaxing. My day at work had been long and hard. I looked up from the newspaper I was reading. I saw a huge truck. It sped by, and it covered me with filthy exhaust. I prayed the bus would come soon.

As you read this paragraph, you realize that you haven't emphasized your most important ideas and that your style is choppy and monotonous. Therefore, you decide to rewrite by combining sentences through subordination (you can review ways to do this by rereading pages 228–229):

> I had been waiting at the bus stop for 20 minutes. Because the afternoon air was hot, thick, and humid, I became uncomfortable and soon began to perspire. Wishing I were home, I thought about getting under the shower, cooling off, and relaxing. My day at work had been long and hard. As I looked up from the newspaper I was reading, I saw a huge truck, which sped by and covered me with exhaust. I prayed the bus would come soon.

In combining some sentences, you've made your writing smoother and more interesting because you've created sentences of different lengths. What's more, some ideas have gained emphasis.

Compounding   This method involves putting subjects, verbs, adjectives, and adverbs together in the same sentence as long as they relate to one another logically.

Sometimes, ideas that are very similar seem awkward and boring if expressed in separate sentences. For example: "Egbert has been transferred to Minneapolis. Rowena has also been transferred to that city." Notice how much more interesting these short sentences become when you combine their subjects: "Egbert and Rowena have been transferred to Minneapolis." Here are a few more examples:

> **Original:** The doctor rushed into the emergency room. She went immediately to a patient who had been bitten by wasps.
> **Compound verb:** The doctor rushed into the emergency room and went immediately to a patient who had been bitten by wasps.
>
> **Original:** The weather around here is sometimes unpredictable. Sometimes it becomes treacherous.
> **Compound adjective:** The weather around here is sometimes unpredictable and treacherous.
>
> **Original:** Grieving over the loss of her child, the woman wept openly. She wept uncontrollably.
> **Compound adverb:** Grieving over the loss of her child, the woman wept openly and uncontrollably.

CREATE VARIETY BY CHANGING SENTENCE PATTERNS

As you know, all complete sentences contain a subject, a verb, and a complete idea; many also contain modifiers (adjectives, adverbs, prepositional phrases, and the like) and other elements. However, there is no rule that all sentences must begin with a subject, that a verb must follow the subject immediately, or that everything else must be placed at the end of a sentence. Depending on their purpose, good writers create as many patterns as they need to make their writing interesting and effective. Here are a few ways you can vary the basic patterns of your sentences.

Begin with an Adverb   *Adverbs* modify verbs, adjectives, or other adverbs. They help explain *how, when, where,* or *why.* The following examples begin with adverbs or with groups of words that contain and serve as adverbs (shown in italics):

> *Soon* the rain stopped and the sun reappeared.
>
> *High above the spectators,* the hot air balloon drifted peacefully.
>
> *Slowly* and *confidently,* Maria rose to the speaker's platform.

Near the ancient Egyptian city of Thebes, pharaohs built monuments to their wealth and power.

Begin with an Infinitive

As you learned earlier, an *infinitive* is the present tense of a verb with the word *to* in front of it. Infinitives acting as nouns often make good beginnings for sentences:

To study archaeology was her childhood dream.

To defend unpopular ideas takes courage.

To call him a coward is unfair and inaccurate.

Begin with a Preposition or Prepositional Phrase

Prepositions connect or show relationships between nouns or pronouns and the rest of a sentence. *Prepositional phrases* contain prepositions, a noun or pronoun, and any words that modify that noun or pronoun.

Without love, life is empty.

Between the mountains ran a bright, clear stream.

Before the spectators stood a Mayan priest ready to perform the harvest ritual.

To a large temple, the worshippers carried flowers, candles, and statues.

Inside the barn, Freda found tools that dated from the Revolution.

Begin or End with a Participle or Participial Phrase

A *participle* is a verb turned into an adjective. Many participles end in "ed" or "ing." But words like *caught, lost, found, brought,* and *drawn,* which are formed from irregular verbs, can also be participles. A *participial phrase* is a group of words containing a participle.

Screeching, the infant birds told their mother they were hungry.

Exhausted, I fell asleep as soon as my head touched the pillow.

Caught in the act, the thief gave up easily.

I stayed home that night, *having nowhere else to go.*

Suddenly, the old bicycle broke apart, *scattering spokes and bits of chain everywhere.*

Jamie wept openly, *his dream destroyed.*

Ask a Rhetorical Question

You learned in Chapters 3 and 4 that asking a question is a good way to begin a paragraph or an essay. Rhetorical questions—those to which the writer knows the answer or to which no answer is expected—can also emphasize important points and create variety. Take this example from a speech condemning television by Federal Communications Commission head Newton Minow at a meeting of television executives in 1961:

You will see a procession of game shows, violence, audience participation shows, formula comedies about totally unbelievable families, blood and thunder mayhem, violence, sadism, murder, Western badmen, Western good men, private eyes, gangsters, more violence and cartoons. And endlessly, commercials—many screaming, cajoling, and offending. And, most of all boredom. . . .

Is there one person in this room who claims that broadcasting can't do better?

Reverse the Position of the Subject and the Verb   Say that you write, "Two small pines grew at the crest of the hill." When you read your rough draft, you realize that this is the kind of pattern you've used in many other sentences. To vary the pattern, simply reverse the position of your subject and verb: "At the crest of the hill grew two small pines."

Create Variety by Using a Colon

Use a Colon after an Independent Clause to Introduce Information That Names or Explains Something in That Clause   Such information can be expressed in a word or phrase, a list of words, or even a sentence.

> **Word:** He was motivated by one thing and one thing only: greed.
> (*"Greed" names "thing."*)

> **List:** He has three loves: his dog, his car, and his stomach.
> (*"His dog, his car, and his stomach" name his "loves."*)

> **Sentence:** Please follow these instructions: Find the nearest exit, walk to it quickly, and help other passengers who need assistance.
> (*The sentence after the colon explains "instructions."*)

Use a Colon to Introduce a Quotation   Using a colon is a good way to introduce someone else's words and at the same time use a different sentence pattern. Let's say you wanted to quote from President Kennedy's Inaugural Address. You might write:

> Today we would do well to remember JFK's exhortations to his fellow Americans: "Ask not what your country can do for you—ask what you can do for your country."

Visualizing Sentence Structure

To see how some of the principles you have just learned work in professional writing, read these paragraphs from Pete Hamill's autobiography, *A Drinking Life*. Comments in the left margin explain how Hamill created emphasis. Those on the right discuss variety. Hamill is writing about World War II.

EMPHASIS   *VARIETY*

*Colon
introduces
list explaining
"special way."*

*Repeats "our"
for emphasis,
parallelism.*

*Divides
sentence
into segments
to increase
emphasis.*

We lived in the rhythms of the war. Years later, we even marked time in a special way: Before the War, During the War, After the War. The war was in our comics, our movies, our dreams. The radio was filled with it. Every evening, my mother listened to Edward R. Murrow and Gabriel Heatter, and in school we followed the war on maps. There was North Africa. And Tobruk. And somewhere in all that yellow emptiness El Alamein.

*Varies
sentence
length.*

*Follows a
simple
sentence
with a
compound
sentence.*

*Subordinates
one idea
to another.*

*Coordinates
two equally
important
ideas.*

*Creates
emphasis
through
repetition.*

At Holy Name, I heard about the war from new teachers every year, each of them rolling down the maps and showing us the places that were in the newspapers and on the radio. There was so much excitement when the Allies landed in Sicily because the parents of most of the Italian kids were from that island. They wanted the Americans to win. They had brothers in our army, and some of the brothers died in those first battles. All of them said their parents were worried. I got an aunt there, said Vito Pinto. My grandmother is there, said Michael Tempesta. I got an uncle over there, said George Poli. The war went on and on.

*Ends
sentence
with
participle
phrases.*

*Follows long
sentence with
short one.*

*Follows simple
sentence with
compound
sentence.*

Revising to Create Variety and Emphasis

Read these two versions of paragraphs from Alice Wnorowski's "A Longing," which appears in this chapter. Although the rough draft is correct, Wnorowski knew that revising it would allow her to give important ideas the appropriate emphasis and to bring variety to her writing style.

Wnorowski—Rough Draft, Paragraphs 3 and 4

Vary length?

The morning dew chilled my naked feet. I stopped on the sandy lane. From out of the corner of my eye, I suddenly caught a movement. Something was moving in the wide, open hay field that lay before me. Five deer, three does and two fawns, were grazing

Vary structure?

in the mist-filled dips of the roller-coaster landscape. I sat down in the damp earth to watch them. I got my white nightdress all brown and wet.

What is being emphasized in this one-sentence paragraph?

The deer casually strolled through the thigh-high grass, stopping every other step to dip their heads into the growth and pop them back up again with long, tender timothy stems dangling from the sides of their mouths.

Too long?

Wnorowski—Final Draft, Paragraphs 3 and 4

Combines sentences through coordination, subordination, and compounding.

The morning dew chilled my naked feet, and I stopped on the sandy lane. From out of the corner of my eye, I suddenly caught a movement in the wide, open hay field that lay before me. In the mist-filled dips of the roller-coaster landscape grazed five

Creates variety by reversing subject

deer: three does and two fawns. I sat down
in the damp earth to watch them and got my
white nightdress all brown and wet.

and verb.
Uses colon
to introduce
a list.

Divides
paragraph
into two
sentences;
emphasizes
both ideas.

   The deer casually strolled along through
the thigh-high grass, stopping every other
step to dip their heads into the growth and
pop them back up again. Long, tender
timothy stems dangled from the sides of
their mouths.

Practicing Combining Sentences

The two paragraphs below lack emphasis and variety because the sentences
they contain are similar in length and structure. Use techniques explained in
this chapter to rewrite the paragraphs in the spaces that follow them. Combine
sentences, remove words, add details, choose new vocabulary, or make any
other changes you wish to create more interesting and effective paragraphs.

Ramses II

Ramses II was a pharaoh [ruler] of Egypt.
He lived approximately 3,300 years ago. He
took the throne when he was only 24. He
ruled for 66 years. He died at about age
90. He had a huge family. He had more than
100 children. He is thought to be the
pharaoh when Moses led the Hebrews from
bondage in Egypt. He is also remembered for
his many important building projects. He
was an industrious and resourceful king. He
left his mark on the Egyptian landscape. He
built temples and other magnificent

monuments in every major city of his

kingdom. His projects included expanding

the famous temples at Karnak and at Luxor.

1

He is buried in the Valley of the Kings.

This place is near Luxor. Luxor used to be

2

called Thebes.

_____

_____

_____

_____

_____

3

_____

_____

4

_____

_____

_____

5

_____

6

_____

_____

7

_____

Trinity

The prefix "tri" means three. Traditional

8

Christianity teaches that God exists in a

trinity, three persons. These are the

Father, the Son, and the Holy Spirit.

9

Christianity is not the only religion that

has a trinity. Hinduism also has a trinity.

It is called the Trimurti. "Murti" means

shape in Sanskrit. Sanskrit is the ancient

```
language of India.  Many classical religious

and literary works are written in this

language.  The Hindu trinity has three

members.  They are Brahma, Vishnu, and

Shiva.  Brahma is the creator.  Vishnu is

the preserver.  Shiva is the destroyer.
```

———————————————————————————————————

———————————————————————————————————

———————————————————————————————————

———————————————————————————————————

———————————————————————————————————

———————————————————————————————————

———————————————————————————————————

———————————————————————————————————

———————————————————————————————————

———————————————————————————————————

———————————————————————————————————

———————————————————————————————————

The following selections will help you develop the ability to create sentences that are both varied and emphatic. As you read on, try to apply the techniques you're learning in this chapter to your own writing. Don't hesitate to reread important sections in the introduction to this chapter when you need to.

The Vices of Age*

Malcolm Cowley

Poet, critic, historian, and literary editor of New Republic *magazine, Malcolm Cowley (1898–1989) remained energetic and productive well into old age. He is the author of* Exile's Return, *an important book about the "lost generation" of American writers, such as Hemingway and Fitzgerald, who lived in Paris during the 1920s. The paragraphs that follow are taken from "The View from 80," an article that Cowley wrote for* Life *magazine in 1978 and that he later used in a book of the same title.*

Preparing to Read

1. One of the people discussed in this selection was an "admiralty lawyer." He practiced law governing naval, shipping, and other maritime matters.
2. Cowley's title prepares us for what is to come. What are "vices"?
3. Should Cowley have entitled this essay "The Vices of Old Age"?

Vocabulary

avarice (noun)	Greed.
dismantled (verb)	Took apart.
dismaying (adjective)	Disappointing.
immoderate (adjective)	Extreme, unreasonable.
intruders (noun)	Trespassers.
lethargy (noun)	Sluggishness, lack of energy.

The Vices of Age

Malcolm Cowley

Among the vices of age are avarice, untidiness, and vanity. . . . 1

Untidiness we call the Langley Collyer syndrome. To explain, Langley 2 Collyer was a former concert pianist who lived alone with his 70-year-old brother in a brownstone house on upper Fifth Avenue. The once fashionable neighborhood had become part of Harlem. Homer, the brother, had been an admiralty lawyer, but was now blind and partly paralyzed; Langley played for him and fed him on buns and oranges, which he thought would restore Homer's sight. He never threw away a daily paper because Homer, he said,

---

*Editor's title.

might want to read them all. He saved other things as well, and the house became filled with rubbish from roof to basement. The halls were lined on both sides with bundled newspapers, leaving narrow passageways in which Langley had devised booby traps to catch intruders.

On March 21, 1947, some unnamed person telephoned the police to report that there was a dead body in the Collyer house. The police broke down the front door and found the hall impassable; then they hoisted a ladder to a second-story window. Behind it Homer was lying on the floor in a bathrobe; he had starved to death. Langley had disappeared. After some delay, the police broke into the basement, chopped a hole in the roof, and began throwing junk out of the house, top and bottom. It was 18 days before they found Langley's body, gnawed by rats. Caught in one of his own booby traps, he had died in a hallway just outside Homer's door. By that time the police had collected, and the Department of Sanitation had hauled away, 120 tons of rubbish, including, besides the newspapers, 14 grand pianos and the parts of a dismantled Model T Ford.

3

Questions for Discussion

1. What sentences in this selection are periodic? Explain the ideas they emphasize.
2. What other methods discussed in this chapter does Cowley use to create emphasis? For instance, find an example of parallelism.
3. These paragraphs illustrate ways to create variety. Where does Cowley use participial phrases? In what other way(s) does he create variety?
4. Identify one or two of the vivid images the author uses to show us the kind of life Langley and Homer Collyer led. What words make these images effective?
5. Is Cowley's attitude toward the aged negative? Explain by making reference to specific words and sentences.

Thinking Critically

1. In the first sentence, Cowley mentions three vices of age. Name three vices of youth. Then explain one of these by using examples of people you know or have read about. Put your ideas in writing.
2. What kind of old age will you have? Before you answer, consider your personality—your habits, your virtues, your faults, your temperament, the people and things with which you surround yourself, the kinds of things you save, and so on. Then, use this information to predict the kind of person you will be at age 80 or 90. Take notes as you go through this process. Then, put the results into a paragraph or two.

Suggestions for Journal Entries

1. People of all ages have vices. Do you know someone who is particularly greedy, sloppy, vain, lazy, or jealous, or who suffers from another bad quality or habit? What does this person say or do to illustrate this vice? Use brainstorming or focused freewriting to record these details. If possible, recall incidents from your subject's life to show how seriously he or she has been affected by this vice. Incidentally, a good subject for this assignment might be a relative, a close friend, or even yourself.

2. Are all elderly people like those Cowley describes? Think about someone about age 80 whom you admire. List details to show that, far from being eccentric or strange, he or she keeps up with the times, is active and alert, or contributes much to the lives of others. Once again, recall an incident or two that explain why you think highly of this person.

Gettysburg Address

Abraham Lincoln

Perhaps the best-loved American president, Abraham Lincoln was a model of what a leader should be: decisive, principled, hard working, and compassionate. He was also among the most eloquent of public speakers. His Second Inaugural Address and Gettysburg Address are landmarks of American oratory. In November 1863, Lincoln came to Gettysburg, Pennsylvania, to dedicate a cemetery at the site of the Civil War's bloodiest battle. The turning point of the War, the Battle of Gettysburg had raged for four days and killed 50,000 Americans, both Union and Confederate, before Southern forces under General Robert E. Lee withdrew. Lincoln's Gettysburg Address is an eloquent and powerful statement of his belief that "all men are created equal"; of his grief over the death of his countrymen on both sides; and of his faith that "government of the people, by the people, for the people, shall not perish from the earth." Incidentally, Lincoln did not rely on a speech writer; he composed the Gettysburg Address himself.

Preparing to Read

1. Note that Lincoln makes excellent use of repetition. One word in particular is used seven times in this short speech. Look for and underline it each time.

2. Lincoln begins with a reference to the past, moves to the present, and ends with the future. Such references help organize the speech. Read the speech once; then, reread it to spot these references.

3. Another technique used to hold this speech together and give it greater emphasis is parallelism. Look for examples of this technique throughout the Gettysburg Address.

4. In the last sentence, Lincoln describes a "great task remaining before us." Read this important sentence several times to make sure you understand it fully.

Vocabulary

conceived (adjective)	Created.
consecrate (verb)	Bless, sanctify, make holy.
dedicate(d) (verb/adjective)	Set aside for a purpose, sometimes to honor or worship.
detract (verb)	Take away from, lessen, decrease.
hallow (verb)	Make holy or sacred, sanctify.
in vain (adjective)	For no reason or purpose.
measure (noun)	Amount.
proposition (noun)	Idea, principle.
resolve (verb)	Decide, determine.

Gettysburg Address

Abraham Lincoln

FOUR SCORE AND seven years ago our fathers brought forth on this continent   1
a new nation, conceived in Liberty, and dedicated to the proposition that
all men are created equal.

Now we are engaged in a great civil war, testing whether that nation, or   2
any nation so conceived and so dedicated, can long endure. We are met on a
great battlefield of that war. We have come to dedicate a portion of that field,
as a final resting place for those who here gave their lives that that nation
might live. It is altogether fitting and proper that we should do this.

But in a larger sense, we can not dedicate—we can not consecrate—we   3
can not hallow—this ground. The brave men, living and dead, who struggled
here, have consecrated it, far above our poor power to add or detract. The
world will little note, nor long remember what we say here, but it can never
forget what they did here. It is for us the living, rather, to be dedicated here
to the unfinished work which they who fought here have thus far so nobly
advanced. It is rather for us to be here dedicated to the great task remaining
before us—that from these honored dead we take increased devotion to that
cause for which they gave the last full measure of devotion—that we here
highly resolve that these dead shall not have died in vain—that this nation,
under God, shall have a new birth of freedom—and that government of the
people, by the people, for the people, shall not perish from the earth.

Questions for Discussion

1. What examples of repetition appear in this speech?
2. The most obvious example of parallelism in the Gettysburg Address
   appears at the very end: "government of the people, by the people,
   for the people, shall not perish from the earth." What other examples
   of parallelism do you find?
3. Most sentences in this speech are long, but Lincoln does vary
   sentence length. Where does he do this?
4. What two participial phrases does Lincoln use at the end of the first
   sentence? Would it have made better sense to put the information
   they convey into another sentence? Why or why not?
5. Where in paragraph 2 does Lincoln use a participial phrase?
6. What effect does repeating the word "dedicate" or "dedicated" have?
   Does the word have any religious significance?
7. Where else does Lincoln use words that have a religious significance?
   What is he trying to tell us by using such vocabulary?
8. What is Lincoln's central idea? What devices does he use to maintain
   coherence?

Thinking Critically

1. In Preparing to Read, you learned that Lincoln makes reference to the past, to the present, and to the future. Find places in which he does this. What is he trying to accomplish by setting up this pattern other than helping to organize the speech? What does he accomplish each time he references a specific time?

2. Reread the last sentence. Is there a pattern in Lincoln's resolving that "these dead shall not have died in vain," that "this nation, under God, shall have a new birth of freedom," and that democracy "shall not perish from the earth"? What is that pattern, and why would such a pattern be so effective in a speech?

Suggestions for Journal Entries

1. In what ways do you think the government should be "for the people"? What rights, and/or services should it guarantee us? Use clustering, draw a subject tree, or freewrite for about 10 minutes on this question. After you have completed your journal entry, read it to classmates or friends. Together, brainstorm for a few minutes to collect more ideas.

2. Many speeches in American history have served as sources of inspiration from decade to decade, from generation to generation. With the help of your instructor or your college librarian, locate a speech that you'd like to read or reread. Then analyze this speech. Pick out examples of parallelism, repetition, and other techniques the writer has used to create emphasis. Here are a few speeches you might choose from:
   Abraham Lincoln, Second Inaugural Address
   Franklin Delano Roosevelt, First Inaugural Address
   Adlai Stevenson, Eulogy for Eleanor Roosevelt
   Dwight D. Eisenhower, Farewell Address
   John F. Kennedy, Speech at the Berlin Wall
   Martin Luther King, Jr., Speech at the Lincoln Memorial ("I Have a Dream")
   Ronald Reagan, Speech at Moscow State University

3. Using as many paragraphs as you like, rewrite Lincoln's speech in your own words. Make sure that you express his central idea clearly and that you emphasize his other important ideas through parallelism, repetition, or any of the other techniques you've learned for creating emphasis.

A Longing
Alice Wnorowski

"A Longing" is a tender, almost dreamlike recollection of a beautiful childhood experience that continues to haunt the author. Wnorowski wrote this short essay in response to a freshman English assignment designed to help students learn to use concrete detail. However, it also illustrates several important principles about sentence structure discussed earlier in this chapter. Wnorowski began her studies at a community college. She has since earned a B.S. with honors in engineering.

Preparing to Read

1. You've learned that coordination can be used to create sentences in which two or more ideas receive equal emphasis and that subordination can be used to create sentences in which one idea is stressed over others. Look for examples of coordination and subordination in this essay.

2. The author puts variety into her writing by using techniques discussed earlier in this chapter. They include beginning sentences with an adverb and a prepositional phrase and using participles to vary sentence structure and length.

3. Remember what you learned about using details in Chapter 5, especially those that appeal to the five senses. Identify such details in "A Longing."

Vocabulary

acknowledge (verb)	Recognize.
conceived (verb)	Understood.
yearn (verb)	Desire, long for.

A Longing
Alice Wnorowski

AN EASY BREEZE pushed through the screen door, blowing into my open face   1
and filling my nostrils with the first breath of morning. The sun beamed warm rays of white light onto my lids, demanding they lift and acknowledge the day's arrival.

Perched in the nearby woods, a bobwhite proudly shrieked to the world   2
that he knew who he was. His song stirred deep feelings within me, and I was overcome by an urge to run barefoot through his woods. I jumped up so

abruptly I startled the dog lying peacefully beside me. His sleepy eyes looked into mine questioningly, but I could give him no answer. I only left him bewildered, pushing through the front door and trotting down the grassy decline of the front lawn.

The morning dew chilled my naked feet, and I stopped on the sandy lane. From out of the corner of my eye, I suddenly caught a movement in the wide, open hay field that lay before me. In the mist-filled dips of the roller-coaster landscape grazed five deer: three does and two fawns. I sat down in the damp earth to watch them and got my white nightdress all brown and wet.

3

The deer casually strolled along through the thigh-high grass, stopping every other step to dip their heads into the growth and pop them back up again. Long, tender timothy stems dangled from the sides of their mouths.

4

The fawns were never more than two or three yards behind their mothers, and I knew a buck must not be far off in the woods, keeping lookout for enemies. Suddenly, a car sped along the adjacent road, disrupting the peace of the moment. The deer jumped up in terror and darted toward the trees. They took leaps, clearing eight to ten feet in a single bound. I watched their erect, white puffs of tails bounce up and down, until the darkness of the woods swallowed them up and I could see them no more.

5

I don't think that at the simple age of eleven I quite conceived what a rare and beautiful sight I had witnessed. Now, eight years later, I yearn to awaken to the call of a bobwhite and to run barefoot through wet grass in search of him.

6

Questions for Discussion

1. Find a few examples of both coordination and subordination in this essay.
2. Identify some adverbs, prepositional phrases, and participles Wnorowski uses to create variety.
3. In which sentence are the normal positions of the subject and verb reversed?
4. In paragraph 5, the author varies the length and structure of her sentences to make her writing more interesting. What methods discussed in this chapter does she use?
5. To which of our five senses do the details in this essay appeal?
6. What is the meaning of Wnorowski's title? Why is it appropriate?
7. What techniques does the writer use to maintain coherence in and between paragraphs?

Thinking Critically

1. This selection reveals as much about the writer as about the experience she recalls. From what you have just read, what can you say about Wnorowski's personality?
2. For anyone living in or near a rural area, seeing a family of wild animals is not an unusual event. Why, then, is this event so special to the writer?

Suggestions for Journal Entries

1. Think back to an experience you would like to relive. Make a list of the things that made this experience memorable and that will explain why you have such "a longing" to relive it.
2. Use the brainstorming technique discussed in "Getting Started" to list details about a natural setting (for example, a meadow, mountain, seashore) that you experienced recently or remember vividly.

The Buried Sounds of Children Crying

Harrison Rainie

On a quiet April morning in 1995, terrorists set off a 5,000-pound bomb at a federal office building in Oklahoma City. Among the 170 people killed were many infants and small children. It is a tragedy that has been burned into the American consciousness and that will cause us pain for generations to come. Harrison Rainie writes for U.S. News & World Report, *where this essay was published shortly after the bombing.*

Preparing to Read

1. In paragraph 3, Rainie quotes lines from William Shakespeare's *King John.* In this play, Arthur, the king's nephew, is captured in battle and is killed while attempting to escape. Constance, Arthur's mother, goes mad with grief and kills herself.

2. This essay contains examples of language that shows, which you learned about in Chapters 5 and 6. Look for concrete and specific nouns, vivid verbs, adjectives, and adverbs. Make a special effort to find figures of speech.

Vocabulary

distraught (adjective)	Troubled, upset, worried.
embodiment (noun)	Realization, manifestation.
gracious (adjective)	Gentle, tender, lovely.
implication (noun)	Indication, suggestion.
incessant (adjective)	Without end.
ineffable (adjective)	Indefinable, indescribable.
instinctive (adjective)	Inbred, natural.
molecular level (noun)	The most basic level, the smallest part of our being.
nourish (verb)	Feed.
nurturing (adjective)	Caring for, feeding, supporting.
pluck (noun)	Boldness, nerve, courage.
prevails (verb)	Exists, is the rule.
qualifiers (noun)	Describers.
riveting (adjective)	Captivating, engaging.
roguishness (noun)	Friskiness.
vacant (adjective)	Empty.

The Buried Sounds of Children Crying

Harrison Rainie

Almost to a person, the searchers who combed the ruins at the Alfred P.   1
Murrah Federal Building said they had one thought after finishing their work: They wanted to go home and hug their kids. The most chilling fact about the Oklahoma City bombing was that it struck at children eating breakfast and playing in a day-care center one floor above the street. And the only way to respond to the ache the incident created is to clasp all surviving children tightly—even those thousands of miles from harm's way—and pour out a fearful love.

While there was much talk about the meaning of this attack on "Amer-   2
ica's heartland," its biggest impact was on the soul's heartland. We are fixed at the molecular level to respond to children. Some famous experiments have shown that their faces have been designed to draw instinctive nurturing from us; their noises are especially riveting to adult ears. Give a mother a pile of dozens of identical T-shirts, as one researcher did, and she can pick out the one her child wore by its scent.

The death of such precious beings violates the order and meaning of life.   3
The only way to understand it is to describe the incessant pain of the loss, as the distraught Constance does in Shakespeare's *King John:* "Grief fills the room up of my absent child, / Lies in his bed, walks up and down with me; / Puts on his pretty looks, repeats his words, / Remembers me of all his gracious parts, / Stuffs out his vacant garments with his form." Adults nourish this grief the way they would the child himself, psychologist Louise Kaplan says.

The tragedy of the children's deaths in Oklahoma City is compounded   4
by the loss of many adult lives and the implications of the bombing's occurrence in a heartland city. Oklahoma holds a spot in the American imagination as the embodiment of normality, a gritty wholesomeness, an appealing streak of roguishness and pluck, as a place where a pretty happy coexistence prevails among American Indians, Northern Methodists whose ancestors entered through Kansas, Southern Baptists whose kin came from Texas and many newcomers in the past generation.

Its capital city is a festival of Americana, home of the National Cowboy   5
Hall of Fame and Western Heritage Center, the National Softball Hall of Fame and a nice firefighters' museum. That, though, did not prevent it from being devastated by an evil force—and an alien one, no matter what its origin is. "You don't have terrorism in Middle America," insisted firefighter Bill Finn. Now we do. And the city will be long haunted by the sounds described by Red Cross worker Jennifer Harrison: "As we helped people on the street, we could hear children crying, like blowing in the wind. You couldn't see them. You just heard their voices."

In our language, we use parental terms in inventive ways as qualifiers: 6
We can live in fatherlands, speak in mother tongues, measure things by Father Time and exist in Mother Nature. But our attachment to children is so

ineffable, we don't use it to describe other ideas. Child love is the essence of life, and we have all been orphaned by the slaughter of children in Oklahoma City.

Questions for Discussion

1. What function does the colon serve in the first sentence of paragraph 1?
2. Where else in this essay does the author use a colon? What function does it serve in those places?
3. Find examples of parallelism in this essay.
4. Explain how Rainie maintains variety in paragraph 2.
5. Paragraph 5 contains a three-word sentence. Should this sentence have been combined with another sentence? Why or why not?
6. Find a periodic sentence in paragraph 5.
7. Where does Rainie use images to communicate his feelings? Discuss two examples.
8. Where does Rainie use personification?

Thinking Critically

1. In your own words write a summary of the quotation from *King John* in paragraph 3.
2. Read (or reread) "The Last Safe Haven," an essay in Chapter 3 (page 109), which also discusses violence in America. In what way is its message similar to that in "The Buried Sounds of Children Crying"?
3. In paragraph 3, we read: "The death of such precious beings violates the order and meaning of life." Explain this statement.

Suggestions for Journal Entries

1. "We are fixed at the molecular level to respond to children," Rainie says in paragraph 2. He then provides a few brief examples to explain what he means. Reread this paragraph. Then, use freewriting to recall at least one example from your own experience or observation that would support or explain this idea.
2. Use any prewriting method explained in "Getting Started" to discuss your reaction to the Oklahoma City bombing or to any other event that shocked the nation or your community, campus, or family. Don't be content to list a few words such as *stunned,* or *angry,* which will describe your immediate reaction only. Instead, explore the thoughts and feelings you have had about this event since learning about it.

The Band from Hell
Cal Thomas

Social critic and columnist Cal Thomas is among the most widely read journalists in the United States. His syndicated columns appear in over 350 newspapers, and over 100 radio stations carry his commentaries on politics, morality, and values in contemporary America. He is the author of nine books, including The Death of Ethics in America *and* Uncommon Sense. *"The Band from Hell" appeared in a collection of essays entitled* The Things That Matter Most, *published in 1994.*

Preparing to Read

Thomas mentions a number of people and trends important to his central idea:

1. Glenn Miller was a very popular band leader in the 1930s and 1940s. Serving in the army during World War II, Miller was killed when his plane was shot down.
2. The term *bobby-soxers,* for teenage fans, comes from the ankle socks worn by young women in the 1940s and 1950s.
3. Charles Manson was the leader of a ritual cult that brutally murdered Sharon Tate Polanski and five of her friends at her Bel Air, California, home on August 10, 1969. Hours later, they killed Leno and Rosemary LaBianca. Manson and his accomplices are serving life sentences.
4. Joycelyn Elders was surgeon general during President Clinton's first term. Janet Jackson is a rock star.

Vocabulary

catechism (noun)	Book summarizing the basic principles of a religion.
deemed (adjective)	Judged to be, considered to be.
disproportionate (adjective)	Uneven, unequal, lopsided.
emblematic of (adjective)	Representative, indicative, or characteristic of.
emulate (verb)	Imitate, copy, follow.
epitaph (noun)	Inscription memorializing a dead person.
epithet (noun)	Title or term that describes the nature of a person or thing.
impotent (adjective)	Powerless.

nihilistic (adjective)	Relating to a belief that nothing has value or meaning.
perversion (noun)	Vice, depravity.
profanities (noun)	Swear words, curses, blasphemies.
rampant (adjective)	Uncontrolled, unruly, raging.
vulgarities (noun)	Indecencies, obscenities.

The Band from Hell

Cal Thomas

THERE ARE THOSE who contend that violence in music and on film does not influence people to emulate what they see and hear. If that is true, why do advertisers pay so much money (nearly $1 million a minute during the Super Bowl broadcast) in an effort to influence behavior in favor of beer, tires, automobiles, and shaving cream?

1

Violence and illicit sex, when seen regularly on television and in movies and music, give a type of cultural permission for people to behave as their entertainment role models behave. How could it be otherwise? Bobby-soxers in the forties did not become serial killers after watching Frank Sinatra at the Paramount Theater in New York or listening and dancing to a Glenn Miller tune.

2

The sixties tore away the veil of decency that had kept entertainment respectable, if not always responsible. As the values and beliefs of a generation were discarded, the new generation needed music and other forms of entertainment that would reflect its increasingly nihilistic worldview.

3

From the now relatively tame Elvis and the Beatles, we have regressed to the band from Hell, Guns N' Roses, a group for whom perversion would be a step up. David Geffen, the former president of the label that produced Guns N' Roses' *Use Your Illusion I* and *II,* summed up the catechism of modern entertainment when he said, "When you give people what they want, they'll show up in droves." A fine, fine, epitaph for a generation.

4

The Guns N' Roses albums are so packed with profanities and vulgarities that the *band* requested a parental advisory label be pasted on the album cover. The warning label could use a warning label. It states, "This album contains language some listeners may find objectionable. They can F—— off and buy something from the New Age section." One album contains a song written by convicted murderer Charles Manson.

5

It gets worse, as difficult as that may be to comprehend. If there is entertainment for the damned in Hell, Guns N' Roses will be the opening act. Axl Rose, the foul-mouthed lead "singer," even calls his mother by a sexual epithet that only pornographic magazines and *Rolling Stone* would print. He's the kind of guy you would want your daughter to date, if you were a pervert.

6

Rolling Stone reviewed the album and saw beyond the band's "thousand points of spite" to a core political message that, we are told, "however inde-

7

fensible at times, is emblematic of a greater adolescent cancer: an almost total loss of hope compounded by blind, impotent rage and the perverted Reagan-Bush morality in which the actual cloth of the Stars and Stripes is deemed more holy than the freedom and humanity for which it stands."

That's a lot of message for two albums. But the core in this number— indeed, in most numbers these days—is loss of hope, and rage at that loss of hope. Reagan and Bush didn't cause us to lose hope. It was on the way out before they came in. The sixties people promised us paradise. They polluted the paradise we already had and were incapable of building another one in its place.   8

So many of the children of the children of the sixties barely know their parents. Many of these parents, in numbers disproportionate to those of other generations, are either divorced (sometimes more than once) or work all the time, having little time for meaningful relationships with those they helped to create.   9

For role models, many have turned to rock stars, who become teachers of the moral code they follow. Just one issue of *Rolling Stone* magazine often contains the concentrated philosophy of a generation, and the poison now infects and affects a second generation. Read Janet Jackson, interviewed on sex (*Rolling Stone,* September 16, 1993), and ask yourself whether she or another black woman—Surgeon General Joycelyn Elders—is likely to have the greater influence.   10

What is the answer, then? Rampant censorship? No, but labeling records, a practice once advocated by Tipper Gore and Susan Baker through their Parents Music Resource Center, is a good idea. If we can force food manufacturers to label products as to fat and caloric content, why not force the manufacturers of products that cause hardening of the intellectual and spiritual arteries to come clean about the content of their products? This isn't censorship, but the opposite. It would give parents more information about what their kids want to hear and a discussion could ensue that would benefit all concerned.   11

Questions for Discussion

1. What is Thomas asking in paragraph 1? Does this question make for a good introduction?

2. Where else in this essay does Thomas use rhetorical questions, and what function do they serve?

3. In paragraph 4, the author intentionally uses a fragment. Why didn't he express this idea in a complete sentence such as "This is a fine, fine epitaph for a generation"?

4. Where in paragraph 6 does Thomas use a periodic sentence? What is the effect of this sentence on the reader?

5. Reread paragraph 8. How does the author maintain sentence variety?

6. Find one example of each of the following in paragraphs 9 and 10:
   A sentence that begins or ends with a participial phrase.
   A sentence that begins or ends with a prepositional phrase.
   A compound sentence.

7. What pattern or patterns in the essay's conclusion echo what we see in the introduction?

8. Find at least two examples of figurative language in this essay.

Thinking Critically

1. Reread the essay by George Bush in Chapter 1. Then, explain *Rolling Stone* magazine's play on words when it refers to a "thousand points of spite" in paragraph 7.

2. What objection is *Rolling Stone* making to the morality of the Reagan-Bush years (1981–1993)? What is Thomas's answer to that objection (paragraph 8)?

3. Explain the analogy Thomas makes in his conclusion.

Suggestions for Journal Entries

1. Think of a particular artist or group that uses language or behavior you find offensive or objectionable. Freewrite about this artist or group for as long as you can, but produce at least one full paragraph. Whenever possible, quote lyrics or describe behavior to which you object.

2. Go to the library and find *Rolling Stones'* interview of Janet Jackson in the September 16, 1993, issue. Summarize Jackson's views on sex.

3. Thomas explains that forcing record manufacturers to label their products is the same as requiring food manufacturers to label their products. List a few other manufacturers required to list the ingredients or potential dangers of their products.

Suggestions for Sustained Writing

1. Malcolm Cowley describes the horrible deaths of two old gentlemen as a way to explain one of the "vices" of old age. But we all have vices, whatever our age. Consider someone you care about who suffers from a particular vice, such as laziness, greed, vanity, sloppiness, or even a more serious problem such as sexual promiscuity or drug or alcohol abuse. Write this person a letter that recalls two or three startling incidents from

his or her life. In other words, show your reader how seriously this vice is affecting him or her.

You might begin the letter by explaining how much better life could be if your reader overcame the problem. You might conclude by offering your help, advice, and friendship.

Before you start writing, look at the journal notes you made after reading Cowley; you may have already gathered important information for this assignment. Then, draft the first version of your letter. When you revise, make sure to emphasize important ideas. Like Cowley, for example, use parallelism and include periodic sentences. At the same time, ask your reader a few rhetorical questions.

2. The second item under Suggestions for Journal Entries after "The Vices of Age" asks you to gather information about an elderly person you admire. If you responded to this suggestion, read your journal entry now and add any new detail that comes to mind.

Next, organize what you've written into the paragraphs of an essay. Place your thesis in an introductory paragraph that compares or contrasts your subject with others, that begins with a startling remark, or that uses another technique for writing introductions discussed in Chapter 4. Make sure your thesis states why you admire your subject. Explain that you respect this individual because of his or her accomplishments, or simply name particular character traits you find admirable. Then, in *each* of the paragraphs that follow, discuss one accomplishment or character trait in detail.

Like Cowley, vary the length and structure of your sentences, use rhetorical questions, and practice parallel structure. Don't forget to revise your paper and to edit it carefully.

3. Read the notes you made in response to the first of the Suggestions for Journal Entries following Lincoln's "Gettysburg Address." (If you haven't completed this short assignment, do so now.)

Next, focus on three or four of the rights and/or services that democratic governments should guarantee their people. Choose those you believe are essential. Define each of these items in one or two sentences; then arrange them in a list that ends with the one item you consider most important of all.

Use this list as a blueprint or outline for an essay that explains, develops, and supports each of these ideas (rights/services) in a separate paragraph or group of paragraphs. When you begin revising your rough draft, write an introductory paragraph that contains a thesis and captures the reader's attention. Also, write a concluding paragraph based upon one of the techniques explained in Chapter 4. As you rewrite this and subsequent drafts, create variety and emphasis by using the advice in this chapter. The next step, of course, is to edit and proofread your work.

4. One of the Suggestions for Journal Entries after Alice Wnorowski's "A Longing" asks you to think about an experience you would like to relive. If

you responded to this suggestion, you've made a list of effective details that will help explain why you have such a longing to repeat this experience.

Add to your notes, and expand them into an essay that shows what made the experience so memorable. Develop your thesis in concrete detail, and make your writing unified and coherent by using techniques discussed in Chapter 2.

After you've written your first draft, read your essay carefully. Should you do more to emphasize important ideas or to maintain your reader's interest? If so, revise your paper by using techniques for creating emphasis and variety explained in the introduction to this chapter. As usual, edit and proofread the final draft of your paper.

5. The second item in Suggestions for Journal Entries after "A Longing" invites you to begin listing details about a natural setting—a forest, meadow, seashore, mountain, river—that you visited recently or remember vividly.

    Follow the advice in item 4 of Suggestions for Sustained Writing above, and turn these notes into a short essay.

6. In the first suggestion for journal entries after Rainie's "The Buried Sounds of Children Crying," you were asked to provide an example to support the idea that "We are fixed at the molecular level to respond to children," which appears in paragraph 2. Reread that paragraph. Then, read your journal notes. Next, add at least two other examples that will help prove this point. Discuss each of these examples in a separate paragraph of an essay that uses the quotation above as its thesis.

    Make sure the quotation and your explanation of it appears in your essay's introduction. You might also use a contrast, a definition, or an anecdote in the beginning of your paper. A good way to conclude is to refer to your thesis or to make a call to action. In any case, review the methods of writing introductions and conclusions in Chapter 4 before you begin to draft your essay.

7. Read the entries you made after reading Thomas's "The Band from Hell." If you responded to the first suggestion for journal writing, expand the paragraph you wrote into a full-length essay that explains what you object to in the lyrics or behavior used by musical artists or groups. Make sure that the reasons behind your objections are made clear. In fact, you might state them in your thesis.

    You can focus your entire essay on the artist or group you began writing about in your journal, or you might write about others as well. When you revise your paper, incorporate some of the effective techniques for creating emphasis seen in Thomas's essay, for example, rhetorical questions and periodic sentences. Also, vary sentence length and structure. If your rough draft contains too many short, simple sentences, combine them by using coordination, subordination, or compounding.

    Asking a question, using a startling remark, or quoting directly from a song that offends you might make a good introduction. To conclude, try making reference to your thesis, looking to the future, or like Thomas, making a recommendation. As a final step, edit and proofread your work.

8. If you responded to the second of the Suggestions for Journal Entries after Thomas's "The Band from Hell," you have already summarized the *Rolling Stone* interview with Janet Jackson. Write an essay in which you explain whether or not you find Jackson's views on sex objectionable. Be specific by focusing on three or four opinions she states (quote them directly) and by answering each one in a detailed, well-developed paragraph. You need not express the same view on each of Jackson's opinions. In fact, you can agree with some and disagree with others.

When you revise your rough draft, combine sentences to avoid choppiness and repetition, vary the length and structure of sentences, insert questions to maintain the reader's interest, and use periodic sentences and parallelism for emphasis. Once again, finish up by doing a thorough job of editing and proofreading.

Writing to Learn: A Group Activity

Cal Thomas's "The Band from Hell" discusses the possibilities of attaching warning labels to music recordings in much the same way that food and drug manufacturers label their products. Thomas's essay is part of a long-time debate about the appropriateness of rating or controlling various forms of expression, including music, film, television, printed matter, and the Internet.

The First Meeting

Ask each member of your group to choose one of the five media or forms of expression listed above and to search the library or the Internet for one article that argues for at least some regulation of that medium and one that argues against regulation.

Research

Group members might start searching their library's electronic databases or the Internet by entering phrases such as *free speech, free speech and cyberspace, recording industry ratings, media policy, parents music resource center, Tipper Gore, TV parental guidelines,* or *V-chip.* Once you have located articles for and against regulating the particular form of expression you are researching, summarize their main points and make copies of both your notes and the original articles for distribution.

The Second Meeting

Distribute, discuss, and evaluate each other's articles and summaries. Students who have submitted less than complete or effective summaries should be asked to revise their work or find other articles. At the end of this meeting, ask each group member to use the ideas and information discussed to write the rough draft of a paper that argues in favor of or against regulating one or more of the forms of expression considered by your group. Ask everyone to bring copies of his or her draft to the next group meeting.

THE THIRD MEETING

Read and evaluate each other's drafts. Offer your peers suggestions for revision as well as information or ideas that might help them support their opinions better. In keeping with what you have learned in this chapter, also offer pointers about combining sentences or using other techniques that might improve sentence variety and emphasis.

Description

This section's two chapters show how to develop verbal portraits—pictures in words—of people, places, and things you know well. The more specific you make any piece of writing, the more interesting, exciting, and effective it will be. And this is especially true of descriptive writing. Successful descriptions require a lot of specific details.

Knowing Your Subject

Gathering descriptive details becomes easier when you know the person, place, or thing you're describing. If you need to learn more about your subject, spend some time observing it. Use your five senses—sight, hearing, touch, taste, and smell—to gather important information. And don't be afraid to take notes. Write your observations, reactions, and impressions in your journal, on note cards, or at least on scratch paper. They will come in handy as you sit down to put together your verbal portrait.

Using Language That Shows

As you learned in Chapter 5, using language that shows makes any writing you do far more *concrete, specific,* and *vivid* than simply telling your readers what you mean. Such language is vital to description.

For instance, it's one thing to say that your mother "came home from work looking very tired." It's quite another to describe "the dark shadows under her eyes and the slowness of her walk as she entered the house."

In the first version, the writer uses a weak abstraction to get the point across. But "looking very tired" can mean different things to different people. It doesn't show the reader exactly what the writer sees. It doesn't point to things about the subject—the dark shadows under her eyes, the slowness of her walk—that *show* she is tired.

Use Concrete Nouns and Adjectives

The next thing to remember is to make your details as concrete as possible. For example, if you're describing a friend, don't just say that "He's not a neat dresser" or that his "wardrobe could be improved." Include concrete nouns and adjectives that will enable your readers to come to the same conclusion. Talk about "the red dirt along the sides of his scuffed, torn shoes; the large rips in the knees of his faded blue jeans; and the many jelly spots on his shirt."

The same is true when describing objects and places. It's not enough to claim that your 1979 convertible is "a real eyesore." You've got to *show* it. Describe the scrapes, scratches, dents, and rust spots; mention the cracked headlights, the corroded bumpers, and the bald tires; talk about the fact that the top is faded.

Include Specific Details

After you've chosen a number of important details that are concrete—details that show rather than tell something about your subject—make your description more specific. For instance, revise the description of your friend's attire to "Red clay was caked along the sides of his scuffed, torn loafers; his knees bulged from the large rips in his faded Levi's; and strawberry jelly was smeared on the collar of his white Oxford shirt."

When describing that 1979 convertible, don't be content simply to mention "the scratches and scrapes on the paint job." Go on to specify that "some of them are more than an inch wide and a half inch deep." Make sure your readers know that those "corroded bumpers" are made of "chrome" and "are scarred with thousands of tiny pockmarks and rusty blemishes." Finally, don't say that the top is "faded"; explain that "the canvas top, which was once sparkling white, has turned dirty gray with age."

Create Figures of Speech

In Chapter 6 you learned that one of the best ways to make your writing clear and vivid is to use figures of speech, expressions that convey a meaning beyond their literal sense. Writers rely heavily on figures of speech when they need to explain or clarify abstract, complex, or unfamiliar ideas. Metaphor, simile, and personification can be used to compare an aspect of the person or thing being described to something with which readers are already familiar. In "If at First You Do Not See . . . " which appears in Chapter 8, Jesse Sullivan describes trees that seem "to bow their heads in sorrow," their branches "twisted and ill-formed, as if poisoned by the very soil in which they are rooted."

In addition, figures of speech make it possible for writers to dramatize or make vivid feelings, concepts, or ideas that would otherwise have remained abstract and difficult to understand. If you read Emanuel di Pasquale's "Joy of an Immigrant, a Thanksgiving" (Chapter 6), you might remember that the poet compares his journey to America with the flight of a bird to a land where he "can build a dry nest" and where his "song can echo."

Rely on Your Five Senses

Earlier you read that a good way to gather information about any subject is through observation. Observation is often thought of as seeing, and the most common details found in description are visual. However, observing can also include information from the other four senses. Of course, explaining what something sounds, feels, smells, or tastes like can be harder than showing what it looks like. But the extra effort is worthwhile. In fact, whether you describe people, places, or things, the greater the variety of details you include, the more realistic and convincing your description will be.

Next to sight, hearing is the sense writers rely on most. In Chapter 8, Gordon Parks describes a boy holding a "bawling naked baby in his arms." He goes on to mention that the boy "whacked" the baby's bottom and that, later, two of the family's daughter's "burst into the shack, screaming and pounding on one another." In that same chapter, Mary Ann Gwinn imitates the "mournful and chilling" cry of a wounded bird by creating her own words: "Whooooooh, Whooooh, Whoooh." It is "something between a cry, a whistle and a sob," she says.

When writers describe rain-covered sidewalks as "slick," scraped elbows as "raw" or "tender," or the surfaces of bricks as "coarse" or "abrasive," they appeal to the sense of touch. Another example appears in Mary Ann Gwinn's "A Deathly Call of the Wild," in Chapter 8, when she writes that some of the oil spilled onto the shores of Alaska had the "consistency of chocolate syrup."

Tastes and smells are perhaps the most difficult things to describe. Nonetheless, you should include them in your writing when appropriate. Notice how well Mary Taylor Simeti does this when describing the Easter picnic she and her family make of take-out food from a hillside restaurant in Sicily:

> . . . [Our] obliging host produces [brings out] three foil-covered plates, a
> bottle of mineral water, and a round kilo loaf of fragrant, crusty bread. We
> drive back along the road a little way to a curve that offers space to park and
> some rocks to sit on. Our plates turn out to hold spicy olives, some slices of
> *prosciutto crudo* [cold ham] and of a peppery local salami, and two kinds of
> pecorino [sheep's milk] cheese, one fresh and mild, the other aged and
> sharper. With a bag of oranges from the car, the sun warm on our backs, the
> mountains rolling down at our feet to the southern coast and the sea beyond,
> where the heat haze clouds the horizon and hides Africa from view, we have
> as fine an Easter dinner as I have ever eaten. (*On Persephone's Island*)

Being Objective or Subjective

Describing something objectively requires the writer to report what he or she sees, hears, and so on as accurately and as thoroughly as possible. Subjective description allows the writer to communicate his or her personal feelings or reactions to the subject as well. Both types of description serve important purposes.

Most journalists and historians try to remain objective by communicating facts, not opinions about those facts. In other words, they try to give us the kind of information we'll need to make up our own minds about the subject.

This is what student Meg Potter does when she describes one of the thousands of homeless living on the streets of our cities:

> This particular [woman] had no shoes on, but her feet were bound in plastic
> bags that were tied with filthy rags. It was hard to tell exactly what she was

wearing. She had on . . . a conglomeration of tattered material that I can
only say . . . were rags. I couldn't say how old she was, but I'd guess in
her late fifties. The woman's hair was grey and silver, and she was beginning
to go bald.

As I watched for a while, I realized she was sorting out her bags. She
had six of them, each stuffed and overflowing. . . . I caught a glimpse of
ancient magazines, empty bottles, filthy pieces of clothing, an inside-out
umbrella, and several mismatched shoes. The lady seemed to be taking the
things out of one bag and putting them into another. All the time she was
muttering to herself. ("The Shopping Bag Ladies")

Potter never reveals her feelings about her subject. She simply explains
what the shopping bag lady looks like and what she does. Even words like
conglomeration and *filthy,* while vivid, tell us more about what the writer sees
than how she feels about her subject. As a result, we are left to make up our
own minds about what we read.

In some cases, however, writers find it useful to reveal their feelings
about the person, place, or thing they are describing, so they take a subjective
approach. Doing so often adds depth and interest to their work. In "The
Temptress," for example, student Dan Roland includes details from his senses
and creates figures of speech to communicate various feelings about a golf
course he visits:

A friendly sun peeks out from behind the green hills, revealing a giant coat
of glistening frost on a silent land. At this hour, even the birds still sleep.
The howling wind's savage teeth bite deeply, and the cold air grips me by
the throat. The steaming coffee goes down easily, warming my insides and
making the frigid environment almost bearable. I peer over an elegant landscape. As far as I can see, all is calm. Manicured fairways reach out across
the land, and ponds of glass reflect the sun's red glow. There are trees everywhere, from delicate symmetrical pines that line the fairways to majestic,
spiteful oaks that eat my golf balls for breakfast, lunch, and dinner.

Watch for examples of objective and subjective description as you read
the poems and essays in Chapters 8 and 9. At the same time, identify concrete and specific details and figures of speech, which will help you better appreciate and understand what goes into writing vivid, interesting, and effective description.

CHAPTER 8

Describing Places and Things

The introduction to Section Three explained several ways to increase your powers of description regardless of the subject. This chapter presents several selections that describe places and things. It also explains two techniques, introduced earlier, that will help you make your subjects as interesting and as vivid to your readers as they are to you: using proper nouns and effective verbs.

Using Proper Nouns

In addition to filling your writing with concrete details and figures of speech, you might also want to include a number of *proper nouns,* which, as you know, are the names of particular persons, places, and things. Here are some examples: Arizona, University of Tennessee, Lake Michigan, Farmers and Merchants' Savings and Loan, First Baptist Church, Spanish, Chinese, Belmont Avenue, Singer Sewing Machine Company, Harold Smith, San Francisco Opera House, *Business Week* magazine, and Minnesota Vikings.

Including proper nouns that readers recognize easily can make what you are describing more familiar to them. At the very least, it makes your writing more believable. Notice how Alfred Kazin's recollection of his childhood home is enriched by the names of places and things (shown in italics) he uses in this passage from "My Mother in Her Kitchen":

> In the corner next to the toilet was the sink at which we washed, and the square tub in which my mother did our clothes. Above it, tacked to the shelf on which were pleasantly arranged square, blue-bordered white sugar and spice jars, hung calendars from the *Public National Bank* on *Pitkin Avenue* and the *Minsker Progressive Branch* of the *Workman's Circle;* receipts for the payment of insurance premiums and household bills on a spindle; two little boxes engraved with *Hebrew* letters. One of these was for the poor, the other to buy back the *Land of Israel.*

Using Effective Verbs

We know how important verbs are to narration, but effective verbs can also add much to a piece of description. Writers use verbs to make descriptions more specific, accurate, and interesting. For instance, "the wind had chiseled deep grooves into the sides of the cliffs" is more specific than "the wind had made deep grooves." The verb *chiseled* also gives the reader a more accurate picture of the wind's action than *made* does.

In the introduction to Section Three, you've just read about how to enrich the description of a friend's clothing by adding specific details. Returning to that sentence, notice that lively verbs (in italics) make as much of a difference as do concrete nouns and adjectives:

> Red clay *was caked* along the sides of his scuffed, torn loafers; his knees
> *bulged* from the large rips in his faded Levi's; and strawberry jelly *was*
> *smeared* on the collar of his white Oxford shirt.

Something similar can be said about the verbs Robert K. Massey uses in a portrait of the Russian countryside that opens his biography of Peter the Great:

> Around Moscow, the country *rolls* gently up from the rivers *winding* in sil-
> very loops across the pleasant landscape. Small lakes and patches of woods
> *are sprinkled* among the meadowlands. Here and there, a village *appears,*
> *topped* by the onion dome of its church. People *are walking* through the
> fields on dirt paths *lined* with weeds. Along the riverbanks they *are fishing,*
> *swimming* and *lying* in the sun. It is a familiar Russian scene, *rooted* in cen-
> turies. (*Peter the Great*)

Including Action and People in the Description of a Place

Narration and description are closely related, and they often appear together. Storytellers describe places where their narratives take place. Writers of description often reveal the character or atmosphere of a place by narrating events that occur in it or by describing people who appear in it.

A selection in this chapter that shows how actions and the people who perform them can help reveal the character of a place is Gordon Parks's "Flavio's Home." In the following passage, Parks reveals the hopelessness and poverty that fills the da Souza home when he tells us about the fear, sadness, and anger with which the family's children conduct themselves:

> Maria's eyes flashed anger. " . . . I'll beat you, you little bitch." Liza threw a
> stick at Maria and fled out the door. Zacarias dropped off to sleep.
> Mario . . . slouched in the corner and sucked his thumb. Isabel and Albia
> sat on the floor, clinging to each other with a strange tenderness. Isabel held
> on to Albia's hair and Albia clutched at Isabel's neck. They appeared frozen
> in an act of quiet violence.

Visualizing Details That Describe Places and Things

The following paragraphs are from John Ciardi's essay "Dawn Watch," in which the author describes the sights, sounds, and smells of sunrise in his backyard.

The traffic has just started, not yet a roar and stink. One car at a time goes by, the tires humming almost like the sound of a brook a half mile down in the crease of a mountain I know—a sound that carries not because it is loud but because everything else is still.

Appeals to senses.

Uses simile.

The lawns shine with a dew not exactly dew. There is a rabbit bobbing about on the lawn and then freezing. If it were truly a dew, his tracks would shine black on the grass, and he leaves no visible track. Yet, there is something on the grass that makes it glow a depth of green it will not show again all day. Or is it something in the dawn air?

Includes action.

Our cardinals know what time it is. They drop pure tones from the hemlock tops. The black gang of grackles that makes a slum of the pin oak also knows the time but can only grate at it. They sound like a convention of broken universal joints grating up hill. The grackles creak and squeak, and the cardinals form tones that only occasionally sound

Relies on concrete, specific nouns.

Uses metaphor.

Uses simile.

Appeals to senses.

Reveals subjective reaction to cardinals and grackles.

through the noise. I scatter sunflower seeds
by the birdbath and hope the grackles won't
find them.

Revising Descriptive Essays

Read these two versions of three paragraphs from Jessie Sullivan's "If at First
You Do Not See . . . ," a student essay that appears later in this chapter in
its entirety. Though the rough draft is powerful, Sullivan's revision smooths
out rough spots, improves wording, and provides additional detail that
makes her writing even more vivid and effective.

Sullivan—Rough Draft

I live in an apartment on the outskirts of
New Brunswick, New Jersey. To the right of
my building is Robeson Village, a large low-
income housing project with about two-
hundred apartments facing each other on
opposite sides of a wide, asphalt driveway
that runs the length of the complex. In this   *Wordy?*
driveway, drug dealers and buyers congregate
daily, doing business in front of anyone who
cares to watch. Sometimes, children who have
witnessed these transactions look over
paraphernalia the dealers and their   *What kind of paraphernalia?*
customers have left in their wake.

   To the left of my building is Henry
Street, a street that has grown to be
synonymous with illegal drugs over the
years. It is truly a pathetic sight. The
block consists of a half dozen vacant and   *If "vacant," how can they be*
condemned buildings, all of which are still

"inhabited"?

Wordy?

<u>inhabited</u> by addicts and dealers who have set up store there in much the same way a legitimate business <u>owner decides on a particular</u> location where business will be most profitable.

. . .

Whose eye?

<u>To the eye</u>, the community appears to be in a state of depression. Even trees, which traditionally symbolize life and vitality

Make this more vivid?

What kinds of "pungent odors"?

reflect this. <u>Pungent odors</u> are made worse by the stench of rotting food, spilled from overturned garbage cans onto the sidewalk and cooking in the heat of the sun.

Make this image more active, lively?

Sullivan—Final Draft

I live in an apartment on the outskirts of New Brunswick, New Jersey. To the right of my building is Robeson Village, a large low-income housing project with about two-hundred apartments facing each other on opposite sides of a wide, asphalt driveway that runs the length of the complex. <u>Here</u>, drug dealers and buyers congregate daily, doing business in front of anyone who cares to watch. Sometimes, children who have witnessed these transactions look over the <u>crack vials</u>, <u>hypodermic needles</u>, <u>syringes</u>, and other paraphernalia the dealers and their customers have left in their wake.

Substitutes one word for three.

Adds specific detail to define "paraphernalia."

To the left of my building is Henry

Uses fewer words than original. Street, which <u>has become</u> synonymous with illegal drugs. It is a pathetic place. The

Changes wording to be more accurate. block consists of a half dozen condemned buildings, all of which are <u>lived</u> in or <u>frequented</u> by addicts and dealers. The

latter have set up stores there in much the

Uses fewer words than original. same way legitimate merchants choose locations where they think business will be profitable.

. . .

To the eye <u>of the visitor</u>, the community *Adds detail.*

Adds effective adjective. appears to be in a <u>chronic</u> state of depression. Even trees, symbols of life and vitality, seem to bow their heads in sorrow. *Uses personification to create a vivid image.* Rather than reaching up in praise, their branches are twisted and ill-formed, as if poisoned by the very soil in which they are

Uses specifics to explain what kinds of odors. rooted. The pungent odors of <u>urine</u>, <u>feces</u>, and <u>dead</u>, <u>wet leaves</u> are made worse by the stench of rotting food, which <u>spills</u> from *Uses verbs to make image active, lively.* overturned garbage cans onto the sidewalk and <u>cooks</u> in the heat of the sun.

Practicing Techniques That Describe Places and Things

Write a three- or four-sentence paragraph on each of the topics below. You may want to write the rough draft of each paragraph on a piece of scrap paper first, then write the final draft in the spaces provided.

Ways to make your writing rich and vivid are suggested, but use whatever techniques you think will work best.

1. **Topic:** An eating area in your student center or a reading area in the library.
   Suggestions: Appeal to the senses; include information about people and their behavior.

   _____

   _____

   _____

   _____

   _____

   _____

   _____

   _____

2. **Topic:** A wedding or other type of ceremony.
   Suggestions: Describe the people in attendance; use simile or metaphor.

   _____

   _____

   _____

   _____

   _____

   _____

3. **Topic:** An animal (or type of animal) you like or dislike.
   Suggestions: Use simile, metaphor, or personification; appeal to the senses.

   _____

   _____

   _____

   _____

   _____

   _____

   _____

4. **Topic:** The inside of a coffee shop, bar, restaurant, or other small public place.
   Suggestions: Appeal to the senses; include information about people and their behavior.

   _____

   _____

   _____

   _____

   _____

   _____

5. **Topic:** The inside of your car, your bedroom, your family's kitchen, or any other room in which you spend a great deal of time.
   Suggestions: Appeal to the senses; use simile.

   _____

   _____

   _____

   _____

   _____

   _____

   _____

Enjoy the five selections in this chapter. Each describes its subject in a unique way, but all will show you how to make your writing more vivid, interesting, and moving.

Watching the Reapers*

Po Chü-i

Perhaps one of the most productive of all Chinese poets, Po Chü-i lived between 772 and 846. Many of his works, though seemingly simple in content, reveal a profound concern for others. Some of them, aimed at the consciences of the ruling class, recall the social evils of his day. Others use description as a tool for exposing guilt, heartache, or other strong emotion in the poet. "Watching the Reapers" does all of these things.

Preparing to Read

1. In the introduction to this chapter, you learned that including action is a good way to capture the character of a place or scene. "Watching the Reapers" makes good use of this technique.

2. Description can have many uses. Here it becomes a tool for self-reflection as well as social commentary.

3. The "fifth month" in line 2 refers to midsummer. In lines 19 and 20, Po mentions that the reapers have paid a tax to the state equal to the amount of grain they had raised themselves. This statement is a clear indication that one of the purposes of this poem is to expose a political and economic evil. In line 23, Po tells us that, as a government official, he is paid in "stones," which are measures of grain.

Vocabulary

glean (verb)	Gather.
grudging (adjective)	Resenting.
lingered (verb)	Remained, stayed around.

Watching the Reapers

Po Chü-i

> Tillers of the earth have few idle months;
> In the fifth month their toil is double-fold.
> A south wind visits the field at night;
> Suddenly the ridges are covered with yellow corn.
> Wives and daughters shoulder baskets of rice,   5

---

*Translated by Arthur Waley.

Youths and boys carry flasks of wine,
In a long train, to feed the workers in the field—
The strong reapers toiling on the southern hill,
Whose feet are burned by the hot earth they tread,
Whose backs are scorched by the flames of the shining sky.   10
Tired they toil, caring nothing for the heat,
Grudging the shortness of the long summer day.
A poor woman with a young child at her side
Follows behind, to glean the unwanted grain.
In her right hand she holds the fallen ears,   15
On her left arm a broken basket hangs.
Listening to what they said as they worked together
I heard something that made me very sad:
They lost in grain-tax the whole of their own crop;
What they glean here is all they will have to eat.   20
And I today—in virtue of what desert
Have I never once tended field or tree?
My government-pay is three hundred stones;
At the year's end I have still grain in hand.
Thinking of this, secretly I grew ashamed   25
And all day the thought lingered in my head.

Questions for Discussion

1. What concrete nouns does Po use in this poem?
2. Where does he use effective verbs and adjectives?
3. Explain how Po's description of the reapers helps him describe the fields in which they toil.
4. One of Po's objectives is to make us aware of how hard a life the reapers have. How do his descriptions of the fields, the wind, and other natural objects help him do this?
5. Why does Po make sure to include action in this poem?
6. What emotion does Po reveal in his conclusion?

Thinking Critically

1. If Po were writing in our day, what would he say about the way our society treats its workers? As you think about this topic, focus on a particular industry, business, or trade.
2. Jump ahead to Chapter 11 and read Carl Sandburg's "Child of the Romans." In what ways are its message and content similar to those of Po's poem?
3. Reread line 12. What does Po mean by the "shortness of the long summer day?"

Suggestions for Journal Entries

1. Use listing, clustering, or freewriting to begin gathering concrete details about a place that you have worked in and that you have found interesting. You don't have to have liked this place; you need only have found it interesting. Try to remember the kind of people and activities that one would normally find there, but keep your information factual and objective. Do not include details that would reveal your feelings about the place.

2. Read over your response to Suggestion 1. Now, be subjective. Through freewriting, explain your feelings about this workplace, the people in it, and the kind of work that goes on there. Finally, answer this question: Would you recommend this job to one of your friends?

Flavio's Home

Gordon Parks

Gordon Parks (1912) is a film director/producer, author, composer, and photographer. His feature films include Shaft *(1972),* The Super Cops *(1974),* Leadbelly *(1976), and* Moments without Proper Names *(1986). He also made the television documentary* The Diary of a Harlem Family *(1968), for which he won an Emmy Award. Perhaps his most memorable film is* The Learning Tree *(1969), a fictionalized account of his childhood in Kansas.*

Parks is the founder and was the editorial director (1970–73) of Essence *magazine, and he has written many works of nonfiction—including several memoirs and many books on the art of photography—as well as a novel,* Shannon *(1981). Today, however, his fame rests chiefly on his photography and on the writings that accompany his photography collections. In* Voices in the Mirror *(1990), a memoir in which "Flavio's Home" first appeared, Park says that he uses "photography as a weapon against poverty and racism." As a staff writer for* Life *magazine, he was once assigned to complete a photo-essay on poverty in one of the "favelas," or slums, of Rio de Janeiro, Brazil. The essay that follows is based on what he witnessed on that trip.*

Preparing to Read

1. Read Parks's first paragraph several times to determine his purpose.

2. Is the first line of this essay a warning of what is to come?

3. Look for images of and references to death starting with paragraph 2. What do you think "Catacumba," the name of the slum where Flavio lives, means in English? Look up words that begin with "cata" in the dictionary if necessary.

4. Read paragraph 3 carefully. Like other paragraphs, it uses effective language, but it also hints at something we will learn about at the essay's end.

Vocabulary

afflictions (noun)	Troubles, suffering, illnesses.
excrement (noun)	Bodily waste.
hemmed and hawed (verbs)	Hesitated before speaking.
jaundiced (adjective)	Yellowed because of illness or malnutrition.
maze (noun)	Confusing set of passageways in which one gets lost easily.
mobilize (verb)	Put into action.
plankings (noun)	Rough boards.

plush (adjective)	Rich, luxurious.
scurried (verb)	Ran around or hurried nervously.
skepticism (noun)	Lack of trust or faith.
wallowing (adjective)	Rolling around, as a pig does in the mud.

Flavio's Home

Gordon Parks

I'VE NEVER LOST my fierce grudge against poverty. It is the most savage of all human afflictions, claiming victims who can't mobilize their efforts against it, who often lack strength to digest what little food they scrounge up to survive. It keeps growing, multiplying, spreading like a cancer. In my wanderings I attack it wherever I can—in barrios, slums and favelas.   1

Catacumba was the name of the favela where I found Flavio da Silva. It was wickedly hot. The noon sun baked the mud-rot of the mountainside. Garbage and human excrement clogged the open sewers snaking down the slopes. José Gallo, a *Life* reporter, and I rested in the shade of a jacaranda tree halfway up Rio de Janeiro's most infamous deathtrap. Below and above us were a maze of shacks, but in the distance alongside the beach stood the gleaming white homes of the rich.   2

Breathing hard, balancing a tin of water on his head, a small boy climbed toward us. He was miserably thin, naked but for filthy denim shorts. His legs resembled sticks covered with skin and screwed into his feet. Death was all over him, in his sunken eyes, cheeks and jaundiced coloring. He stopped for breath, coughing, his chest heaving as water slopped over his bony shoulders. Then jerking sideways like a mechanical toy, he smiled a smile I will never forget. Turning, he went on up the mountainside.   3

The detailed *Life* assignment in my back pocket was to find an impoverished father with a family, to examine his earnings, political leanings, religion, friends, dreams and frustrations. I had been sent to do an essay on poverty. This frail boy bent under his load said more to me about poverty than a dozen poor fathers. I touched Gallo, and we got up and followed the boy to where he entered a shack near the top of the mountainside. It was a leaning crumpled place of old plankings with a rusted tin roof. From inside we heard the babblings of several children. José knocked. The door opened and the boy stood smiling with a bawling naked baby in his arms.   4

Still smiling, he whacked the baby's rump, invited us in and offered us a box to sit on. The only other recognizable furniture was a sagging bed and a broken baby's crib. Flavio was twelve, and with Gallo acting as interpreter, he introduced his younger brothers and sisters: "Mario, the bad one; Baptista, the good one; Albia, Isabel and the baby Zacarias." Two other girls burst into the shack, screaming and pounding on one another. Flavio jumped in and parted them. "Shut up, you two." He pointed at the older girl. "That's Maria,   5 the nasty one." She spit in his face. He smacked her and pointed to the smaller sister. "That's Luzia. She thinks she's pretty."

Having finished the introductions, he went to build a fire under the stove—a rusted, bent top of an old gas range resting on several bricks. Beneath it was a piece of tin that caught the hot coals. The shack was about six by ten feet. Its grimy walls were a patchwork of misshapen boards with large gaps between them, revealing other shacks below stilted against the slopes. The floor, rotting under layers of grease and dirt, caught shafts of light slanting down through spaces in the roof. A large hole in the far corner served as a toilet. Beneath that hole was the sloping mountainside. Pockets of poverty in New York's Harlem, on Chicago's south side, in Puerto Rico's infamous El Fungito seemed pale by comparison. None of them had prepared me for this one in the favela of Catacumba.

Flavio washed rice in a large dishpan, then washed Zacarias's feet in the same water. But even that dirty water wasn't to be wasted. He tossed in a chunk of lye soap and ordered each child to wash up. When they were finished he splashed the water over the dirty floor, and, dropping to his knees, he scrubbed the planks until the black suds sank in. Just before sundown he put beans on the stove to warm, then left, saying he would be back shortly. "Don't let them burn," he cautioned Maria. "If they do and Poppa beats me, you'll get it later." Maria, happy to get at the licking spoon, switched over and began to stir the beans. Then slyly she dipped out a spoonful and swallowed them. Luzia eyed her. "I see you. I'm going to tell on you for stealing our supper."

Maria's eyes flashed anger. "You do and I'll beat you, you little bitch." Luzia threw a stick at Maria and fled out the door. Zacarias dropped off to sleep. Mario, the bad one, slouched in a corner and sucked his thumb. Isabel and Albia sat on the floor clinging to each other with a strange tenderness. Isabel held onto Albia's hair and Albia clutched at Isabel's neck. They appeared frozen in an act of quiet violence.

Flavio returned with wood, dumped it beside the stove and sat down to rest for a few minutes, then went down the mountain for more water. It was dark when he finally came back, his body sagging from exhaustion. No longer smiling, he suddenly had the look of an old man and by now we could see that he kept the family going. In the closed torment of that pitiful shack, he was waging a hopeless battle against starvation. The da Silva children were living in a coffin.

When at last the parents came in, Gallo and I seemed to be part of the family. Flavio had already told them we were there. "Gordunn Americano!" Luzia said, pointing at me. José, the father, viewed us with skepticism. Nair, his pregnant wife, seemed tired beyond speaking. Hardly acknowledging our presence, she picked up Zacarias, placed him on her shoulder and gently patted his behind. Flavio scurried about like a frightened rat, his silence plainly expressing the fear he held of his father. Impatiently, José da Silva waited for Flavio to serve dinner. He sat in the center of the bed with his legs crossed beneath him, frowning, waiting. There were only three tin plates. Flavio filled them with black beans and rice, then placed them before his father. José da Silva tasted them, chewed for several moments, then nodded his approval for the others to start. Only he and Nair had spoons; the children ate with their fingers. Flavio ate off the top of a coffee can. Afraid to offer us food, he edged his rice and beans toward us, gesturing for us to take some. We refused. He smiled, knowing we understood.

Later, when we got down to the difficult business of obtaining permission from José da Silva to photograph his family, he hemmed and hawed, wallowing in the pleasant authority of the decision maker. He finally gave in, but his manner told us that he expected something in return. As we were saying good night Flavio began to cough violently. For a few moments his lungs seemed to be tearing apart. I wanted to get away as quickly as possible. It was cowardly of me, but the bluish cast of his skin beneath the sweat, the choking and spitting were suddenly unbearable.

11

Gallo and I moved cautiously down through the darkness trying not to appear as strangers. The Catacumba was no place for strangers after sundown. Desperate criminals hid out there. To hunt them out, the police came in packs, but only in daylight. Gallo cautioned me. "If you get caught up here after dark it's best to stay at the da Silvas' until morning." As we drove toward the city the large white buildings of the rich loomed up. The world behind us seemed like a bad dream. I had already decided to get the boy Flavio to a doctor, and as quickly as possible.

12

The plush lobby of my hotel on the Copacabana waterfront was crammed with people in formal attire. With the stink of the favela in my clothes, I hurried to the elevator hoping no passengers would be aboard. But as the door was closing a beautiful girl in a white lace gown stepped in. I moved as far away as possible. Her escort entered behind her, swept her into his arms and they indulged in a kiss that lasted until they exited on the next floor. Neither of them seemed to realize that I was there. The room I returned to seemed to be oversized; the da Silva shack would have fitted into one corner of it. The steak dinner I had would have fed the da Silvas for three days.

13

Questions for Discussion

1. In which parts of the essay does Parks remain objective? Where does he become subjective by reacting to and commenting upon what he witnesses?
2. What references to and images of death can be found in this essay?
3. What other examples of figurative language does Park use?
4. In what parts of the essay does the author appeal to the senses?
5. Analyze paragraphs 2, 3, and 6 carefully. What descriptive techniques discussed earlier in this chapter do they use?
6. Where does Parks use contrast, and to what purpose?

7. Why does the author describe Flavio in such detail? Isn't this supposed to be a description of a place?

8. What happens in a place helps reveal its character. What do the events Parks narrates tell us about Flavio's home? Start with paragraph 7.

9. Why does the author bother to include the names of all the da Silva children? What other proper nouns do you find?

10. Why does he include dialogue—what the people say—in this essay?

11. In what paragraph does Parks prepare us for Flavio's coughing, which we learn about in paragraph 11?

12. Why does the author describe his hotel room?

Thinking Critically

1. What do paragraphs 11 and 12 reveal about the author's character and his purpose for writing this essay?

2. Why does Parks bother to tell us about the lovers kissing in the elevator? How do you react to their ignoring his presence and carrying on with their love-making?

3. Compare this essay to Jesse Sullivan's "If at First You Do Not See . . . ," which also appears in this chapter. In what ways are they different? Is Sullivan's purpose the same as Parks's?

Suggestions for Journal Entries

1. Parks has a talent for piling detail upon detail to paint a vivid and compact word picture of what he describes. In paragraph 6, for example, he tells us that the da Silvas' stove was the "rusted, bent top of an old gas range resting on several bricks." In fact, the entire paragraph shows Parks's ability to accumulate concrete, specific, and vivid detail.

   Try your hand at doing the same by writing a one-sentence description of a common object. For example you might start with an ordinary piece of furniture—perhaps the desk or table you are working on right now—and then add details until you have a list that looks something like this:

   The desk

   The wooden desk

   The large wooden desk

   The large brown wooden desk

   The large brown wooden desk covered with junk

   The large brown wooden desk covered with junk, which squats in the corner of my room

The large brown wooden desk covered with junk, books, and papers, which squats in the corner of my room.

Repeat this process, adding as many items as you can, until you've exhausted your mind's supply of nouns and adjectives. Then review your list. Can you make your description even more specific and concrete? For instance, the above example might be revised to read:

The four-foot-long dark brown oak desk was covered with my math book, an old dictionary with the cover ripped off, two chemistry test papers, today's French notes, a half-eaten bologna sandwich, and a can of diet cola.

2. This essay contains both objective and subjective descriptions of "Catacumba," a symbol for poverty and human misery if there ever was one. Have you ever seen such a place in your own country? If so, begin recording details that might describe it. If this topic doesn't appeal to you, gather details about any public place such as a bus station, amusement park, sports arena or stadium, airport, shopping mall, or waterfront—just to name a few examples.

   Whatever topic you choose, approach this journal entry in two steps. Begin by gathering details that describe the place objectively. Then, record your subjective reaction. Use clustering or listing to gather information that might describe this location.

If at First You Do Not See . . .

Jessie Sullivan

When Jessie Sullivan began this essay for a college composition class, she wanted simply to tell her readers what her neighborhood looked like. As she revised and developed her work, however, she discovered that the place in which she lived had a vibrant character beyond what the eye can see. Slowly, she expanded and refined her purpose until description became a tool for exploring the sorrow and the promise of her world. Sullivan majors in liberal arts and business. She plans to study business administration in graduate school.

Preparing to Read

1. As you learned in Chapter 3, narration and description can sometimes be used to explain ideas. Sullivan uses description to explain what is wrong with her neighborhood but also to reveal her hope for the people and place she loves.

2. In creating the contrast explained above, Sullivan reveals much about herself: her courage, her vision, and her desire to make a difference.

3. You know that this essay uses both description and contrast. Look for examples as well.

Vocabulary

bewilderment (noun)	Astonishment, confusion.
condone (verb)	Make excuses for.
defaced (verb)	Made ugly, disfigured.
diversified (adjective)	Varied, different.
illicit (adjective)	Illegal, prohibited.
infamous (adjective)	Dishonorable, known for evil or wrongdoing.
obscenities (noun)	Words or drawings that are indecent and offensive.
oppressive (adjective)	Harsh, severe, hard to bear.
paraphernalia (noun)	Gear, equipment used in a particular activity.
pathetic (adjective)	Pitiful, wretched, miserable.
preconceived notions (noun)	Prejudices, opinions formed before having accurate information about something.
sober (adjective)	Reliable, serious, steady.
superficial (adjective)	Quick and careless, shallow, on the surface.

If at First You Do Not See . . .

Jessie Sullivan

A LOOK OF genuine surprise comes over some of my classmates when I mention where I live. My neighborhood has a reputation that goes before it. People who have never been there tend to hold preconceived notions about the place, most of which are negative and many of which are true. Those who actually visit my neighborhood usually notice only the filth, the deterioration of buildings and grounds, and the crime. What they fail to see isn't as apparent, but it is there also. It is hope for the future.

I live in an apartment on the outskirts of New Brunswick, New Jersey. To the right of my building is Robeson Village, a large low-income housing project with about two-hundred apartments facing each other on opposite sides of a wide, asphalt driveway that runs the length of the complex. Here, drug dealers and buyers congregate daily, doing business in front of anyone who cares to watch. Sometimes, children who have witnessed these transactions look over the crack vials, hypodermic needles, syringes, and other paraphernalia the dealers and their customers have left in their wake.

To the left of my building is Henry Street, which has become synonymous with illegal drugs. It is a pathetic place. The block consists of a half dozen condemned buildings, all of which are lived in or frequented by addicts and dealers. The latter have set up stores there in much the same way legitimate merchants choose particular locations where they think business will be profitable.

It is this area, three blocks in radius, that is infamous for illicit drugs, prostitution, and violence of every sort. Known as the "Vil," it is regarded as the city's hub of criminal activity and immorality.

With the growing popularity of crack, the appearance of the community has gotten worse and worse, as if it were on a collision course with destruction. Fences that once separated one property from another lie in tangled rusted masses on sidewalks, serving now only as eyesores. Almost all of the buildings are defaced with spray-painted obscenities and other foul messages. Every street is littered with candy wrappers, cardboard boxes, balled-up newspapers, and broken beer and soda bottles.

But Henry Street is undeniably the worst. The road is so covered with broken glass that the asphalt is barely visible. The way the glass catches the sunlight at every angle makes the street look almost magical, but there is nothing magical about it. Henry Street is a dead-end in more than the literal sense. In front of apartment buildings, the overgrown lawns, which more closely resemble hay than grass, are filled with old tires, cracked televisions, refrigerators and ovens with missing doors, rusted bikes, broken toys, and worn chairs and tables without legs. Dozens of abandoned cars, their windows shattered and their bodies stripped of anything of value, line the curbs. The entire block is so cluttered with refuse that strangers often mistake it for the junk yard, which is five blocks up.

To the eye of the visitor, the community appears to be in a chronic state   7
of depression. Even trees, symbols of life and vitality, seem to bow their
heads in sorrow. Rather than reaching up in praise, their branches are twisted
and ill-formed, as if poisoned by the very soil in which they are rooted. The
pungent odors of urine, feces, and dead, wet leaves are made worse by the
stench of rotting food, which spills from overturned garbage cans onto the
sidewalk and cooks in the heat of the sun.

Most people familiar with the neighborhood are aware that the majority   8
of us residents are virtual prisoners in our homes because of the alarming
crime rate. Muggings, rapes, and gang-related shootings, many of which do
not get reported in newspapers, are commonplace. Many residents live in
such fear that they hide in their apartments behind deadbolt locks and
chains, daring to peer out of their peepholes only when a frequent gunshot
rings out.

Many of my neighbors have adopted an I-mind-my-own-business atti-   9
tude, preferring to remain silent and blind to the goings-on around them.
This is the case for so many of them that many nonresidents believe everyone
feels this way. Unfortunately, most outsiders learn about our community
from people who have been here only once or twice and who leave with unfair and dangerous misconceptions about us. They see the filth and immorality, and that is all they see. They take one quick look and assume none of us
cares about the neighborhood or about the way we live.

I see my neighborhood from the inside, and I face all of the terrible 10
things I have mentioned on a day-to-day basis. I also see aspects of my community that cannot be appreciated with a superficial first glance. If you look
at the place closely, you will find small strong family units, like my own, scattered amid the degeneration and chaos. Working together, struggling to free
themselves from oppressive conditions, these families are worth noticing! We
are sober, moral people who continue to live our lives according to the laws
of society and, more important, according to the laws of God Himself.

Look closely and you will find those of us who pick up the trash when 11
we see it scattered on our small lawns, sidewalks, and doorsteps. We discourage our children from disrespecting the area in which they live, and we see to
it that they don't litter or deface public property. We emphasize the importance of schooling, and we teach them about the evils of drugs and crime,
making certain that they are educated at home as well.

Most important, we practice what we preach. We show the children with 12
our actions that we do not condone the immoral and illegal acts around us,
and we refuse to take part in any of them. We call the police whenever we
hear gunshots, see drug transactions, or learn of any other unlawful activity.
The children know that we care and that we are trying to create a brighter future for them.

However, the most visible sign of hope is that young people from my 13
neighborhood—and from many neighborhoods like mine, for that matter—
are determined to put an end to the destruction of our communities. It angers

us that a minute yet very visible group of negative individuals has come to represent the whole. It saddens us that skills, talents, and aspirations, which are so abundant in our communities, should go untapped. Therefore, we have decided to take matters into our own hands; we will get the education we need and solve the problems of our neighborhoods ourselves.

Many of us attend the local county college, where we come together often to share ideas for a better future for our community. We also give each other the moral support we need to achieve our educational goals. Our hope binds us together closely and is itself a sign that things will get better. 14

This May, I was proud to see a number of friends receive associate's degrees and get admitted to four-year colleges and universities for advanced degrees. I hope to do the same soon. We are studying for different professions, but no matter how diversified our goals, we will use our knowledge for the benefit of all. This means returning to the community as doctors, lawyers, teachers, entrepreneurs. We will build programs to assist the people of our community directly: day care centers for children with working mothers; family mental and physical health clinics; job-training and placement facilities; legal service centers; youth centers; and drug/alcohol rehabilitation programs. Given the leadership of educated people like those we will become, such facilities can eventually be operated by community residents themselves. Most important, we intend to serve as visible and vocal role models for our children—for the leaders who will follow us and keep our hope alive. Eventually, we will bring about permanent change and make it impossible for a misguided few to represent a proud and productive community. 15

When friends visit me in my apartment for the first time, they frequently ask in awe and bewilderment, "How can you live in such a bad place?" I always give the same reply: "It isn't where you live, but how you live and what you live for." 16

Questions for Discussion

1. What does Sullivan mean in paragraph 1 when she says that her "neighborhood has a reputation that goes before it"? Does this statement help introduce what follows in the rest of the essay?

2. Where in this essay does Sullivan include proper nouns? How do they help her achieve her purpose?

3. One reason this essay is so powerful is that it uses specific details. Find examples of these in paragraphs 5 and 6. Then find more examples in any other paragraph of your choice.

4. What image does Sullivan create in paragraph 7? What figure of speech does she use to develop this image?

5. Does action play a role in this essay? What is it?

6. Sullivan mentions her neighbors. How do they help define the neighborhood?

7. What sense other than sight does Sullivan appeal to?

8. When does she make use of illustration (examples)?

Thinking Critically

1. Why do you think Sullivan bothers to tell us that many shootings never get reported in the newspapers?

2. Summarize Sullivan's central idea in your own words.

3. This is a thought-provoking essay. What questions might you ask Sullivan about herself or her neighborhood if you were able to interview her? (For example, who or what has been her greatest inspiration?) Write your questions in the right- and left-hand margins.

Suggestions for Journal Entries

1. Make a list of the qualities you admire most about the neighborhood in which you live or grew up. Then make another list of ways it might be improved.

2. Use any technique discussed in "Getting Started" to gather information about what your home, neighborhood, or town might look like to someone seeing it for the first time. Then, go beyond appearances and discuss the real character of the place. Like Sullivan, describe what's on the "inside."

3. Think of a community, a family, or any group of people struggling to grow, improve, or even survive. What makes their life a struggle? What hope do you see for this place or these people?

A Deathly Call of the Wild

Mary Ann Gwinn

Mary Ann Gwinn was among several reporters at the Seattle Times *who wrote about the effects of the Exxon Valdez oil spill on Prince William Sound in 1989. Their stories were so penetrating that they won a Pulitzer Prize in journalism.*

Gwinn's article shows that, in the right hands, description has uses beyond pure observation. In some ways, "A Deathly Call of the Wild" is the kind of writing scientists do: it explains a serious problem by carefully recording the effects of that problem. At the same time, Gwinn uses what she saw to persuade us that we have a lot to learn from nature. However we look at it, she proves that description is a powerful tool for many purposes.

Preparing to Read

1. "A Deathly Call of the Wild" is an example of narration and description working together. Gwinn tells us what she observed on a trip to Prince William Sound. An expert reporter, she also includes a great many direct quotes from people she spoke with. You will learn more about using quoted material and other narrative techniques in Section Four.
2. What does the word "deathly" in the title prepare us for?
3. Although writing straight news stories demands objectivity, journalists are permitted a more subjective approach in columns, human-interest stories, or feature articles like this one.

Vocabulary

cause célèbre (noun)	Important cause or issue.
compelling (adjective)	Urgent, demanding.
compulsively (adverb)	Involuntarily, as if being forced or compelled.
havoc (noun)	Ruin, destruction.
intermittently (adverb)	Now and again.
lacerated (adjective)	Cut, torn, scraped.
mournful (adjective)	Sad, heartbreaking.
plumage (noun)	Feathers.
provoke (verb)	Cause, bring about, induce.
pruned (adjective)	Trimmed, clipped.
rationality (noun)	Reason, intelligence.
sinuous (adjective)	Curved.
vain (adjective)	Useless, futile.
vengeance (noun)	Revenge.
wreaked (verb)	Caused.

A Deathly Call of the Wild

Mary Ann Gwinn

VALDEZ, ALASKA—I had tried to prepare myself for Green Island, but noth- 1
ing can prepare you for the havoc wreaked on the creatures of Prince
William Sound.

From the helicopter that took me there, the 987-foot tanker Exxon 2
Valdez, stuck like a toy boat on Bligh Reef, was dwarfed by the immensity of
the sound. It was hard to believe that we could fly 60 miles, land and walk
right into the ruination of a landscape, so far from that broken boat.

The helicopter landed on the beach of Green Island. Its beaches are 3
broad and slope gently, in contrast to the rocky, vertical shores of many of
the other islands in the sound. For that reason, Green Island is favored by
wildlife. Now the oil has turned the gentle beach into a death trap.

No sooner had the Alaska National Guard helicopter roared away than a 4
black lump detached itself from three or four others bobbing in the oil-
streaked water. It was an old squaw, a sea bird normally recognizable by its
stark black-and-white plumage. The tuxedo plumage had turned a muddy
brown and orange.

It staggered up the beach, its head compulsively jerking back and forth, 5
as if trying to escape the thing that was strangling it. Tony Dawson, a photographer for Audubon magazine, and I watched it climb a snowbank and flap
into the still center of the woods. "They move up into the grass, along the
creek beds and into the woods, where they die," Dawson said. "It's like
they're fleeing an invisible enemy."

Dawson used to be a veterinarian. He said documenting the oil spill 6
makes him feel like a photographer in Vietnam: "Every day, a new body
count." As in that war, helicopters drone across the sky, boats beach on
shore, men land, size up the situation and depart.

Eleven days into the spill, scientists are trying to decide which beaches to 7
clean and which to leave alone, reasoning that disruption would hurt some
more than it would help. Very little actual beach cleanup is taking place.
Most of the animals are going to die, a few dozen or hundred every day, by
degrees.

I walked along the beach, which in some places was glutted with oil like 8
brown pudding; in others, streaked and puddled with oil the consistency of
chocolate syrup. The only sounds came from a few gulls and the old squaw's
mate, which drifted down the polluted channel toward its fate. Far away, a
cormorant spread its wings and stretched in a vain attempt to fluff its oil-
soaked feathers. A bald eagle passed overhead.

It was then that I heard a sound so strange, for a brief moment all my 9
20th century rationality dropped away.

Something was crying in the vicinity of the woods, a sound not quite 10
human. I looked into the trees.

Whooooooh. Whooooh. Whooooh. Up and down a mournful scale.   11
Something is coming out of those woods, I thought, and is going to take
vengeance for this horror on the first human being it sees.

Then I saw a movement in the grass at the end of the beach. It was   12
a loon.

Loons have become something of a cause célèbre to bird lovers. They are   13
beautiful birds, almost as large as geese, with long, sharp beaks, striking
black-and-white striped wings and a graceful, streamlined head. They are a
threatened species in the United States because they need large bodies of
water to fish in and undeveloped, marshy shorelines to nest on, and most
shoreline in this country has been landscaped and pruned.

The most compelling thing about the loon is its call—something be-   14
tween a cry, a whistle and a sob, a sound so mournful and chilling it
provoked the word "loony," a term for someone wild with sorrow, out of
their head.

This was an arctic loon in its winter plumage, brown instead of the strik-   15
ing black and white of summer. It had ruby-red eyes, which blinked in terror
because it could barely move. It was lightly oiled all over—breast, feet, wings,
head—destroying its power of flight. Its sinuous head darted here and there
as we approached. It flapped and stumbled trying to avoid us, and then it
came to rest between two large rocks.

As Dawson photographed it, it intermittently called its mournful call. Its   16
mate swam back and forth, calling back, a few yards offshore.

I could see it tremble, a sign that the bird was freezing. Most oiled birds   17
die because the oil destroys their insulation.

"It's like someone with a down coat falling into a lake," Dawson ex-   18
plained. The breeze ruffled its stiffening feathers. As Dawson moved closer
with the camera, it uttered a low quivering cry.

After 10 minutes or so, I just couldn't watch anymore. It was so beauti-   19
ful, and so helpless and so doomed. We had nothing like a bag, sack or cloth
to hold it in. I walked around the point.

Then I heard Dawson calling. He walked into view holding the furious,   20
flapping loon by its upper wings, set it down on the grass and said, "Come
here and help me. He won't hurt you."

I was stunned by the rough handling of such a wild thing, but it devel-   21
oped that Dawson, the former veterinarian, knew his birds. He had grasped
the loon exactly in the place where his wings would not break. He would tell
me later that most bird rescuers are too tender-hearted or frightened of birds
to contain them, and let a lot of salvageable birds get away.

We had to wait for the helicopter, and Dawson had to take more pic-   22
tures, so I grasped the loon behind the upper wings, pinning them together,
and took up the loon watch. The bird rose, struggled and fell back to earth,
then was still.

I was as afraid of the loon as it was of me in a way that touching a totally   23
wild thing can provoke. But I began to feel its strength. It was warm, it had

energy, and it could still struggle. I could hear it breathing, and could feel its pulse. It turned its red eye steadily on me. We breathed, and waited, together.

Dawson returned, took a black cord from a lens case and neatly looped it 24 around the bird's wings. The helicopter dropped out of the sky and settled on the beach. I held the string as the loon, unblinking, faced the terrific wind kicked up by the machine. Then Dawson neatly scooped up the bird and settled into the helicopter. The loon lashed out with its needle beak until David Grimes, a fisherman working with the state on the spill, enveloped it in a wool knit bag he carried with him. The bird stilled.

Dawson and I were both streaked with oil and blood from the loon's feet, 25 lacerated by barnacles on the beach. He gave me a small black and white feather that had fallen from the bird's wing.

We took the loon to the bird-rescue center in Valdez. I don't know if it 26 will live. Dawson thought it had a good chance. I thought of the mate we had left behind in the water.

Afterward, we talked about whom bird rescues help more, the rescued or 27 the rescuer. Most rescued birds don't make it. And tens of thousands more from the Valdez spill will die before they even get a chance.

I know only that the loon told me something that no one other thing 28 about this tragedy could. If only we could learn to value such stubborn, determined life. If only we could hold safe in our hands the heart of the loon.

Questions for Discussion

1. What makes Gwinn's description of the loon's call disturbing? Why does she say it is "not quite human" (paragraph 10)? Why does she bother to define the word *loony* (paragraph 14)?

2. What is it about the loon's appearance that makes its cry even more "mournful"?

3. To which sense besides sight and hearing does Gwinn appeal?

4. Identify effective verbs she uses to reveal the tragedy in Prince William Sound. Why does she explain how she and her companion reacted; why doesn't she simply focus on the birds?

5. What examples of analogy did you find? How about comparison or contrast?

6. If the article is about the loon, why does Gwinn talk about the "old squaw," the cormorant, and other birds?

7. Does the image in paragraph 23 prepare us for the conclusion of this essay? In what way?

Thinking Critically

1. Explain what the author is suggesting when she wonders "whom bird rescues help more, the rescued or the rescuer" (paragraph 27).
2. Reread paragraph 28. What has the author learned from the loon?
3. What is the purpose of this essay? Does it go beyond criticizing civilization's assault on the natural environment?

Suggestions for Journal Entries

1. We don't need to fly to Prince William Sound to see pollution, nor can we say that protecting nature is the responsibility of big oil companies alone. Focus on a natural scene near your home or campus—a hillside, forest, lake, park, seashore—whose beauty is diminished because of what careless individuals have done. Are there beer bottles, paper bags, and cigarette wrappers around? Have people carved their initials in trees or spray-painted large rocks? Does the water contain old tires or other junk instead of fish, birds, and other wildlife? Can you hear car horns and loud radios? Brainstorm about this place, if possible with someone else who has been there. Gather details that show the effects of human irresponsibility on the environment you are describing.

2. Have you ever had to help an animal in trouble? Think about a lost dog or cat, an injured bird, or even a larger animal like a cow, sheep, or horse that needed assistance. Use listing or focused freewriting to gather details that (1)describe the animal; (2) explain where, when, and how you tried to help it; and (3) reveal how both you and it reacted to the problem. For inspiration, reread some of the more moving paragraphs in Gwinn's article, especially paragraph 23.

3. The essay's title is particularly effective. Think back to a time when you found yourself in a wilderness: a forest, mountain range, desert, large state or national park. How did you react to what you saw, heard, felt, and so on? What word best describes your reaction to being there: *excitement, uneasiness, fear, terror, contentment, peacefulness, happiness, boredom, discomfort?* Use any method for gathering information discussed in "Getting Started" to begin describing this "wild" place and to explain how you felt about being there.

Blindsided by Tetanus

Claire Panosian Dunavan

Claire Panosian Dunavan is assistant professor of medicine and a specialist in infectious diseases at the UCLA Medical Center. She became interested in the study of infectious diseases on a trip to Haiti shortly after her college graduation. Tetanus is a serious infectious disease that causes painful muscle contractions. A common symptom is lockjaw. Although tetanus is easily preventable through inoculations, the disease is still rampant in poor countries where medical care is inadequate. This essay first appeared as a "Vital Signs" column in Discover *magazine in January 2000.*

Preparing to Read

1. What does the word "blindsided" in the title tell you about the discussion that will follow?
2. This essay describes a disease (a thing) and has been included in this book to prepare you for the kind of reading and writing you might encounter in college science courses.
3. Some of the words in this piece are specialized, so be prepared to consult the vocabulary list often. Also, don't get discouraged if you don't fully understand this essay the first time you read it. "Blindsided by Tetanus" may require two or three readings. Then again, most essays worth reading should be read over and over!

Vocabulary

antitoxin (noun)	Medicine used to stop or neutralize effects of a harmful substance in the body.
bacillus (noun)	Type of bacteria.
culled (adjective)	Taken from.
encephalitis (noun)	Inflammation of the brain.
excreted (verb)	Discharged waste.
gurney (noun)	Stretcher on wheels.
induced (adjective)	Caused or brought on by.
laceration (noun)	A cut.
laconically (adverb)	Using few words.
leached (adjective)	Drained.
mute (adjective)	Silent, unable to speak.
neonatal (adjective)	Pertaining to newborns.
pathogens (noun)	Things that cause diseases.
perforated (adjective)	Penetrated, broken through
peritonitis (noun)	Inflammation of the lining of the abdomen.

perpetrator (noun)	Cause, culprit.
plagued (verb)	Caused pain or distress.
provoked (verb)	Caused.
psychosis (noun)	Any mental condition that causes the patient to lose contact with reality.
resident (noun)	Doctor who has been awarded a medical license and is training in a medical specialty at a particular hospital.
spasms (noun)	Abnormal and involuntary muscle movements.
stimuli (noun)	Agents that cause reactions in living things or parts of living things.
toxin (noun)	Poisonous substance
ventilator (noun)	Device to help patients breathe.
vulnerable (adjective)	Capable of being attacked or harmed.
wrenching (adjective)	Painful, either emotionally or physically.

Blindsided by Tetanus

Claire Panosian Dunavan

EDUARDO RUBBED HIS jaw and tried to open his mouth, wondering about the tight muscles in his face and neck that had plagued him all day. Then he noticed the flashing lights of a police cruiser in his rearview mirror. As an illegal alien in a battered pickup without cash, driver's license, or friends, Eduardo felt that this was becoming his worst nightmare.

Charged with weaving across lanes and driving an unregistered vehicle, Eduardo spent the next two days in a holding cell. As the hours passed, his cell mates noticed that he grew stiff, grinned oddly, and ignored his food. Then, one of the guards saw him violently jerk his neck and torso. The guard thought, "This guy's faking seizures to get out of jail." But Eduardo's spasms persisted, and other prisoners began backing away from him. The staff decided to pack him off to the county hospital's psychiatric unit.

During my years as the sole infectious diseases specialist at that small county hospital in southern California, I wasn't called to the psychiatric emergency room often. But when I was, the cases were never boring—like the woman with obsessive-compulsive disorder who swallowed nails, tacks, and the metal springs from ballpoint pens. She came in with a fever and a boardlike abdomen—a textbook case of peritonitis due to a perforated intestine. But that's another story.

Eduardo posed a challenge. As I and the resident both knew—but the police did not—psychosis and overdose were not the only conditions that could produce a rigid neck and torso, a mute smile, and jerking movements. An infection of the central nervous system was another possibility, and we'd recently seen a few cases of mosquito-borne encephalitis in the area.

"¿ *Como esta?*" I asked as I approached the young man lying on a gurney   5
in a curtained cubicle. The greeting was a courtesy. Eduardo was in no shape
to talk. Invisible pulleys had stretched his mouth into a tight smirk. But his
eyes were wide open, alert, and terrified—no sign of confusion or coma.

"Great—you got here fast!" The resident's voice rang out as he flung back   6
the curtain.

The sharp sound and sudden motion startled Eduardo. His head jerked   7
back, his shoulders and trunk arched up, and he gasped in pain. But he remained conscious throughout the 15-second attack. That's not consistent
with spasms induced by brain disorders. This was no ordinary seizure.

Suddenly the diagnosis dawned on me. Twelve years earlier, as a medical   8
volunteer in Haiti, I had watched a rigid yet fully conscious pregnant woman
arch her body in just the same way.

She'd had tetanus.   9

"Get the ICU team here as soon as possible," I said to the resident. I   10
spoke softly to avoid startling Eduardo into another spasm. "The next time
this happens, he could stop breathing," I told the resident. "You make sure he
gets an airway. Meanwhile, I'll order up some antitoxin."

In the specialty of infectious diseases, few physical displays are as dra-   11
matic as the spasms provoked by tetanus. Its cause is a protein toxin so po-
tent that many victims require months to recover from its effects, if they survive at all.

But the toxin is not the ultimate perpetrator of tetanus. That honor is re-   12
served for the bacillus *Clostridium tetani,* which produces the toxin. Excreted
in the feces of animals and widely distributed in soil, mature *C. tetani* resemble tennis rackets, bulging at one end with a hardy spore. It doesn't always
take an old nail puncturing a foot to get these into a human host. All the bacteria need is a minor breach of the skin—a laceration, a burn, or even an in-
sect bite. And if they land in tissue that receives little oxygen, they will
thrive—multiplying and manufacturing their deadly product.

Lockjaw, or trismus, is an early sign of tetanus. It means the toxin has af-   13
fected nerves in the masseters, or chewing muscles. Another early symptom is
risus sardonicus, a term from Roman times for the tetanus victim's telltale
smile, raised eyelids, and wrinkled forehead. The most vivid hallmark of all is
the wrenching spasms, which result when two opposing muscle groups are
simultaneously activated. The spasms can be triggered by anything from a
sudden noise, movement, or draft of air to such internal stimuli as a full blad-
der or a cough.

Fortunately, most people in industrialized countries needn't worry that   14
everyday scratches and scrapes will yield an internal harvest of tetanus toxin.
Because they've received a series of tetanus vaccines in childhood as well as
the occasional tetanus booster, their bodies have plenty of protective antibodies. Reported tetanus cases in the United States often number no more than
100 a year.

But people in the developing world are less likely to receive tetanus vac-   15
cines and they suffer the consequences. Tetanus kills an estimated 300,000
each year; almost all deaths occur in developing countries. Newborns are particularly vulnerable. During the first few weeks of life, their only defense
against pathogens comes from antibodies imported from their mothers's
breast milk. Infants born to nonimmunized mothers are tetanus cases waiting
to happen. One dirty knife or soiled bandage on the umbilical stump is all it
takes. Today neonatal tetanus accounts for over half of the more than
500,000 cases worldwide.

Although Eduardo had no visible signs of infection, at least somewhere   16
in his tissues there must be *C. tetani* pumping out toxin. Penicillin was in
order. The drug would wipe out the toxin-producing bacteria. And we hoped
the antitoxin—antibodies culled from horses or humans immunized against
tetanus—would intercept the poisons in his blood and prevent his symptoms
from getting worse.

Unfortunately, its effects were far from Lazarus-like. Eduardo remained   17
in the ICU for a full month, while the toxin was slowly leached from his spinal
cord and brain. I was hoping for a full recovery, but sometimes tetanus so
damages nerves that muscles are left permanently weakened. Even muscle re-
laxants, low lights, and tiptoeing doctors and nurses couldn't prevent Eduardo's spasms, so we paralyzed his muscles and put him on a ventilator.
Thankfully, he made it through.

Several weeks after his discharge from the hospital, I saw Eduardo at a   18
follow-up visit. He was still thin and leaning on a cane. When I greeted him
in the hall, he seemed to remember me.

"Tetanus vaccine?" he responded laconically to my first eager question. "I   19
don't remember any vaccines in the village where I grew up."

I made a mental note to ask our nurse to vaccinate him. Ironically, so lit-   20
tle toxin is released during an infection that even a full-blown case of tetanus
builds no immunity against future attacks.

"What about an injury?" I persisted. "Usually a wound precedes tetanus."   21

"Ah, the soccer game," he mused, "A few weekends before I started getting   22
stiff, something sharp went right through the sole of my shoe. Glass, I think."

I had one last question. "What was it like when you knew you were sick,   23
but everyone else thought you were crazy?"

"Sorry, he can't talk about that," his brother piped in. "Attorney's   24
orders."

I smiled. Only in America.   25

Questions for Discussion

1. Focus on two or three paragraphs you find especially effective.
   Identify concrete and specific nouns, vivid verbs, adjectives, and/or
   adverbs that reveal Dunavan's skill as a writer of description.

2. Science writers often make comparisons, draw analogies, and use metaphors and similes, especially when addressing nonscientific audiences. Where in paragraph 5 does Dunavan do this? Where else does she do this?

3. Another characteristic of scientific writing is that it contains definitions of terms with which readers might not be familiar, such as *risus sardonicus,* in paragraph 13. What other examples of definition do you find in this essay?

4. Science writing is noted for its objectivity. But in writing for nonscientific audiences, authors sometimes become subjective and reveal their excitement or concern. Find examples of subjective description in this essay.

5. You probably have read that writers often combine methods of development. Where does Dunavan use narration in this essay? Where does she explain causes and effects?

6. To what purpose does Dunavan use dialogue?

7. Why do you think that Eduardo was "weaving across lanes" (paragraph 2)?

8. Eduardo's jailers decided "to pack him off to the county hospital's psychiatric unit" (paragraph 2). How might this fact help describe the effects of tetanus?

9. Comment on the conclusion to this essay? Why is it or isn't it appropriate?

Thinking Critically

1. In paragraph 3, Dunavan begins to tell us about a woman suffering from peritonitis. If, as she says, "that's another story," why does she bother to mention this woman at all?

2. In paragraph 17, we find the term "Lazarus-like." Who was Lazarus? What does this simile mean? Try doing a little research in a concise encyclopedia or in the Bible to answer this one.

3. What is Dunavan's purpose in writing this essay? Is it different from Aronowitz's purpose in "A Brother's Dreams," another essay discussing an illness, which appears in Chapter 3?

Suggestions for Journal Entries

1. Use the clustering technique or other method of gathering information explained in "Getting Started" to record symptoms of a serious disease that you or someone you know has suffered. Don't limit yourself to physical ailments; psychological disorders such as anorexia nervosa, schizophrenia, or another emotional illness might also be an appropriate topic.

2. Consider an illness that is, unfortunately, too common among members of your generation, occupation, race, family, or community. List its causes, symptoms, and methods of treatment or prevention, if any.

3. Have you ever been "blindsided"? In other words, have you ever mistaken a person, thing, situation, or problem for what it was not? For example, you might have had a so-called friend who turned out to be just the opposite. You might have attended an event that fell far short of your expectations and that was hardly worth the money and time you spent attending. Have you ever followed a cause, a principle, or a leader who or which, in hindsight, turned out to be far less noble than you once thought? Have you ever tried to solve a problem only to find out that, all along, you had mistaken the cause of that problem? Use listing or freewriting to gather details that might explain how and why you were blindsided.

Suggestions for Sustained Writing

1. Read over the notes you made in response to both Suggestions for Journal Entries after Po's "Watching the Reapers." If you have not responded to both of these suggestions, do so now.

   Using description as your main method of development, write an essay in which you explain why you would or would not recommend that a good friend take a job at the place you have begun to describe in your journal. Before beginning your rough draft, try making an outline of your paper. For example, you might organize it in three sections, each of which covers a body paragraph or two. The first could describe the physical characteristics of the workplace itself. The second might focus on the kinds of activities—the work—that normally takes place there. The third might describe the people who work in or frequent the place.

   As you begin to draft your paper, remember that you are trying to answer a specific question: Would you recommend this job to a friend? If the answer is no, make sure you include sufficient negative details to support this view and vice versa. One way to introduce this essay is to address the reader directly, ask a question, or make a startling remark. A good way to end it is to restate or summarize some of the points you have made in the body of your essay or offer your reader advice.

   However you decide to proceed, make sure that you provide sufficient detail to make your argument convincing. Then, revise, edit, and proofread.

2. If you responded to the second Suggestion for Journal Entries after "Flavio's Home" by Gordon Parks, turn these notes into a full-length

essay that describes a place about which you have already gathered information. Begin by recording even more details about your subject. If you can, brainstorm with a fellow student who is also familiar with this place.

In the first draft, include details that paint an objective picture of your subject. Talk about the general layout, shape, or dimensions of the place, the colors of walls, ceilings, and floors, the kinds of furniture and other objects it contains. If you're writing about an outdoor place, mention trees, rocks, streams, bridges, park benches, walls, lampposts, and so on. In your next draft(s), add information about what the place looks, smells, and sounds like. If possible, make use of narration to re-create the kind of activity that normally occurs in this place and to introduce your readers to people who frequent it. In the process, begin revealing your subjective reactions. Use concrete details and vivid verbs, adjectives, and adverbs as well as figures of speech to let readers know what you think about this place and of the people you find there. Like Parks, do not be afraid to express your emotions.

After completing your second or third draft, write a thesis stating your overall opinion. Put this thesis in an introductory paragraph designed to capture the reader's attention. Close your essay with a memorable statement or summary of the reasons you are or are not planning to visit this place again. Finally, edit your work by checking grammar, spelling, and sentence structure.

3. If you read "If at First You Do Not See . . . ," follow Sullivan's lead: describe a place you know well by presenting two views of it. For example, one view might be negative, the other positive. Another way to proceed is to describe what newcomers see when they visit this place as opposed to what you see in it. A good place to describe might be your neighborhood or other part of your hometown, your high school or college campus, a run-down but beautiful old building, or the home of an interesting relative or friend.

Although your paper need not be as long as Sullivan's, it should use techniques like those found in hers. For example, appeal to the senses, include action, use figures of speech to create images, or describe the people who live in or frequent the place.

Check the journal entries you made after reading Sullivan's essay. They might help you get started. Once you have finished several drafts, write an introduction that captures the reader's attention and expresses your central idea in a formal thesis statement. Put the finishing touches on your writing by correcting errors that will reduce its effectiveness or distract your readers. Be sure all your spelling is correct.

4. The three journal suggestions following Gwinn's "A Deathly Call of the Wild" provide good starts for longer assignments.

If you responded to Suggestion 1, turn your notes into an essay about the effects of pollution on a natural setting you know well. Explain how civilization has marred or destroyed its beauty, and don't be afraid to give your subjective reaction to what you see, hear, and so on. A good way to begin is to use a startling remark or to contrast what *is* with what *should be*. A good way to conclude is to make a call to action.

If you responded to Suggestion 2 after Gwinn's essay, use this information to write about an incident in which you had to help an animal in trouble. Explain what happened, describing the animal and the scene vividly and concretely. Like Gwinn, however, focus on one thing: what you learned about the animal, about yourself, *or* about your relationship with nature. In fact, summarize what the experience taught you in your thesis statement.

If you responded to Suggestion 3, continue the description of a "wild" place by explaining how you reacted to being there. Again, express the central idea that all of your essay's details will support in a thesis statement. In other words, use your thesis to tell readers how you felt about the experience. Then, in the rest of the essay, include information about the place that will show why you felt that way.

Good luck. Any of these suggestions can lead to an exciting essay. Whichever one you choose, follow a careful process of revising and editing to produce a paper that is well developed, vivid, and free of errors.

5. Like Dunavan in "Blindsided by Tetanus," write an essay in which you discuss the causes, symptoms, and likely outcomes of a disease that you or someone you know well has suffered. Focus on the disease, not on the person. Before you begin, read the journal notes you made after reading Dunavan's essay. If you answered items 1 and/or 2 of the Suggestions for Journal Entries after this selection, you might have already gathered information to get you started.

Now, make an outline of your essay. Here's a sample on which you might want to base your outline:

I. **Introduction:** State the thesis and define the disease. Use one of the techniques for creating effective introductions explained in Chapter 4.

II. Describe the disease's most common symptoms. Appeal to the senses; use vivid verbs, adjectives, and adverbs.

III. Explain the disease's causes. Use concrete/specific nouns, vivid verbs.

IV. Discuss likely outcomes. Explain how it can be treated or cured if possible. If it can't be treated, explain how it develops.

V. **Conclusion:** Explain methods of prevention, if any. Then end your essay by looking to the future, one of the methods for concluding explained in Chapter 4.

Before you begin (or at any stage in the writing process), find more information about the disease you are discussing by researching it in a medical or standard encyclopedia or on the Internet. If you incorporate any information from an outside source, use direct quotations or prepare a summary or paraphrase in your own words. In addition, don't forget to give your sources credit through internal citations and a Works Cited page. You can learn more about how to do this by reading the Appendix to this text, which explains Modern Language Association (MLA) methods for citing sources.

Writing to Learn: A Group Activity

If you read Po Chü-i's "Watching the Reapers," you got a view of labor abuses in ninth-century China. What about such abuses in today's world?

THE FIRST MEETING

Ask each member of the group to find and summarize at least two articles on child labor practices around the world. If this topic doesn't interest your group, try researching subjects such as the enforcement of the minimum wage in the United States, the use and abuse of illegal aliens in U.S. manufacturing, the presence of sweatshops at home and abroad, or even the use of slave labor. Then again, you might ask for suggestions from your English professor or from professors of economics, political science, labor law, history, or business.

Ask each student to focus on a particular aspect of the topic you have chosen. For example, one or two might search for information on child labor practices in Central and South America; others might research child labor in China, Thailand, or another Asian country; one might find material on this subject as it relates to the United States.

RESEARCH

Find articles on the Internet, via the *Readers' Guide to Periodical Literature,* or in one of your library's electronic databases by searching for phrases such as:

Child labor

Child labor laws

Child labor—Central America

Child labor—working conditions

Child labor—imported products

Try to find articles that reveal abuses of children in the work place and that explain what is being done or should be done to eliminate these evils. Make photocopies for every group member.

THE SECOND MEETING

Distribute copies of articles you collected. Read each aloud, with one student recording the most important ideas of each. Then, as a group, agree on an outline for a paper that will list and discuss what you agree are the worst examples of the abuse of child labor that you can find. Call this paper A.

Next, make an outline for paper B, which will list and discuss solutions to the problems in paper A. (You might take some of these solutions from your reading, but you might think of some yourselves.)

Assign half the group to draft paper A, the other half to draft paper B. Make copies for every group member.

THE THIRD MEETING

Distribute copies of both drafts. Discuss them and recommend adding or deleting information, reorganizing paragraphs, rewriting sentences, and making any other content or stylistic changes necessary. Be sure the organization of paper B conforms to that of paper A. In other words, the first solution in paper B should respond directly to the first problem in paper A.

Assign two people to act as editors, one for each paper. Ask them to edit, retype, and proofread these documents before submitting them to your instructor.

CHAPTER 9

Describing People

In Chapter 8 you learned that writers often go beyond physical appearance when describing a place or thing; they reveal its character as well. This is even more true when people are the subjects of description. Writers describe gardens at dawn, summer festivals, or dirty subway stations because they are impressed by what that they see, hear, and so on. More often than not, they describe human beings because they are fascinated by their personalities, values, and motivations as well as by their looks and the sounds of their voices. Of course, many writers start by describing physical appearance—what's on the outside. But they often end up talking about their subjects' characters— what's on the inside.

All the authors represented in this chapter use concrete and specific details (nouns and adjectives) to describe the physical characteristics of their subjects. This is always a good way to begin. You can start off by explaining something about your subjects' physical appearance, the clothes they wear, the sound of their voices, the language they use, or simply the way they walk. Such description might also help you introduce your subjects' personalities to your readers, for someone's physical appearance can reveal a great deal about what he or she is like inside.

You can also communicate a great deal about the people you're describing by telling your readers what you've heard about them from others and even what you've heard them say about themselves; such information is usually conveyed through dialogue (quoted material). Recalling anecdotes about your subjects is still another good way to convey important information about them. Finally, some authors comment directly on their subjects' personalities or use figurative language to make their descriptions more lively and appealing. Remember such techniques when you gather and communicate important information about your subjects.

Describing Your Subject's Appearance and Speech

Physical appearance can show a great deal about a person's character, and writers don't hesitate to use outward details as signs or symbols of what's inside. For instance, how often have you heard people mention deep-set, shifty eyes or a sinister smile when describing a villain? Aren't heavy people often described as jolly? And often, aren't the clothes people wear or the way they comb their hair seen (fairly or unfairly) as a sign of their character?

In "Oma: Portrait of a Heroine," an essay in this chapter, student writer Maria Scamacca describes her subject's appearance to introduce her character:

> When I first met Oma six years ago, she looked about eighty years old, was a few pounds over-weight for her medium frame, and was slightly hunched over. She wore a flowered house dress, a starched white apron, and old, scuffed leather loafers. Oma was deaf in one ear from a neglected childhood ear infection, and half of her face drooped from Bell's palsy. She shuffled her feet and held on to furniture with swollen, scarred hands as she walked.

Another good way to provide insight into someone's personality is to recall what he or she says. Barry Shlachter in his essay later in this chapter makes us aware of Mother Teresa's optimism and faith when he quotes her as having said: "Where there is tragedy, there is salvation. Even when the mother cries, the child finds happiness. It is eternal."

Revealing What You Know about Your Subject

You have learned that narrating events helps capture the character or atmosphere of a place you are describing. Similarly, you can reveal a lot about someone by discussing his or her actions or behavior. One of the best ways to do this is by telling anecdotes, brief stories that highlight or illustrate an important aspect of your subject's personality. For example, Barry Shlachter in "Charisma Fortified by 'Chutzpah' " demonstrates Mother Teresa's ability to inspire others by telling a brief story about her directing relief efforts in a town devastated by a cyclone. Anecdotes like this help us understand how someone reacts to various people, problems, and situations. They say a lot about a person's attitude toward life.

Another good way to reveal character is to tell readers important facts about your subject's life, home, or family. In "Two Gentlemen of the Pines," for example, we learn that Bill's parents abandoned him as a child and that, except for some help from neighbors, he survived alone. This information goes a long way toward accounting for his shyness. In the same selection, we are treated to a good look at the house and yard of Fred Brown, a picture that gives us an understanding of the old man's character beyond learning how he looks and talks.

Revealing What Others Say about Your Subject

One of the quickest ways to learn about someone is to ask people who know this individual to tell you about his or her personality, lifestyle, morals, disposition, and so on. Often, authors use dialogue or quotations from other people to reveal something important about their subject's character. In "Crazy Mary," student Sharon Robertson combines physical description (concrete details) with information she learned from other people (dialogue) to create a memorable and disturbing portrait of an unfortunate woman she once knew:

> She was a middle-aged woman, short and slightly heavy, with jet-black hair and solemn blue eyes that were bloodshot and glassy. She always looked distant, as if her mind were in another place and time, and her face lonely and sad. We called her "Crazy Mary."
>
> Mary came to the diner that I worked in twice a week. She would sit at the counter with a scowl on her face and drink her coffee and smoke cigarettes. The only time she looked happy was when an old song would come on the radio. Then Mary would close her eyes, shine a big tobacco-stained smile, and sway back and forth to the music.
>
> One day an elderly couple came in for dinner. They were watching Mary over their menus and whispering. I went over to their table and asked if they knew who she was. The old man replied, "Aw, dat's just old Mary. She's loonier than a June bug, but she ain't nutten to be afraid of. A few years back, her house caught fire and her old man and her kids got kilt. She ain't been right since."
>
> After hearing this, it was easy to understand her odd behavior.

Other people can make good sources of information. We know from experience, however, that what others say about a person is often inaccurate. Sometimes, in fact, different people express very different—even contradictory—opinions about the same person. For example, what you think about a particular relative, friend, or classmate might differ from the reaction of other people who know that person just as well. Consider how differently supporters and critics of a particular politician or entertainer view their subject. Today, of course, President Abraham Lincoln enjoys the greatest respect among historians and the public alike. When he was alive, however, opinions about him differed; he was seen as a rustic frontiersman by some people, as a crafty tyrant by others, and as an embattled defender of human rights by still others.

Visualizing Details That Describe People

The two short selections that follow use techniques important to describing people. The first, by Dr. Richard Selzer, describes the physical appearance of an AIDS patient in Haiti. The second, by Jade Snow Wong, describes the personality of a man who works in a factory that is run by the author's family and that doubles as their home.

"Miracle" by Richard Selzer

Uses specific details: nouns, adjectives.

A twenty-seven-year-old man whose given name is Miracle enters. He is wobbly, panting, like a groggy boxer who has let down his arms and is waiting for the last punch. He is neatly dressed and wears, despite the heat, a heavy woolen cap. When he removes it, I see that his hair is thin, dull reddish and straight. It is one of the signs of AIDS in Haiti. . . . The man's skin is covered with a dry itchy rash. Throughout the interview and examination he scratches himself slowly, absentmindedly. The rash is called prurigo. It is another symptom of AIDS in Haiti. The telltale rattling of the tuberculous moisture in his chest is audible without a stethoscope. He is like a leaky cistern [tank for liquid] that bubbles and froths.

Uses simile to describe appearance.

Uses vivid adjectives

Conveys action.

Appeals to hearing.

Uses a simile to create an image.

"Uncle Kwok" by Jade Snow Wong

Recalls a recurring action that tells us about Kwok's personality.

After Uncle Kwok was settled in his chair, he took off his black, slipperlike shoes. Then taking a piece of stout cardboard from a miscellaneous pile which he kept in a box near his sewing machine, he traced the outline of his shoes on the cardboard. Having closely examined the blades of his scissors and tested their sharpness, he would cut out a pair of cardboard soles, squinting critically through his inaccurate glasses. Next he removed from both shoes the cardboard soles he had made the day before and inserted the new pair. Satisfied with his inspection . . . he got up . . . disposed of the old soles, and returned to his machine. He had not yet said a word to anyone.

Uses vivid adjectives/adverb to create an image.

Reveals an important aspect of his personality.

Daily this process was repeated. . . .

The next thing Uncle Kwok always did was to put on his own special apron, homemade from double thicknesses of heavy burlap and fastened at the waist by strong denim ties. This long apron covered his thin, patched trousers and protected him from dirt and draft. After a half hour had been consumed by these chores, Uncle Kwok was ready to wash his hands. He sauntered into the Wong kitchen, stationed himself at the one sink which served both family and factory, and with characteristic meticulousness [care], now proceeded to clean his hands and fingernails.

Describes his clothing as a clue to his personality.

Uses a vivid verb.

It was Mama's custom to begin cooking the evening meal at this hour . . . . but every day she had to delay her preparations at the sink until slow-moving Uncle Kwok's last clean fingernail passed his fastidious

Recalls an action to describe Kwok.

[close] inspection. One day, however, the
inconvenience tried her patience to its
final limit.

> Trying to sound pleasantly persuasive,
> she said, "Uncle Kwok, please don't be so
> slow and awkward. Why don't you wash your
> hands at a different time, or else wash them
> faster?"

Explains what someone else thinks of Kwok.

> Uncle Kwok loudly protested . . . "Mama,
> I am not awkward. The only awkward thing
> about my life is that it has not yet
> prospered!" And he strode off, too hurt even
> to dry his hands, finger by finger, as was
> his custom.

Allows Kwok to reveal himself in his own words.

Revising Descriptive Essays

Below are the rough and final drafts of paragraphs from Maria Scamacca's "Oma: Portrait of a Heroine," an essay that describes her husband's grandmother. The complete essay can be found in this chapter. Scamacca knew she was onto something when she wrote a rough draft, and she felt she owed her subject her best effort. Therefore, she revised her essay several times, making excellent use of the descriptive techniques discussed in this and in the previous chapter. If you still have doubts about the importance of revising, compare these two drafts.

Scamacca—Rough Draft

How old? How much over-weight?

> When I first met Oma, she looked very old
> and a bit over-weight. Some wore a house
> dress, an apron, and loafers. She was deaf
> in one ear, and there was something wrong
> with the muscles in her face. Oma shuffled
> when she walked and had to hold on to the
> furniture. Despite her disability, and the

Add details?

What was wrong?

Good, but make more vivid?

fact that she lived alone, Oma's house
looked neat, but there were signs that her
eyes had become weak.

*Clarify?
What signs?*

. . .

Oma was born in Hungary. She was an only

What days? child—rare in those days. Her mother died
when she was in her teens, and she was left
alone. At eighteen, she married a widower
with a young daughter; the couple eventually
had three other children. They lived on a
farm near the Romanian border. Farm life was
hard, but Oma took to it well. In addition
to cooking and housekeeping, she did other
chores. She often told me how she force-fed
geese by stuffing balls of bread down their
long necks.

*Does this
information
reveal her
personality?*

Scamacca—Final Draft

*Provides
specifics;
makes
description
more
accurate,
vivid.*

When I first met Oma six years ago, she
looked about eighty years old, was a few
pounds over-weight for her medium frame, and
was slightly hunched over. She wore a
<u>flowered</u> house dress, a <u>starched</u> <u>white</u>
apron, and <u>old</u>, <u>scuffed</u> <u>leather</u> loafers. Oma

*Shows
what was
wrong.*

was deaf in one ear from a <u>neglected</u>
<u>childhood</u> <u>ear</u> <u>infection</u>, and half of her
face <u>drooped</u> from <u>Bell's</u> <u>palsy</u>. She shuffled
her feet and held on to the furniture with
<u>swollen</u>, <u>scarred</u> <u>hands</u> as she walked.
Despite Oma's disability and the fact that

*Adds specific
details.*

*Explains kind of
childhood she had.*

*Add vivid
details.*

she lived alone, her house looked neat, but

there were small crumbs and stains on the

tables, and particles of food were stuck to

some of the dishes, unnoticed by eyes

weakened with age.

Substitutes details to clarify what was meant by "signs" that her eyes had become weak.

. . .

Oma was born in Hungary. She was an only

child—rare in the <u>early days of this</u>   *Explains "those days."*

<u>century</u>—the only surviving baby of four

pregnancies. Her mother died when Oma was in

her teens, and she was left alone to <u>keep</u>

<u>house for her father</u>. At eighteen, she

Shows that she has been a hard worker from childhood.

married a widower with a young daughter; the

couple eventually had three other children.

Author has added so much information about Oma's personality that she must create two paragraphs.

They lived on a farm near the Romanian

border on which they grew and raised all

their food, even the grapes from which they

made their own wine.

Adds detail to show she is self-sufficient.

Farm life was hard, but Oma took to it

well. In addition to cooking and

housekeeping, she had to tend to the horses

and other farm animals, bake bread, make

sausage, and salt the meats the family would

Adds concrete details that make ideas more convincing.

eat year round. Oma was fond of telling me

how she force-fed geese by stuffing balls of

bread down their long necks with her

fingers. Her geese got so fat they couldn't

fly, but they brought the best prices at the

market, <u>she often reminds me</u>.

Allows Oma to speak for herself, to reveal her pride.

Practicing Techniques That Describe People

1. Write a paragraph that describes your physical appearance. Include
    details that appeal to the senses, and try to use figures of speech. Be
    specific about your height, weight, hair color, eye color, and so on. Write
    the rough draft on scratch paper. Put your final draft on the lines below.

    _____

    _____

    _____

    _____

    _____

    _____

    _____

    _____

2. Write a paragraph that describes your best or worst quality. For example,
    discuss your patience or impatience, your tolerance or lack of tolerance
    for differences in people, your ambition or laziness, or your knack for
    making or losing friends. Show readers what you mean by using
    examples and by recalling what others have said about you. Write the
    rough draft on scratch paper. Put your final draft on the lines below.

    _____

    _____

    _____

    _____

    _____

    _____

    _____

    _____

3. How do others see you? Write a paragraph that explains how someone
    you know well would describe your best or worst quality. Focus on only
    one aspect of your personality. Use any of the techniques for describing
    what you have learned so far. Write the rough draft on scratch paper. Put
    your final draft on the lines below.

    _____

    _____

———————————————————————————

———————————————————————————

———————————————————————————

———————————————————————————

———————————————————————————

———————————————————————————

———————————————————————————

———————————————————————————

Enjoy the selections that follow. Each contains examples of the practices discussed on the previous page, and each provides additional hints to help you make your writing stronger and more interesting.

Photograph of My Father in His Twenty-Second Year

Raymond Carver

Born in Clatskanie, Oregon, Raymond Carver (1938–1988) was a writer of fiction and poetry and winner of several major literary prizes including a National Book Award. He taught English and creative writing at UCLA, the University of Iowa Writer's Workshop, the University of Texas at El Paso, Syracuse University, and Goddard College in Vermont. He is best remembered for Cathedral, *a collection of short stories that was nominated for a Pulitzer Prize. His last work was* A New Path to the Waterfall, *a book of poetry completed just before he died.*

Preparing to Read

1. This is both a physical and psychological portrait. Try to figure out what the physical details that Carver includes tell us about his father's personality.
2. At the end of the poem, Carver reveals things about himself. Ask yourself why he does this.

Vocabulary

bluff (adjective)	Confident, arrogant.
cocked (adjective)	Tilted or turned up.
dank (adjective)	Damp, humid.
hearty (adjective)	Robust, cheerful.
perch (noun)	Freshwater fish.
posterity (noun)	Descendants, future generations.

Photograph of My Father in His Twenty-Second Year

Raymond Carver

October. Here in this dank, unfamiliar kitchen
I study my father's embarrassed young man's face.
Sheepish grin, he holds in one hand a string
of spiny yellow perch, in the other
a bottle of Carlsbad beer.

5

In jeans and denim shirt, he leans
against the front fender of a 1934 Ford.

He would like to pose bluff and hearty for his posterity,
wear his old hat cocked over his ear.
All his life my father wanted to be bold.   10

But the eyes give him away, and the hands
that limply offer the string of dead perch
and the bottle of beer. Father, I love you,
yet how can I say thank you, I who can't hold my liquor either,
and don't even know the places to fish?   15

Questions for Discussion

1. What details does Carver reveal about his father's appearance?
2. Which of these details tell us about his personality?
3. In certain places, Carver interprets the picture from his own point of view. In line 2, for example, he describes his father's face as "embarrassed." Find other places where he does this.
4. Why is it important for us to know what Carver's father is holding?
5. What do we learn about Carver's father in line 14?
6. What has the information in line 15 to do with Carver's father?

Thinking Critically

1. Why can't Carver thank his father? What else can we conclude from this short poem about the relationship between the poet and his father?
2. Why does Carver bother to tell us that the kitchen was "dank" and "unfamiliar"?

Suggestions for Journal Entries

1. Study a photograph of yourself that is at least three years old. Use listing to gather information that will help describe the kind of person you were when the photograph was taken.
2. Study a photograph of a member of your family or a close friend. Use listing or answer the journalists' questions to record information about this person's appearance and character. (The journalists' questions begin with "who," "when," "what," "where," "why," or "how.")

Two Gentlemen of the Pines*

John McPhee

A productive writer with a wide range of interests, John McPhee has been a long-time essayist for The New Yorker. *Among his books are* Rising from the Plains *(1986) and* The Control of Nature *(1989). One of the things McPhee does best is to describe the human character. His portraits of people he meets on his travels are among the most memorable in contemporary American literature. McPhee ran into two of his most interesting subjects on a trip through New Jersey's Pine Barrens, a wilderness whose name he used as the title of a book from which this selection is taken.*

Preparing To Read

1. You know that we can learn a lot about people from what they say. This is very true of Fred, the first of McPhee's subjects, but less true of Bill. Nonetheless, the little that Bill lets slip out provides good clues to his personality.

2. McPhee describes the setting in which he meets his subjects; doing so helps enrich their portraits.

3. Think about the use of "gentlemen" in the title as you read this selection.

Vocabulary

cathode-ray tubes (noun)	Television picture tubes.
dismantled (adjective)	Taken apart.
eyelets (noun)	Holes through which laces can pass.
gaunt (adjective)	Lean, thin, angular.
mallet (noun)	Heavy hammer with a short handle.
poacher (noun)	Someone who uses another's land to hunt or fish there illegally.
thong (noun)	Strip of leather used as a lace.
turfing it out (noun)	Digging out the top layer of soil and grass.
understory (noun)	Underbrush.
undulating (adjective)	Changing, varying, fluctuating.
vestibule (noun)	Small room at the entrance to a building.
visored (adjective)	Having a long brim that shades the sun.

---

*Editor's title.

Two Gentlemen of the Pines

John McPhee

FRED BROWN'S HOUSE is on an unpaved road that curves along the edge of a   1
wide cranberry bog. What attracted me to it was the pump that stands in
his yard. It was something of a wonder that I noticed the pump, because
there were, among other things, eight automobiles in the yard, two of them
on their sides and one of them upside down, all ten years old or older.
Around the cars were old refrigerators, vacuum cleaners, partly dismantled
radios, cathode-ray tubes, a short wooden ski, a large wooden mallet, dozens
of cranberry picker's boxes, many tires, an orange crate dated 1946, a cord or
so of firewood, mandolins, engine heads, and maybe a thousand other things.
The house itself, two stories high, was covered with tarpaper that was peeling
away in some places, revealing its original shingles, made of Atlantic white
cedar from the stream courses of the surrounding forest. I called out to ask if
anyone was home, and a voice inside called back, "Come in. Come in. Come
on the hell in."

I walked through a vestibule that had a dirt floor, stepped up into a   2
kitchen, and went on into another room that had several overstuffed chairs in
it and a porcelain-topped table, where Fred Brown was seated, eating a pork
chop. He was dressed in a white sleeveless shirt, ankle-top shoes, and undershorts. He gave me a cheerful greeting and, without asking why I had come
or what I wanted, picked up a pair of khaki trousers that had been tossed
onto one of the overstuffed chairs and asked me to sit down. He set the
trousers on another chair, and he apologized for being in the middle of his
breakfast, explaining that he seldom drank much but the night before he had
had a few drinks and this had caused his day to start slowly. "I don't know
what's the matter with me, but there's got to be something the matter with
me, because drink don't agree with me anymore," he said. He had a raw
onion in one hand, and while he talked he shaved slices from the onion and
ate them between bites of the chop. He was a muscular and well-built man,
with short, bristly white hair, and he had bright, fast-moving eyes in a wide-
open face. His legs were trim and strong, with large muscles in the calves. I
guessed that he was about sixty, and for a man of sixty he seemed to be in remarkably good shape. He was actually seventy-nine. "My rule is: Never eat
except when you're hungry," he said, and he ate another slice of the onion.

In a straight-backed chair near the doorway to the kitchen sat a young   3
man with long black hair, who wore a visored red leather cap that had dark-
ened with age. His shirt was coarse-woven and had eyelets down a V neck
that was laced with a thong. His trousers were made of canvas, and he was
wearing gum boots. His arms were folded, his legs were stretched out, he had
one ankle over the other, and as he sat there he appeared to be sighting carefully past his feet, as if his toes were the outer frame of a gunsight and he
could see some sort of target in the floor. When I had entered, I had said

hello to him, and he had nodded without looking up. He had a long, straight nose and high cheekbones, in a deeply tanned face that was, somehow, gaunt. I had no idea whether he was shy or hostile. Eventually, when I came to know him, I found him to be as shy a person as I have ever had a chance to know. His name is Bill Wasovwich, and he lives alone in a cabin about half a mile from Fred. First his father, then his mother left him when he was a young boy, and he grew up depending on the help of various people in the pines. One of them, a cranberry grower, employs him and has given him some acreage, in which Bill is building a small cranberry bog of his own, "turfing it out" by hand. When he is not working in the bogs, he goes roaming, as he puts it, setting out cross-country on long, looping journeys, hiking about thirty miles in a typical day, in search of what he calls "events"—surprising a buck, or a gray fox, or perhaps a poacher or a man with a still. Almost no one who is not native to the pines could do this, for the woods have an undulating sameness, and the understory—huckleberries, sheep laurel, sweet fern, high-bush blueberry—is often so dense that a wanderer can walk in a fairly tight circle and think that he is moving in a straight line. State forest rangers spend a good part of their time finding hikers and hunters, some of whom have vanished for days. In his long, pathless journeys, Bill always emerges from the woods near his cabin—and about when he plans to. In the fall, when thousands of hunters come into the pines, he sometimes works as a guide. In the evenings, or in the daytime when he is not working or roaming, he goes to Fred Brown's house and sits there for hours. The old man is a widower whose seven children are long since gone from Hog Wallow, and he is as expansively talkative and worldly as the young one is withdrawn and wild. Although there are fifty-three years between their ages, it is obviously fortunate for each of them to be the other's neighbor.

Questions for Discussion

1. What do details about Fred's and Bill's physical appearances say about them?

2. Think about the way the older man welcomes his visitor. How do such actions reveal his character?

3. The original shingles on Fred's house are made of cedar "from the stream courses of the surrounding forest" (paragraph 1). In what way is this and other information about the house helpful to understanding Fred?

4. Does Fred's claiming there is "something the matter" with him explain the way he views himself?

5. Bill says he goes into the woods in search of "events." What are these events? Should the author have used a synonym for this word instead of quoting Bill directly? Why or why not?

Thinking Critically

1. Why is it important for us to learn about Bills' childhood? In a short paragraph that uses information from "Two Gentlemen of the Pines," explain how learning about Bill the child helps us to understand Bill the man.

2. Pretend that you accompanied McPhee into the pines. What would have been your reaction to Fred and Bill? Reread this selection and make notes in the margins to explain what you might have said or done in response to various events you read about. For example, how would you have reacted to meeting Fred in his undershorts?

Suggestions for Journal Entries

1. As this selection shows, we can learn a lot about people from the places they call home. Use listing to begin describing a place you consider your own: your room, your kitchen, your garage, the inside of your car, for example. You might even describe a place—public or private, indoors or out of doors—that you enjoy visiting. Gather details that show how this place reflects your personality or that explain what draws you to it time and again.

2. Have you ever taken a trip and come upon strangers you found interesting because they were different from most people you know? Use focused freewriting to explain why they captured your attention.

3. McPhee accounts for Bill's shyness by explaining that his parents abandoned him. Do you know someone who experienced an event or set of circumstances that marked his or her personality? Interview this person; learn what in his or her past contributed to a particular characteristic or personality trait. Say your great uncle is thrifty. When you interview him, you find that he was orphaned at age eight, that he lived many years in poverty, and that he is afraid of being poor again. Good subjects for this assignment include anyone with a distinctive personality trait and a willingness to talk about his or her past.

Oma: Portrait of a Heroine

Maria Scamacca

Maria Scamacca graduated from college with a degree in nursing and is now a critical-care registered nurse at a large hospital. "Oma: Portrait of a Heroine" was written in a freshman composition class in response to an assignment that asked students to describe people they found inspiring. After reading Scamacca's essay, it is easy to understand why she chose to write about Oma.

Preparing to Read

1. *Oma* means grandmother in Hungarian. *Opa* means grandfather.
2. You have learned that description and narration often appear together. Here, stories from Oma's life help shed light on her character.
3. Scamacca mentions events from twentieth-century history. During World War II (1939–1945), the Germans conquered much of eastern Europe but were pushed back by the Soviets. At the war's end, Hungary, Romania, East Germany, and other eastern nations became Soviet satellites. In the Korean War (1950–1953), American troops formed the bulk of a United Nations force that defended South Korea from communist North Korea and China.

Vocabulary

black market (noun)   Underground commercial system in which banned or stolen goods are sold or traded.
compensation (noun)   Payment.
displaced (adjective)   Forced to move.
equivalent (noun)   The equal of.
humane (adjective)   Kind, charitable, benevolent.
implores (verb)   Begs.
palsy (noun)   Paralysis.
provisions (noun)   Necessities, supplies.

Oma: Portrait of a Heroine

Maria Scamacca

WHEN I FIRST met Oma six years ago, she looked about eighty years old, was a few pounds over-weight for her medium frame, and was slightly hunched over. She wore a flowered house dress, a starched white apron, and

1

old, scuffed leather loafers. Oma was deaf in one ear from a neglected childhood ear infection, and half of her face drooped from Bell's palsy. She shuffled her feet and held on to the furniture with swollen, scarred hands as she walked. Despite Oma's disability and the fact that she lived alone, her house looked neat, but there were small crumbs and stains on the tables, and particles of food were stuck to some of the dishes, unnoticed by eyes weakened with age.

That's why I was shocked when she led me through the back door to a   2
garden that she boasted of planting and maintaining alone. It was like no garden I had ever seen, an acre of food and beauty. Ready to be picked and eaten were neat and orderly rows of potatoes, carrots, asparagus, onions, peppers, lettuce, lima beans, and string beans. Her garden also boasted strawberries, blueberries, gooseberries, currant, peach trees, watermelons, and many other fruits. And there were flowers everywhere: zinnias, day lilies, marigolds, irises, and petunias. I sensed immediately that this paradise was the creation of a unique energy, courage, and beauty I came to see in Oma.

Each year the impossible garden yields bushels of fruits and berries for   3
the jams and jellies that Oma cooks and jars herself. She also cans fruit and vegetables, and she uses the fruit in the fillings of luscious pastries that, as I was to learn, have made her famous among friends, family, and neighbors. She still does all of her own cooking and had been known, until only recently, to throw holiday dinners for more than twenty people.

From the day I met Oma, I grew to admire her and have looked forward   4
to visiting. Almost every Sunday after church, my husband's family and I gather around her dining room table for fresh coffee, homemade Prinz Regent Torte (a seven-layer cake), Schwarzwälder Kirschtorte (Black Forest cherry cake), warm cookies, and good talk.

Oma dominates the conversation, filling us with stories of her childhood   5
and of World War II; she hardly stops to take a breath unless one of us asks a question or implores her to translate the frequent German or Hungarian phrases that pop out of her mouth. At such times, we play guessing games as Oma tries to explain in broken English a word or expression for which she knows no English equivalent.

Oma was born in Hungary. She was an only child—rare in the early days   6
of this century—the only surviving baby of four pregnancies. Her mother died when Oma was in her teens, and she was left alone to keep house for her father. At eighteen, she married a widower with a young daughter; the couple eventually had three other children. They lived on a farm near the Romanian border on which they grew and raised all their food, even the grapes from which they made their own wine.

Farm life was hard, but Oma took to it well. In addition to cooking and   7
housekeeping, she had to tend to the horses and other farm animals, bake bread, make sausage, and salt the meats the family would eat year round. Oma is fond of telling me how she force-fed geese by stuffing balls of bread down their long necks with her fingers. Her geese got so fat they couldn't fly, but they brought the best prices at the market, she often reminds me.

Her family also raised their own pigs. But when it came time to slaughter the animals, her husband, Opa, asked his neighbor to do it. In return, Opa slaughtered the neighbor's pigs. "He felt bad, you know, killing his own pig," Oma said. At times, Oma and Opa hired outside help, whom they paid with bread and salted meat, but they did most of the work themselves, and they prospered.

8

Then the war came. First her horses were stolen by Russian soldiers. Then the family was removed from their farm, and Oma found herself in a Russian concentration camp. The stories from this period of her life are confusing. I have heard bits and pieces of them repeatedly over the past six years, and I have had to reconstruct them myself. Once in a while I ask Oma to clarify the order of events, but she doesn't get very far until she starts an entirely new story.

9

After the war, the borders of countries were redrawn, and Oma's family was displaced with only a few hours' notice. Allowed to take only the clothes on their backs and whatever they could carry, they were put into a cattle car on a long freight train. The new government provided no compensation for their land and told them to leave all of their possessions behind. The only explanation was that their family had originally come from Germany and that they were required to leave Hungary and return to the land of their ancestors. This was not punishment, the authorities explained; it was "humane displacement."

10

Before they boarded the train, the family had to collect enough grain and other provisions to feed themselves during the long trip. But they saw little of their food; Oma thinks it was stolen and sold on the black market. "There were no bathrooms on the train," Oma explained. "If someone had to defecate or urinate, they were held by others out of the open doors over the side of the moving train. And they call that humane!"

11

When they arrived in Germany, Oma and her family were placed in a room in a run-down building that had holes in the walls and was full of rats. Her husband developed pneumonia. Sick for months, he almost lost the will to live and just lay in bed. When he finally recovered, they moved to America, but they had to leave their daughter behind because she had tuberculosis. Oma still weeps openly whenever she recalls being forced to abandon her child. Luckily, however, things turned out well for "Tante Vicki," who still lives in Germany and now has a family of her own.

12

In time, the family settled in Millstone, New Jersey, and began to build a new life in what was then a small rural community. In the early 1950s, however, Oma and Opa lost their oldest son in the Korean War, so when the other two boys married and moved out of the house, the two old people were on their own.

13

Several years ago, Opa died of lung cancer contracted from many years of working in an asbestos factory. Oma continues to receive a good pension and health benefits from his employer. They come in handy, for over the past few years she has been hospitalized several times. Last summer she got so sick she couldn't even plant her garden, so all of her grandchildren got together to plant it for her. That is the only request she has ever made of them.

14

It is hard to see a woman who was once so strong grow old and weak. At 15 times, Oma feels quite useless, but she can still tell wonderful stories, and we listen avidly. I wonder if there will be a garden this year.

Questions for Discussion

1. What is Scamacca's thesis?
2. Where does the author use details that describe Oma's physical appearance? Do any of these details provide hints about her character?
3. Explain what two or three incidents from Oma's life tell us about her personality.
4. What does Oma reveal about herself?
5. Why does Scamacca tell us about Opa in paragraphs 8 and 12? How does this information help describe Oma?
6. This essay makes fine use of concrete and specific details. Pick out such details in at least two paragraphs.
7. What techniques for writing introductions does Scamacca use? (Review Chapter 4 if you need to.)
8. What technique for writing conclusions does she use? (Review Chapter 4 if you need to.)
9. In Oma, the author sees "energy, courage, and beauty." In what ways is Oma beautiful?

Thinking Critically

1. If you were able to meet Oma, what would you ask her about her life? As you reread this essay, write questions to her in the margins of the text when they occur to you. Then do some creative guessing. On the basis of what you know about Oma, answer your questions in a paragraph or two.
2. Pretend that the government has decided to take almost everything you own and to send you to another country. Would you resist? If so, how? If not, how would you prepare for this drastic change?
3. Reread Maria Cirilli's "Echoes" in Chapter 1. In what ways is this essay similar to Scamacca's? In what ways are these essays different?

Suggestions for Journal Entries

1. Do you have an older relative, friend, or neighbor whose attitude toward life you consider heroic? Choose your own definition of the

word *heroic.* Freewrite for about five minutes about an event from this person's life that might show his or her heroism.

2. Interview the person mentioned above. Try to find out more about his or her attitude toward life. A good way to do this is to ask your subject to tell you about a difficult or depressing time and to explain how he or she dealt with it. Record your subject's comments as accurately as you can; use direct quotations when appropriate.

3. Brainstorm with one or two others who know the person mentioned above. Try to gather facts, direct quotations, and opinions that you could use in a paper that describes your subject as heroic.

Charisma Fortified by "Chutzpah"

Barry Shlachter

Barry Shlachter is a reporter for the Star Telegram *in Forth Worth, Texas. For more than a decade, he worked as a correspondent for the Associated Press, a service that provides news stories to papers around the world, in both Asia and Africa. Shlachter met, interviewed, and has written about Mother Teresa, the subject of this piece, on several occasions. Mother Teresa was born in Macedonia but left her homeland to join an Irish order of Roman Catholic nuns and eventually dedicated her life to serving the poor, the homeless, and the defenseless. She died at the age of 87 on September 5, 1997, in Calcutta, India.*

Preparing to Read

1. Indira Ghandi, mentioned in paragraph 3, was the prime minister of India until her assassination in 1984. Eva Peron was the wife of Argentine dictator Juan Peron. Eva enjoyed a great deal of political power until her death of cancer at age 33 in 1954.

2. *Charisma* means personal warmth, charm, allure, or appeal. The word is often associated with political leaders. *Chutzpah* is a Yiddish word meaning courage and determination. It too is rarely used when speaking of religious leaders, but both terms capture Shlachter's vision of Mother Teresa and play important roles in his title and central idea.

3. "Fortified" is also an important word in the title. Consider its meaning as you read on.

Vocabulary

aimlessly (adverb)	Without purpose or plan, disorganized.
bureaucrats (noun)	Government officials.
clerics (noun)	Priests, nuns, or other members of the clergy.
cynical (adjective)	Critical, skeptical.
epiphany (noun)	Awakening, realization.
fended off (verb)	Fought off, avoided.
habit (noun)	Nun's attire, clothing.
hospice (noun)	Place where terminally ill are cared for.
indifferent (adjective)	Unconcerned, apathetic.
sari (noun)	Indian dress.
understated (adjective)	Subtle.
unfazed (adjective)	Undisturbed.
vestige (noun)	Trace.

Charisma Fortified by "Chutzpah"

Barry Shlachter

S HE WAS A tiny woman who spoke remarkably simple words. Yet Mother
Teresa used that unadorned speech to bend the will of indifferent bureaucrats, cynical journalists and at least one of the world's most despised tyrants.

I know. I watched her.

If she had gone into politics instead of missionary work, I thought after
first meeting her after a 1977 cyclone in India, she would have put an Indira
Ghandi or an Eva Peron to shame. That thought was reinforced upon seeing
her again two years later when she won the Nobel Peace Prize and during the
1984 Ethiopian famine.

Few could resist this woman in the home-spun sari-like habit. Born in
what is now Macedonia of ethnic Albanian parents, she came to India with an
Irish order, became a naturalized Indian and founder of her own Missionaries
of Charity at a time when foreign clerics were seen as an unwanted vestige of
the colonial era. Ministering to the poorest of Calcutta's poor, she won national, then world, fame for her selfless work.

On a stretch of coastal road in south India, she once came upon a group
of government doctors stranded when their vehicle broke down. After she
spoke to them briefly, they unanimously volunteered to join her cyclone relief effort, abandoning their own assignments.

"It's hard to say 'no' to a living saint," explained a relief official who knew
her, a Hindu like the majority of Indians. "Few are left unaffected by her
charisma," a priest told me. It was that understated charisma, fortified with
well-intentioned chutzpah, that helped bring about what she invariably called
"God's miracles."

Her caravan of trucks and cars made its way to Mandapakala, once a
prosperous farming community flattened by the storm. It was piled with
corpses that day Mother Teresa arrived to supervise relief operations. Methodically, she issued instructions on the disposal of bodies, a health hazard
to the living.

"The best thing would be to build a single long trench and lay the bodies
in a file," she crisply told members of her order and a crowd of volunteers she
had attracted along the way. "That, we discovered, was the simplest method
when the floods took their toll in Jalpaiguri in Bengal last year."

Many of the survivors wandered aimlessly about the village or picked
through rubble in search of a pot to hold water or boil rice. A woman called
to Mother Teresa, pointing to her only surviving family member, a 6-year-
old deaf mute, and asked: "What will I do with him? Is he worth anything?"
The boy approached the nun and played with her wooden rosary. Mother
Teresa gathered him in her arms and the child, unable to speak, gurgled
with delight.

"See," she told the distraught mother. "The child is happy."

Turning to those accompanying her, the nun said: "Where there is 11 tragedy, there is salvation. Even when the mother cries, the child finds happiness. It is eternal."

In Ethiopia, I witnessed two small "miracles" during a visit by Mother 12 Teresa—and those were aside from all the life-saving efforts by her missionaries among the starving.

Toward the end of my second or third stint in Ethiopia, an Associated 13 Press colleague based in Zimbabwe flew up to relieve me. The late John Edlin was something of a legend in Africa press circles. A hard drinking New Zealander, he had lost count of the times his wife had thrown him out. Sent to cover Sen. Ted Kennedy's famine tour, Edlin was too pickled to dictate more than two paragraphs each night of what was a major story.

Then he met Mother Teresa.   14

It was an epiphany for Edlin. At first, he considered chucking his job to 15 handle her order's press relations in Ethiopia. (Mother Teresa did this all too well on her own.) In the end, the tough Kiwi became an overnight humanitarian who quietly set up and financed an orphanage for children who lost their parents in the famine. Then he returned to reporting.

If the 1984 drought was of biblical proportions, so was the raw cruelty of 16 the country's dictator, Col. Mengistu Haile Mariam. His Marxist regime killed an estimated 150,000 people, while Mengistu is widely believed to have personally strangled his predecessor, Emperor Haile Selassie.

It is well known that the country's Jews, known as Falasha, were perse- 17 cuted. But Mengistu was equally brutal toward a Lutheran-linked church and to practicing Roman Catholics, said my best source in Addis Ababa, the papal nuncio (the Vatican ambassador). Ordinary people were terrified of Mengistu and would not utter his name.

Unfazed, Mother Teresa requested a meeting with the dictator, telling re- 18 porters she would ask him to hand over the late emperor's palace for use as a hospice. She didn't get the palace, but to the amazement of everyone I ran across, she received a piece of land smack in the middle of the capital.

For a journalist, interviewing Mother Teresa about herself was a task. 19 Not that she fended off such encounters; she just wouldn't say much about herself. Instead, she'd speak of miracles, large and small, that materialized, thanks to God, when they were needed most.

"It's His work, not mine," she told me at the Calcutta home for the desti- 20 tute and dying after winning the 1979 Nobel Peace Prize. "God is our banker, He always provides." She recalled a day at the home when "we found we had nothing, not a single piece of bread to give our people."

"You know what happened? For some mysterious reason, all the schools 21 suddenly closed that day and their bread was sent to us," she said.

"Now who else but God could have done that?"   22

Joe DiMaggio: The Silent Superstar

Paul Simon

Paul Simon (1941) is a musician and composer who has written, performed, and recorded songs that have become classics of American popular music. Simon worked with Art Garfunkel from 1967–1971 to produce award-winning albums such as The Sounds of Silence *(1966);* Parsley, Sage, Rosemary and Thyme *(1968); the soundtrack from* The Graduate *(1968); and* Bridge over Troubled Water *(1972). Simon's subsequent works include* Still Crazy After All These Years *(1975) and* Graceland *(1986), both of which won Grammy Awards.*

Joseph Paul DiMaggio (1914–1999), a native of North Beach, California, played centerfield for the New York Yankees from 1936 to 1951. One of the best fielders and hitters ever to play the game, DiMaggio was named the American League's Most Valuable Player in 1939, 1941, and 1947. He hit safely in 56 straight games in 1941, a record that remains unbroken 60 years later. Sportswriter George Vecsey called him a "staggering blend of power and self-control." He hit 361 home runs but struck out only 369 times in his 16-year career. Many people say that DiMaggio was the best that baseball had to offer. But he was more than a super-athlete. "The Yankee Clipper" was an American hero. The ultimate professional, he was a model for young people, someone to whom they could look for inspiration and example. He stood for values that seem to be rare today, not only in professional sports, but any-where. DiMaggio had integrity, humility, and respect for others. And, in turn, he earned and kept the respect of the American people. After he retired from baseball, he became president of the Mr. Coffee Corporation, for which he ap-peared in television commercials. In the 1970s, he was named in a public sur-vey the most trustworthy person on television. Joe DiMaggio was a gentle, hon-orable, and good man. To the aging baseball fan who is writing this, he will always be a hero.

Preparing to Read

1. Read a little about the life and career of Joe DiMaggio on the Internet or in a sports encyclopedia.
2. Simon mentioned DiMaggio in "Mrs. Robinson," a song featured in *The Graduate* (1967). The film criticizes the kinds of contemporary American values that are in complete opposition to those DiMaggio embraced. If you haven't yet seen *The Graduate*, borrow or rent a video copy
3. In paragraph 10, Simon mentions Mother Teresa and Jeffrey Dahmer. An essay on Mother Teresa appears earlier in this chapter. An essay on Jeffrey Dahmer appears in Chapter 5.

Vocabulary

alluded (verb)	Made an indirect reference.
anointed (adjective)	Divinely chosen, consecrated (here used metaphorically).
antithesis (noun)	Complete opposite.
attribution (noun)	Assignment of.
befouls (verb)	Soils, dirties.
deconstructed (adjective)	Analyzed to such an extent that it loses all meaning.
deify (verb)	Turn into a god.
distortion (noun)	Misrepresentation, falsification.
enthralled (verb)	Enchanted, held spellbound.
icon (noun)	Symbol.
iconoclastic (adjective)	Rebellious, ignoring the rules.
iconographic (adjective)	Relating to images of a hero, legend, or god.
idolatry (noun)	Worship of statues or images (here used metaphorically).
malice (noun)	Ill will, hatred.
neurotic (adjective)	Overly anxious, emotionally off-balance.
petty (adjective)	Mean-spirited, selfish.
scrutinized (adjective)	Analyzed, examined closely.
transgressions (noun)	Sins.
trepidation (noun)	Fear, nervousness.

Joe DiMaggio: The Silent Superstar

Paul Simon

MY OPINIONS REGARDING the baseball legend Joe DiMaggio would be of no particular interest to the general public were it not for the fact that 30 years ago I wrote the song "Mrs. Robinson," whose lyric "Where have you gone Joe DiMaggio, a nation turns its lonely eyes to you" alluded to and in turn probably enhanced DiMaggio's stature in the American iconographic landscape.

A few years after "Mrs. Robinson" rose to No. 1 on the pop charts, I found myself dining at an Italian restaurant where DiMaggio was seated with a party of friends. I'd heard a rumor that he was upset with the song and had considered a lawsuit, so it was with some trepidation that I walked over and introduced myself as its composer. I needn't have worried; he was perfectly cordial and invited me to sit down, whereupon we immediately fell into conversation about the only subject we had in common.

"What I don't understand," he said, "is why you ask where I've gone. I just did a Mr. Coffee commercial, I'm a spokesman for the Bowery Savings Bank and I haven't gone anywhere."

I said that I didn't mean the lines literally, that I thought of him as an American hero and that genuine heroes were in short supply. He accepted the explanation and thanked me. We shook hands and said good night.

Now, in the shadow of his passing, I find myself wondering about that explanation. Yes, he was a cultural icon, a hero if you will, but not of my generation. He belonged to my father's youth: he was a World War II guy whose career began in the days of Babe Ruth and Lou Gehrig and ended with the arrival of the youthful Mickey Mantle (who was, in truth, my favorite ballplayer).

In the 50's and 60's, it was fashionable to refer to baseball as a metaphor for America, and DiMaggio represented the values of that America: excellence and fulfillment of duty (he often played in pain), combined with a grace that implied a purity of spirit, an off-the-field dignity and a jealously guarded private life. It was said that he still grieved for his former wife, Marilyn Monroe, and sent fresh flowers to her grave every week. Yet as a man who married one of America's most famous and famously neurotic women, he never spoke of her in public or in print. He understood the power of silence.

He was the antithesis of the iconoclastic, mind-expanding, authority-defying 60's, which is why I think he suspected a hidden meaning in my lyrics. The fact that the lines were sincere and that they've been embraced over the years as a yearning for heroes and heroism speaks to the subconscious desires of the culture. We need heroes, and we search for candidates to be anointed.

Why do we do this even as we know the attribution of heroic characteristics is almost always a distortion? Deconstructed and scrutinized, the hero turns out to be as petty and ego-driven as you and I. We know, but still we anoint. We deify, though we know the deification often kills, as in the cases of Elvis Presley, Princess Diana and John Lennon. Even when the recipient's life is spared, the fame and idolatry poison and injure. There is no doubt in my mind that DiMaggio suffered for being DiMaggio.

We inflict this damage without malice because we are enthralled by myths, stories and allegories. The son of Italian immigrants, the father a fisherman, grows up poor in San Francisco and becomes the greatest baseball player of his day, marries an American goddess and never in word or deed befouls his legend and greatness. He is "the Yankee Clipper," as proud and masculine as a battleship.

When the hero becomes larger than life, life itself is magnified, and we read with a new clarity our moral compass. The hero allows us to measure ourselves on the goodness scale: O.K., I'm not Mother Teresa, but hey, I'm no Jeffrey Dahmer. Better keep trying in the eyes of God.

What is the larger significance of DiMaggio's death? Is he a real hero? Let me quote the complete verse from "Mrs. Robinson":

Sitting on a sofa on a Sunday afternoon
Going to the candidates' debate
Laugh about it, shout about it
When you've got to choose

Every way you look at it you lose.
Where have you gone Joe DiMaggio
A nation turns its lonely eyes to you
What's that you say Mrs. Robinson
Joltin' Joe has left and gone away.

In these days of Presidential transgressions and apologies and prime-time 13
interviews about private sexual matters, we grieve for Joe DiMaggio and
mourn the loss of his grace and dignity, his fierce sense of privacy, his fidelity
to the memory of his wife and the power of his silence.

Questions for Discussion

1. Why doesn't Simon describe DiMaggio's appearance?
2. Where in the essay does the author use examples to define
   DiMaggio's character?
3. In paragraph 9, we learn that DiMaggio was "as proud and masculine
   as a battleship." Where else does Simon use figurative language?
4. What does the author mean by "moral compass" (paragraph 10)? In
   what way did DiMaggio fit that definition?
5. In paragraph 7, Simon tells us what DiMaggio was not. How does
   doing this help to define him?
6. Reread paragraph 2. What clues do you see about the kind of man
   Simon is about to describe?
7. Why does Simon bring up Elvis Presley, John Lennon, and Princess
   Diana in paragraph 8? How was DiMaggio different from these
   people?
8. In paragraph 9, we read that DiMaggio "never in word or deed
   befouls his legend and greatness." Explain why this statement might
   serve as the essay's thesis.

Thinking Critically

1. Besides DiMaggio's character and athletic ability, what caused the
   public to admire him so much? (Reread paragraph 7.)
2. Consider the essay's title. In what way is "silent" a synonym for
   "humble"? In what way did DiMaggio's silence actually announce his
   professionalism and integrity?
3. DiMaggio was nicknamed "Joltin' Joe" and "the Yankee Clipper."
   Look up the term "Yankee Clipper" in an encyclopedia or unabridged
   dictionary. In what ways might that metaphor apply to a baseball
   player? What is the double meaning of the word "clipper"?

Suggestions for Journal Writing

1. Think of a public figure you consider to be a "moral compass"— perhaps an athlete; a priest, minister, or rabbi; a public servant or politician; someone who has served in the military; an artist; a medical researcher; a scientist or doctor; the head of a charitable or public-service organization; or a philanthropist (someone who raises and gives money to charity). Gather information about this person's life, the difficult choices he or she has had to make, the hardships he or she has faced, and the goals he or she has achieved. Your purpose is to prove that the way this individual has conducted his or her life can serve as a model for others. Use library and/or Internet research to gather information about this individual, or interview a professor who is familiar with your subject.

2. If, as Simon believes, DiMaggio represented "the values of . . . America" in the 1940s and 50s, in what ways might the America of those decades be different from today's America? Use clustering, listing, or freewriting to record your responses. If possible, interview someone who lived during those decades to find out more about American culture and values as they existed then.

Suggestions for Sustained Writing

1. Describe someone you know by focusing on the strongest or most important feature of his or her personality. Here's an example of a preliminary thesis statement for such an essay: "When I think of Millie, what comes to mind first is her faith in people."

    As you draft the body of your essay, tell of something in your subject's past that accounts for this characteristic. For example, explain that Millie has had an unshakable faith in the goodness of people ever since, as a child, she lost her parents and was raised by neighbors. Then, give examples of that faith. Use what you have learned about Millie from personal experience, from people who know her, or from Millie herself. Tell one or two anecdotes (brief, illustrative stories) to convince readers that what you say is true.

    A good way to learn more about the person you are describing is to interview him or her. Take accurate notes. When it comes time to write your essay, try quoting your subject directly; use his or her own words to explain how he or she feels. Examples of how to put direct quotations into your work appear in McPhee's "Two Gentlemen of the Pines." In fact, if you responded to the journal suggestions after this selection, you may already have gotten a fine start on the assignment.

Revise your paper as often as necessary. Make sure it includes enough information and is well organized. As part of the editing process, check that you have used quoted material correctly. If you have doubts, speak with your instructor.

2. The journal suggestions after Carver's "Photograph of My Father in His Twenty-Second Year" asked you to make notes about a photograph of a close friend or family member or of yourself. If you responded to either suggestion, turn your notes into an essay.

Before you begin, review your journal notes, then add details that come to mind as you are reading them. If possible, interview another person who knows your subject well and ask him or her to provide information and quotations that might help describe your subject's character. This is essential if the picture is of you.

Begin drafting by describing the physical appearance of your subject. Like Carver, you might also describe the setting. Then, use this information as a spring-board to discussing your subject's personality. For example, Carver says his father wore "his old hat cocked over his ear" as a sign of his desire to be "bold."

Read your rough draft carefully. As you revise, try to narrate events that might reveal your subject's character. Include quotations and figures of speech when possible. Double-check word choice when you edit your paper for grammar, spelling, and other matters. A good way to introduce this essay is with a startling remark or a question. A good way to conclude it is by using an anecdote or quotation that will stick in readers' minds.

3. Maria Scamacca writes about a brave woman, who has suffered from war, illness, and the loss of children. Do you know people who have faced hardship and disappointment? What do their reactions tell you about their characters?

Describe one such person by explaining how he or she reacts to difficulty and disappointment. Tell interesting facts from his or her personal history to help readers understand the strength (or weakness) of your subject's character. In addition, explain what other people think of this individual, quote him or her directly, or use anecdotes to tell readers about the way he or she faces misfortune.

Summarize the information you have gathered in a thesis statement that expresses your feelings about this person. Of course, you don't need to place the thesis at the very beginning of your essay. Put it anywhere it fits, even at the end. In fact, you can open your first draft simply by describing physical appearance. If you do this, however, try to follow Scamacca's example: choose details that show what your subject looks like and that provide clues to his or her character.

In any case, before you get started, look over the journal entries you made after reading "Oma: Portrait of a Heroine." Then, go through the process of writing systematically. Never remain satisfied with an early draft; for best results, always rewrite and edit.

4. If you haven't done so yet, respond to all three of the Suggestions for Journal Entries after Scamacca's "Oma: Portrait of a Heroine." Now, write an essay that explains to readers why you think the subject you are writing about is heroic.

Narrate events from your subject's life that will show his or her heroism, but also try to include comments—perhaps direct quotations— from your subject and from people who know him or her well. Like Scamacca, you might want to start by describing your subject's physical appearance or by taking readers on a tour of his or her home. Just make sure this information contains clues to your subject's character.

As you go through the revision process, improve word choice by substituting vivid verbs and adjectives as well as concrete, specific nouns for any less effective language. Try creating figures of speech when appropriate. As always, edit and proofread your work.

5. Reread the journal entries you made after reading Barry Shlachter's "Charisma Fortified by 'Chutzpah.' " Then, expand these notes into a full-length essay.

If you responded to the first suggestion you will be describing a person you consider an example for others to follow. To gather more information, discuss our subject with mutual friends, interview your subject directly, or recall anecdotes (brief stories) containing facts to support your belief that this person should be looked up to.

Use the notes you made in response to the second suggestion for journal writing to write an essay explaining how an epiphany (revelation) changed the life or character of someone you know. Like many good papers describing people, yours can rely on anecdotes as well as direct quotations. Begin by explaining what brought on this epiphany. In the rest of your paper, compare your subject's life or character after the epiphany to what it was before.

Whichever topic you choose, begin by making at least a rough outline. Then, go through the writing process carefully, making sure to revise several times and to edit carefully.

6. Review the notes you made after responding to the first journal suggestion after Simon's "Joe DiMaggio: The Silent Superstar." If you have not yet responded to this, do so now. Turn your notes into an essay that explains why the subject you have chosen to describe is a "moral compass" or model for the rest of us. Focus on the hardships this individual has had to overcome, the goals he or she has attained, the things he or she has done for others, and the strengths of character that enabled him or her to accomplish all these things. Write the first draft of your paper by

using the information you have already gathered. As you revise this draft, however, include any new details and ideas that come to mind as you are composing. You might also want to complete more Internet or library research or to interview people who know something about your subject.

7. Most people send friends and relatives store-bought greeting cards on their birthdays. Try something different. Write a birthday letter to a friend or relative whom you love and admire. Begin with a standard birthday greeting if you like. But follow this with four or five well-developed paragraphs that explain the reasons for your love and admiration. Use your knowledge of your reader's past—what you have learned firsthand or heard from others—to recall anecdotes that support your opinion. In other words, show what in his or her character deserves love and admiration.

Not everything you say in this letter has to be flattering. In fact, this is a good chance to do some mild kidding. So, don't hesitate to poke good-natured fun at your reader—and at yourself—as a way of bringing warmth and sincerity to your writing. Just remember that your overall purpose is positive.

This assignment is different from most others. Nonetheless, it demands the same effort and care. In fact, the more you love or admire your reader, the harder you should work at revising and editing this tribute.

Writing to Learn: A Group Activity

You have read Shlachter's essay on Mother Teresa in this chapter. Some say that Mother Teresa should be declared a saint. Whether or not this occurs, few can dispute the fact that this tiny nun was an example of unselfishness worthy of imitation.

THE FIRST MEETING

Assign each student to research another great humanitarian. Here's a list of some figures some might want to learn more about:

Clara Barton	Martin Luther King, Jr.
Carlos Costa	Florence Nightingale
Father Flanagan	Albert Schweitzer
Mohandas Gandhi	Raoul Wallenberg
Dolores Hope	

Of course, you might choose your own subjects. As a matter of fact, one of you might find information on an organization such as the Red Cross, the Red Crescent, Save the Children, or Doctors without Borders. Just make sure that each student researches a different subject.

RESEARCH

Search for information on the Internet, in your library's book catalog, or in a CD or online database for periodicals and newspapers. If you are researching a person, summarize important events in his or her life and list significant contributions he or she has made. If you are researching an organization, define the group's objective and report on the work it is doing. As always, make photocopies of your notes for distribution at your group's next meeting.

THE SECOND MEETING

After distributing copies of everyone's notes, ask each student to explain what he or she discovered. Make recommendations for further research, especially to students whose notes need greater detail. Then ask everyone to turn his or her notes into one or two well-developed, well-organized paragraphs whose purpose it is to prove that his or her subject is an example of humanitarianism. Ask group members to bring photocopies of their work to the next meeting.

THE THIRD MEETING

Distribute and read the paragraphs each group member has brought. Then, ask one person to organize these paragraphs into a coherent essay that defines the term *humanitarianism* by using the subjects your group wrote about as examples. Assign a second person to write an introduction (complete with thesis statement) and a conclusion to this essay. Assign still another to revise and edit it. Finally, ask one other person to type and proofread the final version before submitting it to your instructor.

Narration

The selections in the two chapters of this section have a great deal in common. Their most basic and most obvious similarity is that they tell stories. They do this through *narration,* a process by which events or incidents are presented to the readers in a particular order. Usually, this is done in chronological order, or order of time.

The logical arrangement of events in a story is called its *plot.* Often, writers begin by telling us about the first event in this series, the event that sets the whole plot in motion. And they usually end their stories with the last bit of action that takes place.

But this is not always the case. Where a writer begins or ends depends on the kind of story he or she is telling and the reason or purpose for telling it. Some stories begin in the middle or even at the end and then recall what happened earlier. A good example is Wagner's "Death of an Officer" in Chapter 10. Other stories are preceded or followed by information the author thinks is important. For instance, in Chapter 11, Carl Sagan introduces a story about Frederick Douglass by explaining that children born into slavery were often separated from their parents, a fact significant to events that follow in the essay.

More than 2,300 years ago, the Greek philosopher Aristotle taught that a narrative must have a beginning, a middle, and an end. In other words, a successful story must be complete. It must contain all the information a reader will need to learn what has happened and to follow along easily. That's the most important idea to remember about writing effective narratives, but there are several others you should keep in mind.

Determining Purpose and Theme

Narration can be divided into two types: fiction and nonfiction. Works of nonfiction recount events that actually occurred. Works of fiction, though sometimes based on real-life experiences, are born of the author's imagination and do not re-create events exactly as they happened.

Many nonfiction stories are written to inform people about events or developments that affect or interest them. Newspaper or magazine articles, such as Gaye Wagner's "Death of an Officer" (Chapter 10), are perfect examples. This type of writing is also used by scientists to explain natural processes as they occur step by step over time. In fact, narration can explain complex ideas or make important points about very real situations. Adrienne Schwartz's "The Colossus in the Kitchen" (Chapter 11), for instance, tells a true story that illustrates the evil and stupidity of apartheid, the political system whose effects Schwartz witnessed in South Africa.

Therefore, many narratives are written to dramatize or present an important (central) idea, often called a *theme*. They portray life in such a way as to reveal something important about people, human nature, society, or life itself. At times, this theme is stated in a *moral,* as in Aesop's fables, the ancient Greek stories that teach lessons about living. More often than not, however, the theme or idea behind a story is unstated or implied. It is revealed only as the plot unfolds. In other words, most stories speak for themselves.

As a developing writer, one of the most important things to remember as you sit down to write a narrative is to ask yourself whether the story you're about to tell is important to you in some way. That doesn't mean you should limit yourself to narrating events from personal experience only, though personal experience can often provide just the kind of information you'll need to spin a good yarn. It does mean the more you know about the people, places, and events you're writing about and the more those people, places, and events mean to you, the better able you'll be to make your writing interesting and meaningful to your readers.

Finding the Meaning in Your Story

As explained above, you won't always have to reveal why you've written your story or what theme it is supposed to present. You can allow the events you're narrating to speak for themselves. Often, in fact, you won't know what the theme (central idea) of your story is or why you thought it important until you're well into the writing process. Sometimes, you won't know that until after you've finished.

But that's just fine, for writing is a voyage of discovery. It helps you learn things about your subject (and yourself) that you would not have known had you not started the process in the first place. *Just write about something you find interesting and believe is important.* This is the first step in telling a successful story. You can always figure out why your story is important or what theme you want it to demonstrate later in the process, when you write your second or third draft.

Deciding What to Include

In most cases, you won't have much trouble deciding what details to include. You'll be able to put down events as they happened or at least as you remember them. However, in some cases—especially when you are trying to present a particular theme or idea—you'll have to decide which events, people, and so on should be emphasized or talked about in great detail, which should be mentioned only briefly, and which should be excluded from the story altogether.

In "The Day I Was Fat" (Chapter 10), for example, Lois Diaz-Talty's purpose is to explain how an insult she suffered actually improved her life. The event occurred while she was driving her children to a pool. Of course, the author could have included many different facts about the trip, but she chose to include only those related directly to the insult and its effect on her life.

Making Your Stories Lively, Interesting, and Believable

Once again, good stories dramatize ideas or themes. They do this through actions and characters that seem vivid and interesting, as if they were alive or real.

One of the best ways to keep your readers' interest and to make your writing vivid is to use verbs effectively. More than any other part of speech, verbs convey action. They tell *what happened.* It's important to be accurate when reporting an incident you've experienced or witnessed. You ought to recapture it exactly as you remember and without exaggeration. However, good writing can be both accurate and interesting, both truthful and colorful. You can achieve this balance by choosing verbs carefully.

In "Mid-Term Break" (Chapter 10), for example, the speaker says that his mother "*coughed* out angry tearless sighs." Of course, he could have said that she was so angry she couldn't cry, but that would not have shown us the emotional torture she experienced.

Using adverbs—words that describe verbs, adjectives, and other adverbs—can also make your writing more emphatic, specific, and interesting. Consider these two lines from Pickering's "Faith of the Father" (Chapter 11): " . . . Miss Ida was shy. She read poetry and raised guinea fowl and at parties sat *silently* in a corner. Only on Easter was she outgoing: then like a day lily she bloomed *triumphantly.* . . ."

A good way to make your writing more interesting and believable is to include proper nouns—names of specific persons, places, and things—which will help readers feel they are experiencing the story as they read it. In "Death of an Officer" (Chapter 10), Gaye Wagner writes that the officer's "funeral procession filled the three miles from *Jack Murphy Stadium* to the church with bumper-to-bumper police units. . . . Police cars came from *San Diego,* the *Border Patrol,* the *U.S. Marshals, El Cajon, La Mesa, Chula Vista, National City, Riverside, Los Angeles,* seemingly everywhere."

Showing the Passage of Time

Of course, the most important thing in a story is the plot, a series of events occurring in time. Writers must make sure that their plots make sense, that they are easy to follow, and that each event or incident flows into the next logically.

A good way to indicate the passage of time is to use transitions or connectives, the kinds of words and expressions used to create coherence within and between paragraphs. In his popular essay about future trips to outer space, Kenneth Jon Rose uses a number of such transitional devices (in italics) as he explains what it might be like to leave the earth on a tourist shuttle to the stars. Notice how they keep the story moving and make it easy to follow:

> [While] *looking out your window,* you'll see the earth rapidly falling away, and
> the light blue sky progressively turning blue-black. You'll *now* be about
> 30 miles up, traveling at about 3000 mph. *Within minutes,* the sky will ap-
> pear jet black, and only the fuzzy curve of the earth will be visible. *Then,*
> at perhaps 130 miles above the surface of the earth and traveling at
> 17,000 mph, engines will shut down and . . . you'll become weightless.
> ("2001: Space Shuttle")

If you want to refresh your memory about other effective transitional devices to use in your writing, turn back to Chapter 2.

Describing Setting and Developing Characters

Establishing the setting of your story involves describing the time and place in which it occurs. You've probably done some of that in response to the assignments in Chapter 8, "Describing Places and Things." Developing characters involves many of the skills you practiced in Chapter 9, "Describing People."

In general, the more you say about the people in your narrative and about the time and place in which it is set, the more realistic and convincing it will seem to your readers. And the more they will appreciate what it has to say. Remember that your purpose in writing a narrative is to tell a story. But the kind of characters who inhabit that story and the kind of world in which it takes place can be as interesting and as important to your readers as the events themselves.

As you probably know, an important narrative element is dialogue, the words a writer allows people in the story to speak. You can use dialogue to help reveal important aspects of someone's personality, to describe setting, and even to relate events that move the plot along. In fact, several authors whose selections follow allow their characters to explain what happened or to comment on the story's action in their own words. Usually, such comments are quoted *exactly*—complete with grammatical errors and slang expressions. So, try letting your characters speak for themselves. They may be able to tell your readers a lot about themselves, about other characters, and about the narratives in which they appear.

CHAPTER 10

Personal Reflection and Autobiography

Though different in style and content, the selections in this chapter are similar because they are written in the first person. This is the point of view from which the authors have chosen to tell their stories. In first-person narration, the storyteller, also known as the narrator, participates in the action and recalls the events from his or her personal perspective.

When writers reveal things about other people's lives or talk about events in which they were not involved, they often rely on third-person narration and use the pronouns *he, she, it,* and *they* to explain who did what in the story. Examples of this kind of writing can be found in Chapter 11, "Reporting Events." However, all the selections in Chapter 10 are intended to reveal something important about the lives or personalities of their storytellers. That's why they can be classified as personal reflection or autobiography and are written from the first-person point of view, using the pronouns *I* or *we*.

Visualizing Details and Techniques Important to Personal Reflection and Autobiography

This paragraph from Ralph Ellison's "Battle Royal" recalls a strange event in which Ellison and nine other young black men were made to fight one another blindfolded. The scene is a fight ring in the middle of a hotel ballroom filled with spectators—including "some of the most important men of the town"—anxious to see faces bruised and bloodied. The young fighters are just entering the ring. (Other parts of this story appear later in this chapter.)

We were rushed up to the front of the *Describes setting.* ballroom, where it smelled even more

Shows time passing. strongly of tobacco and whiskey. Then we were pushed into place. I almost wet my

Shows his fear. pants. A sea of faces, some hostile, some amused, ringed around us, and in the center, *Chooses words carefully* facing us, stood a magnificent blonde—stark

Describes setting. naked. There was dead silence. I felt a

345

blast of cold air chill me. I tried to back
away, but they were behind me and around me. *Describes others in the story.*
Some of the boys stood with lowered heads,
trembling. I felt a wave of irrational guilt
Uses action to convey his feelings. and fear. My teeth chattered, my skin turned
to goose flesh, my knees knocked. Yet I was
strongly attracted and looked in spite of
myself. Had the price of looking been *Emphasizes his curiosity.*
blindness, I would have looked. The hair was
yellow like that of a circus kewpie doll,
the face heavily powdered and rouged, as
though to form an abstract mask, the eyes
Shows his subjective reaction. hollow and smeared a cool blue, the color of
a baboon's butt. I felt a desire to spit on
her. I wanted at one and the same time to
run from the room, to sink through the
Shows his conflicting emotions. floor, or go to her and cover her from my
eyes and the eyes of the others. . . .

Revising Autobiographical Essays

Later in this chapter you will read Lois Diaz-Talty's "The Day I Was Fat," which explains how this nursing student turned a painful insult into an occasion for self-reflection. It is no accident that the story is so vivid, convincing, and meaningful. Diaz-Talty revised and edited her work carefully and repeatedly. Compare a few paragraphs from one of her early drafts with those from her final draft.

Diaz-Talty—Rough Draft

I was headed to the pool with Mary Gene and
the children, and I got into an argument   *Who is Mary Gene?*
with a teenager driving behind our car. He

More detail about how he did this?

nearly <u>ran us off the road</u>. I <u>showed my</u>
<u>disapproval</u>, and we began yelling at each
other. He was about 18, with rotten teeth.

How did you show it?

When did this occur?

He pulled into the pool's parking lot behind
us; our argument became heated. Turning to
his friend, he said, "She's fat!"

Is that all? Did more take place?

Once inside the gates to the pool, my
friend advised me to forget the whole
incident. "He was gross," she said.

Will this convince the readers?

But I couldn't get his words out of my
mind. Nobody had ever called me fat before,
and it hurt terribly. But it was true.

On that very day, as I sat at the pool
praying that nobody would see me in my
bathing suit, I promised myself that no one
would ever call me fat again.

Diaz-Talty—Final Draft

Makes time reference.

One summer afternoon <u>in 1988</u>, as I was
headed to the pool with my <u>sister-in-law</u>
Mary Gene and our children, I got into an

Identifies Mary Gene.

Adds details to explain how he "nearly ran us off the road."

argument with a teenager who was driving
fast and tail-gaiting our car. When he
nearly ran us off the road, I turned around
and <u>glared</u> at him to show my disapproval and
<u>my concern for our safety</u>. Suddenly, we

Explains how she showed disapproval. Provides more information.

Explains when this happened.

began yelling at each other. He was about
18, with an ugly, red, swollen face. The few
teeth he had were yellow and rotten. He

followed us to the pool and, as he pulled into the parking lot behind us, our argument became heated.

"What's your problem, bitch?" he screamed.

"You drive like an idiot! That's my problem, okay?"

Adds an effective verb.

When I got out of the car and walked around to get the baby, he <u>laughed</u> to his friend, "Ah, look at 'er. She's fat! Go to hell, fat bitch." And then they drove away.

Adds details and direct quotations to re-create the argument.

Expands Mary Gene's response.

Once inside the gates to the pool, my sister-in-law advised me to forget the whole incident.

"Come on," she said. "Don't worry about that jerk! Did you see his teeth? He was gross."

Captures author's thoughts through direct quotation.

Paragraph is now more convincing.

But I couldn't get his words out of my mind. They stung like a whip. "I'm fat," I thought to myself. "I haven't just put on a few pounds. I'm not bloated. I don't have baby weight to lose. I'm just plain fat." Nobody had ever called me fat before, and it hurt terribly. But it was true.

Adds sentences to explain the

On that very day, as I sat at the pool praying that nobody would see me in my bathing suit, I promised myself that no one would ever call me fat again. That hideous, 18-year-old idiot had spoken the words that

importance
of what just
happened.

none of my loved ones had had the heart to

say even though they were true. Yes, I was

fat.

Practicing Skills of Personal Reflection and Autobiography

Here are two more paragraphs from Ralph Ellison's "Battle Royal." Practice your skills by following the instructions for each paragraph below.

1. In this first paragraph, underline effective words or phrases, especially vivid verbs, adjectives, and adverbs.

   A glove smacked against my head. I pivoted, striking out stiffly as someone went past. . . . Then it seemed as though all nine of the boys had turned upon me at once. Blows pounded me from all sides while I struck out as best I could. So many blows landed upon me that I wondered if I were not the only blindfolded fighter in the ring. . . .

2. Important words have been removed from this second paragraph. Replace them with words of your own. Use only the kinds of words indicated. Avoid *is, are, was, were, have been, had been,* and other forms of the verb *to be.*

   I could no longer control my emotions. I had no dignity. I _____ about

_{VERB}

   like a baby or a drunken man. The smoke had become _____ and with

_{ADJECTIVE}

   each new blow it seemed to _____ and _____ my lungs. My

_{VERB} _{VERB}

   saliva _____ like hot bitter glue. A glove _____ my head,

_{VERB} _{VERB}

   filling my mouth with _____ blood. A blow landed _____ against

_{ADJECTIVE} _{ADVERB}

   the nape of my neck. I felt myself going over, my head hitting the floor. Streaks

   of _____ light filled the _____ world behind the blindfold. I lay

_{ADJECTIVE} _{ADJECTIVE}

   _____ pretending I was knocked out, but felt myself seized by hands

_{ADVERB}

   and _____ to my feet. "Get going, black boy!" My arms were like

_{ADJECTIVE}

   _____; my head _____ from blows. I managed to feel my way

_{NOUN} _{VERB}

to the ropes and held on. A glove landed in my mid-section, and I went over

_____, feeling as though the smoke had become a knife _____
   ADVERB   ADJECTIVE

into my guts. Pushed this way and that by the legs milling around me, I

_____ pulled erect and discovered that I could see the black, sweat-
TRANSITION

washed forms weaving in the blue-smokey atmosphere like _____
                                                                       ADJECTIVE

dancers weaving to the _____ drum-like thuds of the blows.
                                             ADJECTIVE

The reading selections that follow are powerful personal statements about the people who speak through them and the worlds they inhabit. Read them carefully. They may inspire you to create articulate and convincing statements about yourself and your world.

Mid-Term Break

Seamus Heaney

Seamus Heaney (1939–   ) was born in County Derry in Northern Ireland. The son of a farmer, Heaney took a B.A. at Queen's University in Belfast and then began teaching in secondary school. He is now professor of poetry at Oxford University in England and has been a visiting lecturer at Harvard University and at the University of California. Called the greatest living Irish poet, Heaney has won many awards including the Nobel Prize for literature (1995), the most prestigious honor a writer can receive. His poems focus on the land, people, and history of Northern Ireland. Some of his works also discuss the political and religious turmoil that have plagued his country. Collections of Heaney's poetry include Field Work *(1979),* Station Island *(1984), and* The Hero Lantern *(1987).*

Preparing to Read

1. What does the title tell us about the speaker of this poem?
2. As you read the first stanza (verse paragraph), ask yourself why the speaker tells us about spending "all morning in the college sick bay [infirmary]."
3. At the beginning of the poem, the speaker mentions bells ringing. For what might this prepare us?

Vocabulary

gaudy (adjective)   Conspicuous, ugly, in bad taste.
knelling (adjective)   Ringing.
poppy (adjective)   Red or deep orange.
pram (noun)   Baby carriage.
snowdrops (noun)   White flowers that bloom in early spring.
stanched (adjective)   Wrapped so as to stop the flow of blood.

Mid-Term Break

Seamus Heaney

I sat all morning in the college sick bay
Counting bells knelling classes to a close.
At two o'clock our neighbours drove me home.

In the porch I met my father crying—
He had always taken funerals in his stride— 5
And Big Jim Evans saying it was a hard blow.

The baby cooed and laughed and rocked the pram
When I came in, and I was embarrassed
By old men standing up to shake my hand

And tell me they were "sorry for my trouble." 10
Whispers informed strangers I was the eldest,
Away at school, as my mother held my hand

In hers and coughed out angry tearless sighs.
At ten o'clock the ambulance arrived
With the corpse, stanched and bandaged by the nurses. 15

Next morning I went up into the room. Snowdrops
And candles soothed the bedside; I saw him
For the first time in six weeks. Paler now,

Wearing a poppy bruise on his left temple,
He lay in the four foot box as in his cot. 20
No gaudy scars, the bumper knocked him clear.

A four foot box, a foot for every year.

Questions for Discussion

1. What transitional words does Heaney use to move this brief story along.
2. Does this story contain dialogue?
3. Consider the different (and perhaps unexpected) ways in which Heaney's mother and father react to the death. What do their reactions tell us about their characters?
4. Comment upon Heaney's choice of verbs in stanzas 5, 6, and 7. What use of adjectives, especially participles, does he make in this poem?
5. How does Heaney establish setting? Does the setting change?
6. Find examples of figurative language in this poem.

Thinking Critically

1. We are shocked to learn of the death of a child at the end of this poem, but Heaney has prepared us all along. Make notes in the margins where you find clues about the poem's ending.
2. What contrasts does Heaney draw in this poem?

3. Heaney attended St. Columb's College before entering Queens University. What might the word "college" mean as used in "Mid-Term Break"?

Suggestions for Journal Entries

1. In the Questions for Discussion, you were asked to consider the different ways in which Heaney's mother and father reacted to the loss of their child. Some people react differently to death than others. Use freewriting, clustering, or listing to gather details that might help explain how you or someone you know reacted to the death of a loved one. Try to use vivid language and be as detailed as you can as you gather this information.

2. In stanza 6, Heaney writes: "Snowdrops/And candles soothed the bedside." Find out more about "snowdrops" in an unabridged dictionary or concise encyclopedia. Then, using freewriting, compose a detailed picture of what you imagine this scene to be. Base your description on Heaney's words, but go beyond them by adding detail from your own imagination.

Cry: The Story of a Comfort Woman

Razel Ariz Florento

"Cry: The Story of a Comfort Woman" was a winning entry in the 1996–97 Annual Student Achievement Awards for Excellence in Feminist Scholarship. Razel Ariz Florento was a student at Jersey City State College where she majored in English. A Filipino-American, Florento read about "comfort women" in the Filipino Reporter. *The story chronicled the experiences of Maria Rosa Henson who, during the occupation of the Philippines in World War II, was confined to a brothel where she was forced to have sex with Japanese soldiers. Henson was one of the many thousands of the young women in the Philippines, Korea, China, and other parts of occupied Asia who were tortured, raped, and verbally abused to "comfort" their conquerors. "I feel that I am Henson's daughter," Florento says, "a daughter who will never experience her pain, but must remember and understand."*

Preparing to Read

1. Florento takes on Henson's role and speaks in her voice. In other words, she tells the story in the first person (using pronouns such as *I* and *me*) as if Henson herself were speaking.
2. The poem begins in the present, uses a flashback to recall the past, then switches back to the present.
3. What might the term "comfort woman" mean?

Vocabulary

within earshot (adverb)   Close enough to be heard easily.

Cry: The Story of a Comfort Woman

Razel Ariz Florento

"Tanako"
name uttered from my lips
While my husband sleeps
beside me, my children
within earshot of my   5
Nightmares.

The war cancelled my womanhood,
my sanity, my name.
I gave them comfort,
ducking bullets, and kisses   10

that tasted like the damp jungle
from where they came.

I gave them breasts, back, bone.
In turn they tied my right leg
to a nail on the wall—   15
Roasted pig to be devoured by hungry soldiers.

Unlike the pig
I was kept alive.

I do not know
where my anger went.   20

When Tanako was finished
with me, thirty more men
needed comfort I myself
did not possess.
I comforted them, eyes closed   25
dreaming of sleep.

Even while I bathed
they watched my attempts
to get rid of their jungle
scent Coconut and mango dreams   30
only to be delivered to the whiskey of their breaths
and made me cry.

They laughed because
the bullets in my mouth and
between my legs silenced me in shame.   35

I do not know
where my anger went.

I think I keep it in my eyes.

My breasts, my back, my bone,
have long since disappeared.   40
Lost in the jungle barracks
where my father and mother died.

My eyes remember.
Everything.

They put nineteen thousand   45
apologies in my head
Nineteen thousand apologies
for my trouble.
They gave me nineteen thousand
to repair my soul.   50
It is broken.

I remember the pain of
sometimes forgetting.
Forgetting to tell my daughters
of my pain.   55

I cannot look at roasted pig anymore
because it is dead . . .
Coconut and mango dreams
replaced by Tanako's eyes.

Questions for Discussion

1. What words or phrases does Florento include here to show the passage of time?
2. What clues does she give us when she shifts from present to past and from past to present?
3. In addition to plot, narratives normally contain characters, dialogue, and setting. Find examples of each in this poem.
4. Find one or two examples of effective verbs in this selection.
5. Find one or two startling images and at least one figure of speech.
6. Who is Tanako?
7. Why does the speaker mention her parents in line 42?
8. Recall the quotation from Florento in the biographical sketch above. Then, reread lines 52–59 and explain how they reveal the author's purpose.

Thinking Critically

1. In what way is the speaker's recalling her experiences as a comfort woman similar to what Elie Wiesel does in "A Prayer for the Days of Awe" in Chapter 4? In what way is it different?
2. Reread lines 13–16. Explain two ways in which line 16 might be interpreted.
3. Reread "Cry: The Story of a Comfort Woman." Write notes in the margins that would enrich your understanding of what is being said. Pay special attention to lines 27–32, 39–44, and 45–51.

Suggestions for Journal Entries

1. Florento tells the story of a person who continues to suffer years after being degraded and injured by others. Have you or someone you know ever been degraded, humiliated, or hurt by someone who exerted power over you? If so, write down the most important facts of this

story in your journal. Of course, the situation need not be as horrible as the one discussed in "Cry: The Story of a Comfort Woman." One way to gather information is to search your memory through freewriting or clustering or using the journalists' questions. If your subject is someone other than yourself, try interviewing him or her.

2. Near the end of the poem, the speaker makes it clear that she has found the telling of this tale very painful, just as painful as holding it in for so many years. Recall a time in which you debated about telling your loved ones about an incident in your life. Why was the incident painful? Why was telling your loved ones about it painful? Listing, clustering, or freewriting might be the best ways to gather information about this topic.

The Day I Was Fat

Lois Diaz-Talty

When she isn't waitressing part-time or taking care of her family of four, Lois Diaz-Talty studies nursing and writes interesting essays such as the one below. She credits her husband and children for encouraging her academic efforts. Nonetheless, as the essay shows, she is an energetic, determined, and intelligent woman, who is sure to succeed. When asked to write about a pivotal event or turning point in her life, Diaz-Talty recalled an incident that is burned into her memory and that has helped shape her life.

Preparing to Read

1. The significance of the event narrated in this essay is explained in its thesis, which appears near the end.
2. Diaz-Talty's style is conversational, familiar, and often humorous, but her essay is always clear, correct, and focused. Pay particular attention to her use of dialogue, which helps capture the flavor of the moment.
3. Her title is unusual. What does it signal about what is to come?

Vocabulary

condiments (noun)	Seasonings, flavorings.
committed (adjective)	Determined.
ironically (adverb)	Having an effect opposite the one expected.
limber (adjective)	Able to bend easily, flexible.
notorious (adjective)	Shameful, bad.

The Day I Was Fat

Lois Diaz-Talty

I WAS NEVER in great shape. As a child, I was always called "plump," and my 1 friend "Skinny Sherri" was always, well, skinny. I could never sit Indian-style the way other kids did, and when I made the cheerleading squad in eighth grade it was because I had a big mouth and a great smile, not because I could execute limber splits or elegant cartwheels. Although I maintained a respectable weight throughout high school (after all, my "entire life" depended upon my looks and popularity), there was always a fat person inside of me just waiting to burst onto the scene.

Adulthood, marriage, and settling down had notorious effects on my weight: I blew up! The fat lady had finally arrived, saw the welcome mat, and moved right in. No one in my family could tell me I was fat. They knew that I had gained weight, I knew that I had gained weight, and I knew that they knew that I had gained weight. But to discuss the topic was out of the question. Once, my mother said, "You're too pretty to be so heavy"; that was the closest anyone had ever come to calling me fat. Later, my husband teased me because we couldn't lie on the couch together anymore, and I just cried and cried. He never dared to mention it again, but I didn't stop eating.

2

I had just given birth to my first child and was at least fifty pounds overweight. Nonetheless, I remember feeling that that was the greatest time in my life. I had a beautiful new baby, new furniture, a great husband, a lovely house. What more could anyone want? Well, I knew what else I wanted: I wanted to be thin and healthy. I just didn't care enough about myself to stop my frequent binging. I tried to lose weight every day, but I couldn't get started. Diets didn't last through lunch, and I got bigger by the day.

3

One summer afternoon in 1988, as I was headed to the pool with my sister-in-law Mary Gene and our children, I got into an argument with a teenager who was driving fast and tail-gaiting our car. When he nearly ran us off the road, I turned around and glared at him to show my disapproval and my concern for our safety. Suddenly, we began yelling at each other. He was about 18, with an ugly, red, swollen face. The few teeth he had were yellow and rotten. He followed us to the pool and, as he pulled into the parking lot behind us, our argument became heated.

4

"What's your problem, bitch?" he screamed.

5

"You drive like an idiot! That's my problem, okay?"

6

When I got out of the car and walked around to get the baby, he laughed to his friend, "Ah, look at 'er. She's fat! Go to hell, fat bitch." And then they drove away.

7

Once inside the gates to the pool, my sister-in-law advised me to forget the whole incident.

8

"Come on," she said. "Don't worry about that jerk! Did you see his teeth? He was gross."

9

But I couldn't get his words out of my mind. They stung like a whip. "I'm fat," I thought to myself. "I haven't just put on a few pounds. I'm not bloated. I don't have baby weight to lose. I'm just plain fat." Nobody had ever called me fat before, and it hurt terribly. But it was true.

10

On that very day, as I sat at the pool praying that nobody would see me in my bathing suit, I promised myself that no one would ever call me fat again. That hideous, 18-year-old idiot had spoken the words that none of my loved ones had had the heart to say even though they were true. Yes, I was fat.

11

From then on, I was committed to shedding the weight and getting into shape. I started a rigorous program of running and dieting the very next day. Within months, I joined a gym and managed to make some friends who are

12

still my workout buddies. However, in the past seven years, I've done more than lose weight: I've reshaped my attitude, my lifestyle, and my self-image. Now, I read everything I can about nutrition and health. I'm even considering becoming an aerobics instructor. I cook low-fat foods—chicken, fish, lean meats, vegetables—and I serve my family healthy, protein-rich meals prepared with dietetic ingredients. The children and I often walk to school, ride bikes, rollerblade, and run. Health and fitness have become essential to our household and our lives. But what's really wonderful is that, some time between that pivotal day in 1988 and today, my self-image stopped being about how I look and began being about how I feel. I feel energetic, healthy, confident, strong, and pretty. Ironically, the abuse I endured in the parking lot has helped me re-gain my self-esteem, not just my figure. My body looks good, but my mind feels great!

I hope that the kid from the pool has had his teeth fixed because I'm sure 13 they were one source of his misery. If I ever see him again, I won't tell him that he changed my life in such a special way. I won't let him know that he gave me the greatest gift he could ever give me just by being honest. I won't give him the satisfaction of knowing that the day he called me fat was one of the best days of my life.

Questions for Discussion

1. Where does Diaz-Talty express the essay's central idea? In other words, which sentence is her thesis?
2. What purpose does the author's quoting herself serve in this essay? Why does she quote her mother?
3. Why did the author quote the exact words of the 18-year-old who harassed her? Would simply telling us what happened have been enough?
4. Why does Diaz-Talty bother to describe this person? Why does she make sure to reveal her attitude toward him?
5. Reread three or four paragraphs, and circle the transitions used to show the passage of time and to create coherence.
6. Find places in which the author uses particularly good verbs, adjectives, and adverbs.

Thinking Critically

1. Make notes in the margins next to details that reveal important aspects of the author's personality.
2. Were you in the author's place, how would you have reacted to the insult? Now think about an aspect of your personality or lifestyle that needs improvement. Write a paragraph that explains how you might improve it.

Suggestions for Journal Entries

1. Recall a painful experience that changed your life for the better. Answer the journalists' questions to collect details about this event and to explain how it helped you. For example, here is the journal entry Lois Diaz-Talty made in preparation for "The Day I Was Fat":

   When? In 1988, shortly after I gave birth to Tommy.

   What? An argument with a teenager who had been driving behind us. He called me fat.

   Who? I and a rude, 18-year-old stranger, who looked gross.

   Where? On the way to the pool.

   Why important? Because I *was* fat.

   How? His insult shamed me. Made me work harder to lose weight and helped restore self-esteem.

2. Use focused freewriting to gather details about how you reacted to an incident in which someone hurt, insulted, or cheated you, or did something else unpleasant to you. In the process, analyze your reaction to this event. What did it reveal about your character?

Death of an Officer

Gaye Wagner

The author is an officer with the San Diego Police Department. Before joining the force she had worked for seven years in youth services in New Hampshire. Wagner holds both bachelor's and master's degrees. "Death of an Officer" appeared in The American Enterprise *magazine in 1995. Accompanying the article was a list of 161 police officers killed in the line of duty in the United States during 1994.*

Preparing to Read

1. In addition to practicing narrative techniques, the author uses description and verbal images to enrich her story. Look for places where she does so.
2. Included here are letters from children expressing their reactions to the officer's death. Read them carefully.

Vocabulary

apathy (noun)	Indifference, lack of concern.
bizarre (adjective)	Strange.
counteract (verb)	Remedy, work against.
detachment (noun)	Separation.
dimension (noun)	Aspect.
enamored (adjective)	Pleased, enchanted, in love with.
immerse (verb)	Plunge into.
invincible (adjective)	Unbeatable.
mired (adjective)	Stuck in.
mortality (noun)	Certainty of death.
nunchakus (noun)	A hand weapon used in martial arts and police work.
ponder (verb)	Think about, consider.
preoccupied (adjective)	Absorbed by, totally concerned about.
prophecy (noun)	Prediction.
resuscitating (adjective)	Reviving, restoring.
shrouded (verb)	Covered, concealed.

Death of an Officer

Gaye Wagner

WHEN OFFICER Ron Davis was shot in the dark, foggy pre-dawn of September 17, 1991, I momentarily lost my perspective on why I've chosen to do what I'm doing. For a time, I focused on just one dimension of my   1 job as a police officer: the possibility of a violent death, for me or people I care about.

Despite the graphic slides and blow-by-blow descriptions of on-duty deaths that we sat through in the Academy, I still must have believed deep down that I, and those along-side me, were invincible. Then the faceless gloom of mortality took the place of a fallen comrade. The streets became an evil, threatening place.

Before I felt the blow of a co-worker's death, I looked on each shooting, stabbing, and act of violence as any rubbernecker would—with a certain detachment. I was living the ultimate student experience: Social Wildlife 101. What better way to understand problems of crime and justice than to immerse yourself in the 'hood. I was there, but I was still an onlooker peering inside some kind of fence. I watched, probed each tragic or bizarre incident with curiosity, and pondered the problems I faced.

With the death of a comrade, I understood that I was inside the fence. I'm no longer an outsider looking in. The shadow of death stalks all of us who walk in the valley of drugs, guns, alcohol, hopelessness, and hate. Police, addicts, hustlers, parents trying to build futures for their children, good people struggling— we all risk falling into the firing line of desperation, apathy, or corruption.

For a while, my response to the new threats I saw around me was to treat all people like they were the enemy. Since an "us" and "them" mentality can be a self-fulfilling prophecy, some of my contacts with people were a little bumpy. Normally my approach is courteous, in one of several variations: either as sympathizer, "just the facts, Bud" chronicler, or all-ears naïve airhead who can hardly believe that you, yes you, could do a dastardly deed . . . ("how did this all happen, my friend?").

But suddenly I just wasn't as enamored with this job as I had been. Let's face it, a sense of contributing to society, the excitement of racing cars with lights and sirens, helping folks, and the drama of never knowing what's next place a poor second to living long enough to count grey hairs and collect Social Security.

I had trouble getting an impersonal all-units bulletin about someone I knew out of my head. I read these bulletins every day, but the words now stung: "187 Suspect . . . Arrest in Public for 187 P.C.—Homicide of a Police Officer . . . Suspect Description: Castillo, Arnaldo . . . On September 17, 1991, at 05:15 hours, Castillo was contacted by two officers in regard to a domestic violence call. As the officers approached, Castillo opened fire with a .45 cal. automatic weapon, fatally wounding one officer."

It was a routine incident that any one of us could have gone to, in an apartment complex that we've all been to. A victim mired in her own problems—a broken collar bone and a life crushing down around her—forgot to tell officers that her crazed, abusive boyfriend had fled with a gun. What followed happened fast. Thick fog and darkness shrouded the complex parking lot where Davis and his partner stopped to contact a driver backing out of the lot.

Ron took a bullet in the neck as he stepped out of his passenger side door. The bullet bled him faster than any resuscitating efforts could counteract. He died while his partner hopelessly tried to breathe life back into his bloody, weakening body. Medics said that even if they'd been there when it happened, there would have been nothing they could do to save his life.

The next week brought a crush of support for our division. The chief, 10 the field operations commander, psychological services counselors, and peer support counselors all came to our lineups to say we're here, man, and we know it doesn't feel good. The lineup room looked like a wake with its display of food, flowers, and cards that showered in from other divisions, other departments, and the citizens of our division.

Ron's squad was placed on leave, so officers came from other divisions to 11 help us cover manpower shortages. And on the day of the funeral, officers volunteered from all over the city to cover our beats so that everyone in our division could go to the service.

The funeral procession filled the three miles from Jack Murphy Stadium 12 to the church with bumper-to-bumper police units flashing red and blue overhead lights. Police cars came from San Diego, the Border Patrol, the U.S. Marshals, El Cajon, La Mesa, Chula Vista, National City, Riverside, Los Angeles, seemingly everywhere. The sight we made sent chills up my spine.

For the breadth of that three-mile procession, for a few minutes at least, 13 drivers couldn't keep racing in their usual preoccupied frenzy. Traffic had to stop. In those frozen freeway moments, a tiny corner of the world had to take time out to notice our mourning at the passing of Ronald W. Davis, age 24, husband, father of two, San Diego police officer. The citizens held captive by the procession responded with heart. There was no angry beeping, there were no cars nosing down breakdown lanes. Drivers turned off ignitions in anticipation of a long wait and watched patiently. Many got out of their cars and waved or yelled words of sympathy.

The pastor's words at the funeral have stayed with me, because he began 14 stretching my perspective back to a more fruitful, hopeful size. "Life is not defined by the quantity of years that we are on this earth, but by the quality of the time that we spend here."

I never cried at the funeral. I cried three weeks later in front of a second 15 grade class.

Staring at the bulletin board one day drinking my coffee, I noticed a 16 sheaf of papers with big, just-learned-to-write letters on them. The papers were letters to the Officers of Southeastern from Ms. Matthews's second grade class at Boone Elementary:

Dear Friends of Officer Davis, 17

We hope this letter will make you feel better. We feel sad about what happened to Officer Davis. We know he was a nice man and a good cop. We thank you for protecting our neighborhood. We know you try to protect every one of us. We know Officer Davis was a good father. We're sorry.

Your friend,
Jeffrey

Dear Friends of Officer Davis,   18

We feel sorry about Officer Davis. I know you feel sorry for what happened
when the bad guy killed your friend, Officer Davis. Thank you for protecting us. I know that he's dead and I know you feel sorry about it. I'm glad
you got the bad guy. Do you think this would happen again? I'm sure not.
Please protect yourself.

> Your friend,
> Henry

P.S. I live in Meadowbrook apartments. Thank you.

Dear Friends of Officer Davis,   19

We feel sad about Officer Davis being killed. The man that killed Officer
Davis got killed right behind our house. We live in front of Meadowbrook
apartments. It is really sad that Officer Davis got killed. Last year when my
brother was in sixth grade and he was playing basketball with his friends,
two kids came and took the ball away. They broke his basketball hoop. Officers helped find the two kids. We are thankful you are trying to protect us.

> Your friend,
> Travis

Dear Friends,   20

I hope you will feel better. I know how you feel, sad. Was Officer Davis
your friend? Well, he was my friend, too. When I saw the news I felt very
sad for him. When I grow up, I might be a police officer. I'll never forget
Officer Davis. I know how losing a friend is. When you lose a friend you
feel very sad. I know how losing a friend is cause my best friend moved
away to Virginia. They wrote to me once and I still miss her and I miss Officer Davis, too.

> Your friend,
> Jennifer L.

Dear Officers,   21

I hope you feel a little better with my letter. We feel sorry that Officer Davis
was killed. I heard that he got shot on his neck when he was just getting out
of his car. I also heard that Officer Davis was an officer for two years and
that he has two children. That one is one years old and the other five years
old. I want to say thank you for protecting us and for helping us. We all
wish that Officer Davis was still alive.

> Your friend always,
> Arlene

Dear Officers, 22

We were so sad that your friend Officer Davis died. Last night on 9-17-91 I couldn't sleep because I was thinking all about your friend Officer Davis. When I heard about Officer Davis getting shot I was so sad. I know how it feels when a friend is gone. I wish that Officer Davis could hear this but he can't right now. Officer Davis and the rest of the force do a great job.

Sincerely,
Jasper

Those letters brought feelings up from my gut. The next day I visited 23 Room B-17 to deliver thank you notes to the authors. Ms. Matthews was so excited with my visit that she asked me to speak to the class. She explained that the letters were a class exercise to help the students deal with fears they had expressed to her after the shooting. Because many of her students lived in the apartments where Ron was shot, the shooting was very personal to them. Some couldn't sleep, others were afraid to walk to school, and some were shocked at the realization that the "good guys" get killed too.

I hadn't expected to give a speech, and wasn't really ready to give one on 24 this particular topic. When I faced the class, I saw 32 sets of Filipino, Latino, white, and African-American eyes fixed on me. Their hands all sat respectfully in their laps. In those young faces, I saw an innocence and trust that I didn't want to shake.

I thought of the sympathy in their letters; I pictured them passing by the 25 large, dark stain of Officer Davis's blood that still scarred the parking lot pavement; and I wondered what young minds must think when a force of blacked-out SWAT officers sweeps through nearby homes in search of the "bad guy" who shot the "good guy."

I wondered how many of the children had been home looking out their 26 windows when the suspect, Arnaldo Castillo, was shot by a volley of officers' gunfire as he sprung out of his hiding place in the late afternoon of September 17. I couldn't imagine what these children must be thinking, because a second grader growing up in rural New Hampshire in 1962 didn't witness such events. I could only think that second graders of any generation in any place in the world shouldn't have to witness or ponder the senselessness of human violence.

When I finally opened my mouth to speak, my eyes watered and no 27 words would come out. I could say nothing. Each time I tried to push my voice, my eyes watered more. I looked helplessly at Ms. Matthews and the vice principal, who had come to listen to me. Ms. Matthews came to my rescue by starting to talk to the class about strong feelings and the importance of letting feelings out so we don't trap sadness inside ourselves. "Even police officers know that crying can be a strong thing to do." Her reassurances to them reassured me and made me smile at the image of myself, "the big, brave cop" choked up by a second grade class.

We talked for a time about the shooting, about having someone to talk to about scary things, and about how important their thoughtful letters had been in a time of sadness. By the time I left, they were more enchanted with my handcuffs and nunchakus than they were concerned by death. Ahhh, the lure for us kids of all ages conjured up by cops and robbers, catching bad guys, rescuing good guys, and having a belt full of cop toys.   28

Through Ron's death, I grew to have a more mature, realistic view of my job. Through the eyes of the pastor at the funeral and Ms. Matthews's second grade class, I recovered perspective and belief in the value of what I do. It's important for me to live my life doing something I believe is important for this thing we call humanity. And I believe that what I do is important because of people like Henry, Jasper, Jennifer L., Jeffrey, Travis, Arlene, Ms. Matthews, and all of the kids in Room B-17.   29

Questions for Discussion

1. How does Wagner show the passage of time? Reread paragraphs 5–10 to find good examples.
2. Find verbs, adjectives, and adverbs that keep the essay interesting and believable. Reread paragraphs 6–13 for good examples.
3. What use does Wagner make of proper nouns? What effect do they have on her story?
4. What use does the essay make of description?
5. Before this incident, Wagner had looked on violence as "any rubbernecker would—with a certain detachment" (paragraph 3). What does this image tell us? Where else in this paragraph and the next does she use verbal images?
6. All writers must decide to include some things and to exclude others. Why are the children's letters included?
7. Why does Wagner mention "the citizens held captive" by the funeral procession (paragraph 13)? Why does she use the word *citizens*?
8. How did the officer's death change Wagner's view of herself and of her job?

Thinking Critically

1. Why were the students asked to write letters? Is the purpose of their assignment similar to the purpose behind Wagner's writing this essay? Point out similarities by writing notes in the margins of the essay.
2. Is it strange that second graders are writing about violence in their community? What does this tell us about our society? Does "Death of an Officer" echo ideas in "The Last Safe Haven," in Chapter 3? If you

haven't read that short essay, do so now. Write your response in a paragraph or two that make reference to both selections.

Suggestions for Journal Entries

1. The pastor says that "Life is not defined by the quantity of years that we are on this earth, but by the quality of the time that we spend here." Use this idea as the focus of a freewriting exercise. Use examples from your own life and observations to support this idea.

2. Writing is a good tool for dealing with the fear, anger, or sadness that comes from losing someone you care for or respect. Use focused freewriting or listing to explain your immediate and long-term reactions to such a loss. Then explain what the reaction you have just described says about you. Does it reveal something about your personality? Did the experience change you in any way?

3. Because of the death of a fellow officer, Wagner sees herself and her job differently. Recall an event that changed your attitude about your role at school, at work, in your family, in your community, or in any other group or place. Use listing to gather information about the most important aspects of this event.

Suggestions for Sustained Writing

1. If you responded to the first Suggestion for Journal Entries after Heaney's "Mid-Term Break," write an essay in which you explain your reaction or the reaction of someone you know to the death of a loved one. Now, add information to the notes you have already taken on this topic in your journal. If possible, interview or brainstorm with another person who has shared this loss—perhaps another family member or a close friend. Delve into your subject's character by explaining how he or she reacted to the shock, grieved over the loss, and dealt with the grief, if at all. Your narrative might span a few days, a few weeks, or even a few years.

   As you revise your first draft, add concrete details, figures of speech, and vivid verbs and adjectives. When you revise your second draft, try adding dialogue, and make sure you have described the setting and the people in your story well. Finally, check to see if you have included transitional devices and effective verbs to move the story along and to make it easy to follow. Next, edit your work for grammar; sentence structure, length, and variety; word choice; and punctuation and spelling. As always, proofread. This will probably be a powerful story—you don't want to spoil it with silly mistakes in writing or typing.

2. In "Cry: The Story of a Comfort Woman," the speaker tells the story of her humiliation and torture at the hands of enemy soldiers during World War II. If you or someone you know has ever been degraded, humiliated, or hurt in any way by someone who had authority or exerted power over you, tell that story now. Of course, it need not be as horrible as what you read in Florento's poem. You might simply relate how as a child you were harassed by a schoolyard bully or how a friend of yours was mistreated by an employer. Begin by reading the notes you made to the Suggestions for Journal Entries after "Cry: The Story of a Comfort Woman," especially those in response to Suggestion 1.

   You might begin by explaining why this experience was so significant for your subject. A good place to express this idea is in your thesis. Then, you can simply narrate what happened, using transitions to move from one event in the story to the next. Your concluding paragraph might rephrase your thesis or look to the future. As you revise and edit, make sure the information and the vocabulary you include clearly reflect your subject's reaction to or attitude about the experience. Try adding vivid details, figures of speech, and dialogue to increase interest.

3. Use narration to explain what someone did to influence you either positively or negatively. Show how this person encouraged or discouraged you to develop a particular interest or talent; explain what he or she taught you about yourself; or discuss ways he or she strengthened or weakened your self-esteem.

   You need not express yourself in an essay. Consider writing a letter instead. Address it to the person who influenced you, and explain your appreciation or resentment of that influence. Either way, put your thesis—a statement of just how positively or negatively he or she affected you—in the introduction to your essay or letter.

   Before you begin, check the journal entries you made after reading Diaz-Talty. Then, write one or two stories from personal experience that show how the person in question affected you. After completing your first draft, try adding dialogue to your stories. Reveal your subject's attitude toward you by recalling words he or she used when answering your questions, giving you advice or instructions, or commenting on your efforts.

   As you revise your work further, make sure you have explained the results of this person's influence on you thoroughly. Add details as you move from draft to draft. Then, edit for grammar, punctuation, spelling, and other problems that can make your writing less effective.

4. The first of the Suggestions for Journal Entries after Diaz-Talty's "The Day I Was Fat" asks you to gather information about a painful experience that changed your life for the better. Use this information to begin drafting a full-length essay that explains what happened.

   You might begin the first draft by stating in one sentence how this event changed you; this will be your working thesis. You can then tell your story, including only those materials that help explain or prove the thesis. For example, Diaz-Talty says that being called fat helped her regain her self-esteem and her figure; every detail in her story helps prove this statement.

As you write later drafts, add dialogue and descriptive detail about people in your story, just as Diaz-Talty did. If you are unhappy with your introductory and concluding paragraphs, rewrite them by using techniques explained in Chapter 4.

Before you get to your final draft, make certain your paper contains vivid verbs, adjectives, and adverbs, which will keep readers interested. If it doesn't, add them. Then, edit and proofread your work carefully.

5. As Gaye Wagner did ("Death of an Officer"), write the story of an event that significantly changed your attitude about your role at school, at work, in your family, in your community, or in any other group or place. If you responded to the third of the Suggestions for Journal Entries after Wagner's essay, read your notes before you start writing.

Begin your rough draft by explaining how the event you are narrating changed your attitude. Next, summarize that explanation in one sentence, which will act as your working thesis statement. Then tell your story as completely as you can, but include only those details that support or explain your thesis.

Don't hesitate to use dialogue or to describe other people who had important roles in your story. Make sure that your introduction captures your reader's attention and that your conclusion is logical and memorable. If not, rewrite these parts of your essay.

If you have done a good job of introducing, developing, and concluding your paper, you will want to edit and proofread it with care. Working hard to mine diamonds makes no sense if you are not going to polish them.

6. How we face life's hardships, losses, fears, and emergencies says a lot about the people we are. We can see this clearly in Wagner's "Death of an Officer." Tell the story of how you, a close friend, neighbor, or relative dealt with a serious personal problem or concern. As you draft your essay, make sure the events of your narrative reveal the strength or lack of strength in your subject's character. Begin by reviewing the journal notes you made after reading Wagner's essay.

A general overview of your subject's character can make a good introduction to this essay. If you are writing about someone other than yourself, explain how well you know each other or how close you are. Make sure the introduction also includes a statement that clearly expresses the way your subject handles hardship, stress, or adversity. This will be your thesis, the idea that the rest of your essay will illustrate or prove through narration.

After you have completed the second or third draft, read your story carefully and decide whether you have included enough detail to make it convincing. Add information if necessary. At the same time, check that transitions between sentences and paragraphs are clear and logical. As always, polish the final version to catch errors in grammar, spelling, and so on.

Writing to Learn: A Group Activity

In "Cry: The Story of a Comfort Woman," Razel Ariz Florento takes on the voice of a woman who experienced an atrocity during World War II. The story that she tells gives us a good picture of the horror this innocent woman endured.

THE FIRST MEETING

Ask each student to learn about and take notes on the horrors that someone living in a particular place and time might have suffered during war. In doing so, each of you might research what it was like to be one of the following:

- A Polish Jew who had been sent to Auschwitz, one of the most notorious Nazi concentration camps during World War II.
- A Korean "comfort woman."
- A resident of Hiroshima on the day the first atomic bomb was dropped.
- A Londoner who was terrorized by Nazi war planes during the Blitz.
- A young mother caring for an infant during the allied bombing of Dresden, Germany, during World War II.
- A child walking the streets of Guernica, Spain, on the day the city was bombed by forces allied to Franco in the Spanish Civil War.
- A Muslim father trying to shelter his family in Sarajevo, Bosnia-Herzegovina, while the Serbs shelled the city.
- An Armenian who witnessed the genocide of her people at the hands of the Turks at the beginning of this century.
- A Tutsi or Hutu experiencing the horrors of the Rwandan civil war in 1994.

On the other hand, you might choose to research another type of individual who experienced the horrors of another war.

RESEARCH

Library print sources, including an encyclopedia, the *New York Times Index,* and the *Readers' Guide to Periodical Literature,* are good starting points. CD or online databases should also provide you with helpful information. Finally, check the Internet. Photocopy and bring articles and other materials you have found as well as your notes to the next group meeting.

continued

THE SECOND MEETING

Have members of the group share both their notes and copies of the materials they found. For inspiration, reread Florento's "Cry: The Story of a Comfort Woman" aloud. Then, ask each student to write an essay narrating experiences—based on his or her research—that would show what it was like to be a Jew at Auschwitz, a resident of Hiroshima, or any other victim of war. Like Florento, each of you might want to write in the first person, assuming the voice and the personality of your subject.

After completing at least two drafts of your essays, photocopy them in preparation for the next meeting.

THE THIRD MEETING

Ask students to distribute copies of their papers to each other. After each reads his or hers aloud, make comments that will help the writer add to, revise, and refine his or her work before submitting it to the instructor.

Reporting Events

The poems and essays in the preceding chapter are autobiographical; they look inward and explain something important about the narrator, the person telling the story. As you recall, each of them is told from the first-person point of view, using the pronoun *I* or *we*.

The poems and essays you will read in this chapter, on the other hand, look outward. Some may reveal important facts and insights about their storytellers. Nevertheless, they tell us more about the worlds their narrators live in than about the narrators themselves.

Several of these selections re-create incidents from personal experience and show their writers involved in the action in some way. As a result, they, too, are written in first person. An example is Adrienne Schwartz's "The Colossus in the Kitchen," a story about racism in South Africa, told from the perspective of its young narrator.

In Sagan's "Frederick Douglass: The Path to Freedom," on the other hand, the storyteller is not involved in the action. He relates an incident in which he took no part. As a result, he tells the story from a third-person point of view, using *he, she,* and *they* to explain who did what. As you can see, a story's point of view depends on whether the narrator is a participant or an outsider.

Whichever point of view the selections in this chapter use, they provide a sometimes touching, sometimes terrifying, and always interesting account of their authors' reactions to the world around them. In the introduction to Section Four, you read that narration can be used for a variety of purposes. The poems and essays that follow prove that reporting events is one way to make a point about the nature of human beings and the worlds in which they live. Indeed, if you have ever taken a course in psychology or sociology, you know how important narration can be to explaining human and social behavior.

Though not always expressed in a formal thesis statement, the main point in each of these selections comes across clearly and forcefully because of the writer's powerful command of language and of techniques important to telling a story. Use these poems and essays as sources of inspiration for your own work. Reporting events you have heard about, witnessed, or taken part in is an excellent way to continue growing as a writer. It can also help you discover a clearer and more perceptive vision of the world, at least the world you are writing about.

Visualizing Narrative Elements

The paragraphs that follow are from "Padre Blaisdell and the Refugee Children," René Cutforth's true story of a Catholic priest's efforts to save abandoned children during the Korean War. The place is Seoul; the time, December 1950.

Describes setting and introduces the main character.

At dawn Padre Blaisdell dressed himself in the little icy room at the top of the orphanage at Seoul. He put on his parka and an extra sweater, for the Siberian wind was fluting in the corners of the big grey barrack of the school. . . . The water in his basin was solid ice. . . .

His boots clicked along the stone flags in the freezing passages which led to the main door. The truck was waiting on the snow-covered gravel in the yellow-grey light of sunrise. The two Korean nurses stood as usual, ready for duty—pig-tailed adolescents, their moon faces as passive and kindly as cows.

Describes other characters.

Uses a transition to show passage of time.

By the time he reached Riverside Road the padre had passed through the normal first stage of reaction to the wind . . . he was content now in his open vehicle to lie back and admire the effortless skill of the wind's razor as it slashed him to the bone.

Uses a metaphor, action verb.

Uses vivid adjectives and proper nouns to describe setting.

There's a dingy alley off Riverside Street, narrow, and strewn with trodden straw and refuse which would stink if the cold allowed it life enough. This alley leads to the arches of the railway bridge across the Han River. The truck's wheels

crackled over the frozen . . . alley, passed
from it down a sandy track and halted at the
second arch of the bridge [in front of

Uses vivid verbs and adjectives.

which] lay a pile of filthy rice sacks,
clotted with dirt and stiff as boards. It
was a child, practically naked and covered
with filth. It lay in a pile of its own
excrement in a sort of nest it had scratched
out among the rice sacks. Hardly able to
raise itself on an elbow, it still had
enough energy to draw back cracked lips from
bleeding gums and snarl and spit at the
padre like an angry kitten. Its neck was not   *Uses a simile.*
much thicker than a broom handle and it had
the enormous pot-belly of starvation.

Uses a transition to show passage of time.

At eleven o'clock in the morning, when
the padre returned to the orphanage, his
truck was full. "They are the real victims
of the war," the padre said in his
careful . . . colorless voice. "Nine-tenths
of them were lost or abandoned. . . . No one

Uses dialogue to provide information and explain story's purpose.

will take them in unless they are relations,
and we have 800 of these children at the
orphanage. Usually they recover in quite a
short time, but the bad cases tend to become
very silent. . . . I have a little boy who
has said nothing for three months now but
Yes and *No*."

TRACKING THE PASSAGE OF TIME "Padre Blaisdale and the Refugee Children"

We can divide the story roughly into three major sections, each of which is introduced by transitions that relate to time.

"At dawn . . ."
Padre Blaisdale and the nurses leave the
orphanage in search of orphans.

"By the time he reached Riverside Road . . ."
They find the child in the alley.

"At eleven o'clock in the morning . . ."
They return with a truckload of children.

Revising Narrative Essays

The third selection in this chapter, "The Colossus in the Kitchen," was written by Adrienne Schwartz, a student who recalls the racial prejudice aimed at Tandi, a black woman who worked for her family in her native South Africa. Realizing narrative essays require as much care as any others, Schwartz made important changes to her rough draft and turned an already fine essay into a moving and memorable experience for her readers. Compare these excerpts from her drafts.

Schwartz—Rough Draft

```
Our neighbors, in conformity with

established thinking, had long called my

mother, and therefore all of us, deviants,

agitators, and no less than second cousins

to Satan himself. The cause of this
```

Use a quotation to show this?

```
dishonorable labeling was the fact that we

had been taught to believe in the equality

and dignity of humankind.
```

That was why I could not understand the apoplectic reaction of the neighbors to my excited news that Tandi was going to have a baby. After all, this was not politics; this was new life. Tandi's common-law husband lived illegally with her in the quarters

Connect these ideas better?

assigned to them; complying with the law on this and many other petty issues was not considered appropriate in our household. It was the Group Areas Act that had been responsible for the breakup of Tandi's marriage. Her lawful husband, who was not born in the same area as she, had been refused a permit to work in the Transvaal, a

Make smoother?

province in northeastern South Africa, where we lived. In the way of many others, he had *Needed?* been placed in such a burdensome situation and found the degradation of being taken

More vivid?

from his wife's bed in the middle of the night and joblessness more often than he could tolerate. He simply went away, never to be seen or heard from again.

Find a better place for this idea?

The paradox of South Africa is complex in the extreme. It is like a rare and precious stone set amid barren wastes, and yet it feeds off its own flesh.

The days passed, and Tandi's waist got

Slow down? Show passage of time?

bigger and pride could be seen in her eyes.

The child died after only one day.

Schwartz—Final Draft

Our neighbors, in conformity with
established thinking, had long called my
mother, and therefore all of us, deviants,
agitators, and no less than second cousins
to Satan himself. The cause of this

Uses a direct quotation to prove an idea.

dishonorable labeling was the fact that we
had been taught to believe in the equality
and dignity of humankind.

   "Never take a person's dignity away from
him," my mother had said, "no matter how
angry or hurt you might be because in the
end you only diminish your own worth."

   That was why I could not understand the
apoplectic reaction of the neighbors to my
excited news that Tandi was going to have a
baby. After all, this was not politics; this

Moves this information to a more logical place.

was new life. But the paradox of South
Africa is complex in the extreme. The
country is like a rare and precious stone
set amid barren wastes, and yet close up it

Adds vivid details in a metaphor.

is a gangrenous growth that feeds off its
own flesh.

   Tandi's common-law husband lived
illegally with her in the quarters assigned

Adds transition to connect ideas.

to them; complying with the law on this and
many other petty issues was not considered
appropriate in our household. It was the
Group Areas Act that had been responsible

for the breakup of Tandi's marriage <u>in the</u>
<u>first place</u>. Her lawful husband, who was not
born in the same area as she, had been
refused a permit to work in the Transvaal,

Removes
unnecessary
information.

Adds vivid
verbs; makes
sentences
smoother.

and like others placed in such a burdensome
situation, <u>suffered</u> the continuous
degradation of being <u>dragged</u> from his wife's
bed in the middle of the night and of being
<u>denied</u> work more often than he could
tolerate. <u>Eventually</u> he simply <u>melted</u> away,
never to be seen or heard from again, making
legal divorce impossible.

Adds
transitions
to show time
passing.

<u>As the days passed</u>, Tandi's waist
<u>swelled</u>, and pride <u>glowed</u> in her <u>dauntless</u>
eyes.

Uses vivid
vocabulary.

<u>And</u> then the child was born, and he lived
for a day, and then he died.

Expands this
sentence for
dramatic effect.

Practicing Narrative Skills

What follows is an eyewitness account of the last moments of the Titanic, which sank in 1912 after striking an iceberg. The writer views the scene from a lifeboat about two hours after having abandoned ship. Practice your skills by following the instructions for each section of this exercise.

1. Underline words and phrases that make this an effective narrative. Look especially for vivid verbs, adjectives, and adverbs. Also underline transitions.

In a couple of hours . . . [the ship] began to go down . . . rapidly. Then the fearful sight began. The people in the ship were just beginning to realize how great their danger was. When the forward part of the ship dropped suddenly at a faster rate . . . there was a sudden rush of passengers on all the decks towards the stern. It was like a wave. We could see the great black mass of people in the steerage sweeping to the rear part of the boat and breaking through to the upper decks. At a distance of about a mile we could distinguish everything through the night, which was perfectly clear. We could make out the increasing excitement on board the boat as the people, rushing to and fro, caused the deck lights to disappear and reappear as they passed in front of them. [Mrs. D. H. Bishop]

2. Important words have been removed from the following paragraphs. Replace them with words of your own. Use only the kinds of words indicated. Avoid *is, are, was, were, have been, had been,* and other forms of the verb *to be.*

This panic went on, it seemed, for an hour. _____ the ship seemed to

TRANSITION

_____ out of the water and stand there perpendicularly. It seemed to

VERB

us that it stood _____ in the water for four full minutes.

ADVERB

_____ it began to _____ gently downwards. Its speed increased

TRANSITION · VERB

as it went down head first, so that the stern _____ down with a rush.

VERB

The lights continued to burn till it sank. We could see the people

_____ _____ in the stern till it was gone. . . .

VERB · ADVERB

_____ the ship sank we _____ the screaming a mile

ADVERB OF TIME · VERB

away. Gradually it became fainter and fainter and died away. Some of the

lifeboats that had room for more might have _____ to their rescue,

VERB

but it would have meant that those who were in the water would have

_____ aboard and sunk them.

VERB

The five selections that appear in this chapter are very different in style, content, and purpose. But they all make their points in interesting and meaningful ways. More important, they illustrate effective techniques important to narrative and other types of writing that you will use in both your college and professional life.

Child of the Romans

Carl Sandburg

Carl Sandburg (1878–1967) is one of America's best-loved poets and biographers. He is remembered chiefly for his six-volume biography of Abraham Lincoln and his collections of poetry, such as The Chicago Poems, Cornhuskers, *and* The People, Yes, *which reveal a love for the common people. His support for labor is evident in* "Child of the Romans," *a sketch of an Italian immigrant railroad worker. For Sandburg, this "dago shovelman" was typical of the people who built America's factories, railroads, and cities.*

Preparing to Read

1. *Dago* is an insulting term for an Italian. The poem's title refers to the fact that 2,000 years ago Italy was the center of the powerful Roman Empire.
2. Sandburg contrasts the life of the shovelman with those of the people on the train. It is this comparison that serves as the theme of the poem.
3. Verbs and adjectives create a sense of reality in this poem and keep it interesting. Look for them as you read "Child of the Romans."

Vocabulary

eclairs (noun)   Rich, custard-filled pastries topped with chocolate.
jonquils (noun)   Garden plants of the narcissus family with lovely yellow or white flowers.

Child of the Romans

Carl Sandburg

The dago shovelman sits by the railroad track
Eating a noon meal of bread and bologna.
A train whirls by, and men and women at tables
Alive with red roses and yellow jonquils,
Eat steaks running with brown gravy,   5
Strawberries and cream, eclairs and coffee.
The dago shovelman finishes the dry bread and bologna,
Washes it down with a dipper from the water-boy,
And goes back to the second half of a ten-hour day's work
Keeping the road-bed so the roses and jonquils   10
Shake hardly at all in the cut glass vases
Standing slender on the tables in the dining cars.

Questions for Discussion

1. The poem's plot is very simple. What events take place during the shovelman's lunch?

2. Sandburg gets very detailed in listing the various items that the railroad passengers are dining on. How do these contrast with what the shovelman is eating?

3. Why does Sandburg make sure to tell us that the train "whirls" by as the man eats his lunch? How does his description of the movement of the train contrast with what you read in the last three lines of this poem?

4. How long is the shovelman's day? In what way does his work, "keeping the road-bed," affect the passengers?

5. The poem has two very different settings. What are they, and how does the contrast between the two help Sandburg get his point across?

Thinking Critically

1. Earlier you read that Sandburg was a friend to labor and the common people. Underline words or phrases in his poem that support this idea. Does the poem tell us anything about Sandburg's attitude toward the wealthy? If so, what is it?

2. "Child of the Romans" was written in 1916. Would the setting be different if Sandburg were writing this poem today? What else might change?

3. Read a little about the Romans in an encyclopedia. Besides being Italian, in what way is the shovelman a "child of the Romans"?

Suggestions for Journal Entries

1. If you know a hardworking immigrant who has come here in search of a better life, write a story about this person's typical workday.

2. If you have ever had a job in which you provided a service for other people (perhaps as a housepainter, waitress, or salesclerk), narrate one or two events from a typical workday.

3. After reading Sandburg's story of the shovelman's difficult life, many readers are inclined to count their blessings. List some things in your life that make it easier and more hopeful than that of the shovelman.

What the Gossips Saw

Leo Romero

*A native of New Mexico, Leo Romero is among a growing number of contem-
porary Southwestern writers whose poetry and fiction are becoming popular
across the country. Romero studied at the University of New Mexico, where he
took a degree in English. His poems have appeared in several recent collections
of poetry and prose. "What the Gossips Saw" was first published in 1981 in a
collection of his poetry called* Agua Negra.

Preparing to Read

1. This is the story of a community's response to a woman who had her
   leg amputated. What it says about the way society sometimes reacts
   to those who are "different" can be compared with what we learn
   from another piece in this chapter: Schwartz's "The Colossus in the
   Kitchen."
2. Romero chooses to leave out periods and other end marks. Doing so
   sometimes helps poets create dramatic effects. Nevertheless,
   developing writers should always include appropriate punctuation.

Vocabulary

alluring (adjective)	Appealing, tempting.
conjecture (noun)	Guessing, speculation.
hobble (verb)	Limp.
in cohorts (adjective)	In league with, cooperating with.
murmur (verb)	Mumble discontentedly.

What the Gossips Saw

Leo Romero

Everyone pitied Escolastica, her leg
had swollen like a watermelon in the summer
It had practically happened over night
She was seventeen, beautiful and soon
to be married to Guillermo who was working   5
in the mines at Terreros, eighty miles away
far up in the mountains, in the wilderness
Poor Escolastica, the old women would say
on seeing her hobble to the well with a bucket

carrying her leg as if it were the weight   10
of the devil, surely it was a curse from heaven
for some misdeed, the young women who were
jealous would murmur, yet they were grieved too
having heard that the doctor might cut
her leg, one of a pair of the most perfect legs   15
in the valley, and it was a topic of great
interest and conjecture among the villagers
whether Guillermo would still marry her
if she were crippled, a one-legged woman—
as if life weren't hard enough for a woman   20
with two legs—how could she manage
Guillermo returned and married Escolastica
even though she had but one leg, the sound
of her wooden leg pounding down the wooden aisle
stayed in everyone's memory for as long   25
as they lived, women cried at the sight
of her beauty, black hair so dark
that the night could get lost in it, a face
more alluring than a full moon

Escolastica went to the dances with her husband   30
and watched and laughed but never danced
though once she had been the best dancer
and could wear holes in a pair of shoes
in a matter of a night, and her waist had been
as light to the touch as a hummingbird's flight   35
And Escolastica bore five children, only half
what most women bore, yet they were healthy
In Escolastica's presence, no one would mention
the absence of her leg, though she walked heavily
And it was not long before the gossips   40
spread their poison, that she must be in cohorts
with the devil, had given him her leg
for the power to bewitch Guillermo's heart
and cloud his eyes so that he could not see
what was so clear to them all   45

Questions for Discussion

1. What words and phrases in this poem show time passing?
2. What figures of speech does Romero include?
3. Pick out a few vivid verbs and adjectives used in "What the Gossips Saw."

4. The story takes place in a village where life is hard. Why is it important for us to know that?

5. The gossips believe Guillermo "could not see/what was so clear to them all." What does Guillermo see that they don't?

6. How do the gossips explain Guillermo's marrying Escolastica even after she loses her leg? What does this say about them?

7. What can we conclude about the gossips' opinion of men in general?

Thinking Critically

1. Many of us know people like the gossips. Do such people deserve blame or pity? Are they malicious or just ignorant?

2. Schwartz's "The Colossus in the Kitchen," which comes next in this chapter, shows that bad luck can be mistaken by small-minded people as a sign of sinfulness and of God's punishment. Where does this theme appear in Romero's poem? Make notes in the margins to prove your point.

Suggestions for Journal Entries

1. Think of a person or an event that was the subject of gossip in your school or community. Use listing or another method for gathering details discussed in "Getting Started" to explain how much the gossips exaggerated, twisted, or lied about the facts. Try to show how they changed the truth to make the story seem more sensational, startling, racy, or horrible than it was.

2. Not all communities react badly to people who are different. Do you agree? If so, provide evidence from personal experience, from newspapers, or from other sources to support this idea. For example, talk about how quickly people in your city responded when they heard a neighbor needed expensive medical care, or explain how well students at your school accept newcomers from other cultures.

The Colossus in the Kitchen

Adrienne Schwartz

Adrienne Schwartz was born in Johannesburg in the Republic of South Africa, where she now lives. "The Colossus in the Kitchen" is about the tragedy of apartheid, a political system that kept power and wealth in the hands of whites by denying civil and economic rights to nonwhites and by enforcing a policy of racial segregation. Tandi, the woman who is at the center of this story, was Schwartz's nursemaid for several years.

Schwartz wrote this essay in 1988. Since that time, South Africa has abolished apartheid and extended civil rights to all citizens, and Nelson Mandela, a black political leader who had been imprisoned by the white minority government during the apartheid era, became South Africa's first freely elected president.

Preparing to Read

1. The Group Areas Act, which Schwartz refers to in paragraph 7, required blacks to seek work *only* in those areas of the country for which the government had granted them a permit. Unfortunately, Tandi's legal husband was not allowed to work in the same region as she.

2. The Colossus was the giant bronze statue of a male figure straddling the inlet to the ancient Greek city of Rhodes. It was known as one of the seven wonders of the ancient world. More generally, this term refers to anything that is very large, impressive, and powerful. As you read this essay, ask yourself what made Tandi a colossus in the eyes of young Schwartz.

Vocabulary

apoplectic (adjective)	Characterized by a sudden loss of muscle control or ability to move.
ashen (adjective)	Gray.
bestriding (adjective)	Straddling, standing with legs spread widely.
cavernous (adjective)	Like a cave or cavern.
confections (noun)	Sweets.
cowered (verb)	Lowered in defeat.
dauntless (adjective)	Fearless.
deviants (noun)	Moral degenerates.
disenfranchised (adjective)	Without rights or power.
entailed (adjective)	Involved.

flaying (noun)	Whipping.
gangrenous (adjective)	Characterized by decay of the flesh.
nebulous (adjective)	Without a definite shape or form.
prerogative (noun)	Privilege.
sage (adjective)	Wise.

The Colossus in the Kitchen

Adrienne Schwartz

I REMEMBER WHEN I first discovered the extraordinary harshness of daily life for black South Africans. It was in the carefree, tumbling days of childhood that I first sensed apartheid was not merely the impoverishing of the landless and all that that entailed, but a flaying of the innermost spirit.   1

The house seemed so huge in those days, and the adults were giants bestriding the world with surety and purpose. Tandi, the cook, reigned with the authoritarian discipline of a Caesar. She held audience in the kitchen, an enormous room filled with half-lights and well-scrubbed tiles, cool stone floors and a cavernous black stove. Its ceilings were high, and during the heat of midday I would often drowse in the corner, listening to Tandi sing, in a lilting voice, of the hardships of black women as aliens in their own country. From half-closed eyes I would watch her broad hands coax, from a nebulous lump of dough, a bounty of confections, filled with yellow cream and new-picked apricots.   2

She was a peasant woman and almost illiterate, yet she spoke five languages quite competently; moreover, she was always there, sturdy, domineering and quick to laugh.   3

Our neighbors, in conformity with established thinking, had long called my mother, and therefore all of us, deviants, agitators, and no less than second cousins to Satan himself. The cause of this dishonorable labeling was the fact that we had been taught to believe in the equality and dignity of humankind.   4

"Never take a person's dignity away from him," my mother had said, "no matter how angry or hurt you might be because in the end you only diminish your own worth."   5

That was why I could not understand the apoplectic reaction of the neighbors to my excited news that Tandi was going to have a baby. After all, this was not politics; this was new life. But the paradox of South Africa is complex in the extreme. The country is like a rare and precious stone set amid barren wastes, and yet close up it is a gangrenous growth that feeds off its own flesh.   6

Tandi's common-law husband lived illegally with her in the quarters assigned to them; complying with the law on this and many other petty issues was not considered appropriate in our household. It was the Group Areas Act   7 that had been responsible for the breakup of Tandi's marriage in the first place. Her lawful husband, who was not born in the same area as she, had been refused a permit to work in the Transvaal, and like others placed in such a burdensome situation, suffered the continuous degradation of being dragged from his wife's bed in the middle of the night and of being denied work more often than he could tolerate. Eventually he simply melted away, never to be seen or heard from again, making legal divorce impossible.

As the days passed, Tandi's waist swelled, and pride glowed in her dauntless eyes.   8

And then the child was born, and he lived for a day, and then he died.   9

I could not look at Tandi. I did not know that the young could die. I thought death was the prerogative of the elderly. I could not bear to see her cowered shoulders or ashen face.   10

I fled to the farthest corner of the yard. One of the neighbors was out picking off dead buds from the rose bushes. She looked over the hedge in concern.   11

"Why! You look terrible . . . are you ill, dear?" she said.   12

"It's Tandi, Mrs. Green. She lost her baby last night," I replied.   13

Mrs. Green sighed thoughtfully and pulled off her gardening gloves. "It's really not surprising," she said, not unkindly, but as if she were imparting as sage a piece of advice as she could. "These people (a term reserved for the disenfranchised) have to learn that the punishment always fits the crime."   14

Questions for Discussion

1. Why does Schwartz spend so much time describing the kitchen in paragraph 2? Does this help us understand Tandi?

2. What details do we learn about Tandi, and what do they tell us about her character? Why does the author call her a "colossus?"

3. Besides Tandi, who are the characters in this narrative and what do we know about them?

4. Why does Schwartz recall events from Tandi's past (paragraph 7)?

5. The author makes especially good use of verbs in the last half of this essay. Find some examples.

6. Schwartz's use of dialogue allows her to explain important ideas. Where in this essay does she use dialogue, and what does it reveal?

Thinking Critically

1. Apartheid was not "merely the impoverishing of the landless" but also "a flaying of the innermost spirit," says Schwartz. What does she mean by this? If necessary, use the encyclopedia to do a little research on apartheid.

2. Is Schwartz's message or central idea similar to Romero's in "What the Gossips Saw?" Write a paragraph in which you compare (point out similarities between) the central ideas of these selections.

Suggestions for Journal Entries

1. Have you or anyone you know well ever witnessed or been involved in a case of intolerance based on race, color, creed, or sex? List the important events that made up this incident and, if appropriate, use focused freewriting to write short descriptions of the characters involved.

2. Schwartz's essay is a startling account of her learning some new and very painful things about life. Using any of the prewriting methods discussed in "Getting Started," make notes about an incident from your childhood that opened your eyes to some new and perhaps unpleasant reality.

3. Were you ever as close to an older person as Schwartz was to Tandi? Examine your relationship with the individual by briefly narrating one or two experiences you shared with him or her.

Faith of the Father
Sam Pickering

Sam Pickering teaches nature writing and children's literature at the University of Connecticut. He has written many scholarly books and articles and has published in the National Review, Kenyon Review, *and* Sewanee Review, *as well as in other prestigious journals. His essay collections include* The Right Distance, A Continuing Education, *and* May Days.

The humorous tone of "Faith of the Father" makes it different from other selections in this chapter. However, its message is just as serious as theirs. Indeed, Pickering is a master at making important ideas come alive through interesting, sometimes hilarious, characters and events. "Faith of the Father" first appeared in the Southwest Review.

Preparing to Read

Pickering makes references to the Bible and to the Christian faith throughout this essay. Lazarus (paragraph 2) is a figure from the New Testament, whom Christ brought back from the dead. Solomon (paragraph 6) is a king of Israel; in describing the lilies of the field, St. Matthew says that "Solomon in all his glory was not arrayed [dressed] like one of these." The Resurrection (paragraph 11) is the rising of Christ from the dead.

Vocabulary

analysis (noun)	Study of, investigation of.
articled (adjective)	Formal, made up of regulations and procedures.
ascension (noun)	Rise.
chalice (noun)	Cup for sacred wine.
deity (noun)	A god, divinity.
dispassionate (adjective)	Unemotional, without feeling.
emblem (noun)	Sign.
endured (verb)	Lasted through.
erratically (adverb)	Unevenly, not in any pattern.
irascible (adjective)	Ill tempered, cranky.
mourning cloak (noun)	Butterfly with purplish-brown wings.
pretension (noun)	Arrogance, excessive pride.
speculated (verb)	Guessed, wondered.
sustenance (noun)	Support, nourishment.

Faith of the Father

Sam Pickering

ON WEEKDAYS Campbell's store was the center of life in the little Virginia town in which I spent summers and Christmas vacations. The post office was in a corner of the store, and the train station was across the road. In the morning men gathered on Campbell's porch and drank coffee while they waited for the train to Richmond. Late in the afternoon, families appeared. While waiting for their husbands, women bought groceries, mailed letters, and visited with one another. Children ate cups of ice cream and played in the woods behind the store. Sometimes a work train was on the siding, and the engineer filled his cab with children and took them for short trips down the track. On weekends life shifted from the store to St. Paul's Church. Built in a grove of pine trees in the nineteenth century, St. Paul's was a small, white clapboard building. A Sunday School wing added to the church in the 1920s jutted out into the graveyard. Beyond the graveyard was a field in which picnics were held and, on the Fourth of July, the yearly Donkey Softball Game was played.

St. Paul's was familial and comfortable. Only a hundred people attended regularly, and everyone knew everyone else and his business. What was private became public after the service as people gathered outside and talked for half an hour before going home to lunch. Behind the altar inside the church was a stained glass window showing Christ's ascension to heaven. A red carpet ran down the middle aisle, and worn, gold cushions covered the pews. On the walls were plaques in memory of parishioners killed in foreign wars or who had made large donations to the building fund. In summer the minister put fans out on the pews. Donated by a local undertaker, the fans were shaped like spades. On them, besides the undertaker's name and telephone number, were pictures of Christ performing miracles: walking on water, healing the lame, and raising Lazarus from the dead.

Holidays and funerals were special at St. Paul's. Funerals were occasions for reminiscing and telling stories. When an irascible old lady died and her daughter had "Gone to Jesus" inscribed on her tombstone, her son-in-law was heard to say "poor Jesus"—or so the tale went at the funeral. Christmas Eve was always cold and snow usually fell. Inside the church at midnight, though, all was cheery and warm as the congregation sang the great Christmas hymns: "O Come, All Ye Faithful," "The First Noel," "O Little Town of Bethlehem," and "Hark! The Herald Angels Sing." The last hymn was "Silent Night." The service did not follow the prayer book; inspired by Christmas and eggnog, the congregation came to sing, not to pray. Bourbon was in the air, and when the altar boy lit the candles, it seemed a miracle that the first spark didn't send us all to heaven in a blue flame.

Easter was almost more joyous than Christmas. Men stuck greenery into   4
their lapels and women blossomed in bright bonnets, some ordering hats not
simply from Richmond but from Baltimore and Philadelphia. On a farm outside town lived Miss Emma and Miss Ida Catlin. Miss Emma was the practical
sister, running the farm and bringing order wherever she went. Unlike Miss
Emma, Miss Ida was shy. She read poetry and raised guinea fowl and at parties sat silently in a corner. Only on Easter was she outgoing; then like a day
lily she bloomed triumphantly. No one else's Easter bonnet ever matched
hers, and the congregation eagerly awaited her entrance which she always
made just before the first hymn.

One year Miss Ida found a catalogue from a New York store which ad-   5
vertised hats and their accessories. For ten to twenty-five cents ladies could
buy artificial flowers to stick into their bonnets. Miss Ida bought a counter
full, and that Easter her head resembled a summer garden in bloom. Daf-
fodils, zinnias, and black-eyed Susans hung yellow and red around the brim
of her hat while in the middle stood a magnificent pink peony.

In all his glory Solomon could not have matched Miss Ida's bonnet. The   6
congregation could not take its eyes off it; even the minister had trouble concentrating on his sermon. After the last hymn, everyone hurried out of the
church, eager to get a better look at Miss Ida's hat. As she came out, the altar
boy began ringing the bell. Alas, the noise frightened pigeons who had recently begun to nest and they shot out of the steeple. The congregation scattered, but the flowers on Miss Ida's hat hung over her eyes, and she did not
see the pigeons until it was too late and the peony had been ruined.

Miss Ida acted like nothing had happened. She greeted everyone and   7
asked their healths and the healths of absent members of families. People tried
not to look at her hat but were not very successful. For two Sundays Miss Ida's
"accident" was the main subject of after-church conversation; then it was forgotten for almost a year. But, as Easter approached again, people remembered
the hat. They wondered what Miss Ida would wear to church. Some people
speculated that since she was a shy, poetic person, she wouldn't come. Even
the minister had doubts. To reassure Miss Ida, he and his sons borrowed lad-
ders two weeks before Easter, and climbing to the top of the steeple, chased
the pigeons away and sealed off their nesting place with chicken wire.

Easter Sunday seemed to confirm the fears of those who doubted Miss   8
Ida would appear. The choir assembled in the rear of the church without her.
Half-heartedly the congregation sang the processional hymn, "Hail Thee, Festival Day." Miss Ida's absence had taken something bright from our lives, and
as we sat down after singing, Easter seemed sadly ordinary.

We were people of little faith. Just as the minister reached the altar and   9
turned to face us, there was a stir at the back of the church. Silently the minister raised his right hand and pointed toward the door. Miss Ida had arrived.
She was wearing the same hat she wore the year before; only the peony was
missing. In its place was a wonderful sunflower; from one side hung a black

and yellow garden spider building a web while fluttering above was a mourning cloak, black wings, dotted with blue and a yellow border running around the edges. Our hearts leaped up, and at the end of the service people in Richmond must have heard us singing "Christ the Lord Is Risen Today."

St. Paul's was the church of my childhood, that storied time when I thought little about religion but knew that Jesus loved me, yes, because the Bible told me so. In the Morning Prayer of life I mixed faith and fairy tale, thinking God a kindly giant, holding in his hands, as the song put it, the corners of the earth and the strength of the hills. Thirty years have passed since I last saw St. Paul's, and I have come down from the cool upland pastures and the safe fold of childhood to the hot lowlands. Instead of being neatly tucked away in a huge hand, the world now seems to bound erratically, smooth and slippery, forever beyond the grasp of even the most magical deity. Would that it were not so, and my imagination could find a way through his gates, as the prayer says, with thanksgiving. Often I wonder what happened to the "faith of our fathers." Why if it endured dungeon, fire, and sword in others, did it weaken so within me?

10

For me religion is a matter of story and community, a congregation rising together to look at an Easter Bonnet, unconsciously seeing it an emblem of hope and vitality, indeed of the Resurrection itself. For me religion ought to be more concerned with people than ideas, creating soft feeling rather than sharp thought. Often I associate religion with small, backwater towns in which tale binds folk one to another. Here in a university in which people are separated by idea rather than linked by story, religion doesn't have a natural place. In the absence of community ceremony becomes important. Changeable and always controversial, subject to dispassionate analysis, ceremony doesn't tie people together like accounts of pigeons and peonies and thus doesn't promote good feeling and finally love for this world and hope for the next. Often when I am discouraged, I turn for sustenance, not to formal faith with articled ceremony but to memory, a chalice winey with story.

11

Questions for Discussion

1. Where in this essay does Pickering describe setting?
2. What do we learn about Miss Ida's character? Is it important for us to know about her?
3. Why does Pickering mention the names of the hymns the congregation sang at Christmas and Easter?
4. How does he indicate the passage of time in paragraphs 6–9?
5. Does the author include dialogue in this story? Where and for what purpose?
6. What is his purpose in mentioning that, on Christmas Eve at St. Paul's, "Bourbon was in the air" (paragraph 3)?

Thinking Critically

1. Pickering believes religion has more to do with people than with doctrine. What does he mean?
2. Why is the congregation happy about Miss Ida's return (paragraph 9)? How is her story related to the Easter theme?
3. The author doesn't think religion has a "natural place" in colleges and universities. Do you agree?

Suggestions for Journal Entries

1. Answer the journalists' questions to recall information about a humorous event that happened during a celebration—religious or not—that you attended.
2. In paragraph 10, Pickering tells us that his childhood vision of religion was a mixture of "faith and fairy tale." What was your childhood faith like? Recall an incident from those years that might help answer this question. Use listing or answer the journalists' questions to explain what happened.

Frederick Douglass: The Path to Freedom

Carl Sagan

Carl Sagan was a professor of astronomy at Cornell University and the author of many books on science. He worked on several NASA projects and researched the possibilities of life on other planets. As host of the popular television program "Cosmos," Sagan did a great deal to increase public interest in science and mathematics and to increase support for education in these subjects. Among Sagan's most widely read books are The Dragons of Eden, *for which he won the Pulitzer Prize in 1977,* Broca's Brain, Cosmos, *and* The Demon-Haunted World, *from which this selection is taken. Sagan died in 1997.*

Preparing to Read

1. Sagan uses dialogue effectively. Read his direct quotations carefully.
2. The essay begins with remarks that explain the kind of thinking that led to and supported the institution of slavery (paragraphs 1–4). Although not part of the narrative per se, this information sheds important light on the events that led to Douglass's achieving his freedom.
3. What might be "the path to freedom" discussed in this essay?

Vocabulary

antebellum (adjective)	Before the Civil War.
condoned (verb)	Tolerated, excused.
drudgery (noun)	Hard, tedious work.
eluded (verb)	Escaped.
fiendish (adjective)	Devilish.
heart-rending (adjective)	Heartbreaking.
hereditary (adjective)	By birth, genetic.
manifesting (adjective)	Showing.
nil (noun)	Nothing, zero.
prohibitions (noun)	Bans, laws against.
reprieve (noun)	Relief, pardon.
reticent (adjective)	Restrained, quiet.
subversive (adjective)	Rebellious, defiant, revolutionary.
surreptitiously (adverb)	Secretly.

Frederick Douglass: The Path to Freedom

Carl Sagan

FREDERICK BAILEY was a slave. As a boy in Maryland in the 1820s, he had no 1
mother or father to look after him. ("It is a common custom," he later
wrote, "to part children from their mothers . . . before the child has
reached its twelfth month.") He was one of countless millions of slave children whose realistic prospects for a hopeful life were nil.

What Bailey witnessed and experienced in his growing up marked him 2
forever. "I have often been awakened at the dawn of day by the most heart-
rending shrieks of an aunt of mine, whom [the overseer] used to tie up to a
joist, and whip upon her naked back till she was literally covered with
blood . . . From the rising till the going down of the sun he was cursing,
raving, cutting, and slashing among the slaves of the field . . . He seemed to
take pleasure in manifesting his fiendish barbarity."

The slaves had drummed into them, from plantation and pulpit alike, 3
from courthouse and statehouse, the notion that they were hereditary inferi-
ors, that God *intended* them for their misery. The Holy Bible, as countless
passages confirmed, condoned slavery. In these ways the "peculiar institution" maintained itself despite its monstrous nature—something even its
practitioners must have glimpsed.

There was a most revealing rule: Slaves were to remain illiterate. In the 4
antebellum South, whites who taught a slave to read were severely punished.
"[To] make a contented slave," Bailey later wrote, "it is necessary to make a
thoughtless one. It is necessary to darken his moral and mental vision, and,
as far as possible, to annihilate the power of reason." This is why the slave-
holders must control what slaves hear and see and think. This is why reading
and critical thinking are dangerous, indeed subversive, in an unjust society.

So now picture Frederick Bailey in 1828—a 10-year-old African-American 5
child, enslaved, with no legal rights of any kind, long since torn from his
mother's arms, sold away from the tattered remnants of his extended family
as if he were a calf or a pony, conveyed to an unknown household in a
strange city of Baltimore, and condemned to a life of drudgery with no
prospect of reprieve.

Bailey was sent to work for Capt. Hugh Auld and his wife, Sophia, mov- 6
ing from plantation to urban bustle, from field work to housework. In this
new environment, he came every day upon letters, books, and people who
could read. He discovered what he called "this mystery" of reading: There
was a connection between the letters on the page and the movement of the
reader's lips, a nearly one-to-one correlation between the black squiggles and
the sounds uttered. Surreptitiously, he studied from young Tommy Auld's
Webster's Spelling Book. He memorized the letters of the alphabet. He tried to
understand the sounds they stood for. Eventually, he asked Sophia Auld to
help him learn. Impressed with the intelligence and dedication of the boy,
and perhaps ignorant of the prohibitions, she complied.

By the time Frederick was spelling words of three and four letters, Captain Auld discovered what was going on. Furious, he ordered Sophia to stop. In Frederick's presence he explained:

> A nigger should know nothing but to obey his master—to do as he is told to do. Learning would *spoil* the best nigger in the world. Now, if you teach that nigger how to read, there would be no keeping him. It would forever unfit him to be a slave.

Auld chastised Sophia in this way as if Frederick Bailey were not there in the room with them, or as if he were a block of wood.

But Auld had revealed to Bailey the great secret: "I now understood . . . the white man's power to enslave the black man. From that moment, I understood the pathway from slavery to freedom."

Without further help from the now reticent and intimidated Sophia Auld, Frederick found ways to continue learning how to read, including buttonholing white schoolchildren on the streets. Then he began teaching his fellow slaves: "Their minds had been starved . . . They had been shut up in mental darkness. I taught them, because it was the delight of my soul."

With his knowledge of reading playing a key role in his escape, Bailey fled to New England, where slavery was illegal and black people were free. He changed his name to Frederick Douglass (after a character in Walter Scott's *The Lady of the Lake*), eluded the bounty hunters who tracked down escaped slaves, and became one of the greatest orators, writers, and political leaders in American history. All his life, he understood that literacy had been the way out.

Questions for Discussion

1. This essay shows clearly that narration can be used to make a point. Where does Sagan place his thesis?

2. What method for writing conclusions discussed in Chapter 4 does Sagan use?

3. The author keeps the story moving by using transitional words and expressions in important places. Find a few of them.

4. How does Sagan's quoting Frederick Douglass directly help him tell the story?

5. Where in this essay does Sagan establish setting?

6. This is a short selection. What is the author able to reveal about his characters?

Thinking Critically

1. Why does Sagan quote Captain Auld directly in paragraph 7? What is it that Auld unknowingly reveals to Frederick?

2. In *The Demon-Haunted World,* the book from which this essay was taken, Sagan quotes Epictetus, a Roman philosopher who had once been a slave: "We must not believe the many, who say that only free people ought to be educated, but we should rather believe the philosophers who say that only the educated are free." What light does this statement shed on Sagan's essay on Frederick Douglass?

3. In Chapter 2, reread William Bennett's essay "Study Calculus!" about mathematics teacher Jaime Escalante. Explain why Escalante might hold up Frederick Douglass as an example to his students.

Suggestions for Journal Entries

1. Think of a person you know who has had to overcome obstacles to achieve an important goal in life. If you can, interview this person to learn more about his or her struggle.

2. Frederick Douglass taught himself to read without the benefit of formal education. Indeed, his owner did everything he could to keep him from learning. Do you know someone who has been discouraged from educating him- or herself? Do you know someone who had to learn an important skill on his or her own? Use clustering or freewriting to gather information about this individual. You might even brainstorm with older people who are acquainted with your subject.

Suggestions for Sustained Writing

1. Sandburg's "Child of the Romans" contrasts the shovelman's life with those of the railroad passengers. Show how difficult or easy your life seems when contrasted with the life of someone you know. If you made a journal entry after Sandburg's poem, you might have already gathered details for this paper.

    Focus your essay on the other person; recall events that show the kind of life he or she has led. At the same time, remember that setting is important, so include details that reveal where or when these events took place.

    A good way to introduce the essay is to explain how difficult or easy life seems to you. Then, write a thesis statement that contrasts your life with the life of the other person. Put the thesis at the end of your introduction. For example, say you start by complaining about the difficult courses you are taking, the many hours you work as a cashier, or the fact that you drive an old car. The thesis at the end of this introduction might be: "My life may be hard, but I count my blessings when I think about the sacrifices my cousin made to get through college."

However you begin, make the events you narrate in the body of your essay illustrate or prove your thesis. If they don't, revise the thesis or rewrite the body of the paper to include details that relate to the thesis more directly. Conclude your essay by explaining what this assignment has taught you about yourself or your society.

Finally, rewrite and edit the finished product. Make sure your information is well organized, your language is vivid and clear, and your grammar, sentence structure, punctuation, and spelling are correct.

2. Several selections in this chapter are about life's painful realities. "What the Gossips Saw" shows how mean-spirited people can become toward those different from them. "The Colossus in the Kitchen" tells of an encounter with institutionalized racism and human insensitivity. "Frederick Douglass: The Path to Freedom" recalls the horror of slavery.

Use these selections as inspiration, and write the story of an event that taught you something distressing about human behavior or society. Try to include the journal notes you made after reading the works mentioned above.

There are several ways to organize this narrative. Perhaps the easiest is to tell the story from beginning to end, just as you remember it. You need not write a formal introduction unless, like Sagan, you want to share important insights or background information with readers before beginning the story itself. In fact, your central idea can wait until you write a concluding paragraph that summarizes what the events you just narrated taught you.

As always, write several drafts and provide enough details to make your story believable. This is a good time to include proper nouns and write dialogue that will give readers the feeling they are on the scene. As you edit, make sure the story moves smoothly and remains interesting. If not, include words and expressions that show the passage of time and add vivid verbs and adjectives.

3. In "What the Gossips Saw," Romero shows that people who gossip can exaggerate or twist a story so badly that, in their mouths, the truth becomes unrecognizable. Look back to the journal notes you made after reading this poem. Then, begin drafting an essay that tells what happened when gossips spread rumors about a person or event in your school or community.

As with other assignments, there are several ways to organize your thoughts. For example, start by revealing the truth of a story and then explain step-by-step how gossips distorted that truth. On the other hand, you might recall how false rumors began, how they spread, and how they affected people. A good way to end this kind of paper is to tell the truth as you know it.

Whether you use either of these methods or follow one of your own, make the story persuasive. Write several drafts, each of which develops the plot in greater and more vivid detail. In addition, explain what this experience taught you about gossip and about the people who spread it. The best place to do this is in the paper's introduction or conclusion.

This assignment is a good chance to use dialogue and to practice other techniques discussed in Chapter 9 for describing people and their personalities. As you revise your work, rely on such techniques to make the characters in your story interesting and believable. When the time comes to edit, double-check any dialogue you have included for correct punctuation.

4. The selections by Romero, Schwartz, and Sagan speak of the unfair treatment of people. Have you ever been treated unfairly, belittled, or held back because of your race, religion, nationality, physical handicap, personal belief, or any other reason? Tell your story vividly and completely. In the process, explain what the experience taught you about other people or society in general. Express this idea as your thesis statement somewhere in the essay.

Good examples of essays that use narration to develop a strong thesis statement are Schwartz's "The Colossus in the Kitchen" and Sagan's "Frederick Douglass: The Path to Freedom." In her first paragraph, Schwartz defines apartheid as "a flaying of the innermost spirit," then uses the rest of her essay to support that idea. In his conclusion, Sagan tells us that "all his life, [Douglass] understood that literacy had been the way out" of bondage. This is the central idea he develops through the narrative.

Begin working by reviewing journal notes you made after reading the works of the authors mentioned above. Then outline and draft your paper. Like Schwartz and Sagan, you can focus on one event. On the other hand, like Romero, you might narrate two or three events to support your thesis. Either way, include details about the people in your story as you draft or revise. Describe their personalities by revealing what they said or did. Then, as you edit for grammar, punctuation, and spelling, pay special attention to the vocabulary you have chosen. Include proper nouns as appropriate, and make sure your language is specific and vivid.

5. Did you respond to the first of the Suggestions for Journal Entries after "Faith of the Father"? If so, use the details you collected to get started on an essay that tells a humorous incident you witnessed or took part in during a religious, political, academic, or other kind of ritual, ceremony, or formal event.

Like Pickering, describe both the setting and the people of your story. Use dialogue whenever you can, and identify specific places and things—like the hymns in "Faith of the Father"—that will make your writing realistic and convincing.

A good way to introduce this essay is to describe a scene or to make a startling remark. You might conclude by using a quotation readers will remember, looking to the future, or offering advice.

When it comes time to rewrite your first draft, replace flat, uninteresting vocabulary with forceful verbs and vivid adjectives. Add transitions to make your story easy to follow. Use as much detail as needed to help your readers see the event as you did. If you write a truly entertaining paper, share it with your friends and family. First, however, remove any mechanical or stylistic errors that would reduce your essay's effect on them.

6. If you responded to the second journal suggestion after Pickering's essay, expand your entry into a full-length essay. Tell a story that will allow your readers to understand what religion meant for you when you were a child. Like Pickering, you need not have had an active role in the event or events you are narrating. Just make sure that what you write will be vivid and clear enough to explain the part religion played (and perhaps still plays) in your life.

   If you run short on details, try interviewing others who witnessed or took part in what occurred. Otherwise, follow the advice offered in Suggestion 5 above.

7. Have you ever witnessed or experienced a car accident, robbery, mugging, house fire, serious injury, sudden illness, or other violence or misfortune? Tell what happened during this terrible experience and describe the people involved. However, spend most of your time discussing the reactions of people who looked on as the event took place. Were you one of them? What did they do or say? What didn't they do that they should have done?

   You might find inspiration and information for this project in the journal entries you made after reading Romero and Schwartz. Before you write your first draft, however, think about what the event itself and the onlookers' reactions taught you about human nature. Were you encouraged or disappointed by what you learned? Express your answer in a preliminary thesis statement. Write at least two drafts of your story, and make sure to include details that will support this thesis.

   Then revise at least one more time by turning what you have just written into a letter to the editor of your college or community newspaper. Use your letter to explain your approval or disappointment about the way the onlookers reacted, but don't mention their names. If appropriate, offer suggestions about the way your readers might respond if faced with an experience like the one you have narrated. Whether or not you send your letter to a newspaper, edit it carefully, just as if it were going to be published.

Writing to Learn: A Group Activity

Carl Sagan's "The Path to Freedom" explains how Frederick Douglass threw off the chains of slavery. However, there is more to know about Douglass's role in the freeing of other slaves and the abolition of slavery in general. Indeed, Douglass was part of an enormously important movement in American history, the particulars of which should never be forgotten. As such, your writing group might compile a list of people, events, and organizations important to the long struggle that resulted in the abolition of slavery.

THE FIRST MEETING

Assign each student to research four or five people, organizations, or developments that played a role in the struggle to abolish slavery. Limit your searches to topics that can be discussed in two or three paragraphs. Do not try to research complex topics such as the Civil War, for example. Below is a list of people, legal cases, laws, and organizations you might want to learn more about. Of course, you may want to add to this list:

John Brown	Nat Turner	Fugitive Slave Laws
Anthony Burns		Kansas-Nebraska Act
Cassius Marcellus Clay	*Armistad* Case	Missouri Compromise
Frederick Douglass	*Creole* Case	Underground Railroad
William Lloyd Garrison	*Dred Scott* Decision	American Anti-Slavery
Abraham Lincoln	Emancipation	Society
Lucretia Coffin Mott	Proclamation	Free-Soil Party
Harriet Tubman	Fourteenth	Society of Friends
Sojourner Truth	Amendment to the	*The Liberator*
	U.S. Constitution	

RESEARCH

Print sources in your library's reference section should provide you with all the information you will need. However, many sites on the Internet also discuss topics in the list above. You might want to research each of these topics individually or search for terms such as *slavery* or *abolitionist movement*. In addition, your library should have a large variety of books that will help. Here are just five to look for:

Bontemps, Anna, *100 Years of Negro Freedom,* 1980

Blackett, R. J. M., *Beating against the Barriers,* 1986

Du Bois, W. E. B., *The Souls of Black Folk,* first published in 1903

Ebony editors, *Ebony Pictorial History of Black America,*
1971

Hughes, Langston, *A Pictorial History of Black America,*
1956, 1983

You are sure to find others in your library's card or online catalog of books.

Take good notes on each topic you research. Try to focus on information that explains what made that person, organization, or development important to the struggle for freedom. Then put the notes you have taken on each topic into a well-developed paragraph or two. Each topic you discuss will become one entry in the glossary or listing your group is compiling.

Make enough copies of each entry you write to share with members of your group at your next meeting.

The Second Meeting

Distribute and read each other's entries. Make suggestions for improvement in content. Make certain every entry explains the importance of the topic discussed to the eventual abolition of slavery. Assign each student the task of revising his or her work and of bringing copies to distribute at the next meeting.

The Third Meeting

Distribute revised copies of the work you discussed during the second meeting. This time, make suggestions that will help the writer edit and proofread his or her work. Assign one person to collect the finished entries in a few days and to put them in alphabetical order before submitting them to the instructor.

Exposition

Many new writers begin to develop their skills by practicing the kinds of writing found in Sections Three and Four, description and narration. As you learned in previous chapters, description and narration usually involve writing about subjects that are concrete and, often, very specific—people, places, events, or objects that the reader can picture or understand easily. The primary purpose of description, of course, is to explain what someone or something looked like, sounded like, and so forth. The primary purpose of narration is simply to tell what happened, although many short stories and narrative essays do a great deal more.

At times, however, new writers face the challenge of discussing abstract ideas that can't be explained through narration and description alone. In such cases, they must rely on a variety of methods of development and techniques associated with exposition. *Exposition* is writing that explains.

Each essay selection in Chapters 12, 13, and 14 explains an abstract idea by using illustration, comparison and contrast, or process analysis as its *primary* method of development. However, these selections also rely on other methods explained earlier in this book (see Chapter 3). In fact, most writers of exposition combine methods to develop ideas clearly and convincingly. Comparison-and-contrast papers frequently contain definitions, anecdotes, and examples; process analyses include accurate, sometimes vivid descriptions; and illustration essays sometimes use comparisons, anecdotes, and descriptions.

Whatever your purpose and however you choose to develop ideas, you will have to know your subject well, include enough accurate information to make your writing convincing, and present that information in a way that is clear and easy to follow.

Explaining through Illustration

One of the most popular ways to explain an idea is illustration, a method of development you read about in Chapter 3. Illustration uses examples to turn an idea that is general, abstract, or hard to understand into something readers can recognize and, therefore, grasp more easily. As the word implies, an illustration is a concrete and specific picture of an idea that would otherwise have remained vague and undefined.

For instance, if you wanted a clearer and more definitive notion of what your friend meant when she claimed to have met several "interesting characters" since coming to school, you might ask her to describe a few of those characters specifically and to show you in what ways they were interesting. Each of the people she discussed would then serve as an illustration or picture of what she meant by the abstract word *interesting*.

Explaining through Comparison and Contrast

This method of development involves pointing out similarities or differences, or both, between two people, objects, places, experiences, ways of doing something, and the like. Writers compare (point out similarities between) and contrast (point out differences between) two things to make one or both more recognizable or understandable to their readers. Let's say you want to explain a computer monitor to someone who has never seen one. You might compare it with a television set. After all, both have glass screens on which electronic images appear. To make your explanation more complete and accurate, however, you might also need to contrast these two devices by pointing out that only on television can one watch a baseball game, a soap opera, or reruns of *I Love Lucy*. Contrast also comes in handy when you want to explain why you believe one thing is better than another. For example, "Watch the Cart!" an essay in the introduction to Chapter 13, points out differences to explain why the author thinks women are more adept at grocery shopping than men.

There are many reasons for comparing or contrasting the subjects you wish to write about. Whatever your purpose, you may find that comparing or contrasting will help you bring abstract ideas into sharper focus and make them more concrete than if you had discussed each of your subjects separately.

Explaining through Process Analysis

Process analysis is used in scientific writing to help readers understand both natural and technical processes such as the formation of rain clouds, the circulation of blood through the body, or the workings of a CD player, for example. However, it also has a place in nonscientific writing. For example, you might want to use process analysis to explain how U.S. presidents are elected, how money is transferred from one bank to another electronically, or even how your Aunt Millie manages to turn the most solemn occasion into a party.

Process analysis is useful when you need to provide the reader with directions or instructions to complete a specific task. Subjects for such essays might include "how to change the brakes on a Ford Mustang," "how to bake lasagna," or "how to get to school from the center of town."

In each of these examples, the writer is assigning him- or herself the task of explaining, as specifically and as clearly as possible, an idea that might be very new and unfamiliar to the reader. And, in each case, the essay will focus on how to do something or how something is done.

Though it may often seem deceptively simple, writing a process paper is often a painstaking task and must be approached carefully. Remember that your readers might be totally unfamiliar with what you're explaining and will need a great deal of information to follow the process easily and to understand it thoroughly.

As a matter of fact, the need to be clear and concrete often causes writers of process analysis to rely on other methods of development as well. Among them are narration, description, illustration, and comparison and contrast. Of these, writers of process analysis rely most heavily on narration. After all, a process is a story. Like narratives, process papers are often organized in chronological order and explain a series of events. Unlike narratives, however, process essays don't simply tell *what* happens; they also explain *how* something happens or *how* something should be done.

CHAPTER 12

Illustration

You have learned that the most interesting and effective writing uses specific and concrete details to *show* rather than to *tell* the reader something. This goes for all types of writing, including exposition. One of the best ways to show your readers what you mean is to fill your writing with clear, relevant examples. Examples are also referred to as *illustrations*. They act as pictures—concrete representations—of an abstract idea you are trying to explain, and they make your writing easier to understand and more convincing for your readers. Illustration can be used as the primary method to develop a thesis in your expository writing.

Effective illustrations make reference to specific people, places, and things—familiar realities that your readers will recognize or understand easily. Say that you want to convince them that your 1996 Wizbang is an economical car. Instead of being content to rely on their understanding of a vague word like *economical*, you decide to provide examples that show exactly what you think this term means. Therefore, you explain that the Wizbang gets about 65 miles per gallon around town, that its purchase price is $4,000 less than its least expensive competitor's, and that it needs only one $50 tune-up every 40,000 miles. Now that's economical!

Several types of examples are discussed below. The important thing to remember is that the examples you choose must relate to and be appropriate to the idea you're illustrating. For instance, you probably wouldn't cite statistics about the Wizbang's safety record if you wanted to impress your readers with how inexpensive the car is to own and operate.

Specific Facts, Instances, or Occurrences

A good way to get examples into your writing is to use specific facts, instances, or occurrences relating to the idea you are explaining. Let's say you want to prove that the Wizbang does not perform well in bad weather. You can say it stalled twice during a recent rainstorm or that it did not start when the temperature fell below freezing last week. If you want to show that people in your town are community-minded, you might mention that they recently opened a shelter for the homeless, that they have organized a meals-on-wheels program for the elderly, or that they have increased their contributions to the United Way campaign in each of the last five years. If you want to prove that the 1960s were years of turmoil, you can recall the assassinations of John and Robert Kennedy and Martin Luther King, Jr., the antiwar marches, and the urban riots.

The selections in this chapter use specific facts, instances, or occurrences to illustrate and develop ideas. Grace Lukawska's "Wolf" is full of revealing facts about this animal. Specific instances and occurrences can be found in Irina Groza's "Growing Up in Romania" and in Philip K. Howard's "The Death of Common Sense." Michael Barone's "The American Century" uses facts and instances to convince us that the twentieth century was truly America's own.

Statistics

Mathematical figures, or statistics, can also be included to strengthen your reader's understanding of an abstract idea. If you want to prove that the cost of living in your hometown has increased dramatically over the last five years, you might explain that the price of a three-bedroom home has increased by about 30 percent, from $100,000 to $130,000, that real estate taxes have doubled from an average of $1,500 per family to $3,000 per family, and that the cost of utilities has nearly tripled, with each household now spending about $120 per month on heat and electricity. Philip K. Howard's "The Death of Common Sense" makes good use of statistics.

Specific People, Places, or Things

Mentioning specific people, places, and things familiar to the readers can also help you make abstract ideas easier to understand and more convincing. If you want to explain that the American South is famous for the presidents and statespeople it has produced, you might bring up George Washington, Thomas Jefferson, Henry Clay, Lyndon Johnson, Martin Luther King, and Jimmy Carter. If you need to convince readers that your city is a great place to have fun, you will probably mention its amusement park, professional football stadium, brand-new children's zoo and aquarium, community swimming pool, campgrounds, and public golf courses. Specific people, places, and things are mentioned throughout Howard's "The Death of Common Sense."

Anecdotes

As you probably know, anecdotes are brief, informative stories that develop an idea or drive home a point. They are similar to and serve the same purpose as specific instances and occurrences, and they are sometimes used with such illustrations to develop an idea more fully. However, anecdotes often appear in greater detail than other types of examples. Look for anecdotes especially in Groza's "Growing Up in Romania" and Howard's "The Death of Common Sense."

Visualizing Examples

The following paragraphs are from Alleen Pace Nilsen's "Sexism in English: A 1990's Update." They explain interesting facts about etymology, the origins of words.

States her thesis.

. . . in American culture a woman is valued for the attractiveness and sexiness of her body, while a man is valued for his physical strength and accomplishments. A woman is sexy; a man is successful.

A persuasive piece of evidence supporting this view are the eponyms—words that have come from someone's name—found in English.

Creates an interesting contrast.

[After researching this subject] I had a two-and-a-half-inch stack of cards taken from men's names, but less than a half-inch stack from women's names, and most of those came from Greek mythology. In words that came into American English since we separated from Britain, there are many eponyms based on the names of famous

Uses specific instances.

American men: bartlett pear, boysenberry, diesel engine, franklin stove, ferris wheel, gatling gun, mason jar, sideburns, sousaphone, schick test, and winchester rifle. The only common eponyms taken from

Mentions specific people.

American women's names are *Alice blue* (after Alice Roosevelt Longworth), *bloomers* (after Amelia Jenks Bloomer) and *Mae West jacket* (after the buxom actress). Two out of the three feminine eponyms relate closely to a woman's physical anatomy, while the masculine eponyms (except for *sideburns* after General Burnsides) have nothing to do with the namesake's body, but instead honor the man for an accomplishment of some kind.

Although in Greek mythology women played a bigger role than they did in the biblical stories of the Judeo Christian

Mentions specific mythological figures; mentions things readers will recognize.

cultures . . . the same tendency to think of women in relation to sexuality is seen in the eponyms *aphrodisiac* from Aphrodite, the Greek name for the goddess of love and beauty, and venereal disease, from Venus, the Roman name for Aphrodite.

Another interesting word from Greek mythology is Amazon. According to Greek folk etymology, the *a* means "without" as in *atypical* or *amoral* while *mazon* comes from *mazos,* meaning breast as still seen in *mastectomy*. In the Greek legend, Amazon women cut off their right breasts so that

Tells an anecdote.

they could better shoot their bows. Apparently, the story tellers had a feeling that for women to play the active, "masculine" role that the Amazons adopted for themselves, they had to trade in part of their femininity.

Revising Illustration Essays

Before writing "Wolf," student Grace Lukawska had completed a great deal of prewriting in her journal to get started. When she finished her first draft, however, she realized she would have to add more detail and restructure her essay and improve some of her word choices to make her point effectively. By the time she finished, she had written several drafts, but the final product shows that careful revision is always worth the effort. Read these paragraphs from two versions of the complete paper, which appears in this chapter. Information in parentheses refers to Candace Savage's *Wolves,* a book in which Lukawska researched facts about her subject.

Lukawska—Rough Draft

Make introduction more interesting?

Include vivid details and examples to explain misconceptions?

There are still popular misconceptions of the wolf as predator. Many people think that wolves kill for pleasure or just to show their dominance over other animals. However, the truth is that wolves are very fascinating and intelligent.

Their intelligence manifests itself in their behavior. Wolves belong to a group of animals who live in hierarchical groups. According to Candace Savage, a large, well-organized pack consists of an upper class— parents, a middle class—uncles and aunts, a lower class—children, and finally "helpers"

For what? Explain?

who are inexperienced hunters and who depend on the pack (55). Their role is to baby-sit youngsters while the other wolves are hunting (62).

Another example of wolves' aptitude is clear communication. The leader of the

Does this relate to communication?

group, usually the male, establishes regulations so that each animal knows whom it can boss and to whom it must <u>submit</u>.   For instance, a middle-class wolf must obey the leader's orders; children and helpers must <u>submit</u> to their relatives.   These rules help to prevent fights or disagreements in packs.

Say more about their language? Use examples?

Furthermore, wolves have their own language which is based on different sound levels in their voices.   For example, according to Savage, a whimper indicates a friendly attitude; snarls convey warnings and admonitions (58).

Lukawska—Final Draft

For centuries, popular misconceptions have pictured the wolf as a terrifying predator

Creates vivid images that serve as examples.

that kills for pleasure.   The name itself calls up nasty images: the glutton who "wolfs" down his food; the werewolf, who, during a full moon, grows hair all over his body, howls into the night, and claws beautiful maidens to death.   Even in fairy

Mentions specific story, which readers might recognize

tales, such as "Little Red Riding Hood," the wolf is pictured as shrewd and bloodthirsty.

Makes thesis clearer, stronger.

But is the wolf really a cold-blooded killer? Not at all; the wolf is a magnificent animal which displays many of the characteristics we value in human beings.

The intelligence of the wolf manifests itself in its behavior. The wolf's society is well organized and hierarchical.

Mentions title of Savage's book.

According to Candace Savage, author of *Wolves*, a pack consists of an upper class—parents, a middle class—uncles and aunts, a lower class—children, and finally "helpers,"

Becomes more specific.

who are inexperienced hunters and <u>who depend upon the pack for their food</u> (55). Their role is to baby-sit youngsters while the other wolves are hunting (62). Like humans, wolves practice adoption. If parents die, their children are cared for by another family.

New paragraph explains behavior, not communication.

The leader of the group, usually a male, establishes regulations so that each animal knows whom it can boss and to whom it must submit. For instance, a middle-class wolf must obey the leader's orders; children and helpers must submit to their relatives. This rule helps prevent disagreements and fights.

Creates a new paragraph to discuss communication. Expands her discussion.

Another indication of the wolf's intelligence is the ability to communicate. Wolves have their own language, which is based on the use of different intonations. According to Savage, a whimper communicates friendship, snarls convey warnings and admonishments, and a "special chirplike tone expresses sexual interest" (58). Like dogs, wolves also use gestures and facial

Uses description to create examples.

expressions to communicate. By moving their foreheads, mouths, ears, and eyes, they express their emotions and announce their ranks. Frightened wolves keep their teeth covered, "eyes slightly closed, ears flat to the head" (Savage 55). They also bend their legs and tuck in their tails. Wolves that are self-confident, on the other hand, point their ears forward and bare their teeth. Wolves of the highest rank reveal their

Includes concrete, specific vocabulary.

positions by keeping their tails and ears up and by looking directly into the eyes of other animals. Members of the pack show respect for them; like dogs, they keep their ears tucked in, their heads down, and their legs slightly bent.

Practicing Illustration

Examples can be defined as concrete signs of abstract ideas. Below are several topic sentences expressing abstract ideas. Use the spaces below each to write a paragraph relating to each sentence. Develop your paragraph by using at least three examples of the kinds you have just read about. First, however, make a quick list of the examples you will use on a sheet of scratch paper. You can discuss them in detail when it comes time to write the paragraph.

Feel free to reword these sentences any way you like.

1. Wherever you go these days, people seem to be recycling.

_____

_____

_____

_____

_____

_____

_____

_____

_____

2. Some people I know are very materialistic.

_____

_____

_____

_____

_____

_____

_____

_____

3. A friend of mine often engages in self-destructive behavior.

_____

_____

_____

_____

_____

_____

_____

4. _____ succeeds at whatever sport (or other type of activity) he (or
   (name a person)
   she) pursues.

_____

_____

_____

_____

_____

_____

_____

_____

_____

5. Electronic devices play important roles in the modern home.

_____

_____

_____

_____

_____

_____

_____

6. People in my town seem to be getting richer and richer (or poorer and poorer).

_____

_____

_____

_____

_____

_____

_____

The illustrations found throughout this chapter make the abstract ideas they explain more interesting, more believable, and more easily understood. Keep this in mind as you read the essays that follow and especially as you begin to use illustration in your own writing.

Wolf

Grace Lukawska

Born in Boleslawiec, Poland, Grace Lukawska came to the United States in 1986. After studying English for speakers of other languages, she enrolled in a developmental writing course in which she wrote this paper. In Poland, Lukawska had seen many television specials on wild animals. When asked to write about a fascinating animal, she immediately thought of the wolf. Lukawska is now a medical assistant.

Preparing to Read

1. The author develops this essay with examples, but she also uses comparison and description.
2. Pay particular attention to the essay's good organization. Consider what Lukawska has done to keep her essay focused.
3. "Getting Started," the introductory chapter of this book, explains that summarizing written materials is a good way to gather information. Another is to quote directly from a source. Lukawska summarizes and quotes directly from Candace Savage's *Wolves*. She credits this book by indicating in parentheses the pages from which she took information. These entries are called parenthetical (internal) citations. She also provides full bibliographical information about the book at the end of her paper. You can learn more about crediting sources in the Appendix at the end of this textbook.

Vocabulary

admonishments (noun)	Condemnations, rebukes.
attribute (verb)	Associate with, blame for.
glutton (noun)	Someone who eats too much.
hierarchical (adjective)	Arranged by rank or importance.
intonations (noun)	Levels of sound, pitches.
manifests (verb)	Shows.
misconceptions (noun)	Incorrect opinions.
solidarity (noun)	Unity, mutual support, togetherness.

Wolf

Grace Lukawska

FOR CENTURIES, POPULAR misconceptions have pictured the wolf as a terrifying predator that kills for pleasure. The name itself calls up nasty images: the

1

glutton who "wolfs" down his food; the werewolf, who, during a full moon, grows hair all over his body, howls into the night, and claws beautiful maidens to death. Even in fairy tales, such as "Little Red Riding Hood," the wolf is pictured as shrewd and bloodthirsty. But is the wolf really a cold-blooded killer? Not at all; the wolf is a magnificent animal which displays many of the characteristics we value in human beings.

The intelligence of the wolf manifests itself in its behavior. The wolf's society is well organized and hierarchical. According to Candace Savage, author of *Wolves,* a pack consists of an upper class—parents, a middle class—uncles and aunts, a lower class—children, and finally "helpers," who are inexperienced hunters and who depend upon the pack for their food (55). Their role is to baby-sit youngsters while the other wolves are hunting (62). Like humans, wolves practice adoption. If parents die, their children are cared for by another family. 2

The leader of the group, usually a male, establishes regulations so that each animal knows whom it can boss and to whom it must submit. For instance, a middle-class wolf must obey the leader's orders; children and helpers must submit to their relatives. This rule helps prevent disagreements and fights. 3

Another indication of the wolf's intelligence is the ability to communicate. Wolves have their own language, which is based on the use of different intonations. According to Savage, a whimper communicates friendship, snarls convey warnings and admonishments, and a "special chirplike tone expresses sexual interest" (58). Like dogs, wolves also use gestures and facial expressions to communicate. By moving their foreheads, mouths, ears, and eyes, they express their emotions and announce their ranks. Frightened wolves keep their teeth covered, "eyes slightly closed, ears flat to the head" (Savage 55). They also bend their legs and tuck in their tails. Wolves that are self-confident, on the other hand, point their ears forward and bare their teeth. Wolves of the highest rank reveal their positions by keeping their tails and ears up and by looking directly into the eyes of other animals. Members of the pack show respect for them; like dogs, they keep their ears tucked in, their heads down, and their legs slightly bent. 4

Like people, wolves are sociable. In a group, they constantly check one another by sniffing. To show affection, they nuzzle each other as if to kiss. To express hostility, they lick their cheeks, wag their tails, howl, and even stick out their tongues. This kind of behavior serves not only to locate companions outside the pack but also to mark their territory and tell enemies of the family's solidarity (Savage 59). 5

Regardless of rank or age, wolves enjoy playing games with other members of their pack. Even the leader, who may appear to be aggressive and ruthless, takes an active part in these activities, which include chasing one another and rolling over. Another sign of intelligence, such exercises not only give them pleasure, but also help them keep physically fit. 6

Wolves are natural-born strategists and planners. Hunting a large animal like a deer or moose is very dangerous for a single wolf. Therefore, they hunt in groups. After locating a herd, one might act as a decoy to draw males away from the herd while the rest single out and attack the victim. Wolves kill only weak or sick animals, and they never kill more than they need. In case there is any excess, leftovers are buried near their dens.

7

The reputation from which wolves suffer is undeserved and unfair. Wolves can be violent, and they are terrifying hunters. But they kill only to feed and protect their families; they never commit distinctly "human" crimes such as murder, theft, and rape. Wolves are not bloodthirsty monsters that should be feared and eradicated. They are magnificent animals, and they deserve their place on earth.

8

Works Cited: Savage, Candace. *Wolves.* San Francisco: Sierra Club, 1980.

Questions for Discussion

1. In Preparing to Read, you were asked what the author did to keep this essay focused and organized. What is the essay's thesis? What techniques does she use to maintain unity and coherence?
2. What kinds of examples does Lukawska rely on most in this essay? Does she ever refer to specific persons, places, or things?
3. Where in this essay does she use comparison?
4. Where does she create verbal images? Why are they so effective?
5. What techniques for writing introductions and conclusions has Lukawska used? (Check Chapter 4 if you need to review these techniques.)

Thinking Critically

1. Consider another animal that has a bad reputation: a rat, a snake, a bat, a pig, a spider, or some other unpopular beast. Then in a paragraph or two discuss the positive qualities of this creature. For example, many people hate and fear rats, but laboratory rats play an important role in medical research.
2. Reread Lukawska's introduction. Then list other examples that would illustrate the popular misconception of wolves as bloodthirsty monsters.
3. The author suggests that human beings can sometimes be more beastly than the beasts. What does she mean? Do you agree? Can you provide some examples?

Suggestions for Journal Entries

1. Think of an animal or species of animal you know well—your Siamese cat or all domestic cats, the neighbor's German shepherd or all shepherds, a bird that often visits your backyard or all common birds. List important things you know about this creature—anything that would provide clues about its behavior, lifestyle, or personality.

   Then ask yourself what this information tells you. Draw three or more general conclusions about the animal from the details you have listed. Write these conclusions in the form of topic sentences for paragraphs that you might later develop in an essay.

2. Are human families as well organized and as close as the wolf family? Think of your own family. Then write a paragraph in which you use illustrations to evaluate the kind of family to which you belong. Perhaps the best types of illustrations to use are anecdotes taken from your own experiences.

Growing Up in Romania

Irina Groza

When Irina Groza was a girl, Romania was a communist country, where personal freedom and economic opportunity were in short supply. Like other countries behind the iron curtain, Romania made it difficult for people to leave. But Groza was one of the lucky ones, and she was able to immigrate to the United States. Today, she is a registered nurse and is raising a family.

Preparing to Read

1. Groza shows that personal experience can be a rich source of illustrations to develop an abstract idea. She fills her essay with specific instances and anecdotes that explain how horrible life in Romania had become under a tyrannical and incompetent government.

2. Several types of writing can be used together to make a successful essay. Groza relies heavily on examples but also includes narrative and descriptive details.

3. In 1990, communist governments across eastern Europe fell from power. In Romania, dictator Nicolae Ceauşescu, his wife, and several members of his government were tried and executed for crimes against the people they had oppressed for over 30 years.

Vocabulary

brutalize (verb)	Treat cruelly or violently.
classics (noun)	Important and lasting works of literature.
compliance (noun)	Submission, agreement.
cult (noun)	Excessive or unnatural devotion to a person or idea.
egomania (noun)	Extreme pride and self-concern.
flawed (adjective)	Defective, faulty.
ideology (noun)	Ideas, beliefs, philosophy.
impoverishing (noun)	Making poor.
indoctrinate (verb)	Drill into, force to believe.
inflicted (verb)	Imposed.
jeopardy (noun)	Danger, risk.
magnitude (noun)	Size, extent.
prey on (verb)	Persecute, attack, victimize.
purge (verb)	Remove, eliminate.
regime (noun)	Government, rule.
stature (noun)	Standing, reputation.
suppress (verb)	Dominate, control.

Growing Up in Romania

Irina Groza

I GREW UP in a beautiful Transylvanian city called Arad, just a few miles from   1
the Hungarian border. In the mid-fifties, when I was born, Romania was
still recovering from the Second World War, and people were working hard
to rebuild their country. I was in the third grade when our beloved president,
Gheorghe Gheorghiu-Dej, died. He was succeeded by Nicolae Ceauşescu, a
young and ambitious general who promised us a bright future. At his election, no one was able to foresee the magnitude of his egomania, ruthlessness,
and incompetence. The tyranny that followed nearly destroyed Romania and
inflicted widespread suffering on its people for many years.

At the beginning of Ceauşescu's presidency, life was still good. I remem-   2
ber going into town with my mother. The streets were busy places, filled with
people who were smiling and laughing as they went about their business. The
shops contained plenty of food; people stood in line only to buy fresh milk
and bread. Slowly, however, certain foods began to disappear from store
shelves and counters. It became much harder to get meat and fresh vegetables. Consumer goods such as clothing and small appliances became scarce. I
heard my mother complain about the new president, but as a child I did not
find these problems significant.

Then I started noticing a change in our school books. National heroes   3
like Michael Eminescu and George Cosbuc, who had once been glorified,
were deleted from our history texts. George Enescu and other great Romanian writers, artists, and musicians, who had been the symbols of our culture,
were hardly mentioned. Classics were removed from our school library, and
its shelves were overloaded with books about the new president and his
regime. He was portrayed as a hero of the people who had fought for com-
munism, but he was a hero we had never heard of before. School children
had to take courses in politics designed to indoctrinate them with Ceauşescu's
diseased ideology. We were forced to memorize his speeches, which were full
of lies about the progress and prosperity his government had brought to Romania. Before long this sickening personality cult became obvious to everyone, and we knew that our country and our culture were being polluted by
this madman.

Before long, new laws restricting people's personal freedom were put into   4
effect. One of these prohibited travel outside the country, and Romanians
found themselves prisoners in their own country. Another law required every
family to have at least four children. Ceauşescu believed that increasing the
population would make Romania powerful and increase his stature in the
world. All contraceptives were removed from the shelves, and doctors who performed abortions were severely punished. But many people could not afford to
support large families and were forced to turn their children over to state or-
phanages. As shown in recent news releases, these places were badly run and
unsanitary. In fact, many of the children housed there contracted AIDS.

In another attempt to suppress the people and to destroy their spirit, the government began a campaign to discourage church attendance. Celebrations of religious holidays were prohibited, and people who openly expressed their faith put themselves in jeopardy. One day a police officer stopped me and ridiculed me in front of my friends because I was wearing a cross around my neck. I felt embarrassed and angry, but there was nothing I could do. I had heard that many people had been beaten by the police, and we lived in constant fear of them. Those who continued to oppose the system were thrown into jail or put into mental institutions.

As soon as Ceauşescu took office, he began to purge those in the government who might oppose him, and he surrounded himself with his supporters. He also established the *Securitate,* a secret police force, which drew to its ranks many misfits who were greedy for power and who had the stomach to swallow the government's lies. No special training was required of these people, just blind compliance to the will of the regime and a desire to brutalize people. Members of the *Securitate* were privileged: they shopped in their own well-supplied stores, and their salaries were about six times those of medical doctors.

The *Securitate* was Ceauşescu's tool for holding down opposition to a regime that the people knew was a miserable failure and that had succeeded only in impoverishing the country and subjecting us to extreme economic hardship. People worked hard, but the lines at food stores became longer and longer. There were severe shortages of meat, milk, butter, flour, soap, detergent, toothpaste, gasoline, and medical supplies. No one could understand why a country that was so rich in natural resources and that possessed so many acres of fertile farmland was unable to feed its people or supply them with simple necessities.

One reason was that Ceauşescu had broken the people's spirit. Another had to do with his insane plan to crowd Romania's growing population into large cities. On the outskirts of Arad were many private homes, each of which sat on land of between half an acre and an acre. One year, the government decided to take this land from us and to build high-rise apartments on it. Neither we nor our neighbors got paid for our property. On top of everything else, we had to clear the land ourselves by cutting down our many fruit trees. Up to that point, we had been able to supplement our food with the fruits and vegetables we grew in our garden and with the animals we raised. But then the situation became desperate, and we were barely able to feed ourselves. The president's iron hand was felt by everyone, and hatred of him grew in everybody's heart.

Like everyone else, I missed the necessities that Ceauşescu's flawed economic policy had taken from us. But I did not realize how badly the government had mismanaged its finances and how corrupt it had become until my mother became ill. Already retired by the time I left high school, she was suffering from high blood pressure and had a heart condition. In an emergency, when I had to call an ambulance, I was told to lie about my mother's age.

Medical emergency squads had been instructed not to pick up retired people. If they were left to die, the government would no longer have to pay their pensions.

As the economic crisis got worse and shortages of important supplies in- 10 creased, the crime rate began to soar. Alcohol abuse became a problem, as did theft, burglary, and assault. But the *Securitate* were busy searching for people who committed political crimes, and real criminals were given a free hand to prey on decent people. In fact, the police often paid common criminals to act as their informants.

I was seventeen and still in high school when I started working in a huge 11 textile factory. Once in the factory, no one was able to leave before quitting time unless he or she got a special pass from the boss. Every two weeks, we had to stay late to attend Communist Party indoctrination sessions. During these absurd meetings, the factory doors were locked, and no one was permitted to leave.

Our regular work week was six days long, but my boss often required 12 us to work on Sundays as well. In the beginning, I refused the overtime, reminding the boss that, according to our constitution, I had to work only six days a week. He in turn reminded me that if I refused overtime I could be assigned to the worst area in the factory. At this point, I had no choice but to accept the overtime, which paid the same wages as work on any other day.

Each day before we left the factory, we had to go through a room 13 where women guards body-searched us. One day, a guard thought that I was acting suspiciously and brought me to a special room where she asked me to remove all my clothes to see if I was hiding stolen material. I could not have concealed much under the thin summer dress I was wearing. She knew that because she had already body-searched me and had found nothing. I refused to obey. To clear myself, I called on another guard to search me again. At that moment, I felt embarrassment and outrage; I knew that the guard's purpose was only to exercise her power by humiliating whomever she wanted to.

My story is not unique. Ceauşescu's government tried to strip all Roma- 14 nians of their dignity, pride, and freedom. Everyone suffered in some way, and everyone has a personal tragedy to tell. As for me, I could not continue to live under the constant humiliation and the severe restrictions on personal freedom that I have described. I remember looking at the birds and envying them because they were free to go anywhere in the world.

I promised myself I would never have children in Romania because I did 15 not want them to suffer as I had. In 1977, with the help of a brother who was living in the United States, I had the opportunity to leave. The day I emigrated, the course of my life changed for the better though my heart broke for those I left behind. Now, however, new hope blossoms for Romania. In December 1990, as part of the overthrow of corrupt Communist governments across eastern Europe, the people deposed the Ceauşescu regime and established a democracy.

Questions for Discussion

1. Find Groza's thesis statement. What are the three main points she makes about Ceauşescu's government?
2. Which examples in this essay do you think best illustrate each of those three points?
3. How does Groza explain that Romania, a land rich in natural resources, was unable to feed its people?
4. What kind of people did the Ceauşescu government employ to carry out its policies? What examples of such people does Groza provide?
5. Why does she include details about life in Romania before Ceauşescu came to power?
6. How does Groza show that life in Romania was difficult for other people as well as for her?

Thinking Critically

1. In what way is this essay similar to Scamacca's "Oma," a selection that appears in Chapter 9? Does it discuss similar ideas? What might a conversation between Oma and Irina Groza be about?
2. Does this essay discuss ideas similar to those in Howard's "The Death of Common Sense," which appears next? On what points might Groza and Howard find agreement?

Suggestions for Journal Entries

1. The government Groza describes is monstrous. Have you ever lived under, read about, or heard about a government that suppresses personal freedom and keeps its people in fear and poverty as Romania's did? If so, use focused freewriting to record one or two well-developed examples of how that government treats or treated its people.

   Another way to approach this assignment is to interview a person who has lived under a dictatorship. Find out what freedoms and opportunities your subject was denied, and explain his or her reaction to living in a country with such a government.
2. One major difference between a democracy and the communist society Groza describes is the freedom to criticize the government. Think of a law, policy, or practice of your government—federal, state, or local—with which you disagree. Brainstorm with others who share your opinion. Together, discuss the ways this law, policy, or practice affects people you know. Then, write down reasons it should be changed. If this topic doesn't interest you, focus on a school policy or regulation you want changed.

The Death of Common Sense

Philip K. Howard

This essay, which appeared in Reader's Digest, *was excerpted in 1995 from a book by the same title. The book's subtitle, which reveals much about its contents, is* How Law Is Suffocating America. *The author is an attorney who has done a great deal of research on the effect of the growing mass of government regulations on every segment of American society.*

Preparing to Read

1. This essay contains a variety of examples: specific instances and occurrences, statistics, and anecdotes. It also mentions familiar persons, places, and things. Look for such examples as you read it.
2. Find places where Howard uses dialogue. Ask yourself how this helps him make his point.
3. What clues about the essay's thesis and contents does the title provide?

Vocabulary

abode (noun)	Home, residence.
citing (adjective)	Criticizing, finding fault with, penalizing.
deplorable (adjective)	Terrible, distressing.
dictates (noun)	Rules, regulations.
edifice (noun)	Building.
explicitly (adverb)	Clearly, in an outspoken manner.
frailty (noun)	Weakness, fragility.
idiosyncrasy (noun)	Individuality, oddity, irregularity.
mammoth (adjective)	Huge.
pH (noun)	A measurement of acidity or alkalinity used in chemistry.
Providence (noun)	Heaven.
saris (noun)	A kind of dress worn by many women in India and Pakistan.
specific gravity (noun)	The mass of a volume of a substance as compared to the mass of an equal volume of water.

The Death of Common Sense

Philip K. Howard

IN THE WINTER of 1988, Mother Teresa's nuns of the Missionaries of Charity walked through the snow in the South Bronx in their saris and sandals looking for abandoned buildings to convert into homeless shelters. They found two, which New York City offered them at $1 each. The nuns set aside $500,000 for the reconstruction. Then, for a year and a half, they went from hearing room to hearing room seeking approval for the project.

1

Providence, however, was no match for law. New York's building code requires an elevator in all new or renovated multiple-story buildings of this type. Installing an elevator would add upward of $100,000 to the cost. Mother Teresa didn't want to devote that much money to something that wouldn't really help the poor. But the nuns were told the law could not be waived even if an elevator did not make sense.

2

The plan for the shelter was abandoned. In a polite letter to the city, the nuns noted that the episode "served to educate us about the law and its many complexities."

3

What the law required offends common sense. After all, there are probably over 100,000 walk-up apartment buildings in New York. But the law, aspiring to the perfect abode, dictates a model home or no home.

4

Today, laws control much of our lives: fixing potholes, running schools, regulating day-care centers and the workplace, cleaning up the environment—and deciding whether Mother Teresa gets a building permit.

5

Our regulatory system has become an instruction manual, telling us exactly what to do and how to do it. The laws have expanded like floodwaters breaking through a dike—drowning the society we intended to protect.

6

In 1993, at Long Island's John Marshall Elementary School, the local fire chief appeared around Halloween dressed as Officer McGruff, the police dog that promotes safety. He noticed all the student art tacked to the walls. Within days, McGruff had done his duty: the art was gone.

7

Why? The New York State fire code addresses this public hazard explicitly: "[S]tudent-prepared artwork . . . [must be] at least two feet from the ceilings and ten feet from exit doors and . . . not exceed 20 percent of the wall area."

8

No one had ever heard of a fire caused by children's art. The school superintendent, accused of permitting a legal violation, suggested that he had used a rule of thumb "on how much to decorate."

9

Liz Skinner, a first-grade teacher, was confused: "The *essence* of primary education is that children show pride in their work." Now, said one observer, the school looked "about as inviting as a bomb shelter."

10

Government has imposed fire codes for centuries. But only our age has 11 succeeded in barring children's art from school walls.

Safety also was the goal of Congress when in 1970 it created the Occupa- 12 tional Safety and Health Administration. For 25 years OSHA has been hard at work, producing over 4,000 detailed rules that dictate everything from the ideal height of railings (42 inches) to how much a plank can stick out from a temporary scaffold (no more than 12 inches). American industry has spent several hundred billion dollars to comply with OSHA's rules. All this must have done some good.

It hasn't. The rate of workdays missed due to injury is about the same as 13 in 1973. A tour through the Glen-Gery brick factory near Reading, PA, indicates why.

People have been making bricks more or less the same way for thou- 14 sands of years. No hidden hazards have ever been identified. But OSHA inspectors periodically visit the Glen-Gery factory and walk around with measuring tapes. They are especially interested in railings, citing Glen-Gery for having railings of the wrong height.

Glen-Gery has never had a mishap related to railings. But inspectors 15 won't discuss if a violation actually has anything to do with safety. They are just traffic cops looking for violations. "We've done basically everything they asked for the last 20 years," says Bob Hrasok, Glen-Gery's full-time manager in charge of regulatory compliance.

As a result, warnings are posted everywhere. For example, a large "Haz- 16 ardous Material" sign was placed on one side of a storage shed—holding sand. OSHA categorizes sand as a hazardous material because sand—identical to the beach sand you and I sunbathe on—contains a mineral called silica, which some scientists believe under some conditions might cause cancer.

In 1994, Glen-Gery was required to include with shipments of brick a 17 form describing, for the benefit of workers, how to identify a brick (a "granular solid, essentially odorless," in a "wide range of colors") and giving its specific gravity (approximately 2.6). In fact, OSHA issued 19,233 citations in 1994 for not keeping its forms correctly. According to one expert, filling out these forms takes Americans 54 million hours per year.

Solid, objective rules, like the precise height of railings, satisfy lawmak- 18 ers' longing for certainty. Human activity, however, cannot be so neatly categorized. And the more precise the rule, the less sensible the law.

Until recently, Dutch Noteboom, 73, owned a small meat-packing plant 19 in Springfield, OR. The U.S. Department of Agriculture (USDA) had one full-time inspector on the premises and one supervisor who visited regularly. This level of attention is somewhat surprising, since Noteboom had only four employees. But the rules required it. Every day the inspector sat there, "often talking on the phone," says Noteboom. But they always found time to cite him for a violation: one was for "loose paint located 20 feet from any animal."

"I was swimming in paper work," says Noteboom. "You should have seen 20 all the USDA manuals. The regulations drove me out of business."

The Soviets tried to run their country like a puppeteer pulling millions of strings. In our country, government's laws have become like millions of trip-wires, preventing us from doing the sensible thing.

21

On the banks of the Mississippi River in Minneapolis, a mountain of 75,000 tons of lime sludge was built up over 60 years, the byproduct of a nearby plant. By the early 1980s, it sat in the path of a proposed highway.

22

Government rules designate any material with a pH of over 12.5 as "hazardous waste." That may generally make sense, but not for lime, which is used to improve the environment by lowering the acidity of land and water.

23

The mountain of lime, whose alkalinity was also raised by dampness, had a pH of 12.7. The highway was stopped dead in its tracks for many months because Minnesota had no licensed hazardous-waste-disposal site for the lime. Eventually, it was pushed onto adjoining land, where, with the help of the sun, it dried its way into lawfulness.

24

People tend to have their own way of doing things. But law, trying to make sure nothing ever goes wrong, doesn't respect the idiosyncrasy of human accomplishment. It sets forth the approved methods, in black and white, and that's that. When law notices people doing it differently, it mashes them flat.

25

Gary Crissey and a partner have run a tiny coffee shop in New York's Little Italy for years. Recently, some customers were dismayed when served with disposable plates and forks. Crissey explained that restaurant inspectors had stopped by and told him the law would not let him operate if he continued to wash dishes by hand. The code requires an automatic dishwasher or a chemical process. But the idea of using chemicals was unappealing, and Crissey's coffee shop is so small that it has no room for a dishwasher. The only solution was disposables. Now everything is plastic.

26

Today we have a world in which people argue not about right and wrong, but about whether something was done the right way. With enough procedures, it's argued, no bureaucrat will ever again put his hand in the till. And so, by 1994, the Defense Department was spending almost half as much on procedures for travel reimbursement ($1.5 billion) as on travel itself ($3.5 billion).

27

Plato argued that good people do not need laws to tell them to act responsibly, while bad people will find a way around law. By pretending procedure will get rid of corruption, we have succeeded only in humiliating honest people and have provided a cover of darkness and complexity for the bad.

28

By the mid-1980s, Brooklyn's Carroll Street Bridge, built in 1889, was in disrepair. The city budgeted $3.5 million for an overhaul. Under procurement procedures, the renovation was estimated to take seven years.

29

But with the bridge's 100th anniversary approaching, Sam Schwartz, the chief engineer responsible for bridges, thought the bridge should be fixed in time for a centennial party. Eleven months later, at a cost of $2.5 million, the bridge had been fixed. Practically the entire neighborhood participated in the centennial party, by all accounts a wonderful affair.

30

For his leadership in completing the job in one-seventh of the time and 31 at 70 percent of budget, Schwartz received a reprimand.

Our modern legal system has achieved the worst of all worlds: a system of 32 regulation that goes too far—while it also does too little. A number of years ago, two workers were asphyxiated in a Liberal, KS, meat-packing plant while checking on a giant vat of animal blood. OSHA did virtually nothing. Stretched thin giving out citations for improper railing height, OSHA reinspected only once in eight years a plant that had admittedly "deplorable" conditions.

Then three more workers died—at the same plant. The government re- 33 sponse? A nationwide rule requiring atmospheric testing devices in confined work spaces, though many of them have had no previous problems.

Most such legal dictates are stacked on top of the prior year's laws and 34 rules. The result is a mammoth legal edifice: federal statutes and rules now total about 100 million words. The Federal Register, a daily report of new and proposed regulations, increased from 15,000 pages in the final year of John F. Kennedy's Presidency to over 68,000 pages in the second year of Bill Clinton's.

Whenever the rules are eased, however, America's energy and good sense 35 pour in like sunlight through opened blinds. After the 1994 earthquake in Los Angeles toppled freeways, Gov. Pete Wilson suspended the thick book of procedural guidelines and gave incentives for speedy work.

From law's perspective, the Los Angeles repair project was a nightmare of 36 potential abuse. The process wasn't completely objective; almost nothing was spelled out to the last detail. When disagreements occurred, private contractors and state bureaucrats had to work them out. Rather than specifying every iron rod, state inspectors took responsibility for checking that the work complied with general standards. The result? Instead of a 2½-year trudge through government process, the Santa Monica Freeway was rebuilt in 64 days to a higher standard than the old one.

"I'm proud," said Dwayne Barth, a construction supervisor. "It feels good 37 having a stake in rebuilding L.A."

When the rule book got tossed, all that was left was responsibility. No 38 one decided to spite Mother Teresa. It was the law. No one wants to take down children's art. It's the law.

"The idea of law," Yale professor Grant Gilmore cautioned in 1977, has 39 been "ridiculously oversold."

The rules, procedures and rights smothering us are aspects of a legal 40 technique that promises a permanent fix for human frailty. This legal experiment, we learn every time we encounter it, hasn't worked out. Modern law has not protected us from stupidity and caprice, but has made stupidity and caprice dominant features of society.

Energy and resourcefulness are what was great about America. Let judg- 41 ment and personal conviction be important again. Relying on ourselves—rather than the law—to provide answers is not a new ideology. It's just common sense.

Questions for Discussion

1. What is Howard's purpose? What is his thesis? Why did he use illustration to develop it? Would explaining how various laws came into being (process analysis) have been a good way to proceed?

2. Where does Howard cite statistics? Where does he use anecdotes?

3. How does his quoting people affected by overregulation help him achieve his purpose?

4. You know that it is not uncommon to find several methods of development in one essay. Where in this essay do you find comparison?

5. Where does Howard make use of figurative language? What does it say about his attitude toward his subject?

6. Howard's examples refer to a variety of regulations, occupations, people, and sections of the country. Explain how this variety contributes to the essay's success.

Thinking Critically

1. Read Glazer's "The Right to Be Let Alone" in Chapter 15. Explain the similarities between Glazer's ideas and Howard's in a short paragraph.

2. Is Howard against all government regulation? From what he has said, determine the kinds of regulations he might support to ensure workers' safety, to protect the environment, to maintain bridges, to keep schools safe, and so on. Reread the essay and make notes about such regulations in the margins. Then explain one of your examples in a well-developed paragraph.

3. Use the double-entry (summary/response) method you learned about at the beginning of this book in "Getting Started" to analyze and respond to three or four paragraphs in this essay. Don't be afraid to express your disagreement with anything Howard says. If you need to review how a double-entry notebook works, reread pages 5 and 6.

Suggestions for Journal Entries

1. List three laws or rules enforced by your college, community, or state that offend common sense. Then, brainstorm with a friend; gather details to show that these regulations should be changed to meet the needs for which they were intended. If you can't find a partner, do some freewriting or listing on your own.

2. Think of some rules enforced by your college, community, or state that make sense and that meet the needs for which they were

intended. List them, and then explain briefly why you think they should not be changed.

3. Howard claims "people have their own way of doing things. But law, trying to make sure nothing ever goes wrong, doesn't respect the idiosyncrasy of human accomplishment." Freewrite for five minutes to explain what he means. Then list three examples to show that people who "break the rules"—who follow their own dreams instead of doing what they are told—sometimes accomplish a great deal. Take your examples from your own experiences, observations, or reading.

The American Century

Michael Barone

Michael Barone is a senior editor at U.S. News & World Report, *for which he writes a column entitled "On Politics." He has been editor and co-author of the* Almanac of American Politics *for 20 years, and he has written for* Reason Magazine, The American Enterprise *magazine, and* Jewish World Review, *among several other periodicals. In 1990, Barone published* Our Country: The Shaping of America from Roosevelt to Reagan. *He has also been a longtime participant on "The McLaughlin Group," a political roundtable which airs on public television. Barone wrote "The American Century" as a special report for* U.S. News & World Report *in December 1999.*

Preparing to Read

1. The subtitle of Barone's essay was originally "From Movies to Microchips to Military Might, Uncle Sam Has Left His Mark around the World." Consider this sentence as you begin to read. It will help you spot Barone's thesis.

2. In a way, this essay is a history. But Barone is less interested in telling a story than in making a point. He lists American accomplishments as examples to illustrate the idea that the twentieth century has truly been "the American century."

3. Barone names numerous people, phenomena, events, and developments with which you will want to be familiar. If you don't recognize a name or term on the following list, look it up on the Internet or in a concise encyclopedia.

Jimmy Carter	Henry Kissinger	Theodore Roosevelt
Winston Churchill	Henry Luce	Spanish American War
Great Depression	The Marshall Plan	Joseph Stalin
Admiral Dewey	Benito Mussolini	Frederick W. Taylor
Charles Dickens	Richard Nixon	Harry S. Truman
Adolf Hitler	Prohibition	Watergate
The Iron Curtain	Ronald Reagan	
Martin Luther King	Franklin Roosevelt	

Vocabulary

belligerence (noun) — Aggressiveness.
bounteous (adjective) — Plentiful, rich.
buccaneering (adjective) — Thieving, stealing, pirating.

burgeoning (adjective)	Growing.
censored (verb)	Edited and controlled the news.
conciliated (adjective)	Soothed, pacified.
dubbed (verb)	Called, named.
elites (noun)	Snobs, the privileged few.
escalated (verb)	Increased rapidly.
festered (verb)	Decayed; remained open and unhealed, as a wound.
gainsaying (noun)	Arguing against.
import (noun)	Meaning, significance.
leveraged (verb)	Caused, made possible.
malevolent (adjective)	Evil.
manifestation (noun)	Sign.
mantle (noun)	Sign of leadership, cloak of power and authority.
nationalized (verb)	Put under the control and ownership of the government.
obsolescence (noun)	Being out of date, no longer useful.
precepts (noun)	Principles.
prowess (noun)	Strength.
relinquish (verb)	Surrender, give up.
stagnated (verb)	Stopped growing or moving forward.
supple (adjective)	Flexible.
wrought (verb)	Caused, brought about.

The American Century

Michael Barone

O N DEC. 8, 1941, the day after the attack on Pearl Harbor, Franklin 1
D. Roosevelt stood before Congress and called for a declaration of war. "The American people in their righteous might," the president proclaimed, "will win through to absolute victory."

Absolute victory: No compromise, no deals with the enemy. *Righteous* 2
might: Not just a strong America—a virtuous one. *The American people:* A people united, not just the military, or a few elected leaders.

With those 13 words, FDR sketched a history of the 20th century that, if 3
exceedingly short, was also disarmingly accurate. In February 1941, Henry Luce, in his famous "American Century" editorial in *Life,* called on Americans to "accept wholeheartedly our duty and our opportunity as the most powerful and vital nation in the world . . . to exert upon the world the full import of our interests."

And so we have. The most riveting story of the 20th century is the rise of 4
totalitarianism and its defeat at the hands of America. But there are other sto-

ries, other chapters. Luce could have no way of knowing it when he penned his editorial, but Americans literally took him at his word, thrusting upon the world the full import of their interests and energies over the course of these hundred years. At the dawn of a new millennium now, one may look back at the old and find it impossible not to recognize an indelible American imprint in virtually every area of human endeavor—in science and medicine, business and industry, arts and letters—it has been Uncle Sam's century. Over the years, America has been criticized by friend and foe for a dominance both real and perceived. But there is no gainsaying the fact that, if nations were people, Uncle Sam would be the man of the century.

The American legacy is impressive—but it is one no one could have predicted at the dawn of the now departing century. A hundred years ago, America was the largest of the great powers. Its economy had surged ahead of those in Europe. For all of America's sweep and swagger, however, Britain was the dominant world power, with the largest empire and Navy, rivaled only by Germany, with its huge Army and strength in science.   5

America, for many reasons, was unwilling and unready to inherit the mantle of leadership. The United States was united in name only, the wounds of the Civil War still far from healed. Though wages in the North were twice those in the South, few Southerners deigned to cross the Mason-Dixon line. On both sides of the divide, racial segregation was the order of the day. On the borders, meanwhile, immigrants were pouring in—17 million between 1890 and 1914. The new arrivals gave cold comfort to America's elites. The Poles, Jews, Italians, they feared, couldn't possibly become *true* Americans.   6

Happily, the elites were wrong—dead wrong. Before too long, an America that had been "a nation of loosely connected islands," as historian Robert Wiebe called it, was becoming a more cohesive and unified whole. The building blocks of the civic life we take for granted today soon began falling into place. The medical profession standardized the curricula of the nation's medical schools. The practice of law, once open to anyone, was limited to those who had passed state bar exams. Teachers worked from a common curriculum that emphasized English and civics. Education became a transforming engine. The number of kids enrolled in high schools quadrupled from 1890 to 1910. At more rarefied levels, dozens of great research universities were formed.   7

A new order. The way America worked changed, too. Businesses were transformed from buccaneering, seat-of-the-pants outfits run by ragged eccentrics into professionally managed organizations. Factories were increasingly run according to the precepts of "scientific" management. The concept was pioneered by Frederick W. Taylor. His time-and-motion studies reduced each task to single steps, allowing managers to maximize production, even by unskilled laborers. Suddenly, the chaotic and unstable economy of the 19th century was a thing of the past.   8

Nowhere was change so pronounced as in the military. "We are a great nation," Theodore Roosevelt said in 1898, "and we are compelled, whether   9 we will or not, to face the responsibilities that must be faced by all great nations." This was not just rhetoric. In February 1898, as Americans protested Spain's suppression of a revolt in Cuba, Assistant Secretary of the Navy Roosevelt ordered the Pacific fleet to stand ready to attack the Philippines if war came. It did, and before American forces could roust the Spaniards from Cuba, Admiral Dewey sailed into Manila Harbor and destroyed the Spanish fleet. To the surprise and delight of TR, the "splendid little war" sparked enthusiasm among Southerners and Northerners alike. Americans were suddenly possessed of a swaggering new confidence: They could project power far beyond their borders to achieve good ends.

That confidence swelled when Roosevelt, as president, won a treaty to let 10 America build the Panama Canal. American engineers succeeded where the French had failed, bridging jungles and mountains with an elaborate system of interlocking channels; at the same time, Dr. Walter Reed conquered yellow fever. The lesson, taught in textbooks for years after, was simple—and breathtaking: American expertise could make the world a better place.

But the world was an increasingly perilous place, too. No sooner had the 11 Panama Canal opened, in August 1914, than Europe was plunged into war—which leveraged its own kind of change. President Wilson nationalized the railroads and the shipyards. Newspapers were censored. War critics were jailed. In the meantime, Wilson raised a military of nearly 3 million men, and Americans took pride in helping to win "the war to end wars."

After, America boomed economically. But still it declined to take up the 12 mantle of Britain, now exhausted by wartime costs and slaughter. At home Americans disagreed furiously about Prohibition and, in the Scopes trial of 1925, science and religion. Mass immigration was ended in 1924, but the melting pot kept bubbling. Millions of workers bought cars and fled the teeming tenements on new highways. For a brief, shining moment, Americans seemed freed from the workaday worries of the rest of the world.

So they were thoroughly unprepared for the shocks of the second third of 13 the century—worldwide depression and the rise of totalitarianism. Between 1929 and 1933, the nation's economy shrank by nearly half; 1 in 4 workers was unemployed. Abroad, the wounds of World War I festered, the result, Lenin's Soviet Russia in 1918, Mussolini's Fascist Italy in 1922, Hitler's Nazi Germany in 1933.

Instead of dividing the nation, however, these shocks forged new bonds 14 of common purpose. Popular culture helped. Despite the Depression, radio ownership doubled between 1929 and 1932. Americans went mad for movies. In 1930, in a country of 130 million people, movie attendance hit 90 million a week. The big screen created the strongest popular culture since Dickens and defined for the world a characteristic American style—breezy, friendly, open, optimistic.

All the way. But war clouds soon gathered again. The Sudetenland, Aus- 15 tria, Czechoslovakia—Nazi belligerence knew no bounds. Most Americans, however, were unmoved. It would require another president named Roosevelt to change that. In June 1940, as France surrendered to Hitler and Britain prepared for invasion, FDR started selling arms to Britain and boosted defense spending. Facing re-election, he took the politically risky steps of supporting a military draft, then dispatched 50 destroyers to Britain. Americans supported the moves, and Roosevelt was re-elected. Almost immediately, he won more aid for Britain. After Nazi forces attacked the Soviet Union in the summer of 1941, Roosevelt sent arms to Moscow and blocked oil sales to Japan. Again, Americans applauded: If it required war to stop totalitarianism, so be it.

Then came Pearl Harbor. "We are all in it together—all the way," FDR said in his fireside chat, two days later. "Every single man, woman, and child is a partner in the most tremendous undertaking in our American history." Roosevelt built his war effort on cooperation between big government, big business, big labor. America became "the arsenal of democracy," its industrial might churning out the awesome tools of victory: 7,333 ships, 299,000 aircraft, 634,000 jeeps, 88,000 tanks. The top-secret Manhattan Project, which cost $2 billion—the nation's total economic production in 1940 was $99 billion—produced the atomic bomb. The result was victory over Germany and Japan, confirming America's status as the world's dominant military and economic power.   16

Just as the first World War had, the war against the Axis powers wrought extraordinary change at home. Americans got used to working productively, and even creatively, in large organizations. Big business, big labor, and big government—with occasional friction—produced a bounteous economy, not another depression. Postwar America's "organization men" and "conformists" produced the baby boom, the habits of the burgeoning middle class reflected in the new universal culture of 1950s television. Church membership reached new highs. Crime fell to record lows. Confidence in major institutions surged. Americans were bound together by common experiences—the comprehensive high school, the military draft, large corporations, suburbia.   17

This was also Cold War America. In March 1946, Winston Churchill, now out of office, went to Fulton, Mo., with Harry Truman and proclaimed that, because of Joe Stalin, "an iron curtain" had fallen across Eastern Europe.   18

Americans responded boldly. The Truman Doctrine promised to protect all "free peoples of the world." The Marshall Plan provided vast economic aid to Europe. The NATO treaty of April 1949 was America's first peacetime military alliance. In June 1950, Truman sent troops to Korea to stop the Communist invasion. Defense spending increased, and stayed high for years. America was engaged in a "long, twilight struggle," John Kennedy said. And her people paid for it with high taxes for defense and foreign aid, a military draft, air-raid drills, and listening to Soviet threats of nuclear war over Berlin and Cuba. All that is taken for granted today, but in historic perspective it was extraordinary. "Only a society with enormous confidence in its achievements and in its future," as Henry Kissinger wrote later, "could have mustered the dedication and the resources to strive for a world order in which   19 defeated enemies would be conciliated, stricken allies restored, and adversaries converted."

Doubts set in. It didn't last. Halfway around the globe, a commitment 20 that started with just a few hundred Pentagon advisers escalated into a war with more than half a million American troops—a war that could not be won. Aides to Presidents Kennedy and Johnson had devised a military strategy in Vietnam that was incapable of working. Defense Secretary Robert McNamara scornfully dubbed it, "the social scientists' war."

It was a war many affluent Americans did not find important enough to 21 draft their sons for. McNamara's draft system allowed college students to avoid service. Antiwar movements on elite campuses produced a generation of academics and professionals who regarded the United States and the Communists as morally equivalent. By 1968, many of the planners and supporters of the Vietnam War saw it as deeply immoral. They no longer believed, as the Roosevelts did, in American exceptionalism—the belief that this country was uniquely strong and uniquely good.

In other ways, the postwar system was breaking down. Congress had 22 passed civil rights laws in response to the nonviolent movement led by Martin Luther King Jr. But black protesters called for violence in response to white oppression.

Big government produced not only war and riots, but also stagflation— 23 high inflation and low economic growth. Big businesses grew less supple and creative, turning out gas guzzlers with "planned obsolescence." Big labor unions stagnated, then lost membership. And the cultural unity of postwar America was splintering. Families with two television sets and several radios no longer watched the same shows and listened to the same music. The universal popular culture of midcentury soon gave way to rival countercultures, many hostile to old values. Starting in the late 1960s, birth rates fell and divorce and births to unwed mothers rose: "the great disruption," as Francis Fukuyama calls it. Crime and welfare dependency tripled from 1965 to 1975.

As the elites lost confidence in America, the American people lost confi- 24 dence in the elites. Richard Nixon's rhetorical appeals to "the silent majority" rallied only some Americans, and his cool pursuit of geopolitical advantage, the opening to China, and withdrawal from Vietnam failed to engage Americans' yearning for moral purpose, even before his own moral authority was destroyed by Watergate.

Foreign policy elites increasingly saw American strength as malevolent, 25 and were pleased to see it reduced. This was symbolized by the 1977 treaty to relinquish the Panama Canal. Elites, guilty about how America obtained the canal, saw this as necessary to prevent violence in Panama. But most voters still felt pride in this great American achievement, and opposition to the treaty energized Ronald Reagan's nearly successful challenge of President Gerald Ford in 1976.

American pride sank even lower when Iran refused to release 52 Ameri- 26 cans held hostage in the U.S. Embassy in November 1979. Under international law, this was an act of war. But for months President Jimmy Carter refused to use force and tried to negotiate, and his half-hearted seven-helicopter rescue attempt in April 1980 failed. Each Carter policy was approved in the polls. But in the end, voters wanted results. Carter was beaten soundly by Reagan, whose threats to use force resulted in the hostages' release just as he was sworn into office.

Reagan embodied the characteristic American style of the 1930s and 1940s movies in which he himself had been a star. He shared most Americans' pride in their country and rejected the guilt complex of the elites. His tax cuts led to two decades of solid economic growth and low inflation, interrupted by recession briefly in 1990–91. Complacent corporate executives were ousted by leveraged buyouts and directors seeking more profits. Big corporations were challenged by tiny start-ups: IBM was replaced as the major high-tech firm by Microsoft. American computers and high-tech—the latest manifestation of 20th-century Americans' scientific and technological expertise—led the world. The peacetime expansions of the 1980s and 1990s produced 40 million new jobs, while the sputtering economies of Europe and Asia produced virtually none. Ordinary Americans' incomes surged and widespread stock ownership resulted in a stock market boom and real gains in wealth for the masses.   27

Unmatched prowess. Abroad Reagan, despite scorn from the elites, pursued an assertive policy like Harry Truman's. He increased defense spending, sent American troops to Grenada, and supported anti-Communist forces in Central America and Afghanistan. The defense buildup and Reagan's Strategic Defense Initiative convinced Soviet leaders that they could never match the economic and technological prowess of the United States.   28

Like the two Roosevelts, Reagan insisted on proclaiming the superiority of the American system. In London in 1983, he predicted the demise of the Soviet Union. In Berlin in 1987, he demanded, "Mr. Gorbachev, tear down this wall." By October 1989 the wall was history. The Soviet empire soon followed.   29

Today, at century's end, America is unquestionably the world's dominant military, economic, and cultural superpower. This has been the work of the American people. The 76 million of 1900 are now the 273 million of 2000. The descendants of the immigrants who choked the slums in 1900 are now firmly interwoven into the American fabric. The descendants of the blacks who were excluded by segregation in 1900 now have full civil rights and are surging into the middle classes and upper ranks of society. The new immigrants from Latin America and East Asia who have arrived since the 1965 immigration reform are progressing as their counterparts did a century ago.   30

The American traditions of excellence fostered by the elite of the first third of the century and the characteristic American openness depicted in the popular culture of the second third of the century gave the American people the strength and the confidence to forge ahead in the last third of the century when so many in the elite lost confidence in their country. Sharing with   31

Ronald Reagan the belief that this country is "a city on a hill," they have won through to absolute victory over totalitarianism, as Franklin Roosevelt promised, and have made this the American century that Henry Luce envisioned.

Questions for Discussion

1. What is Barone's thesis?
2. What use does Barone make of statistics in this piece?
3. Where does he include specific facts and instances?
4. Of course, Barone's writing is full of references to events. Which of these do you find most effective as examples?
5. What use does he make of direct quotations? Can they be considered examples as well? If so, of what?
6. Reread paragraph 7. The author mentions "the building blocks of the civic life." Explain the examples of such "building blocks" that he uses.
7. What is the importance of the examples Barone uses in paragraphs 9 and 10? What do such examples tell us?
8. What use does he make of comparison and contrast? (Reread paragraphs 18 and 19.)
9. In the beginning of the essay, Barone defines several terms. Why does he do so? Where else does he use definition?
10. The inclusion of exciting verbs maintains reader interest. Find several examples of such verbs and explain how they work.
11. According to the author, how do Americans usually respond to a crisis? Identify specific instances of such responses in Barone's essay.
12. Over all, what is Barone's attitude toward the American public? Cite examples from his essay to support your answer.

Thinking Critically

1. Who are the "organization men" and the "conformists" whom Barone mentions in paragraph 17? What is his attitude toward them? Use the context that Barone creates to draw materials for your answer.
2. In what eras were American enthusiasm and confidence the highest? In what eras were they the lowest? Write notes in the margins to identify these times and to explain the causes for the way people saw them.
3. Barone speaks of several major changes in society and culture as he surveys the twentieth century. Make marginal notes in places where he asserts such changes. Then, in a few short paragraphs, explain what these changes were and what caused them.

4. Barone obviously has pride in America's achievements. Are there any times in this essay when he seems to criticise American society or government?

Suggestions for Journal Entries

1. Choose a twentieth-century public figure—American or not—who you believe has had a significant effect on us. The influence might be positive or negative. Interview a professor who knows about this figure, complete some library research, or search for information about your subject on the Internet. Your aim is to gather information to show that your subject had a significant impact on our society. If you wish, choose one of the people mentioned in item 3 of Preparing to Read.

2. Interview a person who lived through one of the major events that Barone mentions—perhaps a war, the race riots of the sixties, Prohibition, or the Great Depression. Learn all you can about this person's firsthand experiences during this time.

Suggestions for Sustained Writing

1. Take any *simple* idea or statement of fact that you know a lot about. Prove this idea or statement in an essay of four or five paragraphs by using examples like the kinds you have learned about. Start by writing a preliminary thesis that expresses the idea or fact plainly. For instance:

> Winters in my state can be *treacherous.*

> The hurricane that smashed into town last summer *devastated our community.*

> A student's life is *hectic.*

> Doing your own sewing (carpentry, plumbing, car repair, typing, or the like) can *save you a lot of money.*

> Casual sex can be *harmful to your health.*

The main point in each statement is in italics. As you know, the main point in a thesis is what an essay should focus on. Keep this in mind as you write your first draft. Then, review your paper to determine whether each example you have included relates directly to your main point. If not, replace it with a better example or revise your thesis. Add other examples to develop your main point even further as you complete later drafts.

When the time comes to correct spelling, punctuation, and grammar, check for coherence and clarity as well. Strengthen connections between sentences and paragraphs. Replace words and phrases that seem vague, general, or dull with more concrete, specific, and colorful choices.

2. If you responded to the first of the Suggestions for Journal Entries after Lukawska's "Wolf," you have already written three topic sentences that express conclusions about the behavior or personality of a particular animal or species of animal.

   Use these topic sentences in the body paragraphs of an essay that, like "Wolf," expresses your views on the character of this animal. Develop these paragraphs with illustrations. Perhaps some of the information in your journal will serve this purpose. Then, summarize in one statement the ideas expressed in your topic sentences; make this your essay's thesis.

   After completing your first draft, return to your paper and insert additional details and examples that will make it more convincing and clear. In your third draft, work on creating an effective introduction; like Lukawska, try using a startling remark or challenging a widely held opinion. In your conclusion, rephrase your thesis or look to the future. Then, revise the entire paper once more to improve word usage and sentence structure. End this careful process by editing for grammar and by proofreading.

3. Have you ever lived in a land whose government was a dictatorship? Do you know someone who did? Write an essay that uses examples from personal experience—yours or someone else's—to explain what living in that country was like.

   Collect information before starting your first draft. If you are writing about yourself, brainstorm with a family member who remembers as much about that time in your life as you do. If you are writing about someone else, try interviewing this person to gather examples about the kind of life he or she endured. In addition, read your response to the first journal suggestion after Irina Groza's "Growing Up in Romania."

   Like Groza, use anecdotes and specific instances to explain what the government did to limit people's personal and economic freedom. Your essay doesn't have to be as long as hers, but it should be filled with examples that show how difficult living under a dictatorship can be.

   Groza cared enough about her readers and her subject to complete the writing process step-by-step. She made several drafts, each of which developed her thesis in greater and more startling detail. Then she revised and edited her work to make sure it was well organized, coherent, and free of mechanical errors. Follow her example.

4. As an alternative to suggestion 3, write a letter to the editor of a local or college newspaper complaining about a law, regulation, policy, or practice in your community or on campus. Using examples from personal experience, explain why you are against it; show how negatively it affects you and others in your town or school.

Let's say your college library closes on Saturdays and Sundays. You decide to explain that this policy is hard on students who can't go to the library at other times. To develop your central idea, you might:

- Talk about the long trips to other libraries you and friends are forced to make on weekends.
- Discuss your many attempts to find a quiet place to study on Sunday afternoons.
- Explain that 10 of the 20 students in your history class didn't finish their midterm essays on time because they could not get information they needed.

You are trying to convince your readers of a particular opinion. So, pack your letter with examples, but remember that each example should relate directly to that opinion. As always, state your point clearly in a thesis.

Begin this assignment by looking to the journal responses you made after reading Groza's "Growing Up in Romania" and Howard's "The Death of Common Sense." That information might help you complete the first draft of your letter. Once again be thorough and careful when revising and editing your work.

5. Do some of the rules and regulations enforced by your college, community, or state offend common sense? Or do most laws that govern you seem reasonable? Take one or the other side of this issue or argue that some laws make sense while others are ridiculous. Either way, prove your point by discussing three or four laws, rules, or regulations as examples.

In any case, make your central idea clear from the very beginning. For example, argue that common sense, practicality, and the people's best interest should determine law—not some abstract theory or impractical principle. Then, in the body of the essay, show how the rules and regulations you are discussing meet or fail to meet this standard. If you are arguing both sides of the issue, make sure you discuss examples of both reasonable and unreasonable laws.

Before you begin, check the notes you made in your journal after reading "The Death of Common Sense." They should provide useful facts, insights, and examples with which to develop your paper. As always, apply common sense to your writing: revise, edit, and proofread.

6. Review the notes that you made in response to the first suggestion for journal entries after Barone's "The American Century." Use these notes in an essay that proves that your subject has had an important effect on life or society in the twentieth-century. Include statistics, anecdotes, and specific instances and/or occurrences from his or her life to prove your point. Remember, your paper is to be an *illustration* essay. Therefore, like Barone, you might use chronological (narrative) order, but your purpose is not to tell a story. It is to gather *examples* that prove the point you are making about the influence your subject has exerted.

As explained earlier, you may write about someone who has had a positive influence or someone who has had a negative influence—a hero or a villain. After you write your first draft, check to see that you have included enough examples and that each is well developed. If not, do some more research. Add direct quotations from sources you have read or from those you have interviewed, if you can. Of course, you must give all sources of information credit. You can do this by using internal citations in the body of your paper and by listing your sources in a works-cited page. Study the Appendix at the end of this textbook if you need help doing so.

Writing to Learn: A Group Activity

In "Growing Up in Romania," Irina Groza writes about a government that denied people basic human liberties. In 1787, the Framers of the United States Constitution worried that the government they were creating might someday do the same. Therefore, they guaranteed the people certain fundamental rights, which they stated in the first ten amendments to the Constitution, now known as the Bill of Rights.

THE FIRST MEETING

Read and discuss the Bill of Rights (you can find it in any library or on the Internet). Then, choose the three or four amendments that your group believes are of greatest importance today. Ask each student to research one of these. The purpose of this assignment is to gather and present information that will help the group better understand the purpose and importance of each amendment.

RESEARCH

Search the Internet, the *New York Times Index, The Readers' Guide to Periodical Literature,* or an electronic database, such as ProQuest or InfoTrac, for information on the amendment you have chosen. Specifically, find information that will help you:

- Understand and explain what the amendment means. Be aware that experts on law and government disagree about the meaning and scope of certain amendments. This is especially true of the second amendment, the right to bear arms.
- Explain why the Framers of the Constitution thought it important to include the amendment. Briefly discuss one or two events, circumstances, or issues from history that might have influenced their decision.
- Explain why you think the amendment continues to be important. Discuss examples of the kinds of issues, circumstances, events, or problems to which the amendment applies today.

Take careful and complete notes. Then, write a well-developed paragraph responding to each of the three items above. Make copies of your work.

THE SECOND MEETING

Distribute copies of the paragraphs students have written and have them critique each other's work. Pay special attention to the clarity with which the writer explains what the amendment means. Then, evaluate the effectiveness of examples the writer uses in the second and third paragraphs. Offer concrete suggestions for additional research and/or revision. Arrange for one member of the group to collect and duplicate the final drafts of everyone's work before the next meeting.

THE THIRD MEETING

As a group, write one or two summary paragraphs that explain the importance of the Bill of Rights and that prepare readers for a discussion of the particular amendments your group has written about. Use this material as an introduction to a paper that contains each member's final draft. Use simple subheadings, such as **Amendment I,** to separate the three or four major sections of the body of the paper. Finally, assign someone to write a short concluding paragraph that comments on the good sense or perception of the people who wrote these amendments.

CHAPTER 13

Comparison and Contrast

Comparison and contrast are methods of organizing and developing ideas by pointing out similarities and differences between subjects.

A comparison essay identifies similarities—even between subjects that seem different. For example, you might compare the government of the United States with that of ancient Rome; a newly patented drug with an age-old herbal treatment; the methods of building the Egyptian and Mayan pyramids with modern construction methods. A contrast essay identifies differences—even between subjects that seem alike; usually these subjects belong to the same general class or are of the same type. Such is the case in Cowley's "Temptations of Old Age," a selection in this chapter that discusses how two different types of people face the challenges of aging.

Contrast can also be used to explain the pros and cons of a particular question. In "The Militiaman, the Yuppie, and Me," Carolyn Swalina presents two sides to the gun-control issue. Swalina's tone is sarcastic and designed in part to amuse us, but her essay shows that contrast can serve as an effective tool for debate. For example, you might use it to discuss the pros and cons of living in a particular city, the advantages and disadvantages of getting married, or the strengths and weaknesses of your college basketball team. Explaining what you like and dislike about going to college, working at the supermarket, or visiting relatives will also make a good contrast paper. You might even discuss why you both loved and hated a certain film, television program, concert, or novel.

Organizing Comparison/Contrast Papers

One of the greatest advantages of using comparison or contrast is the simplicity with which it allows you to organize information. In fact, putting together a successful comparison or contrast essay doesn't have to be difficult if you follow either of the two standard methods of organization: point by point or subject by subject.

Which of the two methods for organizing a comparison or contrast paper is better for you? That depends on your topic and your purpose. The subject-by-subject method of organization is often used in short pieces. You can see it in Alan Paton's "The Road from Ixopo," a selection containing only a few paragraphs that contrast two places in the same mountains of South Africa. The point-by-point method, on the other hand, works well with essays that compare or contrast several aspects, qualities, or characteristics of two subjects. This arrangement allows readers to digest large quantities of information bit by bit. As such it helps eliminate the risk that they will forget what you said in the first half of your essay before they finish the second half. Stephen Moore's "New Blood for Cities" uses the point-by-point pattern.

Visualizing Methods of Comparison

THE POINT-BY-POINT METHOD

Using the point-by-point method, you compare or contrast one aspect or characteristic of both subjects, often in the same paragraph, before moving on to the next point in another paragraph. For example, if you were showing how economical your 2001 Wizbang automobile is by contrasting it to the 2001 Roadhog, your essay might be organized like this:

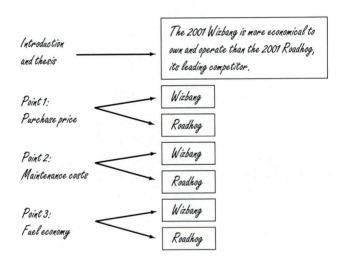

THE SUBJECT-BY-SUBJECT METHOD

Using the subject-by-subject method, you discuss *one* subject completely before going on to compare or contrast it with another subject in the second half of the essay. For example, you might outline the essay about the Wizbang and its competitor like this:

Introduction and thesis	The 2001 Wizbang is more economical to own and operate than the 2001 Roadhog, its leading competitor.
Subject 1: The Wizbang	• Purchase price • Maintenance costs • Fuel economy

Subject 2: The Roadhog

- Purchase price
- Maintenance costs
- Fuel economy

SEEING THE PATTERN IN A COMPARISON/CONTRAST PAPER

Student James Langley's "Watch the Cart!" which appears below, discusses differences between male and female shoppers. It follows the point-by-point pattern, which is often found in longer essays. Notes in the left margin explain how Langley organized his paper. Notes on the right explain how he developed it.

States thesis.

There is nothing similar to the way men and women shop for groceries. Believe me, I know because I work in a major supermarket. After watching scores of people shop for food day in and day out, I have become an expert on the habits of American consumers.

Establishes his expertise.

I have noticed many things about them, but nothing stands out more clearly than the differences between men and women.

First of all, men never know where anything is. Nine times out of ten, it will

Begins with topic sentence.

be a man who asks an employee to find a product for him. I don't know how many guys come up to me in the course of a night to ask

Point 1: How men search for a product

me where something is, but 50% of those who do invariably return to me in five minutes

Includes a statistic.

still unaware of the product's location. Men have no sense of direction in a supermarket. It's as if they're locked up in some life-sized maze. It has always been my contention that men who shop should be provided with specially trained dogs to sniff out the

Uses a simile.

products they desire. It would certainly
save me valuable time too often wasted as I
explain for the tenth time that soup is in
aisle 9.

*Point 1:
How women
search for
a product.*

Women, on the other hand, rarely ask for
an item's location. When they do, it is
usually for an obscure product only they
have heard of and whose name only they can
pronounce. Whenever a woman asks me where
some such item is, I always tell her to go
to aisle 11—the dog-food aisle. Send a man
there, and he'll forget what he was looking
for and just buy the dog food out of
desperation. Send a woman there, and she'll
be back in five minutes with the product in
hand, thanking me for locating it for her.

*Begins
with topic
sentence.*

*Uses an
example.*

*Point 2:
How quickly
men and
women shop.*

Another difference between men and women
is that women shop at speeds that would get
them tickets on freeways, while men shop
with the speed of a dead snail. A woman can
get her shopping done in the same amount of
time every time she goes. A man who shops
just as often gets worse and worse every
time.

*Begins
with topic
sentence.*

*Point 3:
How well
men and
women
manipulate
carts.*

The biggest difference between the sexes
in regard to shopping, however, involves the
manipulation of carts. A woman guides a
cart through the store so fluidly and
effortlessly that her movements are almost

*Begins
with topic
sentence.*

poetic. Men are an entirely different

story. A man with a shopping cart is a

menace to anyone within two aisles of him.

Men bounce their carts off display cases, *Creates a vivid image.*

sideswipe their fellow patrons and create

havoc wherever they go. They have no idea

of how to control the direction of carts.

To a man, a shopping cart is a crazed metal *Uses a metaphor.*

monster designed to embarrass and harass

him.

Conclusion refers to thesis and restates essay's main points. Overall, then, women are far more

proficient shoppers than men. They are

efficient, speedy and graceful; men are slow

and clumsy. I know these things because I

work in a supermarket. I also know these

things because I am a man.

Revising Comparison/Contrast Papers

Carolyn Swalina's "The Militiaman, the Yuppie, and Me" (appearing later in this chapter) contrasts two extreme positions on the issue of gun control. To do this, Swalina created a conversation between two men on each side of the issue. She also managed to reveal some of her own thoughts on gun control and on the zealots involved in this debate. Paragraphs from her rough and final drafts appear below. They show the importance of making sure each side in a pro-and-con paper is developed adequately. They also show that revising to remove unneeded words makes writing more efficient.

Swalina—Rough Draft

As I sat there just sipping coffee, two men

at a nearby table began to catch my *Remove unneeded words?*

attention. One of them was a large man

Describe this man?

wearing camouflage pants and a black tee shirt; he pounded his fist on the table <u>for</u> <u>emphasis</u>? as he spoke to his <u>companion</u>. I labelled the two of these men the "militiaman" and the "yuppie."

Remove unneeded words?

"Listen, there are a lot of crazies out there in this world of ours," said the militiaman. "Besides, having guns is our constitutional right."

"Ever read the second amendment?" <u>said</u> <u>the militiaman</u>. "Washington and the rest of those guys knew what they were doing; they saw what happened when you let the government have all the firepower. The feds will bother you whenever they feel like it. At least, if I still have my guns, they'll think twice before knocking down my door with a tank in the middle of the night."

Combine with previous paragraph? Remove unneeded words?

Allow him more time to explain his opinion on this point?

"I'd rather have a cop knock down my door than some crazy with a gun," said the yuppie.

"Either way, you should have a gun to defend yourself," insisted the militiaman.

Swalina—Final Draft

As I sat there sipping coffee, two men at a nearby table caught my attention. One of them, a large man wearing camouflage pants and a black tee shirt, pounded his fist on the table as he spoke to his companion, who

Has removed unneeded words.

Describes the yuppie.

was wearing khaki slacks, penny loafers, and a button-down shirt. He was sipping club soda. I labelled them the "militiaman" and the "yuppie."

Adds information via a quotation.

Has combined paragraphs to eliminate unneeded words.

"Listen, there are a lot of crazies out there," said the militiaman. "Besides, having guns is our constitutional right. Ever read the Second Amendment? It gives us the right 'to keep and bear arms'. Washington and the rest of those guys knew what they were doing; they saw what happened when you let the government have all the firepower. The feds will bother you whenever they feel like it. At least, if I still have my guns, they'll think twice before knocking down my door with a tank in the middle of the night."

Adds new information to explain yuppie's opinion.

"Yes, I've read the Constitution," said the yuppie. "And the Second Amendment is about 'a well regulated militia', not private ownership. Besides, I'd rather have a cop knock down my door than some crazy with a gun."

"Either way, you should have a gun to defend yourself," insisted the militiaman.

Includes her own opinions in the essay for clarity, interest.

"Who were these guys?" I wondered. "Constitutional lawyers? And what were the chances that the government would drive a tank through my front door?"

Practicing Comparison and Contrast

In the spaces provided, write paragraphs that respond to any four of the following items. Remember that comparison explains similarities while contrast explains differences.

Before you start writing a paragraph, gather details for it and make a rough draft. Before you begin your final draft, make sure the paragraph has a topic sentence.

1. Compare caring for a child and caring for an animal.

_____

_____

_____

_____

_____

_____

_____

2. Compare writing papers for English class and preparing for a mathematics test.

_____

_____

_____

_____

_____

_____

3. Compare the cooking of two different cultures. For instance, compare Chinese with Italian, Indian with Mexican, Caribbean with Japanese, or Eastern European with American.

_____

_____

_____

_____

_____

_____

4. Compare someone you know (perhaps yourself) to an animal. Start by writing "_____ is a snake" or "_____ is a workhorse."

_____

_____

_____

_____

_____

_____

_____

5. Contrast your work or study habits with those of a friend.

_____

_____

_____

_____

_____

_____

_____

6. Contrast the ways you and your parents (sister, brother, or other relative) view sex (marriage, education, religion, money, or your friends).

_____

_____

_____

_____

_____

_____

_____

7. Contrast two hobbies you pursue, two sports you play or follow, or two jobs you have held.

_____

_____

_____

_____

_____

_____

8. Contrast two pieces of music, films, paintings, books, or television shows that are about similar subjects or that have similar purposes.

_____

_____

_____

_____

_____

_____

As you just learned, how you organize a comparison or contrast essay depends on your topic and on the reason you are writing about it. In general, there is no absolutely right or wrong method for arranging the details in such a paper. Sometimes you may simply want to use the pattern which you find easier. Just remember that comparing and contrasting are powerful tools for discovering ideas and expressing them effectively. In fact, the very act of pointing out similarities and differences may lead to important discoveries about your subjects that will make your writing richer in detail and more interesting.

The Road from Ixopo*

Alan Paton

An educator, writer, and vocal opponent of apartheid, Alan Paton (1903–1988) remains South Africa's best-known writer. His most widely read work is Cry, the Beloved Country, *of which this selection is the first chapter. This novel is an eloquent treatment of race and justice in a society tortured by an insane system of segregation. It is also the poignant story of parental love and the pain of loss experienced by two families, one black and one white. Among Paton's other works are* Ah, But Your Land Is Beautiful; Too Late the Phalarope; *and* Tales from a Troubled Land, *a book of short stories.*

Preparing to Read

1. Ixopo is not far from Paton's hometown of Pietermaritzburg, which is in the province of KwaZulu/Natal.

2. The Drakensberg Mountain range runs for about 600 miles in southeastern South Africa. Ingeli and East Griqualand are also place names in the area.

Vocabulary

bracken (noun)	Type of large fern.
forlorn (adjective)	Sad, despairing.
kloof (noun)	Ravine, gorge, cleft.
shod (adjective)	Wearing shoes.
unshod (adjective)	Not wearing shoes, barefoot.
veld (noun)	Open grassland of South Africa.

The Road from Ixopo

Alan Paton

THERE IS A lovely road that runs from Ixopo into the hills. These hills are grass-covered and rolling, and they are lovely beyond any singing of it. The road climbs seven miles into them, to Carisbrooke; and from there, if there is no mist, you look down on one of the fairest valleys of Africa. About you there is grass and bracken and you may hear the forlorn crying of the titihoya, one of the birds of the veld. Below you is the valley of the Umzimkulu, on its journey from the Drakensberg to the sea; and beyond and behind the

1

---

*Editor's title.

river, great hill after great hill; and beyond and behind them, the mountains of Ingeli and East Griqualand.

The grass is rich and matted, you cannot see the soil. It holds the rain 2 and the mist, and they seep into the ground, feeding the streams in every kloof. It is well-tended, and not too many cattle feed upon it; not too many fires burn it, laying bare the soil. Stand unshod upon it, for the ground is holy, being even as it came from the Creator. Keep it, guard it, care for it, for it keeps men, guards men, cares for men. Destroy it and man is destroyed.

Where you stand the grass is rich and matted, you cannot see the soil. 3 But the rich green hills break down. They fall to the valley below, and falling, change their nature. For they grow red and bare; they cannot hold the rain and mist, and the streams are dry in the kloofs. Too many cattle feed upon the grass, and too many fires have burned it. Stand shod upon it, for it is coarse and sharp, and the stones cut under the feet. It is not kept, or guarded, or cared for, it no longer keeps men, guards men, cares for men. The titihoya does not cry here any more.

The great red hills stand desolate, and the earth has torn away like flesh. 4 The lightning flashes over them, the clouds pour down upon them, the dead streams come to life, full of the red blood of the earth. Down in the valleys women scratch the soil that is left, and the maize hardly reaches the height of a man. They are valleys of old men and old women, of mothers and children. The men are away, the young men and the girls are away. The soil cannot keep them any more.

Questions for Discussion

1. What pattern of comparison/contrast does Paton use to organize this selection? Why did he choose this one and not the other?

2. Identify three or four natural objects that the author uses as points of contrast.

3. Find examples of particularly vivid adjectives and verbs in paragraphs 1 through 3.

4. What vivid images does Paton create in paragraph 4? What is happening in each?

5. Besides contrast, what other method of development does Paton use?

6. In Chapter 7, you learned several ways to create emphasis. Find examples of such techniques in this selection, especially parallelism and repetition.

Thinking Critically

1. What important point or points is Paton making in this selection? Why did he use contrast to make it or them?

2. As you have learned, these four paragraphs make up the first chapter of *Cry, the Beloved Country*. This novel is, among many things, an indictment of apartheid (the forced segregation of nonwhites from whites) and of the brutal effects of that political system. Write a paragraph in which you speculate on how this first chapter might be preparing us for what is to come in the novel?

Suggestions for Journal Entries

1. Think of a natural environment you know well that has been damaged. Use listing to gather details that describe the effects of the damage and explain what caused it.

2. Gather details that might describe two different parts of your city, community, state, or campus.

3. In paragraph 2, Paton says "Destroy it and man is destroyed." Think about the information you put down in response to Suggestion 1 above. Now, use listing or clustering to gather details that might show how damaging this environment has affected the people who live in or frequent it.

New Blood for Cities

Stephen Moore

Stephen Moore is an economist at the Cato Institute, a think tank in Washington, DC. He has also worked on the U.S. Congress's Joint Economic Committee. His articles have appeared in The Wall Street Journal *and the* Los Angeles Times, *among other publications. He has appeared on television programs such as* The News Hour with Jim Lehrer *and* The McLaughlin Group, *and he is a contributing editor for* Human Events *and the* National Review. *His book,* Immigration for the Twenty-First Century, *was published in 1994. "New Blood for Cities" appeared in* The American Enterprise *magazine.*

Preparing to Read

1. "Balkanization" (paragraph 1) refers to the division, after World War I, of the area of the Balkan Mountains in southeastern Europe into several smaller nations, many of which were hostile to each other. These included Bulgaria, Greece, and Albania as well as several smaller states such as Serbia, Bosnia, and Croatia. Thus, *balkanization* means "to divide into opposing groups or factions."

2. Alexis de Tocqueville (1805–1859) (paragraph 2) was a French social philosopher. He wrote *Democracy in America* (1835), a book based on his travels in the United States. He believed American democracy would outlast European monarchy.

3. The heart of this contrast essay is paragraphs 5 through 10. But read paragraphs 1 through 4 and 11 carefully. They reveal Moore's purpose and thesis.

Vocabulary

assesses (verb)	Evaluates, measures, appraises.
compelling (adjective)	Impressive, convincing.
demographic (adjective)	Relating to population.
fiscal (adjective)	Financial; in this case, relating to public finances and budgets.
infusion (noun)	A flowing into.
per capita (adjective)	Per person, per head.
refute (verb)	Disprove, rebut.
virtually (adverb)	Essentially, practically.

New Blood for Cities

Stephen Moore

IMMIGRATION, WARNS A recent *New York Times Magazine* story, is leading to the "balkanization" of America's once-mighty industrial cities. "In the last half of the 1980s, for every ten immigrants who arrived in New York, Chicago, Los Angeles, and Houston, nine residents left for elsewhere," the article informs us. Meanwhile, city officials and antiimmigration groups charge that immigrants impose large economic burdens on America's inner cities.

Not so fast, argues a new study from the Alexis de Tocqueville Institution (ADTI) in Alexandria, VA. Certainly immigrants have a profound demographic, economic, and fiscal impact on America's largest central cities. More than half of all immigrants reside in just seven cities: Los Angeles, New York, Chicago, Miami, San Diego, Houston, and San Francisco. And true, immigrants impose special strains on these cities—heavier demands for social services, schools, and housing; language problems; and tighter labor markets. But the benefits of an infusion of fresh blood may offset these costs, the ADTI study suggests.

It assesses the local impact of immigration by contrasting the economic condition of cities with the highest immigration and those with the lowest immigration from 1980–90 (and through 1994 where more recent data is available). The 85 most populous U.S. cities, population 200,000 or more, are examined using Census Bureau data on nine different economic and fiscal measures.

The study's findings challenge much conventional wisdom:

- In the 1980s cities with the highest immigration had a job-creation rate twice as high as cities with the lowest immigration.

- Residents of high-immigrant cities are, on average, 15 percent richer than residents of low-immigrant cities. And incomes grew faster in high-immigrant areas as well. Residents of the cities with the most immigrants in 1980 experienced a 95 percent growth in per capita income that decade, versus an 88 percent growth in income for residents in the cities with the fewest immigrants in 1980.

- Poverty rates were 20 percent higher in 1990 in the cities with the fewest immigrants than in the cities with the most immigrants. The poverty rate from 1980–90 grew almost twice as fast in the cities with fewest immigrants in 1990 as in the cities with the most immigrants.

What about social conditions? No single factor has contributed to the declining livability of America's inner cities more than crime. Since at least the turn of the century, when the great wave of Germans, Italians, and Irishmen arrived through Ellis Island, Americans have often seen immigrants as a source of criminality.

Immigrants and Crime Don't Really Mix

High-Immigrant Cities	Foreign-Born, 1990	Crime Rate, 1991
Hialeah	69%	8 per 1,000
Miami	59	18
Santa Ana	51	8
Glendale	45	5
Los Angeles	38	10
San Francisco	34	9
Anaheim	28	7
New York	28	9
San Jose	27	5
Jersey City	26	9
Average, high-immigrant cities		9

Low-Immigrant Cities	Foreign-Born, 1990	Crime Rate, 1991
Jackson	1%	14 per 1,000
Shreveport	1	10
Birmingham	1	13
Memphis	1	10
Louisville	2	6
Richmond	2	12
Indianapolis	2	7
Mobile	2	13
Nashville	2	9
St. Louis	2	16
Average, low-immigrant cities		11

True or not in the past, crime and immigration do *not* go together today.   9
The table shows that high-immigrant cities in 1990 had a crime rate of 9
per 1,000 residents. Low-immigrant cities had a crime rate of 11—or about
22 percent higher. Only Miami, which has a very heavy concentration of immigrants and also the second highest crime rate of all major cities, is a major
exception to the rule.

The ADTI study does not answer the critical question of whether the im-   10
migrants cause urban conditions to improve, or whether improved urban
conditions cause the immigrants to come. But it does provide compelling evidence to refute the belief that the economic decline of cities is *caused* by immigration. The assertion cannot be true, because, with few exceptions, the
U.S. cities in greatest despair—Detroit, St. Louis, Buffalo, Rochester, and
Shreveport, for example—have virtually no immigrants.

Some 200 years ago James Madison wrote: "That part of America that has 11
encouraged [foreign immigration] has advanced most rapidly in population,
agriculture, and in the arts." That observation may be as true today as it was
at the birth of the nation.

Questions for Discussion

1. Which of the two patterns for organizing comparison/contrast essays
   does this essay use?
2. Moore's introduction is four paragraphs long. What is the function of
   each of these paragraphs?
3. Why does the author mention the *New York Times Magazine* story in
   paragraph 1? How does doing so help him make his point?
4. What kinds of details does Moore use most frequently to support the
   central ideas of paragraphs 5 through 10?
5. Does Moore believe the presence of large numbers of immigrants
   makes living in a place better? If not, what is his thesis?
6. What method for concluding essays explained in Chapter 4 does
   Moore use?

Thinking Critically

1. Explain the effect of Moore's including the table entitled "Immigrants
   and Crime Don't Really Mix." Couldn't he have just summarized this
   information in another paragraph or two?
2. You might agree with everything Moore has to say. Nonetheless,
   there are two sides to every story, even if one is more convincing than
   the other. Reread this essay. Offer an objection or counterargument
   to each of the author's arguments in paragraphs 5 through 10.

Suggestions for Journal Entries

1. Are you an immigrant, the child of an immigrant, or even the
   grandchild of an immigrant? If so, make a list of all of the good things
   people of your family or your ethnic group have contributed to the
   community, the state, or the country in general.
2. Think of other advantages that the presence of immigrants brings to a
   community. For example, you might mention that many new
   Americans start small businesses that provide new products and
   employment opportunities. You might talk about various types of
   music, art, or sports that immigrants have brought to America. Or,
   you could mention how the variety of ethnic restaurants, started by
   immigrants, has made your city a more interesting place to live.

3. For Moore, the notion that immigration is a burden on the cities is
    clearly a misconception. Think of three or four popular
    misconceptions about immigrants in general or members of a
    particular immigrant group. List these in a sentence or two. Then list
    an argument or fact that would refute each of these misconceptions.

Temptations of Old Age*

Malcolm Cowley

Malcolm Cowley (1898–1989) was a writer, editor, literary critic, and historian noted for his energy and productivity up until his death at 90. In the last decade of his life, Cowley wrote The View from 80, *a book that explains his very positive attitude toward aging and that offers excellent advice about the latter stages of life. Another selection from* The View from 80 *appears in Chapter 7.*

Preparing to Read

1. This selection is from a chapter of Cowley's book that discusses several temptations of old age and explains ways to avoid them. Among these temptations are greed, vanity, and a desire to escape life's problems through alcohol. But the greatest temptation, as shown in the following paragraphs, is "simply giving up."

2. Renoir, mentioned in paragraph 4, was a French painter of the nineteenth and twentieth centuries. Goya was a Spanish painter of the eighteenth and nineteenth centuries.

3. What hint about the selection's contents does the word "temptations" provide?

Vocabulary

ailments (noun)	Illnesses, disorders, diseases.
compelling (adjective)	Convincing, strong, valid.
distinguished (adjective)	Well-respected.
distraction (noun)	Amusement, diversion.
infirmities (noun)	Illnesses, weaknesses, ailments.
lithographs (noun)	Prints.
outwitted (verb)	Outsmarted, outmaneuvered.
Rolls-Royce (noun)	Expensive British automobile.
senility (noun)	Forgetfulness and decrease in mental powers affecting some elderly people.
stoical (adjective)	Brave, uncomplaining.
unvanquished (adjective)	Undefeated.

---

*Editor's title.

Temptations of Old Age

Malcolm Cowley

NOT WHISKEY OR cooking sherry but simply giving up is the greatest tempta- 1
tion of age. It is something different from a stoical acceptance of infirmi-
ties, which is something to be admired.

The givers-up see no reason for working. Sometimes they lie in bed all 2
day when moving about would still be possible, if difficult. I had a friend, a
distinguished poet, who surrendered in that fashion. The doctors tried to stir
him to action, but he refused to leave his room. Another friend, once a successful artist, stopped painting when his eyes began to fail. His doctor made
the mistake of telling him that he suffered from a fatal disease. He then lost
interest in everything except the splendid Rolls-Royce, acquired in his prosperous days, that stood in the garage. Daily he wiped the dust from its hood.
He couldn't drive it on the road any longer, but he used to sit in the driver's
seat, start the motor, then back the Rolls out of the garage and drive it in
again, back twenty feet and forward twenty feet; that was his only distraction.

I haven't the right to blame those who surrender, not being able to put 3
myself inside their minds or bodies. Often they must have compelling reasons, physical or moral. Not only do they suffer from a variety of ailments,
but also they are made to feel that they no longer have a function in the community. Their families and neighbors don't ask them for advice, don't really
listen when they speak, don't call on them for efforts. One notes that there
are not a few recoveries from apparent senility when that situation changes. If
it doesn't change, old persons may decide that efforts are useless. I sympa-
thize with their problems, but the men and women I envy are those who accept old age as a series of challenges.

For such persons, every new infirmity is an enemy to be outwitted, an 4
obstacle to be overcome by force of will. They enjoy each little victory over
themselves, and sometimes they win a major success. Renoir was one of
them. He continued painting, and magnificently, for years after he was crippled by arthritis; the brush had to be strapped to his arm. "You don't need
your hand to paint," he said. Goya was another of the unvanquished. At 72
he retired as an official painter of the Spanish court and decided to work only
for himself. His later years were those of the famous "black paintings" in
which he let his imagination run (and also of the lithographs, then a new
technique). At 78 he escaped a reign of terror in Spain by fleeing to Bor-
deaux. He was deaf and his eyes were failing; in order to work he had to wear
several pairs of spectacles, one over another, and then use a magnifying glass;
but he was producing splendid work in a totally new style. At 80 he drew an
ancient man propped on two sticks, with a mass of white hair and beard hiding his face and with the inscription "I am still learning."

"Eighty years old!" the great Catholic poet Paul Claudel wrote in his jour- 5
nal. "No eyes left, no ears, no teeth, no legs, no wind! And when all is said
and done, how astonishingly well one does without them!"

Questions for Discussion

1. Pick out particularly vivid verbs and adjectives in this selection.
2. Where does Cowley signal a transition from one subject to another?
3. Various methods can be combined to develop one idea. Where in this piece does Cowley use examples?
4. Do you think the conclusion of this selection is effective? Why or why not? If necessary, review ways to write conclusions in Chapter 4.
5. Why, according to the author, do some elderly people simply give up?
6. What does he mean when he says that others see "every new infirmity" as "an obstacle to be overcome by force of will" (paragraph 4)?

Thinking Critically

1. Cowley quotes directly from the "unvanquished." Why doesn't he also quote from "those who surrender"?
2. This selection uses the subject-by-subject pattern. Why does the author begin with the "givers-up" and not end with them? Should he have discussed Renoir, Goya, and Claudel first?
3. Would "Temptations of Old Age" have been better organized point by point? Why or why not?

Suggestions for Journal Entries

1. What Cowley says might apply to folks of all ages. Do you know someone who seems to face all the challenges life has to offer? Spend five minutes freewriting about the way this person reacts to such challenges. Then do the same for someone you might call a giver-up. Try to include facts about their lives that will describe their personalities.
2. In what way are you like the people in your family who have come before you? Think about a parent, grandparent, great-aunt, or other older relative. Use listing or focused freewriting to explain what is similar about your personalities, interests, lifestyles, or your opinions about music, politics, other people, or anything else you can think of.

The Militiaman, the Yuppie, and Me

Carolyn Swalina

Carolyn Swalina has studied literature and communications at Wilkes University and the University of Maine. She is currently working on her doctorate in special education at the University of California at Berkeley. Her purpose in this essay is to contrast two extreme views on an issue that in the last few years has been the subject of much debate. She uses the point-by-point method in a fictional dialogue between a pro-gun and an anti-gun advocate. Swalina also creates a persona, or speaker, to express her own, more moderate views on the subject.

Preparing to Read

1. Sal Monella's Brew and Burger, the name of the place in which the dialogue takes place, contains a pun, a play on words. *Salmonella* is a bacteria that causes food poisoning. Using this word sets a humorous and ironic (tongue-in-cheek) tone. Thus, we know from the beginning that what is being said—by the militiaman and the yuppie, at least—does not reflect the author's point of view.

2. The characters in this dialogue quote from the Second Amendment to the U.S. Constitution: "A well regulated Militia, being necessary to the security of a free State, the right of the people to keep and bear Arms shall not be infringed [restricted]."

3. The title prepares us for the three people we will encounter in this essay.

Vocabulary

camouflage (adjective)	Type of military clothing worn when hiding in woods or brush. Usually brown and green to blend in with other natural colors.
impaired (adjective)	Limited, diminished, damaged.
law-abiding (adjective)	Obeying the law.
militiaman (noun)	A member of a private, armed, military-like group. Such groups have no connection with the U.S. government.
raving (adjective)	Very enthusiastic about; it can also mean irrational or delirious. Obviously, both meanings apply in this essay.
scopes (noun)	Optical devices fitted on rifles for long-range shooting.
yuppie (noun)	An acronym (word made up of the first letters of a title) that means young urban professional.

The Militiaman, the Yuppie, and Me

Carolyn Swalina

JUST BEFORE I left school the other night, my journalism professor asked me to write an editorial about gun control for the college newspaper. It would be due the next day.   1

When I got home at 10:30 PM I decided I could think better if I relaxed a bit at Sal Monella's Brew and Burger around the corner. As I sat there sipping coffee, two men at a nearby table caught my attention. One of them, a large man wearing camouflage pants and a black tee shirt, pounded his fist on the table as he spoke to his companion, who was wearing khaki slacks, penny loafers, and a button-down shirt. He was sipping club soda. I labelled them the "militiaman" and the "yuppie."   2

"Listen, there are a lot of crazies out there," said the militiaman. "Besides, having guns is our constitutional right. Ever read the Second Amendment? It gives us the right 'to keep and bear arms.' Washington and the rest of those guys knew what they were doing; they saw what happened when you let the government have all the firepower. The feds will bother you whenever they feel like it. At least, if I still have my guns, they'll think twice before knocking down my door with a tank in the middle of the night."   3

"Yes, I've read the Constitution," said the yuppie. "And the Second Amendment is about 'a well regulated militia,' not private ownership. Besides, I'd rather have a cop knock down my door than some crazy with a gun."   4

"Either way, you should have a gun to defend yourself," insisted the militiaman.   5

"Who were these guys?" I wondered. "Constitutional lawyers? And what were the chances that the government would drive a tank through my front door?"   6

"If guns are banned, what makes you think they're just gonna go away?" the militiaman asked. "Sure, law-abiding citizens will turn theirs in, but what about street gangs and muggers? The only ones with guns will be cops and criminals. No, I'm not going to give up my guns until you can prove that all the criminals and crazies have given up theirs. And it's not just me! Everyone in my militia feels the same."   7

"What's wrong with cops having guns?" I said under my breath.   8

"Yes, but there are simply too many guns," responded the yuppie, sipping his club soda. "I went to visit my mother at the retirement home last week, and she was raving about a seminar she attended on rifle scopes for the visually impaired. She says her hit-to-miss ratio has improved 100% because of those new scopes. They even come in designer colors."   9

"What do you mean, designer colors?" I thought. "Scopes for the visually impaired? And what's your mother doing in a rest home if she can still shoot?"   10

"Good for Mom. She's a true American. She'll go down fighting," said the militiaman pushing his glass aside. "The government keeps taking away people's rights. Look at Waco. Just a few people who want to live in peace and   11 harmony, and the government comes in with heavy artillery to take their guns away."

"Yes, but if you don't have guns, the government won't bother you. After all, we are a country of laws. Guns are dangerous, and it's the government's responsibility to protect us from them. The best way to do that is to outlaw all of them." 12

"So," I thought, "what if someone decides to outlaw fast cars, baseball bats, and kitchen knives? Will people who own those things be criminals too?" 13

"But owning a gun is part of American manhood," said the man in the tee-shirt. "What would John Wayne or Clint Eastwood do without their guns?" 14

John Wayne and Clint Eastwood? I saw Hollywood images of the Alamo and Custer's last stand. But they had nothing to do with real people I knew who use guns to scare away groundhogs and skunks, to hunt, or to protect themselves in rural areas where the nearest police are miles away. 15

"Ah, their movies are just propaganda," said the yuppie. "They have nothing to do with the real problem of violence in this society." 16

The militiaman sneered; the yuppie turned red. He looked up for a moment trying to think about what to say next. "Let me tell you about the cold, hard facts. My son got shot on the playground because he wouldn't give some kid his homework. I've been shot twice: once on the highway after I brake-checked some guy who was tailgaiting me and once when I didn't make change fast enough when boarding a bus. When I walk up my street, I dodge bullets like I'm in a war zone. Sometimes I think I was safer in the army." 17

"You were," I finally broke in. "You had a gun when you were in the army." 18

"No kidding," continued the yuppie staring at me, "My mailman has a gun, the lady who runs the news stand has a gun, and just last week I saw a semi-automatic hanging in the back window of an ice cream truck. I did, I tell you; I did." 19

As he finished, I began to think that there might be some merit in outlawing club soda. 20

I paid for my coffee and walked out into the night air. The editorial was still due. My visit to Sal Monella's hadn't been very fruitful, but it convinced me that, perhaps, there are a lot of "crazies" out there. 21

Questions for Discussion

1. What differences do you see in the personalities of the militiaman and the yuppie? How does Swalina communicate these differences?

2. What is the speaker's attitude toward these men?

3. How does she expose the extremism in the yuppie's anti-gun stance?

4. How does she expose the extremism in the arguments of the militiaman?

5. Why does the author have the militiaman quote one part of the Second Amendment and the yuppie quote the other part? Why didn't she allow one man to quote the whole thing?

6. Do some of the arguments the militiaman and the yuppie use sound familiar? Which ones have you heard before?

7. In what other ways has Swalina made the debate seem believable? For example, does she ever use proper nouns?

8. What is Swalina's central idea?

Thinking Critically

1. Summarize the speaker's views on gun control. Begin by writing notes in the margins where her remarks appear. Then, use your notes to develop a short paragraph that explains her point of view.

2. Use the double-entry journal method to analyze the comments of the militiaman and the yuppie. Remember that this method requires summary and response. So, draw a line down the center of a piece of paper. On one side, summarize what each man says on each point discussed. On the other side, record your reactions to each of the ideas you summarized.

3. Mundie's "The Mentally Ill and Human Experimentation: Perfect Together," a student essay in Chapter 5, also uses irony. Compare and contrast that selection with Swalina's.

Suggestions for Journal Entries

1. Think of other arguments for or against gun control. List them in your journal.

2. Make two lists of arguments—pro and con—that you might use when presenting opposing sides of a controversial question. You can choose an issue in the national media, such as reforming the welfare system, testing student athletes for drugs, enforcing the death penalty, or limiting immigration. Then again, you might discuss something specific to your community or campus. For example, present arguments for and against requiring students to take certain courses or charging them athletic, activity, parking, and other fees along with tuition.

Suggestions for Sustained Writing

1. Did you respond to the second of the Suggestions for Journal Entries after Paton's "The Road from Ixopo"? If so, turn your notes into an essay that details major differences between two parts of your community, city, state, or campus. In the process, explain what accounts for or has created these differences.

   As Paton did in "The Road from Ixopo," try using the subject-by-subject method. In fact, you might use the selection by Paton as a model. Begin by writing an outline containing two major headings under each of which you will discuss one of the areas you are contrasting. Then, under the first heading list several points, topics, ideas, or facts about the area that you will discuss. Under the second heading, list points, topics, ideas, or facts that parallel, mirror, or complement those found under the first.

   Now, using this blueprint, write your rough draft. When you revise this draft, take another tip from Paton. Add the kind of concrete, specific, and vivid language that he uses and that you learned about in Chapters 5 and 6 of this textbook. In addition, draw verbal images that will make your contrast starker and more convincing to your reader. Then, edit your final draft carefully.

2. If you have not responded to all three of the items for journal writing after Moore's "New Blood for Cities," do so now. Then, read over all of your notes and use them to start an essay that contrasts at least three common misconceptions or false ideas about immigrants with the truth about them. You might devote your entire paper to one particular group of immigrants. Then, again you might attack misconceptions about three or more different groups.

   The point-by-point method, which Moore uses, is probably the best way to organize this paper. Begin by making an outline much like the one you see in the diagram that helps explain the point-by-point method on page 450. Like Moore, make sure to write an interesting introduction and a memorable conclusion. State your thesis clearly in the beginning or at the end of your essay.

   You need not rely heavily on statistics, as Moore does. If possible, however, you can include some simple statistics, even those you have gathered through personal observation. Of course, description, anecdotes, and examples might provide all the details you will need to develop your ideas successfully. In any event, use language that is specific and concrete. When revising your work, add vivid verbs and adjectives and create verbal images that will keep the reader's interest. Finally, edit your best draft and proofread your final product.

3. In talking about people who are 80, Malcolm Cowley describes two different types: those who fight on and those who give up. But we see these types in every generation, even our own. In fact, you may have begun

discussing such people in your journal. Use these notes in an essay about people you know who fit Cowley's personality types: those who face life bravely and those who just give up.

On the other hand, if you don't like this topic, you can start from scratch and choose your own basis for contrast. For example, discuss two very different types of students: those who are serious about getting an education and those who are not. Here's an example of a thesis for such a paper:

> While serious students study hard, do extra reading, and compare notes with classmates, those who just want to get by spend much of their time playing cards or watching television.

Cowley uses the subject-by-subject method; you might want to do the same. However you decide to organize your essay, discuss two or three people you know as examples of *each* personality type. Begin with a rough draft, adding details with each revision to make your paper clearer and more convincing. In the process, include an effective introduction and conclusion.

Then, rewrite your paper once more. Make sure it has a clear thesis, is easy to follow, and is free of mistakes in grammar, punctuation, spelling, and the like.

4. Follow Carolyn Swalina's example. Write an essay in which you contrast two extreme views on a controversial subject about which you gathered details in your journal after reading "The Militiaman, the Yuppie, and Me."

If you wish, pattern your paper on Swalina's, and use the point-by-point method. To do this, focus on three or four major points; present two opposing opinions on each point before moving on to the next point. On the other hand, you can use the subject-by subject method by presenting all the arguments on one side of the issue before discussing the arguments on the other side. Either way, remember that, like Swalina, you are exposing two very extreme views. And like Swalina, you may want to express a third, more moderate and more reasonable view of your own. You can conclude your essay with this view by expressing it in a thesis statement near the end of your paper.

This is a complicated assignment. To do it well, you will have to revise your work several times. And any assignment that demands that much work also deserves to be edited and proofread conscientiously.

5. What was your hometown, neighborhood, or street like when you were a child, and what is it like now? Has it changed for the better or for the worse?

Describe important changes in a well-developed essay that uses the subject-by-subject method. If you wish, begin by describing what the place was like before, then discuss what it has become. Rely on your senses, and use language that is specific, vivid, and concrete. Examples of such language are found throughout this chapter but especially in the work of Paton and Cowley. Other selections that describe places and things well appear in Chapter 8.

As you write your first draft, focus on a thesis that expresses your approval or disapproval of the changes you have seen. Put that thesis in your introduction or conclusion. Here are two examples:

> What's happened to the downtown area in the last ten years has convinced me that even the most rundown city can be saved.

> What's happened to Elm Street in recent years has made me an opponent of urban renewal.

If you responded to the journal suggestions after Paton's "The Road from Ixopo," you might already have the information and inspiration to begin this project.

Writing to Learn: A Group Activity

In "New Blood for Cities," Stephen Moore draws our attention to the question of immigration. Should we leave our current immigration policy as is, or should we limit the number of immigrants? What effect—negative or positive—does the current system have on this country's economy, health care, schools, welfare system, and tax rates? Here's your chance to present both sides of the issue.

THE FIRST MEETING

Brainstorm to identify research questions concerning the impact that immigration is having on the country. For example, one of you might research immigration's effects on health care. Another might find information on immigration and the welfare system. Still others might research its impact on education, the economy, or employment. Someone could even learn about the changes immigration is bringing to American culture, especially in cuisine, entertainment, and fashion. Before you adjourn, make sure someone agrees to report on major aspects or regulations of the current U.S. immigration policy.

RESEARCH

Stick to current sources. Check the Internet, but also use your library's online and print databases to find relevant articles in periodicals. For example, try InfoTrac or ProQuest as well as the most recent installments of the *New York Times Index*, the *Readers' Guide to Periodical Literature*, and the *Social Sciences Citation Index*. Find information and opinions on both sides of the question you are researching. Bring your notes and photocopies of pages from your sources to the next meeting.

THE SECOND MEETING

The purpose of this assignment is to present both sides of the issue. Therefore, make sure everyone has gathered enough information to compose a paper that fully explains both the pros and cons of each question researched. Write an outline for a paper that will address each of these questions in a separate section. Then, ask each student to write at least two paragraphs addressing his or her assigned question. Ask the person who researched the current U.S. immigration policy to write an introduction that summarizes that policy and introduces points to be discussed in the rest of the paper.

THE THIRD MEETING

Critique each other's work and offer suggestions for improvement. Make sure everyone has fully discussed both the pros and cons of the question he or she researched. Pick one student to collect the final versions of everyone's writing and put together a draft of a complete paper that will be distributed and reviewed next time.

THE FOURTH MEETING

Distribute and read the draft of the paper. Make revisions as needed. Ask one student to edit the paper and another to type and proofread it.

CHAPTER 14

Process Analysis

Like illustration and comparison and contrast, process analysis is a way to explain complex ideas and abstract concepts. It can be used to show how something works or how something happens. It also comes in handy when you want to give readers instructions.

Organization, Purpose, and Thesis

Process explanations are organized in chronological order, much like narrative essays and short stories. In narration, however, the writer's purpose is to tell *what* happens. In process analysis, it is to explain *how* something happens (or happened) or *how* it is done.

You would be explaining a process if you wrote an essay discussing how the body uses oxygen, how electric light bulbs work, how a CD player produces sound, or how the Grand Canyon was formed. An example of such an essay in this chapter is Carl Sagan's "The Measure of Eratosthenes."

As you can see, process analysis is an important tool in scientific writing. But it can also be applied to topics in history, sociology, economics, the arts, and other subjects. For example, a process paper might be a good way to explain how the U.S. Constitution was ratified, how the stock market works, how people celebrate a holiday or tradition, or how a particular type of music developed. As Kenneth Kohler shows in "How I Came Out to My Parents," this type of writing can even explain how people deal with important personal issues.

Process analysis is also used in writing instructions. Scientists, doctors, engineers, and computer experts, for example, must often write careful directions to show their readers how to use a tool or machine, how to complete a procedure safely, how to conduct a test to achieve accurate results, or how to run complicated computer software. As a beginning writer, you might want to discuss a more limited subject by showing your readers how to change a tire, hang wallpaper, stop smoking, lose weight, study for a math exam, or accomplish another important task or goal. In this chapter, selections that instruct readers are Benjamin Franklin's "Drawing Electricity from Clouds" and Adam Goodheart's "How to Fight a Duel," as well as Triena Milden's "So You Want to Flunk Out of College," which appears in the introduction.

The thesis in a process analysis essay is usually a statement of purpose; it explains why a process is important, why it occurs or occurred, or why it should be completed. For example, if you want to explain how to change the oil in a car, you might begin by saying that changing oil regularly can extend the engine's life. In addition to a statement of purpose, writers often begin with a broad summary or overview of the process so that readers can understand how each step relates to the whole procedure and to its purpose.

Clarity and Directness

As with all types of writing, clarity and directness are important in process writing. You must explain the various steps in your process specifically and carefully enough that even readers who are unfamiliar with the subject will be able to follow each step easily. To be clear and to maintain your reader's interest, keep the following in mind:

1. *Use clear, simple language:* Use words that your readers will have no trouble understanding. If you *must* use terms your readers are not familiar with, provide a brief definition or description. Depending on how much your readers know about how to change a tire, for example, you might have to describe what a lug wrench looks like before you explain how to use it.

2. *Use the clearest, simplest organization:* Whenever possible, arrange the steps of your process in chronological order. In addition, use plenty of connective words and phrases between paragraphs (especially to show the passage of time); this will keep your writing coherent and easy to follow.

3. *Mention equipment and supplies:* Let readers know what equipment, tools, supplies, and other materials are involved in the process. Define or describe items that might be unfamiliar to them. If you are giving instructions, list these materials *before* you start explaining the steps in your process. Otherwise, the reader will have to stop in mid-process to find a needed item. This can be frustrating and time consuming.

4. *Discuss each step separately:* Reserve an entire paragraph for each step in the process; this is especially important when giving instructions. Explaining more than one step at a time can confuse readers and cause you to leave out important information.

5. *Discuss simultaneous steps separately:* If you need to explain two or more steps that occur at the same time, write about these steps in separate paragraphs. To maintain coherence between paragraphs, use connective elements such as "At the same time," "Meanwhile," and "During this stage of the process."

6. *Give all the necessary information:* Always provide enough information to develop each step in the process adequately, and don't forget the small, important details. For instance, if you're explaining how to change the oil in a car, remember to tell your readers to wait for the engine to cool off before loosening the oil-pan bolt; otherwise, the oil could severely burn their hands. On the other hand, the oil should be warm enough so that it all drains off.

7. *Use the right verb tense:* If you're explaining a recurring process (one that happens over and over again), use the present tense. In writing about how your student government works, for instance, say that "the representatives *are elected* by fellow students and *meet* together every Friday afternoon." But if you're writing about a process that is over and done with, such as how one individual ran for election, use the past tense.

8. *Use direct commands:* When giving instructions, make each step clear and brief by simply telling the reader to do it (that is, by using the imperative mood). For example, don't say, "The first thing to do is to apply the handbrake." Instead, be more direct: "First, apply the handbrake."

Visualizing Process Analysis

The following diagram illustrates how you might organize the instructions on removing a flat tire. Transitions are underlined.

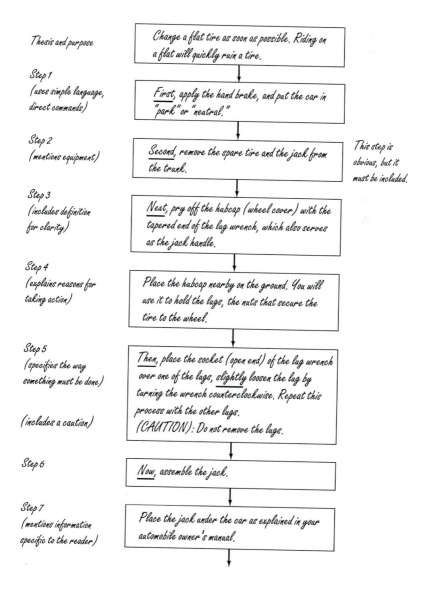

Thesis and purpose — Change a flat tire as soon as possible. Riding on a flat will quickly ruin a tire.

Step 1 (uses simple language, direct commands) — First, apply the hand brake, and put the car in "park" or "neutral."

Step 2 (mentions equipment) — Second, remove the spare tire and the jack from the trunk. — This step is obvious, but it must be included.

Step 3 (includes definition for clarity) — Next, pry off the hubcap (wheel cover) with the tapered end of the lug wrench, which also serves as the jack handle.

Step 4 (explains reasons for taking action) — Place the hubcap nearby on the ground. You will use it to hold the lugs, the nuts that secure the tire to the wheel.

Step 5 (specifies the way something must be done) (includes a caution) — Then, place the socket (open end) of the lug wrench over one of the lugs, slightly loosen the lug by turning the wrench counterclockwise. Repeat this process with the other lugs. (CAUTION): Do not remove the lugs.

Step 6 — Now, assemble the jack.

Step 7 (mentions information specific to the reader) — Place the jack under the car as explained in your automobile owner's manual.

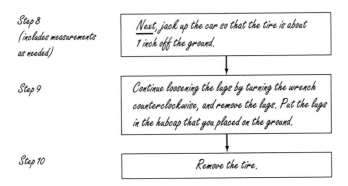

Step 8
(includes measurements
as needed)

Next, jack up the car so that the tire is about 1 inch off the ground.

Step 9

Continue loosening the lugs by turning the wrench counterclockwise, and remove the lugs. Put the lugs in the hubcap that you placed on the ground.

Step 10

Remove the tire.

SEEING THE PATTERN IN A PROCESS ANALYSIS PAPER

The following essay, "So You Want to Flunk Out of College," takes a humorous approach to a serious issue. Student author Triena Milden uses irony by arguing the opposite of what she believes. Nonetheless, her tongue-in-cheek essay illustrates several techniques important to process analysis.

Flunking out of college is a relatively easy task. It requires little effort and might even be considered fun. Though it is hard to imagine why anyone would purposely try to flunk out of college, many people accomplish this task easily. In fact, whatever the reason one might want to flunk out of college, the process is quite simple.

States thesis.

Uses present tense.

First, *do not show up* for classes very often. It is important, however, to show up occasionally to find out when tests will be scheduled; the importance of this will become apparent later in this essay.

When in class, *never raise your hand* to ask questions and never volunteer any answers to the teacher's questions. If the teacher calls on you, either answer incorrectly or

Uses transitions for clear, simple organization.

Uses direct commands.

say "I don't know." Be sure your tone of voice conveys your lack of interest.

Discusses each step separately.

Another thing to avoid is homework. There are two reasons for this. First and most important, completing homework assignments only reinforces information learned earlier, thereby contributing to higher test scores. Second, although teachers credit homework as only part of the total grade, every little bit of credit hurts. Therefore, make sure that the teacher is aware that you are not doing your homework. You can do so by making certain that the teacher sees you writing down the answers as the homework is discussed in class.

Provides all necessary information.

The next area, tests, can be handled in two ways. They can either not be taken or be failed. If you do not take them, you run the risk of receiving an "incomplete" rather than a failing grade. In order to flunk out of college, failing grades are preferable. Therefore, make sure to take and fail all exams. Incidentally, this is where attendance and homework can really affect performance. Attending class and doing homework regularly can be detrimental to obtaining poor test scores.

Uses simple language.

Continues to use direct commands.

Since you won't know the correct answers to test questions, make sure to choose those that are as absurd as possible without being obvious. Even if you guess a few correctly, your overall grade will be an *F* as long as the majority of your answers are wrong. By the way, one sure way to receive that cherished zero <u>is</u> to be caught cheating: all teachers <u>promise</u> a zero for this.

Keeps to the present tense.

The same ideas <u>pertain</u> to any reports or term papers that you are assigned. If you fail to turn them in, you might get an "incomplete." Therefore, hand in all papers, especially if they're poorly written. Make sure to use poor organization, to present information in a confused manner, and to write on the wrong topic whenever you can. The paper should be handwritten, not typed, and barely legible. Misspellings should be plentiful and as noticeable as possible. Smudged ink or dirty pages add a nice touch to the finished product. Finally, try to get caught plagiarizing.

Provides all necessary information.

By following these few simple suggestions, you will be assured of a failing grade. Try not to make it too obvious that your purpose is to fail. However, if a teacher shows concern and offers help, be sure to exhibit a poor attitude as you refuse. Should you decide to put extra effort into failing, you may even

Ends with a memorable conclusion.

finish at the bottom of the class. Someone
has to finish last. Why not you?

Revising Process Analysis Papers

When Kenneth Kohler wrote the first draft of "How I Came Out to My Parents," he used narration. Later, he decided that telling what happened was less important than explaining how it happened. Paragraphs from the draft and revision of his paper show how he changed his narrative into process analysis. They also show that he added information, removed unnecessary words and details, and combined sentences to make his writing more efficient. The entire essay appears later in the chapter.

Kohler—Early Draft

My struggle to "come out of the closet" grew
out of several needs. First, I had a need
to be closer to my parents and to share my
life with them. Second, I had a need to be
honest with them about who I really was.

Combine these two reasons?

And third, I needed to let them know that
there was someone special in my life. By

Is "And" needed?

Remove? Isn't this clear already?

coming out to my parents, I would risk
alienation and rejection for the hope that
they would gain a little more understanding
of the man whom they called their son.

Save for later paragraph?

. . .

I had no idea how my parents might react
when I came out to them. I knew that if my
parents reacted violently or negatively it

Repeats ideas from above. Remove?

could take years to heal the damage that
would be done by their reaction. It was a
chance I had to take. I had to risk telling
them my deepest secret in an attempt to get

Wordy? Remove unnecessary words?

closer to them. It was a risk my brother
never had to take.

Do readers need to know this?

Kohler—Final Draft

My struggle to "come out of the closet" grew
out of several needs. First, I wanted to be
closer with my parents and to be honest

Combines ideas.

about who I was. Second, I needed to let
them know that there was someone special in
my life. Finally, I had agreed to speak at
my church about being gay, and I felt it
important to tell my parents about my
lifestyle before informing my congregation.

Adds information to strengthen and clarify purpose.

Has removed ideas that belong in a later paragraph.

. . .

I had no idea how they might react when I
came out to them. I knew that if they
responded violently or negatively it could
take years to heal the damage. I also knew
that I might never see them again. It was
for this reason that I had avoided coming
out to them before. However, because of my
pending public announcement, the time had
come to let them know.

Adds information important to purpose.

Has removed unnecessary words, details.

I planned what I had to say carefully.
Something so important could not simply be
announced and forgotten. I had actually
begun to prepare for this moment years
before by reading as much as I could about
homosexuality and by talking to gay friends.
It was necessary for me to accept myself as

Adds a paragraph to trace steps in the process.

Step 1

a gay man before expecting others to do so.

I had to develop a positive self-image, and   *Step 2;*
Note
this took several years. <u>Then</u>, in the week   *transition.*

prior to my announcement, I began to

rehearse my lines. I made notes for various

approaches I could take. I wanted to feel

secure in my delivery and didn't want to

appear ashamed of my lifestyle. "Why should

I be?" I thought. I had never felt

differently. I imagined my parents' every
                                                   Step 3
reaction and tried to predict my responses.

I even prepared myself for the worst, afraid

they would tell me to "Get out and never

come back!"

Practicing Process Analysis

Reread Visualizing Process Analysis and the diagram of it on pages 481–482. Use the method you see there to list instructions on doing a simple task. Write these steps in the boxes below, one step per box. Be complete; if you need more boxes, draw them on a piece of paper. As always, make a rough draft first. Here are examples of the task you might write about.

How to brush your teeth.
How to make a pot of coffee.
How to address an envelope.
How to make out a check.
How to start a car.
How to take a two-minute shower.
How to do laundry in a washing machine.
How to heat leftovers in a microwave.

State task's
purpose

Step 1

Step 2

Step 3

Step 4

Step 5

Step 6

Step 7

Step 8

Enjoy the four selections that follow. They are well written and should provide you with effective examples of the techniques found in writing that makes good use of process analysis.

Drawing Electricity from Clouds*

Benjamin Franklin

Printer, scientist, writer, and statesman, Benjamin Franklin (1706–1790) helped to draft the Declaration of Independence, served as special envoy to France during the American Revolution, and negotiated the treaty of peace with Great Britain. He also participated in the Constitutional Convention of 1787. Among his inventions are bifocals and the Franklin stove. His experiments with the kite, which he detailed in a letter to Peter Collison in 1752, proved that electricity was present in the atmosphere.

Preparing to Read

Franklin explains the process of drawing electricity from clouds in one long paragraph. However, each step is easy to distinguish because it is explained separately.

Vocabulary

filaments (noun)   Fibers, threads.
kindled (verb)   Ignited.
phial (noun)   Small bottle; today, typically spelled *vial*.
spirits (noun)   Alcohol solutions.

Drawing Electricity from Clouds

Benjamin Franklin

Sir,

As frequent mention is made in public papers from Europe of the success   1
of the Philadelphia experiment for drawing the electric fire from clouds by means of pointed rods of iron erected on high buildings, etc, it may be agreeable to the curious to be informed that the same experiment has succeeded in Philadelphia, though made in a different and more easy manner, which is as follows:

Make a small cross of two light strips of cedar, the arms so long as to   2
reach the four corners of a large thin silk handkerchief when extended; tie the corners of the handkerchief to the extremities of the cross, so you have the body of a kite, which, being properly accommodated with a tail, loop, and

---

*Editor's title.

string, will rise in the air, like those made of paper, but this, being of silk, is fitter to bear the wet and wind of a thunder-gust without tearing. To the top of the upright stick of the cross is to be fixed a very sharp-pointed wire, rising a foot or more above the wood. To the end of the twine, next to hand, is to be tied a silk ribbon, and where the silk and twine join, a key may be fastened. This kite is to be raised when a thunder-gust appears to be coming on, and the person who holds the string must stand within a door or window or under some cover, so that the silk ribbon may not be wet; and care must be taken that the twine does not touch the frame of the door or window. As soon as any of the thunderclouds come over the kite, the pointed wire will draw the electric fire from them, and the kite, with all the twine, will be electrified, and the loose filaments of the twine will stand out every way, and be attracted by an approaching finger. And when the rain has wet the kite and twine, so that it can conduct the electric fire freely, you will find it stream out plentifully from the key on the approach of your knuckle. At this key the phial may be charged; and from electric fire thus obtained, spirits may be kindled, and all the other electric experiments be performed, which are usually done by the help of a rubbed glass globe or tube, and thereby the sameness of the electric matter with that of lightning completely demonstrated.

B Franklin

Questions for Discussion

1. Process essays often include statements of purpose. Where do we find such a statement in this selection?
2. Where does Franklin include transitional devices?
3. Where does Franklin mention equipment needed? Does he include a warning?
4. Process papers are supposed to use simple, clear language and be easy to follow. Allowing for the fact that Franklin wrote this nearly 250 years ago, does this selection meet those criteria? Explain.

Thinking Critically

1. You learned in the introduction to this chapter that process analysis is used to give instructions as well as to explain how a process occurs. Franklin does both those things in paragraph 2. Explain the differences between the first half and the second half of this paragraph.
2. Franklin put his explanation into one paragraph. Rewrite paragraph 2 using a list format; put each step Franklin explains into its own short paragraph. Add details if you think doing so will improve the original, and use your own vocabulary to modernize the language.

Suggestions for Journal Entries

1. Think about a simple process that you've had to complete at home, at work, or at school. For instance, recall the steps you went through the last time you painted a wall, cooked macaroni and cheese, cut grass, set the table for dinner, ironed a load of laundry, or got dressed for an important date. Make a list of the tools, equipment, utensils, ingredients, or materials you needed to complete this process.

2. After brainstorming with a friend, write a paragraph that briefly discusses steps you go through to complete a common process such as shopping for groceries, polishing shoes, or getting a child ready for bed. You might start by reviewing what you wrote when responding to the Practicing Process Analysis exercise on pages 487–489.

How to Fight a Duel

Adam Goodheart

Adam Goodheart is an associate editor with Civilization *magazine, published by the Library of Congress in Washington, DC. Goodheart writes a column called "Lost Arts" in which he explains how to master arts, skills, or activities from the past. Among these intriguing articles are "How to Host a Roman Orgy" and "How to Fly a Zeppelin." "How to Fight a Duel" appeared in 1996.*

Preparing to Read

1. Tort reform (paragraph 1) is a movement to change laws governing suits brought to gain compensation for injury to one's person, property, or reputation.
2. In paragraph 4, Goodheart mentions a "second." This is a person who accompanied and assisted the duelist and even took his or her place if necessary.
3. As with the other articles in his column, Goodheart explains a serious subject humorously. One way he does this is to mix formal, even exotic, language with everyday vocabulary, including slang.

Vocabulary

à la terre (**adverb**)	To the ground (French).
blunderbuss (**noun**)	A gun with a wide muzzle used at close range.
calumniating (**adjective**)	Slandering, making malicious and untrue statements about.
frock coat (**noun**)	Close-fitting, knee-length coat.
impertinent (**adjective**)	Arrogant, rude, presumptuous.
languid (**adjective**)	Listless, lacking in energy or spirit.
lanky (**adjective**)	Tall and thin.
latitude (**noun**)	Degree of freedom.
litigious (**adjective**)	Given to lawsuits, argumentative.
prescribed (**verb**)	Directed, specified.
prevaricating (**adjective**)	Speaking falsely or in a misleading way.
provoke (**verb**)	Incite, anger.
sangfroid (**noun**)	Cold-bloodedness, coolheadedness (French).
trifle (**noun**)	Something of no importance.

How to Fight a Duel

Adam Goodheart

TORT REFORM IS for wimps. If we really want to fix our litigious society, how   1
about reviving the old-fashioned pistol duel? As the author of *The Art of
Duelling* wrote in 1836, "It is certainly both awful and distressing, to see a
young person cut off suddenly in a duel . . . but the loss of a few lives is a
mere trifle, when compared with the benefits resulting to Society at large"—
such as enforcing good manners. Though you may protest that you don't
know a flintlock from a fife cleaner, the rules for duels are really quite simple.

Equipment

Two (2) smoothbore flintlock pistols.

Gunpowder.

Some round lead bullets and linen patches.

A surgeon's kit.

A frock coat.

A handkerchief.

A mortal enemy.

1. The Challenge.   In the 18th and 19th centuries, elaborate manuals   2
prescribed the exact circumstances under which duels were fought. A slur
against one's wife or mistress was a common motive, though the Irish dueling
code of 1777 ruled such insults justified if they had "the support of ladies'
reputations." (But ladies dueled too; in 1721 the Countess de Polignac
plugged Lady de Nestle over the handsome Duc de Richelieu.)

Still, if the offense has not been obvious, you'll often find it necessary to   3
provoke a challenge by insulting your would-be enemy. Here, more creative
latitude is permitted. Some insults for you to choose from: "impertinent
puppy" (Major Oneby to a Mr. Gower, 1720); "prevaricating, base, calumni-
ating scoundrel, poltroon and coward" (Gen. James Wilkinson to Rep. John
Randolph, 1807); "Baron—of Intellect" (Harry Maury to Baron Henri Arnous
de Riviere, 1858). Or you can bypass such formalities like Lord Cobham
who, in 1750, simply seized Lord Hervey's hat and spat into it.

2. Preliminaries and Precautions.   Once a duel has been agreed   4
upon, it is customary simply to exchange cards and then leave all further
arrangement to your seconds. The challenger's second then calls upon the
challenged party to arrange the confrontation. Such a visit should be cordial
if not exactly friendly; sangfroid, at least, is essential. In an 1870 duel, Prince
Pierre Bonaparte grew flustered and fired a bit prematurely—killing, that is to
say, the unfortunate second who had come to deliver a challenge.

Traditionally, the duel must take place within the next 48 hours—to re-   5
duce practice time—and preferably at dawn. Pick a secluded spot; if there's a
state or national boundary handy, fight near enough to it so you can escape

across if you prove victorious. And be discreet, even with friends and family. In 1898, a Berlin duel was cut short when the opponents' fathers burst out of the shrubbery and began thrashing the young men with canes.

3. Taking the Field. Arrive properly attired in a dark frock coat—one without gilt buttons and with lapels to hide your white collar, since these make easy targets. (In 1806, Andrew Jackson scandalized Kentucky—a tough feat in those days—by fighting Charles Dickinson wearing a loose dressing gown draped over his lanky frame.) Greet your antagonist and take your place. The more serious the dispute, generally, the closer you will stand. Anywhere from 10 to 50 paces is customary, although in 1819 Armistead Mason and John Mc-Carty—they were rival politicians—blasted holes in each other with shotguns at four paces. Before shots are exchanged, the seconds can try to effect a reconciliation. If your thirst for vengeance is implacable, proceed to Step 4.

4. Ready, Aim, Fire. You and your antagonist will fire simultaneously on cue, usually the dropping of a handkerchief. You should be standing sideways to offer as narrow a target as possible—though not if you're built like British politician Charles James Fox, who exclaimed at a 1779 duel, "Why, man, I'm as thick one way as the other!" If you're considering firing into the air, inform yourself as to local custom. While the languid Brits thought it unsporting under any circumstances to take careful aim, the Germans were deeply offended if you didn't shoot to kill.

If both bullets miss, you can either declare the affair settled or go for another round. If you hit your foe, advises *The Art of Duelling,* "An expression of regret should always precede [your] quitting the field." If you're hit, the handbook continues, "treat the matter coolly"; if you happen to die, "go off with as good a grace as possible."

Warning Don't try any fancy stuff. In 1808, two Frenchmen fought a duel with blunderbusses in balloons; M. Grandprée sent M. le Pique plummeting *à la terre.* Late in the century, the "dynamite duel" came into vogue—participants would hurl sticks of TNT at each other. But gentlemen prefer pistols at 10 paces.

Questions for Discussion

1. Earlier in this chapter you read about techniques writers of process analysis use to keep their work interesting and clear. Find examples of such techniques. For example, where does Goodheart use direct commands? What verb tense does he use?

2. As you would expect, Goodheart lists steps involved in a duel in chronological order. Why does he arrange these steps into four separate categories?

3. What does the author propose as the purpose for dueling?

4. What method or methods of development that you learned about in Chapter 3, other than process analysis, does this essay use?

5. Why does the author include a separate list of equipment? Why didn't he just include these items in the text as he went along?

6. You learned in Preparing to Read that Goodheart creates humor by mixing informal and formal language. You can find one such example in paragraph 1. Look for at least one other and explain why it is funny.

Thinking Critically

1. Considering what you have learned about dueling, what can you add to the warning given at the end of the essay?

2. Paragraph 3 reports that Harry Maury called Henri Arnous de Riviere the "Baron—of Intellect." How do you interpret his insult?

3. What does paragraph 5 say about the image of dueling even in the past?

Suggestions for Journal Entries

1. What is worth fighting for? Make a list of people, beliefs, or ideas for which you might risk your well-being or even your life.

2. Defined broadly, a duel could be any confrontation, contest, or encounter between two people. Consider the following:

> Bargaining when buying a car.
>
> Convincing a child to do something he or she does not want to do.
>
> Asking for a raise or time off at your job.
>
> Talking your way out of a traffic ticket.
>
> Convincing someone you dislike to stop calling or annoying you.

These are only a few examples. You can probably think of many more. Focus on one such "duel"; use clustering, freewriting, or brainstorming with a friend to gather information that might explain how to prepare for and fight your particular duel successfully.

The Measure of Eratosthenes

Carl Sagan

Carl Sagan was a professor of astronomy at Cornell University and the author of many books on science. He published "The Measure of Eratosthenes" (er-uh-TAHS-thuh-neez) to honor the Greek thinker who, 17 centuries before Columbus, measured the Earth and proved it was round. Another essay by Sagan can be found in Chapter 11.

Preparing to Read

1. In paragraph 4, Sagan claims that "in almost everything, Eratosthenes was 'alpha.' " Alpha is the first letter of the Greek alphabet.
2. Papyrus, mentioned in paragraph 5, is a plant from which paper was made in ancient times.
3. What might Sagan mean by "measure" in the title?

Vocabulary

cataract (noun)	Large waterfall.
circumference (noun)	Distance around a circle or globe.
compelling (adjective)	Difficult to ignore.
deduced (verb)	Concluded, discovered.
inclined (adjective)	Slanted.
intergalactic (adjective)	Between galaxies.
intersect (verb)	Cross.
musings (noun)	Thoughts.
pronounced (adjective)	Significant.
randomly (adverb)	By chance.

The Measure of Eratosthenes

Carl Sagan

THE EARTH IS a place. It is by no means the only place. It is not even a typical place. No planet or star or galaxy can be typical, because the cosmos is mostly empty. The only typical place is within the vast, cold, universal vacuum, the everlasting night of intergalactic space, a place so strange and desolate that, by comparison, planets and stars and galaxies seem achingly rare and lovely.

If we were randomly inserted into the cosmos, the chance that we would find ourselves on or near a planet would be less than one in a billion trillion

trillion (10^{33}, a one followed by 33 zeros). In everyday life, such odds are called compelling. Worlds are precious.

The discovery that the earth is a *little* world was made, as so many im- 3 portant human discoveries were, in the ancient Near East, in a time some humans call the third century BC, in the greatest metropolis of the age, the Egyptian city of Alexandria.

Here there lived a man named Eratosthenes. One of his envious contem- 4 poraries called him "beta," the second letter of the Greek alphabet, because, he said, Eratosthenes was the world's second best in everything. But it seems clear that, in almost everything, Eratosthenes was "alpha."

He was an astronomer, historian, geographer, philosopher, poet, theater 5 critic, and mathematician. His writings ranged from "Astronomy" to "On Freedom from Pain." He was also the director of the great library of Alexandria, where one day he read, in a papyrus book, that in the southern frontier outpost of Syene (now Aswan), near the first cataract of the Nile, at noon on June 21 vertical sticks cast no shadows. On the summer solstice, the longest day of the year, as the hours crept toward midday, the shadows of the temple columns grew shorter. At noon, they were gone. A reflection of the sun could then be seen in the water at the bottom of a deep well. The sun was directly overhead.

It was an observation that someone else might easily have ignored. 6 Sticks, shadows, reflections in wells, the position of the sun—of what possible importance could such simple, everyday matters be? But Eratosthenes was a scientist, and his musings on these commonplaces changed the world: in a way, they made the world.

Eratosthenes had the presence of mind to do an experiment—actually 7 to observe whether *in Alexandria* vertical sticks cast shadows near noon on June 21. And, he discovered, sticks do.

Eratosthenes asked himself how, at the same moment, a stick in Syene 8 could cast no shadow and a stick in Alexandria, far to the north, could cast a pronounced shadow.

Consider a map of ancient Egypt with two vertical sticks of equal length, 9 one stuck in Alexandria, the other in Syene. Suppose that, at a certain moment, neither stick casts any shadow at all. This is perfectly easy to understand—provided the earth is flat. The sun would then be directly overhead. If the two sticks cast shadows of equal length, that also would make sense on a flat earth: the sun's rays would then be inclined at the same angle to the two sticks. But how could it be that at the same instant there was no shadow at Syene and a substantial shadow at Alexandria?

The only possible answer, he saw, was that the surface of the earth is 10 curved. Not only that: the greater the curvature, the greater the difference in the shadow lengths. The sun is so far away that its rays are parallel when they reach the earth. Sticks placed at different angles to the sun's rays cast shadows of different lengths. For the observed difference in the shadow lengths, the distance between Alexandria and Syene had to be about seven degrees along the surface of the earth; that is, if you imagine the sticks extending down to the center of the earth, they would intersect there at an angle of seven degrees.

Seven degrees is something like one-fiftieth of 360 degrees, the full cir-   11
cumference of the earth. Eratosthenes knew that the distance between Alexandria and Syene was approximately 800 kilometers, because he had hired a man to pace it out.

Eight hundred kilometers times 50 is 40,000 kilometers; so that must be   12
the circumference of the earth. (Or, if you like to measure things in miles, the distance between Alexandria and Syene is about 500 miles, and 500 miles times 50 is 25,000 miles.)

This is the right answer.   13

Eratosthenes' only tools were sticks, eyes, feet, and brains, plus a taste for   14
experiment. With them he deduced the circumference of the earth with an error of only a few percent, a remarkable achievement for 2,200 years ago. He was the first person accurately to measure the size of a planet.

Questions for Discussion

1. What does paragraph 6 tell us about the purpose for which Sagan wrote this essay?

2. Where does Sagan refer to the scientific process of making observations and of drawing conclusions from those observations?

3. Where does Sagan define important terms?

4. You have read that each step in a process should be discussed thoroughly. In what paragraph or paragraphs does Sagan's essay illustrate this principle?

5. Does this essay list separate steps in a process one by one? Explain your answer.

6. What methods of development, other than process analysis, does Sagan use?

Thinking Critically

1. Why does the author tell us so much about the life of Eratosthenes? Explain your answer in a short paragraph.

2. Make notes in the margins that explain each step in the process by which Eratosthenes measured the earth's circumference. Then put your notes into a well-organized paragraph.

Suggestions for Journal Entries

1. Make a brief, informal list of steps you might use to explain how a simple machine or natural process works. Pick something you have had experience with or know a lot about. Here are examples:

Machine	Process
Sling shot	Circulation of the blood
Bow and arrow	Formation of rain clouds
Bottle opener	Photosynthesis
Cork screw	Osmosis
Food blender	Pollination of flowers by bees
Pliers	Transmission of a particular disease
Water wheel	Movement of the tides
Fishing reel	Formation of a fossil

2. Follow the advice in Suggestion 1 for a process that human beings have learned or invented to survive or to improve the quality of their lives. Examples include the process by which a broken bone is set, artificial respiration is given, an incandescent bulb turns electricity into light, solar energy is used to heat a house, a serious disease is treated, or a food crop is grown or harvested.

How I Came Out to My Parents

Kenneth Kohler

When his freshman English instructor encouraged the class to "write from the heart," Ken Kohler decided to explain how he accomplished one of the most difficult and meaningful tasks in his life—telling his parents he was gay. Kohler's recollection of the process by which he came to the decision and finally confronted his parents shows how deeply concerned he was about their feelings and about the kind of relationship he would have with them once they knew of his sexual preference.

This essay represents the best of what process writers can achieve, for it combines the author's emotional commitment to his subject with clear, logical analysis. Ken Kohler is now a computer programmer.

Preparing to Read

1. Like other process essays, "How I Came Out to My Parents" is organized as a narrative. But this is not just another story. What is really important here is not *what* happened, but *how* it happened—the agony Kohler endured to tell his family about his homosexuality.

2. This selection is divided into two sections. The first explains how Kohler made the decision and found the courage to tell his parents he was gay. The second discusses the results of that decision.

Vocabulary

acknowledged (verb)	Admitted.
acutely (adverb)	Greatly, sharply.
alienation (noun)	State of loneliness, exclusion.
congregation (noun)	Church members.
disclosure (noun)	Announcement, revelation.
irreparably (adverb)	Beyond repair.
pending (adjective)	Upcoming, expected.
predict (verb)	Know ahead of time.
rejection (noun)	Disapproval.

How I Came Out to My Parents

Kenneth Kohler

BEING A MINORITY within your own family can be a source of conflict. I had always known that I was different from my brother and my sister. My parents, too, may have sensed the difference, but they never acknowledged it

1

to me. For many years, I had struggled with the idea of letting them know how different I was from my older brother. I was gay and didn't know how they would react if they ever found out.

My struggle to "come out of the closet" grew out of several needs. First, I wanted to be closer with my parents and to be honest about who I was. Second, I needed to let them know that there was someone special in my life. Finally, I had agreed to speak at my church about being gay, and I felt it important to tell my parents about my lifestyle before informing my congregation. 2

Rejection was my greatest fear. At the time, I had friends who had not spoken to their families for years after revealing they were gay. Their parents could not understand how their children could be "fags" or "dykes." These were terms their families had previously applied only to strangers. Some friends even told me about the violent reactions their families had had to the news. One of them said his father chased him around the house with a butcher knife. I had also known people who had used their homosexuality as a weapon against their families. Never did I want to hurt my parents; I merely wanted to break down the barriers between us. 3

I had no idea how they might react when I came out to them. I knew that if they responded violently or negatively it could take years to heal the damage. I also knew that I might never see them again. It was for this reason that I had avoided coming out to them before. However, because of my pending public announcement, the time had come to let them know. 4

I planned what I had to say carefully. Something so important could not simply be announced and forgotten. I had actually begun to prepare for this moment years before by reading as much as I could about homosexuality and by talking to gay friends. It was necessary for me to accept myself as a gay man before expecting others to do so. I had to develop a positive self-image, and this took several years. Then, in the week prior to my announcement, I began to rehearse my lines. I made notes for various approaches I could take. I wanted to feel secure in my delivery and didn't want to appear ashamed of my lifestyle. "Why should I be?" I thought. I had never felt differently. I imagined my parents' every reaction and tried to predict my responses. I even prepared myself for the worst, afraid they would tell me to "Get out and never come back!" 5

I also knew it was possible that none of the negative things that had happened to my friends would happen to me. In fact, I thought my parents might have already suspected I was gay. After all, I had been living with a man for three years. My partner at the time said, "They probably already know about you, the way you swish around!" I knew he could be right, but I was still afraid. Would my disclosure actually draw me closer to them as I had hoped, or would it push me away? Would they accept my partner as they had in the past? How would I cope with the loss of their love? These were just a few of the many questions that swept through my mind as I called my mother to ask if I could visit and talk about something important. 6

My heart was racing and my palms were sweating as I stopped the car in front of their house. I turned off the ignition, took a deep breath, and 7 stepped out. "This is it," I thought. "This is what I've been thinking about doing for years." The walk to the front door had never seemed so long. I was acutely aware of my heartbeat pounding in my ears. My breath seemed suspended in the frigid February night air. Time seemed to stop as I nervously straightened my jacket, threw my shoulders back, swallowed hard, and opened the front door.

My father was sitting in the recliner watching the television. My mother was folding laundry. "Hi, how are you doing?" I said, trying to hide my nervousness. They both looked up and smiled. As I walked over to give each of them a hug, I wondered if they would ever smile at me again.

    8

I took off my coat, sat down next to my mother, and began to help her fold the laundry. We talked about how fast my niece was growing up. While we spoke, I tried to form the words that I feared would hurt them irreparably, but I realized there was only one way to say it. "Mom. Dad. I've been thinking about telling you this for some time now." I swallowed hard and took a good look at them. "I'm not telling you this because I want to hurt you. I love you. Please try to understand." I paused and took a deep breath. "I'm gay."

    9

There was silence. Finally, with much hesitation, my mother asked, "Are you sure?"

    10

There was still no response from my father. I wondered what was racing through his head. His silence was deeper than I could remember. Again my mother spoke. "Are you happy?"

    11

"Yes," I replied with hesitation. I was not sure what would happen next. I could almost hear the silent screams that I imagined howling in each of them.

    12

"Well," she paused, "you've always been good to us, and you've never given us any problems."

    13

"Here it comes," I thought, "the guilt trip."

    14

"I guess if you're happy," she continued slowly as if weighing every word, "then I'll try to understand."

    15

A smile spread over my face as I leaned over and gave her a long, warm hug. Never had I felt so close to her. It was only then that my father piped up, "I hope you aren't sleeping with someone new every night." I assured him that I wasn't as I gave him a hug.

    16

"You know, it's funny," my mother said. "We always thought your friend was gay, but we didn't know you were." I tried hard to keep from laughing as I thought of my partner's remarks. Deep down, I suspected that they had always known but had denied it.

    17

When I explained that I was going to speak at my church about what it was like to be gay, my mother's brow became dark and furrowed. "Do you think you should? What if you lose your job? What if someone tries to hurt you?" she responded.

    18

I tried to assure her that everything would be all right, but I really had no idea what might happen. Of course, I knew my parents would struggle with my gayness just as I had, but I was overjoyed that they were asking such

    19

questions. A great burden had been lifted from my shoulders; I felt like laughing and dancing around the room. I realized I no longer had to hide my private life, to change pronouns, or to avoid questions about whom I was dating. More important, I had discovered how deeply my parents loved me.

Questions for Discussion

1. Why did Kohler feel the need to "come out of the closet"?
2. Discuss the fears he dealt with before deciding to tell his parents he was gay.
3. What steps did he take to prepare *himself* for the moment when he would tell his parents he was gay?
4. What steps did he take to prepare his *parents* for this moment? Should he have done more to get them ready?
5. Why does the author tell us how the parents of his friends reacted when they announced they were gay? Does including this information help him explain a process?

Thinking Critically

1. This essay and Sagan's "The Measure of Eratosthenes" tell us how something was done. What other similarities do you find between these selections? Make notes in the margins of Kohler's essay to identify them.
2. Had Kohler asked you for advice about approaching his parents, what would you have told him? Put your comments in the form of a letter.

Suggestions for Journal Entries

1. Recall a time when you told someone something he or she did not want to hear. Perhaps you had to tell your parents that you had wrecked the family car, or had to persuade a sweetheart that your relationship was over, or had to inform a friend or relative that a loved one had died. Freewrite for about five minutes to explain how hard this was.
2. Kohler's decision to tell his parents he was gay came from a strong desire to be honest with them. Write about a time when you needed to reveal something about yourself to a loved one who might find it difficult to accept. List a few steps that explain how you did this.

Suggestions for Sustained Writing

1. Triena Milden takes an ironic or tongue-in-cheek approach to academic studies in "So You Want to Flunk Out of College," which appears in the chapter's introduction (pages 482–485). You too may be able to provide advice to help someone fail at something important. Write an ironic but complete set of instructions for this purpose. Put them in a letter to someone you know well.

   If you follow Milden's lead, begin your letter by explaining how hard or easy it is to fail at the task you are discussing. Somewhere in your letter, perhaps in the introduction or conclusion, you might also explain why anyone would want to fail at it in the first place. In any case, revise and edit your letter to make sure it's clear, easy-to-follow, and fun to read.

2. If Suggestion 1 doesn't appeal to you, write an essay that explains how *not* to do something. Here are some topics you might choose:

   > How not to study for an important exam.
   > How not to do laundry.
   > How not to light a barbecue grill.
   > How not to start exercising.
   > How not to lie to your parents, children, spouse, or sweetheart.
   > How not to drive a car if you want it to last.
   > How not to become depressed when life gets difficult.
   > How not to become addicted to tobacco, drugs, alcohol, or other substances.
   > How not to get hooked on watching TV or any other activity.

3. Review the journal notes you made after reading the selection by Franklin. Use them in an essay that explains how to complete a simple but important task. Begin by making a scratch outline of the major steps in the process.

   Use as much detail as possible so that even someone who knows nothing about your subject can follow it easily. Pick an activity that is simple, that you are familiar with, and that you can cover well in a short paper. Stay away from topics such as "how to paint a house" or "how to improve your health." Instead, try "how to prepare a small bedroom for painting" or "how to fight a cold." In your introduction, explain the purpose behind completing the process, and describe tools or equipment needed.

   Now, put your instructions to the test. Ask someone to follow them exactly as written. If he or she has trouble, revise your instructions to make them clearer, more logical, or more complete. Then edit and proofread your work.

4. The word *duel* can have many meanings. If you responded to the second journal suggestion after Adam Goodheart's essay, you have probably gathered some pointers on how to prepare for and fight a modern duel (contest, confrontation, or encounter) such as the kind people face every day. Read your notes, and use them as the basis of a paper that provides complete instructions.

   Begin with an outline that, as in Goodheart's essay, divides the process chronologically into major components. Let's say you want to teach your reader how to bargain over the price of a car. You might list headings such as Adopting the Right Attitude, Researching Dealer Costs, Visiting Several Dealerships, Making an Offer, and Closing the Deal. As you write your first draft, list and explain particular steps under each of these headings in detail.

   When you revise your first draft, make sure you have explained each step separately and clearly, used direct commands, and provided all needed information. If necessary, include a list of supplies/equipment in your introduction and a warning in your conclusion. Now, ask a fellow student to read and comment on your work. Revise it once more. Then edit and proofread.

5. Item 2 in the Suggestions for Journal Entries after "The Measure of Eratosthenes" asks you to list steps in a process that human beings have learned or invented to survive or to improve the quality of their lives. If you did not respond to that suggestion, do so now.

   Use your list as the outline to an essay that fully explains the process. Write your first draft by following this outline. As you revise, develop each step in greater detail until you are sure the process is clear and complete. When you are ready to write an introduction, discuss the reason or reasons this process is important, thereby giving your essay an identifiable purpose and focus. In other words, let your readers know from the very start that the essay is worth their time.

   As you edit your final draft, check for coherence—adding connectives and linking pronouns as necessary. Then proofread.

6. Ken Kohler's "How I Came Out to My Parents" explains the painful process of telling people a truth they might not want to hear. Have you ever been in a similar situation? Did you ever have to confess that you smashed up the family car, misplaced an important document or tool at work, or lost your younger brother in a shopping mall? Have you ever said good-bye to a loved one or told somebody a close relative or friend died?

   Write an essay explaining how you did what had to be done. As you draft and rewrite, include details to show how painful the process was. Remember that this is not simply a narrative. Don't just say that you got the courage to face the situation or that you overcame emotional hurdles. Show *how* you did these things step by step.

You can begin by explaining how you got yourself ready. Next, recall the things you did to prepare your listener(s) for the news. Then, tell how you made the announcement, and describe the way your listener(s) reacted. Finally, like Kohler, explain how you felt when the experience was over.

Check your journal for notes that will help you get started. As you write your paper, remember that Kohler's essay is so powerful because he revised and edited it carefully. Do the same with yours.

Writing to Learn: A Group Activity

In his column in *Civilization*, Adam Goodheart gives instructions on "lost arts." Have some fun by writing instructions on how to perform an art, skill, or other activity that today is rarely or no longer practiced.

THE FIRST MEETING

Choose a lost art to research. Here are some suggestions. How to:

Plan and prepare a Christmas dinner for George and Martha Washington.

Make a stained glass window for a church or cathedral.

Build an ancient pyramid (Egyptian, Aztec, or Mayan).

Plan and build a Buddhist pagoda.

Lead a camel caravan across desert trade routes.

Construct an Iroquois long house.

Make and bury a mummy.

Use leeches to treat a patient suffering from a fever or other illness.

After you have decided on a subject, brainstorm to identify questions to research. Let's say your group decides to explain how to construct and use a Roman catapult. One of you might investigate the purpose for which this war machine was developed. Another could find information classifying various types of Roman catapults. Still another could learn about their construction and operation. Someone else might research the dangers of operating a catapult.

RESEARCH

Research the Internet, specialized encyclopedias and other works in your library's reference section, or books listed in the card or online catalog. Bring the notes you take and photocopies of pages from your sources to the next meeting.

continued

THE SECOND MEETING

Make sure the group has gathered enough information to compose a paper that (1) explains the purpose of the process, (2) lists and explains all necessary materials, and (3) provides step-by-step instructions for carrying out the process. Then, write an outline of a paper that addresses each of these items in a separate section. Have each student write two or three paragraphs for one of these sections. You might also ask someone to write an attention-grabbing introduction and a warning paragraph that identifies hazards or dangers involved in the process. Bring photocopies of your work to the next meeting.

THE THIRD MEETING

Critique each other's contributions; offer suggestions for revision. Make sure your work is clear and easy to follow. Assign one student to collect the final versions of everyone's work and to create a draft of a complete paper to be distributed at the next meeting.

THE FOURTH MEETING

Distribute and read the draft of the paper. Make last-minute suggestions for revision. Ask one student to edit the paper and another to type and proofread it.

Argumentation and Persuasion

Argumentation and persuasion are similar, and they often work together. In fact it is rare to find an essay that is pure argumentation without the slightest hint that the author is trying to persuade the readers. It is even rarer to find an effective persuasive essay that is not based on a logical argument. However, argument and persuasion are not identical.

Establishing Purpose

To begin with, a formal "argument" is not a fight, altercation, or heated discussion with tempers flaring and threats being exchanged. *Argument* is the defense of an opinion or of a position on an issue that is supported by concrete evidence and that is presented logically. The purpose of a written argument is limited: to prove a point, a thesis—sometimes referred to as a proposition. Scientists use argument to prove a theory or hypothesis. Historians engage in argumentation when they dispute theories about the causes of a war or of an economic depression. A psychologist might argue that genetic factors caused someone to become a serial killer, and an economist could use argumentation to present theories about the business cycle or the effects of taxation.

Persuasion begins with logical argument. It too uses logic and concrete evidence to make a point, to prove a thesis. However, *persuasion* goes beyond argument and also appeals to the reader's emotions, values, and self-interest. The Declaration of Independence, a classic piece of persuasion, even attempts to inflame our passions. Finally, the purpose of persuasion is not simply to prove a point; it is to get readers to act. Lawyers use persuasion to get judges and juries to rule in favor of their clients. Politicians use persuasion to get voters to support them.

So first of all, you need to decide if your purpose is to argue or to persuade. Your decision will affect the word choices you make, the tone of your paper, and even its content. You would be writing an argument if you tried to convince your readers that the Internet and other electronic means of publishing information will someday replace the printed books and paper journals now on college library shelves. You would also be arguing if you proved that devoting too much time to a job while attending college full-time reduces the chances for academic success. On the other hand, you would be writing persuasively if you tried to convince your college president to reduce the library's book budget and allocate the money to the purchase of CD ROMs or subscriptions to periodical databases. You would also be trying to persuade if you wrote a letter to your college newspaper so as to convince students to reduce their work hours and spend more time on their studies.

Determining Tone and Content

The tone and language of an argument are usually objective, neutral, specific, and rational. The argument might draw on the testimony of experts, on statistics, or on historical or scientific studies. Experts and authorities in a particular field, who have a reputation for evaluating issues fairly are often cited by writers of argument. Argument depends on logic. In persuasive essays, writers also use language that is more personal and emotionally charged. They sometimes involve themselves in the essay by viewing things subjectively; they focus on particular people and incidents more than on abstract studies and statistics; and they usually defend their positions vigorously and even passionately.

Let's say you are writing an argument that victims of violent crime ought to be compensated by the government. You might include Department of Justice statistics on the annual medical bills for victims of crime nationwide. You might remind readers that the government often helps victims of natural disasters and cite specific instances or programs in which such aid has been distributed. You might even describe a program used in another country that forces convicted criminals to work so as to fund a compensation program for crime victims. The tone of your argument would be dispassionate, and your presentation logical.

On the other hand, if you are writing an article to gather support for a rally to get Congress to pass a crime-victims bill, you might describe the long-term emotional and physical effects that specific crime victims are suffering. You might create vivid images of people no longer able to walk, to work, or to live pain-free lives. You might also appeal to the readers' self-interest by asking them to predict the horrors they might endure if ever victimized by some thug. Your language will probably be emotionally charged, and the images you paint will be startling. This is what we see in Angela Brandli's research essay, which appears in the Appendix at the end of this book. So persuasive was the author that she convinced state legislators to pass a bill that increased compensation for victims of violent crime.

Expressing a Voice

Although argument relies on logic and although persuasion can appeal to the reader's emotions as well, the line between pure argument and pure persuasion sometimes gets blurred. In fact, writers of argument frequently reveal their feelings about a topic, if ever so subtly. In "The Right to Be Let Alone" (Chapter 15), Barry Glazer uses emotionally charged language when he asserts that if he were "in the throes of terminal cancer or facing the horror of Alzheimer's disease" he should be allowed to commit suicide. Thus, while his purpose is not to move his readers to action, Glazer does touch our emotions, and we are the more convinced. An effective argument needs to be logical and well supported, but no writer should ever refrain from expressing his or her personal voice in a piece of formal writing, as long as it remains reasonable and restrained.

Being Fair, Accurate, and Logical

You will learn more about specific techniques you can use when writing either argumentation or persuasion essays in the next two chapters. However, whether you are writing argument or persuasion, remember to be accurate and fair. Being persuasive is not a license to mislead your readers. Unfortunately, sometimes both argument and persuasion suffer from logical fallacies. In many cases, writers commit such fallacies unknowingly. Dishonest writers do so intentionally.

Five Logical Fallacies

Errors in logic, though sometimes subtle and hard to detect, appear in political speeches and advertisements, in television commercials, in newspaper editorials, and even in well-written and sincere arguments of bright college students. Here is a list of five logical fallacies that you should look for when reading or listening to argumentation or persuasion and that you should avoid in your own writing.

Generalizations Supported by Insufficient Evidence Writers sometimes draw conclusions not justified by the amount or kind of information they have gathered. Failing to consider enough or the right kind of evidence can lead to faulty generalizations. Here are a few examples of insufficient evidence.

1. My neighbors never finished high school, but they have built a very lucrative plumbing company. Therefore, the claim that education improves one's chances for success is false.
2. The president will veto a bill lowering tax rates for married couples. Obviously, he doesn't want to help families.
3. The directory assistance operator could not find the name or number of a company that I know is listed. The telephone company should train their employees better.
4. The Supreme Court refused to review a lower court's judgment against the tobacco industry. Obviously, the Supreme Court is antibusiness.

The Straw Man As the name implies, the straw man is an argument that is weak and easy to knock down. The straw man comes into play when a writer falsely claims that the opposing side supports an idea that is indefensible. The writer then refutes this obviously bad idea and, in the process, casts the opposition in a bad light. The straw man is a pretense; it has little to do with the point being debated, nor does it represent the opponent's views fairly and accurately. In fact, it is often used only to distract readers from valid arguments of the opposition.

> **Your position:** You argue that we should create a plan to force those convicted of violent crime to compensate their victims and their victims' families. You propose that prisons establish small factories in which prisoners must work so as to earn the money to compensate their victims.
> **Your opponent's position:** Using the "straw man," your opponent argues that you are suggesting a return to the chain-gang system of punishment and that you are in favor of slave labor.

> **Your position:** You argue that people who have no children in the public school system should pay less school tax than those who do.
> **Your opponent's position:** You are an elitist who cares little for public education and is concerned only with educating the children of the rich, most of whom attend private schools.

> **Your position:** You argue that the government should preserve thousands of acres of untouched wilderness that happens to be located upon huge oil reserves.
> **Your opponent's position:** You care more about trees and wildlife than you do about the consumers who would benefit from cheaper heating oil and gasoline prices.

The* Ad Hominem *Argument *Ad hominem* is Latin for "to the person." When writers indulge in this unethical tactic, they attack the person's character rather than his or her position, logic, opinions, or history.

For example, when John F. Kennedy ran for president in 1962, some unscrupulous people attacked him because he was a Roman Catholic. They ignored the fact that Kennedy had on numerous occasions affirmed his commitment to the separation of church and state. When Ronald Reagan ran for governor in California in the 1970s and, again, when he ran for president, some opponents attacked him because he had been an actor, not because of the issues he supported.

You would be arguing *ad hominem* if you claimed that Senator Alvarez cannot represent the interests of families because she is single, or that Representative Kelly will not fight to increase community-college funding because he attended a private university. On the other hand, you would be arguing fairly if you mentioned that Senator Alvarez has consistently opposed pro-family legislation or that Representative Kelly has made several speeches arguing for an increase in community-college tuition so as to decrease state funding for such schools.

Begging the Question   This fallacy occurs when a writer draws an invalid conclusion from a false assumption or an assumption that cannot be proven. Thus, the writer avoids addressing the real issue or question.

For example, you would be begging the question if you argued that, because Angela is a member of Alcoholics Anonymous, she could not have been the one you saw having a beer at Calhoun's Saloon last night. The false assumption here is that members of Alcoholics Anonymous never fall back into their old habits. The argument begs the question: *Did Angela drink a beer at Calhoun's Saloon last night?*

The Red Herring   The red herring distracts the audience from the real issue at hand. It gets its name from a practice used by farmers to protect their newly planted fields from fox hunters and their dogs. Farmers often dragged a red herring along the edge of their fields where it would leave a strong scent. This scent distracted the dogs and kept them and the hunters from trampling the crops.

Most visibly, red herrings can be found in commercials and advertisements. Automobile commercials picture cars and their drivers winding through beautiful mountain passes as they head toward stunning sunsets; exercise machines are pictured against exotic, tropical landscapes populated by people with perfect bodies; soft drinks are promoted through television spots that picture athletic young people engaged in exciting sports such as rock climbing, hang gliding, or surfing. None of these tells us much about the product. They are selling an image that, like the farmer's red herring, is supposed to draw our attention away from what is really being sold.

One commercial goes so far as to portray a four-wheel-drive vehicle as an adult toy. It suppresses the fact that most people really buy cars for one practical reason—safe and reliable transportation. It encourages the notion of "fun" and, red-herring fashion, distracts us from the reality that, in order to pay for this "toy," we will have to work extra hard and, in most cases, tie ourselves to an all-too-real auto loan that takes three, four, or five years to pay off!

CHAPTER 15

Argument

As you have learned in the introduction to Section Six, a formal, written argument is very different from a loud or excited discussion about a point of controversy! In fact, when it comes to writing, *argumentation* is an attempt to prove a point—also known as a thesis or proposition—or to support an opinion through calm if vigorous logic and presentation of evidence.

Mastering Induction and Deduction

Two types of thinking are used in argumentation: *induction* and *deduction.* Both support an opinion or belief the writer expresses in a *conclusion.*

Inductive thinking involves collecting separate facts, reasons, or other pieces of evidence and then drawing a conclusion from that information. Say you come down with a case of food poisoning—cramps, vomiting, a headache, the works. When you call the other five people with whom you shared a pot of stew the night before, each tells the same horrible story about cramps, vomiting, and so on. It's safe to say the stew made you sick. That's your conclusion. Support for that conclusion comes in the form of six separate tales of woe.

As a matter of fact, induction is the kind of thinking behind conclusion and support, one of the methods of developing paragraphs and essays explained in Chapter 3. Papers developed through this method express a conclusion or opinion in a formal thesis statement. A good example is Philip K. Howard's "The Death of Common Sense" in Chapter 12. Howard claims that America is being overregulated. This is his *conclusion,* which he expresses in his thesis. He then goes on to discuss *supportive evidence* from which he drew that conclusion.

Here's an example of a paragraph developed using the conclusion-and-support method. It is based upon information from an essay by Lester Brown:

> In the next century, increases in the levels of air pollution caused by the burning of fossil fuels will force us to seek alternative sources of energy. *Thankfully, such alternatives are plentiful.* Around the equator and in deserts, homeowners and industries will install solar panels on rooftops and on the summits of hills to collect energy that will generate electricity or heat water directly. People living on wind-swept prairies will create their own power by using windmills. Geothermal energy may be tapped by those living in countries around the Mediterranean Sea. Finally, governments might once again fund large-scale hydroelectric projects, such as those created by the Tennessee Valley Authority during the Great Depression.

The second sentence (in italics) in this paragraph is the *conclusion,* which is expressed as the paragraph's topic sentence: "Thankfully, such alternatives are plentiful." This is the point the writer wishes to make, the proposition he wishes to prove. The rest of the paragraph provides evidence to *support that conclusion.*

If induction involves drawing a general idea from specific pieces of evidence, deduction moves from the general to the specific. Using deduction, writers start with a general statement or idea they believe their readers will agree with. Next, they apply a specific case or example to that statement. Finally, they draw a limited conclusion from the two. The logical structure through which this is done is called a syllogism. You would be using deduction to create a syllogism if you argued:

> **General statement:** All full-time students can use the college exercise room free of charge.
> **Specific case:** I am a full-time student.
> **Conclusion:** Therefore, I can use the college exercise room free of charge.

Alice Callaghan uses deductive reasoning in "Desperate to Learn English," an essay that appears later in this chapter. Her argument goes something like this:

> **General statement:** Mastering English is essential to success in school.
> **Specific case:** Bilingual education makes it harder for non-native speakers to learn English.
> **Conclusion:** Bilingual education should be abolished.

Induction and deduction are two different ways of reasoning, but they almost always complement each other. In fact, logical and well-supported arguments often reflect both types of thinking.

Developing Ideas in an Argument

In Chapter 3, you learned that there are several ways to develop a paragraph or essay whether your purpose is to explain or to argue or persuade. One of the most popular is conclusion and support, the method you just learned about. As the selections in this chapter show, however, writers of argument often use a combination of methods to provide evidence that proves a point or supports a proposition (thesis). For example, in "Free Speech on Campus," Nat Hentoff uses comparison, mentions the opinions of others via direct quotations, and includes examples to make his point. Student Barry Glazer appeals to authority in "The Right to Be Let Alone" when he makes specific reference to the U.S. Constitution and quotes Supreme Court Justice Louis Brandeis. Alice Callaghan uses narration and statistics effectively in "Desperate to Learn English."

The most important thing to remember about an effective argument is that it is both *logical* and *well supported*. You can use inductive reasoning, deductive reasoning, or both, but your arguments must be reasonable and easy to follow. You can support ideas with examples, facts, statistics, the knowledge or opinions of experts, analogies, comparisons, definitions, first-hand observations, and the like. But your writing must contain enough supportive information to be clear, convincing, and easily understood.

Establishing Your Authority

Of course, the best way to establish your authority—to show that you are knowledgeable about a subject and that you should be believed—is to amass relevant facts and opinions that show you know what you are talking about. In some cases, there is no need for the author to establish his or her credentials. Nat Hentoff, whose essay "Free Speech on Campus" appears in this chapter, doesn't need to tell us he is an expert on this topic because his reputation as a defender of the First Amendment is widespread. On the other hand, it sometimes helps to remind readers of your credentials and experience. That's what Dudley Barlow does in the beginning of his essay on bilingual education, which appears in this chapter, when he alludes to the fact that he is an experienced teacher.

Anticipating and Addressing Opposing Opinions

It is always a good idea to think about points of view in opposition to your own. Doing so shows that you are open-minded, that you have considered more than one side, that you have thought out your position and others' well, and that you are knowledgeable about your subject. In short, it lends authority to your writing. This is very important when writing persuasion, but it also plays a part in argument. One way to address an opposing opinion is simply to show that it lacks validity, when this is the case. Another effective way is to recognize the validity of your opponent's argument while offering your own as the more realistic or logical alternative. To succeed, each of these tactics requires you to demonstrate to your reader your fair and accurate understanding of the opposing view. Barry Glazer's "The Right to Be Let Alone" and the two essays discussing bilingual education in this chapter illustrate ways in which to deal with opposing arguments.

Visualizing Strategies for Argument

Read the following editorial, published in *USA Today*. Then, read the two discussions that follow it, which show how it uses both deduction and induction.

Drug Tests Fail Schools

Imagine you wanted to go out for your company's softball team and your boss told you: "Pee in this cup—in front of me." 1

Most adults would consider such a demand outrageous. Yet, that's what some public schools were demanding from student athletes in the war against drugs when 12-year-old James Acton came along in 1991. 2

The would-be seventh-grade football player put a damper on such demands. First, he told Vernonia, OR, public school officials that he wouldn't go along. Then he went to court. His claim: The district's drug tests—required of all those trying out for sports—violate Fourth Amendment rights to privacy. 3

Last year, a federal appeals court in San Francisco agreed. In doing so, it made such testing illegal in nine Western states under its jurisdiction. And it discouraged schools elsewhere from starting testing programs until the Supreme Court rules on the case. 4

Today, the high court hears arguments. And if students, schools and taxpayers are lucky, it will kill all such required drug tests for student athletes by next fall. 5

Drug testing can be smart, when it's conducted to protect public safety and security, as with transportation workers and drug enforcement agents. And it may even be sensible when it's done to ensure role models, such as professional and college athletes, don't abuse narcotics. 6

But it wastes money and violates rights when forced upon thousands of youngsters. 7

Vernonia began its program mostly because of increased disciplinary problems. 8

But school officials chose not to focus on the problem kids. They lassoed mostly innocent ones. Of 500 students tested in 4½ years, a mere 12 tested positive, not many for a district claiming huge problems. 9

And who paid for the willy-nilly testing? Not local folks, but deficit-riddled Uncle Sam through the federal drug-free schools program. Vernonia's cut: $7,500 a year. 10

History shows there's a fairer way. Teen drug use was cut substantially during the 1980s, not because a few schools tested students for drugs but because most taught students the dangers of abuse and involved parents in their programs. 11

Schools should do the same today. They should call parents of kids suspected of drug use and get permission for any testing. 12

That would save money, focus the drug fight on those causing problems and not invade the privacy of innocent kids whose only crime is trying out for a sport. 13

Deduction in "Drug Tests Fail Schools" As you have learned, deduction moves from general to specific. The process starts with a general statement, to which a specific case or example is applied. Then, a conclusion is drawn from these two. Here's how deduction works in "Drug Tests Fail Schools":

> **General statement:** Drug testing should be permitted only to protect public safety or to ensure that role models don't abuse drugs (paragraph 6).
> **Specific case or example:** Forcing students to test for drugs only wastes money and violates rights; it does not protect public safety (paragraph 7).
> **Conclusion:** Therefore, forcing students to take drug tests should be stopped.

Induction in "Drug Tests Fail Schools"   Earlier you read that induction is the basis of the conclusion-and-support method for developing a paper. Support for a conclusion comes in the form of evidence or reasons behind it. Here's how induction works in "Drug Tests Fail Schools":

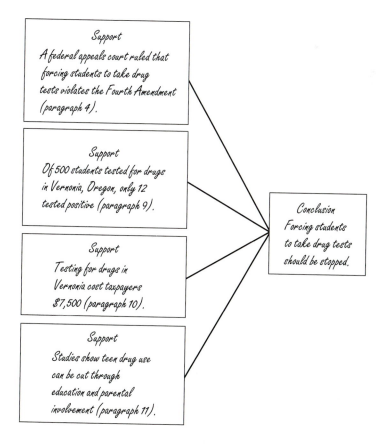

Support
A federal appeals court ruled that forcing students to take drug tests violates the Fourth Amendment (paragraph 4).

Support
Of 500 students tested for drugs in Vernonia, Oregon, only 12 tested positive (paragraph 9).

Support
Testing for drugs in Vernonia cost taxpayers $7,500 (paragraph 10).

Support
Studies show teen drug use can be cut through education and parental involvement (paragraph 11).

Conclusion
Forcing students to take drug tests should be stopped.

Revising Argument Papers

An argument requires logical and clear writing, and such writing takes hard work. Barry Glazer, a student whose essay appears in this chapter, wrote several drafts of a paper on individual rights before he arrived at a version with which he was satisfied. His rough draft contained the germ of an idea and several good examples but by the time Glazer wrote his final draft, the paper had been transformed into a first-rate argument paper. Even the title had changed.

Glazer—Rough Draft

It Ain't Nobody's Business but My Own

Help? In what way?

Government is supposed to help people, not hurt them. Those we elect to public office are there to make things better for everyone. However, many of them are doing

What kinds of things?

things that annoy and frighten me. If I am

not hurting anybody, the government should

Expand? Clarify?

stay out of my private affairs. What I do, if it isn't causing anyone else harm, is no one's business but my own.

If I have a terminal disease, I should be

Support this claim.

allowed to kill myself or get a doctor to help me do so.

If I am driving home late at night the

They don't? Support this claim.

police have no right to stop me just because I am young and look suspicious. Recently, I was walking around the block at three in the morning and the police stopped and questioned me. Yet, all I was doing was taking a late-night stroll.

. . .

*What kinds
of things?*

Yes, we need government to take <u>care of
important things</u>. But the government and
the police should stay out of people's lives
when it is none of their business. They
should just leave us alone.

Glazer—Final Draft

The Right to Be Let Alone.] *Revises
title.*

Government is the instrument of the people,

*Appeals to
authority.*

says the <u>United States Constitution.</u> Those
to whom the people entrust power are charged
with <u>maintaining justice</u>, <u>promoting the</u>

*Explains how
government
"is supposed
to help
people".*

<u>general welfare</u>, and <u>securing the blessings</u>
<u>of liberty for us all.</u> Recent newspaper

*Explains
what he
meant by
"things that
annoy and
frighten
me."*

opinion polls, however, suggest that many
Americans are dissatisfied with the men and
women running our communities, our states,
and our nation. More and more of us have
come to believe that our leaders are
isolated from the realities ordinary people
face. We fear we are losing control.

Instead of helping to alleviate this
feeling of impotence, however, politicians
and bureaucrats continue to make and enforce
regulations that constrain our lives and
constrict our freedoms. To help people
regain a rightful measure of control,
government—whether national, state, or
local—should stay out of our private lives

Appeals to authority.

whenever possible. As Supreme Court Justice Louis Brandeis noted, Americans treasure their "right to be let alone."

Supports claim with convincing details.

There is no reason for the government to interfere in our lives if our behavior does not adversely affect others or if there is no immediate necessity for such interference. Were I in the throes of terminal cancer or facing the horror of Alzheimer's disease, I should be allowed to kill myself. Faced with the agonizing degeneration of my memory and personality, I would probably want to end my life in my own way. But the government says this is illegal. Indeed, were I to call upon a doctor to assist me on this final quest, she would stand a good chance of being charged with murder.

Appeals to emotions.

Supports claim by appealing to authority.

The government should also stay out of an individual's life if there is no reason to believe he is doing wrong. The Bill of Rights protects us from unlawful searches and seizures. Yet, if I drive home from work in the early morning, I stand a reasonable chance of being stopped without cause at a police roadblock. While armed, uniformed officers shine flashlights in my face, I can be subjected to questions about my destination and point of origin. I can

Appeals to reader's self-interest and personal values. be told to produce my papers and to step out of my car. I can be made to endure the embarrassment of performing tricks to prove my sobriety. Allowing the police such powers is hardly in keeping with our government's mission to promote justice, security, and liberty.   *Appeals to emotions.*

. . .

Supports preceding statement.   Clearly, government is a necessity. Without it, we would face anarchy. Yet, those who roam the halls of power should remember from where their power originates and should find ways to reduce the burden of unnecessary regulations heaped on the backs of the American people.   *Appeals to emotions.*

Practicing Strategies for Argument

Practice Deduction   Read the following general statements. Think of a specific case or example that applies to each. Then draw a conclusion. Write your responses in the spaces provided.

1. **General statement:** Students who have had three years of high school mathematics can enroll in Math 101.

   Specific case: _____

   _____

   _____

   _____

   Conclusion: _____

   _____

   _____

2. **General statement:** Students who commute to the college by car must buy parking decals.

Specific case: _____

_____

_____

_____

Conclusion: _____

_____

3. **General statement:** Cars more than five years old must be inspected once per year.

Specific case: _____

_____

_____

_____

Conclusion: _____

_____

4. **General statement:** People whose families have a history of heart disease should have annual coronary examinations.

Specific case: _____

_____

_____

_____

Conclusion: _____

_____

5. **General statement:** People who don't vote should not complain about the way government is run.

Specific case: _____

_____

_____

_____

Conclusion: _____

_____

Practice Induction   Read each group of supportive statements below. Then, using induction, draw a general conclusion from it. Write the conclusion in the space provided.

1.   **Support:** None of the restaurants on the east side of town offers meals for under $30.

   Support: The east side is full of luxury high-rise apartment buildings.

   Support: The east side has no discount clothing, drug, or grocery stores.

   Conclusion: _____

   _____

2.   **Support:** Students who attend Professor Villa's class regularly have a good chance of passing her tests.

   Support: Professor Villa encourages students to come to her office for extra help.

   Support: Professor Villa's assignments are clear and practical.

   Conclusion: _____

   _____

3.   **Support:** The lock on the door had been broken.

   Support: I couldn't find my jewelry.

   Support: Furniture, pictures, and pillows had been moved.

   Conclusion: _____

   _____

4.   **Support:** Serena dragged herself into the apartment and turned on the light.

   Support: There were circles under her eyes.

   Support: In about five minutes, the apartment was dark again.

   Conclusion: _____

   _____

5.   **Support:** Miguel Hernandez plans to attend medical school after getting his bachelor's degree in biology.

   Support: His sister wants to become a dentist.

   Support: His brother is enrolled in a five-year program in architecture.

   Conclusion: _____

   _____

Bilingual Education: Opposing Views

"Desperate to Learn English" by Alice Callaghan
"Melting Pot or Tossed Salad" by Dudley Barlow

A priest in the Episcopal Church, Alice Callaghan directs Los Familias del Pueblo Community Center in Los Angeles, California. "Desperate to Learn English" first appeared on August 15, 1997, on the New York Times *op-ed page.*

Dudley Barlow is a high-school teacher in Canton, Michigan. He writes "The Teachers Lounge" and "Education Resources" for Education Digest, *a research journal in education. "Melting Pot or Tossed Salad" appeared in the March 1996 issue of that journal.*

Preparing to Read

1. In November 1977, *U.S. News & World Report* magazine claimed that a "measure that would virtually eliminate bilingual education in California" would most certainly appear on the ballot in 1998. A referendum limiting state funding for bilingual education was passed by the voters in that year.

2. Analyze each of the titles of the essays presented here. What do the titles tell us about the contents of the essays to which they belong?

Vocabulary

acknowledge (verb)	Admit, recognize.
adios, amigo (verb/noun)	Spanish for "goodbye, friend." Used sarcastically.
advocates (noun)	Supporters
assimilation (noun)	Absorption.
ballot initiative (noun)	Referendum putting a question to a public vote.
compatriots (noun)	Colleagues, co-workers.
confines (noun)	Borders.
critical mass (noun)	Extremely large number, breaking point.
denounced (verb)	Severely criticized, condemned.
entrenched (adjective)	Dug in, securely established.
ethnic (adjective)	Relating to a race or nationality.
havens (noun)	Safe places.
languish (verb)	Lose strength or energy, fade.
lectern (noun)	A podium or platform from which a speaker addresses listeners.
linguistic (adjective)	Relating to language and the study of language.

monoglots (noun)	Speakers of only one language.
proficiency (noun)	Skill, ability.
relinquished (verb)	Gave up, surrendered.

Desperate to Learn English

Alice Callaghan

JUANA AND FLORENCIO left the poverty of their rural Mexican village in 1985 and came to Los Angeles to work in the garment district's sweatshops. In 1996, they pulled their three children—all born in Los Angeles—out of school for nearly two weeks until the school agreed to let them take classes in English rather than Spanish.

Seventy other poor immigrant families joined this school boycott in February 1996, insisting that their children be allowed out of the city's bilingual program, which would not teach English to children from Spanish-speaking homes until they learned how to read and write in Spanish. In the end, the parents prevailed.

Yet, throughout California and elsewhere in the country, many Hispanic parents are worried that bilingual education programs are keeping their children from learning English.

These children live in Spanish-speaking homes, play in Spanish-speaking neighborhoods and study in Spanish-speaking classrooms. With little exposure to English in the primary grades, few successfully learn it later.

This is why many Latino parents are backing a California ballot initiative that would end bilingual education for most children in the state. The measure will be put to vote in June if enough signatures are gathered to put it on the ballot.

School administrators, Latino politicians and other advocates of bilingual education have denounced the measure. Though they acknowledge the failings of the system, they insist they can fix it with time.

Yet after 25 years, bilingual education has few defenders among Latino parents. In a *Los Angeles Times* poll this year, 83 percent of Latino parents in Orange County said they wanted their children to be taught in English as soon as they started school. Only 17 percent of those surveyed said they favored having their children taught in their native language.

One reason bilingual education is so entrenched is money. Bilingual teachers in Los Angeles are paid extra, up to $5,000 a year; schools and school districts receive hundreds of dollars for each child who is designated as having limited proficiency in English. About $400 million in state and Federal money supports bilingual educational programs in California. Because such money is not readily relinquished, students languish in Spanish-language classes.

Moreover, there are not enough bilingual teachers. In Los Angeles, the shortfall has been so severe that the city has granted emergency credentials to people whose only claim to a classroom lectern is their ability to speak Spanish.

Latino parents know that placing their children in English-language 10 classes will not cure the many problems plaguing California schools, where the Latino dropout rate is 40 percent and Latino students have consistently low achievement test scores. Unless these students can learn in English, future school reform efforts will not help them.

Most parents who participated in the school boycott last year labor in 11 garment district sweatshops. Others wait on tables, clean downtown offices or sell fruit or tamales on street corners. All struggle on average monthly incomes of $800.

Education is their only hope for a better future for their children. The 12 first step is learning English.

Melting Pot or Tossed Salad

Dudley Barlow

IT WAS A student named Brian, during my first year of teaching, who intro- 1 duced me to Hyman Kaplan, the main character in Leonard Q. Ross's wonderful little book, *The Education of H*y*m*a*n K*a*p*l*a*n.* The character is a German Jewish immigrant in his forties, and he is in Mr. Parkhill's class entitled "American Night Preparatory School for Adults." Kaplan first came to Parkhill's attention when the class turned in an assignment on common nouns and their plural forms. Kaplan's paper read: "house . . . makes . . . houses, dog . . . makes . . . doggies, library . . . makes Public library, cat . . . makes . . . Katz."

Throughout the book, we watch as Kaplan plunges enthusiastically into 2 this puzzle of a new and difficult language. On the final exam, he writes Parkhill a note because, "In the recass was som students asking if is right to say Its Me or Its I . . . a planty hard question, no? Yes."

Kaplan has the whole puzzle neatly solved. "If I am in hall and knok, 3 knok, knok; and I hear insite (insite the room) somebody hollers 'Whose there'—I anser strong *'Its Kaplan'!!*

"Now is fine! Plain, clear like gold, no chance mixing up Me, I, Ect. 4

"By *Thinking* is Humans making big edvences on Enimals. This we call 5 Progriss."

Kaplan came to my mind as I started writing this column. He was fortu- 6 nate to be able to struggle with this new language in the company of the long-suffering Parkhill. A few weeks ago, I saw a news story on television about two non-English speakers who were not so fortunate.

The story concerned a bar owner somewhere in the state of Washington 7 who refused to serve two Mexican patrons because they did not speak English. I believe she even went so far as to have the two men thrown out of the establishment. On the wall of the bar was a sign that said something like, "If you don't speak English, adios, amigo." When the TV reporter covering the story asked the woman about the incident, she said, "I thought this was America. In America, we speak English."

This woman reminded me of something my wife's uncle, Joe Zadzora, once told me. Joe was born in a coal town in Pennsylvania in the early 1920s, and he worked in the mines before joining the army during World War II. He told me about the ethnic groups—including Poles, Slavs, Russians, Irish, and Hungarians—who mined the coal and lived in the company town above the shafts. They had come to this country for the same reasons that immigrants have always come here: There was work to be had in America, and if they worked hard at difficult and sometimes dangerous jobs, maybe they could make it possible for their children to have better jobs and better lives.

8

Many, perhaps most, of them did not speak English. They did not need it. They could cut, blast, and shovel coal below ground with their compatriots, and above ground they lived in ethnic neighborhoods where the languages of their homelands worked just fine. But for their children, it was a different story. They went to school to learn, among other things, how to speak English to fit into this new land. English was the first key to assimilation into the broader culture beyond the company town.

9

The first generation born here would speak two languages with ease: the old world language used at home and English in the larger world. The next generation would have a new mother tongue, but would still be able to understand their grandparents. By the third generation, though, they would be monoglots again, and their ancestral languages would be lost.

10

This has been pretty much the normal course of events for immigrant families here. Big cities with their ethnic neighborhoods sometimes provided linguistic havens where the old languages could hang on for generations. Foreign-born folks less adventuresome than Hyman Kaplan could find everything they needed within the confines of a few blocks and within the familiar tongues of their former homes.

11

Ultimately, though, assimilation was what everyone wanted. Immigrants wanted to acquire our language to be able to partake of the American Dream, and we knew that they were right in wanting to be like us.

12

Now, though, things are changing. In some parts of our country, in the Southwest in particular, non-native English speakers are reaching a critical mass which has weakened the arguments for learning English.

13

The melting pot is becoming a tossed salad in which the various elements are mixed together but retain their individual identities. So, how do we respond to this new situation? What do government printing offices do? Does the Internal Revenue Service print forms in Spanish as well as English? What about road signs: Do cities in California, Arizona, and Texas print directions in both languages?

14

And how do those of us in the education business respond to this new situation? What are schools where Spanish-speaking students outnumber English-speaking students to do?

15

Some policymakers would respond the way the owner of that Washing- 16
ton pub did, and insist that "In America, we speak English." This "English
only" approach would have all lessons taught only in English to force non-
English speakers to learn our language.

Others would have us offer bilingual instruction designed to communi- 17
cate with students in the language with which they are most familiar while
trying to equip them with the language that would carry them beyond the
confines of their own ethnic group.

There must also be a third group that would argue that, if a class is made 18
up entirely or even predominantly of Spanish speakers, the lessons should be
taught entirely in Spanish. To force these students to abandon Spanish for
English, this group would argue, is a form of linguistic racism.

My sympathies are with the second group. If a school has a student pop- 19
ulation made up primarily of Spanish speakers, I think it would be foolhardy
not to communicate with them in the language they understand best. At the
same time, we need to recognize (and these students need to understand)
that the language of commerce—the language of the widest range of opportunities in our country—is English. For this reason, these students also need to
acquire English language skills.

And what about the road signs and IRS forms? We need to take a cue 20
from business here. The instructions telling me how to set up my computer came in English and Spanish, and the instructions in a box of film or
cough syrup come in several languages. As Kaplan would say, "This we call
Progriss."

As a footnote, one final comment about the Washington bar owner who 21
refused to serve the patrons who did not speak English. I believe her name
was Orlander. Something tells me that her first ancestors to reach American
soil didn't speak English, either. Someone must have served them.

Questions for Discussion

1. Where in her essay does Callaghan use statistics?
2. Does Callaghan rely on authority to support her opinions? Where?
3. How does she anticipate arguments of the opposition?
4. Comment on Callaghan's introduction. What purpose does it serve?
5. Find examples of deductive reasoning in Callaghan's essay.
6. Explain how Callaghan tries to appeal to our emotions.
7. What methods of development does Barlow use in "Melting Pot or Tossed Salad"?
8. Where does Barlow address opposing arguments?
9. Why is Barlow's introduction so long?
10. Why does he quote Hyman Kaplan so extensively?
11. What is the thesis of "Melting Pot or Tossed Salad"?

12. How does the author's contrasting the metaphors of the "melting pot" and the "tossed salad" describe the current U.S. population?

13. Why does Barlow mention three different positions on bilingual education (paragraphs 16, 17, and 18)? Why doesn't he limit himself to the two opinions in paragraphs 16 and 17?

Thinking Critically

1. Is Callaghan being fair in her criticisms of the bilingual-education establishment (paragraph 8 and 9)? Why or why not?

2. Early in "Desperate to Learn English," we learn that 71 families joined in the school boycott. Is this statistic convincing? Why or why not?

3. What does Barlow mean when he claims that "non-native speakers are reaching a critical mass, which has weakened the arguments for learning English"? Do you agree with this statement?

4. If these two authors met in a debate, on what points would they definitely disagree? Are there any points on which they might agree?

Suggestions for Journal Entries

1. What's your opinion? Should we abolish bilingual education, keep it as it is, or change it in some way? Interview educators (including those who teach in bilingual programs, if possible) to gather insights.

2. Think of a particular change we should make in public education and list arguments that would support that change. Here are some examples of changes one might advocate:

> Increase services for learning-disabled students.
> Increase or decrease the number of electives high school students can take.
>
> Grant tax credits to parents whose children attend private or parochial schools.
>
> Require foreign-language study from first through twelfth grade.
>
> Fund all public schools in America by allocating the same amount of tax money for every student regardless of the community or state in which he or she lives.

The Right to Be Let Alone

Barry Glazer

Barry Glazer became interested in writing when he enrolled in a basic-skills composition class during his first semester in college. He went on to major in history and English, to become editor of his college newspaper, and to take a bachelor's and a master's degree.

Preparing to Read

1. This essay is logical, clear, and well developed, but it goes beyond pure argument and often appeals to the emotions.
2. Glazer organizes his work around three principles by which he would restrict the government's ability to interfere with our lives. Identify these principles as you read "The Right to Be Let Alone."
3. Louis Brandeis, mentioned in paragraph 2, was associate justice of the United States Supreme Court (1916–1939). He was a champion of individual rights.

Vocabulary

adversely (adverb)	Negatively.
alleviate (verb)	Reduce, lessen, relieve.
anarchy (noun)	Chaos, disorder, lawlessness.
bureaucrats (noun)	Government officials.
constrain (verb)	Restrain, hold in check, bind.
constrict (verb)	Bind, choke, squeeze.
endure (verb)	Suffer, bear, submit to.
entrust (verb)	Give to for safekeeping.
impotence (noun)	Lack of power.
reflect (verb)	Think.
refrain from (verb)	Stop, cease, avoid.
throes (noun)	Agony, pain.

The Right to Be Let Alone

Barry Glazer

GOVERNMENT IS THE instrument of the people, says the United States Constitution. Those to whom the people entrust power are charged with maintaining justice, promoting the general welfare, and securing the blessings of liberty for us all. Recent newspaper opinion polls, however, suggest that many Americans are dissatisfied with the men and women running our communities, our states, and our nation. More and more of us have come to believe that our leaders are isolated from the realities ordinary people face. We fear we are losing control.

Instead of helping to alleviate this feeling of impotence, however, politicians and bureaucrats continue to make and enforce regulations that constrain our lives and constrict our freedoms. To help people regain a rightful measure of control, government—whether national, state, or local—should stay out of our private lives whenever possible. As Supreme Court Justice Louis Brandeis noted, Americans treasure their "right to be let alone."

There is no reason for the government to interfere in our lives if our behavior does not adversely affect others or if there is no immediate necessity for such interference. Were I in the throes of terminal cancer or facing the horror of Alzheimer's disease, I should be allowed to kill myself. Faced with the agonizing degeneration of my memory and personality, I would probably want to end my life in my own way. But the government says this is illegal. Indeed, were I to call upon a doctor to assist me on this final quest, she would stand a good chance of being charged with murder.

The government should also stay out of an individual's life if there is no reason to believe he is doing wrong. The Bill of Rights protects us from unlawful searches and seizures. Yet if I drive home from work in the early morning, I stand a reasonable chance of being stopped without cause at a police roadblock. While armed, uniformed officers shine flashlights in my face, I can be subjected to questions about my destination and point of origin. I can be told to produce my papers and to step out of my car. I can be made to endure the embarrassment of performing tricks to prove my sobriety. Allowing the police such powers is hardly in keeping with our government's mission to promote justice, security, and liberty.

Finally, the government should refrain from creating unnecessary burdens for the American people. It should stay out of a person's private business if such involvement burdens the individual unnecessarily or unfairly. Recently, my faithful dog Linda was dying. Because of years of abuse at the hands of her previous owner, she was no longer able to walk and had to be carried in my arms. At that time, the dog warden knocked on my door and threatened me with fines for my continued refusal to license the animal. When I told him that Linda was unable to walk, let alone leave my property, he threatened to return with the police.

Similarly, when I wanted to convert my garage into a den, I was over- 6
whelmed by official red tape. The cost of construction permits and of measures to meet complex building codes cost more than the lumber, wall board,
and other supplies for the project. Another example of governmental red tape
became evident when I attempted to enroll in a Japanese language course at a
community college. I was told the state required that I take a mathematics
placement test or pass a course in elementary algebra first!

Clearly, government is a necessity. Without it, we would face anarchy. 7
Yet those who roam the halls of power should remember from where their
power originates and should find ways to reduce the burden of unnecessary
regulations heaped on the backs of the American people.

Questions for Discussion

1. What one sentence in this essay best expresses Glazer's purpose and
   central idea?
2. In Preparing to Read, you learned that the author defends three
   principles by which he would limit government interference. What
   are these principles?
3. What method of development does Glazer rely on most?
4. Pick out vocabulary that appeals to the reader's emotions.
5. Why does Glazer bother to tell us that Justice Brandeis is the source
   of the quotation in paragraph 2 (and of the essay's title)?
6. Find examples of deductive and inductive reasoning in this essay.
7. Where does the author address an argument that an opponent might
   use to dispute his?

Thinking Critically

1. What side would Barry Glazer take in the debate over mandatory
   testing of school-age athletes as expressed in the selection earlier in
   the chapter "Drug Tests Fail Schools"? Support your answer with
   reference to both reading selections.
2. Read or reread "The Militiaman, the Yuppie, and Me" in Chapter 13.
   Then imagine what Glazer might argue in regard to the gun-control
   issue.

Suggestions for Journal Entries

1. Glazer calls up several examples from experiences similar to those you or people like you might have had. Use focused freewriting to narrate an incident that explains how a government rule or regulation interferes with the right of privacy. Interpret the word *government* broadly; write about the federal, state, local, or college regulation you most disagree with. You might even address a rule followed by your family, your athletic team, or other group to which you belong.

2. Play the role of Glazer's opponent by responding to at least one of the examples he uses to support his thesis. Explain why requiring licenses for all dogs is reasonable; why strict building codes are important; why the police should have the right to stop and question drivers; why doctors should not be allowed to help terminally ill patients commit suicide; or why states should set academic standards in public colleges.

3. Even if you agree with Glazer, you may know of instances in which people welcome government "interference." List as many examples of such beneficial interference as you can.

Free Speech on Campus

Nat Hentoff

Nat Hentoff (1925–   ) is one of the most important defenders of free speech in America. He writes a regular column for The Village Voice, *a New York weekly, and he contributes regularly to prestigious newspapers, magazines, and journals across the country. A native of Boston, Hentoff attended Northeastern and Harvard Universities as well as the Sorbonne in Paris, where he studied on a Fulbright fellowship. Although he writes on many subjects, his reputation rests chiefly on his defense of the First Amendment of the U.S. Constitution and his consistent opposition to censorship. Among his books is* The First Freedom: The Tumultuous History of Free Speech in America *(1989).*

Hentoff is generally considered a liberal in politics, but when it comes to free speech he is nonpartisan. In recent years, he has found fault with the Left for its attempts to silence those whose opinions it finds offensive or distasteful. This essay is excerpted from a longer piece, which first appeared in The Progressive *(1989).*

Preparing to Read

1. The First Amendment to the U.S. Constitution states that "Congress shall make no law respecting the establishment of religion, or prohibiting the free exercise thereof; or abridging the freedom of speech, or of the press; or the right of the people peaceably to assemble, and to petition the Government for a redress of grievances."

2. The Fourteenth Amendment (paragraph 21) guarantees due process and equal protection under the law. Due process (paragraph 13) allows citizens to defend themselves in both criminal and civil actions against accusations that can have legal, financial, or other serious consequences.

3. Lenny Bruce, Richard Pryor, and Sam Kinison, who are mentioned in paragraph 13, have used language that some might find offensive or even obscene in their comedy acts.

4. Affirmative action (paragraph 16) is the name given to government regulations that set goals for the admission of minorities to educational institutions and for the hiring of minorities in both the private and public sectors.

5. "Politically correct" is a term used by critics of the Left. They accuse liberals of insisting that only certain beliefs and behaviors are legitimate despite Constitutional and other legal guarantees.

6. Oliver Wendell Holmes was a U.S. Supreme Court Justice famous for his writings on the First Amendment.

Vocabulary

aggravated (adjective)	Heightened, made worse.
condemnation (noun)	Blame, censure.
constitute (verb)	Make up or equate to.
derogatory (adjective)	Degrading, disdainful.
dissented (verb)	Refused to conform or obey.
inquiry (noun)	Questioning, exploration, debate.
knownothingism (noun)	A term that has come to mean intolerance and bigotry. The Noknowthing Party of the nineteenth century wished to close U.S. borders to further immigration.
malignancies (noun)	Cancers.
orthodoxy (noun)	Strict adherence to a doctrine or set of beliefs.
pall (noun)	Gloom, sadness.
pariah (noun)	Social outcast, renegade.
perpetuate (verb)	Continue, keep alive.
pietistic (adjective)	Solemn, but in an affected or false way.
resurgence (noun)	Rebirth.
sanctions (noun)	Punishments.
scant (adjective)	Little.
secular (adjective)	Worldly.
short shrift (noun)	Little attention.
stifling (adjective)	Suffocating.
tempered (adjective)	Balanced, controlled.
ukase (noun)	Proclamation, decree, order.

Free Speech on Campus

Nat Hentoff

A FLIER DISTRIBUTED at the University of Michigan some months ago proclaimed that blacks "don't belong in classrooms, they belong hanging from trees." 1

At other campuses around the country, manifestations of racism are becoming commonplace. At Yale, a swastika and the words WHITE POWER! were painted on the building housing the University's Afro-American Cultural Center. At Temple University, a White Students Union has been formed with some 130 members. 2

Swastikas are not directed only at black students. The Nazi symbol has been spray-painted on the Jewish Student Union at Memphis State University. And on a number of campuses, women have been singled out as targets of wounding and sometimes frightening speech. At the law school of the State University of New York at Buffalo, several women students have received anonymous letters characterized by one professor as venomously sexist. 3

These and many more such signs of the resurgence of bigotry and   4
knownothingism throughout the society—as well as on campus—have to do
solely with speech, including symbolic speech. There have also been physical
assaults on black students and on black, white, and Asian women students,
but the way to deal with physical attacks is clear: call the police and file
a criminal complaint. What is to be done, however, about speech alone—
however disgusting, inflammatory, and rawly divisive that speech may be?

At more and more colleges, administrators—with the enthusiastic sup-   5
port of black students, women students, and liberal students—have been answering that question by preventing or punishing speech. In public universities, this is a clear violation of the First Amendment. In private colleges and
universities, suppression of speech mocks the secular religion of academic
freedom and free inquiry.

The Student Press Law Center in Washington, D.C.—a vital source of   6
legal support for student editors around the country—reports, for example,
that at the University of Kansas, the student host and producer of a radio
news program was forbidden by school officials from interviewing a leader of
the Ku Klux Klan. So much for free inquiry on that campus.

In Madison, Wisconsin, the *Capital Times* ran a story in January about   7
Chancellor Sheila Kaplan of the University of Wisconsin branch at Parkside,
who ordered her campus to be scoured of "some anonymously placed white
supremacist hate literature." Sounding like the legendary Mayor Frank ("I am
the law") Hague of Jersey City, who booted "bad speech" out of town, Chancellor Kaplan said, "This institution is not a lamppost standing on the street
corner. It doesn't belong to everyone."

Who decides what speech can be heard or read by everyone? Why, the   8
Chancellor, of course. That's what George III used to say, too.

University of Wisconsin political science professor Carol Tebben thinks   9
otherwise. She believes university administrators "are getting confused when
they are acting as censors and trying to protect students from bad ideas. I
don't think students need to be protected from bad ideas. I think they can
determine for themselves what ideas are bad."

After all, if students are to be "protected" from bad ideas, how are they   10
going to learn to identify and cope with them? Sending such ideas underground simply makes them stronger and more dangerous.

Professor Tebben's conviction that free speech means just that has be-   11
come a decidedly minority view on many campuses. At the University of Buffalo Law School, the faculty unanimously adopted a "Statement Regarding Intellectual Freedom, Tolerance, and Political Harassment." Its title implies
support of intellectual freedom, but the statement warned students that once
they enter "this legal community," their right to free speech must become
tempered "by the responsibility to promote equality and justice."

Accordingly, swift condemnation will befall anyone who engages in "re-   12
marks directed at another's race, sex, religion, national origin, age, or sex
preference." Also forbidden are "other remarks based on prejudice and group
stereotype."

This ukase is so broad that enforcement has to be alarmingly subjective. Yet the University of Buffalo Law School provides no due-process procedures for a student booked for making any of these prohibited remarks. Conceivably, a student caught playing a Lenny Bruce, Richard Pryor, or Sam Kinison album in his room could be tried for aggravated insensitivity by association.

When I looked into this wholesale cleansing of bad speech at Buffalo, I found it had encountered scant opposition. One protester was David Gerald Jay, a graduate of the law school and a cooperating attorney for the New York Civil Liberties Union. Said the appalled graduate: "Content-based prohibitions constitute prior restraint and should not be tolerated."

You would think that the law professors and administration at this public university might have known that. But hardly any professors dissented, and among the students only members of the conservative Federalist Society spoke up for free speech. The fifty-strong chapter of the National Lawyers Guild was on the other side. After all, it was more important to go on record as vigorously opposing racism and sexism than to expose oneself to charges of insensitivity to these malignancies.

The pressures to have the "right" attitude—as proved by having the "right" language in and out of class—can be stifling. A student who opposes affirmative action, for instance, can be branded a racist.

At the University of California at Los Angeles, the student newspaper ran an editorial cartoon satirizing affirmative action. (A student stops a rooster on campus and asks how the rooster got into UCLA. "Affirmative action," is the answer.) After outraged complaints from various minority groups, the editor was suspended for violating a publication policy against running "articles that perpetuate derogatory or cultural stereotypes." The art director was also suspended.

When the opinion editor of the student newspaper at California State University at Northridge wrote an article asserting that the sanctions against the editor and art director at UCLA amounted to censorship, he was suspended too.

At New York University Law School, a student was so disturbed by the pall of orthodoxy at that prestigious institution that he wrote to the school newspaper even though, as he said, he expected his letter to make him a pariah among his fellow students.

Barry Endick described the atmosphere at NYU created by "a host of watchdog committees and a generally hostile classroom reception regarding any student comment right of center." This "can be arguably viewed as symptomatic of a prevailing spirit of academic and social intolerance of . . . any idea which is not ' politically correct.' "

He went on to say something that might well be posted on campus bulletin boards around the country, though it would probably be torn down at many of them: "We ought to examine why students, so anxious to wield the Fourteenth Amendment, give short shrift to the First. Yes, Virginia, there are racist assholes. And you know what, the Constitution protects them, too.

Not when they engage in violence or vandalism. But when they speak or write, racist assholes fall right into this Oliver Wendell Holmes definition—

highly unpopular among bigots, liberals, radicals, feminists, sexists, and college administrators: "If there is any principle of the Constitution that more imperatively calls for attachment than any other, it is the principle of free thought—not free only for those who agree with us, but freedom for the thought we hate."

The language sounds like a pietistic Sunday sermon, but if it ever falls 23 wholly into disuse, neither this publication nor any other journal of opinion— right or left—will survive.

Questions for Discussion

1. What use of expert testimony and opinion does Hentoff make?
2. What use of anecdotes does he make? Of contrast?
3. Analyze the essay's introduction. What techniques are used here to draw our attention?
4. What is the question Hentoff asks in paragraph 4? How does this question help him introduce his essay?
5. In what way is symbolic speech similar to speech? Why does Hentoff bother to mention symbolic speech?
6. What distinction does the author draw between speech and action? Why is this distinction important to his thesis? What is his thesis?
7. Why does Hentoff quote Professor Carol Tebben (paragraph 9) and David Gerald Jay (paragraph 14)? What do their words add to the author's argument?
8. You learned earlier that, at times, writers of argument reveal their feelings about an issue, if only subtly. Where does Hentoff do this?
9. Where does the author address opposing opinions?
10. Describe the intended audience for this piece.

Thinking Critically

1. Reread Barry Glazer's essay, which appears earlier in this chapter. How might Hentoff respond to Glazer's arguments?
2. Reread Hentoff's essay. Then, using deduction, summarize it into a syllogism. In your own words, state its major premise, its minor premise, and its conclusion.

Suggestions for Journal Entries

1. Can you think of any circumstances when you might agree that speech should be censored? Make a list of such circumstances; then, explain why each might warrant limitations on free speech.

2. Are you in favor of unlimited free speech under all circumstances? If so, explain your reasons. As a way to anticipate arguments opposed to your own, explain how and why you would defend the rights of people to speak—verbally or symbolically—in ways that you might find distasteful, immoral, abhorrent, or even dangerous.

3. Consider an issue on your campus that you feel strongly about. It doesn't have to have earth-shaking consequences. The benefits of keeping the library open all night, the need for more parking spaces, or the advantages of majoring in a particular subject area might make fine topics for argumentation. Use freewriting or clustering to gather information you might later use to argue your position and to anticipate opposing arguments in a formal, full-length essay.

No Place like Home

David Gergen

David Gergen is Editor-at-Large for U.S. News & World Report *magazine, for which he wrote this editorial in June 2000. Gergen also works as a television commentator, journalist, and interviewer for PBS's* The Newshour *and for that program's website, the* Online Newshour. *He has spent 10 years in public service as an advisor to four U.S. presidents: Nixon, Ford, Reagan, and Clinton. A North Carolina native, Gergen holds an A.B. from Yale University and a law degree from Harvard University. He regularly teaches at Duke University as a visiting professor.*

Preparing to Read

1. What does the title of this essay reveal about Gergen's topic and his stand on that topic?
2. In paragraph 8, Gergen mentions "charter schools" and educational "vouchers." Research these terms on the Internet.

Vocabulary

accorded (verb)	Given
anecdotal (adjective)	Relating to individual stories or events used to illustrate a point.
anonymity (noun)	State of being unknown or unacknowledged.
evangelicals (noun)	Members of fundamentalist Christian churches.
fringe (adjective)	On the edge, extreme.
insightful (adjective)	Perceptive, clear sighted.
leeway (noun)	Space, room, tolerance.
median (adjective)	Middle, midpoint.
scrutiny (noun)	Inspection, examination.
siblings (noun)	Sisters and brothers.

No Place like Home

David Gergen

A YEAR AGO, a young man by the name of Jedediah Purdy surprised the book   1
world with the publication of his first major work, *For Common Things: Irony, Trust, and Commitment in America Today.* The book was an insightful, well-written call for a return to core values and an abandonment of an ironic stance toward life.

Critics wondered: Just who is this 24-year-old kid who has given a fresh voice to the Y generation? It turns out that Purdy is a graduate of Harvard and is now studying law, environment, and social values at Yale. But the twist that caught people's attention was the fact that Purdy grew up in the ragged foothills of West Virginia and, until he became a young man, was taught at home by his parents.

Until then, "homeschooling" had been brushed aside by many as a fringe movement, encouraged mostly by white evangelicals who have never been accorded the social respect they deserve. Purdy forced critics to take another look at the issue. Was something going on there that they were missing?

This month, the answer came in: Yes indeed, homeschooling is a phenomenon that deserves a far more serious look. The evidence piled up at the 73rd Scripps Howard National Spelling Bee, an annual event that attracts some of the smartest kids in the nation. This year, there were 248 participants at the national run-off; some 27 were homeschoolers, up from 19 last year.

Ahead of the class. The winner was George Abraham Thampy, age 12, a homeschooler from the St. Louis area who, just a week earlier, had finished second in a national geography competition. Thampy's parents are both from Kerala, India, and they began homeschooling their son, along with six siblings, after an incident of school violence scared them away from public education. Notably, the second- and third-place winners were also homeschoolers.

Jed Purdy and George Thampy have both written moving accounts of their educational experiences. It is easiest to call them "homeschoolers," says Purdy. "Really, though, our parents did something more radical. They freed us to learn."

Educators do not yet have enough data from homeschooling experiments to draw definitive conclusions. The National Home Education Research Institute reports that between 1.3 million and 1.7 million school-age children— about 3 percent—are currently homeschooled. Apparently, these children have not been as closely studied as they should be. But the data we do have show that the numbers are growing rapidly, from 7 percent to 15 percent a year. Lawrence Rudner, of the University of Maryland, has found that the median income for homeschool families ($52,000) is higher than that of all families with children ($36,000). Further, about a quarter of homeschool students are enrolled one grade or more above their age-level peers, and their median scores on tests are "well above" those of public- and private-school students.

While these results may not be definitive, they certainly suggest some obvious implications for public education. We have entered a period of great experimentation in the way we teach the young—"a thousand flowers are blooming"—and we ought to push forward on as many fronts as we can. The more leeway the public school authorities and the unions give to education, the better. Home schools are joining the ranks of charter schools and vouchers as critical paths toward a better educational environment.

The anecdotal evidence from homeschooling also serves as a strong rein- 9 forcement for a point that Theodore R. Sizer and Nancy Faust Sizer make in their recent book, *The Students Are Watching: Schools and the Moral Contract*. Two of the most respected figures in education, the Sizers argue that both the classroom and, importantly, the school itself should be small enough that a kid can receive individual attention.

Most high schools are organized like factories, discouraging a personal re- 10 lationship between students and teachers. The Sizers write: "The loads per teacher are normally heavy—100 to 175 young people during each semester— and the rapid reassignment of students from course to course makes it likely that a large percentage of students are not known well. This creates a situation which is, unfortunately, welcomed by many students: anonymity means their freedom from all sorts of scrutiny and obligation."

It's a long distance from anonymity in a classroom to a child working 11 alongside an adult each day, but it's a path that we must learn to travel. The future will belong to those children who, like Jed Purdy, are "freed to learn."

Questions for Discussion

1. What is the proposition that Gergen is defending?
2. The author writes that 27 of 248 participants in the Scripps Howard National Spelling Bee—a little more than 10 percent—were homeschoolers (paragraph 4). Why is this statistic significant?
3. Where else does he use statistics to support his point?
4. What use of direct quotations does Gergen make? Where does he include the testimony of experts?
5. Would this essay have been as convincing had the author relied solely on the anecdotal evidence presented through the cases of Jed Purdy and George Thampy?
6. Why does Gergen use questions in this piece?
7. What does Jed Purdy mean in paragraph 6 when he claims that his parents "freed us to learn"? Might this idea relate to what Gergen tells us about George Thampy in paragraph 5? How do these ideas relate to Gergen's thesis?
8. Reread paragraph 8. How would you characterize Gergen's attitude about the future of education?

Thinking Critically

1. What might Gergen be alluding to when he mentions "a return to core values" and "an abandonment of an ironic stance toward life"? What are "core values" to you? How would you characterize "an ironic stance toward life"?

2. Write a paragraph that might express Barry Glazer's reaction to Gergen's ideas. (Glazer's essay, "The Right to Be Let Alone," appears in this chapter.) Then, reread James Keller's "Exile and Return," which appears in Chapter 3. Would Keller agree with Gergen's claim that "most high schools are organized like factories" (paragraph 10)? Explain why or why not.

Suggestions for Journal Entries

1. Do you agree with Gergen's claim that "most high schools are organized like factories" (paragraph 10)? Use your own memories of high school and of your high school teachers to provide you with relevant details. Use freewriting or listing to gather your thoughts.
2. Make a list of some of the advantages of homeschooling. Then, make a list of some of the disadvantages. Brainstorm with fellow students if you have trouble gathering ideas.

Suggestions for Sustained Writing

1. Read the notes you made in response to the second of the Suggestions for Journal Entries after the essays by Callaghan and Barlow. (If you have not responded, do so now.)

   Add to your notes, and write a preliminary thesis statement for an essay that would argue for a particular change in public education. Make sure you limit yourself to a specific question. For example, don't argue that all students should learn more about the fine arts. Instead, argue that a year of art appreciation and a year of music appreciation be required of all high school graduates.

   As you draft your paper, make sure to anticipate and address opposing arguments. You can do this by exposing those arguments as unsupported, illogical, or untrue; or you can admit that they have value while arguing that yours make even better sense. If you wish, use your introduction to accomplish this. Then, devote the body of your paper to supporting your own point of view.

   Revise your paper several times, adding information as needed, and make sure your opinion is clear, logical, and well supported. Conclude your work on this project with meticulous editing and proofreading.
2. Like Barry Glazer, many of us have strong opinions about the right of privacy. Perhaps you discussed some of your own in your journal after reading "The Right to Be Let Alone."

Write an essay arguing that some government regulations interfere unnecessarily with the way we live. Use examples of federal, state, or local laws you think limit our freedom. If you interpret the word *government* broadly, you can even focus on rules enforced by your college, your family, or another group to which you belong.

One way to introduce this essay is to show readers that you are reasonable. Begin by admitting that some rules are necessary and should be fully enforced. For example, voice your support for tough laws against child abuse, rape, and drunk driving. At the end of your introduction, however, state your thesis forcefully: explain that some rules enforced by the government, by your family, or by another group are inappropriate and should be abolished. Then, like Glazer, develop your essay with examples from your experiences or from those of people you know or have read about.

Read your first draft carefully, adding details as you go along to make your opinions clear and convincing. In later drafts, try including language and information that appeal to the reader's emotions. Then, edit your work thoroughly.

3. Read "The Right to Be Let Alone" again. Then, write an essay in which you play Glazer's opponent. Argue that, although some government regulations are inappropriate, the ones he criticizes should be strictly enforced.

One way to organize your paper is to defend the regulations Glazer attacks in the same order he presented them. As such, you might outline the body of your essay like this:

> Terminally ill patients should not have the right to commit suicide.
>
> Police have the right to stop and question motorists at random.
>
> Pets should be licensed.
>
> Strict building codes are necessary.
>
> Colleges should enforce academic requirements.

Develop each of these points in concrete and convincing detail using any of the methods mentioned earlier in this chapter. After completing several drafts, write a conclusion that restates your thesis or that uses one of the methods for closing explained in Chapter 4. As always, be sure your final draft is organized and edited well.

4. Reread the notes that you made in response to the first two Suggestions for Journal Entries after Nat Hentoff's "Free Speech on Campus." Turn these notes into a full-length essay in which you argue one of the following:

> Some circumstances allow for limiting free speech.
>
> Free speech should be limited under no circumstances.

If this assignment doesn't interest you, write an essay based on the notes you made in response to Suggestion 3 after Hentoff's essay.

Whichever option you choose, be as complete and convincing as you can by gathering sufficient information to support your proposition. You might want to gather additional details, ideas, and opinions by brainstorming with fellow students or interviewing professors who can offer expert testimony. Also, try looking for more information on the Internet. If possible, use direct quotations.

Whether you organize your essay primarily around deduction or induction, check to be sure that you have not committed any of the logical fallacies discussed in the introduction to Section Six. You can do this when you revise your first draft. Also, make sure that your thesis is clearly stated and that your paper is well organized and easy to follow. As with other papers, edit and proofread carefully. Grammar, mechanical, spelling, and other such errors weaken an argument's effectiveness and lose your reader's trust.

5. If you responded to item 1 of the Suggestions for Journal Entries after Gergen's "No Place like Home," expand your notes into a full-length essay that argues for or against the proposition that most high schools are "like factories" in that they discourage "a personal relationship between students and teachers." Start by adding information to your journal entry. Rely on your own recollections of high school and of the people who taught you there. In addition, however, try brainstorming with classmates or friends whose views on this question agree with yours. If possible, interview a high school teacher for additional insights.

If this assignment leaves you cold, write an essay in which you argue that homeschooling is or is not more effective than the traditional approach. If you responded to the second of the journal suggestions after Gergen's essay, you might have already gathered relevant information for this project. Add to this information through library or Internet research. Whichever side you favor, make certain to address opposing arguments and, while recognizing their validity, show that yours is the best.

If neither of these options interests you, write an essay that points out advantages of homeschooling for a particular kind of student. Describe or define this type of student in detail.

If you include researched material, use internal citations and include a works-cited page at the end of your paper. Doing so will enable you to give credit to the sources from which you borrowed information. Use the Modern Language Association style for incorporating researched material. You can learn about it by reading the Appendix at the end of this textbook.

Writing to Learn: A Group Activity

Should institutions of higher learning regulate speech? If so, to what extent should they regulate it? What kinds of speech should be prohibited, if any, and for what reasons? And who should do the regulating? As a group, review and critique at least two college or university speech policies. (Note: a *critique* is not necessarily a criticism of a document; it is an evaluation.) Begin by finding and photocopying your own school's speech code if it has one. If it doesn't, find the policies of two other schools that are similar to yours or that are located in your county or state. You can do this by searching for these institutions' websites on the Internet. Make copies of both policies for everyone.

The First Meeting

Distribute copies of the policies. Read and discuss them as a group. Most speech policies are not long, so you might be able to do this during your meeting. Then, come to a consensus about the contents of each policy, item by item or point by point. Does the group agree or disagree with each of the points? (If you can't reach a consensus, rely on a majority vote.) Then, decide if you agree or disagree with the overall philosophy and purpose of the documents under discussion.

Research

Ask each group member to search the Internet and/or the library's periodical indexes for articles (online or on paper) that discuss free speech on college campuses. One source you might find effective is the American Civil Liberties Union's website (http://www.aclu.org). Take notes on and bring copies of informative articles to the next meeting.

The Second Meeting

Invite each group member to share his or her research by distributing copies of the materials found and by summarizing important points and ideas orally. After discussing these points and reading from relevant portions of useful articles, start discussing the speech policies you began to consider at your last meeting. Have your views on these policies changed in light of the research?

Whatever your answer, use both the group's reactions to the policies and the insights gained through research to list major points you might develop in a critique of the policies. Ask one student to write a draft of an essay that critiques the first policy and another to write a draft of an essay that critiques the second. Remind them to:

- Address the points the group has agreed to develop.
- Make frequent reference to their primary sources (the policies themselves).
- Include information and insights gathered through research.

Finally, ask them to bring photocopies of the completed drafts to the next meeting, enough for each group member.

The Third Meeting

Distribute copies of the drafts. Then, revise the critiques by adding or deleting information, clarifying ideas, and making the structure of the essays easier to follow. When you are finished, assign a third student to combine all of this into a single essay and to write an appropriate introduction and conclusion. Also, ask this person to write a thesis statement that expresses the group's opinion of the speech codes or of speech codes in general. As before, remind the writer to photocopy this draft.

The Fourth Meeting

Distribute copies of the draft mentioned above and, together, revise it for logic, clarity, and development. Next, edit it for grammar, sentence structure, punctuation, and other language considerations. After the group has agreed to all changes, assign a fourth student to type, proofread, and photocopy a final draft. Submit the original to the instructor and distribute copies to the group members. (You might even want to send a copy to the editor of your college paper for publication.)

CHAPTER 16

Persuasion

As you learned in the introduction to Section Six, effective persuasion always begins with a solid argument based on evidence that is presented logically. However, persuasion goes beyond pure argument. Writers engage in persuasion not only to prove a point but also to convince readers to adopt their point of view and to act on it.

So, if you want to convince readers that your stand on a controversial issue has merit or that a conclusion you have drawn about a complex issue is correct, a strong argument is probably enough. If you need to change people's attitudes or urge them to action, on the other hand, logic and evidence might not be enough to get the job done. You will need to be persuasive. Thus, while remaining clear-headed and fair, you might also want to appeal to the reader's values, pride, emotions, and even self-interest. Before doing so, you will have to consider the attitudes and opinions of your audience.

Appealing to the Reader's Values and Pride

Let's say your college is having a problem with litter, which makes the campus unsightly and even causes minor sanitation problems. As a member of the Student Senate, you are asked to write an open letter to the student body. Your letter will appear on the front page of the college newspaper accompanied by pictures of a parking lot where people have emptied ashtrays or left empty bottles, of a lunchroom table covered with trash, and of classrooms in which papers, used pens, a stray sneaker, and other refuse have been left behind.

Your job is to persuade students to clean up after themselves and to stop trashing the campus. You begin by explaining that common courtesy and concerns over health and sanitation demand that people deposit their garbage properly. The campus is a public place, you argue, and as such it demands that those who use it respect it and keep it clean for others. You also explain that keeping the grounds clean is easy if only everyone participates.

After reading your letter, you decide that your opinions are reasonable and fair. No one would disagree with them. In fact, your letter might be the very model of an effective written argument. However, you realize that it would not convince people to act on your recommendations—it simply does not go far enough.

The next step is to appeal to your readers' values and pride. You start by addressing their sense of fellowship, their pride in being members of an academic community. Remind them that they are college students, not adolescents who need to be taught table manners. You can also appeal to their self-image by explaining that the way students behave reflects their respect—or lack of respect—for the college, for professors, for classmates, and for themselves.

Appealing to the Reader's Emotions

If you are dealing with an especially hard-to-convince group, ask them to put themselves into the shoes of other students, of faculty, and of visitors—not to mention the janitorial staff—who enter the cafeteria to find tables and floors covered with soiled plates and napkins, half-eaten sandwiches, and dirty coffee cups. Express your disgust over the cigarette butts, empty bottles, and paper bags dumped in the parking lots. Complain about yogurt containers, aluminum cans, and other debris left in student lounges. In the process, use colorful images, concrete nouns, and strong verbs, adjectives, and adverbs to get your point across and shake up your audience. Use figures of speech: ask your readers not to turn the place into an academic "pigsty"; or compare the cafeteria at day's end to a "small village that has been looted and trashed by invading barbarians." You will see several excellent examples of speech that appeals to the emotions in Wilfred Owen's "Dulce et Decorum Est," a poem that appears in this introduction.

Appealing to the Reader's Self-Interest

Often this is the only way to move an especially obstinate audience. Try arguing that the dirtier the campus, the more unpleasant it is to be there, and remind your fellow students of the amount of time each of them spends on campus. You might even suggest that it is easier to study and to learn in a clean, attractive setting than in a dump! More important, explain that a dirty campus must be cleaned up and that this increases the cost of janitorial services. Of course, higher operating costs translate into higher tuition levels, so students might have to work longer hours to pay for college, or their parents might have to sacrifice a bit more to send them there.

Anticipating and Addressing Opposing Opinions

You learned in Chapter 15 that anticipating and responding to an opposing argument is important to making your point. Doing this is even more important when engaging in persuasive writing. When you argue, you need show only that, while other opinions have merit, your case is the strongest. When it comes to persuasion, on the other hand, you are asking readers to make a choice and to act on that choice. If they have any doubt that your opinion stands out as the strongest and wisest, they will not follow your lead, and they may, in fact, decide to do nothing. As you read the selections that follow, try to find places where writers address and respond to opposing arguments. More important, make use of this practice whenever you write to persuade.

Establishing Your Authority

Again, you read in Chapter 15 that, when writing argument papers, it is important to gain the confidence of your readers by convincing them you know what you are talking about. This is even more important when writing persuasively. If readers are going to follow your lead and act as you suggest, they will have to trust in your knowledge. As with all writing, the best way to show you are knowledgeable is to use concrete facts—hard evidence—to support your opinions. In addition, however, you might want to explain the source of your knowledge of a particular topic or problem. In "Education Is the Priority," student Nicholle Palmieri persuades her readers that working too many hours can often interfere with one's studies. She establishes her authority by explaining that, while working in the dean's office, she encountered too many students who had failed to make academics their priority and, as a result, were about to flunk out!

Visualizing Strategies for Persuasion

The following antiwar poem was written by Wilfred Owen (1893–1918), a British soldier who witnessed the horror of trench warfare in World War I. The title is Latin for "It is sweet and fitting." The last lines, taken from the Latin poet Horace, translate to "It is sweet and fitting to die for one's country."

Dulce et Decorum Est — *Uses an ironic title.*

Bent double, like old beggars under sacks,

Knock-kneed, coughing like hags, we cursed through sludge, — *Opens with a startling image; uses figures of speech.*

Till on the haunting flares we turned our backs

And towards our distant rest began to trudge.

Men marched asleep. Many had lost their boots

But limped on, blood-shod [shoed in blood]. All

went lame; all blind;

Drunk with fatigue; deaf even to the hoots

Of tired, outstripped Five-Nines that dropped behind.

Includes vivid verbs and adjectives.

Gas! Gas! Quick, boys!—An ecstasy of fumbling,

Fitting the clumsy helmets just in time;

Startles readers with the soldiers' cries.

Narrates action vividly. But someone still was yelling out and stumbling,

And floundʹring like a man in fire or lime...

Dim, through the misty panes and thick green light,

As under a green sea, I saw him drowning.

Creates an extended metaphor to describe the horror of a gas attack.

In all my dreams, before my helpless sight,

He plunges at me, guttering, choking, drowning.

Uses adjectives to evoke an emotional response.

Addresses readers directly to get them to change their minds. If in some smothering dreams you too could pace

Behind the wagon that we flung him in,

And watch the white eyes writhing in his face,

His hanging face, like a devilʹs sick of sin;

If you could hear, at every jolt, the blood

Come gargling from the froth-corrupted lungs

Obscene as cancer, bitter as the cud

Of vile, incurable sores on innocent tongues,—

My friend, you would not tell with such high zest

To children ardent [eager] for some desperate glory,

The old Lie: *Dulce et decorum est*

Pro patria mori.

Continues direct address; persuades readers to stop glorifying war.

Obviously, this is a message to stir our passions. Startling words, images, and figures of speech appeal to the emotions and create in us the sense of the horror that Owen experienced. The poem's central idea is, of course, that war is *not* sweet and fitting and that we must stop lying about it to children. In the last stanza (verse paragraph), the poet addresses his readers directly. He does this first in order to make his argument strike home more directly, to make it more compelling. He appeals to the readers' self-interest; after all they too might be asked to send their sons to war. He also does this so as to answer an opposing argument offered by people who have not seen war close up. We lie to children—"ardent for some desperate glory"—when we romanticize war. In no way is it sweet and fitting to die for one's country, and the poet demands that we stop telling them it is.

Revising Persuasion Papers

Revising any kind of paper takes hard work, but persuasion papers often ask the reader to accomplish tasks or goals or to change deeply held views, so it is important that they be as clear, logical, well supported, and strong as possible. Student Nicholle Palmieri rewrote "Education Is the Priority," which appears in this chapter, to make it the kind of paper she thought would get her fellow students to decrease the emphasis they placed on work in favor of their real goal—to get a college education.

Palmieri—Early Draft

Education Is the <u>First</u> Priority] *Redundant.*

About a year ago, I quit my full-time job to return to college. Despite all of the

Wordy. [obstacles <u>that stood</u> in my way, I was lucky

enough to find <u>a job in the office of Dean</u>] *More information needed.*

<u>Russell</u>. I say "lucky" for many reasons.

The dean and her administrative assistant,

Karen Gormish, are two of the <u>nicest people</u>

<u>on the face of the earth</u>, not to mention the] *Cliché.*

fact that I don't have to worry about my job

interfering with my studies. I am able to

fit my work hours around my class schedule,

and I still manage to get in enough hours to sufficiently cover my bills.

Vague.

Working there, though, has been quite a learning experience. Almost every day, at least one student comes into the office, their eyes scared, pleading to be taken off academic probation. I am often the first

Language seems flat, unappealing. Wrong pronoun agreement.

Wordy.

person that greets them and, therefore, I have the privilege of seeing their appeals firsthand. Most of these students have failed to make their educations their top

Redundant.

priority, and they are paying for it dearly, and there is one claim that almost all have in common their hours at work have taken

Fused sentence.

precious time away from their college studies. Mind you, most of these kids (I

Develop the notion of their being "kids"?

say "kids" because that is what the majority of them are) are living at home and taking about 15 credits per semester. Most of them occupy menial positions at fast-food

Use language that appeals to emotions.

restaurants or retail stores. They take orders from tough supervisors and work long hours toward their future in hopes of

Add details about their situations? Appeal to the emotions.

someday having a real job. From what I understand, most of these students work such hours under threat by their managers of being fired if they refuse.

I find fault with this whole scenario. Fifty years ago, it was unheard of that

Smooth out syntax.

> full-time college students should even work
> two hours a week let alone forty, and that

Support this with research?

was for a good reason.

Palmieri—Final Draft

Education is the Priority *Removes redundancy.*

About a year ago, I quit my full-time job to

Eliminates wordiness.

> return to college. Despite all of the
> obstacles in my way, I was lucky enough to

find a job as a work-study assistant in the

office of Dean Bernadette Russell. I say

Adds information about her job.

"lucky" for many reasons. The Dean and her

administrative assistant, Karen Gormish, are

supportive of students and are willing to

accommodate their needs. Because of their

Replaces cliché with fresher language.

support and flexibility, I don't have to

worry about my job interfering with my

studies. I am able to fit my work hours

around my class schedule—not the other way

around—and still manage to work enough hours

Adds emphasis.

to pay my bills.

Working in the Dean's office has taught

me a great deal about college students and

their priorities. Almost every day, at

Uses language that is clearer, more specific.

Uses language that is more evocative.

> least one of them comes into the office,
> eyes fraught with desperation. They plead
> to be taken off academic probation,
> restriction, or suspension. Some beg to
> have their dismissals lifted and to be
> allowed to re-enroll.

Adds important information.

Eliminates wordiness.

I am often the first person who greets them and, therefore, I see their appeals first. Most of these students have failed to make education their priority, and they are paying for it dearly. In fact, there is one claim that almost all have in common: their hours at work have taken precious time away from their college studies. Mind you, most of these kids (I say "kids" because that is what the majority of them are) are living at home and taking about 15 credits per semester. It is not as if they are seasoned adults who have worked at full-time jobs for fifteen years, have learned to manage their time, and are able to squeeze in a course or two in the evenings and weekends. On the contrary, most of them work at menial positions in fast-food restaurants or retail stores. They take orders from demanding, unreasonable supervisors, and they work asinine, exhausting hours that no human being should have to work—certainly not someone who is attending college classes full-time and devoting hours of endless study toward earning an education and entering a rewarding career. From what I understand, most of these students work such hours under threat of being fired by their managers if they refuse.

Removes redundancy.

Inserts colon to correct fused sentence.

Defines notion of "kids" by contrasting them to "seasoned adults."

Adds words and information that appeal to emotions.

Smooths out syntax.

I find the whole scenario appalling. Fifty years ago, it was unheard of that full-time college students should even work two hours a week, let alone forty, and that was for a good reason. According to the website of the Division of Student Affairs at Virginia Polytechnic Institute and State University, being a successful college student requires "about two hours of preparation for each hour in the classroom. This means that [a student carrying fifteen credits] has at least a forty-five hour work week, and is consequently involved in a full-time occupation" (1). At Newbury College, incoming freshmen are advised to attend classes regularly ("This is a must!"), seek help at the Academic Resources Center, visit their professors regularly during office hours, enroll in "the Academic Enrichment Program," and join a student study group (1). These activities take time—the bulk of your time—but in order to be successful in college you must commit to them. That also means that you will have little time for work outside your studies. For a full-time student, most college counselors recommend no more than 15 hours of work per week. Consider this: If you fail to nurture your education, you will

Finds supportive information through research.

Adds direct quotations from authorities on succeeding in college.

```
find yourself on academic probation,

restriction, or suspension.  Even worse, you

might get yourself dismissed, a blow from

which it is hard to recover even if you

manage to transfer to another college.
```

Practicing Strategies for Persuasion

Reread Wilfred Owen's poem, "Dulce et Decorum Est," on pages 553–554. Pay close attention to the language Owen uses to stir our emotions and appeal to our self-interest. Now use vivid, moving language in a *persuasive* paragraph or two responding to each of the following:

1. Describe the effects of cigarette smoking to persuade someone to kick the habit.

   _____

   _____

   _____

   _____

2. Explain the dangers of drinking and driving to a group of teenagers so as to get them to choose a designated driver whenever they attend parties where alcohol is served.

   _____

   _____

   _____

   _____

3. Discuss the serious, even dangerous effects of promiscuous and/or unprotected sex to a group of 18-year-old males. Your ultimate purpose is to persuade them to abstain from sex until marriage.

   _____

   _____

   _____

   _____

4. Explain the effects of a high-fat diet and a lack of physical exercise to convince a friend to change his or her lifestyle.

   _____

   _____

_____

_____

5. Allow readers to visualize the long-term consequences of marrying a particular person, entering a particular career, or making another important life decision. You can either defend or attack this decision.

_____

_____

_____

_____

Review your responses to the five items above. Then, in each case, write a paragraph that addresses an appropriate opposing argument.

In addition to the four selections that follow, you can find another piece of persuasive writing in the Appendix at the end of this textbook. This persuasive essay is entitled "Victims of Violent Crime: Equal Treatment under the Law." Written by student Angela Brandli, "Victims of Violent Crime" was first drafted as a letter to legislative leaders in New Jersey. It was so persuasive that Brandli was asked to draft a version of a bill to increase compensation for crime victims in that state. The bill was passed by the state legislature and signed by Governor Christine Todd Whitman in 1999, and it has come to be known as the "Brandli Bill."

In the last few pages, you have read a lot about how to write persuasively. As with all kinds of writing, the most important ingredient in persuasion is your knowledge of the subject. Think of yourself as a lawyer. To argue a case or defend a client effectively, you will need to know the evidence well. Otherwise, you will have a hard time convincing judge or jury. Wise readers approach new opinions cautiously. Some will be open to persuasion. Others may even be eager to accept your point of view. But all will expect you to present evidence logically, clearly, and convincingly before they make your opinions their own.

Education Is the Priority

Nicholle Palmieri

Nicholle Palmieri wrote this essay as a letter to the editor of her college news-paper. As a work-study assistant in the office of the Dean of Liberal Arts, Palmieri came into contact with many full-time students who were doing poorly in their studies because they had not made education a priority. The vast majority of these had underestimated the amount of time a successful col-lege career demands, and they were spending too many hours at their jobs. Some of them even held full-time jobs while attending college full-time.

Much of what Palmieri discusses here was inspired by her own experi-ences. As a junior in high school, she held a job as a sales clerk at a store in a large shopping mall. When she told her boss that she could not work overtime because she had to study for an exam the next day, he threatened to fire her. But this student knew her priorities, and she quit before he could do so. Palmieri is now an English major at Douglass College. She plans to pursue a career in publishing after graduation.

Preparing to Read

1. Palmieri's title is, essentially, her thesis. As you learned above, she wrote this selection as a letter to her college newspaper. What does this tell you about her purpose and her audience?

2. The biographical note on this student author reveals something about her personality. What might that be? How will this character trait be reflected in the selection that follows?

3. Palmieri appeals to the reader's emotions, values, and self-interest. Underline places where she does this as you read her essay.

4. The author uses the terms academic "probation," "restriction," and "suspension" to designate the statuses of students whose grades need immediate improvement. "Dismissal" occurs when a student's grades are so low that he or she is asked to leave the college.

Vocabulary

accommodate (verb)	Meet or serve.
appalling (adjective)	Shocking.
asinine (adjective)	Foolish, idiotic.
fraught with (adjective)	Accompanied by, filled with.
menial (adjective)	Low level.
nurture (verb)	Care for, provide for, nourish.
priority (noun)	Item of greatest importance.

scenario (noun)	Situation.
seasoned (adjective)	Experienced.
serf (noun)	Slave, someone bound to the land or to a master.

Education Is the Priority

Nicholle Palmieri

ABOUT A YEAR ago, I quit my full-time job to return to college. Despite all of the obstacles in my way, I was lucky enough to find a job as a work-study assistant in the office of Dr. Bernadette Russell, Dean of Liberal Arts at my college. I say "lucky" for many reasons. The Dean and her administrative assistant, Karen Gormish, are supportive of students and are willing to accommodate their needs. Because of their support and flexibility, I don't have to worry about my job interfering with my studies. I am able to fit my work hours around my class schedule—not the other way around—and still manage to work enough hours to pay my bills.

Working in the Dean's office has taught me a great deal about college students and their priorities. Almost every day, at least one of them comes into the office, eyes fraught with desperation. They plead to be taken off academic probation, restriction, or suspension. Some beg to have their dismissals lifted and to be allowed to re-enroll.

I am often the first person who greets them and, therefore, I see their appeals first. Most of these students have failed to make education their priority, and they are paying for it dearly. In fact, there is one claim that almost all have in common: their hours at work have taken precious time away from their college studies. Mind you, most of these kids (I say "kids" because that is what the majority of them are) are living at home and taking about 15 credits per semester. It is not as if they are seasoned adults who have worked at full-time jobs for fifteen years, have learned to manage their time, and are able to squeeze in a course or two in the evenings and weekends. On the contrary, most of them work at menial positions in fast-food restaurants or retail stores. They take orders from demanding, unreasonable supervisors, and they work asinine, exhausting hours that no human being should have to work—certainly not someone who is attending college classes full-time and devoting hours of endless study toward earning an education and entering a rewarding career. From what I understand, most of these students work such hours under threat of being fired by their managers if they refuse.

I find the whole scenario appalling. Fifty years ago, it was unheard of that full-time college students should even work two hours a week, let alone forty, and that was for a good reason. According to the website of the Division of Student Affairs at Virginia Polytechnic Institute and State University, being a successful college student requires "about two hours of preparation

1

2

3

4

for each hour in the classroom. This means that [a student carrying fifteen credits] has at least a forty-five hour work week, and is consequently involved in a full-time occupation"(1). At Newbury College, incoming freshmen are advised to attend classes regularly ("This is a must!"), seek help at the Academic Resources Center, visit their professors regularly during office hours, enroll in "the Academic Enrichment Program," and join a student study group (1). These activities take time—the bulk of your time—but in order to be successful in college you must commit to them. That also means that you will have little time for work outside your studies. For a full-time student, most college counselors recommend no more than 15 hours of work per week. Consider this: If you fail to nurture your education, you will find yourself on academic probation, restriction, or suspension. Even worse, you might get yourself dismissed, a blow from which it is hard to recover even if you manage to transfer to another college.

Why would anyone want to do that to herself for the sake of some no- 5 brainer, dead-end job that pays $5.05 per hour? I understand that many students need money because they have bills to pay, not the least of which might be tuition. However, there comes a point when enough is enough. I too have bills to pay, and I manage to pay them by working 15 hours a week or less. I could not possibly devote sufficient time to my studies if I worked a minute more, and my supervisor understands this. Managers who don't understand this aren't worth working for, and they would do students in their employ a favor by firing them.

No words can overemphasize the importance of education. Without one, 6 the "kids" I mentioned earlier might be condemned to work as under-paid, under-appreciated, underrespected cashiers and stock clerks for the rest of their lives. It is time college students put their educations first and told their supervisors at McDonald's or Burger King to find another serf if they don't like it. This is a free country. There is nothing—least of all a dead-end job or a cranky fast-food manager—that can deprive you of your right to a quality education and to a successful future.

Works Cited

Division of Student Affairs Home Page. Division of Student Affairs, Virginia Polytechnic Institute and State University. 4 Mar. 2000 <http://www.ucc.vt.edu/stdysk/htimesch.html>.

How to Be a More Active Learner at Newbury College. Newbury College. 4 Mar. 2000 <http://www.newbury.edu/support/active.htm>.

Questions for Discussion

1. What is Palmieri's thesis? Where does she state it most clearly?
2. Does this selection illustrate the uses of deduction, which you learned about in Chapter 15? Explain Palmieri's thinking by creating a syllogism in your own words: start with a general statement, apply a specific case to that statement, and then draw a conclusion.

3. Where in this essay does the author rely on induction, which you also learned about in Chapter 15?

4. Where does the author appeal to her audience's values? To their self-interest?

5. What use does she make of testimony of experts on her subject? Why did she choose these sources to quote directly? Why not include direct quotations from students "fraught with desperation," whom she met in the dean's office?

6. Palmieri chooses her persuasive vocabulary well. Identify and analyze a paragraph or two in which her language appeals to our emotions.

7. Does the author anticipate and answer opposing arguments? Where?

8. Why does Palmieri tell us so much about herself in this essay, especially in her introduction?

Thinking Critically

1. Reread "Study Calculus" by William J. Bennett in Chapter 2 and "Burger Queen" by Erin Sharp in Chapter 3. How might each of them react to Palmieri's essay?

2. Palmieri criticizes employers who do not accommodate students who work for them. How might an employer respond to her comments?

Suggestions for Journal Entries

1. Think about the opposing argument Palmieri addressed in paragraph 5. Can you make a case for this argument? Are there other reasons for working more than 15 hours per week while carrying a full academic load? Brainstorm with two or three classmates to gather relevant information you might use later on to write a rebuttal to Palmieri's essay.

2. Think about an issue that is crucial to student success in college and that you might write about in a letter to the editor of your student newspaper. Palmieri's essay focuses on making education, not work, the priority. Yours might discuss study habits, time management, stress management, participation in community service projects, the dangers of alcohol or drug abuse among students, or any other issue you believe is important to your fellow students. If you need inspiration picking a topic, visit either of the two Internet sites Palmieri mentions in her works-cited list, or go to the websites of other colleges and universities.

I Have a Dream

Dr. Martin Luther King, Jr.

After graduating from Morehouse College at nineteen, Martin Luther King, Jr. (1929–1968), entered the seminary and later became a minister in Atlanta's Ebenezer Baptist Church, where his father was pastor. In 1957, he founded the Southern Christian Leadership Conference, a civil-rights organization. Influenced by the philosophy of human-rights activist and pacifist Mahatma Gandhi, King led several important demonstrations against racial segregation in the South and in the North. Among the most famous was the march in Birmingham, Alabama, in 1963, for which King was arrested. It was during this imprisonment that he wrote "Letter from Birmingham Jail," a landmark in the literature of American human rights. In that same year, King made a stirring speech during the great March on Washington. Delivered before 200,000 people assembled at the Lincoln Memorial, the text of this speech has come to be known as "I Have a Dream." King won several awards for his work in support of human rights, including the Nobel Prize for Peace in 1964. On April 4, 1968, Dr. King was assassinated while he spoke with other civil-rights leaders on a motel balcony in Memphis, Tennessee.

Preparing to Read

1. King refers to the Declaration of Independence and the U.S. Constitution as a "promissory note to which every American was to fall heir." If you haven't done so already, read these documents. You can find them in any college or public library or on the Internet.

2. Look up Martin Luther King, Jr., and/or the American Civil Rights Movement in a library reference book or on the Internet to familiarize yourself with some of the issues and events that King refers to in this speech.

3. Given the fact that King was a Christian minister, what allusions and references might he use in this speech to support his advocacy of civil rights and to move his audience?

Vocabulary

defaulted (verb)	Failed to pay a debt.
devotees (noun)	Disciples, those who believe in.
hallowed (adjective)	Holy, sacred.
inextricably (adverb)	Permanently, unable to be removed.
interposition (noun)	Attempts to stop the enforcement of laws, in this case those guaranteeing civil rights.

jangling (adjective)	Clanking, clattering.
languishing (adjective)	Lying weak and ill.
manacles (noun)	Handcuffs.
militancy (noun)	Aggressiveness, willingness to do battle.
momentous (adjective)	Extremely important, weighty.
nullification (noun)	Refusal to enforce or recognize laws, in this case those guaranteeing civil rights.
redemptive (adjective)	Redeeming, saving.
unalienable (adjective)	Natural, undeniable.
withering (adjective)	Decaying, dying.

I Have a Dream

Dr. Martin Luther King, Jr.

FIVE SCORE YEARS ago, a great American, in whose symbolic shadow we stand, signed the Emancipation Proclamation. This momentous decree came as a great beacon light of hope to millions of Negro slaves who had been seared in the flames of withering injustice. It came as a joyous daybreak to end the long night of captivity. 1

But one hundred years later, we must face the tragic fact that the Negro is still not free. One hundred years later, the life of the Negro is still sadly crippled by the manacles of segregation and the chains of discrimination. One hundred years later, the Negro lives on a lonely island of poverty in the midst of a vast ocean of material prosperity. One hundred years later, the Negro is still languishing in the corners of American society and finds himself an exile in his own land. So we have come here today to dramatize an appalling condition. 2

In a sense we have come to our nation's capital to cash a check. When the architects of our republic wrote the magnificent words of the Constitution and the Declaration of Independence, they were signing a promissory note to which every American was to fall heir. This note was a promise that all men would be guaranteed the unalienable rights of life, liberty, and the pursuit of happiness. 3

It is obvious today that America has defaulted on this promissory note insofar as her citizens of color are concerned. Instead of honoring this sacred obligation, America has given the Negro people a bad check; a check which has come back marked "insufficient funds." But we refuse to believe that the bank of justice is bankrupt. We refuse to believe that there are insufficient funds in the great vaults of opportunity of this nation. So we have come to cash this check—a check that will give us upon demand the riches of freedom and the security of justice. We have also come to this hallowed spot to remind America of the fierce urgency of *now*. This is no time to engage in the luxury of cooling off or to take the tranquilizing drugs of gradualism. *Now is* 4 the time to make real the promises of Democracy. *Now* is the time to rise from the dark and desolate valley of segregation to the sunlit path of racial justice. *Now* is the time to open the doors of opportunity to all of God's children. *Now* is the time to lift our nation from the quicksands of racial injustice to the solid rock of brotherhood.

It would be fatal for the nation to overlook the urgency of the moment 5 and to underestimate the determination of the Negro. This sweltering summer of the Negro's legitimate discontent will not pass until there is an invigorating autumn of freedom and equality. Nineteen sixty-three is not an end, but a beginning. Those who hope that the Negro needed to blow off steam and will now be content will have a rude awakening if the nation returns to business as usual. There will be neither rest nor tranquility in America until the Negro is granted his citizenship rights. The whirlwinds of revolt will continue to shake the foundations of our nation until the bright day of justice emerges.

But there is something that I must say to my people who stand on the 6 warm threshold which leads into the palace of justice. In the process of gaining our rightful place we must not be guilty of wrongful deeds. Let us not seek to satisfy our thirst for freedom by drinking from the cup of bitterness and hatred. We must forever conduct our struggle on the high plane of dignity and discipline. We must not allow our creative protest to degenerate into physical violence. Again and again we must rise to the majestic heights of meeting physical force with soul force. The marvelous new militancy which has engulfed the Negro community must not lead us to a distrust of all white people, for many of our white brothers, as evidenced by their presence here today, have come to realize that their destiny is tied up with our destiny and their freedom is inextricably bound to our freedom. We cannot walk alone.

And as we walk, we must make the pledge that we shall march ahead. 7 We cannot turn back. There are those who are asking the devotees of civil rights, "When will you be satisfied?" We can never be satisfied as long as the Negro is the victim of the unspeakable horrors of police brutality. We can never be satisfied as long as our bodies, heavy with the fatigue of travel, cannot gain lodging in the motels of the highways and the hotels of the cities. We cannot be satisfied as long as the Negro's basic mobility is from a smaller ghetto to a larger one. We can never be satisfied as long as a Negro in Mississippi cannot vote and a Negro in New York believes he has nothing for which to vote. No, no, we are not satisfied, and we will not be satisfied until justice rolls down like waters and righteousness like a mighty stream.

I am not unmindful that some of you have come here out of great trials 8 and tribulations. Some of you have come fresh from narrow jail cells. Some of you have come from areas where your quest for freedom left you battered by the storms of persecution and staggered by the winds of police brutality. You have been the veterans of creative suffering. Continue to work with the faith that unearned suffering is redemptive.

Go back to Mississippi, go back to Alabama, go back to South Carolina, 9 go back to Georgia, go back to Louisiana, go back to the slums and ghettos of our northern cities, knowing that somehow this situation can and will be changed. Let us not wallow in the valley of despair.

I say to you today, my friends, that in spite of the difficulties and frustrations of the moment I still have a dream. It is a dream deeply rooted in the American dream.

I have a dream that one day this nation will rise up and live out the true meaning of its creed: "We hold these truths to be self-evident; that all men are created equal."

I have a dream that one day on the red hills of Georgia the sons of former slaves and the sons of former slaveowners will be able to sit down together at the table of brotherhood.

I have a dream that one day even the state of Mississippi, a desert state sweltering with the heat of injustice and oppression, will be transformed into an oasis of freedom and justice.

I have a dream that my four little children will one day live in a nation where they will not be judged by the color of their skin but by the content of their character.

I have a dream today.

I have a dream that one day the state of Alabama, whose governor's lips are presently dripping with the words of interposition and nullification, will be transformed into a situation where little black boys and black girls will be able to join hands with little white boys and white girls and walk together as sisters and brothers.

I have a dream today.

I have a dream that one day every valley shall be exalted, every hill and mountain shall be made low, the rough places will be made plain, and the crooked places will be made straight, and the glory of the Lord shall be revealed, and all flesh shall see it together.

This is our hope. This is the faith with which I return to the South. With this faith we will be able to hew out of the mountain of despair a stone of hope. With this faith we will be able to transform the jangling discords of our nation into a beautiful symphony of brotherhood. With this faith we will be able to work together, to pray together, to struggle together, to go to jail together, to stand up for freedom together, knowing that we will be free one day.

This will be the day when all of God's children will be able to sing with new meaning

> My country, 'tis of thee,
> Sweet land of liberty,
>   Of thee I sing:
> Land where my fathers died,
> Land of the pilgrims' pride,
> From every mountain-side
>   Let freedom ring.

And if America is to be a great nation this must become true. So let freedom ring from the prodigious hilltops of New Hampshire. Let freedom ring from the mighty mountains of New York. Let freedom ring from the heightening Alleghenies of Pennsylvania!

Let freedom ring from the snowcapped Rockies of Colorado! 22

Let freedom ring from the curvaceous peaks of California! 23

But not only that; let freedom ring from Stone Mountain of Georgia! 24

Let freedom ring from Lookout Mountain of Tennessee! 25

Let freedom ring from every hill and molehill of Mississippi. From every 26 mountainside, let freedom ring.

When we let freedom ring, when we let it ring from every village and 27 every hamlet, from every state and every city, we will be able to speed up that day when all of God's children, black men and white men, Jews and Gentiles, Protestants and Catholics, will be able to join hands and sing in the words of the old Negro spiritual, "Free at last! free at last! thank God almighty, we are free at last!"

Questions for Discussion

1. King's central idea is expressed most forcefully in the sentences that begin "I have a dream . . ." Of these, which has the greatest effect on you?

2. Where in this speech does King appeal to written authority?

3. Where does he use facts to support his point of view?

4. Why does King mention so many Southern states by name?

5. In what parts of this address does the speaker appeal to his audience's values?

6. Where does he appeal to the self-interest of the African-Americans in his audience?

7. Where does he appeal to the self-interest of whites?

8. The speaker uses parallelism to evoke our emotions. Find examples of this rhetorical technique. If necessary, review what you learned about parallelism in Chapter 7.

9. Another way King rouses our emotions is by using figures of speech. Find several examples of figurative language.

10. King addresses two sets of opposing arguments in this speech. Explain how he does this.

Thinking Critically

1. Reread paragraphs 2 and 3. Explain the extended metaphors used in them.

2. Turn back to Chapter 7 in this book, and read Lincoln's Gettysburg Address. Pay particular attention to the word "hallowed," used in paragraph 2 of that document. This is the same word King uses in

paragraph 4 here. What other similarities can you identify in these two addresses?

3. Who is King's audience? Is it only the 200,000 people assembled at the Lincoln Memorial?

Suggestions for Journal Entries

1. Have we made progress in guaranteeing the civil rights of minorities since Dr. King spoke these words? Make a list of the most important advances. Start by reviewing "I Have a Dream" and deciding if the wrongs mentioned there have been dealt with. You might want to do some Internet research on the history of the American Civil Rights Movement—as already suggested in Preparing to Read—to gather facts. You might also want to interview a professor of history, literature, or government at your college to find out more about this question.

2. Do you have your own dream for the world? What major problem affecting the United States or another country would you like to see solved in the next few decades? Perhaps you might address poverty, illiteracy, drug abuse, or teenage pregnancy in America, the AIDS epidemic in Africa, or famine in any of several parts of the world.

    Again you might have to do some library or Internet research or interview a professor who is knowledgeable about the issue you are addressing.

The Media's Image of Arabs

Jack G. Shaheen

Jack Shaheen's parents came to the United States from Lebanon, a country with a large Arabic population. Although he focuses on the stereotype through which the American media pictures Arabs, Shaheen helps us understand the danger in all stereotyping regardless of the group. This essay first appeared in Newsweek in 1988.

Preparing to Read

1. In paragraph 3, Shaheen creates an analogy by calling TV wrestling "that great American morality play." Used in the Middle Ages to teach people morality, such plays portrayed the forces of good and of evil battling for possession of someone's soul.

2. In paragraph 5, Shaheen asks if it is "easier for a camel to go through the eye of a needle" than for the media to portray Arabs fairly. This is a variation on the New Testament's "It is easier for a camel to pass through the eye of a needle than for one who is rich to enter the kingdom of God."

3. The Semites, mentioned in paragraph 8, are people of the eastern Mediterranean; both Jews and Arabs are Semites. At the end of this paragraph, Shaheen asks that we "retire the stereotypical Arab to a media Valhalla." In Nordic mythology, Valhalla was a heaven to which warriors killed in battle were sent.

Vocabulary

caricatures (noun)	Images or pictures that exaggerate and poke fun at the subject's features or qualities.
cliché (noun)	Saying so overused it becomes boring and often meaningless.
conspires (verb)	Schemes, connives.
deplore (verb)	Criticize, lament.
mosques (noun)	Muslim houses of worship.
neutralize (verb)	Act as balance to, counteract.
nurtures (verb)	Feeds, nourishes.
prevail (verb)	Predominate, command our attention.
swarthy (adjective)	Dark-skinned.

The Media's Image of Arabs

Jack G. Shaheen

AMERICA'S BOGYMAN IS the Arab. Until the nightly news brought us TV pictures of Palestinian boys being punched and beaten, almost all portraits
of Arabs seen in America were dangerously threatening. Arabs were either bil-
lionaires or bombers—rarely victims. They were hardly ever seen as ordinary
people practicing law, driving taxis, singing lullabies or healing the sick.
Though TV news may portray them more sympathetically now, the absence
of positive media images nurtures suspicion and stereotype. As an Arab-
American, I have found that ugly caricatures have had an enduring impact on
my family.

 I was sheltered from prejudicial portraits at first. My parents came from
Lebanon in the 1920s; they met and married in America. Our home in the
steel city of Clairton, PA, was a center for ethnic sharing—black, white, Jew
and gentile. There was only one major source of media images then, at the
State movie theater where I was lucky enough to get a part-time job as an
usher. But in the late 1940s, Westerns and war movies were popular, not
Middle Eastern dramas. Memories of World War II were fresh, and the screen
heavies were the Japanese and the Germans. True to the cliché of the times,
the only good Indian was a dead Indian. But when I mimicked or mocked the
bad guys, my mother cautioned me. She explained that stereotypes blur our
vision and corrupt the imagination. "Have compassion for all people, Jackie,"
she said. "This way, you'll learn to experience the joy of accepting people as
they are, and not as they appear in films. Stereotypes hurt."

 Mother was right. I can remember the Saturday afternoon when my son,
Michael, who was seven, and my daughter, Michele, six, suddenly called out;
"Daddy, Daddy, they've got some bad Arabs on TV." They were watching that
great American morality play, TV wrestling. Akbar the Great, who liked to
hear the cracking of bones, and Abdullah the Butcher, a dirty fighter who
liked to inflict pain, were pinning their foes with "camel locks." From that
day on, I knew I had to try to neutralize the media caricatures.

 It hasn't been easy. With my children, I have watched animated heroes
Heckle and Jeckle pull the rug from under "Ali Boo-Boo, the Desert Rat," and
Laverne and Shirley stop "Sheik Ha-Mean-Ie" from conquering "the U.S. and
the world." I have read comic books like the "Fantastic Four" and "G.I. Combat" whose characters have sketched Arabs as "lowlifes" and "human hyenas."
Negative stereotypes were everywhere. A dictionary informed my youngsters
that an Arab is a "vagabond, drifter, hobo and vagrant." Whatever happened,
my wife wondered, to Aladdin's good genie?

 To a child, the world is simple: good versus evil. But my children and
others with Arab roots grew up without ever having seen a humane Arab on
the silver screen, someone to pattern their lives after. Is it easier for a camel to

go through the eye of a needle than for a screen Arab to appear as a genuine human being?

Hollywood producers must have an instant Ali Baba kit that contains   6
scimitars, veils, sunglasses and such Arab clothing as *chadors* and *kufiyahs*. In the mythical "Ayrabland," oil wells, tents, mosques, goats and shepherds prevail. Between the sand dunes, the camera focuses on a mock-up of a palace from "Arabian Nights"—or a military air base. Recent movies suggest that Americans are at war with Arabs, forgetting the fact that out of 21 Arab nations, America is friendly with 19 of them. And in "Wanted Dead or Alive," a movie that starred Gene Simmons, the leader of the rock group Kiss, the war comes home when an Arab terrorist comes to the United States dressed as a rabbi and, among other things, conspires with Arab-Americans to poison the people of Los Angeles. The movie was released last year.

The Arab remains American culture's favorite whipping boy. In his   7
memoirs, Terrel Bell, Ronald Reagan's first secretary of education, writes about an "apparent bias among mid-level, right-wing staffers at the White House" who dismissed Arabs as "sand niggers." Sadly, the racial slurs continue. At a recent teacher's conference, I met a woman from Sioux Falls, SD, who told me about the persistence of discrimination. She was in the process of adopting a baby when an agency staffer warned her that the infant had a problem. When she asked whether the child was mentally ill, or physically handicapped, there was silence. Finally, the worker said: "The baby is Jordanian."

To me, the Arab demon of today is much like the Jewish demon of yes-   8
terday. We deplore the false portrait of Jews as a swarthy menace. Yet a similar portrait has been accepted and transferred to another group of Semites—the Arabs. Print and broadcast journalists have started to challenge this stereotype. They are now revealing more humane images of Palestinian Arabs, a people who traditionally suffered from the myth that Palestinian equals terrorist. Others could follow that lead and retire the stereotypical Arab to a media Valhalla.

It would be a step in the right direction if movie and TV producers de-   9
veloped characters modeled after real-life Arab-Americans. We could then see a White House correspondent like Helen Thomas, whose father came from Lebanon, in "The Golden Girls," a heart surgeon patterned after Dr. Michael DeBakey on "St. Elsewhere," or a Syrian-American playing tournament chess like Yasser Seirawan, the Seattle grandmaster.

Politicians, too, should speak out against the cardboard caricatures. They 10
should refer to Arabs as friends, not just as moderates. And religious leaders could state that Islam like Christianity and Judaism maintains that all mankind is one family in the care of God. When all imagemakers rightfully begin to treat Arabs and all other minorities with respect and dignity, we may begin to unlearn our prejudices.

Questions for Discussion

1. Shaheen draws the evidence for his argument from personal experience, observation, and reading. Identify examples of information that come from each of these sources.

2. Why does the author tell us that "the Arab demon of today is much like the Jewish demon of yesterday" (paragraph 8)? What other comparison does he make, and how does it contribute to his argument?

3. Why does he recall what his mother said when he "mimicked or mocked the bad guys" (paragraph 2) of movies in the 1940s?

4. As you learned in Preparing to Read, paragraph 3 contains an analogy. In what other paragraph does the author place an analogy?

5. Shaheen could have directed his remarks to Arab-American readers, but he chose to address a far more comprehensive audience. How do we know that?

6. Shaheen concludes by asking politicians and religious leaders to speak out against negative stereotyping. Is his ending appropriate to an essay that criticizes the media?

Thinking Critically

1. This essay was written several years ago. Is its message still current? As you begin thinking, recall that immediately after the bombing of the federal building in Oklahoma City in 1995, some law enforcement officials and members of the media speculated that this was the work of Arab terrorists. In a few days, of course, the world learned conclusively that no one of Arab nationality or descent had anything to do with it.

2. Shaheen attacks the media, at least on its portrayal of Arabs. On what issues would you criticize the television, movie, or music industries? On what issues might you applaud them?

Suggestions for Journal Entries

1. Describe the way movies, television, music videos, radio, billboards, newspapers, and popular magazines portray a particular ethnic group. Is the portrait of this group flattering or negative? Examples of a group you might write about include African-Americans, Jews, Hispanics, Native Americans, Asian Indians, Chinese, Poles, Hungarians, Russians, Scandinavians, Italians, or even white Anglo-Saxon Protestants. Good ways to gather details for this journal entry are focused freewriting and brainstorming.

2. Not all stereotyping is based on race, religion, or ethnic background. Members of certain occupations—police officers and politicians, for example—sometimes suffer from bad media images. As a matter of fact, some of the worst stereotyping is based on age, sex, or sexual preference. Think about a group of people—other than a racial, religious, or ethnic group—that you think suffers from an unfair and inaccurate media image. Use focused freewriting or listing to gather examples of the way these people are portrayed on television, in movies, and so forth. Here are some groups you might want to choose from:

Housewives	Secretaries
Teachers	Factory workers
Beauticians	Bachelors
Senior citizens	College students
Homosexuals	Husbands
Grandparents	Intellectuals
Scientists	Athletes
Auto mechanics	Nurses
Musicians	Single women

What's Wrong with This Picture?

Gloria Steinem

Gloria Steinem is consulting editor and frequent contributor to Ms. *magazine, which she co-founded in 1972. A leading feminist and pioneer in the movement for women's rights, Steinem has written for a number of important periodicals, including* Vogue *and* Life. *Among her full-length works are* Marilyn: Norma Jeane *(1986),* A Revolution from Within *(1993), and* Moving Beyond Words *(1994). "What's Wrong with This Picture?" was published in* Ms. *in spring 1997.*

Preparing to Read

1. Freedom of speech figures prominently in this selection. In the United States, it is guaranteed by the First Amendment to the Constitution, as follows: "Congress shall make no law respecting an establishment of religion, or prohibiting the free exercise thereof; or abridging the freedom of speech, or of the press; or the right of the people peaceably to assemble, and to petition the Government for a redress of grievances."

2. *Aryan* (paragraph 11) is a word used by the Nazis to refer to members of their so-called master race.

3. In paragraph 12, Steinem uses the adjective *Orwellian,* which is derived from George Orwell, the author of *1984.* In this novel, Orwell exposes the kind of self-contradictory language and arguments totalitarian governments often use to defend themselves.

4. Jerry Falwell (paragraph 7) is the evangelical minister and former head of the Moral Majority who brought suit against *Hustler* magazine.

Vocabulary

abiding (adjective)	Lasting, enduring, persistent.
advocated (verb)	Argued for, supported.
avert (verb)	Turn away.
biopic (noun)	A biography shown in a film or television show, often with fictionalized parts added.
depicted (verb)	Showed.
sanitized (adjective)	Made clean or sanitary.

What's Wrong with This Picture?

Gloria Steinem

Q: YOU ARE someone who cares deeply about . . . animal rights. . . . If 1
Hustler magazine made its reputation . . . publishing pictures of animals strapped to the bumpers of hunters' cars, would you still have wanted to do this role?"

A: "Well, you know, certainly not." 2

The interviewer was Matt Lauer on NBC's *Today* show. The interviewee 3
was Woody Harrelson, star of *The People vs. Larry Flynt*. His answer said it all: if Larry Flynt published a magazine that portrayed animals in pain, bound and in chains, with objects shoved up their genitals, being tortured and even murdered—which is how *Hustler* has portrayed women—this movie would almost certainly never have been made.

And make no mistake, images like these are the specialties of *Hustler,* the 4
biggest mass-distributed hard-core pornographic magazine in the world. It also includes such racist ones as muscular black men with small heads and huge penises having sex with eager or terrified white women; or a man forcing his wife to sit spread-legged while her genitals are invaded by marching cockroaches. There are photo stories like the one in which a handcuffed woman is raped and apparently killed by guards in a concentration camp–like setting.

Of course, Hollywood's glamorized, sanitized biopic shows none of this. 5
As written by Scott Alexander and Larry Karaszewski, produced by Oliver Stone, and directed by Milos Forman, *Hustler* is all about sex and nudity, not violence and humiliation. The movie doesn't deal with *Hustler* features like "Dirty Pool," which, in January 1983, depicted a woman being gang-raped on a pool table. Months later, a woman *was* gang-raped on a pool table in New Bedford, Massachusetts. Flynt's response was to publish a postcard, of another nude woman on a pool table, inscribed "Greetings from New Bedford, Mass., the Portuguese Gang-Rape Capital of America."

I'm sorry to bring you these *Hustler* images, but many of us avert our 6
eyes from the $10 billion-a-year pornography industry, if only to preserve some sense of dignity and safety. That's why this prestigious film, expected at press time to be nominated for more than one Academy Award, has been able to con many moviegoers and media critics into believing that Flynt is a tacky but charming rebel who deserves our gratitude for strengthening free speech.

That last idea hangs on the slender thread of Flynt's legal victory against 7
Jerry Falwell, who sued over a *Hustler* parody in which he "confessed" to having sex with his mother. The Supreme Court, in an easy, unanimous ruling, upheld long-standing case law that allowed public figures to be parodied, if the result can't be taken as fact.

In fact, the Nazis who marched in Skokie, Illinois, and the Klansmen 8
who advocated violence in Ohio achieved more substantive First Amendment victories than did Flynt. Yet no Hollywood movie would have glamorized a

Klan or Nazi publisher as a champion of free speech, much less described him as "the era's last crusader," which is the way Columbia Pictures describes Flynt.

Several people who know Flynt are angered by the long lie of this movie. The sister of Althea Leasure, Flynt's fourth wife, says that rather than being the abiding soul mate depicted in the movie, Leasure tried to escape from Flynt several times, but couldn't because he controlled her finances. His oldest daughter, Tonya, 31, joined picketers at the movie's San Francisco opening. "Freedom of speech wasn't used when he was violating me," she reportedly said, "He just told me this is what little girls do with their fathers." Flynt denies all the charges.

9

Perhaps worst of all, Larry Flynt is presented in the movie as a man who loves women. In reality, Flynt is like a lesser, but more influential version of the serial killer who sees all women as prostitutes deserving death; he seems to see all women as deserving the humiliation and violence he depicts.

10

So we must consider some questions: Would Milos Forman, a refugee from the Nazis, make a movie glorifying an anti-Semitic publisher? He defends himself by pointing out that the Nazis censored pornography, but doesn't seem to remember that they also created pornography of Jewish women as prostitutes, and of Jewish men as rapists of Aryan women to justify violence—much as Flynt does.

11

Why can feminists speak against everything from wars and presidents to tobacco companies, yet if we use our free speech against pornography, we are accused, in Orwellian fashion, of being against free speech?

12

Why do images of violence and bigotry that would be socially condemned, even though legally protected, become off-limits when disguised as sexuality?

13

I think much of the answer lies in the power of the multibillion dollar international pornography industry. We've made progress in explaining that rape is violence, not sex; that sexual harassment is power, not sex; but not in explaining that pornography, from the Greek word *pornoi,* is about female slaves—the women who were considered the lowest of the low among prostitutes—while erotica, from *eros,* is about sexuality and pleasure.

14

Fortunately, each of us has the First Amendment right to protest. We don't have to let hate masquerade as love, violence as sex, or Larry Flynt as a defender of our freedom.

15

Questions for Discussion

1. What is Steinem's purpose? What is her thesis?
2. How does the author anticipate and defend against the charge that she is arguing for limiting freedom of speech?
3. Throughout the essay, Steinem uses induction to support her thesis. Which piece of evidence do you find most convincing? Which do you find least convincing?

4. Does Steinem ever use deduction to advance her argument? Where?

5. Where and to what end does she use rhetorical questions?

6. Does she ever appeal to the reader's emotions? In what way?

7. Why does the author distinguish between various terms in paragraph 14? Why does she bother to define *pornoi*?

8. What is Steinem getting at in paragraph 7?

Thinking Critically

1. Rephrase paragraph 6 using deduction. In other words, create a general statement, a specific case or example, and a conclusion that will accurately reflect the thinking in that paragraph.

2. Explain why Steinem believes the "Nazis who marched in Skokie, Illinois, and the Klansmen . . . achieved more substantive First Amendment victories than did Flynt" (paragraph 8).

3. Read or reread Cal Thomas's "The Band from Hell" in Chapter 7. How do you think Thomas might respond to Steinem's essay? How would Steinem respond to Thomas's?

Suggestions for Journal Entries

1. If possible, rent and view a copy of *The People vs. Larry Flynt*. Then, write a paragraph in which you evaluate the validity of Steinem's comments about the film.

2. Steinem never argues that *Hustler* magazine or *The People vs. Larry Flynt* ought to be censored, cut, or kept from public view. Her essay simply argues against aspects of the magazine, of the film, and of Flynt himself that she finds offensive. Think of a television show, movie, CD, magazine, newspaper, show-business personality, or other product or personality of the entertainment or communications industries that you find offensive. Use clustering, freewriting, or brainstorming to express your ideas and feelings about this subject.

Suggestions for Sustained Writing

1. Write an essay that tries to persuade your readers that working more than 15 hours a week while pursuing a full-time academic career is reasonable. You might explain that working longer hours is necessary if you are to pay your expenses. You might also explain that some full-time students

are so organized or talented that they can handle more than 15 hours of work. If this idea does not interest you, write an open letter to your fellow students trying to persuade them to adopt a particular behavior or attitude concerning an issue important to them. For example, offer advice on time or stress management, persuade them to change their study habits, encourage their participation in community service, or warn them about the dangers of alcohol abuse. If you responded to either of the journal suggestions after Palmieri's essay, look over the notes you made before you begin this assignment.

Another alternative is to write an essay in which you try to persuade your fellow students to devote 100 percent of their time to school and to quit even the least demanding part-time job. Of course, you will have to suggest alternative sources of income—such as scholarships, loans, and other types of financial aid—that students might tap to pay tuition and living expenses.

Like Palmieri, try to support your arguments with the testimony of experts and present your arguments logically. However, remember that this is a persuasive assignment. Use language that will appeal to your fellow students' pride, self-interest, and emotions. Try to rouse them if you can! In addition, however, make sure to raise and to address opposing arguments. If you are using researched materials, credit your sources with internal citations, as Palmieri did, and include a list of works cited. More information on how to do this can be found in the Appendix of this book. It discusses documentation principles used by the Modern Language Association.

2. Look back to the journal notes you made after reading Dr. King's "I Have a Dream." Whether you responded to item 1 or 2 in the Suggestions for Journal Entries, expand your notes into a persuasive address that you might deliver to a large group of people if you had the opportunity.

If you responded to item 1, you might be satisfied by relating the progress the United States has made in the decades since Dr. King spoke at the Lincoln Memorial. In the process, you could take the position that we have done enough in this area, and that further measures will simply be redundant and even counterproductive. Then again, you might argue that not enough has been done, and you could persuade your listeners that we need to take additional steps to assure everyone's civil rights. However you approach this question, try to be as specific and detailed as you can, relying on library or Internet research and/or using information you have acquired through interviews with faculty members on your campus.

If you responded to item 2, write a speech in which you try to persuade your listeners to support measures to solve a serious problem that threatens our people, society, culture, or environment or that affects the people, environment, or society of another part of the world. Again, be as specific and detailed as you can and rely on research.

Make certain to credit the sources of your research by using the conventions recommended by the Modern Language Association. The Appendix at the end of this book explains how to do so.

3. If you responded to Shaheen's "The Media's Image of Arabs" in your journal, you may have begun discussing the way television, radio, movies, magazines, and the like portray a particular group. Express your reaction to this treatment in a preliminary thesis statement for a persuasive essay. Depending on the details you have already gathered, you might write a preliminary thesis like this: "Green-haired carpenters can expect nothing but ridicule from the media."

Now, draft an essay containing three or four detailed illustrations of what you mean. For instance, discuss magazines, movies, television shows and commercials, and billboard advertisements in which green-haired carpenters are ridiculed. End your essay like Shaheen ends his: offer the media advice about how to correct its stereotype of the people you have discussed.

As you rewrite your paper, add details and revise your thesis statement as needed. Edit your best draft for problems in grammar and mechanics.

4. Write a letter to the producers or sponsors of a television show you think unfairly stereotypes people on the basis of age, race, religion, nationality, profession, gender, or sexual preference. Analyze various episodes of the show. Provide details about the characters, plots, dialogue, and issues presented to support your view that the group in question is being treated unfairly.

Then, persuade your readers to make some changes. You can start with the logical approach. For example, explain that many people no longer tolerate unfair stereotyping and that continuing this practice will reduce the show's viewing audience. However, you can also appeal to your readers' sense of fairness and responsibility. Like Shaheen, for example, you might explain that as "imagemakers" they have an important role in molding the character of our society.

As you go through the process of writing, rewriting, and polishing, make sure to provide evidence and use language that will persuade your readers to change their approach. You might find useful materials in the journal entries you made after reading Shaheen's "The Media's Image of Arabs."

5. The second suggestion for journal writing after Steinem's "What's Wrong with This Picture?" asks that you gather information about a product or personality from the entertainment or communications industries to which you take offense. Add to your notes by interviewing others who may or may not share your opinion and by doing some research in your library or via the Internet on your subject.

Now turn your notes into the first draft of a full-length essay that expresses your opinions clearly. Make specific reference to the film, television/radio program, CD, or person you are writing about. Like Steinem, use direct quotations or make clear and specific reference to those aspects of the product or person that you find most offensive. Use logical arguments and evidence to build your case. If your research or interviews revealed opposing arguments, discuss and counter those opinions before or after you state your own.

Finally, don't be afraid to appeal to your readers' emotions. For example, after drafting the body of your paper, write an introduction that uses startling language and information to dramatize your point of view. In your conclusion, you might include vocabulary intended to move your readers to action. In any case, revise and edit your writing carefully. Then, consider submitting it to your college or local newspaper as well as to your instructor.

Writing to Learn: A Group Activity

Freedom of expression, guaranteed by the First Amendment to the U.S. Constitution, is mentioned in Gloria Steinem's "What's Wrong with This Picture?" Although simple on its face, the First Amendment has been the subject of various interpretations and a great deal of debate since it was written. What's your opinion? Should we protect freedom of expression no matter what the circumstances, who is involved, or what the consequences?

The First Meeting

Brainstorm a list of circumstances or situations that might cause you to argue for limiting free speech. The classic example was put forth by Supreme Court Justice Oliver Wendell Holmes. The First Amendment, he argued, does not protect one from falsely shouting "Fire!" in a crowded theater, for doing so would cause panic and endanger lives. More recently, the courts ruled child pornography illegal. However, other restrictions of the freedom of expression are still being debated. Here are some you might use to start brainstorming a list of your own:

Regulating the content of the Internet.

Censoring or rating radio and television shows.

Regulating or rating films, CDs, or other entertainment products.

Enforcing criteria for what is shown, displayed, or performed in public places such as city museums, train stations, public squares, municipal buildings, or public schools.

continued

Setting criteria for what public libraries put on their shelves.

Writing policies or codes governing speech on college campuses.

After you have brainstormed a list of your own issues (include those above if you like), assign each student the task of researching one particular topic. Ask him or her to find information and opinions on both sides of the issue.

RESEARCH

Search the Internet as well as print and online periodical indexes for articles on your topic published in the last five or six years. Bring your notes and photocopies of pages from sources to the next meeting. For general information on the First Amendment, try the American Civil Liberties Union website on the Internet (http://www.aclu.org).

THE SECOND MEETING

Distribute copies of articles students have read and notes they have taken. Make sure each has gathered information on both sides of his or her topic. After the group has read these materials, debate the pros and cons of each question and, if possible, take a group stand or position on it. (Ask each student to take notes on the group's discussion of the question he or she researched.)

Before closing the meeting, ask everyone to write one or two paragraphs explaining both sides of his or her issue and stating the group's position on it. Encourage him or her to incorporate both researched information and the opinions of fellow group members. Finally, remind everyone to bring copies of this work to the next meeting.

THE THIRD MEETING

Distribute, read, and critique each other's writing; offer suggestions for revision. Ask one student to collect the final versions of everyone's work and use them in a draft of a complete paper that takes positions on the free-speech questions members of your group researched. If possible, have a second student write the introduction and the conclusion to this paper.

THE FOURTH MEETING

Distribute and read the draft of the paper. Make last-minute suggestions for revision. Ask a third student to edit the paper and a fourth to type and proofread it.

Writing a Research Paper Using Modern Language Association (MLA) Style

The Modern Language Association (MLA) is a professional organization of teachers and scholars of language and literature. Like many other professional associations, the MLA has created a style sheet for authors who write about subjects in the disciplines it covers. The following pages explain ways to include and cite (identify the sources of) researched material using MLA style in research papers such as the ones you might be assigned in first-year composition classes and in other college courses. You can find out more about MLA style in Joseph Gibaldi's *MLA Handbook for Writers of Research Papers,* 5th ed., 1999.

Identify the Source of All Researched Information

Most college research papers contain some of the student's own ideas and first-hand knowledge. However, research papers also rely on information, ideas, and direct quotations taken from other sources including books, professional journals, newspapers, pamphlets, and online resources, to name only a few examples. All materials taken from a source other than yourself must be identified as such in the body of the paper. This is known as citing, a process by which you (1) identify the source of the words and/or materials you have researched and (2) provide readers with information they can use to locate this source on their own.

Three ways to take information from a source other than yourself is to:

- **Use a direct quotation:** A direct quotation uses the source's exact words and is indicated by quotation marks ("/") except when quotations of more than three lines are used. In such cases, the quotation is double spaced and indented 10 spaces from the left margin.
- **Paraphrase:** When paraphrasing, the writer uses the source's ideas but expresses them in his or her own words.
- **Summarize:** A summary is like a paraphrase, but when summarizing, the writer condenses a large amount of information from the source into a sentence or two. Again, the writer expresses that material in his or her own words.

A common mistake among beginning writers is to think that only direct quotations need citations. This is NOT TRUE. In fact, whether you quote from, paraphrase, or summarize someone else's work, you must include a citation. In other words, you must identify and give credit to the source. Otherwise, you might be committing plagiarism.

AVOID PLAGIARISM

Plagiarism is a form of academic dishonesty, and it is as serious a matter as copying answers from someone else's test paper or having a friend write an essay and submitting it as your own work. Remember that words and ideas taken from a source other than yourself need to be cited and that direct quotations must be indicated by quotation marks.

Of course, plagiarism when writing a research paper can sometimes be done unintentionally. When paraphrasing, for example, you might accidentally incorporate some of your source's original vocabulary or sentence structure into your notes without using quotation marks. When writing your paper, you might just forget to include an internal citation for ideas you have summarized, or you might simply neglect to type quotation marks around the quoted words or sentences. This is no excuse. Whether intentional or unintentional, plagiarism is a serious misuse of someone else's words or ideas because it presents those words and ideas as if they were your own.

It is especially important to remember that when paraphrasing or summarizing, you need to guard against letting a few of the author's exact words or phrases slip into your own writing without quotation marks. You must also try to avoid following the source's exact sentence structure, plugging your own words into a pattern he or she has already established.

In a paraphrase or summary, the words you use and the order that you present them in should be yours alone. The following sample paragraphs illustrate this idea.

ORIGINAL PARAGRAPH FROM H. L. MENCKEN'S ESSAY "THE PENALTY OF DEATH"

Of the arguments against capital punishment that issue from uplifters, two are commonly heard most often . . .

1. *That hanging a man (or frying him or gassing him) is a dreadful business, degrading to those who have to do it and revolting to those who have to witness it.*
2. *That it is useless, for it does not deter others from the same crime.*

> ## PARAPHRASE OF MENCKEN CONTAINING SOME PLAGIARISM
>
> *According to Mencken, there are two arguments most commonly made against capital punishment. One is that it degrades the executioners and revolts those who witness it; the second is that it does not deter others from the identical crime.*

The problem here is that the paraphrase uses some of Mencken's own words and even his sentence/paragraph structure.

> ## ACCEPTABLE PARAPHRASE
>
> *According to Mencken, opponents of the death penalty claim that it debases those who must administer it. They also claim that it is ineffective in lowering the murder rate.*

Note that this *acceptable* paraphrase must now be *cited*.

Identify Sources through Parenthetical Citations

Using MLA style, you identify the source of quoted, paraphrased, or summarized material by using parenthetical (internal) citations. They are called "parenthetical" because they identify the source within parentheses ( ). Ordinarily, the information within parentheses is brief and includes the author's name and the page number of the book, article, or other sources from which the researched material was taken. However, the form of parenthetical citations can vary depending upon the kind of document being cited and the way the material is introduced. The information in an internal citation must be accurate, for it will lead readers to your Works Cited page (this is usually the last page of your paper), which lists each source you have used in alphabetical order according to the author's last name. Each entry in this list contains all the publication information your readers will need to locate the source on their own. Instructions on completing a Works Cited page appear later in this Appendix.

Cite Researched Information in the Body of Your Paper: Using Parenthetical Citations

The way that you cite a source in the body of your paper depends on whether you are paraphrasing/summarizing or quoting directly. It also depends upon the source from which you are taking information. Study the following examples:

Citing Paraphrased or Summarized Material

The most direct way to cite materials you have paraphrased or summarized is to write the author's last name followed by the page number in parentheses directly after the paraphrase or summary. In the following example, a student paraphrases information from a book by the columnist George F. Will:

> Imposing term limits on members of the U.S. Congress would increase the public's respect for our legislators and encourage more ordinary citizens to run for office (Will 7).

The citation above includes the author's last name and the number of the page from which the student took this information.

Introducing a Direct Quotation with the Author's Last Name

A good practice when quoting directly is to introduce the quotation with the author's last name in a phrase such as "Dr. Lee says . . ."; "According to Professor Gonzalez, . . ."; or "Robinson believes that. . . ." The following example uses a direct quotation from an article by Terry Eastland:

> Commenting on the U.S. Constitution, Eastland argues: "The framers designed and empowered the presidency so that it would provide the energy that the government under the Articles of Confederation lacked" (72).

Introducing a Direct Quotation without the Author's Last Name

If you have mentioned a name only a few lines before and want to avoid repetition, you might introduce another direct quotation from that author without mentioning his or her name. In such cases, simply place the author's name in parentheses followed by the page number. For example, take this direct quotation from Marc Breslow's article, which appeared in *Dollars and Sense:*

> The debate on how to overcome poverty in America continues. One economist believes that government spending is the answer: "To the degree that the War on Poverty failed, it was because we spent too little on it, not too much" (Breslow 121).

Combining a Direct Quotation with Your Own Sentence

You can combine a direct quotation with your own sentence by placing quotation marks ("/") in the appropriate places. Make sure that the quotation fits with your words naturally and correctly. Then, indicate the author's last name and the page number in parentheses.

> Anti-gun-control advocates believe that "guns don't increase . . . crime and violence—but the continued proliferation of gun-control laws does" (Polsby 54).

Note: The ellipses (. . .) that come between "increase" and "crime" indicate that the writer of the paper has removed words from the quotation. This practice is appropriate as long as it does not change the meaning or intent of the quotation.

Using a Direct Quotation Longer than Three Lines

MLA format requires that quotations longer than three lines be double spaced and indented 10 spaces from the left margin. Don't place quotation marks around this material (the indentation takes their place) except where the material already contains quotation marks of its own.

> In *On the Make: The Rise of Bill Clinton,* Meredith L. Oakley explains one of the reasons for Clinton's victory in the 1992 presidential election:

> > A fighter, a survivor, a crusader: It was this image, not that of a draft-dodger, womanizer, prevaricator, and opportunist, that was supposed to emerge in the 1992 presidential campaign, and for the most part, it did. The complete portrait of Bill Clinton was never presented to the American public by reporters who covered him; presidential campaigns and the men and women who chronicle them move too superficially and too fast, and ever since the Gary Hart fiasco, all concerned have been content to let the tabloids deal with the seamier side of history. (16–17)

Note: With a long, *indented* quotation, the page numbers in parentheses come *after* the period; for a short quote that is not set off, the citation goes *before* the period.

Including Material for Which No Author Is Named

If no author is named, place the title of the source within parentheses followed by the page number. If the title is long, you can use only the first two or three words, but make sure to provide enough information so that your readers can easily find this source in your Works Cited page. The following quotation was taken from "Finding Deals, Small Businesses Buy More Online," which appeared on page C4 of *The New York Times* on May 15, 2000:

> According to a survey report in *The New York Times*, "small-business owners are going online in droves looking for deals, particularly on computer equipment, office supplies, and travel reservations . . . " ("Finding Deals" C4).

Including a Quotation Found in Another Source

If you are using information that contains a direct quotation from yet another source, use the phrase "qtd. in" for "quoted in" in the parenthetical citation:

> According to Charles de Gaulle, "the graveyards are full of indispensable men" (qtd. in Byrne 35).

Including Information from a Selection in an Anthology

An anthology is a collection of individual works (essays, poems, short stories, etc.) selected and arranged by an editor. Cite information from individual works by using the name of the selection's author, not the name of the anthology's editor.

> In "Unfair Game," Susan Jacoby defines the "code of feminine politeness," which she says "is no help in dealing with the unwanted approaches of strange men" (303).

Taking Information from Two or More Works by the Same Author

If you are using two or more works by the same author, introduce the material by including the author's name in the text of your paper. Then, write the name of the work (in an abbreviated form, if necessary) in the internal citation along with the page number:

> Jonathan Kozol claims that the cause of homelessness in the United States is not the "deinstitutionalization" of mental patients but the lack of affordable housing for the poor ("Distancing the Homeless" 1).
>
> In his study of homelessness in America, Kozol claims that "early death or stunted cognitive development" as well as "severe

emotional damage" are common in homeless children in the United States (*Rachel and Her Children* 83).

Using Material from the Bible

Indicate the book, chapter, and verse(s) when referencing the bible. You can do this in the body of the text or in a parenthetical citation. In the following example, the book, Proverbs, is mentioned in the text; chapter (18) and verse (24) are mentioned in the parenthetical citation.

> Proverbs shows us two sides of friendship: "Some friends bring ruin upon us, but a true friend is more loyal than a brother" (18: 24).

Using Material from a Corporate Author

If authorship is claimed by an organization, use the name of the organization to introduce the information or include the name in parenthetical citation:

> President Herbert Hoover personally supervised the removal of important government documents from the Oval Office during a fire on Christmas Eve 1929 (White House Historical Association 147).

Including Ideas from an Entire Work

To include ideas from an entire work, just indicate the author's name in the text or parenthetical citation. Obviously, no page number can be given. Take this example that references Pete Hamill's autobiography, *A Drinking Life.*

> Although the book depicts the life of a popular American journalist, *A Drinking Life* also chronicles many of the events, trends, and philosophies that helped shape New York City in the 1930s, 40s, 50s, and 60s (Hamill).

Including Information from a Work That Is Not Paginated

You need not worry about including page numbers if the work you are citing is not paginated. Instead, simply use paragraph numbers:

> Tortorice's explanation of the formation of the aquifer accounts for several properties attributed to the region's groundwater (paras. 4–7).

Using Material from Two Different Authors with the Same Last Name

Make sure to indicate each author's first name when you include information from his or her work:

"The endless struggle between the flesh and the spirit found an
end in Greek art" (Edith Hamilton 65).

Including Information from Two Works in the Same Sentence

Use a semicolon to separate that author and page number(s) of each work in
the parenthetical citation.

A few important differences marked the religious practices of the
Greeks and the Romans even though the gods they worshipped
were essentially the same (Romero 52; Christiansen 184).

Including Material from a Source Whose Author Is Unknown

If the author's name is not available, use the title of the work to introduce the
information or include it in the internal citation. If you choose the latter, you
may abbreviate the title.

The National Woman's Conference held in Houston, Texas, in
1977, produced a "25-point, revised national Plan of Action,"
which was to set the agenda from the Woman's Rights Movement
for the next decade (*70 Years in Review*).

Incorporating Material from a Work in More than One Volume

If you take information from one volume in a multivolume work, indicate the
volume number in the parenthetical citation. Separate the volume and page
numbers with a colon.

In *The Encyclopedia of Philosophy,* Arthur Wooldruff explains that
the British chemist and physicist Michael Faraday (1791–1867)
became interested in science while he was apprenticed to a
bookbinder (3: 18).

Prepare a Works-Cited Page

As you learned above, a Works-Cited page is a list of sources from which you
took information and which are cited (identified) in your paper. Arranged al-
phabetically (by author's last name, in most cases), each item in this list contains all of the publication data readers of your paper will need to locate the
source mentioned.

Typically, a works-cited page is the last thing a research-paper writer
completes, and it appears at the very end of the paper. However, before you
begin even to take notes from a particular book, article, or other source, be
certain to record all pertinent publication information about that source. You
can do this on a index card (3″ × 5″ should be large enough), one source per
card. Sometimes called "bibliography cards," they will come in handy when it
comes time to compile your list of works cited. For a book, the information

on such a card would contain the author's or authors' full names, the full title of the book, the place and date of publication, and the name of the publisher. For a magazine article, it would include the author's name, the title of the article, the title of the magazine, the date of publication, and the number(s) of the page(s) upon which the article appeared. Here is an example of a bibliography card for a magazine article:

Zinmeister, Karl.	*Name of author*
"Divorce's Toll on Children."	*Title of article*
<u>Current</u>	*Title of magazine in which article appears*
February 1997	*Date of publication*
Pages 29–33	*Pages on which article appears*

The Modern Language Association uses various formats for items in a Works-Cited page depending upon the type of source being referenced. Below is a comprehensive list of such formats for the kinds of sources you might use. However, the overall organization of a Works-Cited page follows three principles:

1. Items appear in alphabetical order according to the author's last name or according to the first major word in the title if no author is indicated (short newspaper articles often do not carry the author's name). Items by more than one author are alphabetized according to the author whose name appears first.
2. Items are double spaced, and are separated from each other by two lines.
3. Each item begins at the left margin. If more than one line is needed to complete the entry, subsequent lines are indented five spaces.

Sample Entries for a Works-Cited Page—Print Sources

A Book by a Single Author

MacLean, Harry. *In Broad Daylight.* New York: Harper & Row, 1988.

What This Entry Contains	
MacLean, Harry.	*Name of author, last name first, followed by a period*
<u>In Broad Daylight</u>.	*Title of book, underlined or in italics, followed by a period*
New York:	*Place of Publication, followed by a colon*
Harper & Row,	*Publisher, followed by a comma*
1988.	*Date of publication, followed by a period*

A Book with a Subtitle

A subtitle follows the main title and a colon (:).

> Westervelt, Saundra D. *Shifting the Blame: How Victimization Became a Criminal Defense.* New Brunswick, NJ: Rutgers UP, 1998.

Note: Except when the source has been published in a major U.S. or world city such as Atlanta, Berlin, Boston, Chicago, Dallas, London, Los Angeles, Miami, Montreal, New York, Toronto, Washington, DC, and so on, you should indicate the state, province, or country in which the city is located. In the item above, "NJ" indicates that New Brunswick is in New Jersey. The "UP" stands for "University Press."

A Book by Two Authors

Type the first author's name, last name first, followed by a comma and the word "and." Then type the second author's name, first name first. In the next example, the authors are Gilbert Geis and Leigh B. Bienen.

> Geis, Gilbert, and Leigh B. Bienen. *Crimes of the Century: From Leopold and Loeb to O. J. Simpson.* Boston: Northeastern UP, 1998.

A Book by Three Authors

Type the first author's name, last name first, followed by a comma. Then type the second author's name, first name first, followed by a comma and the word "and." Then type the third author's name, first name first, followed by a period. In the next example, the authors are Mark Umbreit, Robert B. Coates, and Boris Kalanj.

> Umbreit, Mark, Robert B. Coates, and Boris Kalanj. *Victim Meets Offender: The Impact of Restorative Justice and Mediation."* Monsey, NY: Criminal Justice P, 1994.

A Book by More than Three Authors

Type the name of the first author, last name first, followed by "et al." This is the abbreviation for "et alia," a Latin phrase meaning "and others."

> Malikin, David, et al. *Social Disability: Alcoholism, Drug Addiction, Crime, and Social Disadvantage.* New York: New York UP, 1973.

Two or More Works by the Same Author

List works in alphabetical order according to the first major word in their titles. Type the author's name, last name first, in the first entry. Type three hyphens (---) in place of the author's name in subsequent entries.

> Kelleher, Michael. *Murder Most Rare: The Female Serial Killer.* Westport, CT: Praeger, 1998.
>
> ———. *New Arenas for Violence: Homicide in the American Workplace.* Westport, CT: Praeger, 1996.

A Book in a Series

Type the series name and the series number, if any, between the editor's name, which follows the title, and the publication information. Do not underline or italicize the name of the series.

> Dickens, Charles. *Great Expectations.* Ed. Janise Carlisle. Case Studies in Contemporary Criticism. Ser. 4. Boston: Bedford/St. Martin's, 1996.

A Book in More than One Volume

Treat such a work as you would any other book, but indicate the number of volumes the book contains immediately after the title.

> Norwich, John Julius. *The Normans in Sicily.* 2 vols. London: Penguin, 1970.

Note: If you are taking information from only one of the volumes, type the number of that volume. Then, type the total number of volumes at the end of the entry.

> Norwich, John Julius. *The Normans in Sicily.* Vol 1. London: Penguin, 1970. 2 vols.

The Bible

Ordinarily, the Bible does not appear in a Works Cited page, but you might want to indicate a specific version of the Bible in the internal citation.

An Editor of a Book

If you are using information from a book's editor (anthologies and collections are normally put together by editors, who introduce and comment on the selections), use the abbreviations "ed." or "eds." as in the following example:

> Curtis, Lynn A., ed. *Policies to Prevent Crime: Neighborhood, Family, and Employment Strategies.* Newbury Park, CA: Sage, 1987.

An Edited Book

If you are using information from the author of a book that has been edited, indicate the author's name first, followed by the title, followed by the name of the editor or editors preceded by the abbreviation "Ed." or "Eds."

> Twain, Mark. *A Connecticut Yankee in King Arthur's Court.* Ed. Allison E. Ensor. New York: Norton, 1982.

A Later Edition

If you are referencing a work that has been republished in a later edition or editions, indicate the number of the edition you are using.

> Gibaldi, Joseph. *MLA Handbook for Writers of Research Papers.* 5th ed. New York: Modern Language Association, 1999.

A Foreword, Introduction, or Afterword of a Book

Forewords, introductions, and afterwords to a book are often written by someone other than the book's author. If you are using information from such a section in a book, start with the name of the author of the foreword, introduction, or afterword. Then type the word "Foreword," "Introduction," or "Afterword" followed by the title of the book. Continue by typing the name of the book's author (first name first). Finally, indicate place of publication, publisher, and date of publication.

> Smith, Elmer W. Foreword. *Social Disability: Alcoholism, Drug Addiction, Crime, and Social Disadvantage.* By David Malkin, et. al. New York: New York UP, 1973.

A Translation

> Dostoyevsky, Fyodor. *Crime and Punishment.* Trans. Sidney Monas. New York: New American Library, 1980.

A Work by an Association, Organization, or Corporation

Type the name of the organization or corporation first, followed by a period. Then type the title of the work. Then, type the name of the publisher, even if the publisher and the author are the same.

> White House Historical Association. *The White House: An Historic Guide.* Washington, DC: White House Historical Association, 1982.

A Work by an Unknown Author

Begin the entry with the title of the work.

> *A History of Crime in Bucks County.* Philadelphia: Cyclops, 1957.

A Signed Article in a Magazine

> Mackenzie, Dana. "The Shape of Madness." *Discover.* Jan. 2000: 79–83.

What This Entry Contains

Mackenzie, Dana.	*Name of author, last name first, followed by a period*
"The Shape of Madness."	*Title of the article in quotation marks, followed by a period*
Discover.	*Title of Magazine underlined or in italics, followed by a period*
Jan. 2000:	*Date of publication (Discover is a monthly magazine), followed by a colon*
79–83.	*Pages in magazine on which article appears, followed by a period*

An Unsigned Article in a Magazine

Begin with the title of the article in quotation marks.

"United States: Defining Hate." *Economist.* 10 April 1999: 27.

A Signed Article in a Scholarly Journal with Continuous Pagination within a Volume

Libraries often bind monthly, bimonthly, or quarterly issues of journals together in yearly or half-yearly volumes. Some scholarly journals, such as the one in the following example, use continuous pagination through a volume. The number 42 in the example below is the volume number. The article appears on pages 215–227 of that volume.

Umbreit, Mark S. "Victim-Offender Mediation in Canada: The Impact of an Emerging Work Intervention." *International Social Work.* 42 (1999): 215–227.

A Signed Article in a Scholarly Journal with Separate Pagination for Each Issue within a Volume

Some scholarly journals paginate each issue of a volume separately. For example, if issue 1 of volume 23 runs from page 1 through page 129, issue 2 of volume 23 starts with page 1, not with page 130. Therefore, it is important to include the issue number as well as the volume number when listing such journals.

Eden, Kathy. "Great Books in the Undergraduate Curriculum." *Academic Questions.* 13: 2 (2000): 63–69.

Note: This article appears in volume 13 of issue number 2 of the journal *Academic Questions.*

An Article in a Weekly or Biweekly Magazine

Use the same format that you use for a monthly magazine, but indicate the day as well as the month and year of publication.

Gladreeper, Robert. "Siren Song." *New Republic.* 19 April 1999: 8–10.

A Signed Article by Multiple Authors in a Scholarly Journal

Type the name of the first author last name first, followed by a comma. Type the names of subsequent authors first name first.

Belknop, Joanne, Bonnie S. Fisher, and Francis T. Cullen. "The Development of a Comprehensive Measure of the Sexual Victimization of College Women." *Violence Against Women* 5 (1999): 185–214.

An Unsigned Article in a Scholarly Journal

"Victims." *Columbia Journalism Review* 37 (1999): 12–13.

An Article in an Edited Collection

Hattemar, Barbara. "Cause and Violent Effect: Media and Our Youth." *Our Times: Readings from Recent Periodicals.* Ed. Robert Atwan. Boston: Bedford, 1995: 241–249.

A Signed Newspaper Article

Purdy, Matthew. "Extending a Hand, Not Cuffs." *New York Times* 2 Feb. 2000: A5.

An Unsigned Newspaper Article

"Mexican Drug Cartel May Be Linked to 3 US Dead." *The Los Angeles Times* 12 May 2000: 5.

An Editorial in a Newspaper

Since editorials are normally unsigned, you can use the same format as you would for an unsigned article except that you must type the word "Editorial" immediately after the title.

"The Gun Windmills." Editorial. *The Wall Street Journal* 13 Dec. 1999: A34.

A Letter to the Editor

Miller, Thomas V. Letter. *The Washington Post* 20 Oct. 1999: M04.

A Book Review

Preston, William J. "The Politics of Hysteria." Rev. of *Many Are the Crimes: McCarthyism in America,* by Ellen Schrecker. *The Los Angeles Times* 31 May 1998: Book Reviews 6.

An Entry from a Reference Book

"Crime." *the Encyclopedia Britannica: Micropedia.* 15th ed. 1991.

Motion Picture or Video Cassette

Victory at Sea: Full Fathom Five: Videocassette. Video Treasures, Inc., 1986. 20 min.

A Personal or Telephone Interview

Cornell, Matthew. Personal Interview. 9 June 1998.

Sample Entries for a Works-Cited Page—Electronic Sources

An Article from an Online Magazine

Cullen, David. "Overruled." *Salon* 28 Oct. 1999. 3pp. 3 May 2000 <http://www.salon.com/news/feature/1999/10/28/laramie/index.html>.

What This Entry Contains

Cullen, David. ----------------------*Author's name, last name first, followed by a period*

"Overruled." -----------------------*Title of the article in quotation marks, followed by a period*

Salon ------------------------------*Title of magazine, underlined or in italics*

10 Oct. 1999. ---------------------*Date of publication, followed by a period*

3pp.----------------------------------*Number of pages, paragraphs, or other numbered sections if indicated*

3 May 2000-----------------------*Date you accessed the article*
<http://www.salon.com/news/
feature/1999/10/28/laramie/
index.html>.-----------------------*URL in angle brackets with period at the end*

Note: If some of the needed information is not available, follow the advice of the Modern Language Association: include what is readily accessible. Just make sure that your readers will be able to find the article you are citing.

Article from an Online Professional Journal

Iribarren, Carlos MD, et. al. "Association of Hostility with Coronary Artery Calcification in Young Adults." *Journal of the American Medical Association* 283. 19 (May 17, 2000). 7 pp. 25 May 2000 <http://jama.ama-assn.org/issues/v283n19/full//joc91868.html>.

Note: Include the date of publication (May 17, 2000) as well as the date you accessed the article (25 May 2000).

Article from an Online Newspaper or News Service

Babinek, Mark. "Railroad Killer Gets Death Penalty." *San Francisco Examiner* 22 May 2000: 3pp. 27 May 2000 <http://examiner.com/ap_a/AP_Railroad_Killer.html>.

Article from an Online Database

Brown, Thea, et al. "Problems and Solutions in the Management of Child Abuse Allegations." *Family & Reconciliation Courts Review* Oct. 1998: 36. Online. EBSCOhost, item 1121380. 18 Dec. 1998.

Note: This entry lists an article first published in print but accessed online. Such sources should be treated as if they were accessed from print, except that you must:

1. Add a reference to the publication medium, "Online," near the end of the entry.
2. Include the name of the online database and/or computer service (EBSCOhost, for example) from which the article was accessed along with any identification or item numbers provided.
3. Include the electronic publication date (18 Dec. 1998).

Article from a Portable Database

> Halloway, Marguerite. "On the Trail of Wild Elephants." *Scientific American.* December 1994: 48–50. *Expanded Academic ASAP.* CD-ROM. New York: Information Access Company. April 2, 1995.

Book on the WWW

> Hardy, Thomas. *Jude the Obscure.* London 1895. *Project Gutenberg.* Ed John Hamm. Aug 1997. 28 May 2000 <http://promo.net/pg/history.htm>.

Note: This book was originally published in 1895. The date of its electronic publication is August 1997. The electronic producer of the text is Project Gutenberg, a public database of books on the WWW.

CD-ROM in a Single Edition

> "Criminology." *Encyclopedia Britannica.* CD-ROM. London: Encyclopedia Britannica, Inc., 1998.

CD-ROM Issued Periodically

CD-ROM databases are updated periodically. Treat articles in such databases the same way you would printed versions. However, add the name of the database ("SIRS Government Reporter," for example), the medium (CD-ROM), and the company that maintains the database ("SIRS, Inc."). End with the date that the article was published electronically, followed by a period.

> Gilreath, James. "History of a Book: Madison Council Told of First Book Printed in America." *Library of Congress Information Bulletin* 1 May 1995: 200–202. SIRS Government Reporter. CD-ROM, SIRS, Inc. Fall 1998.

Poem on the WWW

> Frost, Robert. "Birches." *Mountain Interval.* New York, 1921. *Representative Poetry Online.* Ed. Ian Lancashire. 1997. U of Toronto. 26 June 1998 <http//www.library.utoronto.ca/ utel/rp/poems/frost6.html>.

Posting on a Forum

> Harrington, J. K. "Publishing." Online posting. 19 May 2000. The
> Writing Life: Inkspot Writers' Community Forums. 25 May
> 2000 <http://writers-bbs.com/inkspot/threads.cgi?action=
> almsgs&forum=writing life>.

Note: Forums are open to people who may or may not be experts in their fields. As with all researched information, make sure of the appropriateness and validity of the source.

Professional Site on the WWW

> *ERIC Clearinghouse on Urban Education Page.* 12 Dec. 1998.
> Columbia U. <http//.eric-web.tc.columbia.edu/home_files/
> eric_cue_desc.html>.

Note: Additional information on creating entries for electronic sources using MLA style can be found at the following Web address: http://www.mla.org/main_stl.html (Modern Language Association website)

EVALUATE THE USEFULNESS OF INTERNET SOURCES

Like all other materials you use, those found on the Internet need to be evaluated for accuracy and timeliness. The Internet is a wonderful tool, which allows everyone to publish his or her ideas and opinions on a system that reaches hundreds of millions of people. Be aware, however, that not everyone who publishes on the Internet is an expert on the topic he or she discusses. For example, in searching for information on Sir Thomas More, you might come upon a piece by Richard Marius, the noted Harvard biographer of this sixteenth-century lawyer. Then again, you might find a research paper on More written by a high-school senior. Which one would be more authoritative?

Also be aware that many people who publish electronically, like those who publish on paper, may not have an unbiased view on an issue, may have done faulty research, or may simply be inaccurate. Here are some questions you might ask to help you evaluate Internet sources:

1. Who is the author and what are his or her credentials? Can you tell if this person has worked in the field about which he or she is writing? Is he or she connected with a university, prominent think tank, government agency, professional journal?

2. Who is the website sponsor? Is it an educational institution, arm of government, business, or professional organization. Or is this just a personal website?

continued

3. Are the website author and sponsor unbiased? For example, you could have confidence in the impartiality of an article on the effects of chewing tobacco appearing in the website of the *New England Journal of Medicine.* Could you put as much confidence in an article on the same subject appearing on a website sponsored by the Down Home Tobacco Growers' Association?

4. Is there any overt bias in the material you have read? Does the author make claims that are unsubstantiated or unconvincing? Does the author contradict him- or herself?

5. Has the author provided a list of sources from which he or she has taken information? Are these sources reputable and unbiased? Are there hyperlinks to other sites? Do you find that materials in those sites seem reasonable, unbiased, and accurate? Who are the authors and sponsors of those sites?

6. Can you tell if the site is updated regularly? Is the data the author relies on current? Are links to other pages and sites current?

7. Is the material well written, or are there grammatical and spelling errors. Does the author rely heavily on flashy graphics rather than on hard data and convincing prose?

8. Was the document published in a print version as well as on the Web? If not, could it have been?

Other Sources

Government Publication

Ordinarily, the government (whether federal, state, or municipal) is considered the author of such works. After typing the name of the government, type the name of the specific agency that published the work.

> United States. Bureau of the Census. *Historical Statistics of the United States: Colonial Times to 1970.* Bicentennial ed. Washington: GPO, 1975.
>
> New Jersey. Division of Youth and Family Services. *Children at Risk 1995–96.* Trenton: NJ Division of Youth and Family Services, 1998.

Pamphlet

As with a book, begin the entry with the author's name if known. If the author is unknown, treat the pamphlet as a book whose author is unknown.

> Webrogan, Signe I. *Projections of the Population of States by Age, Sex, and Race: 1989–2010.* Washington: GPO, 1990.

Published Dissertation

Treat a published doctoral dissertation as a book. However, add the abbreviation "Diss." after the title as well as the name of the university that granted the doctorate and the year the dissertation was completed. End with the publication information as usual.

> Edwards, Flora Mancuso. *The Theater of the Black Diaspora: A Comparative Study of Black Drama in Brazil, Cuba, and the United States.* Diss. New York University, 1975. Ann Arbor: Xerox University Microfilms, 1987.

Unpublished Dissertation

Begin with the author's name, followed by the title of the dissertation in quotation marks. Then type the abbreviation "Diss." as well as the name of the university that granted the doctorate and the year that the dissertation was completed.

> Dann, Emily. "An Experimental Pre-Statistics Curriculum for Two-Year College Students." Diss. Rutgers University, 1976.

Abstract of a Dissertation

Begin with the author's name, followed by the title of the dissertation in quotation marks. Then, type the abbreviation "Diss." and the name of the university at which the dissertation was written, followed by the date of its completion. End with the abbreviation *DA* or *DAI* (*Dissertation Abstracts* or *Dissertation Abstracts International*), followed by the volume, year of publication, and page number.

> Szabo, Lydia. "America in the Making: History and the Hybrid Poetics of Emily Dickinson, Gertrude Stein, and William Carlos Williams." Diss. Duquesne University, 1997. *DAI* 5912A (1998): 4430.

Published Interview

Begin with the name of the person interviewed. Follow with the title of the interview, if any, in quotation marks. If the title of the interview does not include the word "interview" or if the interview has no title, simply type "Interview" after the subject's name.

> Johnson, Paul. "Live with TAE: Interview with Paul Johnson." *The American Enterprise.* Sept./Oct. 1998: 20–23.

Musical Composition

Begin with the composer's name, followed by the title of the work. Underline or italicize the titles of operas, ballets, and works that have a name, as in the first of the following; note that there are no italics for the second:

> van Beethoven, Ludwig. *Eroica.*
>
> Mendelssohn, Felix. Piano Concerto no. 1 in G. op. 25.

Personal Letter

Begin with the writer's name, followed by "Letter to the author" and the date.

> Cornell, Matthew Robert. Letter to the author. 9 June 1998.

Lecture or Address

Begin with the speaker's name, followed by the title of the presentation in quotation marks and the name of the sponsoring organization. End with the place and date of the presentation.

> Partopillo, Alessandro. "Giotto and the Dawn of the Italian
> Renaissance." Art League of Madison. Eagle Hotel, Madison,
> OR. 8 May 1999.

Live Performance of a Play

Begin with the title of the play, underlined or in italics, followed by the name of its author. Next, indicate the names of the director and the principal actors. End with the name of the theater, its location, and the date of the performance you saw.

> *The Iceman Cometh.* By Eugene O'Neill. Dir. Howard Davies. Perf.
> Kevin Spacey and Tony Danza. Brooks Atkinson Theater,
> New York. 22 June 1999.

Map or Chart

Treat such a document as you would a book by an unknown author. Begin with the title underlined or italicized, followed by the word "Map" or "Chart." Then include publication data.

> *Rocky Mountain National Park, Colorado.* Map. Washington DC:
> GPO, 1996.

Radio or Television Interview

Begin with the name of the person interviewed followed by the word "Interview." Then include the title of the program underlined or italicized. End with the name of the network and city, and the date the program was aired.

> Bush, George W. *Hardball.* Interview. CNBC: New York. 29 June
> 1999.

Radio or Television Program

If you are drawing information from a titled episode of a program, begin with the title of that episode in quotation marks. If not, begin with the name of the program underlined or italicized. Then, indicate the name of the host, narrator, or director, if available. Next, type the name of the network, the city, and the date of the broadcast.

> "The Great Chain." *The American Revolution.* Host William
> Curtis. The History Channel. New York. 3 July 1999.

Sound Recording

Begin with the name of the composer or speaker, followed by the title of the work. Then, include the name of the conductor, orchestra, chorus, and leading performers. Conclude by naming the manufacturer of the recording and the date of its publication.

> Puccini, Giacomo. *La Boheme.* Perf. Luciano Pavarotti, Mirella
> Freni, Elizabeth Hardwood, and Gianni Maffeo. Opera of
> Berlin Chor. and Berlin Phil. Orch. Cond. Herbert von
> Karajan: London, 1972.

Work of Art

Begin with the artist's name, if known, followed by the title of the work, underlined or italicized. Next, type the name of the institution and the city in which the work is housed.

> Hopper, Edward. *Nighthawks.* Art Institute. Chicago.

A Student Research Paper

Victims of Violent Crime: Equal Treatment under the Law

by Angela Brandli

A former community college student, Angela Brandli is majoring in public health at Rutgers University. When asked to choose a topic for a freshman composition research paper, Brandli picked something with which she was intimately familiar. Having been a victim of a violent crime that left her severely injured. Brandli decided to research and argue for victims' rights.

This project eventually led Brandli to petition the New Jersey State Legislature to establish a Catastrophic Injury Fund granting $25,000 to victims severely injured as a result of violent crime in order to help with the cost of rehabilitation. In fact, she even drafted a version of a bill that was passed by the New Jersey Senate and the Assembly and signed into law by Governor Christine Whitman on July 15, 1999.

Her research paper illustrates the best of what academic research papers should be: a natural blending of the author's own knowledge and insights with those taken from authorities on the subject through careful and accurate research. Brandli's works-cited page shows that she conducted research both in the library and online. She also gained a great deal of information through a personal interview with an expert in the field.

VICTIMS OF VIOLENT CRIME: EQUAL TREATMENT UNDER THE LAW

Angela Brandli

Victims of violent crime are a growing minority in the United States. However, despite significant progress made by the Victims' Rights Movement, little assistance is available for the rehabilitation of violent-crime victims. In   5
fact, while more and more rights seem to be extended to violent criminals, the rights of law-abiding citizens victimized by these individuals have received little real attention from the government.   10

The Bill of Rights was added to the U.S. Constitution to secure certain individual rights and to protect the citizenry from injustices committed by government. Relying on the ideas of Beccaria and other philosophers of the   15
Enlightenment, the framers of the Constitution desired to protect the rights of the accused prior to conviction. For example, the Fourth Amendment guarantees that no citizen shall be liable to search, seizure of goods, or arrest   20
without probable cause. The Fifth Amendment

---

ll. 4–5: Brandli prepares us for her thesis statement, which appears at the end of the second paragraph, lines 30–35.

ll. 11–32: Brandli quotes from and references various Amendments to the United States Constitution. No internal citations are needed here. Moreover, the Constitution and its Amendments need not be mentioned in the works-cited page, for only one official version of these documents exists.

ensures that "no person . . . shall be deprived
of life, liberty, or property without due
process of law . . . ," and the Sixth Amendment
guarantees the accused "speedy and public trial   25
by an impartial jury . . . ." Moreover, should
the accused be found guilty, the Eighth
Amendment demands that the punishment adminis-
tered be fair and humane. *At the same time, how-*
ever, the Fourteenth Amendment certifies that no   30
state can deny any person equal protection under
the law, thereby supporting the notion that the
government owes victims of violent crime as much
as, if not more than, it provides the perpetra-
tors of such crime.   35

    Nonetheless, over the last decades, extending
equal protection under the law seems to have
done more to provide loopholes for the guilty
than to protect the innocent. We have allowed
rights once designed to protect us from a tyran-   40
nical justice system to become sources by which
law-abiding citizens can be victimized. Although
perpetrators of violent crimes violate and even
kill members of the community, it is that same
community that must bear the expense of provid-   45
ing for their personal needs and must often assume many of their familial responsibilities
after incarceration. Our prisons are full of

---

ll. 30–35: The writer states her thesis.

criminals demanding that they be treated in ac-
cordance with the rights afforded free citizens,   50
and too many politicians and bureaucrats oblige
them. Yes, they are entitled to humane treatment, but by virtue of their crimes they have
forfeited their claim to civil rights afforded
those who obey the law (Long 29).   55

　　According to constitutional scholar Gary
McDowell, confusion over the origins of the
rights of the accused have, ironically, caused
the courts—the protectors of everyone's rights—
to weaken the Constitution's role in protecting   60
the civil liberties of the law-abiding (262).
Indeed, prisoners are often provided with unnecessary services and comforts that taxpayers,
working long and hard, can sometimes ill-afford
to provide themselves. But the greatest irony is   65
that victims and/or their families actually help
fund these expenses involuntarily through taxes,
while little is done to compensate these people
for their suffering.

　　Family advocates argue that the family of a   70
criminal should not have to suffer for his or

---

l. 55: Brandli uses an internal citation to reveal the source (Long) of summarized material found in this paragraph. This information comes from page 29 of Long's book, whose title and publication information appear on Brandli's works-cited page.

l. 56: Brandli introduces a paraphrase of information from an article (found on her works-cited page) by constitutional scholar Gary McDowell by using his name. On line 61, she indicates the page number (262) of the article from which the information was taken. She does not need to repeat the source's name, for it was mentioned only five lines above.

ll. 62–69: Brandli adds her own ideas to those she has researched.

her wrongdoing, that spouses and children of
criminals are victims too. This argument has
merit, but it has been taken to an extreme. Some
states provide assistance to a criminal's family   75
if the offender's incarceration results in financial hardship--this is in addition to funding
programs to assist indigent families with de-
pendent children. In essence, then, they give
preferential treatment to the families of the   80
incarcerated. Yet this assistance is not available to the family of the criminal's victim--
even in murder cases. If a criminal's children
should not be made to suffer for his or her
crime, should this suffering be then visited   85
upon the victim's children? In many cases, the
victim's family is even more affected than the
criminal's family, yet only the latter is entitled to government assistance. Clearly, granting
aid to some victims while ignoring others is   90
discriminatory and violates the right to fair
and equal treatment under the law.

    The U.S. crime victims' movement began in the
1960s. California was the first state to set up
a victims' compensation program in 1965, but it   95

---

ll. 70–81: The writer drew these insights from her reading of several different written sources
and from studying several state laws. Thus, this information may be considered common
knowledge and does not require a citation.

ll. 93–102: The information in these lines comes from "Crime Victims' Rights," a journal article
for which no author is indicated. Therefore the source is cited by title.

wasn't until the early 1970s that victims' rights groups, led by feminists and rape victims, made their appearance. It took an additional ten years for victims' rights reform to reach the federal level. Finally, Congress passed the 1984 Victims of Crime Act ("Crime Victims' Rights" 634). This law established the Crime Victims' Fund to provide grants to the states for their victims' compensation funds. Financed through fines paid by federal criminals, the fund can be accessed only at the state level. Monies from the fund can be applied to a wide range of expenses incurred as a direct result of crime but only if insurance and other recovery sources are unavailable (United States Office for Victims of Crime). What's more, the amount of compensation a victim of violent crime can receive varies from state to state. Nine states offer more than $25,000; twenty-one states offer a maximum of $25,000; and twenty states provide up to $10,000. The only thing that all the funds clearly have in common is that they limit the amount of assistance a victim can access ("Crime Victims' Rights" 637).

l. 111: The information in the previous two lines is taken from a pamphlet called the *Office for Victims of Crime Fact Sheet.* The author is a government agency, the U.S. Office for Victims of Crime, and the publisher is the Department of Justice.

l. 119: The source for this information is "Crime Victims' Rights," the same article cited earlier in this paragraph. Since additional information from another source has intervened, however, a second citation for "Crime Victims' Rights" with the appropriate page number is necessary.

The establishment of a federal Crime Victims'   120
Fund has been viewed by many politicians as well
as the general public as a victory for crime
victims. But the program emerged ostensibly to
satisfy the needs of victims before the scope of
their needs was even determined (Elias 349).   125
This might be a victory for politicians but not
for victims!

Some states are making progress in aiding
crime victims. In Wisconsin, for example, a
Victim's Crime Amendment was added to the state   130
constitution, providing several services to
crime victims. The website of the Wisconsin
Victim Resource Center lists the following:

- Telephone counseling.
- Information and referrals for crime   135
  victims who are experiencing problems.
- Problem-solving assistance relative
  to victimization.
- Victim/witness assistance services in
  matters the Attorney General's Office   140
  is prosecuting and when no other
  services are available.

---

ll. 120–125: Brandli paraphrases from page 349 of an essay by Robert Elias, which is listed in the works-cited page.

ll. 134–151: This information comes from page 1 of the website of the Wisconsin Office of Crime Victim Services. Notice that the list of services, which is a direct quotation and which is longer than three lines, is indented 10 spaces from the left margin and is double spaced. The source has been named in the text of Brandli's paragraph and the page number of the website follows the quoted list. Brandli includes this information to show that some progress on victims' rights is being made. In this way, she attempts to give opponents to her argument a fair hearing. At the same time, she uses this information both to argue that what is being done is still not enough and to show that she has researched the question thoroughly, thereby making her argument even more convincing.

- Resource person to district attorneys in counties with no victim/witness program.
- Informational materials on topics such as sexual assault, child sexual abuse and victims' rights in Wisconsin.
- An advocate for victims in exercising their state constitutional rights.
- Crime victim compensation assistance.
- Victim Appellate Notification Services.(1)

Nonetheless, as reported by Renee Lane of the New Jersey Violent Crime Compensation Board, financial compensation to victims and their families remains limited. The NJ Criminal Injuries Act (1971) addresses the rights and services of victims and witnesses, and it provides protection and reimbursement to witnesses incurring expenses while testifying at trials or otherwise cooperating with the courts. There are no stated limits to reimbursement pertaining to witnesses, but violent crime compensations are limited to $25,000. Surviving victims and members of murder victims' families are eligible to apply to the Violent Crimes Compensation (VCC) Board, which handles claims. On the other hand, family members of surviving victims are not eligible to

---

l. 152: Brandli introduces information she took from a personal interview by indicating her source. Since interviews obviously have no pages, no internal citation of a page number is needed here.

apply even if the crime results in financial
hardship to the victim's spouse and/or children.

Awards are made with the understanding that   170
if the claimant is successful in recovering
money from any other source, he or she must
notify the Board to arrange for reimbursement.
On the other hand, none of the money granted
for the assailant's defense, care, and rehabili-   175
tation has to be repaid, even if his or her
circumstances later change. Tax dollars that
support criminals are spent and forgotten
(Lane).

Furthermore, no programs exist to pay for the   180
rehabilitation of victims, and, as stated above,
victims may be required to repay any limited
compensation awards they receive. Such awards
are funded by fines imposed upon criminals, but
they are subject to availability. Currently,   185
over $15 million owed New Jersey's fund remains
uncollected (Lane). No wonder compensation
awards must be limited!

In short, then, the compensation some victims
of violent crime receive thorough the VCC   190
Program is grossly inadequate and does not sat-

---

l. 179: The internal citation indicates that the information has been taken from an interview with Renee Lane. An internal citation is necessary in this paragraph because the information being cited in this paragraph was not introduced by the source's name.

l. 187: This internal citation again indicates that Lane is the source of the information.

ll. 189–234: All of the information in these lines is taken from personal experience and common knowledge. No citation is necessary.

isfy the state's responsibility of providing
fair and equal treatment under the law. The fact
that the program was designed to be funded by
fines against offenders--hardly reliable sources   195
of income--displays a lack of concern for crime
victims. It is a bone thrown to appease victims'
rights advocates. Indeed, if tax dollars can
fund programs that assist flood, fire, hurricane
and other victims, why can't they be used to as-   200
sist victims of violent crime? Excluding crime
victims and their families from tax-funded assistance violates the Fourteenth Amendment. It
is clearly another act of discrimination against
a minority group.   205

    The needs of violent crime victims vary de-
pending upon the nature of the crime and the seriousness of the injury. However, I have learned
from personal experience that the injury is
often only the beginning of the nightmare. In   210
1990, I sustained a spinal cord injury in a
nearly fatal stabbing. The pain I suffered and
my ongoing recovery cannot be comprehended fully
by anyone who has not had a similar experience.
But my government's failure to assist me ade-   215
quately in confronting the challenges I face
while fighting to rebuild my life has been the
cruelest blow. No government agency funds my rehabilitation. I spend hours developing strategies to combat one insurance cut after another,   220

and I live with conditions that restrict my independence because I lack the funds to provide
an adapted environment that meets the needs of
my disability. Consequently, my family has had
to take on the burden of my care. The one-time   225
compensation grant of $25,000 that the New
Jersey Violent Crime Compensation Board granted
me was a good beginning, but it fell short of
providing the resources to rebuild my life. I
have learned first hand that fair and equal   230
treatment is a concept that America only claims
to provide its people. The reality is that fair
and equal treatment has a dollar limit imposed
at the discretion of our government.

    Admitting that more must be done to help fi-   235
nance the needs of crime victims, the U.S. House
of Representatives voted 431 to 0 on February 8,
1995, for a bill requiring federal convicts to
pay restitution to their victims. Unfortunately,
the Victim Restitution Act applies only to fed-   240
eral violations and not to most assaults, rapes,
and violent street crimes, which are state of-
fenses (Seelye). As reported by Laurie Asseo in
SF Gate News, an online news service, this concept was underscored by a recent U.S. Supreme   245

---

l. 243: The information in the first part of this paragraph comes from Katherine Seelye, whose *New York Times* article appears on the works-cited page.

l. 243: Brandli introduces a direct quotation by using the name of the author: Laurie Asseo. The page number of the Web source follows the quote on line 249.

Court decision declaring unconstitutional "a key

provision of the 1994 Violence Against Women

Act," which "let rape victims sue their as-

sailants in federal court" (1). However, even if

the Victim Restitution Act covered assaults,   250

rapes, and violent street crimes, it is unlikely

that victims would see a single dollar of com-

pensation. In fact, as Bruce Shapiro, himself a

violent-crime victim, argues, federal courts

might be jammed up with new waves of damage   255

claims with jailed criminals claiming that the

government had acted unconstitutionally by cre-

ating "debtors' prisons" (451). In August 1994,

Shapiro and seven other people were stabbed

while they sipped coffee in a Connecticut café   260

near his home. He remains skeptical as to the

effectiveness of victims' compensation laws:

> On the surface it is hard to argue with
>
> the principle of reasonable restitution--
>
> particularly since it implies community   265
>
> recognition of the victim's suffering.

---

ll. 249–258: Brandli both paraphrases and quotes directly from an article by Bruce Shapiro. Since she introduces this information with the name of the author, only the page number appears in the internal citation. Note that the words "debtors' prisons" are in quotation marks. At times, you might want to quote only a word or short phrase and include it along with a paraphrase. In such cases, quotation marks are still required.

ll. 263–272: Brandli quotes directly from Shapiro. Since the quotation is more than three lines long, she indents 10 spaces from the left margin and double spaces the quotation. No quotation marks are necessary in such cases. However, the page number(s) from which this material is taken must appear in parentheses at the end of the quotation and after the final period. Note that Brandli adds the words "crime victims" in brackets [/] for clarity. These are her own words. Adding them to the quotation is permissible for clarity as long as the intent of the quoted material is not affected.

> But I wonder if these laws really will
> end up benefiting [crime victims]--or if
> they are just empty, vote-getting de-
> vices that exploit victims and could ac- 270
> tually hurt our chances of getting
> speedy, substantive justice. (451-452)

Victims of violent crime are being denied
their rights, and their inability to obtain ade-
quate assistance endangers the health and wel- 275
fare of them and their families. The public's
indifference to their severe needs and the denial of public funds to help them address monu-
mental obstacles resulting from their victimization amount to unconstitutional discrimination. 280
Unless we recognize our responsibility to provide victims of violent crime with viable av-
enues for both compensation and rehabilitation,
we will have done many innocent people a great
disservice while, ironically, succoring the very 285
criminals who victimized them.

Works Cited

Asseo, Laurie, "Court Rejects Law Allowing Rape Victims to Sue
  Attackers in Federal Court." *SFGate* 15 May 2000: 4 pp.
  26 May 2000 <http://www.sfgate.com/cgi-bin/article.cgi?file-
  /news/archive/2000.../national1017EDT0545.DT>

"Crime Victims' Rights." *The CQ Researcher* 4:27 (1994): 625-648.

Elias, Robert. "The Politics of Victimization." *Taking Sides:
  Clashing Views on Controversial Issues in Crime and
  Criminology.* Ed. Richard C. Monk. 2d ed. Guilford, CT:
  Dushkin, 1991: 344-350.

Lane, Renee. Personal Interview. 9 Jan. 1996.

Long, Hamilton A. *The American Ideal of 1776: The Twelve Basic American Principles.* Philadelphia: Heritage, 1976.

McDowell, Gary L. "The Supreme Court Has Distorted the Meaning of the Bill of Rights." *The Bill of Rights: Opposing Viewpoints.* Ed. William Dudley. San Diego: Greenhaven, 1994: 257–267.

Seelye, Katherine O. "House Backs Bill to Require Restitution from Criminals." *New York Times* 8 Feb. 1995: A16.

Shapiro, Bruce. "One Violent Crime." *Nation* 3 April. 1995: 437, 446–452.

United States. Department of Justice. *National Victims Resource Center.* Washington, DC: Department of Justice, 1991.

United States. Office for Victims of Crime. *Office for Victims of Crime Fact Sheet.* Washington: Department of Justice, 1993.

Wisconsin Victim Resource Center. 6 May 2000. State of Wisconsin Office of Crime Victim Services. <http://www.doj.state.wi.us/cvs/vrc.htm>.

abstract language   Words that represent ideas rather than things we can see, hear, smell, feel, or taste. The word *love* is abstract, but the word *kiss* is concrete because we can perceive it with one or more of our five senses. (See Chapters 5 and 6.)

allusion   A passing reference to a person, place, event, thing, or idea with which the reader may be familiar. Allusions can be used to add detail, clarify important points, or set the tone of an essay, a poem, or a short story.

analogy   A method by which a writer points out similarities between two things that, on the surface, seem quite different. Analogies are most often used to make abstract or unfamiliar ideas clearer and more concrete. Chapters 3 and 4 contain examples of analogy.

anecdote   A brief, sometimes humorous story used to illustrate or develop a specific point. (See Chapters 9 and 12.)

argument   A type of writing that relies on logic and concrete evidence to prove a point or support an opinion. (See Chapter 15.)

central idea   The idea that conveys a writer's main point about a subject. It may be stated explicitly or implied. Also known as the *main idea* or *controlling idea,* it determines the kinds and amount of detail needed to develop a piece of writing adequately. (See Chapter 1.)

chronological order   The arrangement of material in order of time. (See Section Four.)

coherence   The principle that writers observe in making certain that there are logical connections between the ideas and details in one sentence or paragraph and those in the next. (See Chapter 2.)

conclusion   A paragraph or series of paragraphs that ends an essay. Conclusions often restate the writer's central idea or summarize important points used to develop that idea. (See Chapter 4.) A conclusion can also be defined as a principle, opinion, or belief a writer supports or defends by using convincing information. (See Chapters 3 and 15.)

concrete language   Words that represent material things—things we can perceive with our five senses. (See *abstract language* above, and see Chapters 5 and 6.)

coordination   A technique used to express ideas of equal importance in the same sentence. To this end, writers often use compound sentences, which are composed of two independent (main) clauses connected with a coordinating conjunction. "Four students earned scholarships, but only three accepted them" is a compound sentence. (See Chapter 7.)

deduction A kind of reasoning used to build an argument. Deductive thinking draws conclusions by applying specific cases or examples to general principles, rules, or ideas. You would be thinking deductively if you wrote: All students must pay tuition. I am a student. Therefore, I must pay tuition. (See Chapter 15.)

details Specific facts or pieces of information that a writer uses to develop ideas.

emphasis The placing of stress on important ideas by controlling sentence structure through coordination, subordination, and parallelism. (See Chapter 7.)

figurative language (figures of speech) Words or phrases that explain abstract ideas by comparing them to concrete realities the reader will recognize easily. Analogy, metaphor, simile, and personification are types of figurative language. (See Chapter 6.)

image A verbal picture made up of sensory details. It expresses a general idea's meaning clearly and concretely. (See Chapter 5.)

induction A kind of reasoning used to build an argument. Inductive thinking draws general conclusions from specific facts or pieces of evidence. If you heard the wind howling, saw the sky turning black, and spotted several ominous clouds on the horizon, you might rightly conclude by induction that a storm was on its way. (See Chapter 15.)

introduction A paragraph or series of paragraphs that begins an essay. It often contains a writer's central idea in the form of a thesis statement. (See Chapter 4.)

irony A technique used by writers to communicate the very opposite of what their words mean. Irony is often used to create humor. An effective example of irony can be found in Milden's "So You Want to Flunk Out of College," which appears in the introduction to Chapter 14.

linking pronouns Pronouns that make reference to nouns that have come before (antecedents). They are one of the ways to maintain coherence in and between paragraphs. (See Chapter 2.)

main point The point that a writer focuses on in a thesis or topic sentence. (See Chapter 1.)

metaphor A figure of speech that, like a simile, creates a comparison between two things to make the explanation of one of them clearer. Unlike a simile, a metaphor does not use *like* or *as*. "The man is a pig" is a metaphor. (See Chapter 6.)

parallelism A method to express facts and ideas of equal importance in the same sentence and thereby to give them added emphasis. Sentences that are parallel express items of equal importance in the same grammatical form. (See Chapter 7.)

personification A figure of speech that writers use to discuss animals, plants, and inanimate objects in terms normally associated with human beings: for example, "Our neighborhoods are the *soul* of the city." (See Chapter 6.)

persuasion   A type of writing that supports an opinion, proves a point, or convinces the reader to act. (See Chapters 3 and 16.)

point of view   The perspective from which a narrative is told. Stories that use the first-person point of view are told by a narrator who is involved in the action and who uses words such as *I, me,* and *we* to explain what happened. Stories that use the third-person point of view are told by a narrator who may or may not be involved in the action and who uses words such as *he, she,* and *they* to explain what happened. (See Chapters 10, and 11.)

simile   A figure of speech that, like a metaphor, compares two things for the sake of clarity and emphasis. Unlike a metaphor, however, a simile uses *like* or *as.* "Samantha runs like a deer" is a simile. (See Chapter 6.)

subordination   A technique used to emphasize one idea over another by expressing the more important idea in the sentence's main clause and the other in its subordinate clause. (See Chapter 7.)

syllogism   The logical structure through which a writer uses deduction. To create a syllogism, a writer makes a general statement, then applies a specific case or example to that statement, and then draws a limited conclusion from the two. You would be using deduction in a syllogism if you wrote:

> **general statement:** All lifeguards must know how to swim.
>
> **specific case:** Marvin does not know how to swim.
>
> **conclusion:** Marvin cannot be a lifeguard.

thesis statement   A clear and explicit statement of an essay's central idea. It often appears in an introductory paragraph but is sometimes found later in the essay. (See Chapter 1.)

topic sentence   A clear and explicit statement of a paragraph's central idea. (See Chapter 1.)

transitions (connectives)   Words or phrases used to make clear and direct connections between sentences and paragraphs, thereby maintaining coherence. (See Chapter 2.)

unity   The principle that writers observe in making certain that all the information in an essay or paragraph relates directly to the central idea, which is often expressed in a thesis statement or topic sentence. (See Chapter 2.)

ALBRECHT, ERNEST. From "Sawdust" by Ernest Albrecht. Reprinted by permission of the author.

ARONOWITZ, PAUL. "A Brother's Dream" by Paul Aronowitz, New York Times, January 24, 1988. Copyright © 1988 by The New York Times Company. Reprinted by permission.

BALDWIN, JAMES. From "Sonny's Blues" by James Baldwin collected in Going to Meet the Man. Copyright © 1965 by James Baldwin. Copyright renewed. Published by Vintage Books. Reprinted by arrangement with the James Baldwin Estate.

BENNETT, WILLIAM J. Reprinted with the permission of Simon & Schuster from The Devaluing of America by William J. Bennett. Copyright © 1992 by William J. Bennett.

BUSH, GEORGE. "Still on the Point" by George Bush as appeared in Newsweek, April 28, 1997. Reprinted by permission of the author.

CALLAGHAN, ALICE. "Desperate to Learn English" by Alice Callaghan, New York Times, August 15, 1997. Copyright © 1997 by The New York Times Co. Reprinted by permission.

CARVER, RAYMOND. From Fires by Raymond Carver, copyright © 1983. Reprinted by permission of Capra Press, Santa Barbara.

CIARDI, JOHN L. "Dawn Watch" from Manner of Speaking by John L. Ciardi. Copyright © 1972 Rutgers University Press, New Brunswick, New Jersey. Reprinted by permission of the Ciardi Family Publishing Trust.

COOKE, RUSSELL. From "Old, Ailing, Abandoned," by Russell Cooke. Reprinted by permission from The Philadelphia Inquirer, March 12, 1995.

COWAN, RUTH SCHWARTZ. From "Less Work for Mother?" by Ruth Schwartz Cowan in American Heritage of Science and Technology, Spring 1987. © 1987 Forbes, Inc. Reprinted by permission of American Heritage Magazine, a division of Forbes, Inc.

COWLEY, MALCOLM. "The View from 80 by Malcolm Cowley as appeared in Life, December, 1978. Reprinted by permission of The Estate of Malcolm Cowley.

CUTFORTH, RENE. From "Padre Blaisdell and the Refugee Children" by Rene Cutforth from Eyewitness to History by John Carey, 1990.

DI PASQUALE, EMANUEL. "Joy of an Immigrant" and "Giovanni Iacono." "Joy of an Immigrant" originally published in M.C. Livingston (ed.) Thanksgiving Poems. Reprinted by permission of the author, Emanuel di Pasquale.

ELLISON, RALPH. From Invisible Man by Ralph Ellison. Copyright 1948 by Ralph Ellison. Reprinted by permission of Random House, Inc.

FLORENTO, RAZEL ARIZ. "Cry" by Razel Ariz Florento, one of ten winning submissions to the new Jersey Project's Eighth Annual Student Achievement Awards for Excellence in Feminist Scholarship and appeared in the Vol. of 1996–97 Award-Winning Papers. The Volume is available from The New Jersey Project, William Paterson University, 300 Pompton Rd., Wayne, NJ 07470. Reprinted by permission of the author.

FOX, STEPHEN. From "The Education of Branch Rickey" by Stephen Fox. First appeared in Civilization magazine, September/October 1995. Copyright © 1995 by Stephen Fox. Reprinted by permission of the Robin Straus Agency, Inc., as agent for the author.

FRIEDMAN, DORIAN. From "El Nino" by Dorian Friedman, U.S. News & World Report, September 29, 1997. Copyright © 1997 U.S. News & World Report. Reprinted by permission.

FU, SHEN C. Y. From "A Closer Look at Chinese Calligraphy" by Shen C. Y. Fu. Courtesy of Freer Gallery of Art, Smithsonian Institution, Washington, DC.

FULGHUM, ROBERT. From All I Really Need to Know I Learned in Kindergarten by Robert L. Fulghum. Copyright © 1986, 1988 by Robert L. Fulghum. Reprinted by permission of Villard Books, a division of Random House, Inc.

GOODHEART, ADAM. "How to Fight a Duel" by Adam Goodheart. Reprinted by permission from the May/June 1996 issue of Civilization.

GWIN, MARY ANN. "A Deathly Call of the Wild" by Mary Ann Gwin from *The Seattle Times*. Reprinted by permission of The Seattle Times.

HAMILL, PETER. From *A Drinking Life* by Pete Hamill. Copyright 1994 by Deidre Enterprises, Inc. Reprinted by permission of Little, Brown and Company.

HAYDEN, ROBERT. "Those Winter Sundays" copyright © 1966 by Robert Hayden, from *Angle of Ascent: New and Selected Poems* by Robert Hayden. Reprinted by permission of Liveright Publishing Corporation.

HEANEY, SEAMUS. "Mid-Term Break." From *Poems 1965–75* by Seamus Heany. Reprinted by permission of Farrar, Straus, and Giroux, and by Faber and Faber, Ltd.

HERMAN, MARC. From "Searching for El Dorado" by Marc Herman as appeared in Civilization, June/July 1997. Reprinted by permission of the author.

HOWARD, PHILIP K. From *The Death of Common Sense* by Philip K. Howard. Copyright © 1994 by Philip K. Howard. Reprinted by permission of Random House, Inc.

JAROFF, LEON. From "Crazy About Comets" by Leon Jaroff, *Time,* March 17, 1997. © 197 Time, Inc. Reprinted by permission.

KAZIN, ALFRED. Excerpt from "The Kitchen" in *A Walker in the City,* copyright 1951 and renewed 1979 by Alfred Kazin, reprinted by permission of Harcourt Brace and Company.

KING, JR, MARTIN LUTHER. From "I Have a Dream" by Martin Luther King, Jr. Reprinted by arrangement with The Heirs to the Estate of Martin Luther King, Jr., c/o Writers House, inc., as agent for the proprietor. Copyright 1963 by Martin Luther King, Jr. Copyright renewed 1991 by Coretta Scott King.

LAURENCE, MARGARET. From "Where the World Began" from Heart of a Stranger by Margaret Laurence. Copyright © 1976 by Margaret Laurence. Reprinted with the permission of New End Inc. and McClelland & Stewart, Inc., The Canadian Publishers.

LEE, LI-YOUNG. "The Gift" copyright © 1986 by Li-Young Lee. Reprinted from *Rose* with the permission of BOA Editions, Ltd., 260 East Ave., Rochester, NY 14604.

LEO, JOHN. "Of Famine and Green Beer" by John Leo, *U.S. News & World Report,* March 24, 1997. Copyright © 1997 U.S. News & World Report. Reprinted by permission.

MARIUS, RICHARD. "Writing and Its Rewards" and "Writing Things Down" by Richard Marius. Copyright Richard Marius. Reprinted by permission of the author.

MASSIE, ROBERT K. From *Peter the Great: His Life and World* by Robert K. Massie. Copyright © 1980 by Robert K. Massie. Reprinted by permission of Alfred A. Knopf, Inc.

MCPHEE, JOHN. Excerpt from "The Woods from Hog Wallow," from *The Pine Barrens* by John McPhee. Copyright © 1967, 1968 by John McPhee. Reprinted by permission of Farrar, Straus, & Giroux, Inc. Published in Canada by Macfarlane, Walter & Ross, Toronto. Used by permission.

MOORE, STEPHEN. From "New Blood for Cities" by Stephen Moore. Reprinted from *The American Enterprise,* a Washington-based magazine of politics, business and culture, September/October 1997 with permission.

MULLER, GILBERT and HARVEY WIENER. "On Writing" from *A Short Prose Reader, 4* by Gilbert Muller and Harvey Wiener. Copyright © 1987 by The McGraw-Hill Companies. Reprinted by permission of The McGraw-Hill companies.

NILSEN, ALLEEN PACE. From "Sexism in English: A 1990's Update" by Alleen Pace Nilsen. Reprinted by permission of the author.

PARKS, GORDON. "Flavio's Home" by Gordon Parks from *Voices in the Mirror,* © 1990.

PARSHALL, GERALD. "Freeing the Survivors" by Gerald Parshall, *U.S. News & World Report,* April 3, 1995. Copyright © 1995, U.S. News & World Report. Reprinted by permission.

PATON, ALAN. Reprinted with the permission of Scribner, a Division of Simon & Schuster from *Cry, the Beloved Country* by Alan Paton. Copyright 1948 by Alan Paton; copyright renewed © 1976 by Alan Paton.

PICKERING, SAMUEL F. "Faith of the Father" from *Still Life* by Samuel Pickering. © 1990 by University Press of New England. Reprinted with permission.

RAINIE, HARRISON. "The Buried Sounds of Children Crying" by Harrison Rainie, *U.S. News & World Report,* May 1, 1995. Copyright © 1995, U.S. News & World Report. Reprinted by permission.

ROBERTS, ROBIN. From "Striking Out Little League" by Robin Roberts as appeared in *Newsweek*, 1975. Reprinted by permission of the author.

RUSSELL, BERTRAND. Excerpt from *Autobiography* by Bertrand Russell. Reprinted by permission of Routledge.

RYAN, MICHAEL FORD. From "They Track the Deadliest Viruses" by Michael Ryan, *Parade*, April 23, 1995. Copyright © 1995 by Michael Ryan. Reprinted by permission of the author and Parade.

SAGAN, CARL. From *The Demon-Haunted World* by Carl Sagan. Copyright © 1996 by Carl Sagan. Reprinted by permission of Random House, Inc.

SAGAN, CARL. "The Measure of Eratosthenes" by Carl Sagan, *Harvard* Magazine, September/October 1980. Copyright © 1980 by Harvard Magazine. Reprinted by permission of Harvard Magazine and the author.

SCHROF, JOANNIE M. "The Last Safe Haven" by Joannie M. Schrof from *U.S. News & World Report*, December 26, 1994. Reprinted by permission.

SELZER, RICHARD. From *Mask on the Face of Death* by Richard Selzer. Copyright © 1987 by Richard Selzer. Reprinted by permission of Georges Borchardt, Inc. for the author. First appeared in *Life* Magazine.

SHABECOFF, PHILIP. From "Congress Again Confronts Hazards of Killer Chemicals" by Philip Shabecoff, *New York Times*, October 11, 1987. Copyright © 1987 by The New York Times Company. Reprinted by permission.

SHAHEEN, JACK. "The Media's Image of Arabs" by Jack Shaheen as appeared in *Newsweek*, 1988. Reprinted by permission of the author.

SHARP, ERIN. "Burger Queen" by Erin Sharp from *The American Enterprise* magazine.

SHLACHTER, BARRY. "Charisma Fortified by 'Chutzpah'" by Barry Shlachter, KRT News Service, September 7, 1997. Reprinted with permission of Knight-Ridder/Tribune Information Services.

SIMON, PAUL. "Joe DiMaggio: The Silent Superstar," *New York Times*, March 9, 1999. © 1999 by The New York Times Company.

STEINBECK, JOHN. From "Flight" by John Steinbeck, copyright 1938, renewed © 1966 by John Steinbeck, from *The Long Valley* by John Steinbeck. Used by permission of Viking Penguin, a division of Penguin Books USA, Inc.

STEINBECK, JOHN. From "The Chrysanthemums" by John Steinbeck, copyright 1937, renewed © 1965 by John Steinbeck from *The Long Valley* by John Steinbeck. Used by permission of Viking Penguin, a division of Penguin Books USA, Inc.

STEINEM, GLORIA. "What's Wrong with this Picture?" by Gloria Steinem, *Ms.* Magazine, March, 1997. Copyright © Gloria Steinem. Reprinted by permission of the author.

SUAREZ, MARIO. From "El Hoyo" by Mario Suarez. Reprinted from *Arizona Quarterly*, 3.2 (1947), by permission of the Regents of the University of Arizona.

THOMAS, CAL. "The Band from Hell" from *The Things That Matter Most* by Cal Thomas. Copyright © 1994 by Cal Thomas. Reprinted by permission of HarperCollins Publishers, Inc.

USA TODAY. "Drug Tests Fail Schools," *USA Today*, March 28, 1995. Copyright © 1995, USA Today. Reprinted with permission.

WAGNER, GAYE. "Death of an Officer" by Gaye Wagner is reprinted by permission from the May/June 1995 *The American Enterprise*, published by the American Enterprise Institute in Washington, D.C.

WALEY, ARTHUR. "Watching the Reapers" by Po Chu-yi from *Chinese Poetry* translated by Arthur Waley, 1962. Reprinted by permission of The Arthur Waley Estate.

WALL STREET JOURNAL. From "Affirmative Reaction," *The Wall Street Journal*, April 20, 1995.

WALLIS, CLAUDIA. From "How to Live to Be 120" by Claudia Wallis, *Time*, March 6, 1995. © 1995 Time, Inc. Reprinted by permission.

WARD, GEOFFREY. From "India: 50 Years of Independence" by Geoffrey Ward, *National Geographic*, May, 1997. Reprinted by permission of the National Geographic Society.

WELLSTONE, PAUL. Excerpt from "If Poverty Is The Question" by Paul Wellstone. Reprinted by permission from the Aprtil 14, 1997 issue of *The Nation* magazine.

WHITEHEAD, BARBARA DAFOE. "All is Not Well with the Women of Generation X." Copyright @ 1998 by *The American Enterprise* magazine.

WIESEL, ELIE. "A Prayer for the Days of Awe" by Elie Wiesel, *New York Times,* October 2, 1997. Copyright © 1997 by The New York Times Company. Reprinted by permission.

WILLIAMS, WILLIAM CARLOS. Excerpt from *The Doctor Stories* by William Carlos Williams. Copyright © 1938 by William Carlos Williams. Reprinted by permission of New Directions Publishing Corporation.

WONG, JADE SNOW. From *Fifth Chinese Daughter* by Jade Snow Wong. Copyright © 1950/1989 by Jade Snow Wong. Used by permission of the University of Washington Press.

ZANOZA, DANIEL. "Back from the Brink" by Daniel Zanoza. Reprinted from *The American Enterprise,* a Washington-based magazine of politics, business and culture, September/October 1997 with permission.